Contemporary Latin American Social and Political Thought

Latin American Perspectives in the Classroom
Series Editor: Ronald H. Chilcote

Contemporary Latin American Social and Political Thought

An Anthology

Edited by
Iván Márquez

ROWMAN & LITTLEFIELD PUBLISHERS, INC.
Lanham • Boúlder • New York • Toronto • Plymouth, UK

ROWMAN & LITTLEFIELD PUBLISHERS, INC.

Published in the United States of America
by Rowman & Littlefield Publishers, Inc.
A wholly owned subsidary of The Rowman & Littlefield Publishing Group, Inc.
4501 Forbes Boulevard, Suite 200, Lanham, Maryland 20706
www.rowmanlittlefield.com

Estover Road, Plymouth PL6 7PY, United Kingdom

British Library Cataloguing in Publication Information Available

Library of Congress Cataloging-in-Publication Data

Contemporary Latin American social and political thought : an anthology / edited by
Iván Márquez.
    p. cm. -- (Latin American perspectives in the classroom)
 Includes bibliographical references and index.
 ISBN-13: 978-0-7425-3991-4 (cloth : alk. paper)
 ISBN-10: 0-7425-3991-1 (cloth : alk. paper)
 ISBN-13: 978-0-7425-3992-1 (pbk. : alk. paper)
 ISBN-10: 0-7425-3992-X (pbk. : alk. paper)
 1. Social sciences—Latin America. 2. Political science—Latin America.
 3. Humanities—Latin America. I. Marquez, Ivan, 1965-
 H62.5.L3C65 2008
 320.098--dc22
                                        2007040862

Printed in the United States of America

Contents

PART IV: GUERRILLA REVOLUTION AND SOCIALIST UTOPIA

**PART V: FROM SOCIALIST REVOLUTION TO
DEMOCRACY, NEOLIBERALISM, AND
GLOBALIZATION: POST–COLD
WAR SOCIAL AND POLITICAL THOUGHT**

Acknowledgments

Chapter 1 excerpted from Elena Poniatowska, *Massacre in Mexico*, trans. Helen R. Lane (Columbia: University of Missouri Press, 1992), 3–19, 200–224. Reprinted by permission.

Chapter 2 excerpted from Rigoberta Menchú, *I, Rigoberta Menchú: An Indian Woman in Guatemala*, ed. Elisabeth Burgos-Debray, trans. Ann Wright (London: Verso, 1984), 122–130, 141–149, 163–171. Reprinted by permission.

Chapter 3 excerpted from Domitila Barrios de Chungara, *Let Me Speak!: Testimony of Domitila, a Woman of the Bolivian Mines*, trans. Victoria Ortiz (New York: Monthly Review Press, 1978), 194–206. Reprinted by permission.

Chapter 4 excerpted from José Ignacio López Vigil, *Rebel Radio: The Story of El Salvador's Radio Venceremos*, trans. Mark Fried (Willimantic, CT: Curbstone Press, 1994), 3–11, 140–144, 177–179, 195–215. Reprinted by permission.

Chapter 5 excerpted from *Liberation Theology: A Documentary History*, ed. and trans. Alfred T. Hennelly, S.J. (Maryknoll, NY: Orbis Books, 1990), 62–76. Reprinted by permission.

Chapter 6 excerpted from Leonardo Boff, *Church: Charism and Power: Liberation Theology and the Institutional Church*, trans. John W. Diercksmeier (New York: Crossroad, 1985), 22–46, 125–130. Reprinted by permission.

Chapter 7 excerpted from Ernesto Cardenal, *The Gospel in Solentiname*, trans. Donald D. Walsh (Maryknoll, NY: Orbis Books, 1976), 25–32, 170–184. Reprinted by permission.

Chapter 8 excerpted from Enrique D. Dussel, *Philosophy of Liberation*, trans. Aquilina Martinez and Christine Morkovsky (Maryknoll, NY: Orbis Books, 1985), 181–200. Reprinted by permission.

Chapter 9 excerpted from Paulo Freire, *Pedagogy of the Oppressed*, trans. Mayra Bergman Ramos (New York: Continuum, 1970/1993), 52–67. Reprinted by permission.

Chapter 10 excerpted from Eduardo H. Galeano, *Open Veins of Latin America: Five Centuries of Pillage of a Continent*, trans. Cedric Belfrage (New York: Monthly Review Press, 1973), 145–148, 219–224, 240–244, 248–268. Reprinted by permission.

Chapter 11 excerpted from Raúl Prebisch, *Change and Development—Latin America's Great Task: Report Submitted to the Inter-American Development Bank* (New York: Praeger, 1971), 3–20. Reprinted by permission.

Chapter 12 excerpted from Enzo Faletto and Fernando Henrique Cardoso, *Dependency and Development in Latin America*, trans. Marjory Urquidi (Berkeley: University of California Press, 1979), 8–28. Reprinted by permission.

Chapter 13 previously appeared in *The American Economic Review* 60 (May 1970): 231–236. Reprinted by permission.

Chapter 14 excerpted from Plinio A. Mendoza, Carlos Alberto Montaner, and Alvaro Vargas Llosa *Guide to the Perfect Latin American Idiot*, trans. Michaela Lajda Ames (Lanham, MD: Madison Books, 2000), 37–62. Reprinted by permission.

Chapter 15 excerpted from *Che: Selected Works of Ernesto Guevara*, eds. Rolando E. Bonachea and Nelson P. Valdes (Cambridge: MIT Press, 1969), 155–169. Reprinted by permission.

Chapter 16 excerpted from *Urban Guerrilla Warfare in Latin America*, eds. James Kohl and John Litt (Cambridge: MIT Press, 1974), 81–86. Reprinted by permission.

Chapter 17 reprinted from EZLN, "Sixth Declaration of the Selva Lacandona" <http://www.ezln.org/documentos/2005/sexta1.en.htm> (19 Oct. 2005). Reprinted by permission.

Chapter 18 excerpted from *Cultures of Politics, Politics of Cultures: Re-Visioning Latin American Social Movements*, eds. Sonia E. Alvarez, Evelina Dagnino, and Arturo Escobar (Boulder: Westview Press, 1998), 46–63. Reprinted by permission.

Chapter 19 excerpted from Jorge G. Castañeda, *Utopia Unarmed: the Latin American Left After the Cold War*, (New York: Vintage, 1993), 298-325. Reprinted by permission.

Chapter 20 reprinted from *Challenge* 42.1 (January/February 1999): 14–33. Reprinted by permission.

Chapter 21 excerpted from Hernando de Soto, *The Other Path: The Economic Answer to Terrorism* (New York: Basic Books, 1989/2002), xi–xxxix. Reprinted by permission.

Preface

Latin America is a place where thought and action are often seen as going to-gether. The line between thinkers and doers is not easily demarcated. The word and the deed, in many cases, go hand in hand. And many times, words are seen as deeds. Obviously, there are academic communities in Latin America where discourses driven by the imperative of truth for the sake of truth and argumenta-tive debate among a community of scholars is the default model. But there is this other side of thought in Latin America, the one intrinsically connected to action and the expression of a dynamic lived experience, be it personal or collective. Many Latin Americans use the word *praxis* to identify this thinking for/about/in action, and in many cases, this kind of active thought or thoughtful act is further regarded as transformative or liberatory. Latin America also has a penchant for the expression of lived experience, which becomes manifest in the importance bestowed upon the personal essay, the narrative medium, in general, and the first-person testimonial, in particular.

The main aim of this anthology is to document this pervasive—it could be argued even principal—but nonetheless mostly neglected side of Latin American thought. The anthology includes selections of theoretical-analytical texts, gener-ated for the purpose of capturing what is regarded as a holistic, dynamic process of thinking-acting, and selections of essays and narratives, where the personal is never relegated to second place and the expression and understanding of the complex and messy dimension of lived experience is primary.

Since the 1960's Latin America has produced an impressive body of socio-political texts that can be grouped in five interrelated categories: (1) narratives of resistance and liberation, (2) liberation theology, philosophy, and pedagogy, (3) dependency theory, (4) guerrilla revolution and socialist utopia, and (5) democ-racy, neoliberalism, and globalization. These texts are the discursive component of processes of transformation that have taken place in Latin America at least for the past 40 years. These processes include: (1) the student movement com-ing out of many of the "autonomous" university campuses throughout Latin America, (2) the continued organization of indigenous groups, at different levels, surely going back to the time of the Spanish and Portuguese discovery, conquest, and colonization of Central and South America and the Caribbean, (3) the guerrilla movements, some say coming out of radicalized or disillusioned members (depending on who tells the story) of the student movement, the labor unions, the Catholic Action groups, and the peasantry, (4) the emergence of Christian base ecclesial communities organized in accordance to perspectives emerging out of the Latin American priests' adaptation of certain aspects of the Catholic Council of Vatican II in light of the realities of Latin America, (5) the expansion of the State and the increase of its power for centralized organization, regulation, planning, especially of the economy and education, (6) the emergence of international and extranational organizations such as UN-based organizations, IMF, World Bank, and Inter-American Development Bank, focusing on different aspects of Third World nations' development and operating with different agendas, (7) the U.S.'s continued and increased economic and political involvement in Latin America as transnational foreign investor and as sovereign Nation-State player in the global political economy, and (8) the expansion and increased access of communication media in all sectors of Latin American society.

This anthology is a sourcebook of not readily available English translations of key texts in Latin American social and political thought, representative of these diverse but interrelated and sometimes implicated processes. All of the texts are autochthonous, i.e., Latin Americans living in Latin America produced them. Therefore, contrary to most English anthologies on Latin America, this one is not only on Latin America but also from and of Latin America.

The anthology is divided into parts that are isomorphic to the five categories presented above. Part I is a selection of narratives of liberation and resistance describing (1) defining experiences of the student movement, (2) self-organizing among indigenous people, (3) intercultural and interclass (mis)communication among feminists, and (4) the use of media as a political and social force of communication, organization, and change. Part II is a selection of texts on liberation theology, philosophy, and pedagogy elaborating critical perspectives on (1) the Church's option for the poor in Latin America and all its theological, institutional, social, ecclesial, and practical implications, (2) the philosophical notion of praxis and its relevance to the development of a philosophy of liberation in Latin America, and (3) alternative notions of pedagogy geared toward individual and collective consciousness-raising and empowerment. Part III is a selection of economic texts on development theory, a.k.a., Latin American political economy, (1) showing how it can be seen as a critical reading of First World economic hegemony, (2) tracing its origins and development as a reformist critique or radical rejection of developmentalism in economics (depending on who tells the story), and (3) demonstrating its own subjection to a neoliberal critique. Part IV is a selection of texts about guerrilla socialist revolution, (1) sketching out the vision of a socialist society, (2) describing the strategies and tactics of rural and urban guerrillas, emphasizing their complementarity within a revolutionary process, and (3) reflecting on the place of guerrilla social movements within the new context of neoliberalism and globalization. Part V is a selection of texts pointing to the sociopolitical challenges brought by the post–Cold War era defined by neoliberalism, democracy and globalization, (1) emphasizing the increasing role of cultural movements as agents of social change, (2) sketching out a reformulation of nationalism in Latin America adequate for a world of global capital and free trade between economically unequal nations, (3) proposing a progressive, democratic model of a market economy for present-day Latin America as an alternative to both neoliberal and social democratic models, and (4) demonstrating how capitalism can be adapted to the economic, political, and social realities of Latin America in ways that can lead to the decrease in the power and appeal of terrorism.

All selections come from previously published translations of original Spanish and Portuguese texts.

Iván Márquez

I

NARRATIVES OF
RESISTANCE AND LIBERATION

❶

Massacre in Mexico (1971)

Elena Poniatowska

Elena Poniatowska (b. France, 1932) is a Mexican journalist-author and one of the founders of the Cineteca Nacional, the newspaper La Jornada, Siglo XXI, *one of Mexico's most prestigious publishing houses, and* Fem, *Mexico's first feminist magazine. In 1979 she became the first woman to win the Mexican National Award for Journalism. She is also a university lecturer and political activist. Most recently, she has led the civic resistance movement against the impeachment of Andrés Manuel López Obrador in Mexico's disputed 2006 election. This selection relates the events of the 1968 Tlatelolco Massacre in Mexico City and exemplifies "testimonial writing" at its best and most experimental.*

TAKING TO THE STREETS

> **PEOPLE, UNITE, DON'T ABANDON US, PEOPLE, UNITE,**
> **PEOPLE, DON'T ABANDON US, PEOPLE, UNITE.**
> *Banners at the demonstration of August 18, 1968*

They are many. They come down Melchor Ocampo, the Reforma, Juarez, Cinco de Mayo, laughing, students walking arm in arm in the demonstration, in as festive a mood as if they were going to a street fair; carefree boys and girls who do not know that tomorrow, and the day after, their dead bodies will be lying swollen in the rain, after a fair where the guns in the shooting gallery are aimed at them, children-targets, wonder-struck children, children for whom every day is a holiday until the owner of the shooting gallery tells them to form a line, like the row of tin-plated mechanical ducks that move past exactly at eye level, click, click, click, "Ready, aim, fire!" and they tumble backward, touching the red satin backdrop.

The owner of the shooting gallery handed out rifles to the police, to the army, and ordered them to shoot, to hit the bull's-eye, and there the little tin-plated creatures were standing, open-mouthed with astonishment and wide-eyed with fear, staring into the rifle barrels. Fire! The sudden blinding flash of a green flare. Fire! They fell, but this time there was no spring to set them up again for the next customer to shoot at; the mechanism was quite different at this fair; the little springs were not made of metal but of blood; thick, red blood that slowly formed little puddles, young blood trampled underfoot all over the Plaza de las Tres Culturas.

These youngsters are coming toward me now, hundreds of them; not one of them has his hands up, not one of them has his pants around his ankles as he is stripped naked to be searched; there are no sudden blows, no clubbings, no ill treatment, no vomiting after being tortured; they are breathing deeply, advancing slowly, surely, stubbornly; they come round the Plaza de las Tres Culturas and stop at the edge of the square, where there is a drop of eight or ten feet, with a view of the pre-Hispanic ruins below; they walk on toward me again, hundreds of them, advancing toward me with their hands holding up placards, little hands, because death makes them look like children's hands; they come toward me, row on row; though they are pale, they look happy; their faces are slightly blurred, but they are happy ones; there are no walls of bayonets driving them off now, no violence; I look at them through a curtain of raindrops, or perhaps a veil of tears, like the one at Tlatelolco; I cannot see their wounds, for fortunately there are no holes in their bodies, no bayonet gashes, no dum-dum bullets; they are blurred figures, but I can hear their voices, their footsteps, echoing as on the day of the Silent Demonstration; I will hear those advancing footsteps all the rest of my life; girls in mini-skirts with their tanned young legs, teachers with no neckties, boys with sweaters knotted around their waists or their necks; they come toward me, laughing, there are hundreds of them, full of the crazy joy of walking together down this street, our street, to the Zócalo, our Zócalo; here they come; August 5, August 13, August 27, September 13; Father Jesús Pérez has set all the bells of the cathedral to ringing to welcome them, the entire Plaza de la Constitución is illuminated; there are bunches of *cempazúchitl* flowers everywhere, thousands of lighted candles; the youngsters are in the center of an orange, they are the brightest burst of fireworks of all. Was Mexico a sad country? I see it as a happy one, a marvelously happy one; the youngsters are marching up Cinco de Mayo, Júarez, the Reforma, the applause is deafening, three hundred thousand people have come to join them, of their own free will, Melchor Ocampo, Las Lomas, they are climbing up through the forests to the mountaintops, *Mé-xi-co, Li-ber-tad, Mé-xi-co, Li-ber-tad, Mé-xi-co, Li-ber-tad, Mé-xi-co, Li-ber-tad, Mé-xi-co, Li-ber-tad.*

Elena Poniatowska

I didn't "join" the Student Movement; it had been an intimate part of my life for a long time. What I mean is, I'm from Poli;[1] I live in a house there; that's where my pals, my neighbors, my work are. . . . My kids were born there. My wife is from Poli, too. The Movement has been very close to our hearts for many years. It's not a whim of the moment, or a joke or "good vibes," or anything like that. That's not what it is at all. It's a question of fighting for everything we believe in, for the things we've always fought for, things that our fathers and our fathers' fathers fought for before us. . . . We come from working-class families, people who have always worked hard for a living.

Raúl Álvarez Garín, theoretical physicist, ESFM;[2]
professor at the National School of Biological Sciences
of the IPN; CNH[3] delegate; prisoner in Lecumberri

MÉ-XI-CO—L I-B ER-TAD—MÉ-XI-CO—LI-BER-TAD—MÉ-XI-CO
Chant at demonstrations

I joined the Student Movement simply because one day the *granaderos[4]* turned up at the INBA[5] with police dogs and chains and hauled everybody off to jail. And the INBA hadn't even come out and said whether it supported the Movement or not! (I'm rather inclined to think it didn't, right?) This arbitrary invasion made many of us actors and actresses aware of what was happening, and we decided to join the students and help them, *really* help them, not just march arm in arm in demonstrations or yell at the top of our lungs in meetings. . . . So then we formed an actors' brigade.

Margarita Isabel, actress

PEOPLE UNITE—PEOPLE UNITE—PEOPLE UNITE
Chant at demonstrations

The decision confronting us was not whether to join the Movement but whether to get out of it or stay in it. We had a rather good idea what was going to happen from the very beginning—we suspected, quite rightly, that repression, mass arrests, and clubbings were in the offing—so we had a choice. We could either "go underground," meaning buy a plane or a train ticket or whatever and get out, or stay in the city and wait and see what would happen. . . . We were all in our schools, Raúl in Theoretical Physics, I in Philosophy, and we were already involved in student affairs. The concrete problems in my school, for instance, were: a preparatory program for working-class students, flunk-outs, freeing Vallejo,[6] the curriculum and other academic problems, the independence of the School of Psychology, etc. I was elected president of the student body in 1967, but now I'm just an ordinary alumnus. . . . Everything changed after the twenty-sixth of July. . . . I'm not the same now; we're all different. There was one Mexico before the Student Movement, and a different one after 1968. Tlatelolco is the dividing point between these two Mexicos.

Luis Gonzalez de Alba, CNH delegate from the Faculty of
Philosophy and Letters, UNAM;[7] prisoner in Lecumberri

"Going underground" means doing nothing.

Gilberto Guevara Niebla, CNH delegate from the
Faculty of Sciences, UNAM; prisoner in Lecumberri

I think that repression was responsible for the effectiveness and the importance of the Student Movement. More than any political speech, the very fact of repression politicized people and led the great majority to participate actively in the meetings. It was decided that classes would be suspended in each school, and that was what got us to thinking about forming brigades and action committees in each department. The members of the brigades were students who engaged in all sorts of activities, from collecting money to organizing "lightning meetings" in the streets, in the most isolated working-class districts. Mass demonstrations were one of the most effective political weapons of the Movement.

*Carolina Pérez Cicero, student at the
Faculty of Philosophy and Letters, UNAM*

Mexico had never seen such huge and such enormously enthusiastic spontaneous demonstrations as the ones organized by the students. There was one demonstration, in support of the Cuban Revolution, some years ago, but it was not nearly as wide in scope. The Student Movement really shook Mexican society to its foundations, and that's why the government began to be so afraid of it.

*Félix Lucio Hernández Gamundi, CNH delegate from ESIME,[8] IPN;
prisoner in Lecumberri*

At most, fifteen thousand demonstrators took part in the marches in Mexico City. But six hundred thousand people, from every walk of life, and young people in particular, gathered to show their support. When have we ever seen anything like that? How could the government put up with something like that? It had every reason to go off its nut.

*Salvador Martínez de la Roca ("Pino"), of the Action Committee of the
Faculty of Sciences, UNAM; prisoner in Lecumberri*

They couldn't stand the thought that a veritable multitude, between three hundred and six hundred thousand people, had marched down the principal streets of Mexico City, the Paseo de la Reforma, Juárez, Cinco de Mayo, bearing banners and placards that made fun of the "principle of authority." They were forced to put down the student protest undermining the status quo, the PRI,[9] fake labor unions, and leadership by "mummies."

*Eduardo Valle Espinoza ("Owl-Eyes"), CNH delegate from the
National School of Economics, UNAM; prisoner in Lecumberri*

By marching through the streets, we were more or less avenging all the students in the provinces who had been the victims of repression before our turn came: the students of Puebla, Tabasco, Chihuahua, Sinaloa, Guerrero, Sonora, and in a certain sense, the victims of oppression in Morelia, Hermosillo, and Monterrey.

*Ernesto Hernández Pichardo, student at the
National School of Economics, UNAM*

DON'T SHOOT, SOLDIER: YOU'RE ONE OF THE PEOPLE TOO
Banner at the August 27 demonstration

Mexico today has a population of forty-eight million, scattered over a territory of two million square kilometers. Its rate of population growth is 3.6 per annum (at any rate that is what Dr. Loyo tells us), and since this rate of growth increases every year, there will be ninety million people in our country in 1990. Seventy per cent of them will be under twenty-three years of age.

I mention this because I believe that young peasants, workers, and students are facing a very dim future, since job opportunities are being created for the benefit of special interests rather than society as a whole. We are continually told, "You are the future of the country." But we are constantly denied any opportunity to act and participate in the political decisions that are being made today. . . . We want to and ARE ABLE TO participate today, not when we are seventy years old.

> *Gustavo Gordillo, CNH delegate from the*
> *National School of Economics, UNAM*

PEOPLE, DON'T ABANDON US—PEOPLE, UNITE!
Chant at the August 13 demonstration

I didn't join the Movement; I was part of it from the day I was born. It's my medium, the very air I breathe, and to me the Movement meant protecting my home, my wife, my children, my comrades.

> *Ernesto Olvera, teacher of mathematics at*
> *Preparatory 1,[10] UNAM; prisoner in Lecumberri*

FREE-DOM FOR POLITICAL PRISONERS!
FREE-DOM FOR POLITICAL PRISONERS!
Chant at the August 13 demonstration

The 1968 Student Movement was not suddenly born that same year; it did not come about by spontaneous generation. Countless revolutionary political organizations and important student groups had previously made the same demands. In Mexico freedom for political prisoners is a demand that goes back as far as political imprisonment itself. The same is true of the fight to do away with Article 145, which establishes penalties for "social dissolution," and the fight to do away with the *granaderos*. The 1968 Movement took up all of these demands and not only pressed for the six reforms on its list but also became the spokesman for the reforms most urgently sought by Mexican students, workers, and intellectuals.

In many parts of the country, students had previously led the entire nation in protest movements whose general tenor was very much like that of the 1968 Movement. The most important movements of this sort were those in Puebla in 1964, Morelia in 1966, and Sonora and Tabasco in 1967. Moreover, the demonstrations in support of Cuba, Vietnam, and the Dominican Republic mobilized large groups of students, particularly in Mexico City, and the awareness of the oppression of other peoples greatly raised their level of political consciousness and their awareness of their own strength. This was quite evident in the student protests in Morelia during 1962 and 1963; the movement for university reform in Puebla in 1962; the UNAM strike in 1966; the frequent student strikes for economic and academic reforms in various parts of the country (in particular in the rural normal schools); the student movement in the School of Agronomy in Ciudad Juárez, Chihuahua, which was supported by the other schools of agronomy and by the students of the IPN, and many other student protests.

I do not believe that these protests are isolated incidents. On the contrary, I believe that after the national strike in April 1956 there was a sharp escalation of student protest movements. The Teachers' Movement in 1958, the Railway Workers' Movement in 1958-1959, and the demonstrations in support of the Cuban revolution all contributed to this process, which reached its peak in 1968. Doubtless the Student Movement has hopes that workers and peasants will carry on the struggle.

Pablo Gómez, student at the National School of Economics,
UNAM; member of the Communist Youth; prisoner in Lecumberri

Every year the "fish,"[11] the little fishes, organize two demonstrations that are always the same: one for Cuba and another for Vietnam. They gather in front of the Teatro Xola or go to the Juárez Hemiciclo, let out a few shouts and a few *vivas* and a very few *mueras*, hold up three banners, and at eight o'clock sharp the demonstration ends, as punctually as it began; they fold their banners, put away their placards, and go back home. That's all they ever do! I can't imagine why they keep doing the same old stuff!

Salvador Martinez de la Roca (Pino), of the
Action Committee of the Faculty of Sciences, UNAM

DIA-LOGUE—DIA-LOGUE—DIA-LOGUE—DIALOGUE—
DIA-LOGUE—DIA-LOGUE—DIA-LOGUE
Chant at the August 13 demonstration

The railway workers were alone in 1958. We aren't.

Luis González de Alba, of the CNH

PEOPLE, OPEN YOUR EYES!
Street poster

The conflict is very different from the one in May in France. In Mexico there were practically no demands for changes in the schools and universities, only political petitions: freeing the political prisoners, abolishing the *granaderos*, firing the mayor of the city [*sic*], the head of the security police. . . .

Can we really talk about solid democratic traditions when in fact there is only one political party? When candidates of any other party are not seated in either house of the legislature or only a few are seated to give the appearance of an opposition? And what can we say of the solid tradition of the *tapado*, the next presidential candidate whose name is kept a secret by the president in office and his advisors till the very last minute and then announced through the official Party, the PRI? Everyone in Mexico knows that in the space of just a few weeks, the *tapado*, who often has been a complete unknown up until then, suddenly becomes the most talented, the most capable man imaginable; his portrait begins to appear on every wall, on all the billboards, on lampposts draped in the colors of the national flag, on neon signs full-face, profile, half-profile; his monogram, the initials of his name are painted on every fence, they are carved more or less indelibly into the sides of mountains: scars, stigmata defacing the land. Millions of pesos are wasted on this sort of propaganda to hoodwink the ignorant and gullible masses into believing that the candidate proposed by the PRI has exceptional virtues. What can opposition parties do in the face of this sort of enslavement of the masses, these astronomical expenditures? Either join the other side, or carry on a very modest campaign, a few speeches that blow away in the wind. . . .

These political tricks, these trappings are what have disgusted young students who find every door closed to them and all the jobs set aside for politicians of the PRI, unless they "fall in line" and "get on the bandwagon."

Professor M. Mayagoitia, letter to Le Monde, Paris, October 7, 1968

WE DON'T WANT OLYMPIC GAMES! WE WANT A REVOLUTION!

Chant by students at a number of meetings

DOWN WITH MUMMIES!

Student slogan

There is no doubt that students at the University and the IPN, with their disturbances in the streets and their rowdy behavior in their schools, gave the police every reason to intervene. There were many hold-ups by students. Public warnings and threats of possible punishment had come to have no effect at all. Discipline inside the schools was practically nil. The student "victory" that forced Rector Ignacio Chávez to resign had obviously brought on a tense and demagogic atmosphere within the National University that forced the authorities to covertly adopt the policy of "Agree that the student is right, even though he's not." Many of us remember how a member of the Supreme Court, who was also acting president of the Board of Regents of the University, Attorney José Caso Estrada, referring to the group of "fossils"[12] and gangster-like student leaders at the University, declared that historically the victors (the loser was Rector Chávez) always carry off the spoils. And the spoils in this case turned out to be control of the University. The new authorities were all in favor of catering to the students' demands. University Reform was looked upon as a panacea, and the sorcerers' apprentices heated up their test tubes and their cauldrons, concocted their magic mixtures, announced that the University would be run democratically with the participation of the student body, called on these young people to help decide on the curriculum, plans for improvement, and appointments of teachers and directors. They even went so far as to raise the question "Why not have a student as rector?" Any sort of disciplinary rules were automatically regarded as bad pedagogy. We would have to be understanding and sympathetic and kowtow to these young people whose possible faults or feelings of confusion were due only to the sins and the bewilderment of their elders. We would have to pay for our sins like good Christians. The hour of repentance had come. Fathers have the sort of sons they deserve. *Mea culpa, mea culpa, mea culpa.*

Gerardo Hernández Ponce, teacher at Preparatory 2, UNAM

My father keeps telling me what a good son *he* was and all that. . . . And then I start thinking, "Good Lord, am I some strange sort of creature, or neurotic, or what?" Grownups are so anxious to set exemplary standards for us that they make themselves out to be absolutely perfect, abstract models we should imitate, and bang! that's the end of any communication between us. I get to thinking, "Jeez, to hear my old man talk, he did everything right, and I'm doing everything all wrong!" That's why I can't communicate with him, no matter how hard I try. When my old man begins with that business of "When I was your age . . ." I feel like going off to bed.

Gustavo Gordillo, of the CNH

Young people are angry. They have a right to build the world they live in. They have every reason to be angry. We must humbly admit that this is so, because that is one way of remedying our defects and shortcomings. Our traditions are bad; our attitude toward life couldn't be worse. We have fathered a rebellious, misunderstood generation of young people, who have no free choice as to the sort of present and future they would like to have. We older people ought to become young in heart again, beg these youngsters to accept us, dye our gray hair and cover up our wrinkles with cosmetics, get in on the action, try out this new dance step and do our best to hide the fact that it leaves us panting. Show them that we understand, that we're sorry, and above all do what we can to maintain our position with them, or better yet, improve it. Our deepest, most heartfelt desire is to be popular with young people, to be accepted by them. We *must* succeed in doing this, but the question is how.

Pedro Tamariz, teacher at the Erasmo Castellanos Quinto School

Hey there, you with the long hair, didn't I put money in your collection box for a haircut?

Juan López Martínez, father of a family

Everybody shuts himself up in his own little world. Adults look on anything young people do as an attack on their principles and their moral code. That's the reason behind their illogical hostility toward long hair. What does long hair have to do with decency or whether a kid's good or bad? I like having long hair, but that doesn't mean I'm a homosexual or feminine or who knows what all. Adults try to make the length of your hair the one measuring rod of your sexual normality or your moral decency.

Gustavo Gordillo, of the CNH

My old man and my old lady regard their principles as immutable.

Gabriela Peña Valle, student at the Faculty of
Philosophy and Letters, UNAM

Why do you wiggle your behind like that? What's more, you don't know how to sit properly. I'd sooner die than wear a skirt like that.

Mercedes Fernández de Cervantes, mother of a family

A hundred and fifty pesos for a skirt like that! And it's not even twenty inches long!

Elsa Treviño de Zozaya, mother of a family

Why don't you just go around stark naked?

Sofía Arrechiga de Toscano, mother of a family

Enrollment at the National University and the Polytechnical Institute is snowballing. The number of students in both institutions is already much larger—proportionally—than in any other part of the world. The standard of work accomplished in these institutions is discouraging, for both the quality and the quantity couldn't possibly be any lower.

There is, of course, no single, clear-cut cause for this situation—which has gotten no better and in fact is getting worse all the time. The reasons are both numerous and complex, and if I list a few of them, it is not with the intention of indicating their relative importance, nor do I maintain that they are the only ones: prostitution as a public activity and an effective means of controlling the government, workers, and peasants; bad students and worse teachers; the passivity and the lack of exemplary models of behavior within the family; the lack of attractive political parties that would promote independent points of view in public life; social inequalities with scandalous extremes of wealth and poverty; an inexorable colonial dependence that deeply influences, debases, and distorts every aspect of our development; the extremely painful image of an overall international situation that is chaotic, unjust, and bloody.

In short, a complex state of affairs where nothing is clear-cut, where the few positive forces are slow-moving and inadequate. Hopes that continually come to nothing, because a painful, ever present, desolating reality brands our souls with its stigmata. This has been, and continues to be, the daily bread of young and old. What can we expect of our young people? What do we dare demand of them? What are we older people giving and receiving?

The 1968 Student Movement in Mexico admittedly lost its bearings, and the sudden violent turn it took seemed disproportionate to the street incident that gave rise to it. But which of the rest of us knew where we were heading? What do we have to offer and what are we seeking? If we do not find the right road soon, we must face up, in all honesty, to one fact at least: tragedies such as that on October 2 in the Plaza de las Tres Culturas in Tlatelolco will blindfold us even more, and the lack of hope will lead to more bloodshed still.

Pedro Ramírez Arteaga, professor of philosophy,
Llnitlersity of Hermosillo, Sonora

My folks are pompous asses, and so are my teachers.

Vera Pomar Bermúdez, student at the School of Dentistry, UNAM

The only time I get along well with my parents is when we go to the movies, because nobody talks then.

Victoria Garfias Madrigal, student at the Faculty of Engineering, UNAM

You see now why I'm a hippie.

Eduardo Parra del Río, hippie

I'm delighted by young people today—their fashions, their songs, their freedom, their lack of hypocrisy, their way of looking at love and living it. I prefer the Beatles to Beethoven. How can I explain the difference between John Lennon's "I, Me, Mine" or Paul McCartney's "The Fool on the Hill" and the romantics of my day? I spent my entire youth sitting on Augustín Lara's[13] white brocade sofa, with my tiny foot, as slender as a needlecase, resting on a little cushion; the boys sang "Mujer, mujer divina" in my ear, and you wouldn't believe how bored stiff we were. I don't know what 1 would have given to have them say to me, "See you later, alligator, after while, crocodile," instead of humming, "You've become timid and fearful," and I only wish that when we broke up we'd have merely said,

Bye bye love
Bye bye happiness
Hello loneliness
I think I'm gonna cry.

Luz Fernanda Carmona Ochoa, mother of a family

We had no spirit at all; "I'd like to but I can't" was our motto; when we liked a boy we pretended we didn't; we spent our days fretting, exchanging little notes, gossiping, playing footsie under the table, putting on an act, telling the boys "hands off," making "deals" not worth two cents. We did everything on the sly and it seems to me that's how I lived my whole life, on the sly, getting what I wanted in secret, the way a little girl steals jam from the cupboard, hurriedly closing the door, terrified that somebody might have seen me. . . . That's why I like the way young people live now; the life my daughter leads seems a thousand times better to me than the one I led. I know my daughter doesn't lie to me.

Yvonne Huitrón de Gutiérrez, mother of a family

I come from a working-class family. My parents are too tired at night to talk about anything. We eat and go to bed. The people I talk to are my pals at night school.

Elpidio Canales Benítez, messenger boy at Ayotla Textil

My folks don't even talk to each other. Nobody says much around our house. Why would they talk to us?

Hermelinda Suárez Vergara, operator at Esperanza Beauty Salon

We've got a television set at home.
Rodolfo Nieto Andrade, student at Vocational 1,[14] IPN

Communicate with my old man and my old lady? Are you kidding?
Javier Garza Jiménez, student at the Faculty of Political Sciences, UNAM

At Poli I never heard expressions like "mummies," "squares," people "on the right wave length," and so on. Nobody ever talked about the "sandwich" generation, our parents' generation, crammed in between their children and their own parents like a slice of head cheese. Maybe they use that kind of language at the UNAM, but it seems more like the jargon of intellectuals or small groups hankering to be part of the Movement, to be "in." When we talk among ourselves at Poli, we use the crudest sort of language, bricklayers' language.
Raúl Álvarez Garín, of the CNH

We foresaw the clubbings and the mass arrests, we more or less expected to be thrown in jail, but we didn't foresee that some of us would be murdered.
Gilberto Guevara Niebla, of the CNH

During the Movement, when there was one violent incident after another, many comrades suddenly disappeared, bunches of them were thrown in jail, there were fewer and fewer meetings, lots of people dropped out, there were tanks and bayonets all over the place—this was after the attack on the Santo Tomás campus, the bloodiest and most frightening incident before Tlatelolco. The students took their wounded to the School of Medicine so they wouldn't be hauled off to jail and the *granaderos* and soldiers would go away; I was terribly down in the dumps that day. All of a sudden the thought came to me, "What in the world am I doing here?" . . . I'm lying there on the bed, looking at the ceiling, and suddenly I decide that I don't give a damn whether there's going to be a dialogue with the government or not, whether anybody starts spouting absurd arguments against it, whether they fire Cueto[15] and free the prisoners or not. You're far away right now, and you have no idea what's happening here; I could be with you, I could be like you, devoting my whole life to my profession, concentrating on one tiny little area that I would be thoroughly familiar with, poring over the latest research and the most recent findings published in the professional journals. . . . I felt that day that those areas in my life that had been most important to me in the last few years were falling to pieces.

Luis González de Alba, of the CNH

A fine thing, setting their dogs on us like that! All because we want what's guaranteed in the Constitution, the right to protest, the chance for everyone to go to school, an end to the sort of poverty I see in the towns my mom takes us to visit.

After what happened at Tlatelolco, me and my buddies are going to carry sticks and stones around with us, and if we come across a *granadero* or a soldier by himself, we'll let him have it!

Rodolfo Torres Morales, eleven years old, in his first year of junior high school

To me, the most horrifying thing was realizing that such a thing was possible in a civilized country: Tlatelolco, killing people, irrational behavior, throwing people in prison, but on the other hand, I also realized how many sources of strength a woman has when she loves a man.

Artemisa de Gortari, mother of a family

It's sad to have to die so young! If you hadn't been an agitator and gotten mixed up in all this, you'd be free and not have a care in the world right now!

An Army officer, to the CNH delegate from the Chapingo School of Agriculture, Luis Tomás Cervantes Cabeza de Vaca, at Military Camp 1

THE NIGHT OF TLATELOLCO

We must bear witness to our surprise and indignation at the events that night at Tlatelolco, when barbarism, primitive savagery, hatred, and the most vicious impulses held sway.

Francisco Martínez de la Vega, in an article entitled "Where is Our Country Heading?", El Día, October 8, 1968

Headlines in the Major Daily Papers in Mexico City on Thursday, October 3, 1968

EXCÉLSIOR:
SERIOUS FIGHTING AS ARMY BREAKS UP MEETING OF STRIKERS.
20 Dead, 75 Wounded, 400 Jailed: Fernando M. Garza, Press Secretary of the President of the Republic.

NOVEDADES:
SHOTS EXCHANGED BY SHARPSHOOTERS AND THE ARMY IN CIUDAD TLATELOLCO.
Figures Thus Far: 25 Dead and 87 Wounded: General Hernández Toledo and 12 Other Soldiers Wounded.

EL UNIVERSAL:
TLATELOLCO A BATTLEFIELD.
Serious Fighting for Hours Between Terrorists and Soldiers. 29 Dead and More Than 80 Wounded; Casualties on Both Sides; 1000 Arrested.

LA PRENSA:
MANY KILLED AND WOUNDED ACCORDING TO GARCÍA BARRAGÁN.
Army and Students Exchange Gunfire.

EL DÍA:

CRIMINAL PROVOCATION AT TLATELOLCO MEETING CAUSES TERRIBLE BLOODSHED.
Fight with Army at Tlatelolco Results in Many Dead and Wounded: General Hernández Toledo and 12 Other Soldiers Wounded. One Soldier Dead. Number of Civilians Killed or Wounded Still Not Known.

EL HERALDO:

BLOODY ENCOUNTER IN TLATELOLCO.
26 Dead and 71 Wounded; Sharpshooters Fire on Army Troops. General Toledo Wounded.

EL SOL DE MÉXICO (a morning paper):

FOREIGN INTERLOPERS ATTEMPT TO DAMAGE MEXICO'S NATIONAL IMAGE.
The Objective: Preventing the Nineteenth Olympic Games from Being Held. Sharpshooters Fire on Army Troops in Tlatelolco. One General and 11 Soldiers Wounded; 2 Soldiers and More Than 20 Civilians Killed in a Terrible Gun Battle.

EL NACIONAL:

ARMY FORCED TO ROUT SHARPSHOOTERS: GARCÍA BARRAGÁN.

OVACIONES:

BLOODY GUN BATTLE IN THE PLAZA DE LAS TRES CULTURAS.
Dozens of Sharpshooters Fire on Troops. 23 Dead, 52 Wounded, 1000 Arrested, and More Vehicles Burned.

LA AFICIÓN:

STUDENT MEETING IN TLATELOLCO RESULTS IN HEAVY GUNFIRE

All witnesses agree that the sudden appearance of flares in the sky above the Plaza de las Tres Culturas at the Nonoalco-Tlatelolco housing unit was the signal that unleashed the hail of bullets which turned the student meeting of October 2 into the Tlatelolco tragedy.

At five-thirty p.m. on Wednesday, October 2, approximately ten thousand people were gathered on the esplanade of the Plaza de las Tres Culturas to hear the student speakers of the National Strike Committee, who were standing on a balcony on the fourth floor of the Chihuahua building addressing a crowd consisting mainly of students, men, women, children, and oldsters sitting on the ground, street vendors, housewives with babies in their arms, tenants of the housing unit, and spectators who had dropped by to watch out of curiosity, the usual idlers and bystanders who had merely come to "have a look." The mood of the crowd was calm despite the fact that the regular police, the Army, and the *granaderos* were out in full force. Men and women students were passing out handbills, collecting money in boxes labeled CNH, and selling newspapers and posters, and on the fourth floor, in addition to the Mexican reporters covering national events, there were foreign journalists and photographers who had come to Mexico to report on the Olympic Games that were scheduled to begin in ten days.

A number of students addressed the crowd: a young boy introduced the speakers, another student from UNAM announced, "The Movement will continue despite everything," and another from the IPN said, ". . . the consciousness of our Mexican family has been aroused and it has become politically aware"; a girl who I remember particularly because she was so young spoke of the role the brigades were playing. The speakers criticized the politicians and several newspapers, and proposed a boycott of the daily *El Sol*. The people up there on the fourth-floor balcony spied a group workers entering the Plaza carrying a banner that read: RAILWAY WORKERS SUPPORT THE MOVEMENT AND REJECT THE ROMERO FLORET-ORDAZ TALKS. This contingent of workers received an enthusiast round of applause. This group of railway workers then announced series of escalating strikes, beginning "tomorrow, October 3, in support of the Student Movement."

Just as a student named Vega was announcing that the scheduled march on the Santo Tomás campus of the IPN would not take place because the Army had been called out and there might be violence, flares suddenly appeared in the sky overhead and everyone automatically looked up. The first shots were heard then. The crowd panicked, and despite the fact that the leaders of the CNH up on the fourth-floor balcony of the Chihuahua building kept shouting into the microphone, "Don't run, all of you, don't run, they're just shooting in the air . . . . Stay right where you are, stay where you are, don't panic," the crowd started running in all directions. Everyone was terror-stricken, and many of them fell to the ground there in the Plaza, or leaped down into the pre-Hispanic ruins in front of the church of Santiago Tlatelolco. We could hear heavy rifle fire and the chatter of machine guns. From that moment on, the Plaza de las Tres Culturas was an inferno.

The report on the events at Tlatelolco that appeared in *Excélsior* the following day, October 3, stated, "No one could say precisely where the first shots came from, but the great majority of the demonstrators agreed that the Army troops suddenly began shooting without warning. . . . There were shots from all directions, from the top of a building in the housing unit and from the street, where the military forces fired round after round from the machine guns mounted on their light tanks and armored transports." *Novedades, El Universal, El Día, El Nacional, El Sol de México, El Heraldo, La Prensa, La Afición*, and *Ovaciones* all reported that the Army was forced to return the fire from sharpshooters stationed on the roofs the buildings. As proof of that statement, they mentioned the fact that General Jose Hernández Toledo, who was directing the operation, received a bullet wound in the chest and stated to reporters following the operation he subsequently underwent, "It's my opinion that if it was bloodshed they wanted, the blood I've shed is more than sufficient" (*El Día*, October 3, 1968). According to

Excélsior, "It is estimated that approximately 5000 Army troops, and many police security agents, the majority of whom were dressed in civilian clothes, were involved. All of the latter had white handkerchiefs wrapped around their right hands so that the others could identify them, for in order to protect themselves in case the students attacked, only a very few of them were wearing badges.

"The heavy gunfire lasted for twenty-nine minutes. Then the hail of bullets tapered off, though there were still sporadic bursts of gunfire."

The rifle fire came from many directions and machine-gun bullets whizzed all over the Plaza. As a number of journalists reported, it is quite likely that many of the police and the soldiers killed or wounded each other. "Many soldiers must have shot each other, since as they surrounded the crowd and closed in, bullets were flying in all directions," the journalist Félix Fuentes reports in his story in the October 3 issue of *La Prensa*. The army employed a pincers movement to take over the Plaza de las Tres Culturas, that is to say, the five thousand troops closed in from two directions, firing automatic weapons at the buildings, Fuentes adds. "On the fourth floor of one building, from which three speakers had delivered inflammatory speeches against the government, flashes from firearms were seen. Apparently the federal security agents and the Federal District police had opened fire on the crowd from up there.

"Many people tried to escape by way of the east side of the Plaza de las Tres Culturas, and a large number of them managed to get out, but hundreds of persons came face to face with columns of armed troops pointing their bayonets at them and shooting in all directions. Seeing that escape was impossible in that direction, many people in the crowd fled in terror and sought refuge inside the buildings, but others ran down the narrow little streets in the housing unit and eventually reached the Paseo de la Reforma near the Cuitláhuac Monument.

"This reporter was caught in the crowd near the Secretariat of Foreign Relations. A few steps away a woman fell to the ground–she had either been wounded or had fainted dead away. A couple of youngsters tried to go to her rescue, but the soldiers stopped them."

General José Hernández Toledo stated later that in order to avoid bloodshed he had given the Army troops orders not to use the heavy-caliber weapons they had been armed with (*El Día*, October 3, 1968). (General Hernández Toledo had previously been in command of Army troops occupying the University of Michoacán, the University of Sonora, and UNAM, and has under his command paratroopers who are considered to be the best-trained assault troops in the country.) Nonetheless Jorge Avilés, a reporter for *El Universal*, wrote in the October 3 issue of that daily, "We have now seen the Army troops in all-out action: using all sorts of armaments, including heavy-caliber machine guns mounted on twenty jeeps or more, they fired on all the areas controlled by the sharpshooters." And *Excélsior* added, "Some three hundred tanks, assault troops, jeeps and troop transports have surrounded the entire area, from Insurgentes to the Reforma, Nonoalco, and Manuel González. No one is being allowed to enter or leave this area, unless he can produce absolute proof of his identity" ("Terrible Gun Battle in Tlatelolco. The Number of Dead Not Yet Determined and Dozens Wounded," *Excélsior*, Thursday, October 3, 1968). Miguel Ángel Martínez Agis reported, "An Army captain was on the telephone, calling the Department of Defense, reporting on what was happening: 'We're fighting back with every weapon we have. . . .' We could see that the troops were armed with .45's and .38's, and 9-mm. pistols" ("Chihuahua Building, 6 p.m.," *Excélsior*, October 3, 1968).

> General Marcelino García Barragán, the Secretary of National Defense, stated, "When the Army approached the Plaza de las Tres Culturas it was met with rifle fire from sharpshooters. There was a general exchange of gunfire that lasted approximately one hour. . . .
> "There are both Army troops and students dead and wounded: at the moment, I can't say exactly how many there are."
> "Who in your opinion is the leader of this movement?"
> "I only wish we knew who was behind it."
> [This would seem to indicate that General Barragán had no proof that it was students who were to blame.]
> "Are there any wounded students in the Central Military Hospital?"
> "There are some in the Central Military Hospital, in the Green Cross Hospital, and in the Red Cross Hospital. They've all been placed under arrest and will be available for questioning by the Attorney General's office. We're also holding a number of them in Military Camp 1, where they will be available for questioning by General Cueto, the Chief of Police of the Federal District."
> "Who's in charge of the Army operations?"
> "I am."
> (Jesús M. Lozano, in a story entitled "Freedom Will Continue to Reign," *Excélsior*, October 3, 1968. The secretary of defense then provided an analysis of the situation.)

The Mexico City Chief of Police denied, however, that he had asked the Army to intervene in Tlatelolco, as the secretary of defense had previously reported. In a press conference early that morning, October 3, General Luis Cueto Ramírez made the following statement: "Police officials informed National Defense the moment they received reports that gunfire had been heard in the buildings next to the Secretariat of Foreign Relations and Vocational 7, where troops have been on duty around the clock." He explained that as far as he had thus far been able to determine, no foreign agents had been involved in the student disturbances which had been going on in the city since July. The majority of the arms confiscated by the police were manufactured in Europe and were the same models as are used in the socialist bloc, according to General Cueto. He also declared that he had no evidence that Mexican politicians were involved in the situation in any way, and that he knew of no United States citizens who had been arrested. "Among the prisoners, however, are one Guatemalan, one German, and another foreigner whose nationality I don't recall at the moment," he stated (*El Universal, El Nacional*, October 3, 1968).

No photographs of the dead bodies lying in the Plaza de las Tres Culturas were taken because the Army troops would not allow it (reported in a story with the heading "Many Killed and Wounded Last Night," *La Prensa*, October 3, 1968). On October 6, in a manifesto addressed "To the Mexican People," published in *El Día*, the CNH declared, "The final list of those killed and wounded in the Tlatelolco massacre has not yet been drawn up. Thus far we know of some 100 dead—those whose bodies were removed from the Plaza. There are thousands of wounded." That same day, October 6, the CNH announced that it would hold no more demonstrations or meetings, since the attack by the forces of repression "has caused the death of 150 civilians and 40 soldiers," In his book *The Other Mexico* Octavio Paz quotes the figure that the English daily paper *The Guardian* considered most likely, after "careful investigation": 325 dead.

It is quite certain that even today the precise death toll has not yet been determined. On October 3, the figures quoted in the headlines and news reports in the papers varied from twenty to twenty-eight. The number of wounded was much larger, and two thousand people were jailed. The shooting in the Tlatelolco area stopped around midnight. But the buildings in the housing unit were searched from top to bottom, and some thousand prisoners were taken to Military Camp 1. Around a thousand other persons arrested were taken to Santa Marta Acatitla Penitentiary, in Mexico City. The Tlatelolco area continued to be barricaded by Army troops. Many families abandoned their apartments, taking all their belongings with them, after having been subjected to a rigorous search and interrogation by the troops. Platoons of eleven soldiers each entered the buildings in the nearby suburbs to inspect every dwelling. Apparently they had orders to make a house-to-house search.

At present (early in 1971) those still imprisoned in Lecumberri number about 165.

We shall probably never know what motive lay behind the Tlatelolco massacre. Terror? Insecurity? Anger? Fear of losing face? Ill-will toward youngsters who deliberately misbehave in front of visitors? Together with Abel Quezada,[16] we may ask ourselves, WHY? Despite all the voices that have been raised, despite all the eyewitness testimony, the tragic night of Tlatelolco is still incomprehensible. Why? The story of what happened at Tlatelolco is puzzling and full of contradictions. The one fact that is certain is that many died. Not one of the accounts provides an over-all picture of what happened. All the people there in the Plaza—casual bystanders and active participants alike—were forced to take shelter from the gunfire; many fell wounded. In an article entitled "A Meeting That Ended in Tragedy," which appeared in the Mexico City *Diario de la Tarde* on October 5, 1968, reporter José Luis Mejías wrote, "The men in white gloves drew their pistols and began indiscriminately firing at close range on women, children, students, and riot police. . . . And at that same moment a helicopter gave the signal for the Army to close in by setting off a flare. . . . As the first shots were fired, General Hernández Toledo, the commander of the paratroopers, was wounded, and from that moment on, as the troops raked the crowd with a furious hail of bullets and pursued the sharpshooters as they fled inside the buildings, no one present was able to get an over-all picture of what was happening. . . ." But the tragedy of Tlatelolco damaged Mexico much more seriously than is indicated in a news story entitled "Bloody Encounter in Tlatelolco," which appeared in *El Heraldo* on October 3, 1968, lamenting the harm done the country's reputation. "A few minutes after the fighting started in the Nonoalco area, the foreign correspondents and the journalists who had come to our country to cover the Olympic Games began sending out news bulletins informing the entire world of what was happening. Their reports—which in a number of cases were quite exaggerated—contained remarks that seriously endangered Mexico's prestige," the story read.

The wound is still fresh, and Mexicans, though stunned by this cruel blow, are beginning to ask themselves questions in openmouthed amazement. The blood of hundreds of students, of men, women, children, soldiers, and oldsters tracked all over Tlatelolco has dried now. It has sunk once again into the quiet earth. Later, flowers will bloom among the ruins and the tombs.

Elena Poniatowska

We ran down one floor after another in the center wing of the Chihuahua building, and on one of them, I don't remember which one it was, I felt something sticky underfoot. I turned around and saw blood, lots of blood, and I said to my husband, "Just look at all this blood, Carlos! They must have killed lots of people here!" Then one of the corporals said to me, "It's obvious, *señora*, that you've never seen very much blood. You're making such a fuss over a few little drops of it!" But there was lots and lots of blood, so much of it that my hands felt sticky. There was also blood all over the walls; it seems to me that the walls of Tlatelolco are drenched with blood. It reeks of blood all over Tlatelolco. Lots of people must have bled to death up there, because there was much too much blood for it to have been that of just one person.

Margarita Nolasco, anthropologist

On October 2, Professor Leonardo Pérez González, a teacher at Vocational 7 and a member of the Coalition of Secondary and College Teachers for Democratic Freedoms, was shot to death in the Plaza de las Tres Culturas.

Abelardo Hurtado, professor at the National School of Biology, IPN

Yesterday, October 2, I was put in command of two sections of cavalry troops, numbering seventy-five men, all of whom were attached to the 18th and 19th Cavalry Regiment, and given orders to take these two sections to the Tlatelolco housing unit, with my men and myself dressed in civilian clothes but wearing a white glove so that the authorities would be able to identify us, and upon arriving there we were to guard the two entrances to the Chihuahua building in the aforementioned housing unit and mingle with the crowd that had gathered there for unspecified reasons. Immediately upon sighting a flare in the sky, the prearranged signal, we were to seal off the aforementioned two entrances and prevent anyone from entering or leaving.

Ernesto Morales Soto, Captain, First Class, 19th Cavalry Regiment,
attached to the Olimpia Battalion, under the command of Colonel
Ernesto Gómez Tagle, in an official notarized statement,
no. 54832168, filed in the office of the Public Prosecutor

They're dead bodies, sir. . . .

A soldier, to José Antonio del Campo, reporter for El Día

The dead bodies were lying there on the pavement, waiting to be taken away. I counted lots and lots of them from the window, about seventy-eight in all. They were piling them up there in the rain. . . . I remembered that Carlitos, my son, had been wearing a green corduroy jacket, and I thought I recognized his dead body every time they dragged another one up. . . . I'll never forget one poor youngster, about sixteen or so, who crawled around the corner of the building, stuck his deathly pale face out, and made a V-for-Victory sign with two fingers. He didn't seem to have the least idea what was happening: he may have thought the men shooting were also students. Then the men in the white gloves yelled at him, "Get the hell out of here, you dumb bastard! Can't you see what's happening? Clear out of here!" The kid got to his feet and started walking toward them, as though he didn't have a care in the world. They fired a couple of shots at his feet, but the kid kept right on coming. He obviously didn't have the slightest idea what was going on, and they shot him in the calf of his leg. All I remember is that the blood didn't immediately spurt out; it just started slowly trickling down his leg. Meche and I started screaming at the guys with the white gloves like a couple of madwomen: "Don't kill him! Don't kill him! Don't kill him!" We ran to the door, but the kid had disappeared. I have no idea whether he managed to escape despite his wound, whether they killed him, or what happened to him.

Margarita Nolasco, anthropologist

They started firing from the helicopter, and I began to hear rifle reports overhead. Those idiots were shooting like crazy. That's why the Chihuahua building caught fire, because of the shots from the helicopter.

Estrella Sámano, student

The Plaza de las Tres Culturas is an esplanade quite a bit higher than street level, with several flights of steps leading up to it, and on one side it drops off sharply, giving visitors a good view of the recently restored pre-Hispanic ruins down below. A little church—Santiago de Tlatelolco—was built above these ruins in the sixteenth century.

Luis González de Alba, of the CNH

From the speakers' platform where we were standing, we could see the blue caps of the railway workers below us.

Graciela Román Olvera, student at the Faculty of Medicine, UNAM

I was handing out leaflets and collecting money for the CNH when the three green flares suddenly appeared in the sky behind the church. A lady who was searching in her purse for change to give me started looking for a place to take cover. "Don't panic, they're just trying to scare us a little, don't panic," I said to her. Several people ran past me and I shouted to them, "Don't run, you're in no danger, they're just firing in the air, don't run." Suddenly one of the Movement people ran by and I called to him, "Where are you going? We have to calm the crowd down so they won't panic and start running." But he turned on his heel like a robot and headed for the middle of the Plaza. When I realized after a while that he hadn't come back, 1 thought to myself, I wonder what the hell's happening; he hasn't come back.

José Ramiro Muñoz, engineering student at ESIME, IPN

When I realized that the helicopter had come down dangerously low, circling right above the heads of the crowd in the Plaza de las Tres Culturas and firing on everybody—we could see the gray streaks of tracer bullets in the sky—I was so dumfounded I said to myself, I can't believe it—it's like in a movie! I've never seen anything like this except in the movies. Those just can't be real bullets! I wandered around in a daze, as though I'd gone out of my mind, until finally somebody grabbed me by the arm and stopped me.

Elvira B. de Concheiro, mother of a family

Ever since then, whenever I see a helicopter, my hands start trembling. For many months after I'd seen that helicopter fire on the crowd like that—as I was sitting there in my car—I couldn't write, my hands trembled so.

Marta Zamora Vértiz, secretary

Two helicopters overhead patrolling the student meeting descended and the crews inside started firing on the sharpshooters stationed on the roofs of the buildings.

It has been reported that the co-pilot of one of the helicopters received a bullet wound in the arm when a sharpshooter fired at him repeatedly from the Chihuahua building. The helicopter then took off immediately in the direction of the International Airport.

News story entitled "Many Killed and Wounded
Last Night," La Prensa, October 3, 1968

The helicopter had come down so close that I would be able to identify the man who was firing on the crowd from inside it.

Ema Bermejillo de Castellanos, mother of a family

When the shooting began, people immediately headed for the stairs at the front of the Chihuahua building, shouting, "The Committee, the Committee!" Their one thought was to defend their leaders. Then the units of secret agents posted around the building began shooting at the crowd, driving them off with a hail of bullets.

Raúl Álvarez Garín, of the CNH

I couldn't understand why the crowd kept heading back toward where the men in the white gloves were shooting at them. Meche and I hid there behind a pillar watching the crowd coming toward us, shouting and moaning, being fired on, running away in the opposite direction, and then immediately coming back our way again, falling to the ground, running away again, and then coming back and falling to the ground again. The whole thing just didn't make sense: whatever were they doing? A whole great crowd was running first in one direction and then another: they'd run away and then head back our way again, and more of them would fall on the ground. I thought they should all have sense enough to keep away from the men who were shooting at them, but they kept coming back. I found out later that they were also being shot at from the other side of the Plaza.

Margarita Nolasco, anthropologist

The Army units approached from all directions and encircled the crowd in a pincers movement, and in just a few moments all the exits were blocked off. From up there on the fourth floor of the Chihuahua building, where the speakers' platform had been set up, we couldn't see what the Army was up to and we couldn't understand why the crowd was panicking. The two helicopters that had been hovering over the Plaza almost from the very beginning of the meeting had suddenly started making very hostile maneuvers, flying lower and lower in tighter and tighter circles just above the heads of the crowd, and then they had launched two flares, a green one first and then a red one; when the second one went off the panic started, and we members of the Committee did our best to stop it: none of us there on the speakers' stand could see that the Army troops below us were advancing across the Plaza. When they found themselves confronted by a wall of bayonets, the crowd halted and immediately drew back; then we saw a great wave of people start running toward the other side of the Plaza; but there were Army troops on the other side of the Plaza too; and as we stood watching from up there on the speakers' stand, we saw the whole crowd head in another direction. That was the last thing we saw down below, for at that moment the fourth floor was taken over by the Olimpia Battalion. Even though we had no idea why the crowd had panicked and was running first in one direction and then in the other, those of us who had remained there at the microphone till the very last found ourselves looking down the barrels of machine guns when we turned around. The balcony had been occupied by the Olimpia Battalion and we were ordered to put our hands up and face the wall, and given strict orders not to turn around in the direction of the Plaza; if we so much as moved a muscle, they hit us over the head or in the ribs with their rifle butts. Once the trap they had set snapped shut, the collective murder began.

Gilberto Guevara Niebla, of the CNH

NOTARIZED DEPOSITION, NO. 54832/68

DEPOSITION BY ONE OF THE WOUNDED—MEXICO CITY, D. F. *At nine-thirty p.m. (21:30) on October 3, 1968 (nineteen hundred sixty-eight), the undersigned, in pursuit of his official duties, legally entered the Emergency Ward of the Central Military Hospital and recorded the statement of the patient in Bed 28 (twenty-eight). After being duly informed of his rights, as provided by law, the said patient declared that his name was* ERNESTO MORALES SOTO, *that he was 35 (thirty-five) years of age, a widower, a Catholic, with an education, a Captain of Cavalry, First Class, in the Mexican Army, born in Xicotepec de Juárez in the State of Puebla, residing in this City in Military Camp Number* ONE. *With regard to the events currently under investigation, the deponent* DECLARED: *That he holds a commission as a Cavalry Captain, First Class, in the 19th Regiment, stationed in the City of Múzquiz, in the State of Coahuila, and at the present time is attached to the Olimpia Battalion in this City, under the command of Colonel* ERNESTO GÓMEZ TAGLE, *which has been assigned the special duty of preserving public order during the Olympic Games; that yesterday he was placed in command of two sections of Cavalry, numbering 65 (sixty-five) men, attached to the 18th and 19th Cavalry Regiments, and ordered to proceed to the Tlatelolco housing unit with his men, all of whom were to be dressed in civilian clothes and wear a white glove so that the authorities would be able to identify them, and upon arriving there they were to guard the two entrances to the Chihuahua building of the aforementioned housing unit and mingle with the crowd that had gathered there for unspecified reasons; that immediately upon sighting a flare in the sky, the prearranged signal, his unit was to station itself at both entrances and prevent anyone from entering or leaving; that after the aforementioned flare was set off, they began to hear a great many shots being fired, both from the top of the aforementioned building and from the windows, aimed at the crowd of people gathered below, who attempted to protect themselves by hugging the walls of the building; that a number of people in the crowd attempted to enter the building, whereupon the unit under the command of the deponent, in accordance with the orders they had received, fired in the air to disperse the crowd, these events having occurred at approximately four-forty p.m. (16:40 hours); that one of the shots from the top of the building wounded the deponent in the right arm, whereupon one of his men notified his superior, who ordered the deponent transferred to the Hospital, where he is at present a patient; that upon being wounded, he lost consciousness and therefore does not know what happened subsequently, and that owing to the fact that he is not familiar with that particular area of the city, he is unable to state precisely what streets the entrances to the Chihuahua building are located on, and does not know who the persons were who fired the shots or how many persons were wounded; that for the present this is the sole testimony that lie has to offer. After reading the above deposition, the deponent attested to it by stamping it with his right thumbprint, since the wound in his arm made it impossible for him to sign his name.*

STATEMENT ATTESTING TO WOUNDS INCURRED—The undersigned, in pursuit of his official duties, visited Bed 28 in the Emergency Ward of the Central Military Hospital, where he personally examined the patient occupying said bed, who declared that his name was ERNESTO MORALES SOTO, and in witness whereof the undersigned states: that the said SOTO has the following wounds: a jagged bullet wound on the anterior surface of his right elbow, measuring one centimeter in diameter, and a second wound where the bullet exited, presenting the same characteristics and measuring two centimeters in diameter, on the posterior surface of the elbow, indicating a probable fracture. —Wounds of such a nature as not to endanger the life of the victim and requiring more than two weeks to heal. —Case covered by PART TWO of Article 289 of the Penal Code presently in effect. —Hospitalization not required. —The same wounds attested to and described in the certificate signed by Dr. ALFREDO NEME DAVID, the original of which has been examined and annexed to the present statement. . . . HEREWITH ATTESTED TO:

GERMÁN VALDEZ MARTÍNEZ, *Attorney*
Official Notary, Office of the Public Prosecutor

ALBERTO LÓPEZ ISLAS
LÁZARO RODRÍGUEZ MORALES
Witnesses

A heavier rain of bullets than any of the ones before began then, and went on and on. This was genocide, in the most absolute, the most tragic meaning of that word. Sixty-two minutes of round after round of gunfire, until the soldiers' weapons were so red-hot they could no longer hold them.

Leonardo Femat, in an article "A Tape Recording That Tells the Whole Story," Siempre!, no. 79 (The Night of Tlatelolco), October 16, 1968

I left the University with a group of comrades. We arrived at the Plaza de las Tres Culturas, and it started to rain. We all assembled in our various groups, and I was carrying a banner that read, THE LAW SCHOOL REPRESENTED HERE TODAY. There were other banners, one for instance that said, "The blood of our brothers will not have been shed in vain." I was sitting on the steps in front of the Chihuahua building when suddenly I saw the flares go off, and a few seconds later I heard what I found out later were machine guns firing on the crowd. Our comrade on the speakers' stand shouted, "Don't move, anybody! Keep calm! Sit down!" So I sat down, holding onto my banner. I had no idea what was happening, or rather, I didn't realize how serious the situation was, so 1 just sat there clutching my banner till a comrade shouted to me, "Get rid of that thing!" because I was a perfect target sitting there with my banner. I threw it down and started running with Tita. We ran to where the flags were flying, the flagpoles in the Plaza de las Tres Culturas, over to one side of Vocational 7, and Tita and I tried to get under cover. Then I heard a girl begging for help: "Oh, God, please help me!" I also heard voices shouting things like "My purse, my purse, where's my purse?" At one point we leaped over those pre-Hispanic walls there and fell into a sort of ditch. I lay there on the ground, and other people started falling on top of me. We heard shouts and groans and cries of pain, and I realized then that the gunfire was getting heavier and heavier. Tita and I crawled out of there and ran toward the Calle Manuel González, and the soldiers yelled to us, "Get thc hell out as fast as you can!" As we ran out of the Plaza, a white Volkswagen full of students drove by, and they shouted to us, "Come on! Climb in!" I can't remember if they called us by name: "Come on, Nacha, Tita, get in!" and one of the funny things about the whole bit is that I don't remember how we managed to pile into that car that was already crammed full of a whole bunch of students. We lit out down the Paseo de la Reforma to the Avenida de la República de Cuba, and then Tita climbed out because everybody knew her by sight and she would have been recognized instantly. We all said as much. "You're so big they'd spot you half a mile away," we told her. I went back in that same car with two Movement people from Theoretical Physics at Poli—I don't know who they were—to see if we could find a couple of comrades we had no idea what had happened to. The boys stopped the car somewhere near the Secretariat of Foreign Relations—I don't know the name of the street because I'm not from Mexico City, I'm from Taxco, in the state of Guerrero. They got out and said to me, "Stay here in the car," and I staved there in the car waiting for them all by myself, but as the minutes ticked by, I got more and more nervous; the shooting still hadn't stopped, it was worse in fact, and ambulances were drawing up with their sirens screeching, more and more soldiers were going by, tanks and convoys of troops armed to the teeth. An ambulance drew up right in front of me, and the attendants put a student in it: his head was all bloody; he was dripping blood from head to foot. I was sitting there in the car no more than ten or twelve feet away, and seeing that student in that shape turned my stomach. Then a whole bunch of people ran by shouting, "They've set fire to the Chihuahua building!" I looked up and saw smoke. A high-tension wire fell down then, and everyone running past that Volkswagen I was in was screaming. I was suddenly frightened and scrambled out of the car in a panic and started running. I must have run for a much longer time than I realized, because I suddenly found myself at Sanborn's, on Lafragua. An acquaintance of mine stopped me there on the street. "What's the matter?" he asked me. 1 realized then that I'd been crying and my mascara was running down my cheeks. I felt as though I didn't have one ounce of strength left—I was really in terrible shape. Some kids went into Sanborn's and brought me out some coffee because I was trembling so. "Take it easy, take it easy," they kept saying. Then some more kids came to the door. The only thing I could blurt out was, "They're killing the students!" These same kids then took me to an apartment on the Avenida de Coyoacán, where I was living with Tita and another girl friend.

Ana Ignacio Rodríguez (Nacha), of the Action Committee, UNAM

It never occurred to us that the government might attack us on October 2, because a few days before there had been a meeting at Tlatelolco and in the morning several members of the CNH—the ones who had the most sense and the most savvy, though I never mention names, you know—went to the Casa del Lago to talk with Caso and de la Vega, and we thought that a sort of tacit truce had been arranged, since it looked as though the government was about to reach an agreement with the students. So we scheduled another meeting, but at the same time we decided to cancel the march on the Santo Tomás campus, which had been occupied by Army troops, so we wouldn't be accused of stirring up more trouble. This was announced from the speakers' stand almost immediately after the meeting began. . . . No, I wasn't on the speakers' stand; I stayed down below on the esplanade with Nacha. . . . But then they started shooting—and got their own asses shot off.

Roberta Avendaño Martínez (Tita), CNH delegate from UNAM

There was lots of blood underfoot, lots of blood smeared on the walls.

Francisco Correa, physicist, and professor at IPN

I put my hands over the back of my neck to protect it, with my cheek and my belly and my legs pressing against the floor of the room. I was one of the ones closest to the door of the apartment, almost right next to it. The reports of all sorts of firearms frightened me, and I asked my comrades there in the room to move over and let me share the minimum shelter offered by the partition dividing off the front part of the apartment where we were.

I heard people outside shouting, "We're from the Olimpia Battalion, don't shoot, we're from the Olimpia Battalion!"

My comrades lying there on the floor moved over and I managed to crawl over to the partition. I lay there for some time—I don't know how long exactly—and I kept thinking, The dirty sons of bitches, the filthy murdering bastards.

None of us said much, except once in a while a couple of swear words of the same sort that had been running through my mind broke the impressive "silence" where all we could hear was bullets whizzing all around us. I'd also lost my glasses.

I heard a sob from time to time from one or another of my men or women comrades, and 1 remember hearing someone say (or perhaps I only imagined it), "Don't cry, this is no time to cry, to shed tears: this is the time to engrave what's happening in letters of fire in our very heart of hearts so we'll remember it when it comes time to settle the score with the people responsible for this." Maybe I dreamed it.

At one point the shooting died down a little, and we made our way on our hands and knees into two other rooms in the back of the apartment. As I crawled back there, I saw several of my comrades from the CNH: all of them had a very odd expression on their faces. It wasn't terror, or even fear; it was a gleam of intense hatred in their eyes, plus a look of pain at being so completely helpless.

We all crawled into one little bedroom, and a few seconds later there was another heavy burst of gunfire. We lay down on the floor again, but it was covered with a film of water, and our clothes got soaked. It turned cold as night fell. Amid the continuous burst of rifle fire, we suddenly heard even louder rounds of gunfire, and immediately afterward it began to pour. We were even more concerned at that point, because the building had started swaying when this very loud gunfire began. It could all be summed up in two words: "A tank."

Eduardo Valle Espinoza (Owl-Eyes), of the CNH

Am I losing much blood?

Pablo Berlanga, to his mother, Rafaela Cosme de Berlanga

There was nothing we could do but keep running. They were firing at us from all directions. We ran six or eight feet, keeping under cover, and then ten or twelve feet out in the open. Rifle fire sounds very much like a jet taking off. There was nothing to do but keep running. We heard the display windows of the shops on the ground floor of the Chihuahua building shatter, and we suddenly decided we ought to make a run for the stairway. As I stood down there, babbling all sorts of nonsense, I also suddenly remembered all my many friends and comrades at the meeting and got terrible cramps in my stomach. I remembered names, faces. As I reached this stairway that the people from the CNH who were going to speak had been going up and down all during the afternoon, I met Margarita and Meche, who said to me in the most despairing tone of voice, "María Alicia, our children are up there on the fourth floor!"

For the first time I had the feeling I might be able to do something useful amid all this confusion and suffering, despite my sense of utter helplessness, and I said to them, "I'll go up there with you."

The youngster who had saved my life—by leaping on me and throwing me to the floor there on the speakers' stand when they first started shooting at us—went upstairs with us: he was my armor, my cape, my shield. I have no idea who he was. I have a photographic memory, but I can't remember his face at all. . . . The three of us started up the stairs, and on the first landing we met another youngster. I had seen him on the speakers' stand there on the fourth floor of the Chihuahua building, too, talking with various Movement people as though he knew them very well. I remember him particularly because he'd apparently been wounded in the right wrist and had a white handkerchief wrapped around his hand.

"Don't leave, *señora*, it'll all be over soon," he said to me.

I was about to go downstairs again, because I'd spied some girl friends of mine down on the esplanade. But the boy took me by the arm and very solicitously helped me up the stairs. I was touched by this courageous behavior on the part of yet another student hero, and went upstairs with him.

Then Mercedes shouted, "*Señor*, my children are there upstairs!"

Margarita shouted that her children were up there too, and I stopped there on the stairs and looked at the youngster escorting me, thinking that the courage of those kids is really incredible sometimes. Many hours later, I discovered that my escort was one of the assassins guarding the stairway so that none of the CNH people would escape. He took us back downstairs then, and I remember that we were caught up in a whole crowd of people and shoved to the corner of the Chihuahua building, and that meanwhile there was a steady hail of bullets from the buildings.

A girl came by shouting, "You murderers, you murderers!" I took her in my arms and tried to calm her down, but she kept screaming, louder and louder, until finally the youngster behind me grabbed hold of her and started shaking her. I noticed then that her ear had been shot off and her head was bleeding. The people in the crowd kept piling one on top of another, seeking shelter from the rain of bullets; we were all right on each other's necks, and I felt as though I were caught in the middle of a riot or squeezed in a sardine can.

I stood there staring at the tips of the coffee-colored shoes of some woman. Several rounds of machine-gun bullets suddenly raked the spot where we were standing, and I saw one bullet land just a few inches from that woman's shoe. All she said was, "Oh, my goodness!" and another voice answered, "Make a run for it. If you stay here you'll be even worse off; you're sure to get hurt here." We all started running again and just then I spied a red Datsun with a young girl at the wheel. She'd been shot, and I saw her collapse on top of the steering wheel; the horn kept blowing and blowing. . . . The youngster kept saying, "Don't look, don't look." We ran on toward one of the buildings behind Chihuahua.

María Alicia Martínez Medrano, nursery-school director

Then I heard voices shouting things like "We're wearing white gloves, don't shoot, don't shoot!" And then other voices shouting, "We need a walkie-talkie here, don't shoot us, contact us by walkie-talkie!" There were desperate cries, coming either from down below us on the third floor, or from up above on the fifth or sixth floor: "Olimpia Battalion!" And then I heard whistles blowing. . . . "Olimpia Battalion, line up over here! . . ." And then all I heard was "The eighth and the fourteenth . . ." "The eighth . . . are you all here?" "The fourteenth . . . how many are missing in the fourteenth?" Then voices shouted, "Have the ones from the elevator turned up?" and then more whistles blowing: "Olimpia Battalion, Olimpia Battalion, over here, all of you! Olimpia Battalion, answer!" There were desperate shouts from the police for a long time: "Don't shoot! . . . They're wearing white gloves!" This will give you some idea of how absolutely chaotic the whole affair was, on one hand, and also how it took on proportions that the organizers hadn't expected and got completely out of control. I can assure you that the whole thing was obviously planned in advance; the authorities knew exactly what they were up to. They were trying to prevent any sort of demonstration or student disturbance before the Olympics and during the games. The flares were the signal to start shooting, and they began firing from all directions at once. As for the supposed "sharpshooters," I can assure you—because those of us who were there saw it with our own eyes and know it's true beyond the shadow of a doubt—that the sharpshooters were agents playing their part in the government's plan.

Mercedes Olivera de Vázquez, anthropologist

The authorities said, "Stop all this, right now." They hadn't counted on the fact that the *granaderos*, the soldiers, the security agents would act entirely on their own initiative—they've always had a mind of their own.

Roberta Ruiz García, grade-school teacher

One agent got scared stiff and started shooting. That's what started the whole thing.

Luis Argüelles Peralta, geology student at ESIME, IPN

Hundreds of persons on the fourth floor of the Chihuahua building saw that after arresting the people they had found up there, the plainclothesmen wearing white gloves began firing on the crowd attending the meeting and also on the troops that were moving forward. Immediately thereafter, as the soldiers answered their fire, the agents in civilian clothes took cover behind the cement balustrade, their guns still aimed at the prisoners, who continued to stand there with their hands up, directly in the line of fire. The first shots the soldiers fired landed on the roof, but as the troops moved forward across the Plaza they began aiming lower and bits of plaster started falling off the wall. Then the agents ordered the prisoners to lie down, and as a hail of bullets struck the Chihuahua building, the men in the white gloves, a number of whom had shouted that they were from the Olimpia Battalion, began yelling in chorus to make themselves heard over the heavy gunfire: "We're the Olimpia Battalion, don't shoot!" As the rifle fire grew heavier and heavier and the high-power machine guns mounted on the tanks began to chatter, the men in the white gloves started desperately searching about for a walkie-talkie. One of them, apparently the leader of the battalion, ordered the others to stop shooting. Shouts of "Stop shooting, let's get a walkie-talkie!" were heard. Amid all the shooting they had recognized the burst of small bombs being launched from the tanks to clear openings in the walls for the troops to shoot through. The men with a white glove or a white handkerchief on their left hand kept crawling by, very cautiously, on their hands and knees. Apparently they had no way of communicating with the troops that were firing on everyone in the Plaza. We were surprised it was taking them so long to kill all of us.

Félix Lucio Hernández Gamundi, of the CNH

We lost sight of Reyes and I heard a shout from my brother: "Don't let go of my hand." We clutched each other's hand and headed toward the right, trying to reach the park with the ruins. There were lots of people down there, trying to find cover from the terrible hail of bullets coming from all directions. We could hear shells exploding over all the other noise; the ruins were being shattered by the bullets, and bits of stone started raining down on our heads. I was still clutching my brother's hand, despite the fact that there were other people between us, and I tried to pull him closer to me. Some students were lying there on the ground between us, some of them dead and others wounded. There was a girl right next to me who had been hit square in the face with a dum-dum bullet. It was ghastly! The entire left side of her face had been blown away.

The shouts, the cries of pain, the weeping, the prayers and supplications, and the continuous deafening sound of gunfire made the Plaza de las Tres Culturas a scene straight out of Dante's *Inferno*.

Diana Salmerón de Contreras

"A doctor, please, I beg you, in the name of everything you hold most dear, get me a doctor!"

Olga Sánchez Cuevas, mother of a family

They wouldn't even let the Red and Green Cross ambulances through! They pulled up with their sirens screeching. They were told to turn off their sirens and their lights.

Berta Cárdenas de Macías, tenant in the Tlatelolco housing unit

I warned all of them that the Plaza was a trap—I told them. There's no way out of it, I warned them. But they thought they knew it all. I told them they would have no way of getting out of the Plaza, that we'd be surrounded there, boxed in, like cattle in a corral. I kept telling them that, but they paid no attention.

Mercedes Olivera de Vázquez, anthropologist

I love love.

Hippie button found in the Plaza de las Tres Culturas

I tugged at my brother's arm. "Julio, what's the matter?" I asked him. I tugged at his arm again; his eyes were half closed and there was a very sad look in them. And I heard him murmur the words "I think . . ."

My mind was a total blank. The tremendous crush of people screaming in panic made it hard for me to hear what he was saying. I thought later that if I'd known, if I'd realized that Julio was dying, I would have done something absolutely crazy right then and there.

Later some of the soldiers who had been shooting at the buildings around the Plaza came over to us. The smell of gunpowder was unbearable. Little by little people made room for me so I could kneel down beside Julio.

"Julio, Julio, answer me, little brother," I said to him.

"He must be wounded," one woman said to me. "Loosen his belt."

When I loosened it, I could feel a great big wound. I found out later at the hospital that he had three bullet wounds: one in the stomach, one in the neck, and another in the leg. He was dying.

Diana Salmerón de Contreras

NOTES

1. Instituto Politécnico Nacional (The National Polytechnical Institute [IPN], Mexico City).

2. Escuela Superior de Físico-Matemáticas (School of Theoretical Physics at the IPN).

3. Consejo Nacional de Huelga (National Strike Committee).

4. The riot police.

5. Instituto Nacional de Bellas Artes (the National Institute of Fine Arts).

6. Demetrio Vallejo, leader of the railway union, imprisoned from 1959 to 1970 for leading an illegal strike. (Translator's note.)

7. Universidad Nacional Autónoma de Mexico (Autonomous National University of México).

8. Escuela Superior de Ingeniería Mecánica y Eléctrica (School of Mechanical and Electrical Engineering).

9. Partido Revolucionario Institucional (Institutional Revolutionary Party, the official Mexican government party).

10. University high school.

11. Members of the Communist Party (PC) are often called this in Mexico because "los PCes" is pronounced the same as "los peces," the fish. (Translator's note.)

12. "Professional students," who spend years at the University without getting a degree—often political agitators. (Translator's note.)

13. Writer of sentimental Mexican popular songs. (Translator's note.)

14. Vocational high school.

15. The Mexico City Chief of Police.

16. A famous Mexican editorial cartoonist, who after Tlatelolco drew a now celebrated cartoon in *Excélsior* with the caption WHY? (Translator's note.)

2

I, Rigoberta Menchú: An Indian Woman in Guatemala (1983)

Rigoberta Menchú

Rigoberta Menchú (b. Guatemala, 1959) is a Quiché-Maya advocate of indigenous and women's rights, and ethnocultural reconciliation. In 1991, she participated in the preparation of the United Nations declaration of the rights of indigenous people. She received the 1992 Nobel Peace Prize and the 1998 Prince of Asturias Award of International Cooperation, and she is a UNESCO Goodwill Ambassador. Recently she became president of the company Salud para Todos (Health for All) to provide low cost medicines to poor Guatemalans and has announced her candidacy for the 2007 Guatemalan presidential elections. This selection traces Menchu's personal development and emergence as a young woman activist within a process of organizing of indigenous communities in Guatemala.

SELF-DEFENCE IN THE VILLAGE

"They began to fulfill the destiny which was concealed in the marrow of their bones. . . . "

—Popol Vuh

My time working as a maid, my long stay in the *finca* without going home, and my parents' problems, made me very confused. Yes, I was very confused. I went through a sort of painful change within myself. It wasn't so difficult for the rest of them at home to understand what was real and what was false. But I found it very hard. What did exploitation mean to me? I began to see why conditions are so different. Why do they reject us? Why is the Indian not accepted? Why was it that the land used to belong to us? Used our ancestors to live here? Why don't outsiders accept Indian ways? This is where discrimination lies! Catholic Action too submitted us to tremendous oppression. It kept our people dormant while others took advantage of our passivity. I finally began to see all this clearly. And that's when I started working as an organiser. No-one taught me how to organise because, having been a catechist, I already knew. We began forming groups of women who wanted to join the struggle. And I saw that teaching the children how to act when the enemy came was part of the struggle too. The moment I learned to identify our enemies was very important for me. For me now the landowner was a big enemy, an evil one. The soldier too was a criminal enemy. And so were all the rich. We began using the term "enemies," because we didn't have the notion of enemy in our culture, until those people arrived to exploit us, oppress us and discriminate against us. In our community we are all equal. We all have to help one another and share the little we have between us. There is no superior and inferior. But we realized that in Guatemala there was something superior and something inferior and that *we* were the inferior. The *ladinos* behave like a superior race. Apparently there was a time when the *ladinos* used to think we weren't people at all, but a sort of animal. All this became clear to me.

I threw myself into my work and I told myself we had to defeat the enemy. We began to organise. Our organisation had no name. We began by each of us trying to remember the tricks our ancestors used. They say they used to set traps in their houses, in the path of the *conquistadores*, the Spaniards. Our ancestors were good fighters, they were real men. It's not true what white people say, that our ancestors didn't defend themselves. They used ambushes. Our grandparents used to tell us about it, especially my grandfather when he saw that we were beginning to talk about defending ourselves against the landowners, and wondering if we had to rid ourselves of the landowners before we'd be left in peace. We said: "If they threaten us, why don't we threaten the landowner?" My grandfather gave us a lot of support. There was always a lot of discussion in our house, because my brothers reached their own conclusions, I reached mine, and everyone came to their own conclusions. My grandfather said: "Yes, my children, you have to defend yourselves. Our ancestors defended themselves. The white men are telling lies when they say we are passive. They fought too. And we, why don't we fight with the same arms the landowners use?" If an elderly person tells us this, then it must be true.

The first step the community took was to have my father, the village leader, living in the centre of the community. Everyone felt my father should live in the centre. When Kjell Laugerud divided our small pieces of land into plots, some people had to go and live on one side of the village, some on the other, in different plots. So we were some way away from our neighbours. What my brothers and I decided (my father happened to be with us at the time too) was that we would share the piece of land we had on the flat ground, on the plain. All the members of the community who lived some way off could come down and we'd live together, or with our houses close together so that we could call to each other when the landowners' people came. This was the first step we took. But what were we going to tell people? They knew we had to defend ourselves against the landowners, but they didn't understand that one day the repression would reach us and large numbers of us would be killed. We held a meeting and discussed it with everybody. We talked about sharing out the piece of land behind our house so that our neighbours could live closer. We also asked other neighbours to share their land too. We said that in two months we could have all our neighbours' houses near ours. This proposition was put to the community: "Are you willing to leave your houses and live near us so that when the landowners come, we'll all be together?"

We were making these plans when a village near ours got a taste of the repression. The repression reached San Pablo, a village nearby. They kidnapped the community's leaders—the elected representatives, the chief catechist, and their families. They took away some other catechists too. Men, women and children were taken. They too were fighting a landowner, but they weren't organised yet. This served as an example for us, and my brothers and I, and our neighbours began dividing up the work to be done. Everyone went to cut palm leaves to build the new houses. Some prepared the ground for the houses, others collected leaves, and others cut poles for the walls. We shared the work out. We built the houses close together.

And one day a troop of soldiers arrived. It was the first time we'd seen so many troops in the village; there were ninety of them. We couldn't resist but we did nothing to provoke them either. The community knew more or less what to do if any one of us was taken. The idea from the beginning was that they either left us alone or they'd have to kill all of us. We wouldn't let a single *compañero* be taken away from the village. That's what we did. The soldiers stayed for two weeks and used the community house where we carried out all our ceremonies, and held our meetings. They lived there. At night they went into our maize fields to dig up our potatoes, cut off the maize cobs and young beans, and ate very well. They cut any cobs they wanted. For us this was violating our culture, because we Indians have to perform a ceremony before picking the cob, the fruit of the earth and of the peasants' labour. We were very angry but we didn't show our anger because there were ninety of them, capable of massacring us all. They were armed.

One night around ten o'clock, we were getting ready to go to sleep when my mother saw something black moving around at the back of our house, where we have a little patch of potatoes. She thought it was one of our neighbour's animals and began throwing sticks at it. It was a soldier stealing potatoes. That was the first time my mother got aggressive with any of the soldiers; without a thought to whether she'd be killed or not. She had all our dogs with her. We had a lot of dogs then because all our neighbours had decided to buy another dog each to defend themselves with. So my mother went out with her dogs and her sticks. The soldier said: "No, no, don't, I'm a person." And my mother said: "If you want to eat, why don't you go and work? You're protecting the rich and they don't even feed you. Here we've worked hard for our crops, young man. Leave my things alone or I'll beat you with this stick." So the soldier left the potatoes and went running off in a hurry. The next day they left. They went away.

After they left, the village got together to decide what to do with our maize fields. We would forget our customs, our ceremonies, for a while, and plan our security first. Afterwards we'd go back to the things we want to do. The community decided: "No one must discover our community's secret now, *compañeros*. It's secret what we are doing here. The enemy must not know, nor must our other neighbours." Everyone agreed. We began teaching our children to be discreet. They're usually discreet anyway, but we advised them not to say a single word to any children who weren't from our village about what their parents were doing. We prepared our signals. Our signals were to be all the everyday things we use, all natural things. I remember that we performed a ceremony before beginning our self-defence measures. It was a village ceremony where we asked the Lord of the natural world, our one God, to help us and give us permission to use his creations of nature to defend ourselves with. The ceremony was conducted with a lot of feeling, because, well, we knew that it was up to the community, up to our measures of self-defence, whether two, three, four, or five of our members would be kidnapped, tortured or murdered. The following day everyone came with ideas of how to defend themselves. Some brought stones, others machetes, others sticks, others their work tools. The women brought salt, hot water, etc. We put all our ideas together. How would we use them? One *compañero* would say: "I think that this is useful for defence. How can we use it?" Another would say: "This is what I have in mind. . . ." And he explains what *he* would do if they came. Each person contributed something. Then we organised very carefully who would plan the best ways to use the community's ideas and who would teach them. How would we teach the children? Which duties would the children have? Who would be in charge of seeing that the women played their special part? When would we hold a general assembly to evaluate all this? We began to get a much better idea of how to organise our community.

I was enthralled by all this. As I said before, when the government parcelled the land out and tried to create divisions within the community—everyone with their own plot, their own bit of land—there wasn't enough land for us all to live in one place together. They gave us plots which were very separate, a long way from each other, and many neighbours lived quite a distance away, and the houses were very far apart. We lived like this with the land divided up for about two or three years. They used this method to separate us but the little plots of land weren't big enough to work. We had barely a *manzana* of land each. It was all divided up. What all the neighbours did was to give some of their land to the community as a whole, but even so our houses were still very far apart. So when the repression started coming closer, we realized we had to put our houses together to confront the soldiers when they came to repress our village. It wasn't only the villages nearest to us which had been attacked, there'd been massacres in other communities too. Chajul, Bebaj, Cotzal, were the first to suffer the repression.

We had to build houses for our neighbours between us, and it took about two or three months before everyone was living together. We did it so as to make our self-defence measures more effective. When they were finished, we started developing our security system and each member of the community had special duties to carry out. The children, the women, the young people, the adults, and even the old people had their role to play. Our animals, especially the dogs, help us with our defences too. That's when we started preparing things we had to do secretly, like the traps. No one must know about the traps in our villages. But we all had to know where our neighbours' traps were, otherwise they might capture one of us instead of a soldier or a landowner's bodyguard. One of our *compañeros*, or perhaps a group, took charge of checking the traps which were already there and putting them in working order. These traps were initially meant for catching the mice which eat the cobs, and for the mountain animals which come down and eat our maize. We gave these traps another use—catching the army. They were usually large ditches with invisible nets so that neither animals nor soldiers could see them. They might also be something metal to stop the army. In any case, we know the army can't come in lorries, or bicycles or cars because there are no roads as far as our village. They have to come on foot along the one path. We'd already seen that the army was cowardly and didn't dare come too far into the mountains. They're frightened because they think there are guerrillas there. Those poor soldiers, they don't even know what a guerrilla is, so they imagine he is a monster, like a fierce bird or a sort of animal. This makes them afraid of going into the mountains. They have to come along paths and we set traps on all the main paths leading to our village. We don't set only one trap, we set several because one might fail. This was our first experience with traps so we had to set three or more on every path. In addition to the traps on the path, there were more traps in each house, so that if the army gets as far as the village by another path, he will still get a shock in each *compañero*'s house. Each house also had an emergency exit for every *compañero*, every one of us.

I was helping with the security measures, by setting traps and all the other things for our defence. But at the same time I was involved in organising and educating the *compañeros*. We had to do whatever work the community wanted, what was most needed at the time. And that was teaching many of the *compañeros* to do the same job we did. We tried to avoid all working at the same thing and changed round all the time so that everyone got experience of the different duties. We began organising the children, the women, the men. We started using our safety measures, the emergency exits for example. We decided who'd leave first, who second, third and last, if the army took the village. At first, when we hadn't much experience and hadn't much idea of how to confront the enemy, we planned that the women should leave first with their children—all the kids—and that the men should stay until the last. But we found that in practice that system proved not to be very effective and we were constantly changing our ways of escaping. What happened was that the women and children were safer than the men because the army showed them a bit more respect. It was usually the men they kidnapped, especially the village leaders. So because of this, our men would leave first the women would stay behind to take the beatings. It wasn't that we had a set plan, with a theory and each role worked out, and that was that. No, we were putting new ideas into practice the whole time and practising the things we had to do together. And then, when people were least expecting it, we'd cause some confusion in the village to see how we'd react. We tested our traps and our emergency exits. We realized that, when the army arrived, it wouldn't be very sensible to escape into the mountains in single file along the paths. So we dug large ditches and underground paths. Whenever a village leader gave the signal, we'd all leave and gather in one place. We broke with many of our cultural procedures by doing this but we knew it was the way to save ourselves. We knew what to do and most of the village was ready to follow us. The community elects its leader but everything he does has to be approved by the others. What the community does not approve cannot be carried through. Everyone plays an equal part: men, women, and the children as well. One of the first decisions taken was that there should be a signal for when we were to leave the village. That is a very serious signal. It's only given when the enemy is close by. And the signal will change according to which side the enemy is approaching from. There is one signal for the day and another for nighttime, because at night we can't see where the enemy is coming from. We got together with other villages and built a house at each of the four corners from which the enemy could approach. Some of us would take it in turns to keep watch at night and others would keep watch during the day.

This is something that happened while I was in the village; it was the first time we put our self-defence measures into practice. The soldiers who'd stayed in our village for fifteen days left, but they left with the idea that we were organised. They were already suspicious of certain things while they were in the village, in spite of the fact that our organisation was totally secret. They came back one night and our whole network of information was already in operation. We'd built a camp for the village so that if, at any time, we couldn't live in the village, we could go to the camp. That's when we found our friends from the natural world even more useful—the plants, the trees, and the mountains. Our community began getting used to an even harder life in case we couldn't go back to the village for fifteen or twenty days. It was better than being massacred. We began practising going to the camp to sleep at night whether there were any enemies or not. Our *compañeros* would give us the signal, from far away. So, we'd set traps on the path, and the traps in the houses, and get all the preparations ready. And also on each path, one *compañero*'s house was empty, except for the dogs. If the soldiers came at night, the dogs would bark and follow them. As long as the dogs kept on barking, we knew that the soldiers were still there. That's how our dogs help us. We knew when the army was in the village. They barked whatever time or day the army left. That was the signal that the army had left the village.

That first night they arrived, they went into the houses and found no-one. They beat the dogs, killed some of them, and left. We said to ourselves: "They went into our houses and they are going to go on looking for us. So now we have good cause to find new methods." That's how the community itself looks for ways of improving certain things that weren't any good. We did everything together because there were no longer specific tasks for men and others for women. Now, going to the fields or building a neighbour's house, or anything, was all done communally. We didn't have our own individual things, because this would disperse the community and when the enemy came, he'd be able to kidnap some of us. So we worked together. The women took turns with the men to keep watch at night. Before doing any of these tasks, we had to be sure how we were going to do them. We thought of what would happen if at any time, we couldn't use our traps, or rather that they didn't work. If we couldn't use our escape route or any other of our security measures, we should at least have our weapons ready—the weapons of the people: machetes, stones, hot water, chile, salt. We found a use for all these things. We knew how to throw stones, we knew how to throw salt in someone's face—how to do it effectively. This could only be against the paramilitary forces, from the regiment, because we knew that we had no answer for machine guns. But if the police came with their guns, our weapons can be effective. We've often used lime. Lime is very fine and you have to aim it in a certain way for it to go into someone's eyes. We learned to do it through practice; we practised taking aim and watching where the enemy is. You can blind a policeman by throwing lime in his face. And with stones for instance, you have to throw it at the enemy's head, at his face. If you throw it at his back, it will be effective but not as much as at other parts of the body. These are things we're practising the whole time in our village. And if we're stuck in our homes, we can resort to throwing hot water at them. The whole village must be prepared, in one place and with all their materials for self-defence ready. The whole family must know where an uncle's or a neighbour's things are in case they can't use their own. We need to be on the constant lookout for new techniques. But everything must have a reason or we might do things we want to, but without knowing why we're doing them. Our main weapon, however, is the Bible. We began to study the Bible as a text through which to educate our village. There are many wonderful stories in the Bible.

[. . .]

ATTACK ON THE VILLAGE BY THE ARMY

"Don't wait for strangers to remind you of your duty, you have a conscience and a spirit for that. All the good you do must come from your own initiative."

—Popol Vul

I was free in those days. My father told me: "You are independent you must do what you want to, as long as you do it for our people." That was my father's idea. I was absolutely free to decide, to leave for another village. So I said: "I'm going away." I went because they hadn't kidnapped anyone, nor raped anyone, in our village. But in other villages they had, and I couldn't bear so many women—hundreds of women, young girls, widows—being pregnant because the soldiers had used them sexually. I was ashamed to stay safely in my village and not think about the others. So I decided to leave. My father knew and he said: 'Where you are going, you may not have control over your life. You can be killed at any time. You could be killed tomorrow, the day after tomorrow, or any time.' But I knew that teaching others how to defend themselves against the enemy was a commitment I had to make—a commitment to my people and my commitment as a Christian. I have faith and I believe that happiness belongs to everyone, but that happiness has been stolen by a few. That was what motivated me. I had to go and teach others. That's why I went to the villages most in need, the one most threatened. I had friends there already, I'd met many *compañeras* from that community down in the *fincas*. I'd also met them when we went to the river to collect these little animals—*jutes*—to sell in the town. Those girls were collecting them as well. The animals are like little snails. We sell them in the market and people like eating them very much because they come from the mountains. So every Saturday, my mother used to go to the river and fish for *jutes*, and the next day she'd take them to market to sell. Women do it more than men because on Saturdays they are fixing the animal pens or doing other little jobs around the house, things that they don't have time for the rest of the week. So we spent a lot of time fishing for *jutes*. At the same time, we women felt a lot of affection for the river. It's a lovely feeling down by the river, even if we have to spend the whole day in the river looking for *jutes* among the stones. I enjoyed it very much. I made these friends there and we became closer friends later on when we worked together down in the *fincas* picking cotton. They were still only little. Cotton picking has three "hands," as we say in Guatemala. Cotton is like sponge, like snow. The first "hand" is picked by adults, and they pick the second "hand" too. But the third "hand" is picked by children because they can get in underneath the bushes. A cotton bush is not very tall, only about three feet high. The tallest ones would be only five or six feet. So the children get in under the bush to pick the bits which are left; we mustn't miss a single bit or they don't pay us what they owe us. So with these friends, because I was big and they were little, we'd agreed that I'd pick the second "hand" and they would do the third "hand." They went underneath and I went on top. So we'd talk to each other while we were picking cotton. We became friends.

When I heard from neighbours the news that so-and-so and so-and-so had been raped by the army, I was very angry thinking about my friends—pretty, humble girls. That's really what made me decide to go. I said, "I can't possibly stay here at home while that is happening there." Of course, our region hadn't been liberated and we were still in constant fear of the enemy, with its more and more modern machines, modern weapons, and there could be a massacre in my village at any time. Nevertheless, I felt a greater need to be in the other village and I moved over there to be close to my friends. They told me of their despair at having been raped. There were four of them. Two of them were pregnant by soldiers and the other two not. But they were ill too because they'd been raped by five soldiers who'd come to their house. While I was living in the house of one of my friends who was pregnant, she told me: "I hate this child inside me. I don't know what to do with it. This child is not my child." She was very distressed and cried all the time. But I told her: "You must love the child. It was not your fault." She said: "I hate that soldier. How can I feed the child of a soldier?" The *compañera* aborted her child. She was from a different ethnic group than ours. Her community helped her by telling her that it wasn't unusual, that our ancestors did the same when they were raped, when they had children without wishing to, without any love for the child. But my two friends suffered very much. I didn't know what to do, I felt helpless.

I spoke the same language as they did in that village. What happens in Guatemala is that the Quiché language is the most common. The main languages are Quiché, Cakchiquel and Mam, and from these three mother languages spring all the other languages found here. However one ethnic group doesn't all speak the same language. For instance, the Ixiles are Quichés but they don't speak Quiché and their customs differ from those of the Quiché. So there's a conglomeration of ethnic groups, languages, customs and traditions, and even though there are three mother languages, that doesn't mean we all understand each other. We don't. It was the same with my four *compañeras*. They were from another people, another community, and we just understood each other but with many deformations of the same language. I must say it's unfortunate that we Indians are separated by ethnic barriers, linguistic barriers. It's typical of Guatemala: such a small place but such huge barriers that there's no dialogue between us. We Indians say: "This is my group and this is where I must be." The government takes more and more advantage of these barriers. The two who'd been raped but weren't pregnant must have been about fourteen. They were very ill, but I didn't really know what was the matter with them. One couldn't walk very well and the other had very bad stomach pains. She said her stomach hurt but, honestly, I had no knowledge of things like that. The two who were pregnant rejected their babies and didn't want to mother soldiers' children. It made me feel so helpless. I didn't know what to do. I felt so much pity for them. Their situation was very difficult. But my staying with them did them a lot of good because I spent time with them and talked to them as we'd done when we were young, when we were little girls.

We started setting traps in that village, the same traps as ours but in slightly different ways. The community had many things hidden that they hadn't used out of respect for those objects. But we decided that we needed to use them, because life is worth more than objects even if it means revealing many of our Indian secrets. We started to use them. Another community nearby, the village of Cotzal, was very persecuted. It had been very badly repressed in 1960. From then on there'd been many massacres, many women raped, many men tortured. While I was in the village, a woman arrived, a very old woman. As my father said, unfortunately we don't live very long in Guatemala these days. We usually live to about sixty, that's the life expectancy. People die early because of the conditions we live in. But this woman was extraordinary. She was an exceptional case in this village. She must have been about ninety. They had just killed her last son. First they'd killed her husband. He'd gone to town and hadn't come back. One of her sons went to look for him and he didn't come back. Another went and didn't come back either. The others were all kidnapped from their house. So this woman was left all alone. She was looking for a refuge. I was in the village and my *compañeros* said there was a very old woman who wanted to join our community. She thinks she should stay here. I said: "Of course, she must. We must all help each other and defend ourselves to the very last person."

With all the *compañeros*, we'd installed a self-defence system like the one in my village, using this village's own traps. We said that if the army were to arrive during the night it was good for the very old woman to be with us. We decided that before it got dark, we'd all go and sleep in the mountains. We kept combined watches during the night—a young girl with a boy or a man. This way we'd protect the community throughout the night. That was different from the way we'd done it, but the village wanted to combine the duties for a reason. Keeping watch at night meant turning ourselves into tree trunks, without moving, or else we'd be cannon fodder for the army. The girl would be on another side making herself look like something different from the man. That was this village's idea. Their traps were different and their weapons were different. Everything was the way the *cornpaneros* of the village were used to doing things. Nevertheless, they accepted me. We set to work and I was accepted because of all the help I gave the village.

The army raided the village at night. When they heard the dogs, they fired wildly into the air. They fired everywhere but there was no-one at home. The whole village had taken all their belongings out of their houses and carried them to the camp. So even though the army wanted to steal things, there was nothing there. And even though they burned the houses, it didn't matter very much because the mountains were sheltering the community. We spent two, three, four nights like this. The old lady got really fed up. She couldn't stand the cold. It rained and rained. When it started to pour with rain during the night, the water gushed down through the camp and we got soaking wet. That old lady couldn't bear the cold and one day decided: "Let them kill me if they want, but I'm not going with you to the mountains." It was hard for us to accept the idea of leaving that dear old lady there. She'd taught us many things and often helped us through the experience of her years. The community said they wouldn't agree to her staying in her hut. But she said: "No, I'm staying. I must stay here. If they kill me, they kill me. Anyway, I've no children, no grandchildren, all my grandchildren have been taken away and I've nobody left. If I have helped in any way, it was only my duty." So, with a great deal of sadness, and pain, we had to leave her in her house.

When night came, we all left for the mountains. We left one by one and met up in the mountains. We'd left traps at the doors of all the houses. The trap consisted of a pole and a big, big pit, about as deep as the distance between the floor and the roof. We put the pole across the pit and a board on the pole so that whoever stood on it would fall in. We take it off during the day and set it at night. Everyone in the village knew each others' traps so none of us would fall in. The old lady set her trap. She set the trap and prepared her axe, her machete, her hoe and her stones. She got everything she needed to defend herself ready and went to sleep. We saw our lookout giving the signal from far away and we left. We always have *compañeros* on watch at the main entrance to the village. They signal with their torches. They light it and indicate the number of soldiers approaching by the number of times they wave it. And when the soldiers leave, the *compañero* also has to tell us if they've all gone or not. Everyone was distressed, and I most of all, because I was sure they were going to kill the old lady or rape her. I knew those murderers were so criminal they didn't respect anyone's life, neither old people nor children. They like raping old people and children. At around two in the morning the dogs began to bark and there was shooting and everything, but we didn't hear any shouts from the old woman. We were quite a way away from the village but, all the same, we could pick up all the noises from there. But we didn't hear anything. We thought they'd killed the poor woman. At about half past three, the lookout gave the signal that the army had left the village. He indicated how many had left. Some were still there. We didn't know what to do. So we waited until dawn to see if we should go back to the village or stay in the mountains. At about half past five, when dawn was just breaking, we saw the old woman coming towards us. How could she possibly have escaped death? She stopped and said: "I have a surprise for you," and she was laughing and crying at the same time. But she was crying with joy. There was also anxiety written on her face, however, and we immediately thought that she was an "ear."

There have been "ears" in a lot of villages—people who sell themselves to the government. But I think it's not always their fault. They have to, they are forced to sell themselves, because they are threatened and see no alternative. The government uses them to get information from the community and this causes many deaths. So we thought this old lady was an "ear" although we could hardly believe it of such an honest person. But we took it very seriously because at that time we were very clear about what we had to do. We didn't like violence but if it was the only way of saving our lives, we would use it with justice. Although it hurt us, if this woman had sold herself, we would have to execute her. But she says: "I've got a surprise for you. I've killed a soldier." "I've killed a soldier," she says. But nobody believed her. Well, how could we believe it because, first of all, she was very old and, second, she could hardly see, and third, she didn't have the sort of arms the enemy did. But she kept saying: "I'm so happy. I don't want to die, I want to live again. I killed a soldier." Still no-one believed her. "I'm telling the truth," she said, "look, here are his guns." She was carrying the soldier's rifle and his pistol. She was happy. "Show me, show me how to use it," she said. To me it was like a dream, like a comic strip, hardly believable. She told us: "What happened was that they came into my house, they all managed to jump over the trap, all of them. I hid and crept out of the house on the other side, trying to get away from the house because I thought they'd catch me. The only thing I had with me was my axe. There was a soldier standing at the door looking in, I hit him on the head with my axe and he fell to the ground. The others thought it was guerrillas. They were in such a rush to get out that one of them fell in the trap and the other was rolling around on the ground. The other soldiers shot their wounded comrade. He was trying to escape."

He was old, and afterwards we saw that the wound wasn't serious, not enough for them to have to kill him. But the other soldiers had killed him and left. And that's why we'd been sent the signal that they weren't all there, and why we were so suspicious when the old lady arrived at the camp. We knew that not all the army had left the village. I was so overjoyed, so overjoyed. I said: "This is a great victory for our secrets, no-one has discovered them. We must go on doing this because it is not right that our lives should be worth less than a bird or anything else, and that they can kill us as they wish." The old lady deserved a big reward. But we didn't know what to give really, just our thanks for what she had done. The old lady made a promise: "I want to live, I want to go on with you." She was almost dancing. "Now we have something to defend ourselves with. If we learn to use this, we'll have a weapon like theirs. This is what killed my children," she said. Well, it was something special for her. But it was for us too.

What should we do with the soldier? He'd fallen into the trap with his guns and everything. He had grenades as well. He was very well equipped. We carried the dead body out of the village and put him on a path where they could see him, but which didn't put the community at risk (although they knew he had been there anyway). The other one wasn't dead. He was alive in the trap. We didn't know what to do with him because if we went up to the trap, he'd probably shoot us. In the end, we told him to give up his weapons. We threw a rope down into the pit, talking to him from some way away, telling him that if he sent his weapons up, we'd let him live but that if he refused, he'd die. The soldier must have been pretty miserable in that hole and he said yes, and tied his guns to the rope and we pulled them up. But who could be sure he didn't have another gun? That was very worrying, but some of the community said: "Even if he has a gun, he can only kill one of us, not all of us." So we threw the soldier a rope and we all pulled. He came out and it was true he was unarmed. He'd given up all his weapons.

We did the same with this soldier as we'd done with the one in the village. Here they asked him as well: "How could a soldier be like that?" The *compañeras* who were pregnant told him they were carrying a soldier's child but that they couldn't give birth to a child with blood like a soldier's blood. For an Indian it was like a monster, something unbearable. The soldier began to cry and said: "It's not my fault. They give me orders. They forced us to come here and if we don't obey, they kill us." He said: "We take orders from a captain, and we do what this captain says. If I go into the army, I'm an enemy of the people anyway, and if I lay down my arms, I'm the army's enemy. If one side doesn't kill me, the other will. I don't know what to do." So we told him that if it was difficult for him, from now on he should hide or find something else to do, but that he must stop being evil, like the army. And he told us a lot about how they tortured in the barracks. He said: "From the first day I arrived in the barracks, they told me that my parents were stupid,"—he was an Indian too—"that they were stupid because they couldn't speak and that they'd teach me how people should speak. So they started teaching me Spanish. They gave me a pair of shoes which I found very hard to wear but they beat me into wearing them anyway. They hit me until I got used to them. Then they told me I had to kill the communists from Cuba and Russia. I had to kill them all and then they gave me a gun." But we asked him: "And who do you kill with this gun? Why are you hunting us? Do they say that if your father or mother are on the other side, you must use this gun to kill them too?" "I use this gun the way they tell me to use it. I'm not to blame for all this, they just grabbed me in the town." He cried and we felt sorry for him, because we are all human.

By that time I understood the position very well. I knew it wasn't the fault of the soldiers. The government force our people to be soldiers too. That soldier talked and told us everything they did. This time we were a bit more aware because, as I said, the first time we only begged the soldier to help us, we didn't even ask him the things he did. Now the second time we got a lot of information from him about how they treat the soldiers in the army. "We have to obey the captain. The captain is always behind us and if we don't obey, he shoots us." We asked him: "And why don't you get together then if there's only one captain." "Well, not all of us think the same," he said, "many have come to believe in what we're doing." And we asked him: "And what are you defending? Where are these communists?" The soldier didn't even know what communists were. We asked him: "What do communists look like?" And he said: "Well, they tell us they're in the mountains, that they don't look like people, and things like that." He had no idea of what he was doing. Then we said to him "You are defending the rich. You are defending authority. You're not defending your own people." "It's true," he said, "from now on I'm not going back. I promise you, I swear, I'm not going back to the barracks." And we said to him: "If you are a true son of your people, if you really remember the advice of our ancestors, you must go and make a life where you can, but stop being a criminal. Don't go on killing." The soldier went away convinced. And we heard that he didn't go back to the barracks but went and hid. Perhaps they've killed him now or he might be alive, but anyway that soldier didn't go back to his camp.

That was my second experience of organising work in my people's struggle. My dream was to go on fighting and getting to know my people more closely.

At the same time I was very concerned that everything handed down from our ancestors should still be practiced. And even though the tortures and kidnappings had done our people a lot of harm, we shouldn't lose faith in change. This is when I began working in a peasant organisation and went on to another stage of my life. These are other things, other ways.

POLITICAL ACTIVITY IN OTHER COMMUNITIES: CONTACTS WITH LADINOS

> "We have revealed our secrets to those who are worthy. Only they should know the art of writing and no-one else."
>
> —Popol Vuh

We went on organising our people in 1979. I remember that I hadn't heard anything of my parents since the farewell in the community. I didn't know where they were. They had no news of me either. We didn't see them for a long time. I went to the *fincas*, I went to other areas, but 1 couldn't go back to my village because I was a fugitive like my parents. We lived with other people, with *compañeros* from other Indian groups, and with the many friends I made in the organisation. It was almost as if I were living with my brothers and sisters, with my parents. Everyone showed me so much affection. So we organised the majority of workers on the South coast, in the sugar, coffee and cotton plantations. And they agreed to carry on the political work when they returned to the *Altiplano* so that everybody would be organised. Most of the workers were Indians and poor *ladinos*, and we didn't need to hold courses explaining the situation since it was all around us. Our work went very well. And soon there just wasn't enough time for everything; we had to rush from one place to another, carrying documents, carrying everything. The reason for this was so that others wouldn't put themselves at risk; we were already in danger, the enemy knew us. I travelled from region to region, sleeping in different houses.

All this gave me a lot to think about, a lot, because I came across the linguistic barriers over and over again. We couldn't understand each other and I wanted so much to talk to everybody and feel close to many of the women as I was to my mother. But I couldn't talk to them because they didn't understand me and I didn't understand them. So I said: "We can't possibly go on like this. We must work to help people understand their own people, and be able to talk to one another." From then on I concentrated on getting to know my *compañeros* closely and teaching them the little I knew, so that they too could become leaders of their communities. I remember we talked of many things: of our role as women, our role as young people. We all came to the conclusion that we hadn't had a childhood, nor had we ever really been young because, as we were growing up we'd had the responsibility of feeding little brothers and sisters—it was like having a lot of children ourselves. I sometimes stayed with other Indians in their houses.

I remember the village of Huehuetenango very well, where I stayed in the house of a *compañero* who had ten children. I made a mistake there, it was something that I hadn't realized, thinking that we'd all had the same experiences. The mistake was not to have brought a blanket with me for this journey. I only had a sheet with me for the night. I arrived at that village in the *Altiplano*, and it was so cold, so incredibly cold. You can't believe how cold it was. So I hoped these people would lend me some clothes or a shawl to put over me. But at night I saw that they didn't even have anything for themselves and it made me very sad. How were we going to sleep? It was so cold! The dogs came in and out of the little house all the time because it was open. I asked: "Tell me, are we going to stay here?" I thought we could get leaves from the mountain to warm ourselves with. It was rather late to think of that but they collected quite a lot of leaves . . . . And so they all lay down round the fire; they were all sleeping and I wondered, well, where should I go. And I lay down next to them. By midnight it was so cold that we were almost frozen! The cold woke the parents up. "How cold it is," they said. "Yes," I said, and my jaw was almost stiff with cold. I'd never felt so cold before. Although my home is in the *Altiplano* too, the cold there doesn't compare with this. The parents got up for a while and then went to sleep again. I began to wonder how human beings can stand so much. We often say we can't bear something but we do bear it. The children were all right, quiet on the floor. Since the parents were very fond of me and thought of me as a leader, they said: "Look, here is a mat. Sit on this." But for my part, I couldn't use the mat because I was too ashamed, and also because I felt we were all equal and that they had as much right to the mat as I had. I told my host that I was ashamed by the special treatment they gave me because I was poor too, I was from the mountains too, from the same conditions, and that if we are fighting for equality for everyone, we must begin by sharing everything we have. I didn't mind sharing the mat with the children but I didn't deserve the mat for myself. It made me think a great deal because I said: "In our house we have a mat each." This meant that I'd never suffered as they had here. And I began to discover many things that I hadn't experienced but that many others had. And this made me really angry. I thought, so many rich people wasting even whole beds—one mattress isn't enough for them, they have two or three on their beds. And here there isn't even a mat to sleep on. This gave me lot to think about. This happened with many people. I used to sleep one, two, three nights in one place, then I'd move on to another place for my work. I was happy.

Something I want to tell you, is that I had a friend. He was the man who taught me Spanish. He was a *ladino*, a teacher, who worker with the CUC. He taught me Spanish and helped me with many things. We used to meet secretly because we couldn't meet openly where he lived. That *compañero* taught me many things, one of which was to love *ladinos* a lot. He taught me to think more clearly about some of my ideas which were wrong, like saying all *ladinos* are bad. He didn't teach me through ideas, he showed me by his actions, by the way he behaved towards me. At that time, we used to talk through the night. It was when we began supporting the struggle of peasants in general, and carrying out coordinated actions. For instance, if we call a strike, it's for all workers. If we call an assembly, we listen to the views of all the masses. It was my job to sound out the views of all the *compañeros* I was in contact with in the area I happened to be in, and send them to the regional coordinating body. Then they'd be sent to the national coordinating body to be discussed by the *compañeros* there. Anyway, the example of my *compañero ladino* made me really understand the barrier which has been put up between the Indian and the *ladino*, and that because of this same system which tries to divide us, we haven't understood that *ladinos* also live in terrible conditions, the same as we do.

That's when I became very attached to my *compañeros ladinos* and we began to talk a lot. Our organisation includes Indians and poor *ladinos*, so we began putting this into practice. I remember having lengthy discussions with *ladinos*. I especially remember the times for criticism and the self-criticism which, I think, all revolutionary struggles go through to make the change more profound. The first time I pointed out an error by one of the *ladinos*, I felt terrible. Well, I'd never ever criticized a *ladino* before. I know deep inside what it is to feel humiliated, to have always been called "dirty Indian." "She's an Indian," they'd say as an insult. So for me criticizing a *ladino* was like putting on a mask and doing something shamelessly. Nevertheless, my criticism was constructive. I criticized the *compañero* but accepted his criticism too. These were the first things I found difficult to accept in our struggle.

As I was saying, I'm an Indian*ist*, not just an Indian. I'm an Indianist to my fingertips and I defend everything to do with my ancestors. But I didn't understand this in the proper way, because we can only understand when we start talking to each other. And this is the only way we can correct our ideas. Little by little, I discovered many ways in which we had to be understanding towards our *ladino* friends and in which they had to show us understanding too. Because I also knew *compañeros ladinos* with whom we shared the worst conditions, but who still felt *ladino*, and as *ladinos* they didn't see that our poverty united us. But little by little, both they and I began discussing many very important things and saw that the root of our problems lay in the ownership of the land. All our country's riches are in the hands of the few.

My friend was a *compañero* who had taken the side of the poor, although I have to say that he was middle class. He was someone who'd been able to study, who had a profession and everything. But he also understood clearly that he had to share these things with the poor, especially his knowledge. He preferred to help the CUC rather than become a member because he said: "I don't deserve to be called a peasant. I'm an intellectual." He recognized his inability to do or know many things that peasants know, or the things poor people know. He said: "I can't talk about hunger the way a peasant can." I remember that when we said the root of our problems was the land, that we were exploited, I felt that being an Indian was an extra dimension because I suffered discrimination as well as suffering exploitation. It was an additional reason for fighting with such enthusiasm. I began thinking about my childhood, when we used to go to the market. They used to cheat us when they bought our things because we didn't speak Spanish. Sometimes they'd say they'd paid for our beans or our plants in the market but when we got home and did our sums, the money didn't add up. So in this sense, they exploited us but, at the same time, they discriminated against us because we were ignorant.

So I learned many things with the *ladinos*, but most of all to understand our problem and the fact that we had to solve it ourselves. Sometimes we'd have very heated discussions because the Indians and *ladinos* didn't understand each other. In Guatemala the division between Indians and *ladinos* has contributed to our situation. And it's certain that in our hearts this has affected us very badly. *Ladinos* are *mestizos*, the children of Spaniards and Indians who speak Spanish. But they are in the minority. There is a larger percentage of Indians. Some say it is 60 per cent, others that it's 80 per cent. We don't know the exact number for a very good reason—there are Indians who don't wear Indian clothes and have forgotten their languages, so they are not considered Indians. And there are middle-class Indians who have abandoned their traditions. They aren't considered Indians either. However this *ladino* minority thinks its blood is superior, a higher quality, and they think Indians as a sort of animal. That's the mark of discrimination. The *ladinos* try to tear off this shell which imprisons them—being the children of Indians and Spaniards. They want to be something different, they don't want to be a mixture. They never mention this mixed blood now. At the same time, there are differences between *ladinos* too; between rich *ladinos* and poor *ladinos*. The poor are considered lazy, people who don't work, who only sleep and who have no enjoyment in life. But between these poor *ladinos* and Indians there is still that big barrier. No matter how bad their conditions are, they feel *ladino*, and being *ladino* is something important in itself: it's *not* being an Indian. That's how they have separated the way they act, the way they think. The *ladinos* want to improve their situation, they're looking for a way out of their shell, because even though the *ladino* is poor, even though he's exploited as we are, he tries to be something better than an Indian. In the market, for example, no *ladino* would steal from another *ladino* as he would from an Indian. A *ladino* would even insult a lady but an Indian could never do that. The *ladino* has many ways of making his voice heard—if he goes to a lawyer, he doesn't need an intermediary. He has more channels of access. And so that's why the poor *ladino* rejects the Indian. If a *ladino* gets on a bus, that's normal. If an Indian gets on, everyone is disgusted. They think we are dirty, worse than an animal or a filthy cat. If an Indian goes near a *ladino*, the *ladino* will leave his seat rather than be with the Indian. We feel this rejection deeply. If you examine the conditions of poor *ladinos* and our conditions, you'll see they are the same. There is no difference. When I was little I used to think about this a lot. What is it? What does the *ladino* have that we don't? I compared myself with them. Is it that some parts of his body are different? And the system feeds this situation. It separates the Indian from the *ladino*. The radio, all the radio stations speak Spanish. Indians have no access to radio. So although we were all poor, we did not understand each other.

That's when I started being more aware of the situation. I understood that my bitter experiences, my affection for my *compañeros*, for my people, had made it difficult for me to accept certain things. I identified certain of my attitudes—very rigid ones. Discrimination had made me isolate myself completely from the world of our *compañeros ladinos*. I didn't express certain of my attitudes but they were nevertheless there, like a thorn in my heart, from having repeated so many times: "They are *ladinos*, they can't understand because they are *ladinos*." But slowly, through our discussions, we understood each other. There came a time when the two of us had to carry out tasks together. A *compañero ladino* and me, an Indian. For me it was unbelievable to walk with a *ladino*. I'd been told that Indians were separate for so long. It was like a dream for me, and it made me very reserved with the *compañero*. But that was in the early days and little by little as we talked we learned more. To bring about change we had to unite, Indians and *ladinos*. What they valued most in me was my knowledge of self-defence, my knowledge of our traps, and escape routes. I could teach other *compañeros*. And later on, through my involvement in the struggle—through my participation as a woman, as a Christian, and as an Indian—I was given responsibilities which recognized my abilities as well. So I had a lot of responsibility.

It was the same with my father. On the rare occasions we saw each other he used to tell me of his experiences and say: "Now I'm charge of a whole town. I'm responsible for *ladinos* and Indians. I can't read or write. And my Spanish isn't very good. I've often felt inadequate. Nevertheless, I know my experience is valuable and that I must share it with others." And this confirmed my certainty that the justification for our struggle was to erase all the images imposed us, all the cultural differences, and the ethnic barriers, so that we Indians might understand each other in spite of different ways of expressing our religion and beliefs. Our culture is still the same. I discovered that all Indians have a common culture in spite of the linguistic barriers, ethnic barriers and different modes of dress. The basis of our culture is maize. I was by now an educated woman. Not in the sense of any schooling and even less in the sense of being well-read. But I knew the history of my people, and the history of my *compañeros* from other ethnic groups. I'd got to know many of the groups closely and they'd taught me a lot, including some things which I'd forgotten.

So we come to 1979. We carried out important tasks on the South coast and in the *Altiplano*, directing the people's struggle. Our organisation was no longer a tiny seed. It had won the hearts of the majority of Guatemalans: Indian peasants or poor *ladino* peasants. We travelled all over the *Altiplano*, we went down to the South coast, and we also began working in the East. The important thing to remember is that in the East there are no Indians now. The Indians there have forgotten their costumes, their languages. They no longer speak Indian languages. Just a few old folk speak a little *chorti*. It made me very angry that they should forget their customs and culture. They were workers in the *fincas* too. Or else they were overseers, administrators, soldiers or police. I thought about this a lot. They didn't want to do that but they'd been brutalized. I remember my father telling us: "My children, don't aspire to go to school, because schools take our customs away from us." These people in the East had more access to lower schools but not to any further training. A few have money but the majority only reach second, third or sixth grade in primary school. But they already think differently: although they are still poor they think differently since we Indians have never even seen a teacher. So I thought: "Thank God our parents didn't accept teachers or schools in our community to wipe out what is ours." Sometimes I'd hear how those teachers taught and what education was like in the villages. They said that the arrival of the Spaniards was a conquest, a victory, while we knew that in practice it was just the opposite. They said the Indians didn't know how to fight and that many of them died because they killed the horses and not the people. So they said. This made me furious, but I reserved my anger to educate other people in other areas. This taught me that even though a person may learn to read and write, he should not accept the false education they give our people. Our people must not think as the authorities think. They must not let others think for them.

We can select what is truly relevant for our people. Our lives show us what this is. It has guaranteed our existence. Otherwise we would not have survived. We have rejected all the aims governments have tried to impose. It wasn't only me who did this, of course. I'm saying we did it together. Those are the conclusions my whole community came to. It was the community who taught me to respect all the things which must remain secret as long as we exist, and which future generations will keep secret. That is our objective anyway. When we began to organise ourselves, we started using all the things we'd kept hidden. Our traps—nobody knew about them because they'd been kept secret. Our opinions—whenever a priest came to our village we all kept our mouths shut. We women covered ourselves with our shawls and the men kept their heads bowed. We pretend we're not thinking of anything. But when we're all together, amongst ourselves, we discuss, we think, we give our views. What happens is that, since we've never been given the opportunity to speak, express our opinions, or have our views considered, we haven't bothered to make ourselves heard just for the fun of it. I think as far as this is concerned, we have selected what is relevant for us and have fought for this. As I said before, the life of any single animal means a lot to us. And so much more so the life of a human being. And so when we have to protect our lives, we are ready to defend them even if it means revealing our secrets.

This is why Indians are thought to be stupid. They can't think, they don't know anything, they say. But we have hidden our identity because we needed to resist, we wanted to protect what governments have wanted to take away from us. They have tried to take our things away and impose others on us, be it through religion, through dividing up the land, through schools, through books, through radio, through all things modern. This is why we maintain the rites for our ceremonies. And why we don't accept Catholic Action as the only way to God, and why we don't perform only Christian ceremonies. We don't want to because we know that they are weapons they use to take away what is ours.

3

Let Me Speak! Testimony of Domitila: A Woman of the Bolivian Mines (1977/1978)

Domitila Barrios de Chungara (b. Bolivia, 1937) is a community organizer known in the 1960s and 70s as a leader of the Housewives' Committee of the Mining Center Siglo XX in its efforts to improve the working and living conditions of mining workers and their families. During these years Domitila engaged in several effective hunger strikes and was subjected to prison, torture, and exile. Domitila now lives in Cochabamba, where she directs an Escuela Móvil de Educación Popular. This itinerant school visits rural villages and poor neighborhoods to provide education about legal and human rights, unionization, and the history of the struggle of Bolivian people. She was nominated for the 2005 Nobel Peace Prize. This selection describes and argues for the shift in transnational feminism from a focus on rights and entitlements, leading to strict equality with men, to a struggle to empower women as agents of change.

AT THE INTERNATIONAL WOMEN'S YEAR TRIBUNAL

In 1974, a Brazilian movie director came to Bolivia, commissioned by the United Nations. She was traveling through Latin America looking for women leaders, to find out their opinions about women's conditions, how much and in what way they participate in bettering their situation.

With regard to Bolivia, she was very intrigued by the "housewives' front" which she'd heard about abroad and, also, she'd seen the women of Siglo XX acting in the movie *El Coraje del Pueblo* (The Courage of the People). So, after asking for permission from the government, she went into the mines. And she came to visit me. She liked what I said and she said it was important that everything I knew should be told to the rest of the world. She asked me if I could travel. I said I couldn't, that I didn't have money to even travel in my own country.

So she asked me if I'd agree to participate in a women's congress that was going to take place in Mexico, if she was able to get money for me. I had just found out that there was an International Women's Year.

Although I didn't really believe it much, I said yes, in that case I could go. But I thought it was just a promise like so many others and I didn't pay much attention to it.

When I got the telegram saying that I was invited by the United Nations, I was quite surprised and disconcerted. I called a meeting of the committee and all the *compañeras* agreed that it would be good for me to travel, along with one more *compañera*. But there wasn't enough for two of us to go. The next day I went before a meeting of union leaders and rank-and-file delegates and gave them my report and they agreed that I should participate in the event and they even helped me economically so that I could begin making the arrangements.

So with some other *compañeras* I went to La Paz and we looked into the details, we got guarantees, and I stayed there alone to finish the arrangements. Several days went by. It got to look like I wouldn't be able to make the trip because they didn't want to give me the travel permit.

And it turns out that some Siglo XX leaders arrived in La Paz and were surprised to see I hadn't left. So they went with me to the secretariat of the Ministry of the Interior. And they asked: "What's happening with the *compañera*? Why isn't she in Mexico already? The International Women's Year Conference opens today. What's happened here? Is it or isn't it International Women's Year? Do our wives have the right to participate in this conference, or can only your wives go there?"

And they told me: "Well, *compañera*, since they don't want to let you go, let's leave. Even though you have an invitation from the United Nations, they don't want to let you go to that conference. So we're going to complain to the United Nations. And not only that: we're going to have a work stoppage in protest. Come with us, *compañera*."

They were all set to take me out of the ministry when the guys there reacted: "But . . . why didn't we start there in the first place! One moment, one moment, don't get so hot and bothered. If the lady has an invitation from the United Nations, we should have started there. Where's the invitation?"

The invitation! Every single day, at every turn, I was asked for the copy. And with the experience the miners have, they'd made lots of copies of it. So of course, one copy would get lost and I'd make another. And so on. And the original, well, the leaders themselves had it, because if the first copies got used up, they could make others.

I gave them one more copy; and after an hour, more or less, they gave me my documents. Everything was okay, everything was ready. The plane left the next day at nine in the morning.

When I was about to board the plane, a young lady from the Ministry of the Interior came over to me. I'd seen her there on various occasions, hanging on to her papers. She came over and said: "*Ay, señora!* So, you got your pass? I'm so happy! You deserve it. I congratulate you! How I'd like to be in your shoes, so I could see Mexico! Congratulations!"

But then, very mysterious, she went on: "*Ay*, but *señora*, your return to the country depends a lot on what you say there. So it's not a question of talking about any old thing . . . you've got to think it out well. Above all, you've got to think of your children who you're leaving behind. I'm giving you good advice. Have a good time."

I thought about my responsibility as a mother and as a leader and so my role in Mexico seemed very difficult to me, thinking of what that young lady had said to me. I felt I was between the devil and the deep blue sea, as we say. But I was determined to carry out the mission the *compañeros* and *compañeras* had entrusted me with.

From La Paz we went to Lima, then to Bogotá, and finally to Mexico.

During the trip I thought . . . I thought that I'd never imagined I'd be traveling in a plane, and even less to such a far-off country as Mexico. Never, for we were so poor that sometimes we hardly had anything to eat and we couldn't even travel around our own country. I thought about how I'd always wanted to know my homeland from corner to corner . . . and now I was going so far away. This made me feel happy and sad at the same time. How I would have liked other *compañeras* and *compañeros* to have the same opportunity!

In the plane, everyone was speaking in other languages, chatting, laughing, drinking, playing. I couldn't talk to anyone. It was as if I wasn't even there. When we changed planes in Bogotá, I met a Uruguayan woman who was also going to Mexico to participate in the Tribunal and so then I had someone to talk to.

When we got to Mexico, I was impressed by the fact that there was a bunch of young people talking all different languages and they were there to meet all of us who were arriving. And they asked who was coming to the International Women's Year Conference. They made it easy for all of us to get through customs. Then I went to the hotel they told me to go to.

In Bolivia I'd read in the papers that for International Women's Year there'd be two places: one, the "Conference," was for the official representatives of the governments of all the countries, another, the "Tribunal," was for the representatives of the nongovernmental organizations.

The Bolivian government sent its delegates to the Conference. And these women traveled making fancy statements, saying that in Bolivia more than in any other place, women had achieved equality with men. And they went to the Conference to say that. I was the only Bolivian woman invited for the Tribunal. There I met other Bolivian *compañeras*, but they were living in Mexico.

So I had this idea that there'd be two groups: one, on the government level, where those upper class ladies would be; and the other, on the nongovernment level, where people like me would he, people with similar problems, you know, poor people. It was like a dream for me! Goodness, I said to myself, I'll be meeting peasant women and working women from all over the world. All of them are going to be just like us, oppressed and persecuted.

That's what I thought, see, because of what it said in the papers.

In the hotel I made friends with an Ecuadorian woman and went with her to the place where the Tribunal was being held. But I couldn't go till Monday. The sessions had already begun on Friday.

We went to a very big hall where there were four or five hundred women. The Ecuadorian said: "Come on, *compañera*. Here's where they talk about the most important problems women have. So here's where we should make our voices heard."

There were no more seats. So we sat on some steps. We were very enthusiastic. We'd already missed a day of the Tribunal and we wanted to catch up, get up to date on what had been happening, find out what so many women were think-ing, what they were saying about International Women's Year, what problems most concerned them.

It was my first experience and I imagined I'd hear things that would make me get ahead in life, in the struggle, in my work.

Well, at that moment a *gringa* went over to the microphone with her blond hair and with some things around her neck and her hands in her pockets, and she said to the assembly: "I've asked for the microphone so I can tell you about my experience. Men should give us a thousand and one medals because we, the prostitutes, have the courage to go to bed with so many men."

A lot of women shouted "Bravo!" and applauded.

Well, my friend and I left because there were hundreds of prostitutes in there talking about their problems. And we went into another room. There were the les-bians. And there, also, their discussion was about how "they feel happy and proud to love another woman . . . that they should fight for their rights. . . ." Like that.

Those weren't my interests. And for me it was incomprehensible that so much money should be spent to discuss those things in the Tribunal. Because I'd left my *compañero* with the seven kids and him having to work in the mine every day. I'd left my country to let people know what my homeland's like, how it suffers, how in Bolivia the charter of the United Nations isn't upheld. I wanted to tell people all that and hear what they would say to me about other exploited countries and the other groups that have already liberated themselves. And to run into those other kinds of problems . . . I felt a bit lost. In other rooms, some women stood up and said: "men are the enemy . . . men create wars, men create nuclear weapons, men beat women . . . and so what's the first battle to be carried out to get equal rights for women? First you have to declare war against men. If a man has ten mistresses, well, the woman should have ten lovers also. If a man spends all his money at the bar, partying, the women have to do the same thing. And when we've reached that level, then men and women can link arms and start struggling for the liberation of their country, to improve the living condi-tions in their country."

That was the mentality and the concern of several groups, and for me it was a really rude shock. We spoke very languages, no? And that made it difficult to work in the Tribunal. Also, there was a lot of control over the microphone.

So a group of Latin American women got together and we changed all that. And we made our common problems known, what we thought women's progress was all about, how the majority of women live. We also said that for us the first and main task isn't to fight against our *compañeros*, but with them to change the system we live in for another, in which men and women will have the right to live, to work, to organize.

At first you couldn't really notice how much control there was in the Tri-bunal. But as the speeches and statements were made, things started to change. For example, the women who defended prostitution, birth control, and all those things, wanted to impose their ideas as basic problems to be discussed in the Tribunal. For us they were real problems, but not the main ones.

For example, when they spoke of birth control, they said that we shouldn't have so many children living in such poverty, because we didn't even have enough to feed them. And they wanted to see birth control as something which would solve all the problems of humanity and malnutrition.

But, in reality, birth control, as those women presented it, can't be applied in my country. There are so few Bolivians by now that if we limited birth even more, Bolivia would end up without people. And then the wealth of our country would remain as a gift for those who want to control us completely, no? It's not that we ought to be living like we are, in miserable conditions. All that could be different, because Bolivia's a country with lots of natural resources. But our government prefers to see things their way, to justify the low level of life of the Bolivian people and the very low wages it pays the workers. And so they resort to indiscriminate birth control.

In one way or another, they tried to distract the Tribunal with problems that weren't basic. So we had to let the people know what was fundamental for us in all of that. Personally, I spoke several times. Short speeches, because we could only use the microphone for two minutes.

The movie *La Doble Jornada* (The Double Day), filmed by the Brazilian *compañera* who invited me to the Tribunal, was also useful in orienting people who didn't have any idea of what the life of a peasant woman or working woman is like in Latin America. In *La Doble Jornada* they show the women's lives, especially in relation to work. There you see how women live in the United States, in Mexico, in Argentina. There's a big contrast. But even more so when you see the part about Bolivia, because the *compañera* interviewed a worker in Las Lamas who was pregnant. In the interview she asked her: "Why aren't you taking it easy since you're expecting a baby?" The working woman said that she couldn't because she had to earn a living for her children and her husband too, because he's retired[1] and his pension is very small. "And the pension?" asked the Brazilian woman. Then the miner's wife explained that her husband had left the mine absolutely ruined physically and that all the money from the pension was spent trying to cure him. And that's why now she had to work, her children too, in order to support her husband.

Well, that was pretty strong stuff, and dramatic, no? And the *compañeras* at the Tribunal realized that I hadn't lied when I spoke about our situation.

When the movie was over, since I'd also been in it, they asked me to speak. So I said the situation was due to the fact that no government had bothered to create jobs for poor women. That the only work women do that's recognized is house-work and, in any case, housework is done for free. Because, for example, they give me 14 pesos a month, in other words, two-thirds of a dollar a month, which is the family subsidy that's added to my husband's wage. What are 14 Bolivian pesos worth? With 14 pesos you can buy two bottles of milk or half a box of tea. . . .

That's why—I told them—you have to understand that we won't be able to find any solution to our problems as long as the capitalist system in which we live isn't changed.

Many of those women said that they'd only just begun to agree with me. Several of them wept.

The day the women spoke out against imperialism, I spoke too. And I said how we live totally dependent on foreigners for everything, how they impose what they want on us, economically as well as culturally.

In the Tribunal I learned a lot also. In the first place, I learned to value the wisdom of my people even more. There, everyone who went up to the microphone said: "I'm a professional person, I represent such and such organization. . . ." And bla-bla-bla, she gave her speech. "I'm a teacher," "I'm a lawyer," "I'm a journalist," said the others. And bla-bla-bla, they'd begin to give their opinion.

Then I'd say to myself: "Here there are professionals, lawyers, teachers, journalists who are going to speak. And me . . . what am I doing in this?" And I felt a bit insecure, unsure of myself. I couldn't work up the guts to speak. When I went up to the microphone for the first time, standing before so many "titled" people, I introduced myself, feeling like a nothing, and I said: "Well, I'm the wife of a mine worker from Bolivia." I was still afraid, see?

I worked up the courage to tell them about the problems that were being discussed there. Because that was my obligation. And I stated my ideas so that everyone in the world could hear us, through the Tribunal.

That led to my having a discussion with Betty Friedan, who is the great feminist leader in the United States. She and her group had proposed some points to amend the "World Plan of Action." But these were mainly feminist points and we didn't agree with them because they didn't touch on some problems that are basic for Latin American women.

Betty Friedan invited us to join them. She asked us to stop our "warlike activity" and said that we were being "manipulated by men," that "we only thought about politics," and that we'd completely ignored women's problems, "like the Bolivian delegation does, for example," she said.

So I asked for the floor. But they wouldn't give it to me. And so I stood up and said: "Please forgive me for turning this Tribunal into a marketplace. But I was mentioned and I have to defend myself. I was invited to the Tribunal to talk about women's rights and in the invitation they sent me there was also the document approved by the United Nations which is its charter, where women's right to participate, to organize, is recognized. And Bolivia signed that charter, but in reality it's only applied there to the bourgeoisie."

I went on speaking that way. And a lady, who was the president of the Mexican delegation, came up to me. She wanted to give me her own interpretation of the International Women's Year Tribunal's slogan, which was "equality, development, and peace." And she said: "Let's speak about us, señora. We're women. Look, señora, forget the suffering of your people. For a moment, forget the massacres. We've talked enough about that. We've heard you enough. Let's talk about us . . . about you and me . . . well, about women."

So I said: "All right, let's talk about the two of us. But if you'll let me, I'll begin. Señora, I've known you for a week. Every morning you show up in a different outfit and on the other hand, I don't. Every day you show up all made up and combed like someone who has time to spend in an elegant beauty parlor and who can spend money on that, and yet I don't. I see that each afternoon you have a chauffeur in a car waiting at the door of this place to take you home, and yet I don't. And in order to show up here like you do, I'm sure you live in a really elegant home, in an elegant neighborhood, no? And yet we miners' wives only have a small house on loan to us, and when our husbands die or get sick or are fired from the company, we have ninety days to leave the house and then we're in the street.

Now, *señora*, tell me: is your situation at all similar to mine? Is my situation at all similar to yours? So what equality are we going to speak of between the two of us? If you and I aren't alike, if you and I are so different? We can't, at this moment, be equal, even as women, don't you think?"

But at that moment, another Mexican woman came up and said: "Listen you, what do you want? She's the head of the Mexican delegation and she has the right to speak first. Besides, we've been very tolerant here with you, we've heard you over the radio, on the television, in the papers, in the Tribunal. I'm tired of applauding you."

It made me mad that she said that, because it seemed to me that the problems I presented were being used then just to turn me into some kind of play character who should be applauded. I felt they were treating me like a clown.

"Listen, *señora*," I said to her. "Who asked for your applause? If problems could be solved that way, I wouldn't have enough hands to applaud and I certainly wouldn't have had to come from Bolivia to Mexico, leaving my children behind, to speak here about our problems. Keep your applause to yourself, because I've received the most beautiful applause of my life, and that was from the callused hands of the miners."

And we had a pretty strong exchange of words.

In the end they said to me: "Well, you think you're so important. Get up there and speak."

So, I went up and spoke. I made them see that they don't live in our world. I made them see that in Bolivia human rights aren't respected and they apply what we call "the law of the funnel": broad for some, narrow for others. That those ladies who got together to play canasta and applaud the government have full guarantees, full support. But women like us, housewives, who get organized to better our people, well, they beat us up and persecute us. They couldn't see all those things. They couldn't see the suffering of my people, they couldn't see how our *compañeros* are vomiting their lungs bit by bit, in pools of blood. They didn't see how underfed our children are. And, of course, they didn't know, as we do, what it's like to get up at four in the morning and go to bed at eleven or twelve at night, just to be able to get all the housework done, because of the lousy conditions we live in.

"You," I said, "what can you possibly understand about all that? For you, the solution is fighting with men. And that's it. But for us it isn't that way, that isn't the basic solution."

When I finished saying all that, moved by the anger I felt, I left the platform. And many women came up to me, and at the exit from the hall, many were happy and said I should go back to the Tribunal and represent the Latin American women who were there.

I felt ashamed to think I hadn't been able to evaluate the wisdom of the people well enough. Because, look: I, who hadn't studied in the university, or even gone to school, I, who wasn't a teacher or a professional or a lawyer or a professor, what had I done in the Tribunal? What I'd said was only what I'd heard my people say ever since I was little, my parents, my *compañeros*, the leaders, and I saw that the people's experience is the best schooling there is. What I learned from the people's life was the best teaching. And I wept to think: how great is my people!

We Latin American women issued a document about the way we see the role of women in underdeveloped countries, with everything we felt was important to say on that occasion. And the press published it.

Another thing that I got out of the Tribunal was meeting *compañeras* from other countries, especially the Bolivians, Argentines, Uruguayans, Chileans, who'd been in similar situations to those I'd experienced in prisons, jails, and all those problems. I learned a lot from them.

I think I fulfilled the mission that the *compañeras* and *compañeros* from Siglo XX gave me. In the Tribunal we were with a lot of women from all over the world, and we made everyone who was represented there aware of my country.

It was also a great experience being with so many women and seeing how many, many people are dedicated to the struggle for the liberation of their oppressed peoples.

I also think it was important for me to see once again—and on that occasion in contact with more than five thousand women from all over—how the interests of the bourgeoisie really aren't our interests.

MEETINGS WITH EXILES

During my stay in Mexico, I had the opportunity to meet several Bolivians and spend time with them. Some were exiles who'd left the country in 1971. Many of them had been in prison and then expelled from the country, others had fled, others had sought asylum in the embassies. Of the ones I met there, I only knew one from before, who had come with some students to the mine.

I was impressed to see all those professionals there. I didn't find workers or peasants. Of course, I know there are some exiled in other countries, but, really, the people who leave the country are mostly professionals, no?

I noticed in the exiles very good intentions; they act in solidarity with the people of Bolivia, they don't forget their people.

Personally, they treated me very well, they gave me their help, they made me very comfortable, they had my knee operated on, they even helped me get my teeth fixed which had been broken the second time I was in jail. There wasn't a single *compañero* or *compañera* who didn't show me solidarity.

The Bolivians also helped me get in touch with the people I had to see. In Mexico I had all the comforts I don't have here. I had a bed with mattress, I had a bathroom for myself, I had water and electricity in the house, I had my meals cooked.

But despite all the comfort I found in Mexico, I never felt the desire to stay and have all that, as long as the people in Bolivia are suffering so much. Instead of feeling happy, I thought about how in the mine the people have to walk, how the women, even when they're pregnant, have to carry such heavy loads along such long roads. I thought about the miners of San Florencio who have to go all the way to Siglo XX to buy things. I thought about the women who have to travel several kilometers to reach home after having sold something in the market, and only then start to get some food ready. All that made me feel uncomfortable; me, who'd come to Mexico as a leader invited to the International Women's Year Conference, to speak as a representative of poor and working women.

Of course, I dream of the day when I'll have all those comforts. Yes, I like comfort, but I want it for everyone, for all my people. I don't want it for me alone. I'd like to have all that comfort, but I can't accept it while my people are dying of hunger, living in misery, working so hard. I can't. When we all have comfort, good living, then we'll all be happy, because we won't have to think maybe the neighbor isn't eating today or can't get over a sickness. No longer will we feel ashamed of having a nice new outfit while the rest can't.

That's why in Mexico I missed my people and my environment so much, and I wanted to get back home soon.

A man told us we are like fish who need to be in the water and that die out of the water. And the day that we, the leaders, the ones who are on our way, aren't in the heart of the masses, then that day we'll die. And I really believe that it's easy to die apart from them. Because if a leader isn't with his or her people, that person can't feel happy. And I believe that all who call themselves revolutionaries or are so called, have the obligation to return to the people and fight by their side.

And while they're outside the country, the revolutionaries who've fought for their country shouldn't forget the people who continue fighting in Bolivia in the mines, in the countryside, in the factories, facing the repression which still goes on. They shouldn't forget this and instead should try to prepare themselves as much as possible for their return, in order to respond to the demands the people will make on them.

Those who remain outside calmly, without doing anything, waiting for us to win the victory, those are really traitors to the people, aren't they?

And it's always possible to do something during the time one can't return home. I mean that we, the revolutionaries, shouldn't believe in borders, and wherever a revolutionary is, he or she should transmit the experience of our people to others who are interested in it, especially to the working class and peasants.

NOTE

1. As an invalid. For the majority of miners, the invalid condition is caused by silicosis.

4

Rebel Radio: The Story of El Salvador's *Radio Venceremos* (1991)

José Ignacio López Vigil

José Ignacio López Vigil (b. Cuba, 1945) was born in Cuba and has lived in various Latin American countries, teaching and doing radio broadcasting. For several years he was Programming Director of Radio Santa María y Radio Enriquillo in the Dominican Republic. He was Coordinator of the Training Division of the Latin American Association of Radio Education (ALER), Director of Training of the Nicaraguan Broadcasting Corporation (CORADEP), and of the Latin American and Caribbean Regional Office of the World Association of Community Radio Stations (AMARC). He has taught courses and conducted workshops in radio production throughout the region. Presently he is Production Coordinator for Radialistas Apasionados y Apasionadas *in Lima, Peru. He has written several polemical radio series and several books including the* Manual Urgente para Radialistas Apasionados, *considered to be the bible of radio production by many in Latin America. This selection is a first hand account of the use of the medium of radio as a primary information, communication, consciousness-raising, and organizing tool of a social and political movement in Latin America. In particular, it shows how an underground radio station,* Radio Venceremos, *became an integral part of the Farabundo Martí National Liberation Front's (FMLN) struggle during El Salvador's Civil War (1981–1992).*

THE GENERAL OFFENSIVE

Enter the Viking

Jonás[1] turned up at my house in Mexico.

"We've got to have a radio station," he said. "We'll bust our balls to get it."

In El Salvador at that time, at the end of the seventies, things had turned black as ants. The repression was brutal. Print media was no longer effective. If you had a leaflet in your bag, it could cost you your life. Was it worth risking the lives of those handing leaflets out, to say nothing of those accepting them? Maybe that's why the idea of a radio station took root—they can't frisk you for a voice.

There was no place for us in the media. The left-wing papers had been closed down. *La Crónica del Pueblo* and *El Independiente* had both been bombed. They had begun to dynamite Monsignor Romero's[2] radio station. Journalists were being threatened, murdered, gagged, no one could tell anyone about anything. Our brief takeovers of radio stations were something, but not much.

"We need technical support," Jonás insisted.

I had a few contacts at the University of Guadalajara. That's where we found Toño, an electrical engineer, a dreamer, one of those people who never makes any money because he spends his life looking for meaning in what he does.

Toño worked in a cockroach-infested hole behind an auditorium. There he had all sorts of old equipment: half-built television sets, stripped-down tape recorders, a shitload of tangled wires and, presiding over the disorder, his desk.

"We need a radio station in El Salvador," Jonas told him. "An AM station that can be heard right in the capital city. That's our idea."

Toño fell in love with the project. Before we'd even finished telling him about it, he was looking for a map of El Salvador to study the mountains, calculate distances, heights, valleys, the topography of our little country. The first task we faced wasn't so much learning the ropes as getting hold of equipment. There were legal complications. You can't simply buy a radio transmitter just like that. You need a permit, a licence, a lot of stuff. And since we figured they would try to jam it, Toño suggested we try a shortwave communications radio, which he would try to adapt for AM broadcasting by crystallising the end of the hand. . . .

"Whatever, but let's do it now," Jonas interrupted.

From that moment on, Toño spent every waking hour searching for equipment. Through contacts he had—and he never told us who—he got hold of an old transmitter, a very old transmitter, but a good one. He took it out of a fishing boat. A *Valiant Viking*. It had a viking stamped right there on the metal cover. It was small, but solid, weighed a good sixty pounds. And it was reliable, as we discovered later on.

Once he had the transmitter, Toño set to work to adapt it. He shut himself away in his workshop, hooking up buttons and soldering circuits, and managed to adjust it for AM. Then he began doing tests. He'd put on music and go off in his car to tune in and test the signal's reach and the quality of the sound. That guy was having the time of his life, it was written all over his face.

"How are you doing?" I greeted him one day.

"It's ready;" he said. "The Viking works. It's going to talk more than an old parrot."

"Toño, how does it work?" I asked, worried already.

You see, neither Jonás nor any of us knew anything about electronics. Nothing at all. We had trouble turning on a transistor radio. So he began trying to train us. That is, to train me. The first time, Toño was just like every other technician. They start giving you instructions and talking about ohms and resistance and watts and volts, and they keep you sitting there as if you knew what was going on, as if you had the same background. At last I admitted: "I don't understand anything."

So we agreed he would explain each step so that even a little kid could do it. On the Viking's side there were a whole slew of buttons. He put a number on each one. And in a notebook he wrote: "First, you push such-and-such a switch up. Second, you push such-and-such a switch down." And so on. Because down there no one was going to understand it any other way. Those little numbers travelled down with the transmitter, and they were still there years later, when the Viking fell into enemy hands. We never took them off.

Then we had to figure out how to ship it. I bought a small trailer and did some alterations. For the transmitter I built a hiding place: a box with a sink bolted to the top. Since I couldn't trust a carpenter to do it, I sawed it myself. I took the exact measurements, and the hollow box with its fake sink turned out really splendid. All set? Well, no, because when it came time to pack it up, it wouldn't fit. The Viking was nice and square, but in the back it had a thing that stuck out, like an old plug. This can't be important, I thought. Zip, I pulled it out, and the transmitter fitted perfectly. Problem resolved, I set off for El Salvador. My buddy and I were happy as could be, driving down to the place, still in Mexican territory, where we handed it over to others.

"Be careful when you wash your hands!" I joked with the guy I gave it to.

We weren't going to cross the border. The plan was to get others who weren't Salvadoran to take in the transmitter. I'd travel down later by plane. Once the equipment was safely in the country, I'd turn up with the infamous manual, because I was to be the instructor! It was my job to explain how the hell to run that sucker.

At last, months later, the day we were waiting for arrived. We all met on a farm in Quezaltepeque. Everyone from the party who had anything to do with the radio station was there—Joaquín first in line. We put the transmitter in a small empty house. We hung the aerial from one tree to another—a bipolar aerial that was so long it almost reached beyond the edge of the farm. Then we connected up the cables. Everything was perfect. The moment of truth had arrived. I went into action. The first step. . . . The second step. . . . With the manual in my hand, I gave the orders.

"Ready?" asks Joaquín.

"Ready." I say.

"But this isn't working. Nothing's happening."

"Nothing's happening?"

"Nix."

I kept looking through that manual and everyone kept looking at me. Joaquín, Jonas, half the national directorate. I started getting anxious. And what tends to happen in such circumstances happened: everyone knows, everyone gives an opinion, everyone sticks his finger in.

"Look, that tube barely gives off any light."

"No, *hombre*, it's not the tube. It's this thing over here."

"Tighten that screw, look how loose it is."

Do this, do that, nobody paid me the slightest heed. I stuffed the manual in my pocket so they wouldn't even remember to ask me.

"It's the tube," someone decided. "Stop the chatter and let's change the tube."

"What if that burns it out?" said another.

"Listen brother, if you don't play, you can't win."

In a little while, someone was off to San Salvador with the "bad" tube to buy another. He went and returned. They changed the tube on the Viking and it still didn't work. So they continued debating what might be wrong with the machine, and decided it was broken. That's when I remembered the little thing I'd pulled off in Mexico. The truth is I didn't dare mention it. But I couldn't keep quiet either.

"Look, I took something off it, a plug, because it didn't fit in the box. But I don't think that shitty little piece."

I was dying. Luckily, no one thought what I said mattered. They kept on pushing and pulling on the machine, trying it and getting more and more frustrated. It gave no sign of life. All our great plans had been crushed.

"César," Joaquín says to me, "what did you say about a plug? Could that be it?"

I don't think he'd even finished asking, and I was already getting ready to go back to Mexico. When I explained the disaster to Toño, he laughed: "You've got to be kidding, that's a bridge. The bridge that completes the circuit! It's like taking the spark plugs out of a car! Okay, where did you put it?"

For some reason, I hadn't thrown the little bridge away. I found it and sent it to San Salvador, and they tell me—I wasn't there to see for myself— that the Viking worked beautifully.

Broadcasting under Blankets

The very first broadcasts took place in 1979. We painted graffiti calling on people to tune in to our new station on Tuesdays and Fridays, and ran off leaflets announcing that the Salvadoran people now had their own voice, their own station, the People's Revolutionary Radio.

At first we went up on a little hill near the city to go on air. There was no other way. We hooked up at six in the afternoon—for how long? Ten minutes, maybe fifteen. A mix of commentary, revolutionary music and combative messages: agitation.

By 22 January, 1980 we were transmitting from the National University. That day we'd organised the first big demonstration of the recently created Revolutionary Coordinating Body of the Masses. Damn, it was incredible! Over 300,000 people in the street, the largest mobilisation ever. People began gathering at eight in the morning in Cuscatlán Park. They just kept coming, a sea of men, women, youth, unionists, militants with banners asking for democracy and attacking the Christian Democrats and their civilian-military junta, imposed by the gringos.

At about 9:30 am the crowd started to march, but since there were so many it moved very slowly. When the ones in front reached the National Palace near the cathedral, the ones at the back were still at the El Salvador del Mundo statue. The march didn't go straight downtown, it snaked all around the side streets—it must have been ten kilometres long, more or less. And there were people on the sides. All along the march there were cars with loudspeakers tuned in to our station so that everyone could hear.

We were back at the university broadcasting. Every so often a comrade would phone to tell us how the demonstration was going. We also listened to what the other stations were saying. That was the way we worked back then, pirating off other correspondents because the RRP, our station, was completely clandestine.

Transmitting from the university required some complicated manoeuvring. We usually went on air at six o'clock when the most students would be around. We'd put the aerial up on the roof and connect everything. Then we'd slip through a back door into a little room—a little closed off corner on the first floor, like a storeroom. We'd leave a tape recorder outside playing loud music to distract people, and several of us would keep watch to make sure no one came near. Then those of us with the loudest voices would take the microphone and begin the programme. We had to cover ourselves with blankets to muffle our chants, otherwise they carried into the hallway outside. It was boiling hot anyway, so broadcasting under wool blankets, like ghosts, was a real ordeal.

On the 22nd it was my turn to be the fan. The Viking overheated a lot, it wasn't made to transmit for such long periods. But with the excitement of all that was going on, we stayed on air an hour at a time. Our first hour-long programme! And there I was with a piece of cardboard fanning the Viking so that it wouldn't pass out. When the announcers stuck their heads up for air I'd fan them too. Mariana[3] was there, full of enthusiasm, announcing, reading messages, greeting all the organisations represented on the march.

Then a helicopter circled overhead and we thought they'd located us, so we turned off the transmitter and ended the broadcast.

"Let's go out into the street," I said, "and see what's happening."

What was happening was a terrible massacre. When we got to the US Embassy, we met people streaming the other way.

"They're killing!" they screamed. "Don't go down there!"

But since we were armed, we went on anyway.

"We're going to get it sooner or later anyway," one *compa* said. "Let's blow them to pieces!"

"Don't even think about it. They're shooting from the rooftops."

It was inexcusable—criminal. That huge mass of defenceless people targeted by sharpshooters firing from the roof of the National Palace itself. Other snipers were on top of the theatre and other buildings nearby. Even people who ran to the church got machine-gunned. Some died in their blood on the cathedral steps, others were trampled by the crowd. About a hundred were killed that day, never mind the wounded.

"You've got to take the station elsewhere," the leadership told us. "Increase its signal so that it reaches the whole country. Add short wave so that the whole world will know about the murderers who run this country."

We spent the rest of the year looking for a technician who could adapt the equipment, and a secure place to broadcast from. We found it in Morazán.

Inspired by the Monsignor

Monsignor Romero's radio station[4] was across the street from the archbishopric. Father Rogelio Pedraz was the director and he asked Goyo[5] if he knew of anyone trustworthy who could install a ten-kilo piece of equipment that had just been donated.

Goyo said, "My brother Apolonio just finished studying electronics in Germany."

Yes, I returned with my diploma and landed a good job in the communications department of CEL,[6] but it didn't mean anything to me. I wanted to give the technical things I'd studied overseas some social content. So after I met Rogelio and began to help out at YSAX, I was happy. At least I was doing something, supporting those who could do more than me.

That's when Rubén, another technician, a friend I'd met in Germany, came back to the country.

"It's Sunday," I told him. "Let's go to the cathedral."

"Are you drunk?" he asked. "Since when do you go to mass?"

"You should hear Monsignor Romero's homily. He's going to speak today."

Rubén was awestruck when he heard the Monsignor fearlessly chastise the forces of repression, raising his voice to condemn the attacks, speaking for those who could not speak. He decided to help me. The Monsignor's brave words were like a little motor that kept us going at his station, despite the friends and relatives who'd tell us, "You'd better get out of AX."

The noose was tightening day by day, but we felt we had to keep helping the Monsignor reach thousands of homes in the capital and in much of the country each Sunday. What affection and admiration that man evoked; you could listen to his sermon as you walked down the street, hearing it through the windows of every house, as if it were the only station in San Salvador!

The connections that happen in life: besides Goyo, I had another brother, Rafi, who had already joined the guerrillas. And just then the *compas* were looking for a technician to run the Viking they'd brought from Mexico. They wanted to set up a clandestine radio station to transmit from the university campus. So Jonás contacted me and asked if the bipolar aerial they had was appropriate. I told them it would work, but since the equipment had been adapted for broadcasting in AM between 1580 and 1540 KHz, the aerial ought to be about 90 metres long. And it would be no mean feat to hang such a huge aerial off the roof of the university!

Well, I helped them do it. A whole group of us went along because you need a lot of muscle-power to stretch taut such a long cable. We took the measurements and found it would fit across the roofs of the three buildings of engineering school. One group climbed up on the middle building carrying the middle of the aerial, where the insulator was. Two other groups went up on the other rooftops to pull it tight. We bolted one end down and then stretched it from the other end. We used a board to push and push until it was straight. Then we bolted it down. And we left it there. When it was time to transmit all we had to do was thread a cable onto the female connector at the centre and throw it down to where the Viking was hidden. Afterwards, just unthread it and that was that. That's how we were able to broadcast the historic march of 22 January.

Later on I couldn't continue working with the organisation because CEL sent me abroad on a training course. Rubén, my friend, stayed to help out at YSAX. Since by then I'd met Marianella[7] and had done translations at the Human Rights Commission, I took a lot of material with me about the situation in my country to spread the word overseas.

I returned to El Salvador a few days after the assassination of Monsignor Romero. The news hit me between the eyes. I could neither believe nor accept it. I was a pacifist. I worked in YSAX because I was convinced that the Monsignor could find a way out of the country's disastrous crisis. A whole lot of people shared that same hope. When they killed him, that was when I said yes to everything the *compa* proposed. I said yes to armed struggle. The death of the Monsignor helped clarify my beliefs. Not only in my case. I think the same thing happened to many others.[8]

I went to work on the transmitter. Mateo, who was my contact, brought me a huge box in the parking lot of a supermarket. Inside was the Viking. I had to adapt it for short wave because they had already decided to take it to Morazán. In those days I lived in an apartment near the zoo. I took the equipment home, looked it over, and realised that it could work perfectly well on other bands. The Mexican technician had changed the crystals so that it would work only on AM, but the equipment had everything it needed to broadcast on short wave. Only the tuner was broken, creating a short circuit. I had to repair it and than guess how it all worked, because there was no manual or anything. The instructions that César had brought from Mexico had been lost. My brother Rafi helped me and, between the two of us trying all the switches, we managed to figure it out.

I had still not gone underground. When I went out to the CEL office, I'd hide the transmitter under my bed. Or rather I'd put the bed on top of the transmitter, because to hide the Viking I had to build myself a special bed out of wood, one that would fold up like a big sandwich. When I came home, I'd open it up, take out the equipment, and Rafi and I would get to work testing it. Rafi would go out with his short wave radio, I'd put on classical music and he'd check the reception.

"It's buzzing over here," he'd tell me.

"Now you can't hear shit," he'd say next.

Day after day we worked at adjusting it until we got a good sound. The *compas* were thrilled when we told them the equipment worked fine. But it would work even better if we had a 300-watt amplifier, since the Viking could only put out 50 watts.

So we bought one in Panama, and while I was there I also bought several walkie-talkies, planning already for military communications on the two-metre band. Then I had to bring them all through customs at the Comalapa airport!

"What's this?" the customs agents asked, pointing to the walkie-talkies, which I had taken apart so that only the keypads were visible.

"They're remote controls for TVs."

"And what's this?" they asked, pointing to the amplifier which was so well packed and repacked that all you could see were a few buttons.

"A sound system for a party, *hombre*. Are you going to tell me you've never seen one before?"

"Show us the receipts."

"I haven't got them. I was robbed in Panama"

Of course I did have them, but well hidden. Imagine—on the receipt it said "Communications equipment". They kept me there for about an hour, hanging around and growing desperate. They wanted a bribe, of course.

"What's the story?" I pretended to be angry, "If there are taxes, then tell me how much. But I don't have the receipts."

"But to work out the taxes we need the receipts."

"So how can we settle this? Listen, I work at CEL, understand? For the government! The people from the company are waiting for me outside. Call them in here, ask them, see what ought to be done, but let's get on with it!"

Since they couldn't get either a receipt or a bribe out of me, they had to let me go.

I grabbed my bags and didn't look back. The *compa* waiting for me outside was as pale as I was.

"I've got everything," 1 told him happily.

To the car and home to unpack the treasure. Now we had an amplifier for the Viking! Before sending it to Morazán, two *compas*, Chefe and a girl, came to be taught how to use it. I'd numbered all the switches with little paper tags, and written up a manual explaining each step from turning it on to turning it off. I made it all very simple, thinking of the people who were going to be using it, and I took the precaution of making a photocopy.

We were also on the lookout for enough equipment to start a military communications network on the fronts. Since we couldn't buy these things, we figured we would requisition them. I walked the streets looking at the rooftops and wherever I saw a communications aerial I'd note down the address. Later, the commandos would go and take them. Everything ended up at my apartment, which was looking more and more like a storeroom: the Viking, six little Honda generators (one for each front), Yagi aerials, aluminium tubes, coaxial cables. . . . Now we had all the implements, but we had to train the implementers. So we planned a course in military communications for future radio operators, to be held on the last days of the year.

A nun arranged for us to stay in a house on the outskirts of San Salvador. We spent 30 and 31 December there. We had the liberated radios, the walkie-talkies from Panama, the homemade aerials. They got a blackboard for us, and we held the classes in a nice cool corridor. Everything was as clean and orderly as could be.

"Boys and girls," they used to call us, "lunch is ready."

We ate in a spotless room with white tablecloths. They stuffed us full, we talked for a while, and then back to class. At three in the afternoon, they'd be back: "Boys and girls, would you like a snack?"

They brought us coffee and cookies. It was fantastic.

The eve of the 31st—New Year's Eve—was just what the doctor ordered. While the fireworks were going off in the street, we were inside doing tests. With so much noise, it was a perfect simulation of a battle. One student would take a radio to one corner of the house, another to the other.

"Eastern Front calling the Guazapa Front," one would say. "Do you read me? Over."

"The shit's coming down hard!" answered the other. "Shout louder, sonofabitch!"

Abel and Mauricio, who already knew something about radio and electronics, led the classes along with me. The participants included Oscar, Babyface and

Samuel, who's now in the South, and a nun who went on to do political work in San Vicente. . . . There was also another nun learning to be a radio operator and encoder who was killed a few days later in Cutumay Camones.

The course was over. At the beginning of January 1981, with plans for the offensive under way, we said good-bye. From my apartment things disappeared one by one: the Honda generators, the radios, the aerials . . . Everything went to the front lines.

BACK TO BASICS

Pols and Listeners' Circles

So where did Venceremos end up in all this? What role would the station that had accompanied the BRAZ in the great battles play during the stage of dispersal? How could we adjust the station's work to fit the new tactics?

The essence of the new strategy lay in turning each guerrilla into a political organiser, and developing all the skills of our fighters. To do grassroots organising you had to have your own head organised first, so Venceremos concentrated on contributing to that objective by broadcasting political debate.

"The idea," Atilio said, "is to arm our people with arguments. Just like you have to train to have good aim with a rifle, you have to sharpen your political judgement to be an organiser. The station has to provide a lot of information, and analysis for digesting that information. That's the bottom line."

We'd painted it ourselves on a wall in Ciudad Barrios:

To be uninformed is like being unarmed.
Listen to Radio Venceremos!

How is a group of four or five guerrillas dispersed about the country, working alone in a zone, going to stay informed? Suppose they show up at a house and an old man invites them in for coffee: "Come on in, *hombre*. Come in and let's talk. Isn't it something that Duarte's going to the United Nations to propose a dialogue with the FMLN? Or don't you folks want to dialogue?"

The combatants lived in what was perhaps a very small world, very local, with some national vision and not much awareness beyond that. So here was a man kicking the ball at us and if we didn't get into the net fast, he'd score a goal. What reliable source could they count on? Where could they find out about things and be sure they weren't being tricked? The other media twisted the news; they made Duarte out to be the last bottle of Coca-Cola in the desert. Our men knew that wasn't the truth, but they needed arguments both to explain it to themselves and to convince that old man.

"The first priority is radios!" the commanders declared. "Every guerrilla unit needs a radio receiver right away, no matter what the cost."

The organisation made the effort, and the political officers of every guerrilla unit were given a radio as an indispensable piece of their equipment. They were little Phillips radios, sealed up in brown plastic. Besides being good and cheap, they withstand storms, dust, thumps—they were made for guerrillas. All the political officers—all the pols as we called them in guerrilla lingo—have those radios hanging around their necks. If you go to Perquín and meet up with a group of guerrillas, and you want to know who the political officer is, all you have to do is see who has the radio. That's him. For a political officer, that little radio with the Venceremos frequency is an umbilical cord linking him to the entire organisation and its political line. It's also a very practical tool for working with people.

"Hello!" a pol arrives at a little house he's never visited.

"Hello," the peasant woman tells him, "come on in where it's swept clean."

"How is it going, *señora*? How are the kids?"

That's how you start up a conversation, asking about the kids, about the fire-wood getting wet from so much rain, whatever. Pretty soon the pol, who always makes sure he shows up more or less in time for the Venceremos broadcast, says casually: "Gee, you haven't heard Venceremos today? It must be on already."

"No, we don't have a radio."

"Ah, but look at this little radio I've got, it's really good."

He starts talking and they turn to the station, and then they talk about what they hear.

The image of the pol with his radio says a lot about the role the station played during this decisive stage. Making sure of communications with our listeners was vital in keeping the organisation together. How could you disperse hundreds and hundreds of units throughout the country without ensuring you had a way of guiding their approach to the work, without some channel for direct communication? From then on, to this very day, Venceremos has been the means of communication and political education for the entire FMLN family dispersed across the country.

We also used the pol's radio to encourage people to set up listeners' circles. In part this was a practical response to the lack of both radios and batteries, but we were also interested in getting people into the habit of listening to the station in groups, so that after the show they could debate the issues we raised and understand them better. We encouraged these circles not only among guerrilla units, but among friends in unions, among the lads in the street, among neighbours, among the women of a *barrio*. Listen to the editorial, we'd say, and then discuss it. Listen to the editorial and you'll find the elements you need to analyse society correctly. During this stage we considered the editorials to be more important than ever. The trouble was we were so meticulous about saying everything clearly that we ended up confusing it even more. In the end, what were we saying? Could anyone understand our oh-so-brainy editorials?

Listen to what happened to me once. On Venceremos we were always talking about the listeners' circles: form them, meet together, but I'd never been able to take part in one. When I got hepatitis and had to be taken to Tancredo, I got the chance. Tancredo is where the sick and anaemic guerrillas go for a rest: rest and eat, sleep and eat. Of course, the schedule includes a Venceremos listeners' circle, so at six o'clock, yellow or not, there I was running the discussion and getting a new shock every day.

"What was the most important thing on today's programme?" I'd begin.

"Well, they laid an ambush in . . . "

"Not the military news. The important political message."

"Ummmm . . . "

"What was the issue they took up today?"

"Gee, I don't remember."

"Damn! So you weren't paying attention."

"No, well, yes I was paying attention, but I can't remember now."

"You can't remember anything?"

"Of course I do. They laid an ambush in El Semillero that . . . "

"Forget about the ambush. What was the editorial about?"

"Sorry pal, it's that . . . I've got this disease that makes me forget what I've heard."

"Does everybody have the same disease?"

The experience cured my vocabulary as much as my liver. That's where I realised we had to change the way we did editorials. People didn't understand them. If during the editorial I said "Open your ears! Today's message is important!" then you could see them concentrating, listening carefully, overcoming whatever technical problems or interference we had, and above all trying to overcome the worst interference of all: language. That's right, we'd act like college boys and use some sociological jargon, far-out abstractions that even when understandable, were never very pleasant to listen to. Of course, people's commitment and militancy were serious enough to overcome the tedium. People knew they needed to grow politically in order to improve their organising. When you haven't got fresh bread, you eat stale old loaves, and despite everything, those editorials that were so inappropriate for radio ended up feeding the pols and everybody else.

That's where the other side of the problem lay. What do you do if you have a lot of saints, but only one candle? Which one do you light up? We had only the one radio station, one station and one programme to reach very different audiences. In the editorials we had to give orientation to our fighters, but the same editorials were an arena for debating with the enemy. Even though you have the pols as a captive audience, you can rest assured that the enemy officers are listening too. Not the soldiers, they're not allowed to, but the officers, following the basic principle of know thy enemy, all have to tune in. How could you waste such an opportunity to argue with them? The buzz words, the language had to be very different for them.

The language had to be different again for influential personalities like Father Ignacio Ellacuría, for example. The rector of the UCA[9] was a man whose opinion mattered, not only to his students but to the guerrillas as well. He always deserved our respect, even though we didn't agree on a lot of things—and we agreed on many others—we had excellent relations with him. At times debating with Ellacuría was important, and you couldn't debate with him using some *campesino* fable; you had to use more academic language. That day we'd have to plan: "This editorial is for Ellacuría." He couldn't listen to the station, but he read transcripts of Venceremos, and the next day he'd respond, giving his opinion on the issue.

In other words, on our one and only programme we had to speak to the pol and the peasant woman he was organising, and Ellacuría, and the shameless colonel—and they were all priorities. If we'd had a weekly magazine or a big daily newspaper, we could have done some pieces with more depth, others with less, but Venceremos had to be a station for both the masses and the elite, for the organised and the unorganised. It was the only media we had, though that's no excuse for the yawns we provoked with our notoriously boring editorials.

One Pole, Two Poles, Three Poles . . .

The target audience of Venceremos is quite varied. The station addresses friends and enemies, kids on the street and soldiers, peasants, the bishop and the gringo ambassador. Venceremos talks to them all, and all of them, if they wish or if they dare, can talk on the radio. But Venceremos *belongs* to the combatants. The *compas* feel that it's theirs. It *is* theirs! So if you receive a war dispatch via radio and you stick it in your bag and forget about it when it's time to do the programme, you'll have the radio operator from that zone calling you up the next day: "Listen, what happened to the dispatch we sent you? About the electrical pole . . . "

"Oh yeah, *hombre*, we didn't have time. We'll put it on tomorrow."

Then with all the comings and goings and your bag stuffed with papers, you forget again.

"Look, what happened? I didn't hear it yesterday either."

"Yes, *hombre*, forgive me, what happened was . . . "

They won't let you go. Like a dog nipping at your ankle, they won't leave you in peace until you broadcast a report of their action, even if it's nothing to speak of. The same thing happens if you make a mistake and instead of saying "in the village of Juilijuiste," you say "Juilijueste."

"What were you thinking of? It's Juilijuiste!"

And a little while later: "It wasn't one pole, *hombre*. It was two!"

The *compas* carry out an action. When the radio reports it, the mission is completed, but until then, it's as if they hadn't done a thing. For the fighters, a military action is only over when it goes out over the radio, when everyone knows about it. Even if COPREFA reports it, if Venceremos doesn't it doesn't count.

When the militia began to grow, Fidel, the commander of the Torola zone, told us the story of a few new *compas* who went to Carolina to dynamite a couple of electrical poles. They came back about 5:30 in the afternoon.

"We did it," the boys reported, and without telling anyone else, they turned on the radio and sat down to listen to the programme. When it was over, they went to complain to Fidel: "Why didn't they mention the poles?"

"What poles?"

"The ones we just knocked over."

"But did you write to Venceremos?"

"No."

"First you have to write the dispatch and send it to Venceremos!"

They thought it was automatic, that the radio wasn't only the voice of the people, but the all-seeing eye. The relationship between the station and the fighters got so intense that they don't say "This happened in February of '85" or "in March of '86". They'll say: "It was during Idiot One", because once when the army launched an operation called "Victory One," Santiago called it "Idiot

One." The next he called "Idiot Two." Even their frame of reference for time is set by the names the station uses for operations or the stages of the political or military struggle.

The way the fighters identified with the station was undoubtedly very encouraging, but it brought complications. The same old story: how to edit so much information? The electrical poles are a good example. When we launched a campaign to sabotage the electrical system, you can imagine how many guerrilla units and how many militia members were mobilised across the country to leave it in the dark. The next day a mountain of dispatches started arriving, and all of them were more or less the same. Of course we had to tighten up the information, to make it more fluid, more digestible, not least because it literally would not fit in the space we had.

What did we do? First, since we don't have computers or anything of the sort, Marvin came up with a system. We put them on little papers all cut the same size and filed in different boxes. Everything about poles went here; engagements went over there; ambushes in this other box and so on. Just before the programme began, we'd grab the pile of "poles" and order them by front. Then we'd summarise: on the eastern front, 17; on the central front, 20; on the paracentral front . . . a total of 96 poles knocked down in such and such regions. Did that do the trick? No way, it was no good.

"What about my pole?" the first complaint would come in. "We blew it up at three o'clock in the morning at the turn-off for Yucuaquín."

We couldn't collectivise it, but what a deadly programme reading a series of 96 dispatches on sabotage actions against electrical poles, all of them the same. The final sabotage was against us, for the crime of boredom! Lately we've lengthened the show to over an hour and spiced it up with other things, but it doesn't make any difference. Now it isn't 96 poles they knock over, it's twice that, so our show is just as bad or worse.

If an electrical pole arouses so much expectation, what happens with a casualty? Never mind an ambush! If you forget to read it on air, they might strangle you, and the *compas* are right. Suppose you were a member of the militia: You leave your house today, catch a few hours bad sleep in the woods, march through the middle of the night, lay an ambush with your unit, spend the whole day hiding. You've left your wife with all the kids, your brother taking care of everything on the farm, you've had to make up half a novel to get away from your village without anyone suspecting. Now there you are in the bush, your stomach grumbling, getting eaten alive by mosquitos, scared but working up your courage . . . and at last you pull off the ambush! Then after so much effort some jerk on the radio forgets and all that effort doesn't get recognised, doesn't get aired so that everyone will know, so that all the militia who took part can hear it and say, "I was there."

The political officers tell us that the section we do on the military map, when we read out all these small heroic deeds, helps them a lot. Above all, it helps them consolidate the new recruits. We don't simply give the information cold just like that. We greet the *compañeros*, congratulate them for the courage they showed. Flattery for a *macho*, that's what it is, but when we complain that that long sausage of a section isn't a very journalistic way of doing things, they shut us up right away: "Who is the programme for? For the press or for the fighters?"

If we compress the information it isn't of any use to them, because when it's time for the next ambush and the political officer goes to the militia man's house, he'll find him a bit reluctant: "Brother, I'll see you tonight at such and such a place. You know what for."

"Look, I . . . I can't. My kid's sick."

"Don't tell stories, *hombre*. What's the matter?"

"Well . . . I knocked over a pole and Venceremos didn't say a thing!"

ON TO THE CITIES

A Typical Day at Venceremos

At 5:30 in the morning everybody's awake. Ready? We stand in formation. We do calisthenics for about half an hour. An icy bath in the river and a cup of hot coffee.

* * *

Coffee is a ritual in Morazán. No matter what time it is, there's always coffee. At three in the morning they put on the first pot. You fill up your gourd and serve the whole crowd.

* * *

From six to eight in the morning we do the monitoring. We listen to all the stations in the country, the TV channels, the Voice of America and the Honduran stations, which usually have a lot of news. The camp is a beehive of activity, a pile of radios all turned on, every one of us in his or her tent, deep into our assigned station, taking notes. If you want to find out what's happening in the world, go to Venceremos and ask any of these journalists without diplomas.

Those of us on the broadcasting side get together for a few minutes to decide on the day's work plan. We divide up the tasks: I'll do the editorial, you finish the soap opera, he'll help Chiyo do the monitoring.

* * *

In the camp you could find everything from *Revolutionary Theory* to *Love in the Time of Cholera*. From Marx to Márquez, whatever you wanted. The newspaper comes every day. The country's political magazines like *ECA*, the *New York Times* every so often, *Newsweek*, Omar Cabezas's novels, Sergio Ramirez's latest, *Perestroika* by Kiva Maidanik, *Perfume* by Suskind. . . . The library is quite large—only for long periods we have to hide it or split it up among several locales.

* * *

At eight o'clock we have breakfast. If you've got a deadline to meet, someone will bring you *tortillas*, but it's better to go down to the kitchen, because it's the heart of the camp, the best spot to be. There we have another cup of coffee and get the latest gossip, we run into Atilio, talk about the news, we run into Luisa, we laugh, and we don't go back up to work until old Germán tells us what he saw in the night.

* * *

We built Vietnamese kitchens which have a system of underground tubes that cool off the smoke and dissipate it near the ground as if it were mist. That's the first rule if you want to keep the helicopters from seeing you from up above.

* * *

Nine in the morning and the sacred monitoring meeting. The entire staff gets together and each one reads out his news. Let's see, you, YSU. If there is something worth discussing, we stop and discuss it. Remember that the monitoring was being done by peasant boys and girls who didn't even know the earth is round, yet there they were debating Reagan's foreign policy or the foreign debt. Once, one of them got Lebanon all mixed up. He had the Palestinians fighting the Italians and the French—an awful mess, nobody understood a thing. Somebody suggested we drop it and go on to other items.

"Just a minute!" the *compa* protested. "If you don't explain Lebanon to me, I can't continue monitoring."

Incredible discussions and long-winded explanations make the meetings interminable, but these daily debates are the best political school by far. They force us to dig up the sources if we're going to explain, among other things, what the devil is happening in Lebanon.

* * *

The monitoring team liked to have its idols. When Tripoli got bombed, Khaddafi was the hero. At Venceremos people talked a lot about Khaddafi and it was like touching God's ass. When the war against Nicaragua was really hot, Humberto Ortega was the man. Khaddafi had already fallen from grace because he vacillated at the meeting of the Non-Aligned Nations. After that, everything was Humberto. Then Humberto went to Sapoá for talks with the contras. Sure, we tried to explain to the *compas* about the need for flexibility, but even so Humberto fell off his pedestal—and Gorbachev climbed up. Everybody started talking about Gorbachev, and since we have a lot of names that start with "ch," people started saying Gorbachiyo, Gorbacheje, Gorbachila, Gorbachela—a whole fan club. Heroes were rising and falling fast! Alan García was the star for a short while. Alfonsín had a few points in his favour, but lost them quickly. Several heroes always held their stature: Fidel Castro, for example. All the *compañeros* on the monitoring team really admire and respect Fidel.

* * *

At that meeting we decide on the programme: the subject of the editorial, the military news, news from the popular movement . . . Since we don't have many typewriters or enough time to transcribe it all, we just staple together the handwritten pages from the monitoring team, write up a summary to go on top and send it all to Atilio. If he doesn't get to read everything, at least the summary gives him an overview, and if a story interests him, he can dig it out from the pile. It's all there: opinion pieces from the U.S. press, commentaries from Radio Havana, summaries of panel discussion shows, the national and international news—a daily mountain of information.

There was a time when Atilio would stop whatever he was doing at twelve sharp to meet the broadcasting team, go over the programme, and discuss all the issues. He'd give us his opinion on the political approach to take, but how we actually did it was our problem. As the war became more complex, the meeting got shorter and shorter. Sometimes he'd just check the programme over with Marvel and delegate more to the team, but if you read over the scripts at five o'clock and thought something might cause political problems, you could always go to Atilio and he'd take the time to read them over and suggest another approach. Venceremos always has access to Atilio.

Once we get the green light from Atilio, we have lunch.

* * *

In the kitchen there are two big pots. One is where they cook up the corn for *tortillas*—there's always plenty of corn. The other pot is for what we call the "withwhat." You've got to eat *tortillas* with something, haven't you? You don't eat something with *tortillas*; it's the other way around. *Tortillas* are the meal. That's how *campesinos* (and guerrillas) eat: our diet is *tortillas*. The withwhat could be beans, rice, cheese, meat, vegetables, whatever. But the proportions are always a lot of *tortillas* and a little withwhat. Isra can put away six or eight *tortillas* in a single sitting, depending on the work he's been doing. We've got one *compa* we call Juanito Twelve Chengas. A *chenga* is the same as a *tortilla*, only *chengas* are thick and the size of a dinner plate. Juanito would chow down with a dozen at every meal. You've got to be a horse to eat a dozen *chengas*.

* * *

After lunch, some of us nap for half an hour. Then at 2:00 or 2:30, each of us scuttles off like a crab to his cave to write up his piece for the show. To write in a guerrilla camp is no mean feat. Forget about having a desk where you turn on the lamp and sit down to pound the keys of a typewriter. What you do is pick up a pencil, find a rock to sit on, and start scribbling. When it rains it's a disaster. The paper gets wet, you can't find anywhere to sit, everything gets muddy, even your thoughts, and you can't remember what you were going to write about.

We don't only write. Somebody goes out to do an interview, another makes up jingles, or attends to the comments of some visitor.

* * *

Jonás turns up one day and says: "So how are the apparatchik today?"
"What apparatchik?"

"You. You're a bunch of old fogies. Squares! Venceremos is boring!"

"The best criticism you can make of a river is to build a bridge, don't you think?"

"Precisely. That's why last night I dreamed up something that'll be a lot of fun. Here's the script. Let me know if you like it."

"A script for what?"

"Well, it's a series. A series, but it's not serious. It's called 'The Little Squirrels.'"

"What's it about?"

"There are two characters: a little squirrel who's very political, and another who thinks he's hot shit."

"We can't do that. Which of us can talk like a squirrel?"

"Jesus! You're not even apparatchik. You're just a piece of shit! Don't you have a tape recorder with a speed control?"

"Yeah."

"Well, record the voices normally and then speed it up so it sounds like squirrels talking. Let's do it, *hombre*!"

"But you see . . . "

"Go jump in the river!"

Before Jonás became a guerrilla, he studied art. He was an actor on the stage and taught acting technique. He's a fierce critic of the straight-laced thinking that often comes across on Venceremos.

* * *

At five o'clock everything should be ready. It has to be. Those of us on the broadcasting team get together to decide who will read what, what music we'll use, any last-minute news. We organise the programme and check the scripts one last time. We all agree on what to do—or we start fighting.

* * *

We called Yaser "Menéndez y Pelayo"[10] because he reads the dictionary and he's a real master of syntax, metaphors, parasynthetic adjectives . . .

"People aren't going to understand that word, Yaser."

"What word?"

"That one, 'plaudits.'"

"You're nuts."

"Nor this one, 'uberous'. I don't even know what it means."

"Go look it up in the dictionary."

"Where are the listeners going to look it up?"

"You underestimate the people. You think they're all ignorant."

"It's not that. People don't know what uberous means."

"They should learn. That way they'll get educated."

"You just said they weren't ignorant. Who has to get educated, them or us?"

"Simple language makes people stupid!"

"Flowery language makes them think they're stupid!"

"Come on, cut the bullshit. It's almost six—and the programme's going to come out shituberous!"

* * *

Six o'clock. On air. The national anthem. Every one at his post. Ready? "This is Radio Venceremos, voice of the workers, peasants and guerrillas!" Broadcasting live for an hour straight is really stressful. Not only because a bomb might drop on you, but because the responsibility weighs on your shoulders. After all, this is not just any old radio station. You've got to choose every word with care, because you know the next day the Voice of America is going to reply. You have to make sure the tone is right for psychological warfare. You have to improvise knowing full well that the enemy is monitoring you and will take advantage of any slip-up, and above all, the *compas* are listening and if you show any lack of conviction it affects their combat morale.

Afterwards we do a quick evaluation and then go to supper.

* * *

All of Radio Venceremos's programmes—from 10 January, 1981 to this day—have been saved and are safely stored somewhere in the world. Not one cassette has been lost. We've got thousands of hours of tape of leaders dead and alive, interviews with combatants, the daily military news . . . The oral history of the revolution is right there! We just have to write it up. Anyone fancy the job?

* * *

At night we have a few things left to do, the most important being to waste time gabbing with our friends, but sometimes there is a political meeting, or we have to monitor foreign broadcasts. We usually all get together to watch the eight o'clock news, which is one of the best. For me, and I think for everybody, sitting there watching television with everyone is the best part of the day.

"Listen to that bastard Ponce[11]!"

"His ears will burn tomorrow, because we'll answer him right back!"

"Are you recording that shit?" Atilio asks.

"Yes"

"Let's do a Guacamaya with Ponce. He deserves it!"

Then everybody comes up with a joke or an idea. It's a lot of fun.

* * *

Some people go to roost early with the chickens. Or because of the chick waiting in his tent! Others stay up to watch a movie on the betamax or to tell stories about *La Ciguanaba*. For a while, when Luisa was in charge of the station, we were up all night playing a card game called *matraca*. Playing that game with Luisa was really tricky because she played to win. You could hear us shouting all the way to the mountains of Honduras. Isra would get mad as hell at all the noise and laughter, but what else could we do? *Matraca* is the official game of Venceremos. Anybody who doesn't play it doesn't love his mother.

★ ★ ★

Too bad for the guy who has to stand watch. Good night, tomorrow's another day.

The Last Shy Guerrilla

Love begins with messages by courier. That's the rule among lovers in Morazán—so much so that the desire to write your own messages became one of the greatest motivations to learn to read and write for our peasant *compas*. I'm glad they learned because I couldn't find the time to write all of theirs as well as my own.

"Well it's that . . . listen, I . . . " Servando says one night. "It's that I'd like you to do me a favour."

"A message, right?"

"But don't tell anybody."

It's always got to be a secret. Even though most of the time everybody already knows, you've got to have a touch of mystery and the complicity of a procuress. Or a procurer, in my case.

"Who's it for?" I ask in a whisper.

"For Butterfly, *hombre*," Servando breathes. "Lately I can't sleep for thinking about her."

"Okay, go ahead."

Servando dictates and I fill up the lines of a page of my notebook. Sometimes the wooer will ask you to write in big letters, easy to read, so the sweetheart won't miss even a comma.

"You don't think it's a bit pushy to say 'my dear comrade'?"

"It depends."

"Then take it out, would you? Better later on when the mango's ripe."

The letters are written studiously, weighing the implication of each and every word. They're long, kilometric, filled with country-and-western romanticism and words borrowed from the radio soaps. They're also illustrated.

"Do you know how to draw birds?"

It's a very common question in Morazán. You see, love letters are supposed to have two birds in the corner of the page, their beaks kissing, and hearts with arrows through them.

"Will you fold it for me, or should 1 find someone else who knows how?"

There are two ways to fold a letter. There is the utilitarian way you use if you're telling Luisa to send some cassettes up to Venceremos. Then there is the other way, the artistic way, for when a man is in love. How you fold the paper is part of the message: like a flower, like a little *tamale*, in the shape of a heart, so that when your lady-love opens it she feels the first flush of heat. It unfolds like a rose and inside she finds the nectar of your words: "*Compañera*, please forgive my being so forward, but ever since that afternoon when I saw you in Perquín, my days have been without sun, my compass without a north, my *tortillas* without salt."

If they answer your letter, there's hope. You sprout wings. That Sunday, early in the morning, you meet Servando by the stream. He's washing his things.

"So, it worked."

He wants to look good because he's off on a visit. He bathes, combs his hair, puts on his clean clothes, his tight shirt. All resplendent, he sets his cap or his hat on his head just right. A man can't go out bare-headed. I spent several years with my head uncovered until my girlfriend couldn't stand it any more: "I can't go on with you like that."

"I've got a big head. No hat will fit me."

So she went to a tailor and ordered one made to my size. You see, a man without a hat is worth nothing. The first thing a man gets and the last thing he loses is his hat. To go bareheaded in the countryside is like going barefoot in the city.

"Good luck, Servando!"

The usual thing is to make like a cat. The beloved goes to the camp where the girl is staying. He doesn't say he's going to see her of course. He's come to talk with one of his buddies, or any excuse at all. He yacks on and on, and it gets late. They invite him to eat and it gets later. Once night falls, he makes like a cat. As a good guerrilla, a good *campesino*, he knows where the girl sleeps and how to get there surreptitiously in the dark, to the tent where she awaits him. In absolute silence—because a lot of people are sleeping nearby—he goes inside, stays with her, then he leaves. Nobody finds out, only the guard. You've got to be a hell of a good cat to get by the guard unnoticed, since he's a guerrilla and a *campesino* just like you!

* * *

Is there time for love among the guerrillas? It should be the other way round: Could you possibly do this without love? No way. We love like crazy in the guerrilla camps. Love here is as common as bullets flying by, and there are good reasons for it. Going off into the mountains is a supreme act of rebellion for a young kid. By going against established society, he or she assumes a lot of responsibility from a young age. Responsibility about life, about death, about political decisions. They know that what they are doing will determine the future of the country, no matter whether we win or lose. They feel they are part of something so big it can change the course of the entire country. Some do this more consciously than others, but everyone shares in this feeling of absolute rebelliousness.

So what happens when you're 14 or 16 and you discover that you are in control of your life and your actions? Who is going to tell you yes or no? Your father and older brother can't rule your life any more, so you can love with incredible freedom. You break free of all the social conventions, all the prejudices, all the proper ages for doing one thing or another. You break free and that liberates your capacity for love. Among the guerrillas, you're always in love with someone, and you're always trying to get someone to fall in love with you. Always, day in day out, there's someone waiting for you who wants to make love to you.

This freedom we've won meets up with the oldest of traditions and it's quite a mix. You see, all the moral crap about courtship—sin and staying a virgin and sleeping with somebody else—all that gets buried in the great act of rebellion, but the beautiful rite of love remains. The peasant way of being remains, the little birds in the corners of the page.

* * *

You get all kinds, from the most romantic to the most pragmatic—and the shy.

The romantics go and stand by the wall. I don't know how it is, but when people fall in love there's always a stone wall and she always manages to be sitting there with her eyes lost on the horizon, and he's there, at a prudent distance, rhythmically pounding the mouth of his rifle with the palm of his hand.

"Well yeah, at home we had a little cow . . . You know, once it got worms and we didn't know what to do."

Our Romeo talks on and on, telling stories, waiting for the decisive moment to declare his love.

"Well you know, I've been thinking about you a lot and I'd like for us to be together, that is if you would too."

Acompañarse. That's the matrimonial word. To become *compañeros.* Father Rogelio might even end up involved if it's a formal *acompañamiento*, which is the guerrilla equivalent of a wedding. The romantics always use that strategy, promising a stable relationship and eternal love, no matter whether such a thing is at all feasible in this crazy shit.

Not the pragmatics. The pragmatics skip the protocol and get right down to business.

"Okay, let's both go in this column, then I'll come by your place tonight. Tell me where you're going to be."

"Jesus!" she gets a bit frightened. "Who do you think you are?"

"I don't have a partner and neither do you, right? I'll be there."

"Hang on, don't be in such a hurry."

"But that's the way things are. I'm a man and you're a woman. Why say no, eh?"

"I haven't said that."

It's a form of wooing imposed by the war. We're here today, tomorrow who knows? The man doesn't mince words. The only problem is if she doesn't like the guy. If she does, if he's sparked a feeling, it doesn't matter if his approach is romantic or pragmatic.

Then there are the shy ones. I'm in that category, but I don't know if anyone else is. If there were others, they didn't stay that way for long. Really, I think I may be the only shy man left in this war. Or rather I was, because something as surprising as it was unstoppable happened to me. Want to hear about it?

* * *

Then there's the other side of it, the fierce competition. Among the guerrillas, love is always a wrestling match. You see, in the military force there are far fewer women than men. Among the rank-and-file supporters, in the communities depopulated by repression or unemployment, women predominate, but in a guerrilla column the proportion is seven men for every woman. Seven snipers have got that woman in their sights. Seven crocodiles ready to fight over her in the war of love, the little war within the larger one.

In reality, since the supply is so much greater than the demand, it's not the men who decide. She does. The woman selects the one she'd like to *acompañarse*. That's the way it is. It's matriarchal, feminist, and detestable, but what else can we do? They pick one and leave six. Among the guerrillas, women have all the luck.

★ ★ ★

So, one fine day after five years of working together at Venceremos, of learning all the good, the bad, and the ugly about each other, of her being the party rep in the radio collective, the one charged with bending our minds to the right path, after five years with her as my boss and political officer, Leti stood before me as a woman. I was getting some papers ready for the afternoon show, and when I looked up I saw her and her two big boobs. Leti didn't say a thing and neither did I, but she made me feel her presence. You haven't stopped to look at me the whole war, have you? Well, from now on you're going to have to notice me, understand? Because what's standing before you, above all, is a woman. All that I photographed in her shining eyes.

Down that path I went, my thoughts caught up in the vertigo of my shyness, terrified of putting my foot in my mouth. Was I mistaken? After five years, why does she do this to me? That very evening, I had to take a truck to Perquín because the army was threatening to launch another operation. On the way back, at a crossroads, I ran into Leti. She was waiting for some mules to take the radio equipment up into the mountains. I stopped the truck.

"Don't you look elegant!" she said to me. "I knew you could drive, but I've never seen you at the wheel before. Bye-bye!"

My confusion was growing, I had a bunch of spaghetti between my ears. Could it be true? Suppose I send her a letter and she tells me to go to hell? I could never stand the humiliation!

The next day, I was the one who got a letter. As soon as I saw it folded, my heart started pounding. It could only be her.

Remember, you've got to take along the Venceremos hook-up and change the frequency every other day.

It started off with a rather obvious comment, since I'd been doing that for five years and I didn't need anyone to remind me of anything. I carried that equipment in my sleep. The letter went on and right in the middle of the pretext she slipped in a phrase:

You looked so elegant last night! I wish I could have gone with you.

Then on it went giving directions for the hook-ups and the cables, but by then I was already thinking about other hook-ups and connections.

The army operation turned out to be a false alarm, so the commanders brought us all together in El Manzanal, at the foot of Gigante Hill. That's a lovely camp, filled with apple trees, not the apples they have in other countries, but little yellow fruit that here we call fart-apples because they're full of air and when you bite into them—pppfff—they sound like a fart. Well, it was there in that Salvadoran paradise, under those huge green leafy trees, that Eve tempted me with her apple, even if it was a fart-apple. Right there Leti launched her final offensive. It began in the morning in the Venceremos air-raid shelter, a very narrow tunnel where only one person can enter or leave at a time. On my way out—what a coincidence—I met Leti coming in. I clung to one side and as she passed by with her eyes on the ground, her tits brushed against me, just the nipples. Two boobs this big! I was left breathless, my mouth dry. I still didn't know what to do because I wasn't sure. Suppose she laughs at me, suppose she answers me with a guffaw? I was so shy I wanted to bury myself in that air-raid shelter and never come out until the war was over.

Later on, when I was putting up my tent, Leti came by: "It's a pretty tent, Marvel. Big for one person, small for two."

You could have knocked me down with a feather! I was going nuts. That night I made up some excuse and went to see her. She shared her tent with Dina, so we just talked in whispers killing time until the other girl fell asleep. Once Dina was snoring—or pretending to snore, I'll never know—I took Leti's hand in mine. It was electric, like picking up a live wire. She pulled me towards her and we kissed a long French kiss that was more like a bite, panting too loudly all the while.

"What's the matter?" Leti whispered. "When you taught me broadcasting you didn't take so long."

Shit! But the other girl was right there. How could we do it? Of the three of us, one had to go, so I got up and went outside. I went back to my tent to sleep all alone and dream about the stars.

At dawn a letter arrived:

Let's talk. You must be wondering about things.

More than wondering, I was horny as hell. I was sure I wasn't wrong.

"I want one thing to be clear," Leti began. "It's crazy what we're going to do. As for me, I want to do it. If you do too, great, but don't get the idea that we're going to stay together."

"Whatever you want," I said. "At this point in the championship, any penalty will do."

The worst thing was that the second night Isra was on guard duty. To sneak by without Isra knowing is like asking for the moon. Isra hears things a kilometre away, he sees in the dark, neither special forces nor elves can get by him. But I had to get around him because—and I haven't mentioned this so far—at that time Leti was Mauricio's girlfriend, and Mauricio, the technician, was my good friend, a friend who had the bad luck of being sent to another front for a few months.

The TV news was over. Everybody went off to their tents and all the lights went out. Alone at last, we started kissing passionately, but we were right next to the television, in the camp's meeting place.

"Let's get out of here," she says, already burning.

"Yeah, let's go."

"Where are we going?"

"Oh . . . I don't know."

"You haven't thought of where we're going?"

"Afraid not."

How shameful! The tomcat is supposed to have everything planned out, the time and the place, but just having kept my nerves in check enough to do my usual tasks was plenty for me. Luckily, the she-cat saved the day.

"I know a place," Leti told me. "Isra won't see us. Come on."

She took me to her place, and there we hugged, made love, bit each other, we let loose . . . All the verbs and all the dirty stuff that I'm too shy to tell you.

* * *

There's no movies for the guerrillas, no cafés and no discotheques. Love is what there is. Love is what helps you find, not meaning—you've got meaning—but colour in life. Love and the whole drama leading up to it: did she look at me, she said yes, yesterday I got a letter, today I touched her foot under the table, I put my finger here. . . . All that give and take gets you excited. It makes you happy to be alive.

We don't have Mondays here, or Tuesdays, or Sundays, or anything else. Every day the monitoring at six in the morning, every day the programme at six in the afternoon, every day the enemy might get you. Day or night, in mountains or plains, you live with the terror of a helicopter assault. You live in a brutal, violent world where you've always got to be ready for whatever comes, where you're not at home. You live with death at your side. So a girl bathing in a stream, a well-put compliment, a button poorly fastened, puts colour back in your day. It makes it different.

In my diary I wrote up a vision. One day I was sitting on a stone watching Lidia de Licho and two other women bathing. I was there for an hour, as if watching a movie. The *compas* were pouring water on themselves, laughing, soaping up their naked bodies, no bras. They weren't flirting with me nor did I have any desire to go after anyone. I was just watching. Watching a woman. Watching beauty and forgetting the gunpowder and screams.

* * *

I'm from the asphalt city of Caracas, educated in London. I've visited a hundred cities, but I had no idea what a peasant woman from Morazán is like when she makes love. I've seen a lot, but in all my wanderings about the globe Leti is the most erotic woman I've ever known. Erotic. No inhibitions. She can enjoy a relationship, enjoy sex in a way I hadn't found in any other woman I'd ever met: She's from the *barrio* of Azacualpa. Her most cosmopolitan experience to date had been selling clothes between San Miguel and Usulután, but Leti knew infinitely more about love than I. She knew, among other things, about the importance of words. With Leti, love is spoken, the entire love-act is filled with words. Sensual words referring to this love and to a love we might invent, to shapes, to smells, to tastes. With Leti, love is never limited to hands or mouths or anything else. I never imagined this peasant woman's way of making love. It destroyed my preconceptions—and put an end to my shyness.

In the morning, while we were drinking coffee, Isra winked at me: "You look tired, Marvel," he said and I knew right then that he knew, and that I could count on his silence.

* * *

Here, people have dropped all their traditional ways of behaving. Nobody cares if a woman has had several husbands. Why should it matter? If today she breaks off with one and tomorrow she starts up with another, does that diminish her moral qualities, her capacity to be a good person? It's not a question of promiscuity. I understand promiscuity to be when a woman sleeps with her husband's son, where everybody's getting it on with everybody else. That doesn't happen on the front. If Santiago is with Ana Lidia, she isn't going to lay a finger on me. Somebody's girlfriend is his girlfriend, and people respect that.

People respect homosexuality too. Take the case of Nando, the tailor who made uniforms for half the BRAZ. Nando asked permission like everyone else and made like a cat to be with his friend. Nobody reproached him for being gay. The only problem with Nando was when he wanted to measure you for a pair of trousers—careful with that hand! There was one guy here who called himself Lucha Villa. The *cuilios* would come and he'd shoot at them like everybody else. There were lesbians. Who didn't know about the turbulent love affairs between Trini and whatever her name was? So what? Pluralism has to be the rule in love too.

* * *

I discovered how to find eggs, cut bunches of bananas, ripen sapodillas. I learned to make the best tents in the camp; I learned which poles should be bent and which shouldn't. I got hold of a big nylon sheet—matrimonial size. Even though it weighed a ton in my pack, with it we could make love all the way up and down and to either side, and we didn't fall out. Our tryst under the fart-apple trees led to a steady relationship. Leti and I became a couple, publicly acknowledged. What we never institutionalised was love itself. In the mountains, there is always a place to make love, and we always want to.

Backroom Heroes

I've never liked the Venceremos posters. Most of them are pictures of the broadcasters, or at most, of the production team, but there are hundreds of other people who are involved in this project and who make it possible.

The station is a collective project. What the hell could Santiago use to start up the generator if Odilón didn't bring the gasoline? No matter if we have tons of gasoline, where the fuck could Mauricio hang the aerial if there weren't people ready to give their lives to defend it? And where would we find people ready to give their lives to defend others if there weren't mothers who had read the Bible with Miguel Ventura or Rogelio, and who decided to raise their children to be so generous?

These are the people who don't go on air and aren't on the posters. The logistics team, for example. Let's not worry about the *tortillas* or the medicine or the thousand other things you have to have on a guerrilla front. Let's just talk about gasoline. How do we get gasoline for Venceremos? Little by little, we built up a network of young men who buy a bucketful in Osicala, peasants who carry a litre in their shoulder bag, drivers who store a few gallons in a house in the town of

Sociedad. . . . They have to work with small quantities, like ants, because there's no way to hide or justify taking a whole barrel up to Perquín.

Quincho was the first one to weave the network. He trained Odilón, Roque, all his loyal troops. Then as the war grew more complex, so did Venceremos. We needed more and more gasoline. On top of our six o'clock show, we started doing another at eight. Later on, we added one at six in the morning, then a fourth at noon. From a half-hour programme we went to forty-five minutes, then an hour, and at one god-awful point we were doing an hour and a half or two hours straight. From a small generator we went to a big gasoline-driven one, then to a big diesel generator, plus the FM generator, and another little one to charge the batteries for all the FM repeating stations. It became a big operation, but the logistics were always based on grassroots organising, on an immense machinery of people who made sure each little cog worked.

When the BRAZ was strong our gasoline operation wasn't so humble. Once, during the campaign when the butcher Medina Garay was killed, we set up a barricade on the Pan-American Highway at a place near El Semillero. Hundreds of vehicles got held up, among them two big tanker trucks, one full of gasoline, the other carrying diesel and kerosene. When we went to take that treasure, the drivers didn't even get mad.

"Take whatever you like. It doesn't belong to us."

With the sort of brazenness typical of the BRAZ, we left the battle in a caravan of twelve buses carrying our troops, a jeep in front, another behind, and a third for the logistics chief guarding his two tanker trucks. Just like a regular army!

Since kerosene is the fuel peasants use for their lamps, we handed it out along the way. Every time we came to a town we started yelling: "Kerosene! Come and get it! It's free!"

The whole village turned out, lines of people with buckets. The diesel also became a party. We filled up all the buses and cars we came across, any Christian on wheels. The gasoline, of course, was ours. We took it to Carolina on the banks of the Torola River, and from there our immense grassroots network took over. We had drums stored in the homes of dozens of supporters who risked their lives to make sure Venceremos could go on air.

Other people who don't go on air are the *compas* of the security team: Walter's men, Ismael's, German's—these people are there one hundred percent. They've become incredibly efficient. We arrive somewhere and in the time it takes you to have a catnap they've already set up the infrastructure for the radio and the command post to function. They believe that every minute lost is a gift to the enemy.

It takes years of experience to pick the best place for a camp. It has to have enough routes of escape. It has to fulfil certain conditions for cover and communications. For example, Germán and Isra might go out early in the morning because we have to move. They head off and soon they're hack.

"How do you like the spot?" Manolo asks them.

"It's pretty, very pretty."

"What kind of trees does it have?"

"Oak."

"Have they lost their leaves?"

"No. They've got them."

"Did you test the television?"

"Yes."

"Can you get all the channels?"

"Yes."

"How does channel two come in?"

"It's the worst of them, but you can see it."

"We won't have problems with the monitoring?"

"No."

These are requirements that Che would never have dreamed of, right? Guerrillas with television sets!

Once a site has been selected, we start moving in. First comes the kitchen. Germán takes an advance team to set it up. Then we dig the air-raid shelters: two enormous holes about three by five metres and two-and-a-half metres deep—one for Venceremos, with its built-in table and bench, the other for strategic communications. You lay a double row of tree-trunks and earth on top so even a rocket couldn't cave it in. Then you dig trenches for all the fighters. L-shaped trenches so that if a bomb falls into it the shrapnel won't get everyone. Digging trenches is exhausting work, but the security squad finishes them off in no time. Later on, while everyone pitches their tents, they finish setting up the Vietnamese kitchen, the table for the command post, the place for the television set, all the while making sure that the camp can be taken down as fast as it was put up, or even faster, and that the enemy won't be able to tell who was here.

That's the other condition. When we leave a place, we can't leave behind any clues. The smell of gasoline is suspicious. A miserable little piece of paper with Santiago or Marvel's handwriting means that Venceremos camped here. We've meted out serious punishments for having wiped our asses with a monitoring sheet. That's absolutely prohibited because the first thing the enemy does when they find an abandoned camp is to dig out the latrine and search for papers with writing. If they find out it was us, they'll follow our tracks. That's why the policy is never to leave a camp in place.

Everything has to be left as we found it. The security squad even marks off paths for walking which you can't go off, and when we leave you have to cover them with the same sticks and dry leaves that were there before and that we piled up at the edge of each path. It's impossible to leave it so they won't know someone was there, but they shouldn't know who or how long ago.

Of the original Radio Venceremos security squad, only Isra is left. The rest have all died in combat defending the station, or in other battles defending the people. I have especially fond memories of the Pericas. Minchito, the youngest, was a kid I watched grow up, from the station's messenger to a special forces volunteer. He died heroically in an attack on the base at Gotera. Just before that, his brother Julito died when we were attacked at Arambala. Just after that, his other brother Payín died covering the retreat of several *compañeros*. A few months later Chepito, who was our first cook at Parra de Bambú, died.

Of the Pericas, only the women are left: Marinita, a hard worker who's with Marcela in the press office; and the sixth sibling, the youngest, in Colomoncagua with her parents. Halfway through the war she fulfilled the dream of all young girls who grow up in the refugee camps in Honduras and who listen to Venceremos from afar: She became old enough to return as a guerrilla, to become a radio operator on the front lines.

Six brothers and sisters, six revolutionaries. The Pericas' commitment was made as a group; the father, who was from a very Christian family in La Laguna de Villa El Rosario, volunteered with all his children, all his family, all his cousins and friends. Everything he had, including his life, he gave to God, in other words, to the revolution.

There are many families like them in Morazán and all over the country, and overseas there are innumerable brothers and sisters who work in solidarity: Germans, Swiss, French, North Americans, Nicaraguans, Mexicans and Swedes, a pack of white folks who have helped us generously. What would we have done without the German friends who for ten long years sent us the tubes for the transmitter, each of which costs 3,000 dollars?

All of them, outside the country and in, those who died and those who still fight, they are the ones who have made this station possible. They are Radio Venceremos.

Multi-media Revolution

Right from the start we worked with an array of different media. Even before we had the station, in the days of the COMIN international committee, we made videos and put out the magazine *El Salvador*. Of course we did all this outside the country, though we had a small telex inside for sending information overseas.

Once the station got under way, COMIN focused on supporting whatever Venceremos was doing in Morazán, with the station coordinating all the publicity work. That's when we launched the magazine *Señal de Libertad*, an international Radio Venceremos review, which was even published in German, and lasted for quite a few issues before we suspended publication under an agreement with the other forces of the FMLN.

We also started making movies—features and shorts so people could follow the war as it developed. They've all been documentaries, but a kind of documentary that broke with the classic form of a narrator stringing together a series of images. We worked with a group called *Cero a la izquierda*. The reality they filmed was so eloquent and the montage so well done that no narration was necessary. Check out "Letter from Morazán," "Will to Win," "Time of Audacity." The cineastes gathered in Havana for the Tenth Latin American Film Festival were so impressed with this way of making documentaries that, in addition to the prizes they had awarded us in previous years, they gave Venceremos' productions special recognition. Documentaries about the Salvadoran revolution, which revolutionised the genre.

For the movies and videos, people on the inside—Skinny Gustavo and his team—would work with others who came from overseas to help with the filming and then went back outside the country to edit. The commanders always made a lot of time for them. Maria, Chico, all the big-shots got involved in writing the scripts, reviewing the clips, the whole process.

The videos weren't only for foreign consumption. They were often shown right in the camps and when we took over towns. Later on the Venceremos Cultural Brigade added skits and dances with Los Torogoces musical group. We even took photo exhibits on bamboo stands all over Morazán. You didn't know which to admire more, the incredible pictures of the combatants or the faces of the combatants looking at themselves; actors and spectators at the same time.

Of course, the station always came first, demanding the greatest effort and the most resources. We didn't only broadcast on shortwave. To reach an audience in the cities, since 1982 we broadcast on FM. In 1984–1985, right in the midst of the dispersal of the guerrilla forces, we decided to disperse the station too. The idea was to have a lot of small FM stations connected up to the main Venceremos transmitter. They weren't to be just repeating stations—we'd tried that already with the Devil's chain and the four hookups—this time each was to have its own local 15 minute programme. The challenge was to reproduce the same interplay of political and military elements, the double dimension of having a real presence and doing mass communications, at the level of guerrilla units. We even had a slogan for that stage, *Venceremos is on your front!*

Apolonio and his German friends figured out how to adapt some tiny little FM transmitters which could put out about 100 watts. They were incredibly compact, wonderful little gadgets. Some day they'll be on exhibit in a revolutionary museum. But we ran into a lot of problems with such small autonomous stations. It's not enough to have the equipment, you've got to train the people who are going to do the broadcasting and produce the local shows. We also had to turn a thousand pirouettes to evade the goniometers. What was worse, the war escalated. In Guazapa, for example, the saturation bombing during Operation Phoenix put an end to our efforts to reach the capital via FM. It all became so complicated that we opted for a powerful FM transmitter hidden in Morazán that could reach the whole country.

* * *

The large FM transmitter is a big responsibility for Ricardo, Toni and Marcela's cousin who's called Chiri. Chiri and his team keep that FM substation going with nothing but their halls. They have their own supply network for gasoline, their own logistics operation, their own base of support, their own security system. We don't often see them because even though they are in Morazán, they aren't close to us. Where are they? I'll tell you about the miracle, but not the saint. Let the enemy find them with their fancy goniometers!

They're underground, of course, like armadillos, but don't think it's just a little air-raid shelter; it's a whole underground room, with ventilation, a generator, a transmitter—a real feat of engineering. The only thing outside is the armadillo's tail, that is, the aerial, or rather the mess of aerials, because there's one that receives from us, another that transmits, one that bounces the shortwave signal, another for internal communications, still another hookup we use, and a new aerial we're going to install soon to boost our FM signal so we can reach the youth of the city who don't listen to shortwave because of the damned interference or because it just isn't their thing.

And television. The plan to have a TV Venceremos hasn't been shelved forever, not at all. Any day now we'll surprise you because we've already learned
that we don't need fancy long-range equipment. Do you know how we'll do it?
With simple equipment, but installed in a mobile unit. It's possible. That way
you can broadcast a television signal right from San Salvador, right in the belly
of the capital, and the enemy won't detect you since you're in constant motion
from one side of the city to the other.

As for the radio station, we have plans for that too. Now we have FM equipment that's very portable and quite powerful. There are thousands of ways to
hide it in the city: You could put it in a park, or inside a tape recorder and broadcast with the recorder's aerial; the equipment could be a booby-trap at the same
time. You could install one of those gadgets inside a police car and they wouldn't
even notice! There's also a way to put a clock inside so that several small stations
can broadcast in sequence, like a relay. The first one transmits for five minutes
and, while the enemy is trying to find it, it stops and the second one continues
the broadcast on the same frequency but from another site, and then comes the
third, then the fourth. . . . The *cuilios* will go nuts playing blind man's buff, while
the audience won't even notice that what they heard on one channel was a dozen
different broadcasts. With brains you can do anything!

* * *

We keep a close relationship with our sister station in Chalatenango, Radio
Farabundo Martí. Farabundo went on air a year after we did, on 22 January,
1982, to accompany the FPL's[12] struggle on the central front. They've developed a different communications system to promote their work, using telexes,
very professional press releases, cassettes, solidarity festivals—truly audacious
initiatives.

On several occasions we set up a simultaneous broadcast. Either we broadcast their programme live or they broadcast ours, but hooking up like that was
not easy. We had to adjust the aerials, find better heights for receiving the FM
signal, and expose ourselves to the goniometers.

In any case, both stations, each in its own way, one in Morazán and the other
in Chalate, played an extremely important role, not only for the combatants and
their supporters inside the country, but also for the refugees. In El Salvador there
was a commercial that said "It's a fact that you can't live without a radio." For
people in exile that's the truth. The stations have been umbilical cords keeping
people on the outside in touch for ten years.

* * *

In '80 a group took over the Panamanian Embassy in San Salvador. They
were protesting against the repression and since they were going to be repressed
as well, the takeover ended up in asylum. About a month later they managed to
leave for Panama. There were a lot of them, about 300. Torrijos[13] was very hos-
pitable, but he sent them to live in the middle of nowhere in the jungle on the
Atlantic Coast.

"Salvadorans are like ants," the general said. "Wherever they go, they make their way."

Sure enough, when Torrijos went to visit them a few months later, the Salvadorans had built wooden houses, planted corn, fixed up a runway, the place had come to life.

"What do you call the town?" the general asked.

"Ciudad Romero. For the Monsignor."

"What do the people of Ciudad Romero want?"

"Give us a shortwave radio so we can hear Radio Venceremos"

"I'll send you three, but listen to me: when you get nostalgic, don't come tell me you want to go back. I won't let you go!"

Torrijos laughed, but it was true. The station has fulfilled a social and emotional function beyond keeping people informed. All the refugees have family on the fronts. They hear on the station when their relatives die—did you listen to Venceremos? Juancito died, Doña Mela's son. In the cooperatives, in the refugee camps, people listen to the station every night to stay abreast of the overall situation and to find out about their small circle of friends. Of course it makes them nostalgic, but it also cheers them up, it reminds them that they are Salvadoran. Because after ten years outside your country, without any news of what's happened, anyone could lose interest in returning. Instead, these people are like the day they left, with their suitcases packed.

* * *

Though we had a lot of problems, we managed to set up a support and marketing network overseas. Venceremos's correspondents acted as distributors for the products of the whole system: radio, video, film, music. Several of our people in France established a relationship with the free radios in that country, who produced their own programmes in French calling themselves Radio Venceremos. It caused a diplomatic row because the Salvadoran government protested vehemently to the French. How could France allow subversive groups to install aerials on its soil? They thought we had an international link-up, when it was just a few crumby cassettes that a handful of people broadcast over the free radios!

We also did good work in Mexico. We even had a PO Box there, 7907, where we got letters from listeners all over the world, including people who wrote to us from inside the country, since they had no other way to reach us. We announced that box over Venceremos every day. Later on we couldn't keep it because the political situation in the region changed.

We've done exchanges with community radio stations in Quebec and Vancouver in Canada, and with a few local stations in Los Angeles and San Francisco, who rebroadcast Venceremos programmes for their Latino audience. The relationship with progressive stations in Latin America has been more difficult, because they are very exposed to repression from the government, the army or other powerful groups.

NOTES

1. Commander Jorge Meléndez, head of the Francisco Sánchez Eastern Front and member of the political commission of the Party of the Salvadoran Revolution (PRS).

2. Oscar Arnulfo Romero was archbishop of San Salvador from 1977 until his assassination in 1980.

3. Commander Ana Sonia Medina, member of the PRS political commission.

4. YSAX, known as AX.

5. Monsignor Gregorio Rosa Chávez, auxiliary bishop of San Salvador, and currently chief of the Department of Social Communications of the Latin American Episcopal Conference (DECOS-CELAM).

6. Lempa River Hydroelectric Commission.

7. Marianella García-Villas, president of the Human Rights Commission of El Salvador, murdered by the death squads on 14 March 1983.

8. On 18 February, 1980, the White Warrior's Union (UGB) of then Captain Roberto D'Aubuisson dynamited Monsignor Romero's radio station. On 23 March, YSAX was on the air again, thanks to spontaneous donations. That was the Sunday that the Monsignor called on soldiers to disobey orders. The following day, 24 March, the military high command announced that the archbishop had placed himself outside the law. That afternoon, while he celebrated mass in the chapel of a cancer ward, where he had a room, Oscar Arnulfo Romero was assassinated with a bullet in the heart.

9. Universidad Centroamericana "José Simeón Cañas," a Jesuit–run college in San Salvador.

10. Marcelino Menéndez y Pelayo, a twentieth-century scholar of the Spanish language.

11. Gen. René Emilio Ponce, head of the Salvadoran High Command.

12. Popular Liberation Forces, one of the member organizations of the FMLN.

13. Panamanian President Gen. Omar Torrijos.

II

LIBERATION THEOLOGY, PHILOSOPHY, AND PEDAGOGY

5

Toward a Theology of Liberation
(July 1968)

Gustavo Gutiérrez

Gustavo Gutiérrez (b. Peru, 1928) is a theologian, Dominican priest, and the founder of liberation theology. He has spent most of his life teaching and lecturing at many universities worldwide and as parish priest in Rimac, a slum area of Lima near where he grew up. He founded the Instituto Bartolomé de las Casas de Lima in 1974 to disseminate information and coordinate efforts to help the Peruvian poor. He has published in and been a member of the board of directors of the international journal, Concilium. *In 1983 Cardinal Ratzinger, now Pope Benedict XVI, of the Vatican Congregation for the Doctrine of Faith, accused Gutierrez of politically interpreting the Bible and supporting a temporal messianism. He was inducted into the American Academy of Arts and Sciences in 2002 and received the Prince of Asturias Prize for Communications and Humanities in 2003 for his concern for the poor and the integrity of his message. Currently, he holds the John Cardinal O'Hara Professorship of Theology at the University of Notre Dame. This selection is the foundational text on liberation theology. It redefines theology in light of the Second Vatican Council, by establishing an explicit connection between the theological meanings of faith, salvation, and the Kingdom of God, and human emancipation in the social, political, and economic orders.*

As Christians come in contact with the acute problems that exist in Latin America, they experience an urgent need to take part in solutions to them. They run the risk, however, of doing this without a reexamination of their own basic doctrinal principles, a situation that can lead to dead ends and to action that is ultimately sterile.

In this talk I will distance myself from concrete issues in order to analyze these basic doctrinal principles. Actually, the distancing is only apparent, since the following reflections can only be understood within a broader and richer approach that includes pastoral action and even political action.

INTRODUCTION

First of all, let us examine what we mean by *theology*. Etymologically speaking, theology is a treatise or discourse about God—which really does not tell us very much. The classic meaning of theology is an intellectual understanding of the faith—that is, the effort of the human intelligence to comprehend revelation and the vision of faith. But faith means not only truths to be affirmed, but also an existential stance, an attitude, a commitment to God and to human beings. Thus faith understands the whole of life theologically as faith, hope, and charity.

If, then, we say that faith is a commitment to God and human beings, and affirm that theology is the intellectual understanding of faith, we must conclude that faith is an understanding of this commitment. It is an understanding of this existential stance, which includes the affirmation of truths, but within a broader perspective.

Faith is not limited to affirming the existence of God. No, faith tells us that God loves us and demands a loving response. This response is given through love for human beings, and that is what we mean by a commitment to God and to our neighbor.

Consequently, when we speak about theology, we are not talking about an abstract and timeless truth, but rather about an existential stance, which tries to understand and to see this commitment in the light of revelation.

But precisely because faith is above all an existential stance, it admits a differentiation according to circumstances and the different approaches to the commitment to God and human beings. To say that faith is a commitment is true for all ages, but the commitment is something much more precise: I commit myself here and now. The commitment to God and to human beings is not what it was three centuries ago. Today I commit myself in a distinctive manner.

When we speak of theology, we mean a theology that takes into account its variation according to time and circumstances. From this we can deduce three characteristics:

1. Theology is a progressive and continuous understanding, which is variable to a certain extent. If it were merely the understanding of abstract truth, this would not be true. If theology is the understanding of an existential stance, it is progressive, it is the understanding of a commitment in history concerning the Christian's location in the development of humanity and the living out of faith.

2. Theology is a reflection—that is, it is a second act, a turning back, a reflecting, that comes after action. Theology is not first; the commitment is first. Theology is the understanding of the commitment, and the commitment is action. The central element is charity, which involves commitment, while theology arrives later on.

This is what ancient authors said with regard to philosophy: "Primum vivere, deinde philosophare—first you must live, and then philosophize." We have interpreted this as first *la dolce vita*, and then some reflection if I have time. No, the principle is much more profound: philosophy, like theology, is a second act.

The pastoral consequences of this are immense. It is not the role of theology to tell us what to do or to provide solutions for pastoral action. Rather, theology follows in a distinctive manner the pastoral action of the church and is a reflection upon it.

3. If it is the intellectual understanding of a commitment, theology is an endeavor that must continuously accompany that commitment. The pastoral action of the church will be a commitment to God and the neighbor, while the-

ology will accompany that activity to provide continual orientation and animate it. Every action of ours must be accompanied by a reflection to orient it, to order it, to make it coherent, so that it does not lapse into a sterile and superficial activism.

Theology, therefore, will accompany the pastoral activity of the church—that is, the presence of the church in the world. It will accompany that activity continuously, to help it to be faithful to the word of God, which is the light for theology.

But, I insist, the first and fundamental objective is the commitment of Christians. One should not ask of theology more than it can give. Theology s a science, and like any discipline, has a modest role in the life of human beings. The first step is action. As Pascal expressed it: "All the things in this world are not worth one human thought, and all the efforts of human thought are not worth one act of charity."

Theology is on the level of thought and reflection, and there is no theology that is the equivalent of an act of charity. The central issue is charity, commitment, action in the world. All this is what we understand by theology.

There is talk today of a theology of human liberation. Using this or other expressions, the theme has become a major preoccupation of the magisterium of the church in recent years.

If faith is a commitment to God and human beings, it is not possible to live in today's world without a commitment to the process of liberation. That is what constitutes a commitment today. If participation in the process of human liberation is the way of being present in the world, it will be necessary for Christians to have an understanding of this commitment, of this process of liberation.

This process constitutes what has been called since the council a "sign of the times." A sign of the times is not primarily a speculative problem—that is, a problem to be studied or interpreted. For the reasons noted above, a sign of the times is first of all a call to action and secondly a call to interpretation. A sign of the times calls Christians to action.

The process of liberation is a sign of the times. It is a call to action at the same time that it is a new theme for reflection, new because it is a global term for the problems contained within it. Thus there is a certain deficiency in the attempts that are being made with regard to a theology of liberation, which is clearly evident in the conclusions of the meetings at Mar del Plata and Itapoan, both of which leave me dissatisfied.

We will have to be much more concrete, but we will also be dependent on the progress of the science of economics for a more precise knowledge regarding the national and Latin American reality. A genuine theology of liberation can only be a team effort, a task which has not yet been attempted.

I will limit myself therefore to a sketch, to recalling a few paths of inquiry, as is suggested by my title, "Toward a Theology of Liberation." It really is *toward*. I believe we will have to go much further, but we can only achieve that through collaboration as a number of concepts become more precise.

We understand theology, then, as an intellectual understanding of the faith. But faith is above all a commitment to God and the neighbor. Although it implies the affirmation of truths, Christian truth nevertheless has the particular character of being a truth that is thought but that first of all is done. "To do the truth," the gospel text requires, and that is proper to Christian truth.

In this sketch we will consider three areas along the following lines:

1. the statement of the question
2. human liberation and salvation
3. the encounter with God in history.

1. THE STATEMENT OF THE QUESTION

The gospel is primarily a message of salvation. The construction of the world is a task for human beings on this earth. To state the question of a theology of liberation means, therefore, to ask about the meaning of this work on earth, the work that human beings perform in this world vis-à-vis the faith. In other words, what relationship is there between the construction of this world and salvation?

A theology of liberation, then, will have to reply first of all to this question: Is there any connection between constructing the world and saving it? The question is an old one and has an answer that can be considered the traditional one. Perhaps it is also the one we received in our Christian training and is more or less the following:

The world is a stage on which the drama of salvation takes place, where we are placed to decide if we will be saved or not. Consequently, human life is a "test," and we save or condemn ourselves by our actions. In this perspective the nature of the act itself is secondary.

A work is good if it functions religiously, if it "edifies," as we used to say. For example, a novel is good if it has a "religious" value—that is, if it teaches a religious or moral principle. The question of the book's literary value is secondary, since what is important is that it is useful in teaching its readers to be more moral, more chaste, and the like. A film is good to the extent that it has a "religious" purpose, to the extent that it "edifies."

College libraries used to contain books that were very deficient from a literary standpoint, but "helped" to understand the gospel. That and not their literary value was the important thing. We arrived at the extreme position of condemning as morally evil works that the rest of the world considered to be good and of high literary quality. The authentic works were in our view "evil," while the poor works, which nobody read, were considered good because they "edified." What was important in this approach was to do things for the love of God, as we see in this act of charity, which we still read in prayer books: "to love my neighbor as myself for love of You." The fundamental objective was to place oneself in the presence God, for this automatically gave value to the work. It did not matter if one was an economist or a beautician, as long as everything was done for love of God. The content of the act was of no concern, since the important thing in this life was to say yes or no to the Lord and to live in a moral way.

Work from this perspective had value if it was a sacrifice; the more sacrificial, the greater the value. The more useless it was, the more sacrificial, since even one's intelligence was sacrificed. A God who crushes us, a life in the beyond that devalues the present life, a supernaturalized theology that swallows up natural values, all this is what we have lived for a long time. This has prevented us from appreciating the things of this world. But that is precisely the question: Do these things have a value in themselves? Is there a relationship between the kingdom of God and human work as such?

Father Häring remarks on this point: "Christian morality has been dominated by occasions of sin and complicity." The world is full of complicity and occasions of sin; that is the real world. Fear of this has led Christians to lose interest in their earthly tasks, since preoccupation with the absolute has left no place for the ephemeral, the contingent, and the temporal. We well aware that the Marxist and humanist critique of contemporary Christianity points out that there is something contradictory in our attitude. We have always said that we have only one economy of salvation for human beings, that we have a global view of the human person, that as the pope said at the United Nations and repeated in *Populorum Progressio*, the church is an expert in humanity. But often Christians, with their gaze fixed on the world beyond, manifest little or no commitment to the ordinary life of human beings.

We say that the human person is our fundamental concern, but the contemporary non-Christian humanist believes correctly that Christianity not interested in human values. In a well-known text, Engels says:

> Christianity and socialism proclaim the proximate liberation of humanity from slavery; but Christianity proclaims it in the next life, not here on earth. That is the difference. We are both agreed that humanity has to be liberated; however, for Christians it is later on, while for us it is now.

The absolute salvation provided by God in the hereafter, which diminishes the present life, has led to a very peculiar outlook: human institutions will be considered important if they are oriented to the hereafter. All other institutions have no value because they will pass away.

The church as institution is oriented to the hereafter, to the absolute. Only that which favors religion is considered good. A government is considered good if it aids the church, or if it provides money to build churches and schools. Goodness is measured by generosity to the church, because the church, as an instrument of salvation in the hereafter, is the only thing that will remain. In a somewhat paradoxical manner, therefore, we have a church that preaches "my kingdom is not of this world" ending up very comfortably ensconced in that world.

This position, this way of looking at reality, constitutes a brake on the presence and action of human beings in this world. But in our time we are in a new situation, which has been adopted by the Vatican Council. I believe that there are basically two factors that have created this new situation.

The first is the rise of science in the fifteenth and sixteenth centuries. Previously, nature has appeared to human beings fundamentally as a reflection of the glory of God. It was also seen as a kind of participation in the transcendence of God, so that nature received the same kind of reverent fear that was proper to God. At the present time, however, nature appears as dominated by science and technology as well as by human beings, so that, as the Vatican Council expressed it, "many benefits once looked for, especially from heavenly powers, man has now enterprisingly procured for himself" (*Gaudium et Spes*, no. 33). All this entails an enormous change in our outlook.

A second factor, derived from the first one, is that the human person has become the agent of his or her own destiny and the one responsible for his or her own development in history. This realization has occurred at approximately the same time as the growth of science. It begins with the reflection of Descartes, "I think, therefore I am," a reflection that starts with the human person.

While previous philosophy began with the object, exterior to humanity, Descartes begins with the human being. This tendency is accentuated by Immanuel Kant, for whom the world is a chaos, where the human being creates order by means of the well-known categories. This process will be referred to as a Copernican revolution, with the emphasis placed on the human being. As the affirmation of human subjectivity, it is tremendously important.

A key figure for understanding our era is certainly Hegel, who takes up the affirmation of subjectivity and brings it one step further: the human person is the agent of history, but, even more, history is nothing else than the process of human liberation. Since it is a history of human emancipation, the human being creates history by self-liberation. To liberate oneself, to emancipate oneself, is to create history. This idea will be taken up by Karl Marx within an economic framework,

Father Teilhard de Chardin provides a very beautiful image to describe its process. He sees the history of humanity more or less in the following way. In an early stage, people were in the hold of a ship, but they did not know they were in a ship. They had never left the hold, but remained in its obscure depths. What did they do there? They quarreled among themselves until one day someone climbed the stairs, went to the bridge, and discovered that they were in a machine that moved, that had a motor. It was at that moment that human beings became aware of an active role in history. From that moment on, they said, it was not a question of drifting, but of piloting. That is, human beings had learned that it was necessary to pilot the ship, not to drift in history but to direct it.

It is a question, then, of human liberation, of human emancipation throughout history, which will pass through radical social change, revolution, and even beyond these. Therefore, the question changes. It is not merely a matter of knowing the meaning of earthly action, but of knowing the meaning of human liberation in the perspective of faith, and what faith can say not only to human action in this world but to human liberation. What relationship exists between the kingdom of God and human emancipation?

A text from *Populorum Progressio* is very significant in this respect: "It is a question, rather, of building a world where all persons, no matter what their race, religion, or nationality, can live a fully human life, freed from servitude imposed on them by other human beings or by natural forces over which they have no control" (no. 47). Thus it is a question of constructing a world where human beings are free and in which freedom is not an empty word.

It means that theology faces the sign of the times, which is human liberation, and scrutinizes it profoundly. This leads us to take a definite perspective in judging economic and political domination. When we talk of economic domination, we touch the sore point, especially if we say that what is important is to free the human person, as the pope says, from every form of domination, whether it be natural or human. Economic and political domination not only imprison people economically, but they also prevent them from being human. Thus we must commit ourselves with respect to this great sign of the times.

Perhaps we are not sufficiently attentive to the completely new language of *Populorum Progressio*, which asserts that a global view of humanity is something proper to the church. If you ask Christians what is proper to the church, they will say: grace, the sacraments, but not the global vision of humanity. Are we passing from a theocentric theology to one that is anthropocentric? I think it is much more exact to say that we are passing from a theology that concentrated excessively on a God located outside this world to a theology of a God who is present in this world. That would be a Christian anthropocentrism. One would have to agree with the Protestant theologian Karl Barth, who said: "From the moment God became man, the human being is the measure of all things."

One of the classic texts of Paul VI, presented December 7, 1965, concerned anthropocentrism. In reply to the accusation that the council was excessively anthropocentric, the pope replied that it was a question of God present in history and present in the midst of human beings.

Thus our own question is posed. The theology of liberation means establishing the relationship that exists between human emancipation—in the social, political, and economic orders—and the kingdom of God.

2. HUMAN LIBERATION AND SALVATION

Pope Paul VI said that what the church can appropriately contribute is a global vision of the human being and of humanity, a vision that situates the process of development within the human vocation. This had been affirmed by *Gaudium et Spes*, and a reading of the texts will show us the theological progress that was accomplished by *Populorum Progressio*.

Gaudium et Spes, no. 34, reads: "Throughout the course of the centuries, human beings have labored to better the circumstances of their lives through a monumental amount of individual and collective effort. To believers, this point is settled: such human activity is in accord with God's will." This text shows that all that we do is a response to the will of God.

But Paul VI goes much further. In *Populorum Progressio* he adds clarity and profundity to the conciliar text: "In the design of God, all human beings are called upon to develop and fulfill themselves, for every life is a vocation" (no. 15). Human beings are called upon to develop themselves. In this perspective, we understand development as liberation, with all that implies, even in the economic sphere.

Human emancipation is included within this vocation. The vocation, as we know, is to communion with God, to being a child of God—it is to this that we have been called (Eph. 1:5). To have a vocation means to have been created and chosen to be children of God.

But the pope is careful to say that it is not a question of an individual vocation or of individual salvation. Rather, all human beings are called to this full development, which in the strong biblical sense we call convocation. Human beings are convoked and the process of development lies within that convocation. "All are called to this fullness of development" (*Populorum Progressio*, no. 17).

If this is true, if full, integral, and authentic development liberates human beings, then it is included within the human vocation. Development, therefore, is not a stage previous to evangelization, which we refer to with the incorrect word, "preevangelization." Rather development (and this is the new theological contribution of *Populorum Progressio*) is situated within one's vocation and thus of one's communion with God. It is not a previous step, but forms part of the process of salvation, because it is a vocation. Salvation, therefore, affects the whole human being.

The call of God includes all of reality and provides us with a radical change of outlook, a new way of evaluating the things of this world. This world is not a trampoline to leap upward to God, nor is it a stage on which to play a role—that is, a reality that does not interest us but allows us to be spiritual beings and to choose within it to be good or evil. No. If development is human fulfillment, it is part of our vocation, and all things have value.

There are not static obligations of charity that are somehow independent of the content of my actions of love. The world is not a "test," nor is it a stage. The work of constructing the world, the work itself which is brought to realization, has a salvific value. If development exists within our vocation, it has the value of salvation. Not only what is done for the love of God, but everything which contributes to growth in humanity, as *Populorum Progressio* says, everything which makes a person more human and contributes to human liberation, contains the value of salvation and communion with the Lord. In other words, and this vocabulary is new in the church, integral development is salvation.

What *Populorum Progressio* calls integral development is what we refer to theologically as salvation. Let us consider a text from *Populorum Progressio* (no. 21) which, together with no. 47, is one of the most important the encyclical. Paul VI begins with the definition of development given by Fr. Lebret: it is to pass from less human conditions to more human conditions.

"Less human conditions: the lack of material necessities for those who are without the minimum essential for life, the moral duties of those who are mutilated by selfishness." That is less human. "Less human" also means "oppressive social structures, whether due to the abuses of ownership or the abuses of power, to the exploitation of workers or to unjust transactions." Thus "less human" are oppressive structures, something Christians are generally unaware of. The structure itself is oppressive, although naturally human beings are responsible for it. But let us not say too quickly that we can only change the structures by changing human beings. Faced with contemporary humanism, which desires a change of structures, we are sometimes content to recall that human beings are inclined to sin. Certainly everything is connected, and it is right for a global vision to show the connections between these different aspects. But that global vision should not say that first we must change human beings in order afterward to change the structures. After Marx, it is no longer possible to say first change the human beings and then the structures. Our global vision must be able to see everything in a synthetic way. Human behavior is conditioned by the structures that human beings have created. It is a question, then, of simultaneous action on human beings and structures.

As regards the passage from less human to more human, the pope moves step by step: "More human: the passage from misery toward the possession of necessities, victory over social scourges," in this case scourges not of a personal kind but of structures. Also more human is "the growth of knowledge, the acquisition of culture." More human is "increased esteem for the dignity of others, turning toward the spirit of poverty." I think we have to understand this spirit of poverty correctly. "Poor in spirit," like the word "aggiornamento," are ambiguous expressions. *Aggiornare*, for example, has two meanings: to bring up to date, and to adjourn until tomorrow. Some have labored to "bring the church up to date" and others have tried to adjourn the council "until tomorrow." We could say that Christians today are divided into two sectors, which correspond to the two meanings of aggiornamento. Something similar happens with the phrase "poor in spirit," which I will clarify later on.

More human is "cooperation for the common good, the will and desire for peace." More human, too, is the acknowledgment by human beings of absolute values and of God. Finally and especially, more human is "faith, a gift of God accepted by the good will of human beings and unity in the charity of Christ, who calls us all to share as sons in the life of the giving God, the Father of all" (*Populorum Progressio*, no. 21).

More human is grace, more human is faith, more human is to be a child of God. Consequently, we can say that integral development, authentic emancipation, and human liberation are, for the pope, salvation. Actually, in this section Paul VI is sketching the whole process of development, which proceeds from material and moral misery toward the grace of God. This is development, which is also a task and a call to action.

I emphasize that the work of building the earth is not a preceding stage, not a stepping stone, but already the work of salvation. The creation of a just and fraternal society is the salvation of human beings, if by salvation we mean the passage from the less human to the more human. Salvation, therefore, is not purely "religious."

In all this, the pope and the council are only retrieving the most ancient tradition of the church, which I will now recall and illustrate by two biblical themes that will serve simply as examples.

First of all, there is the relationship between creation and salvation. This is a general theme that is not secondary but in a certain sense dominant throughout the Bible.

In a rather simplistic exegesis, creation is presented as the explanation of what now exists. This is not false, but it is insufficient. In the Bible, creation appears not as a stage previous to the work of salvation but rather as the first salvific act. "God chose us before the salvation of the world" (Eph. 1:3). Creation is included in the process of salvation, which is God's self-communication. The religious experience of Israel is above all a history, but a history that is nothing else but the prolongation of the creative act. Thus the Psalms speak of Yahweh as simultaneously creator and savior (see Psalm 136). The God who has made a cosmos out of chaos is the same one who acts in the history of salvation. The redemptive work of Christ is presented also in a context of creation (John, chap. 1). Creation and salvation have a Christological meaning: in him everything has been created, and everything has been saved (see Col. 1:15-20).

From this perspective, when we say that the human person is fulfilled by prolonging the work of creation through labor, we are affirming that he or she is located first of all within the work of salvation. To subdue the earth, as Genesis prescribes, is a work of salvation. To labor to transform this world is to save it. As Marx had clearly seen, work as a humanizing element normally tends through the transformation of nature to construct a society that is more just and worthy of human beings. The Bible makes us understand the profound meaning of this effort. The construction of the temporal city is not simply a stage of humanization or preevangelization, as theology used to say until recent years. It is to place oneself completely in a salvific process, which includes the whole person. Every offense, every humiliation, every alienation of human labor is an obstacle to the work of salvation.

A second great biblical theme has similar implications. It is the theme of the messianic promises—that is, of the events that announce and accompany the coming of the Messiah. It is not an isolated theme, but like the first one extends throughout the Bible. It has a vital presence in the history of Israel and thus takes its place in the emergence of the people of God.

The prophets announce a kingdom of peace. But peace supposes the establishment of justice, the defense of the *rights of the poor*, the punishment of oppressors, a life without the fear of being enslaved by others. A poorly conceived spiritualization has often made us forget the human task and the power to transform unjust structures that the messianic promises contain. The elimination of misery and exploitation is a sign of the coming of the messiah.

In the Gospel of Luke we read: "The Spirit of the Lord is upon me, because he has appointed me to preach good news to the poor. He has sent me to proclaim release to captives and recovering of sight to the blind." Christ will add later: "Today the Scripture has been fulfilled in your hearing" (4:18). What is it that is being fulfilled? The Spirit has anointed him to preach the gospel to the poor, proclaim liberation to captives, sight to the blind, freedom to the oppressed, and to proclaim the Lord's year of grace.

We have deeply interiorized a framework for interpreting the Bible: as Christians we must understand everything the Old Testament says about the temporal order as belonging to the spiritual plane. This spiritual outlook would begin with the New Testament. Thus we translate "to preach good news to the poor" as meaning that we should tell the poor in spirit that they should hope in God. "To preach liberation to captives" means to speak to the captives about sin. "The recuperation of sight by the blind" means that they do not see God. "Freedom to the oppressed" means those oppressed by Satan.

In reality all these expressions have a meaning that is direct and clear. For example, let us take "to proclaim a year of grace." This becomes clear if we refer to Leviticus 25:10, which says that a just society must be established. *Populorum Progressio* says the same thing: When it is left simply to economic laws freely to organize human life, then we begin to have rich and poor. If the economy is given free rein, the distance between them increases. That is what happened in the past, in the time of Leviticus. For that reason, the "year of grace" was created, when all would have to go back to the starting point, when all would leave aside what they possessed and begin anew.

We have said that everything in the Old Testament was purely secular and thus required transformation into a more religious framework, but this is not true. Certainly there is a religious significance, but the messianic promise means something integral and global, which affects the whole person.

If we understand salvation as something with merely "religious" or "spiritual" value for my soul, then it would not have much to contribute to concrete human life. But if salvation is understood as passing from less human conditions to more human conditions, it means that messianism brings about the freedom of captives and the oppressed, and liberates human beings from the slavery that Paul VI referred to (*Populorum Progressio* no. 47).

The sign of the coming of the messiah is the suppression of oppression: the messiah arrives when injustice is overcome. When we struggle for a just world in which there is not servitude, oppression, or slavery, we are signifying the coming of the messiah. Therefore the messianic promises bind tightly together the kingdom of God and better living conditions for human beings or, as Paul VI said, more human living conditions. An intimate relationship exists between the kingdom and the elimination of poverty and misery. The kingdom comes to suppress injustice.

These are two biblical themes, then, creation/salvation and the messianic promises, which demonstrate the extent to which the encyclical of Paul VI is anchored in revelation and the word of God. Consequently, the pope can say that human development "constitutes a summary of all our duties." If then we can understand integral development as passing from less human conditions to more human conditions, and if within the most human elements we include grace, faith, and divine filiation, then we comprehend profoundly why it can be said that working for development is the summary of all our duties.

3. THE ENCOUNTER WITH GOD IN HISTORY

Gaudium et Spes (no. 45) tells us the following: "The Lord is the goal of human history, the focal point of the longings of history and of civilization, the center of the human race, the joy of every heart, and the answer all its yearnings."

If there is a finality inscribed in history, then the essence of Christian faith is to believe in Christ, that is, to believe that God is irreversibly committed to human history. To believe in Christ, then, is to believe that God has made a commitment to the historical development of the human race.

To have faith in Christ is to see the history in which we are living as the progressive revelation of the human face of God. "Who sees me sees the Father." This holds to a certain extent for every human being according to the important text of Matthew 25, which reminds us that an action on behalf of a human being is an action on behalf of God. If you gave food and drink, you gave it to me; if you denied it, you denied it to me.

The encounter with God takes place in the encounter with our neighbor; it is in the encounters with human beings that I encounter God. Therefore, to have faith is to live in view of tomorrow, which is an encounter with the Lord. To have faith is to journey in history, for the life of faith is a project aimed at the future. To live complacently in the present entails nostalgia for the past and is already growing old.

To use an image from Teilhard de Chardin, God is not at our back, pushing us along on our journey. God is before us, revealed in the thousands of faces of human beings in the different circumstances of life. As Péguy says: "The faith that I love is hope," the hope of encountering God in my encounters with human beings.

Christ is the place of interchange, for in him a human person gives a human face to God and God gives a divine face to human beings. The historic adventure and the meaning of history will be the revelation of God. To believe in Christ, therefore, is to believe at the same time in history. To believe in eschatology, in the final times, is the motor of the historical process.

Faith from this perspective is thus the horizon and also the motivating force of all human behavior at the same time that it divinizes it. The encounter with Christ takes place in the neighbor, so that the key question is: Who is my neighbor?

The parable of the Good Samaritan is clear. Christ is asked: Who is my neighbor? Then the Lord tells a story that on a superficial level teaches that the neighbor is the one who is on the road—that is, the wounded man. But Christ reverses the question at the end: Which of these three was a neighbor to the other? To be a Christian is to draw near, to make oneself a neighbor, not the one I encounter in my journey but the one in whose journey I place myself. The neighbor is the one to whom I draw near, and I am an agent of history.

There are roads in life in which we will always encounter neighbors. If I take the road of human liberation, I will encounter millions of neighbors. The free human person is the one who constructs emancipation and salvation. It is certain that I find God in my neighbor, but as I draw near, I make him or her my neighbor. The last person to pass the wounded man made of him a neighbor.

I leave aside other aspects of the parable, which are interesting in describing this encounter with God, but that is enough. If we are correct, faith energizes and activates within history, since there is no way of encountering God outside history. Christians cannot hide in some dead end of history in order to watch it passing them by.

That the encounter with God occurs in the neighbor is a classic biblical theme. Matthew 25 is a clear text, but the whole Old Testament teaches it: whatever you do for the stranger, the widow, and the orphan has an effect upon God. Those are the three types of the poor: the stranger rejected by a nationalist people, the widow who has no one to support her, and the orphan, left without the aid of parents.

Faith energizes my actions in history and makes me take that history seriously, since it is impossible to be a Christian outside history. At present one should not fear to say that. It is an understanding of what a contemporary commitment is—that is to say, one cannot be a Christian in these times without a commitment to liberation. To be a Christian in our epoch, it is necessary to commit oneself in one way or other in the process of human emancipation.

But at the same time that faith radicalizes my commitment and makes it ever more profound, it also relativizes every human work. There is, therefore, a dialectic between radicalization and relativization.

Faith relativizes human work, because it prevents me from being content with what I am doing or what others are doing. Faith will continually move me further ahead. If God is before us, our journey will never cease. To a certain extent, a Christian remains unsatisfied, for the process of human liberation is never ending.

The radicalization and relativization of my task in history is a dialectical interplay that will comprise my originality as a Christian. It will keep me from falling into sectarianism or being content with my human efforts, but it will also permit me to undertake that task with radical seriousness.

No. 43 of *Gaudium et Spes* poses the question of the relationship between faith and life, and tells us that faith leads us to take our worldly task with great seriousness. It reminds us that faith that is not intertwined with life will be useless. On the other hand, it can be helpful to refer to the second part of no. 43: "Nor, on the contrary, are they any less wide of the mark who believe that religion consists in acts of worship alone and in the discharge of certain moral obligations, and who imagine they can plunge themselves into earthly affairs in such a way as to imply that these are altogether divorced from religious life." Faith should nourish and criticize our commitment in history. We should take up our commitment to the process of change, to revolution, to human emancipation in the light of faith.

CONCLUSION

In closing let us consider two well-known texts in the light of what we have been discussing. The first is from Karl Marx:

> The social principles of Christianity preach the need of a dominating class and an oppressed class. And to the latter class they offer only the benevolence of the ruling class. The social principles of Christianity point to heaven as the compensation for all the crimes that are committed on earth. The social principles of Christianity explain all the viciousness of oppressors as a just punishment either for original sin or other sins, or as trials that the Lord, in infinite wisdom, inflicts on those the Lord has redeemed. The social principles of Christianity preach cowardice, self-hatred, servility, submission, humility—in a word, all the characteristics of a scoundrel [1847, MEGA 1, 6, p. 278].

How could we have presented such an image of Christianity?
The other is a text from Isaiah:

> For behold I create new heavens and a new earth; and the former things shall not be remembered and come into mind. [We will have changed reality in such a way that no one will remember the past. The result is a global change of structures.] But be glad and rejoice forever in that which I create: for behold, I create Jerusalem rejoicing, and her people a joy. I will rejoice in Jerusalem, and be glad in my people; no more shall be heard in it the sound of weeping and the cry of

distress or an old man who does not fill out his days.... They shall build houses and inhabit them; they shall plant vineyards and eat their fruit. They shall not build and another inhabit; they shall not plant and another eat; for like the days of a tree shall the days of my people be, and my chosen shall long enjoy the work of their hands [65: 17-22].

This very concrete reality is the kingdom of God. In it children will not die a few days. The people will not work for others but for themselves, the city will be called a "rejoicing" and her people a "joy."

How could we have transformed this into what was described in the text of Marx? Unfortunately, both images are true, from different perspectives. Although the messianic promises refer to concrete material things, Marx's vision of over a century ago continues to be repeated by human beings today.

The issue, then, is whether we are capable of realizing the prophecy of Isaiah and of understanding the kingdom of God in its integral reality, or whether we are going to give the counter-testimony that is reflected in the statements of Marx. This is precisely what is at stake in our epoch.

6

Church: Charism and Power: Liberation Theology and the Institutional Church (1981)

Leonardo Boff

Leonardo Boff (b. Brazil, 1938) is a theologian, philosopher, writer, and former Franciscan friar and Catholic priest. He has written numerous books and taught and lectured at many universities worldwide, defending liberation theology and, more recently, a systematic ethico-theological perspective on globalization, ecological sustainability, and the promotion of a culture of life, including a discourse on the rights to life and the means to maintain them with dignity. In 1985 Cardinal Ratzinger, now Pope Benedict XVI, of the Vatican Congregation for the Doctrine of Faith, condemned him to "obsequious silence," and he was removed from his editorial functions and suspended from religious duties for one year. In 1992, under renewed threats of a second punitive action by authorities in Rome, he quit the priesthood and the Franciscan order. In 2001 he was honored with the alternative Nobel Prize, the Swedish Right Livelihood Award. Currently he holds the Chair of Ethics, Philosophy of Religion, and Ecology at the State University of Rio de Janeiro (UERJ) and serves as an advisor of social popular movements, such as the Landless Movement and the Base Ecclesial Communities. This selection from Boff's Vatican condemned book argues for a Christian "option for the poor" in a struggle for justice, accuses the institutional Church of aligning itself with the powerful against the disempowered, and advocates a return to the practices of the primitive church, with Christian base ecclesial communities as the central locus of this experience of Church.

THE CHURCH AND THE STRUGGLE FOR JUSTICE AND THE RIGHTS OF THE POOR

Urgency of the Struggle for Justice Today

"From the depths of the countries that make up Latin America a cry is rising to heaven, growing louder and more alarming all the time. It is the cry of suffering people who demand justice, freedom, and respect for the basic rights of human beings and peoples. . . . The cry is increasing in volume and intensity, and at times is full of menace. . . . The situation is one *injustice*" (Puebla, 87, 89, 90, cf.

28). The cry of the Latin American bishops gathered at Puebla is one for justice that, at the same time, denounces social and structural injustices.

Behind this cry lies the true drama. For example, in Brazil, 75 percent of the people live in relative economic marginalization; 43 percent are condemned to a minimum salary in order to survive. A worker from São Paulo, Manuel Paulo, says it best: "What I earn is so little that it only proves that I am still alive." And his wife, Helena, adds: "This is no life for anybody."[1]

Once one of the most promising countries in the world, Brazil serves as an appropriate example: 40 percent of all Brazilians live, work, and sleep with chronic hunger; there are 10 million who are mentally retarded due to malnutrition; 6 million suffer from malaria; 650,000 have tuberculosis and 25,000 suffer from leprosy.[2]

Although the statistics may scandalize some of us, others of us have grown callously used to them. But this dire situation does eat at the conscience of many Christians, giving them no relief. This is the ferment that is giving rise to the growing commitment of more and more churches to the struggle for justice.

Theological Foundation for the Commitment to Justice

There is some basis for the *duty* of every Christian to enter into the struggle for justice. One needs only to look at the recent official documents of the Church. In so doing, one has the security of a doctrine that is obliging upon all Christians. These documents are the various pontifical and episcopal statements that developed the social doctrine of the Church during the 1970s. We will refer here to the 1971 Synod of Bishops' *Justice in the World*, Paul VI's *Octogesima Adveniens* (1971) and *Evangelii Nuntiandi* (1975), John Paul II's *Redemptor Hominis* (1979), and the Latin American bishops' statement at Puebla, *Evangelization in the Present and Future of Latin America* (1979).

Fundamental Affirmation and Central Thesis

In *Justice in the World* the Synod of Bishops said: "Action on behalf of justice and participation in the transformation of the world fully appear as a constitutive dimension of the preaching of the Gospel, or, in other words, of the Church's mission for the redemption of the human race and its liberation from every oppressive situation" (6). "The Gospel message contains . . . *a demand for justice in the world.* This is why the Church has the right, indeed the duty, to proclaim justice on the social, national, and international level and to denounce instances of injustice" (36).

We should note that the bishops do not say that justice is an integral or even central theme but rather a *constitutive* element. Without the preaching of justice there is no Gospel of Jesus Christ. This is not to politicize the Church; it is to be faithful. And if we are not faithful, we mutilate the heart of Jesus' message and we pervert the very mission of the Church. Thus, we understand why the document speaks of "duty." A duty must be fulfilled; unfulfillment of a duty is a sin, even when one who acts is a bishop. For this same reason it is easy to understand the words of Pope Paul VI in *Evangelii Nuntiandi* and often repeated at Puebla: "The Church has the duty of proclaiming the liberation of millions of human beings, many of whom are its spiritual children, the duty of aiding this liberation at its start, of giving witness in its favor, and of accompaning its efforts that it may be achieved. This is not apart from evangelization" (30). Note that duty is mentioned twice, and that the Pope was not speaking only of a spiritual liberation. The sentence immediately preceding this speaks of human oppression: "needs, chronic illnesses, illiteracy, pauperism, injustice in international relations, neocolonialism, etc." (30).

Three Principal Arguments

On what is this duty based? *Justice in the World* adduces two arguments, one from the Old Testament and one from the New. "In the Old Testament God reveals himself to us as the liberator of the oppressed and the defender of the poor, who demands faith in him and justice toward one's neighbor from all. Only in the observance of the duties of justice is God recognized in truth as the liberator of the oppressed" (30). *God is only encountered on the path of justice.* The living God is not a God of prayers, incense, and asceticism. In Isaiah 1:11–18 we learn that what pleases God are not sacrifices and prayers but to "seek what is just, to help the downtrodden, and to do justice to the orphan." Jesus, in the same way, establishes a hierarchy of values: justice, mercy, and faithfulness are more important than religious observance. Love is the core of the biblical message, but in order for it to be true love, justice is presupposed. Thus, the bishops taught that "love implies in fact the absolute demand of justice that consists in the recognition of the dignity and rights of one's neighbor. Justice itself reaches its inner fullness only in love" (34). As such, "love of neighbor and justice cannot be separated" (34). Justice is the minimum requirement without which interpersonal relations cease to be human and become violent.

Because the true God is the God of justice and love, we must denounce the use that is often made by many social systems of the Christian God and Christian tradition. These systems call themselves theistic; in reality, they worship the idols of money, power, and material goods. The true God cannot be found in these realities when they exclude others. Pedro Casaldáliga, the poet-bishop, points out this error in this short poem:

When you say law, I say God.
When you say peace, justice, love, I say God.
When you say God, I say liberty, justice, peace.[3]

God abides in the realities of justice, love, and freedom. He is not automatically present in pious words. If we do not include the realities of freedom, justice, and love when we speak of God, then we are speaking of some idol and not of the living God.

The other argument that underlies the duty to struggle for justice is derived from the New Testament. Summarizing the argument, the bishops say that, due to the incarnation of God in Jesus Christ, "the attitude of man toward other men is integrated in his [or her] attitude toward God" (34). In other words, the truth of our relationship with God is measured by the truth of our relationships with others.

Justice is thus placed at the very heart of religion itself. This is how we understand the eschatological criterion of our final judgment: our relationship to the economic "nobodies" and the human "nobodies" in our daily life (Matt 25:31-46).

Furthermore, the bishops emphasize that Jesus revealed the Father and, at same time, brought God's *intervention of justice* on behalf of the poor and oppressed (Luke 6:20-23: blessed are the poor, the hungry, the sad, the accursed . . .). John Paul II reminded the bishops in Puebla that "Jesus' option was for the most needy." When Luke says, "Blessed are the poor for theirs is the kingdom of God" (6:20), he means, according to the most exacting exegesis, happy are you who are impoverished, you who suffer injustice and violence, because yours is the Kingdom of God, which is the Kingdom of justice, love, and peace.[4] Faced with the injustice that is made concrete in poverty, God himself is indignant. He is being challenged and decides to intervene. Jesus historizes this intervention: God comes and restores justice to the oppressed not because the oppressed person is pious and good but because he or she is a victim of the oppression that has caused his or her situation of poverty.

In a word, justice is so crucial that without its advent there is no coming of the Kingdom of God. The sign that the Kingdom of God approaches and begins to abide in our cities is that the poor have justice done to them, that they participate and share in the goods of life as well as in the life of the community, and that they are raised in terms of their dignity and defended against the violence they suffer at the hands of the current economic and political system.

Another decisive argument that is developed at great length in *Evangelii Nuntiandi* and repeated in many ways by Puebla is the inclusion of justice in the basic content of evangelization (all of part III of *EN* and part II of the Puebla document, chaps. 1 and 2).

The core of evangelization is "salvation in Jesus Christ . . . that had its beginning in this life and will come to total completion in eternity" (*EN* 27). The definition of evangelization developed here contains an explicit message about common life in society, international life, peace, justice, and development—an overwhelmingly powerful message for our day about liberation (*EN* 29). Although the current situation of the oppressed in the world adds nothing to the gospel message, the Pope emphasizes that liberation is part of the essential content of evangelization (*EN* 30. Puebla, 351): from sin and injustice and liberation for the grace of justice and fraternity.

Avoiding Reductionism

In *Evangelii Nuntiandi* Paul VI warns against two types of reductionism in the commitment to justice and liberation, one religious and the other political. Religious reductionism encloses the Church in the sacristy and in sacred gestures: "The Church does not circumscribe its activity to the religious realm as if it were disinterested in the temporal problems of humanity" (34). Therefore, the Church must include the world with its pluses and minuses, in its basic evangelization. The other reductionism is political, trimming the Church's mission by reducing its dimension to a simply temporal concern (32). The Church relates the religious to the political, making public statements of solidarity based on the gospel imperative. The Church does not speak politically about politics but rather speaks evangelically, understanding that politics and the struggle for justice anticipate and make real the Kingdom of God; it transcends politics but at the same time penetrates and assumes it.

Politics and the Struggle for Justice

When one speaks of social justice and liberation, one has already placed oneself in the heart of a situation of political domination. But there is no more ambiguous word than "politics." Reactionary forces within the Church and society take advantage of this ambiguity to free themselves from the struggle for justice. We read headlines such as "The Church must not be involved in politics," "Pope prohibits priests and bishops from involvement in politics," "No politics in the Mass," "No politics in the churches." But what exactly is meant by "politics"?

The Various Meanings of "Politics"

In *Octogesima Adveniens* Paul VI stated: "Under the term 'politics' are many confusions that must be clarified" (46). The bishops at Puebla have helped us to clarify some of these confusions (521-30).

For more than a few people, politics is something dirty, a lie, demagoguery, a prejudice that results from bad political experiences involving corruption, manipulation, and the struggle of special interest groups. However, this is but a pathology of politics which in itself is a highly positive concept such that Aristotle claims that human beings, like it or not, are essentially political animals.

The bishops at Puebla give politics the highest acclaim that it has received in the recent history of the Church: "The necessity for the Church's presence in the political arena flows from the very core of Christian faith" (516). Politics is understood in the context of the lordship of Jesus Christ. He is not the Lord of small places like the heart, the soul, the Church; he is the cosmic Lord, of large spaces like that of politics. Politics has to do with the Kingdom of God because it has to do with justice, a messianic good. Primitive Christians professing "Jesus is Lord" were making a political statement. The second statement of the bishops is to be understood in this context: "[The Church's interest in politics] is a way of worshipping the one God, desanctifying and at the same time sanctifying the world to him" (521: cf. *Lumen Gentium*, 34). To practice politics is to struggle for the justice of all. To struggle for and achieve justice is to give glory to God, the worship that is demanded by Paul in Romans 12:2. *Octogesima Adveniens* teaches: "Politics is the best way—if not the only way—of living out one's Christian commitment, in service to others" (46). Political commitment expresses the love that has found its social dimension of solidarity.

The two meanings of "politics" presented by Puebla are:

1. Politics with a capital *P*: the common search for the common good, the promotion of justice and rights, the denunciation of corruption and violence to human dignity. Politics with a capital *P* "spells out the fundamental values of the entire community—internal harmony and external security—reconciling equal-

ity with freedom, public authority with legitimate autonomy, and the participation of all persons and groups. . . . It also defines the means and ethics of social relations. In this wider sense, Politics is of interest to the Church and, as such, to its pastors, ministers of unity" (521). Politics contains all the ideologies (Marxism, capitalism, the social teaching of the Church) that present the utopic images of humanity and society. The Church has its vision of the world, of the person, of social life, of the distribution of goods, and so on. By proclaiming the Gospel it proclaims the Politics of the Gospel; the Church has an interest in Politics and always has had such an interest.

The Church cannot cease to be involved with Politics; that is, it cannot be indifferent to the justice or injustice of a cause nor can it be silent in the face of the obvious exploitation of any people. There is no neutrality in Politics: one is either for change in the direction of greater social participation or one is in favor of the status quo, which in many countries marginalizes a vast majority of the people.

Apoliticism, lack of interest in the common good and social justice, is formally criticized by Puebla: "The Church must criticize those who would restrict the scope of faith to personal or family life, those who would exclude the professional, economic, social and political orders as if sin, love, prayer, and pardon had no relevance for them" (515). There is an even harsher text:

> There is a manipulation of the Church that may derive from Christians themselves, and even from priests and religious, when they proclaim a Gospel devoid of economic, social, cultural, and political implications. In practice, this mutilation comes down to a kind of complicity with the established order, however unwitting [558].

Neutrality is impossible. We all take stances; it happens that some people have not been conscious of their position. Generally, these people assume the position of the dominant class, of the established order, which in many cases is manifestly antipopular, unequal, and unjust. Attempted apoliticism results in the manipulation and mutilation of the Gospel. We need to become more conscious of the political dimension of the Gospel and our faith.

This dimension is the core of evangelization: "Christianity must evangelize the totality of human life, including the political dimension" (515). It has a place in the pulpit and in the Mass. If our homilies do not touch upon justice, fraternity and participation, if they do not denounce violence, they are mutilating the Gospel and emasculating the message of the prophets and, above all, the good news of Jesus Christ.

2. Politics with a small *p* is all the activity corresponding to the administration or transformation of society through the conquest and exercise of the power of the state. It is the exercise of "political power to resolve economic, political, and social questions according to the criteria or ideology of citizen groups" (523). It is in this sense that one speaks of "party politics" (523). It has to do not with the whole but with a part; it is a faction and fraction of the whole. This does not involve the whole Church but only a part of it, namely, the laity.

Party politics is properly the realm of lay people. Their lay status entitles them to establish and organize political parties, "using an ideology and strategy that is suited to achieving their legitimate aims" (524). However, lay people must observe the minimum requirements for participating in and creating political parties in their role as lay Christians: that of being yeast and salt within the dough of party politics.

Politics and Clarity: Authentic Politicization

Social reality today is extremely sophisticated and unclear, tinted by every type of ideology. There is an especially dangerous ideology, fostered by the ruling classes who control the mass media, that hides the conflicts, slants the news, and thereby paints a rosy picture of a truly tragic reality. The Christian involved in the struggle for justice must be able to avoid such chicanery. For this reason, the Puebla document recommends the use of rational tools to help us see clearly (86, 719, 1046, 1160, 1307, esp. 826). In order to see clearly and act efficaciously we must utilize two primary instruments:

— *Analytical tools.* One must study the mechanisms that generate poverty and violence against human rights; the problem is generally not personal but structural. One must read very technical literature to discover how our society functions, what each person has, how prices and salaries are set and distributed, the importance of multinational corporations, and the nature of existing labor or union legislation.

— *Practical tools.* No desire is efficacious without organization. Thus, there is the importance of organizing centers and offices such as those for legal defense, human rights, justice and peace, and so forth. The Christian must join in the work of these centers as well as participate in unions and neighborhood organizations, thereby joining others in the struggle for justice.

Education is necessary for participation in both Politics and politics. Pope Paul VI speaks of "the importance of an education for life in society" (*Octogesima Adveniens*, 24). Puebla speaks of an education for justice (1029), of liberating education (1026), even though "certain governments have come to consider certain elements of Christian education as subversive" (1017). "Catholic education must produce the agents who will effect the permanent organic change that society needs. This is to be done through a civic and political formation that takes its inspiration from the Church's social teaching" (1033).

This activity is called politicization, which must not be confused with political chicanery. Politicization is a positive concept that signifies an educational activity aimed at social and political coresponsibility. Political chicanery is the utilization of social organizations, created for all, for the sole benefit of a few individuals or the interference of the hierarchy in questions of party politics.

The Distribution of Responsibility within the Church

The Church, fundamentally, is organized into three large bodies: the hierarchy, from the Pope to the deacon; the laity, who are baptized but who do not share in the leadership of the Christian community; and the religious, who are somewhere between the hierarchy and the laity, with elements of both. When it comes to responsibility, religious are considered to be among the hierarchy.

Responsibilities of the Hierarchy

A close reading of the texts of Puebla and *Justice in the World* reveals that it is the responsibility of the hierarchy to *announce* ("a word capable of changing society" [Puebla, 518]) and to *denounce, promote,* and *defend* human rights and dignity. It is their responsibility to be in *solidarity* with lay people and to *encourage* their creativity. They must *interpret* the aspirations of the people of each nation, especially the longings of those whom society tends to marginalize.

The hierarchy does not have a technical responsibility; they do not say *what* to do. They have an ethical responsibility; in the light of the Gospel they may say whether something is just or unjust, whether it favors participation or hinders it. "The service of peace and justice is an essential ministry of the Church" (Puebla, 1304).

Responsibilities of Religious

In *Evangelica Testificatio* Paul VI confronts religious with the "cry of the poor." He states that this cry "must prevent you from committing yourselves to any form of social injustice. It obligates you to awaken your conscience to the drama of misery and the demands of justice found in the Gospel and in the Church" (18). He ends by inviting religious to move closer to the poor in their condition of poverty. Puebla teaches that religious "must also cooperate in the evangelization of the political" (528) but without yielding to the temptation of a commitment to party politics (520).

Responsibilities of the Laity

According to *Lumen Gentium* (33) we must first recognize that the activity of the laity is not an extension of the hierarchy. Lay people have their own place in the Church and they must act within this sphere. The lay person on is not a secular person. He or she is a member of the Church in the secular world and has a direct mandate from Jesus Christ.

According to Puebla the place of lay activity is the world (789). Political activity deserves special emphasis (791). In a world scarred by injustices, lay people "may not excuse themselves from a serious commitment to promote justice and the common good" (793). They must become involved in party leadership (791), including "founding and organizing political parties" (524) with sufficient ideology and strategy (524). They are to do this not only under the direction of the bishops but with their own leadership. The texts of both *Justice in the World* and Puebla are clear on this point: "under the direction of the Gospel spirit and the doctrine of the Church" (*Justice in the World*, 38), "always illuminated by faith and guided by the Gospel and by the social doctrine of the Church, and at the same time by intelligence and ability toward appropriate activity" (Puebla, 793). The bishops emphasize the fact that the Gospel is not enough; clarity is required.

We thus arrive at the conclusion that the laity are exercising a right and a duty when they unite, mobilize, march, and initiate movements for action. peace, and justice. According to the official teaching of the bishops themselves, the laity do not need the backing of their bishop or pastor for their movement to have a "Christian character." These movements have a Christian character because the laity are true members of the Church, and with their dignity as lay people they act in their own milieu, the world and the field of politics, including party politics. According to Puebla the bishops should "demonstrate their *solidarity*, contributing to their formation and their spiritual life and stimulating their creativity that they may seek options ever more in line with the common good and the *needs of the weakest*" (525). "And by developing these activities, they [the laity] act on their own initiative, without involving the ecclesiastical hierarchy in their decisions; in some way, however, this implies the responsibility of the Church, given that they are its members" (*Justice in the World*, 38). Here, the clear distinction is made between Church as hierarchy and Church as the totality of its members.

Two Criteria for the Laity's Commitment to a Political Party

The political party is within the competence of the lay person. However, in the light of faith and the Gospel, not just any political party can be recommended. The Gospel does not point out any particular party, but there are negative criteria that exclude the Christian's participation in some political parties. Criteria have varied throughout history; the bishops in Latin America, given their situation of social injustice and the growing consciousness of the Church there, have offered us two particular criteria for our age.

The entire Church must make a *preferential option for the poor* (Puebla, part IV, chap. 2, 1166–1205), as an expression of its fidelity to the Gospel and to the cry of the oppressed. In close connection with this option, the Church must also make another option for *integral liberation* that seeks the transformation of the present situation toward one that is more fraternal and just (470–506).

These two criteria orient the conscious Christian who wishes to walk with the Church: Which political party best favors the poor? Which one contributes most to integral liberation? These are not simply questions having to do with being *for* the people; the Church must march alongside and *with* the people as they move toward their own complete humanization.

Conclusion: Understanding, Support, Participation

Commissions for peace and justice are springing up all over, linked to the Church's pastoral activity on diocesan, parish, and community levels. The Church must reinforce this way of living the Christian faith toward a fuller humanization of life. Three points deserve mention:

1. Understanding the commitment to justice as a response to the official teachings of the Church and as an expression of the maturity of the laity, incarnating their faith in a reality of conflict.

2. Supporting the movement. To fight for justice is not a bed of roses. It is to enter into a conflict situation and denounce every instance of injustice. It is to live amid tension and to nourish a spirit of peace without being carried away by the instinct of revenge or self-righteousness.

3. Participation in the movement. There is a place for everyone given various levels of commitment and different needs, be it participation on a legal board, research of case studies, doctrine and conscientization, and so on.

"For us today the love of God must become first and foremost a labor of justice on behalf of the oppressed, an effort of liberation for those who are most in need of it" (Puebla, 327). The bishops have given us a powerful mandate.

THE VIOLATION OF HUMAN RIGHTS IN THE CHURCH

There is no institution today that has upheld human dignity more than the Christian community. The Church considers the human person to be an image and likeness of God, believing the individual to be a child of that absolute Mystery, a brother or sister of Jesus Christ, God incarnate, bearer of a nature hypostatically assumed by God himself, and so the Church affirms that human destiny is irreversibly linked to the eternal destiny of the most Holy Trinity. The Church has developed an understanding of the human person that highlights his or her inviolable dignity and sacredness. This anthropological reality forms the basis for inalienable rights that establish unquestionable duties of respect that are so radical that human causes become God's causes.

The theme of basic human rights and privileges has only recently arisen in the consciousness of Christians, but it has always been present in the theoretical understanding of what it is to be human: "The ferment of the gospel, too, has aroused and continues to arouse in man's heart the irresistible requirements of his dignity" (*Gaudium et Spes*, 26). Given this view of humanity, the Second Vatican Council states the following principle in *Dignitatis Humanae*: "The freedom of man [should] be respected as far as possible, and curtailed only when and in so far as necessary" (7). Thus, *Gaudium et Spes* warns citizens to "be on guard against granting government too much authority" (75).

However, the Church is also conscious that freedom, in practice, is limited by personal and social responsibilities shaped by the rights of others, duties toward others, and the common good (*DH* 7). Even so, all forms of discrimination are unjustified: "With respect to the fundamental rights of the person, every type of discrimination, whether social or cultural, whether based on sex, race, color, social condition, language, or religion, is to be overcome and eradicated as contrary to God's intent" (*GS* 29).[5]

Human Rights in the Church: Theory versus Practice

Given the consciousness of human rights within the Church, one might expect that there be a practice commensurate with that theory. However, it is never easy to go from the pristine clarity and internal cohesiveness of theory to practice, with its necessary translations and ambiguities. Nor is every theory reversed by its consequent practice. Theory serves as an imperative and utopic model. The Church is not above this dialectical difficulty; in the Church, as elsewhere, theory is one thing and practice often quite another.

In spite of the inevitable gap between proclamation and implementation, there is today another gap that results from power structures, institutional deficiencies, and distortions—both practical and theoretical—inherited from models that no longer reflect reality. There are violations of human rights within the Church itself. These are not those abuses that are the result of individual abuses of power which are temporal in nature; we refer to those that are the result of a certain way of understanding and organizing the reality of the ecclesial structure—a somewhat permanent state of affairs. In pointing out these abuses, we will confine ourselves to those instances in which there has been a stated commitment to human rights without the resulting practice within the Church itself; we will attempt to explain and understand them, with a view toward improving those practices.

I do not intend to denigrate the Church; this book presupposes an explicit adherence to the sacramental worth of the Church that must not only desire to affirm itself but also to foster self-criticism because "the Church . . . is at the same time holy and always in need of being purified" (*LG* 8). The credibility of its proclamation of human rights and its denunciation of their violations depends upon the respect that the Church itself practices. *Justice in the World* emphasizes this very fact: "While the Church is bound to give witness to justice, she recognizes that anyone who ventures to speak about justice must first be just in their eyes. Hence we must undertake an examination of the modes of acting, of the possessions and lifestyle found within the Church herself" (40).

The purpose of this reflection is to foster a greater and more effective authenticity in the commitment of the local churches to human rights; the contradiction in terms of theory and practice is not found within these churches themselves but in their collision with authority. The prophetic power of these churches must not be weakened.

Practices of the Church

At this point our interest is not so much in the theories of the Church as in its practices, some of which violate human rights as our understanding of them has developed.[6] The principal issues concerning the Church and human rights were brought to the fore and frankly expressed at the Synod of Bishops in 1971 when the document *Justice in the World* was being ironed out.[7] The synod fathers made the attempt to present not only injustices in the world at large but also those within the Church itself.

The Institutional Level

The centralization of decision-making within the Church is well known, the fruit of a long historical process, crystallized in various forms that were perhaps valid at one time but which today conflict with our consciousness of the rights and dignity of the human person.

For example, election to administrative posts within the Church, from the papacy to the priesthood, is not preceded by grassroots consultation of the People of God. When, by accident, such a consultation does take place, it is often disregarded. Leaders are chosen within the strict confines of those who hold ecclesial power; they are imposed on local communities, thrusting to the margins the vast majority of the laity who often possess greater professional, intellectual, and even theological qualifications. The centralization of decision-making inevitably leads to marginalization; this has an effect on basic rights to information and participation in those decisions that affect the responsibility of both the individual and the community. In view of this, *Justice in the World* proposed the correction of the injustice of excluding the laity from ecclesial decisions: "The members of the Church should have some share in the drawing up of decisions, in accordance with the rules given by the Second Vatican Council and the Holy See, for instance with regard to the setting up of councils at all levels" (46).

Even priests are often considered to be incapable of reflection, of being able to organize and make decisions about matters affecting the unity of the Church. It is the bishops who think, act, and speak for the priests in councils, synods, and other ecclesial gatherings. Juridically, priests are auxiliaries to the bishop. Groups of priests have often organized but many times they have been immediately choked by suspicion, gossip, and pressure on the part of their superiors. *Justice in the World* insists on the creation of such groups: "Within the Church rights must be preserved. No one should be deprived of his rights because he is associated with the Church in one way or another" (41).

Another conflict with regard to the basic rights of the human person has to do with the return of priests to the lay state.[8] The desire to leave the ministry is treated practically as a sin, because the encyclical *Sacerdotalis Coelibatus* (written as an open letter) considers these priests as "sadly unfaithful to the vowed obligations of their consecration" (83).[9] Their decision of conscience is not granted moral legitimacy. They are punished with a series of prohibitions, reducing them to a sub-lay status. Among other things, the laicized priest cannot share in the liturgy of any community where his status is known; he may not preach; he is not permitted to exercise any pastoral office; he is prohibited from teaching in seminaries, on theological faculties or any such institution (SEDOC 1971, 308). In a later document, restrictions were outlined that affect the ability to earn a living, not to mention the dangers to the individual's faith and relationship with the visible Church. Those who leave the priesthood are not allowed access to faculties, institutes, schools of religious or ecclesiastical science (e.g., faculties of canon law, missiology, church history, philosophy, pastoral ministry, religious education, catechetics, etc.); nor are they allowed access to any other center of higher studies in which theological or religious disciplines are taught—whether or not the center is directly under ecclesiastical authority. No laicized priest may be trusted with the teaching of theological material or anything closely connected with it such as religious education and catechetics (SEDOC 1973, 1049).

It is not hard to see that such discrimination affects not only the priests themselves but the entire community, deprived of their exceptional training in leadership and the explanation of faith.

Discrimination against women in the Church is one of the most clear examples of the violation of human rights. Women make up at least half of the faithful and women religious are ten times the number of their male counterparts. However, they are juridically considered to be incapable of almost any leadership function, rarely present in secretariats, commissions, and sacred congregations.

Due to cultural tradition as well as the historical expression of the word of God, they are excluded from ministerial duties associated with the sacrament of orders. This tradition was institutionalized as normative doctrine and recently reaffirmed[10] without taking into consideration both exegetical and dogmatic arguments formulated by some of the leading contemporary theologians.[11] The basic argument presented by the statement of the Sacred Congregation for the Doctrine of the Faith stems not from the tradition against the priestly ordination of women, nor from the attitude of Christ, nor from the practice of the apostles, but rather from biology: the biological fact that Jesus was male. The text states:

> It must not be forgotten that Christ is a man. And as such, in spite of wanting to ignore the importance of such symbolism for the economy of Revelation, one must admit that in those actions that demand the character of ordination and in which Christ himself is represented, as author of the covenant and spouse and head of the Church, in the exercise of his ministry of salvation—as takes place to the highest degree in the Eucharist—the role must be fulfilled . . . by a man [p. 7].

Because there is no such being as a man-male in the abstract but only male who are radically determined, linguistically characterized, geographically situated, we ask ourselves if it would not be equally legitimate and consistent with the logic of the above official argument to demand that not just any male may receive the sacrament of orders but, like Jesus, that he be Jewish, born in Galilee, that he speak Aramaic, that he be circumcised. Does the Church not recognize that Jesus chose eleven married apostles and only one bachelor? Does this not carry any weight in the decisions of the Church? The text cited above reserves the word *person* for males, leading one to conclude that women, being unfit for the sacrament of orders, are not persons.

The former archbishop of St. Paul-Minneapolis, during the 1971 synod forcefully declared: "There is no argument that can serve to exclude women from any ecclesial service, especially when it is based solely on masculine prejudice and blind dependency on mere human tradition that reduce the place of women in society to anachronistic representations and Sacred Scripture to fragile interpretation."[12] Paulo Evaristo Arns, cardinal archbishop of São Paulo, affirmed: "How can we not think of the situation of women in society and the Church? It would be very myopic to limit ourselves to the ways and customs of the past without opening new horizons to such a decisive force in the development of humanity."[13]

Freedom of Information and Opinion

Participation is linked to the circulation of information. How can members of the Church help in making decisions if they lack the information necessary to form intelligent opinions? The hierarchy speaks out strongly against censorship practiced by the state and yet the Church exerts almost inquisitorial control of the Catholic means of communication. Any article in theological, scientific, or spiritual journals not in line with a particular ecclesial interpretation, any theological hypothesis that is advanced in view of new problems raised by society, provokes an often violent reaction with threats of submitting the author to a doctrinal trial held by hierarchial superiors.

There are dioceses where a theologian may only speak to women religious groups or to groups of priests after having survived an interrogation that, by its tenor, is almost equivalent to a cross-examination in court. In other places, the simple fact that a person may be a theologian makes him or her suspect of heresy, of defending heretical propositions, of being in opposition to established authority. Many bishops substitute authoritarianism for their own ignorance, an authority based on an unreflected knowledge, monotonously repeating the pronouncements published in *L'Osservatore Romano*.

The servility and silence that characterize Catholic culture is not to be admired. Dom Helder Camara coined an expression that summarizes an entire discourse: a large part of the Catholic press has succumbed to the marriage that introduced the devil to the Church, that of mediocrity wedded to bad taste. Such a spurious wedding results in excessive ideological control over intelligence. *Justice in the World* proclaims: "The Church recognizes everyone's right to suitable freedom of expression and thought. This includes the right of everyone to be heard in a spirit of dialogue which preserves legitimate diversity within the Church" (44).

Doctrine and Discipline

In terms of doctrine the practice of the Church is laden with a long, persistent, and obvious curtailment of basic human rights, to such an extent that a well-known canon lawyer concluded a detailed study on the subject with the following statement: "There is no tradition in the Church that has been helpful for procedures either for the verification of errors of faith or in defense against them. In the western Church, especially, orthodoxy has always enjoyed primacy over orthopraxis."[14]

The Church today lacks the political means for punishing those accused of heresy but the fundamental mentality and proceedings of the past have changed little. Physical torture has been abolished but psychological torture continues: the juridical insecurity of the doctrinal processes; the anonymity of the denunciations; the lack of knowledge as to the reasons behind the charges; the judgments apart from the process; no acknowledgment of offered explanations; repeated accusations to known questions; long intervals between correspondence; the insecurity and uncertainty as to whether the process is being continued or discontinued or whether the procedures have been further refined. All of this, accented even more by the marginalization one suffers in the local church due to the scrutiny of the Sacred Congregation for the Doctrine of the Faith, leads some theologians to the dark night of lonely suffering, psychological worry, and even physical death.

The rules for the examination of doctrine, drawn up by the Sacred Congregation for the Doctrine of the Faith (till 1908 the Congregation of the Inquisition or Holy Office), were published on 15 January 1971. That document curtails a series of sacred human rights that are acknowledged even in manifestly atheistic societies.[15] The process begins without notifying the accused. Later, after those within the Congregation have already taken positions, the accused is informed and requested to respond to the various interrogators. Often, sentences or phrases are taken out of context, truncated, and many times poorly translated from the original into Latin.[16] The accused has no access to the concrete accusations, to the proceedings, or to the various viewpoints of the Sacred Congregation. A *relator pro auctore* is appointed, but the accused is not given his name nor may he choose his own *relator*. This is a Kafkaesque process wherein the accuser, the defender, the lawyer, and the judge are one and the same. There is no right to counsel or any other recourse. Everything is done in secret which, in the absence of any assured rights, gives rise to rumors that are prejudicial against the person and activity of the accused.

The accused's only right is to respond to the solicitation from the Sacred Congregation; he cannot count on any response to questions he may ask or expect to be informed about the course of the proceedings. The incriminating letter has already been written, in condemnatory phrases; the propositions of the accused are labeled "theologically uncertain, dangerous, erroneous, irreconcilable with Catholic doctrine and the rule of faith." Even before he responds to the Congregation, the accused is punished: he may not speak or write about the subject under scrutiny. According to Hans Küng there is no alternative but to sign one's own condemnation.[17] The meeting in Rome to which the theologian is summoned, as his last chance for defense, is held without the juridical assurances evident in civil law: there is no access to the minutes, one may not be assisted by a lawyer. "It appears that a Catholic theologian must travel to Rome like the Czechs for a 'meeting' in Moscow with the Soviet Politburo. . . . A meeting makes sense when there is true dialogue, mutual give and take, and not the dictate by one party that demands the unconditional capitulation of the other."[18]

The ecclesiastical magisterium must present Christian doctrine in a positive way and defend it against possible errors. It is a task and a duty that aids the community of faith and it must include—as *ultima ratio*—eventual doctrinal procedures. The principle of subsidiarity is crucial to such proceedings. First, there should be competent organizations within the episcopal conferences to test the developing theological doctrines that may clash with common doctrine and create conflict among believers. The Sacred Congregation would remain as the final judge, its function linked to that of the national conferences. Second, investigations should be carried out in formal and open fashion in which those bringing charges are distinct from those rendering judgment. The rights of the accused must be guaranteed. Third, from the start, the accused should have the right to present his doctrine and defend it. This presupposes complete access to records and the choice of a competent theological advocate, who can help spell out the doctrine and translate into other words and language understandable to those who must decide the case. There are many scientific, historical, dogmatic, and exegetical problems (the frequent motive for accusations) that could be clarified in this way.[19]

Regula fidei and *doctrina Catholica* (the rule of faith and Catholic doctrine), which it is the function of the Sacred Congregation to uphold, are at the service of faith, faith in the salvation embraced in Jesus Christ. The purpose of theology is to present the essence of faith in such a way that it can be existentially lived by the faithful as well as being plausible to human reason in each age. The rule of faith must preserve the essence of faith but without maintaining it in immutable formulas. What is extraordinary about the Christian faith is that it always maintains its identity throughout its various historical changes and distinct formulations. This was the case with the gospels and will continue throughout history. As our experience of the world changes so do our problems and questions. If theology does not consider these historical factors and does not include them in its presentation of Christian faith, then the rule of faith becomes a caricature of empty, fictional realities.

Great theologians like St. John the Evangelist, St. Paul, Origen, St. Augustine, St. Thomas Aquinas, Johann Adam Möhler, Karl Rahner, and others had the courage to accept the questions of their times and seek answers from the arsenal of faith. This cannot be accomplished with the simple recitation of formulas; there must be the attempt to create new grammar and syntax for faith in each age.[20] Because of possible deviations in this task there is the responsibility for defending the correct understanding of faith by means of the investigation of theological teaching. However, one must proceed in such a way that neither the basic rights nor the dignity of the individual are violated. Thus, *Justice in the World* proclaimed: "The form of judicial procedure should give the accused the right to know his accusers and also the right to a proper defense. To be complete, justice should also include speed in its procedure" (45).

These are only some of the problems that call into question the credibility of the Church in its proclamation of human rights and its struggle for them.

A Possible Explanation

The gap between ecclesial theory and praxis in terms of human rights is a challenge to all who try to interpret it. A shortsighted interpretation would attribute such a contradiction to human deficiencies of those in authority in the Church and of those who are simply cast as victims of a doctrinal understanding of faith or of the primary instincts for power and self-affirmation. This is possible in individual cases because where there is power there may be abuses of that authority. But we must remember that the majority of those in authority in the Church are men of good faith, clear conscience, impeccable personal character.

The problem lies on a deeper level, on the structure that to a great degree is independent of persons. We will approach this problem from various points of view in order to better understand the causes of the contradiction.

Sociohistorical Collision

One explanation is, without a doubt, the power structure in the Church. In terms of decision-making, the pole runs from the Pope to the bishop, to the priests—excluding religious and laity. From a sociological perspective, the Church operates out of an authoritarian system.[21] A system is authoritarian when those in power exclude the free and spontaneous acknowledgement by their subordinates of that authority. The free and spontaneous submission of a group of people to one individual or institution distinguishes authority from power and domination.[22] Without these natural conditions for relationship, authority becomes authoritarian. The system of power within the Church believes itself to come directly from God, and believers must accept it in faith. Socialization through catechesis, theology, and the accepted exercise of its power guarantees the preservation of the structure from generation to generation.[23]

Underlying every true human authority there is divine authority, above all in the case of the Church of Christ. The problem is whether the present *structure* can directly claim divine origin or whether it stems from the insertion of divine authority and the Church in history. Good theology, with help from the New Testament, may be able to uphold the idea that the authority of Christ is present in the entire Church, the body of Christ, in a primary and fundamental manner, and then organically differentiated in the various members of that Church (Pope-bishops-priest-laity). The concrete forms are taken to be the contribution of diverse cultural situations.

The primitive Christian communities felt the powerful need to organize. They inevitably took social and political models from the surrounding world in which to incarnate their authority from God and Christ. The power structure in the Church today is indebted to centuries-old patterns, and two patterns are worth noting in particular: the experience with Roman power and the feudal structure. The Church assumed customs, titles, expressions, and symbols from them. Hierarchy, as a term and as a concept, is a result of this process. This assuming of societal characteristics by the Church was necessary for its continuation in the world and, in the theological sense of incarnation, desired by God. The Roman and feudal style of power in the Church today, however, constitutes one of the principal sources of conflict with the rising consciousness of human rights.

The Roman and feudal style of authority is characterized, first, by a hierarchy with distinct "orders" (Tertullian); second, this hierarchy is personal in nature. The one in power is such for life; his will is law (*lex animata*) within his own "order" but always linked by obedience to the superior "order." Third, it is a sacred and cosmic hierarchy. In other words, its legitimacy comes not from below but from above, from the will of God. The higher someone is in this hierarchy the closer one is to God and so has a greater share in God's divine power. To obey one's superior is to obey God, making obedience a religious act. Fourth, this style of authority is untouchable and not subject to any internal criticism. Criticism from within any of the orders is only possible from a higher authority. A questioning from below would be equal to a revolution in the universe. Thus, any thought of transformation is the same as an attack on God who is author of both the order and structure of sacred power.[24]

This understanding of authority gave meaning to personal and social life. The Church's experience with this structure was so successful that it has continued almost without change, even in the face of the great modern revolutions (French, industrial, socialist, and others) that gave rise to new power structures. With the social transformations of the last centuries, the Church has had to defend itself politically and doctrinally. What the Church defends is not so much its divine authority but the historical form that this authority has assumed. Previously, society recognized the power and authority of the Church; today it has become a ghetto. Society at large does not pay any attention to what happens in the Church, in terms of power, because the Church's presence is no longer decisive in the events that shape the history of a nation.

As we will see later, the Second Vatican Council recognized the historicity of the forms of power within the Church and elaborated a theological understanding of authority that was less monarchical and more congenial, in itself paving the way for new structures of participation in ecclesial life. The Council did this especially through the documents *Lumen Gentium* (on the Church), *Christus Dominus* (on the bishops), *Apostolicam Actuositatem* (on the laity), and *Gaudium et Spes* (on the Church in the modern world).

Analytical Collision

Another explanation of the human rights contradiction arises through an analysis of the Church's consciousness of its own authority. Emile Durkheim asserted: "A society is not simply the mass of individuals that comprises it, nor the territory it occupies, nor the things it uses, nor the movements it carries out, but *above all it is the idea that it has of itself.*"[25] The self-awareness that a group develops about itself is one of the most important factors for explaining its behavior. What self-concept forms ecclesiastical authority? It considers itself to be the principal if not exclusive bearer of God's revelation to the world, with the mission of proclaiming it, explaining it, and defending it.[26] This revelation is found in the sacred Scriptures and interpretation is given by the magisterium of the Church. As such, revelation is doctrinally understood as the collection of truths necessary for salvation.

This is the crux of the problem: the doctrinal understanding of revelation. God reveals necessary truths, some unattainable by reason, to facilitate the road to salvation. The magisterium possesses a collection of absolute, infallible, and divine truths. The magisterium presents an absolute doctrine, free from any doubt. Any inquiry that is born of life and that calls into question a given doctrine is mistaken. Doctrine substitutes for life, experience, and everything from below.[27]

This understanding has grave consequences for the problem of human rights: intolerance and dogmatism. The bearer of an absolute truth cannot tolerate any other truth. As Rubem Alves has noted, "Those who pretend to possess the truth are destined for intolerance." In this understanding, salvation depends on the knowledge of orthodox truth. Having and being coincide: whoever has the truth is saved. Truth is more decisive than goodness. The Inquisition was not bothered by moral crimes but by those related to orthodox truth.[28] One who commits a moral transgression sins but he or she does not jeopardize the understanding and system of truths and power. The sinner contradicts the truth but repents because the truth is recognized. The heretic, on the other hand, denies the validity of the system of truths and proclaims another truth. With a doctrinal understanding of revelation, the heretic is a criminal not only against the unity of the Church but against the very reality of the Church-as-bearer-of-divine-truths. He is like the atheist and is characterized as such by the edict of Constantine (Eusebius. *Vita Constantini* 3, 64). The rigor of the Inquisition was necessitated by the harsh logic of the system itself and even today governs the doctrinal mentality of the Sacred Congregation for the Doctrine of the Faith.

As long as this type of dogmatic and doctrinaire understanding of revelation and salvation continues, there inevitably will be repression of the freedom of thought within the Church. This repression will be carried out with the clean conscience of one fulfilling a sacred duty of preserving the divine right of revelation to which every human right must give way.

Structural Collision

The two previous aspects are not sufficient explanation for the gap between the consciousness of human rights and the fact that they are unrealized historically within the Church. Those aspects are on the level of ideas and models. There is a deeper and more structural level of the concrete practice of those in certain positions of power. Ideas are the products of a concrete life and they serve that life. In other words, in order to understand any phenomenon structurally one must begin not with what is thought and stated but rather with what actions have marked daily life.[29]

Using the model inherited from the Industrial Revolution—one that characterizes modern society—we may speak of the means of production versus the goods and services of that production. In terms of the Church, those who hold the means of religious production, the realm of the symbolic, also hold power and so create and control official discussions. From a sociological point of view there is an undeniable division and inequality is the Church: one group produces the symbolic goods and another consumes them. There are the ordained who can produce, celebrate, and decide and the nonordained who associate with and assist the ordained. The capacity for production and participation in decision-making, although latent in the nonordained, remains untapped. The group that holds the means of symbolic production develops a corresponding theology that justifies, reinforces, and socializes its power by attributing divine origin to its historical exercise of that power. Theology aside, the underlying conflict is one of the power of some over others, a power that will not abdicate its privileges and rights, at odds with the inviolable rights of human persons (participation, symbolic production, free expression, etc.). The Christian lay person is made to believe that, due to being a simple Christian, he or she is faced with divine givens that exclude or subordinate the lay person to a group whose power comes from above. There is nothing left but the acceptance of the fact that although the hierarchy recognizes certain rights they cannot be exercised because they do not fit into the ecclesial organization. The rights of the individual lose their inalienable character and are thus violated.

There is no argument as to the legitimacy of the authority of the Church; it exists and is willed by God. The historical form that it has taken, the ideologically justified imbalance of power among the members of the Church, is called into question.

Paths toward Improvement

How does one overcome or bridge the gap between the Church's theory and praxis? Because of the officially created doctrinal burden that reinforces the interests of those holding sacred power, what will open the path of renewal that will affect the structure itself? There is a reasonable hope that such is possible because of the internal contradiction within the ecclesial consciousness itself. There are practices that limit basic human rights, justified by their corresponding theological theories; there is also another authority, of the Gospel, upon which the Church stands, that constantly criticizes and denounces every abuse of power and calls for respect and service. Jesus' message does not favor the domination of some over others or the curtailment of their rights; the same holds true for the Church that exists because of that message and that incarnates him in the world. On the contrary, these two realities presuppose, guarantee, and promote freedom, fraternity, and mutual and disinterested service. We live under the "law of freedom" (Jas 1:25; 2:12). "That we might be free Christ has freed us" (Gal 5:1). These are the imperatives that foster our hope and lead us to shape practices that strive toward those ideals.

We must first do away with the idealist temptation that is satisfied with raising people's consciousness in order to change the structure of the Church. It is not new ideas but new and different practices (supported by theory) that will modify ecclesial reality. These modifications in turn open the way for a corresponding theory, leading to a new reading of the Gospel and tradition.

We must recognize that in the past few years, especially after Vatican II, extremely important steps have been taken. Just as the Church previously took on Roman and feudal structures, it is now taking on structures found in today's civil societies that are more compatible with our growing sense of human rights. This is the often argued "democratization of the Church." This term does not refer so much to concrete practices and organizations as it does to the intentions and structures of a different type of Church. In this view, the fundamental nature of the Church remains unchanged, with its revelation of Jesus Christ, with the basic doctrines about his life and work, the ethical imperatives implied in his message, and the sacramentality of the Church, but at the same time it favors a free and fraternal community with the participation of the greatest number of people.[30] Those in the hierarchy who favor a centralist feudal model are few; the model for bishops and priests is more that of true shepherds, leaders among their people, in service devoid of all titles, and according to a style that reveals the gospel model of the diaconate. It would take too long and this is not the place to detail the various transformations that are taking on all levels of church power.[31] Not only is established power being modified (and humanized) but new ways of being Church are springing forth, especially in Latin America among the *comunidades eclesiales de base*, such that today we are experiencing a true ecclesiogenesis.

Second, these new church practices, better able to meet the demands of human rights, lead us to a gospel understanding of authority. We are made conscious of the concepts latent in the present conception of ecclesial authority: a metaphysics of creation, the absolute power of the Creator, cosmic harmony—elements that have little to do with the New Testament understanding of service. The authority of the Church stems from the authority of Jesus:

> "Jesus was, or became, authoritative by what he said and did and this is because his words and actions were felt by men to be helpful, liberating, good and beneficial. In other words, Jesus' authority can be defined as *full saving* power." Jesus

did not resort constantly to this full saving power, not did he try to justify it or least of all boast of it in an authoritarian manner. On the contrary, he looked for and tried to provoke human freedom. His methods were those of convincing clarity and insight, rational argument and non-casuistical openness and directness. He had authority because all that he said and did arose from the authority of freedom and love and he gave men the power to create, to love and to be free.[32]

Ecclesial authority that is based on this tradition must be founded upon the equality of brother and sister (Gal 3:26–29: you are one in Christ; Matt 23:8: you are all brothers; Jas 2:2–4: there must be no distinction between you), in a fraternity that is opposed to qualifications such as teacher, father, and so forth (Matt 23:8–9), and in service that is devoid of all domination and pretension to having the final word (Mark 10:42–45; Luke 22:25–27; John 13:14).

Authority was incarnated in many different ways in the primitive Church. In the Pauline communities (Corinth) there was a charismatic structure; in the community at Jerusalem, a synogogal (council of priests) structure. The communities of the pastoral letters had structures centered around the apostolic delegates with their presbyterate, thereby reducing the participation of all baptized Christians who, for Paul, were each bearers of the Spirit. The form mattered little; authority meant service.

However, the historical form of the pastoral letters predominated: the minister with powers that were received through the laying on of hands, giving rise to various *orders* in the Church. This is the root—especially in those cases where the spirituality of service was lacking—for the focus that would one day result in discrimination among the faith community, to such an extent that the ordained kept all power in the Church for themselves. This is certainly against the basic intention of fraternity present in Jesus' message. The centralized form of power is but *one* form that, for historical reasons (in this case, the threat of gnosticism) may be justified but which cannot claim exclusivity through the centuries. The diversity of forms of authority in the New Testament suggests another direction. Authority was congenial before it was monarchical.[33]

The Second Vatican Council, influenced by new styles and practices of authority in the Church, accepted the idea of collegiality not only on the episcopal level but throughout the entire Church. While preconciliar theology excluded the laity from any office because they were not ordained, Vatican II teaches that because of their baptism lay people "are in their own way made sharers in the priestly, prophetic, and kingly functions [*munus*] of Christ. They carry out their own part in the mission of the whole Christian people with respect to the Church and the world" (*Lumen Gentium*, 31). While Pius XII's encyclical *Humani Generis* taught that the hierarchy is solely responsible for the administration of the word of God (18), Vatican II affirms that "lay people announce Christ, explain and spread His teaching according to their situation and ability" (*Apostolicam Actuositatem*, 16).

Finally, an improvement in the doctrinal understanding of revelation and faith is taking place in theology. God, in the first place, did not reveal true propositions *about* himself, man, and salvation. He revealed himself, in his mystery, life and will. Divine life invaded human life. What saves us are not truths formulated in neat sentences but rather God himself who is given as salvation. Faith primarily means the total adherence to the living God, not simply the acceptance of a creed of propositions.

The Church is not only the bearer of revelation and salvation; it also, and rightly, is responsible for doctrine because there may be doctrines and ways of articulating faith that give rise to false representations of God and his love. Doctrines and theologies must always reflect faith. This is the criterion for the correctness of any theology that is presented to the ecclesial community. But the Church must be on guard against dogmatic rigidity and doctrinal fixation, as if doctrine were the ultimate judge. Doctrine is always the historico-cultural translation of God's revelation. We have salvation not through our doctrines but through our practices that follow our encounter with the living and true God.

This existential and biblical understanding of revelation and faith opens the door to various approaches to absolute Truth. This is an eschatological gift; within history our formulations express the absolute Truth but cannot express everything absolutely about the Truth. In everything said there is something left unsaid; every point of view is the view of a point. Therefore, there will always be different ways of articulating faith through doctrines expressed in the words of another culture and even another social class.

Conclusion

The Church recognizes the unfathomable dignity of the human person and so can be the conscience of the world with respect to human rights. But proclamation alone is not enough. The Church will only be heard if it gives witness by its practices, if it is the first to respect and promote human rights within its own reality. Otherwise, one would be right to criticize a Church that sees the speck in the eye of another while ignoring the beam in its own: "Hypocrite, remove the beam from your own eye and then try to remove the speck from your neighbor's eye" (see Matt 7:3-5).

There is a quote from Cardinal Arns, of Brazil, who has become a spokesman in the Church for the defense of human rights, especially those of the nameless, and who because of this knows a great deal about the onerous path of the prophet: "The modern Job has great poems to write. And these poems will not be read except by the heart of God. Do the churches have the courage to be the heart of God in this moment of history?"[34]

THE BASE ECCLESIAL COMMUNITY: A BRIEF SKETCH

Base ecclesial communities (sometimes referred to as basic Christian communities) are a phenomenon that has its origin in Latin America, where they were given their name *comunidades eclesiales de base* because they are communities primarily comprised of lower-class, grassroots people, the base of society, as opposed to the pinnacle of power in the social pyramid. The bishops meeting at Puebla in 1979 hailed them as a "reason for joy and hope" (96. 262, 1309), as "centers of evangelization and moving forces of liberation" (96). To understand this phenomenon that holds so much promise for the future of faith in history, the following sketch is offered. There are five basic points that characterize the base ecclesial community.

1. An Oppressed yet Believing People

The communitarian spirit is a part of modern life. In addition to the large social structures, there are also small groups of people who want to live more immediate and fraternal relationships. The base ecclesial communities are an expression of this desire. There is the added fact that the institution of the Church, in many parts of the world, is in crisis due to the lack of ministers ordained through the sacrament of orders. Without these ministers communities of faith are left to themselves, and run the risk of falling apart and disappearing. The birth of the base ecclesial communities represents a way out of this crisis. In these communities the lay person takes on the task of spreading the Gospel and keeping faith alive. It is also important to note that the members of these communities are generally poor and from the base of society (the lower classes) and from the base of the Church (the laity).

The base ecclesial community is generally made up of fifteen to twenty families. They get together once or twice a week to hear the word of God, to share their problems in common, and to solve those problems through the inspiration of the Gospel. They share their comments on the biblical passages, create their own prayers, and decide as a group what their tasks should be. After centuries of silence, the People of God are beginning to speak. They are no longer just parishioners in their parish; they have their own ecclesiological value; they are recreating the Church of God.

It is true that the Church is Christ's gift which we gratefully receive. Yet the Church is also a human response to faith. The Church is the People of God, born of a believing and, in many parts of the world, oppressed people through the Holy Spirit of God. They are a community of the faithful in which the risen Christ is present. This is the realization of the mystery of the universal Church in the grassroots, in this humble and small group of men, women, and children, often very poor but filled with faith, hope, love, and communion with other Christians. The base ecclesial community makes concrete the true Church of Jesus Christ.

On the one hand is the institutional Church with its dioceses and bishops, with its parishes and sacred ministers, its chapels and churches; on the other is a growing network of base ecclesial communities (especially in Latin America and Brazil in particular, where there are over 70,000 such communities), reaching countless Christians who live out their faith in these communities. These are two expressions of the one Church of Christ and of the apostles. The institutional Church supports and encourages the base ecclesial communities; through them it is able to enter the popular sector and be made concrete by sharing in the painful passion as well as the hopes of the people. These ecclesial communities, in turn, are in communion with the institutional Church; they want their bishop, their priests and religious. In this way, the communities are put in touch with the grand apostolic tradition, guarantee their catholicity, and reaffirm the unity of the Church.

The more the Church is open to the people, the more it becomes the People of God. The more that the poor and oppressed of our societies come together in the name of Christ to hear his word of salvation and liberation, the more they concretely are, in a very real historical sense, the Church of Jesus Christ. There is no real conflict between the ecclesial institution and the ecclesial communities. Conflict does not exist because a large part of the ecclesial institution has joined the communities, including many cardinals, bishops, and pastors. The real tension exists between a Church that has opted for the people, for the poor and their liberation, and other groups in that same Church that have not made this option or who have not made it concrete or who persist in keeping to the strictly sacramental and devotional character of faith.

The base ecclesial community is a blessing from God for our present day and is also the response that faith gives to the challenges of an oppressed and believing people.

2. Born from the Word of God

The Gospel is the calling card of the base ecclesial community. The Gospel is heard, shared, and believed in the community, and it is in its light that the participants reflect on the problems of their life. This is a typical feature of the community; the Gospel is always confronted with life, with the concrete situation of the community. It is not simply a marvelous and consoling message; above all, it is light and leaven. The Gospel is seen as good news, as a message of hope, promise, and joy from the real situations of the poor.

The relationship between Gospel and life takes shape through a slow and difficult process within the community. Initially, the word is brought to bear on the problems of the group, such as the illness of one of the members or unemployment. In time, the group begins to take into account the social question of their surroundings, be it their street or the neighborhood. There may be problems of water, electricity, sewers, paved streets, clinics, schools, and so forth. Later, the group begins to take a political stance toward the social system. The current organization of society is brought into question. At this level of consciousness they begin to participate in the struggles of the people through labor unions, various people's movements, political parties, and the like.

Yet, for the people of the base, faith is the great doorway into social problems. Their social commitment comes from the vision of faith. Their faith is not changed but rather, faced with the facts of life, it is strengthened, doubled, and shows itself for what it is, a leaven of liberation.

The Gospel is shared in absolute freedom in the base ecclesial community. Everyone is given the chance to speak and to give their opinion about a given fact or situation. Surprisingly, the popular exegesis of the community comes very close to the ancient exegesis of the fathers of the Church. It is an exegesis that goes beyond the words and captures the living, spiritual meaning of the text. The gospel passage serves as the inspiration for the group's reflection on life, where the word of God is actually heard.

3. A New Way of Being Church

The base ecclesial community is not only a means for evangelization in popular settings. It is much more. It is a new way of being Church and of concretizing the mystery of salvation that is lived in common. The Church is not only the institution with its sacred scriptures, hierarchy, sacramental structures, canon law, liturgical norms, orthodoxy, and moral imperatives. All of that is important, but the Church is also an *event*. It emerges, is born, and is continually reshaped whenever individuals meet to hear the word of God, believe in it, and vow together to follow Jesus Christ, inspired by the Holy Spirit. This is what happens in the base ecclesial communities. The group may meet under a huge tree and every week they are found there, reading the sacred texts, sharing their commentaries, praying, talking of life, and making decisions about common projects. It is an event, and the Church of Jesus and the Holy Spirit takes shape under that tree.

The principal characteristic of this way of being Church is community. Everyone is a true brother and sister; all share in common tasks. This is the starting point. Everyone is fundamentally equal, yet not everyone can do all the things necessary within the community. Therefore, there are coordinators (often women) who are responsible for order and presiding over the celebrations and sacramental aspects of the community. The Church in the first centuries was understood primarily as *communitas fidelium*, the community of the faithful, with the participation of all members in all things. It slowly became a hierarchical Church, and the possession of sacred power was the basis of its structure, not the community. This organization was historically necessary, but it left no room for the responsible participation of all people in the affairs of the Church. In the base ecclesial community there is the possibility for greater participation and balance in the various ecclesial functions. Lay people are discovering their importance; they, too, are successors of the apostles in that they have inherited the apostolic teachings and are coresponsible for the unity of faith and the community. Apostolicity is not the characteristic only of certain members of the Church, such as the Pope and bishops, but is a characteristic of the entire Church, and this apostolicity is shared in different ways within the Church. Lay people are rediscovering their apostolic and missionary significance through the ecclesial communities. Very often one community establishes other communities and helps them in their growth and development.

The communitarian way of living out faith gives rise to the creation of many lay ministries. In Latin America, these ministries are called services, which is essentially the meaning that Paul gives to "charisms." All services are understood as gifts of the Holy Spirit. There are those who know how to visit and comfort the sick; they are given the task of gathering information and visitation. Others are educated and some teach about human rights and labor laws, some prepare the children for the sacraments, and still others deal with family problems and the like. All of these functions are respected, encouraged, and coordinated in order that everything tends toward service of the whole community. The Church, then, more than an organization, becomes a living organism that is recreated, nourished, and renewed from the base.

4. Sign and Instrument of Liberation

The base ecclesial community is not and cannot be an underground organization or sect. It is a community that is open to the world and society. The reading and common sharing of the Gospel leads the community to social action. All of the problems the members suffer are brought to the base ecclesial community. The group then questions the causes and consequences of these very real problems. In this way, the community serves an undeniably critical and demystifying function. The members of the community learn to live the truth. In the community, it is no longer possible to hide reality. Everything is named for what it is: exploitation is exploitation; torture is torture; dictatorship is dictatorship. The institutional Church has played a great role by conscientizing the people as to their rights, giving them the tools to analyze their situation, and by denouncing the injustices they suffer.

Furthermore, a new type of society is taught within the community. One learns to overcome the unjust relationships that dominate the larger society. How? Through the direct participation of all the members of the group, the sharing of responsibilities, leadership, and decision-making, through the exercise of power as service.

The base ecclesial communities are socially active communities. In some places they are the only channel for popular expression and mobilization. They organize memorials, group projects, community activities, neighborhood credit unions, efforts to resist land takeovers, and many other concerns of the people. Where popular organizations already exist, the base ecclesial community does not try to compete. Rather, it identifies with those movements, sharing members and leadership, support and criticism. The primary concern of the base ecclesial community is *not* the organization of social movements but the formation or strengthening of *popular* movements.

In many places the base ecclesial community poses a threat to the established social order. The communities are repressed, persecuted, and have their saints and martyrs. But this does not seem to have diminished their strength. On the contrary, base ecclesial communities are growing more numerous, stronger, and more courageous because of this consciously accepted suffering.

5. A Celebration of Faith and Life

Christian faith is not only defined in terms of its dimension of commitment and liberation. It has its time for celebrating that liberation. It celebrates the liberation that God achieved for us in Jesus Christ; his presence through the word and the sacraments is celebrated and the faithful are comforted by his promises. The base ecclesial communities have developed this dimension of celebration. Their misery and the seriousness of their struggles have not taken away from the feast where the people breathe freely and enjoy their freedom and joy.

There is a great value placed upon popular religiosity, the devotions to the particular saints of the people, the processions, and other popular feasts. These expressions are not considered to be the deterioration of official, orthodox, and liturgical Catholicism. They are taken to be the way in which the people, within their own categories, have accepted Jesus' message, ruled not so much by the logic of ideas and analytical reasoning as by the logic of the subconscious and the symbolic. Popular religiosity is as valuable as other expressions of faith. It was through this popular religiosity that God visited his poor people. It was through their prayers, their saints, their feasts in honor of the Virgin and the various mysteries of Christ that the people have been able to resist centuries of political and economic oppression and ecclesial marginalization. Through their own religiosity the people, in many parts of the world, have been able to discover the meaning of life, keep their faith alive, and nourish their trust while in a society that has denied them their rights, dignity, and participation. All of this is now leading the Church to reinterpret its traditional pastoral practices that had little appreciation for the religious expressions of the people.

The base ecclesial communities not only strengthen the faith of the people, which would be enough in itself, but also foster creativity in the search for the proper expression of living out faith. The unity between faith and life finds a place in the community and so the presence of God in life is celebrated there. When the community prays, its "prayers of the faithful" recall all of the problems, oppressions, oppressors, hardships as well as victories, successes, and ongoing projects of the community. Not only are the official sacraments celebrated but the sacramental dimension of all life is cause for celebration because the community sees God's grace impregnating the concrete events of its life together. The community has this fine sense of the religious dimension to be found in all stages of human life, and so community gatherings are never completely profane or devoid of God's presence.

Liturgical creativity is also given its place in the community. The people appreciate the canonical, official liturgy but they also create their own rituals, spontaneously enacting the word of God, organizing great celebrations that center around the Bible and include significant regional objects or foods. It is at these times that faith is given its finest expression. A people that knows how to celebrate is a people with hope. They are no longer a wholly oppressed people but a people who march toward their liberation.

NOTES

1. *Folha de São Paulo*, 5/2/76.
2. *O São Paulo*, 2/6–22/74, 3.
3. Pedro Casaldáliga, *Antología retirante* (Rio de Janeiro, 1978), 168.
4. Cf. L. Boff, *Teología do cativeiro e da libertação* (Petrópolis, 1980).
5. The remarks of Friar Bonaventura Kloppenburg (*El cristiano secularizado* [Petrópolis, 1970], 168–69) are right to the point: "The council was very generous in its speech. But this way of speaking is new. Looking at the past history of the Church it is not hard to verify that *diakonia* often became domination and absolutism, that pastoral *munus* took on an authoritarian and imposing character, that the ecclesiastical magisterium became a uniform and intangible theological body, that discipline took the form of rigid and static legalism, that the continuity of the Church turned into an immobile and sacred tradition . . . . Today I read in *Lumen Gentium* 8 that 'the Church is at the same time holy and in constant need of purification'; I read in *Gaudium et Spes* 21 that the Church 'must cease-

lessly renew itself under the guidance of the Holy Spirit'; but I also read in number 6 of the *Mirari vo*s of Gregory XVI that 'it is of the utmost absurdity and highly injurious to say that a certain restoration or regeneration [of the Church] is necessary for it to return to its primitive security, giving it new life, as if to believe that the Church is susceptible to defect, ignorance, or any other human imperfection.' In practice we fell into an ecclesiastical monophysitism that identified human authority with divine authority, making the virtue of obedience the true characteristic of the 'faithful,' which was the simplest designation for a Christian."

6. We will take some examples from the recent history of the Church; the more abundant examples from the past would even better illumine the question that is presented here.

7. *Herderkorrespondenz* 25 (1971): 592–97, esp. 593–95: "Das Thema Gerechtigkeit auf der römischen Bischofssynode"; J. Gremillion, *The Gospel of Peace and Justice* (Maryknoll, NY, 1976), 513–30.

8. "Nuevas normas para la reducción de sacerdotes al estado laical" in SEDOC 4 (1971): 304–11.

9. Ibid., p. 309: "In this same document [*Sacerdotalis Coelibatus*] the Supreme Pontiff, mindful of the motives by which the Church judges it necessary to grant certain priests laicization by dispensing them from the obligation to observe celibacy, admonishes that they 'experience every means of persuasion with the aim of aiding the brother who vacillates to again find peace and trust, to follow the path of repentance, and to return to the fold; it is only when there is no other solution that the Church's unhappy minister is excluded from the exercise of priestly ministry'" (87). The Pope adds that 'if this priest is unable to be saved for the priesthood and yet shows good and serious dispositions for a Christian life as a lay person, the Apostolic See, after having studied all the circumstances and in accord with the local ordinary or with the religious superior, allowing love to triumph over pain, will sometimes grant all the required dispensations.'"

10. The Sacred Congregation for the Doctrine of the Faith, "Declaration on the Question of the Admission of Women to the Ministerial Priesthood" in *L'Osservatore Romano*, 1/30/77.

11. For a synthesis of the theological arguments, see my "O sacerdócio da mulher" in *Convergência* (1973): 663–97.

12. *Herderkorrespondenz* 25 (1971): 593.

13. "Derechos humanos y la tarea de la Iglesia" in CEI Supplement 15: *Direitos Humanos* (Rio de Janeiro, 1976), 28. See the article written by L. Bouyer, writing in the same issue of *L'Osservatore Romano* (1/30/77) in which the document prohibiting priesthood to women was published: "The religion of the Bible, Judaism, and even more so Christianity, has proclaimed the fundamental equality of men and women, but not in the priesthood." Either the right of equality is universal or one cannot speak of equality without cynicism.

14. J. Neumann, "Ketzerverfahren—eine Form der Wahrhietsfindung?" in *Theologische Quartalschrift* 154 (1974): 328–39; here p. 338.

15. Cf. "El Reglamiento para el Examen de la Doctrina" in SEDOC 3 (1971): 1075–76. Cf. also the interview with J. Hammer the secretary for the Sacred Congregation for the Doctrine of Faith in *Herderkorrespondenz* 28 (1974): 238–46; and the critical interviews with the canon lawyer J. Neumann in the same issue, pp. 287–97, and with Hans Küng in issue 27 (1973): 422–27.

16. Cf. the procedure against the Catholic biblical scholar H. Haag and his treatment of original sin: "Ein Verfahren der Glaubenskongregation" in *Theologische Quartalschrift* 153 (1973): 184–92, esp. p. 190.

17. Hans Küng, in *Herderkorrespondenz* 27 (1973): 426.

18. Ibid. The procedure against Ivan Illich became famous for its ideological violence to all rights. The interrogation began like this:

"My name is Illich."

"I know that."

"Monsignor, what is your name?"

"I am the judge."

"I thought I might know your name!"

"That is not important. My name is Casoira."

They wanted to obligate Illich under oath to maintain absolute secrecy as to what was to take place in the halls of the Sacred Congregation, something Illich did not accept. The interrogation mixed trivial questions about his institute with questions about some fifty people, questions of faith, disputed subjects in theology, and "subversive interpretations." These included questions such as "Is it true that you want women to go to confession without the separation of a curtain?": cf. L. Kaufmann, *Schicksal eines Propheten* (Munich, 1970).

19. J. Neumann in *Herderkorrespondenz* 28 (1974): 297.

20. Catholic doctrine is certainly not a rigid and lifeless corpse. It was created; it did not fall out of the sky ready-made; it continues to be shaped, growing and embracing the bottomless wealth of the deposit of faith. Every age, with its questions and anxieties, is important for revealing unsuspected dimensions of the Christian mystery. Theology, along with the entire Church and the supreme magisterium, is called to explore, to translate, and to live the good news of liberation brought by Jesus Christ. There are not only certainties and dogmas; there is also room for hypotheses, for probability, and for healthy pluralism. What is of value for Sacred Scripture has equal value for theology, as stated by the Biblical Commission in 1915: "Everything that Holy Scripture affirms, states explicitly, and insinuates must be taken as affirmed, stated, and insinuated by the Holy Spirit" (*Enchiridion biblicum*, 433). In other words, in the Bible "there is, alongside categorical affirmation, the proposition of a probability, a possibility, a simple conjecture, and even doubt": P. Benoit, *L'inspiration* (Initiation Biblique; Tournai, 1954), 37; P. Grelot, *La Bible: Parole de Dieu* (Paris-Tournai, 1965), 108. This is even more valuable for theology which cannot count on divine inspiration!

21. By system, we mean the definite relation of elements (persons and institutions) that are mutually connected and influenced, forming a more or less ordered body with its particular theories and practices. The Church is considered to be one system with many subsystems (hierarchies, magisterium, proclamation, and the organization of its members). The system of the Church, in turn, is a subsystem of society, influenced by society and in turn capable of exerting influence on that society. The Church is understood only when this reality and its practices are studied together with the principal system, that is, global society.

22. Cf. B. Sauer, "Autoritäre Systeme in der Kirche heute" in *Autorität*, ed. J. Türk (Maguncia, 1973), 114–25; R. Tilmann, "Die Autoritätskrise in den Kirchen" in *Autorität*, 26–40.

23. Cf. the detailed analysis of the system of power in the Church by C. A. Medina and Pedro A. Ribeiro de Oliveira, *Autoridade e participação: Estudo sociológico da Igreja Católica* (Petrópolis, 1973). Also *Macht, Dienst, Herrschaft in Kirche und Gesellschaft*, ed. W. Weber (Freiburg, 1974).

24. Thomas Merton, quoting in *Faith and Violence* (Notre Dame, 1965, 58) from *The Prison Meditations of Father Delp*: "At some future date the honest historian will have some bitter things to say about the contribution of the Churches to the creation of the mass mind, of collectivism, dictatorships and so on."

25. E. Durkheim, *Les formes élémentaires de la vie religieuse* (Paris, 1937), 618 (E.T. *The Elementary Forms of the Religious Life*, 1954).

26. Although doctrinal texts such as *Lumen Gentium, Apostolicam Actuositatem*, and others state that the whole Church (lay and ordained) are responsible for the preservation and integrity of faith and revelation, in practice the hierarchy behaves as if it alone were solely responsible.

27. Freud demonstrated that when there is a conflict between the psyche and reality, the former has the tendency to substitute the latter with words, thereby avoiding real contact with it. "When someone fears contact with reality, words are placed like a veil between what is said and one's surroundings, as well as between what is verbalized and one's own body": N. Brown, *Vida contra muerte* (Petrópolis, 1973; English original: *Love Against Death*). The fear of life comes from the basic structure of life itself, which is dynamic, unforeseeable, and destructive of all pretension. Words, however, are stable, ready-made recipes, generate certainty, and are able to be manipulated.

28. For a brief historical overview of the ideological presuppositions of the institution of the Inquisition, of the Holy Office and the Sacred Congregation for the Doctrine of Faith, see J. Neumann, "Ketzerverfahren," cited in n. 10 above.

29. Clodovis Boff, "Teología e prática" in *Revista Eclesiástica Brasileira* 36 (1975): 789–810, here p. 798: "After Marx, theology could no longer put in parentheses the material conditions of life on the threat of 'mystifying' the reality of iniquitous conditions. The theological word concerning the social realm has no credibility except as a second word, that is, after having done justice to the abovementioned situations. This is precisely the function of socioanalytical study. Against both theoretical pragmatism and epistemological idealism, one must recognize that the practice of theology implies two separate and distinct areas: internal and external. The first is defined by the autonomy of theory, whose rules must be respected. The second corresponds to theology's dependence on the social conditions of production or the economy of social goods, over which the theologian is called to exercise a constant ideopolitical watch."

30. See the entire issue of *Concilium* 63 (1971) entitled *Democratization of the Church*, ed. A. Muller.

31. Cf. the summary of modern changes within the Church in *Autorität*, 26–41, 216ff.; N. Greinacher, "A Community Free of Rule," in *Concilium* 63 (1971): 87–107.

32. R. Pesch, "The New Testament Foundations of a Democratic Form of Life in the Church" in *Concilium* 63 (1971): 58. The opening quote is from J. Blank, *Das Evangelium als Garantie der Freiheit* (Würzburg, 1970), 67f.

33. A. Weiser, "Autorität im Alten und Neuen Testament" in *Autorität*, 60–76; W. Thüsing, "Dienstfunktionen und Vollmacht kirchlicher Ämter nach dem Neuen Testament" in *Macht, Dienst, Herrschaft in Kirche und Gesellschaft*, 61–74.

34. Cardinal Paolo Evaristo Arns, "Derechos humanos y la tarea de la Iglesia," 29 (cited in n. 9 above).

7

The Gospel in Solentiname (1975)

Ernesto Cardenal

Ernesto Cardenal (b. Nicaragua, 1925) is a Catholic priest, liberation theologian, and Nicaragua's preeminent poet. From 1957 to 1959 he studied with Thomas Merton at a Trappist monastery in Kentucky. In 1966 he established a Christian base ecclesial community on the island of Solentiname in Lake Nicaragua that developed various cooperatives, an internationally renowned school of primi-tivist art, a peasant poetry movement, and most importantly, conciousness-raising work based on a revolutionary reading of the Gospels. Cardenal took an active part in the Sandinista revolution that ousted Anastasio Somoza in July 1979, serving as field chaplain for the Frente Sandinista de Liberación Nacional (FSLN), and later, as Minister of Culture in the new government from 1979 to 1988, sponsoring popular workshops in poetry and theatre and promulgating Sandinista political ideals. After leaving the government, Cardenas continued his work as the literary conscience of his country and as virtual international ambassador promoting a political culture of universal love. More recently, he served as vice president of Casa de Los Tres Mundos, a literary and cultural organization based in Managua, Nicaragua. In 2005, he was nominated to re-ceive the Nobel Prize for Literature. Currently he is a member of the advisory committee in the newly launched alternative, pan-Latin American TV station TeleSUR. This selection illustrates some of the conciousness-raising work done by members of the Solentiname Christian base ecclesial community (BEC), providing a rare glimpse at life in an actually existing BEC.

THE SONG OF MARY (*LUKE* 1:46–55)

We came to the Song of Mary, the *Magnificat*, traditionally known by that name because it is the first word in the Latin. It is said that this passage of the Gospel terrified the Russian Czars, and Maurras was very right in talking about the "revolutionary germ" of the *Magnificat*.

The pregnant Mary had gone to visit her cousin Elizabeth, who also was preg-nant. Elizabeth congratulated her because she would be the mother of the Mes-siah, and Mary broke out singing that song. It is a song to the poor. The people of

Nicaragua have been very fond of reciting it. It is the favorite prayer of the poor, and superstitious *campesinos* often carry it as an amulet. In the time of old Somoza when the *campesinos* were required always to carry with them proof they had voted for him, the people jokingly called that document the *Magnificat*.

Now young ESPERANZA read this poem, and the women began to comment on it.

> *My soul praises the Lord,*
> *my heart rejoices in God my Savior,*
> *because he has noticed his slave.*

"She praises God because the Messiah is going to be born, and that's a great event for the people."

"She calls God `Savior' because she knows that the Son that he has given her is going to bring liberation."

"She's full of joy. Us women must also be that way, because in our community the Messiah is born too, the liberator."

"She recognizes liberation. . . . We have to do the same thing. Liberation is from sin, that is, from selfishness, from injustice, from misery, from ignorance —from everything that's oppressive. That liberation is in our wombs too, it seems to me. . . ."

The last speaker was ANDREA, a young married woman, and now ÓSCAR, her young husband, breaks in: "God is selfish because he wants us to be his slaves. He wants our submission. Just him. I don't see why Mary has to call herself a slave. We should be free! Why just him? That's selfishness."

ALEJANDRO, who is a bachelor: "We have to be slaves of God, not of men."

Another young man: "God is love. To be a slave of love is to be free because God doesn't make slaves. He's the only thing we should be slaves of, love. And then we don't make slaves of others."

ALEJANDRO'S MOTHER says: "To be a slave of God is to serve others. That slavery is liberation."

I said that it's true that this selfish God Óscar spoke about does exist. And it's a God invented by people. People have often invented a god in their own image and likeness—not the true God, but idols, and those religions are alienating, an opium of the people. But the God of the Bible does not teach religion, but rather he urges Moses to take Israel out of Egypt, where the Jews were working as slaves. He led them from colonialism to liberty. And later God ordered that among those people no one could hold another as a slave, because they had been freed by him and they belonged only to him, which means they were free.

And TERESITA, William's wife: "We have to keep in mind that at the time when Mary said she was a slave, slavery existed. It exists today too, but with a different name. Now the slaves are the proletariat or the *campesinos*. When she called herself a slave, Mary brought herself closer to the oppressed, I think. Today she could have called herself a proletarian or a *campesina* of Solentiname."

And WILLIAM: "But she says she's a slave of the Lord (who is the Liberator, who is the one who brought freedom from the Egyptian slavery). It's as if she said she was a slave of the liberation. Or as if she said that she was a proletarian or a revolutionary *campesina*."

Another of the girls: "She says she's poor, and she says that God took into account the 'poverty of his slave,' that is, that God chose her because she was poor. He didn't choose a queen or a lady of high society but a woman from the people. Yes, because God has preferred us poor people. Those are the `great things' that God has done, as Mary says."

> *And from now on all generations will call me happy,*
> *for Mighty God has done great things for me.*
> *His name is holy,*
> *and his love reaches his faithful ones*
> *from generation to generation.*

One of the ladies: "She says that people will call her happy. . . . She feels happy because she is the mother of Jesus the Liberator, and because she also is a liberator like her son, because she understood her son and did not oppose his mission. She didn't oppose him, unlike other mothers of young people who are messiahs, liberators of their communities. That was her great merit, I say."

And another: "She says that God is holy, and that means `just.' The just person who doesn't offend anybody, the one who doesn't commit any injustices. God is like this and we should be like him."

I said that was a perfect biblical definition of the holiness of God. And then I asked what a holy society would be.

"The one we are seeking," LAUREANO answered at once. He is a young man who talks of the Revolution or revolutionaries almost every time he comments on the Bible. After a brief pause he added: "The one that revolutionaries want to build, all the revolutionaries of the world."

> *He has shown the strength of his arm;*
> *he conquers those with proud hearts.*

Old TOMÁS, who can't read but who always talks with great wisdom: "They are the rich, because they think they are above us and they look down on us. Since they have the money. . . . And a poor person comes to their house and they won't even turn around to look at him. They don't have anything more than we do, except money. Only money and pride, that's all they have that we don't."

ÁNGEL says: "I don't believe that's true. There are humble rich people and there are proud poor people. If we weren't proud we wouldn't be divided, and us poor are divided."

LAUREANO: "We're divided because the rich divide us. Or because a poor person often wants to be like a rich one. He yearns to be rich, and then he's an exploiter in his heart, that is, the poor person has the mentality of the exploiter."

OLIVIA: "That's why Mary talks about people with proud hearts. It's not a matter of having money or not, but of having the mentality of an exploiter or not."

I said that nevertheless it cannot be denied that in general the rich person is a proud man, not the poor one.

And TOMÁS said: "Yes, because the poor person doesn't have anything. What has he got to be proud of? That's why I said that the rich are proud, because they have the money. But that's the only thing they have we don't have, money and the pride that goes with having money."

> *He pulls down the mighty from their thrones and raises up the humble.*
> *He fills the hungry with good things and he leaves the rich with nothing.*

One said: "The mighty is the same as the rich. The mighty are rich and the rich are mighty."

And another: "The same as proud, because the mighty and the rich are proud."

TERESITA: "Mary says that God raised up the humble. That's what he did to Mary."

And MARIÍTA: "And what he did to Jesus who was poor and to Mary, and to all the others who followed Jesus, who were poor."

I asked what they thought Herod would have said if he had known that a woman of the people had sung that God had pulled down the mighty and raised up the humble, filled the hungry with good things and left the rich with nothing.

NATALIA laughed and said: "He'd say she was crazy."

ROSITA: "That she was a communist."

LAUREANO: "The point isn't that they would just *say* the Virgin was a communist. She *was* a communist."

"And what would they say in Nicaragua if they heard what we're saying here in Solentiname?"

Several voices: "That we're communists."

Someone asked: "That part about filling the hungry with good things?"

A young man answered: "The hungry are going to eat."

And another: "The Revolution."

LAUREANO: "That is the Revolution. The rich person or the mighty is brought down and the poor person, the one who was down, is raised up."

Still another: "If God is against the mighty, then he has to be on the side of the poor."

ANDREA, Óscar's wife, asked: "That promise that the poor would have those good things, was it for then, for Mary's time, or would it happen in our time? I ask because I don't know."

One of the young people answered: "She spoke for the future, it seems to me, because we are just barely beginning to see the liberation she announces."

> *He helps the nation of Israel his servant,*
> *in remembrance of his love;*
> *as he had promised to our fathers,*
> *to Abraham, and to his descendants forever.*

ALEJANDRO: "That nation of Israel that she speaks about is the new people that Jesus formed, and we are this people."

WILLIAM: "It's the people who will be liberated, like before the other people were liberated from the dictatorship of Egypt, where they were treated like shit, changed into cheap hand labor. But the people can't be liberated by others. They must liberate themselves. God can show the way to the Promised Land, but the people themselves must begin the journey."

ÓSCAR asked: "Can you take riches from the rich by force? Christ didn't force the rich young man. He said to him: `If you wish. . . .'"

I thought for a while before answering. I said hesitantly: "You might let him go to another country. . . ."

WILLIAM: "But not let him take his wealth with him."

FELIPE: "Yes, let him take it."

The last remark was from MARIÍTA: "Mary sang here about equality. A society with no social classes. Everyone alike."

THE BEATITUDES (*MATTHEW* 5:1–12)

We read that Jesus went up to a hill, and said to his disciples gathered around him:

> *Blessed are the poor in spirit,*
> *because theirs is the kingdom of heaven.*

I said that in the Bible the poor are often called *anawim*, which in Hebrew means "the poor of Yahweh." They are so called because they are the poor of the liberation of Yahweh, those that God is going to liberate by means of the Messiah. It's like what we now understand as the "oppressed," but in the Bible those poor people are also considered to be good people, honorable, kindly and holy, while their opposites are the oppressors, the rich, the proud, the impious. This word *anawim* was probably the one that Jesus used. In Greek there was no word like that, and when the Gospel of Matthew was translated into Greek that word was translated as "poor in spirit," whereas Luke in his Beatitudes says simply "the poor." This phrase of Matthew, "poor in spirit," has created confusion, and many have believed that it deals with spiritual poverty. And I said that I met a priest who said that the "poor in spirit" were the good rich people.

OLIVIA: "The poor in spirit or the poor in God are the poor, but provided they have the spirit of the oppressed and not of the oppressors, provided they don't have the mentality of the rich."

TOMÁS PEÑA: "Because us poor people can also have pride, like the rich."

ANGEL: "Us poor people can also be exploiters. As for the kingdom of heaven, I say what I've already said other times, that Matthew calls the kingdom of God the kingdom of heaven because of the Jewish custom of not mentioning the name of God out of respect, but that doesn't mean that the kingdom is in 'heaven.' In the other Gospels it is called the kingdom of God. Jesus surely must have used the same words Matthew used, because as a good Jew Jesus would follow the custom of not mentioning the name of God. Because of this expression Christians have for centuries wrongly believed that he's speaking only about a kingdom in the beyond."

And MARIÍTA said: "It's here on earth, but it's also in heaven after death."

Another said: "Yes, because there are so many poor people who die without having any happiness, and why are they called happy then?"

And another: "Like little old Don Chico who just died all alone. When they found him the ants were eating him."

And LAUREANO, who always talks about the Revolution: "But you can't forget that the kingdom is here too. Because they're thinking about heaven, poor people often don't fight."

His cousin ÓSCAR: "Well, if they don't fight for their brothers and sisters and their children they don't get to the other kingdom after they die."

And ÓSCAR'S MOTHER: "It seems to me that the kingdom is love. Love in this life. And heaven is for those who love here, because God is love."

FELIPE: "Jesus said that because he knows the poor are able to put love into practice better, right? — which is the kingdom that God brings us. Then he blesses the poor because they're the ones who are going to make this new society of love."

"And it's because the rich couldn't practice love, then," said JULIO.

I asked why not. And he answered: "Because of their great selfishness, they can't say that they can love. But the poor can, because as oppressed people they do not exploit and they are less selfish."

I said that was true, that the rich in some way always made money at the cost of the poor, making other people work for them, and using the money from that work to make more money at the cost of more work by others. Then, as long as it's that way, as Felipe says, they can't love their fellow human beings, unless they divide up their riches and stop exploiting.

ÓSCAR: "Ernesto, I also think that the poor person can practice love more sincerely, without being afraid, and fight for it, without being afraid of the word of God. But the rich person can't because it doesn't suit him. Even though he may know what's good, he doesn't practice it, because he is always ready to screw people, to exploit them. And that's why I think a rich person can never be sincere, while the poor person can. And God sees the poor person's sincerity and promises him the kingdom of God."

MARCELINO: "The way I see it is that the man who owns a business whether he needs money or doesn't need it, he's always doing business. The poor person says: 'I have a piece of *tortilla* and somebody else doesn't have any, so I'll give him some of my piece.' There is a difference between the spirit of the man who owns a business and the man who doesn't own one. I was talking with a man and I was saying: `What would you do for a man who was in great need and you were selling a boat that cost a thousand *pesos*, would you let him have it for five hundred?' And he said to me: `Why should I? Business is business.' And he's a rich man."

"Well, that's just why he's a rich man," somebody answered.

And ALEJANDRO: "What we see here is that there are two things. One is the kingdom of God, which is the kingdom of love, of equality, where we must all be like brothers and sisters; and the other thing is the system we have, which isn't brand new, it's centuries old, the system of rich and poor, where business is business. And so we see that they're very different things. Then we have to change society so that the kingdom of God can exist. And we're sure that the kingdom will have to be established with the poor, right?"

PANCHO: "With everybody that shares the love, because if there are rich people that share the love, they too can enter the kingdom."

MARIÍTA: "But a rich person that shares love has to share his goods too. That's how he shows that he shares love. Because if he says he has love and doesn't share his goods, how are we going to believe him?"

REBECA: "But it's all the same. Some of us, even though we're poor, we don't inherit the kingdom of God either. If we're poor and don't have love. And there are rich people who have the kingdom of God, if they have love."

ÁNGEL: "That's why it seems to me that we have to interpret carefully. If we just stick to the fact that we're poor and God has said that the kingdom of God is for the poor, then we'd end up saying that, well, since we're poor we already have the kingdom of God and we can do anything! And the rich are going to be condemned because they're rich. So we have to interpret carefully what God says. Let's not think that just because we're poor we already have the kingdom of God."

ÓSCAR: "I think we have to be clear about this. You either love God or you love money. You decide to make money? Well, go love your money, that's your god. Somebody else loves God? He shares his money and is poor. Then he really can live love."

PANCHO: "But there are rich people who share. . . . "

JULIO: "But maybe just a little. And it's to quiet their consciences. Or they give away their money but they give it, maybe, for great temples, for huge churches with good-looking saints, and they don't give a damn for their neighbor, shit on their neighbor. And I don't think that's sharing love, in my thinking."

I said: "Then we're quite clear about what the kingdom of God is, and why Jesus blesses the poor, telling them that that kingdom will be theirs. The other Beatitudes seem to be only other ways of saying the same thing. In all of them the same poor people are spoken of by other names, and what they promise is the same thing."

Blessed are those who are sad in heart, for God will give them consolation.
Blessed are the humble in heart, for they shall inherit the earth that God has promised them.
Blessed are those who hunger and thirst for justice, because they will be fed.
Blessed are those who have compassion for others, for God will have compassion for them.
Blessed are those with pure hearts, for they shall see God.
Blessed are those who bring about peace, for they will be called the children of God.
Blessed are those who suffer persecution for the sake of justice, because theirs is the kingdom of heaven.

First we commented on the sad in heart, who will have consolation.

TOMÁS PEÑA: "I look at, how shall I say it, the relief that Christ gave to the poor when he came, because they felt so alone, and the rich were rich, and the poor were almost an abandoned class. And then when Christ came he gave them that consolation. Us poor people, the poorer we are and the more we suffer, then the happier we must be because we have been chosen for the kingdom. Well, that's what I think. But others think different. And then we don't follow what the Book says here, and maybe we get things confused."

And FELIPE, his son: "Well, it may be something for the poor to be proud of to know that we have been chosen for the kingdom. But we also have to remember that Jesus doesn't want people to go on being oppressed. He carne to liberate humanity, so that the world won't be divided into rich and poor, and he doesn't want everyone to be poor. We can be happy about the news that the kingdom is coming, but we can't be satisfied until it comes."

REBECA: "And he blesses those of humble heart. It seems to me that these are the poor in heart or the humbled. Maybe they were even humbler before (that's my idea anyway) and yet for God they were the most worthy. People shouldn't feel sad, then, even though they are poor, poor in spirit or humbled, because God will bring them into the Promised Land, which is the kingdom. But those of proud heart will not enter."

ESPERANZA, a little girl, asks: "Can there be a humble rich man?"

MARÍA, her sister: "Not unless he shares his wealth."

NATALIA: "Because the first Christians shared everything: land, money, houses, boats."

I said: "And it's clear that the first Christians, as we're told, before they had been given the name of Christians had given themselves the name of *anawim*, because they considered themselves the poor of the Beatitudes. And there were no rich among them because they shared everything, but neither were there any who were in need."

MARCELINO: "He blesses those who hunger and thirst for justice. Hunger and injustice amount to the same thing. Anyone who hungers for food also hungers for justice. They are the ones who are going to make social change, not the satisfied ones. And then they'll be filled with bread and social justice."

Young JULIO: "When there's a revolution in a country the poor aren't hungry anymore, and they are already building, it seems to me, as it says here, the kingdom of heaven among them. As long as there is hunger, injustice, sickness, well it seems to me that the kingdom of heaven is very far off."

ALEJANDRO: "He blesses those who have compassion. I believe that it's those who have compassion for others that become revolutionaries. There are many who are poor, or who are middle-class city people, employees who earn their little salaries but they're not rich, yet they still have the ambition of the rich. And if some time some of them get rich, they might be very cruel. Rebeca pointed out that the poor of Jesus Christ are those who practice love. The poor who are bourgeois, who are opposed to revolutionary changes, they do not have compassion in their hearts, and they are not the poor of the Gospel."

LAUREANO: "A perfect communism is what the Gospel wants."

PANCHO, who is very conservative, said angrily: "Does that mean that Jesus was a communist?"

JULIO said: "The communists have preached what the Gospel preached, that people should be equal and that they all should live as brothers and sisters. Laureano is speaking of the communism of Jesus Christ."

And PANCHO, still angry: "The fact is that not even Laureano himself can explain to me what communism is. I'm sure he can't."

I said to Pancho: "Your idea of communism comes from the official newspaper or radio stations, that communism's a bunch of murderers and bandits. But the communists try to achieve a perfect society where each one contributes his labor and receives according to his needs. Laureano finds that in the Gospels they were already teaching that. You can refuse to accept communist ideology but you do have to accept what you have here in the Gospels. And you might be satisfied with this communism of the Gospels."

PANCHO: "Excuse me, but do you mean that if we are guided by the word of God we are communists?"

I: "In that sense, yes, because we seek the same perfect society. And also because we are against exploitation, against capitalism."

REBECA: "If we come together as God wishes, yes. Communism is an equal society. The word `communist' means community. And so if we all come together as God wishes, we are all communists, all equal."

WILLIAM: "That's what the first Christians practiced, who had everything in common."

PANCHO: "I believe that that communism is a failure."

TOMÁS: "Well, communism, the kind you hear about, is one thing. But this communism, that we should love each other. . . ."

PANCHO: "Enough of that!"

REBECA: "It is community. Communism is community."

TOMÁS: "This communism says: Love your neighbor as you love yourself."

PANCHO: "But every communist speaks against all the others. That means they don't love each other."

ELVIS: "No, man. None of them talk that way, man. They do tell us about their programs. And they're fine."

FELIPE: "The Gospel blesses the poor who have clean hearts. The truth is that they're not all like that, because many have the mentality of the rich. Especially since it's the rich who educate us. On the radio, in the ads, they are forcing their mentality into us; it's completely the rich man's."

WILLIAM: "What Felipe says is quite true. The poor person naturally looks forward to getting out of his misery. But advertising creates false needs in the poor person, making him yearn for what he doesn't need. To build the kingdom of love (and that is to see God) you must be stripped of those ambitions, you must have a clean heart."

MANUEL ALVARADO: "It seems to me that ambition is what makes for disputes and that's why he blesses that kind of poor people, because they don't try to strip anybody of anything. If you're going to take somebody else's land away from him, you need a weapon. That's why there are so many armaments in the country. If I have a worker and I make him work for a wage that doesn't give him enough to eat, I'm not looking for peace, I'm looking for war."

ÓSCAR: "If I'm trying to have one person not exploit the other, I am one who is looking for peace. He says that people who look for peace will be the children of God, because they look for unity, that we should all be brothers and sisters. It's clear that the kingdom of God belongs only to the children of God."

His brother JULIO; "These peacemakers want to put an end to the class divisions that divide humanity, and that's why they fight, but it's not so that they can oppress others but so that nobody will oppress anybody."

ALEJANDRO: "And he says that they are going to be persecuted because they seek justice, and for that also he blesses them. Because it's clear that people who look for this kingdom have to be persecuted. The other day I heard somebody say that there were a lot of people afraid to come to church because there was talk in church against the system. They were afraid they would be informed on, or that something would happen to them, it seems. And they themselves, the next time they see you, they look at you in a certain way. It's not proper to talk about the poor and these things."

I said: "I've just had a visit from a young fellow from the north, from Estelí, from a poor town. He is a *campesino* like yourselves, and he was saying that there, to get together for their Masses first they have to ask permission from the police, and the police captain said that those gatherings were dangerous. The captain is right, for they gather there to talk about the Gospels. Those Christians of the earliest Jewish community, who had taken the name *anawim* before they were called Christians, were so called not only because they were poor but also because they were persecuted. Because `poor of Yahweh' (or `poor in spirit' in these Beatitudes) is the same as saying persecuted."

TOÑO: "That didn't use to happen here because the Masses were in Latin. The priest read these things but he read them in Latin, and he didn't explain them to the people. So the Gospels didn't bother the rich or the military."

And we went on then to the two final verses:

> *Blessed are you, when people insult you and mistreat you*
> *and say all kinds of false things against you because of me.*
> *Rejoice and be glad, because you will receive a reward in heaven;*
> *for like you the prophets that lived before you were persecuted.*

OLIVIA: "Before he talked of people persecuted for looking for justice and now he says 'because of me.' He wants to point out that it's the same thing. Everyone who is persecuted in the cause of justice is persecuted in his cause. Here he is talking of insults and bad treatment, he's not talking of death. It must be because death is only in extraordinary cases (even though it can also happen). The most frequent thing is the insults and bad treatment. We're seeing it right here. They call us communists. To them that means bandits, evil people. Afterwards maybe they'll treat us badly."

JULIO: "We have to speak of injustice, even though they say we're into political maneuvering or communism, and that people shouldn't go to our church now. People who talk like this are getting away from the true Gospel, and they're getting isolated. It seems to me that this is where we ought to feel proud, because we are not into exploitation or evil. We're just spreading the true Gospel."

WILLIAM: "And Jesus compares us with the prophets. The prophets in the Bible were not so much people who predicted the future as people who denounced the present. They were protesting against the celebrations in the palaces, the cheating on the weights and the coins, the things that they bought very cheap from the labor of the poor, the swindles of widows and orphans, the abuses committed by the mafias of priests, the murders, the royal policy that they called prostitution, the dependence on foreign imperialisms. And it's true they also predicted something for the future—the liberation of the oppressed. Christ says that our fate has to be like the fate of those prophets."

And another one (a member of the Youth Club) added: "What Christ says, that they will say 'all kinds of false things against you,' we have already seen it—when that spy was here who informed the Office of Security that a Peruvian was here inciting us to rebellion. And he described these Masses as meetings of conspirators, and he even gave the names of the owners of the boats that came and the number of people that came on each boat, and he said, as if it was a serious thing, that these Masses were attended by a lot of young people. Those prophets were very great men and I think it's a great honor to be compared to them, and so we ought to feel happy. And also happy for the reward we'll have in heaven, which is the same kingdom of heaven that's been promised before."

MARCELINO: "This is what the 'good news to the poor' means. The news that theirs is the kingdom of heaven."

8

Philosophy of Liberation (1980)

Enrique Dussel

Enrique Dussel (b. Argentina, 1934) is an Argentine philosopher, theologian, and historian of the Church and philosophy in Latin America. Exiled in Mexico since 1975, where he teaches philosophy at the UNAM, Dussel is the principal exponent of philosophy of liberation, maintaining a philosophical dialogue about the nature of modernity, Western metaphysics, and ethics with some of the major contemporary philosophers, Kart-Otto Apel, Gianni Vattimo, Jürgen Habermas, Richard Rorty, and Emmanuel Lévinas. The author of more that thirty books, Dussel has lectured and taught at many universities worldwide. He is the General Coordinator of the Association for Philosophy and Liberation (AFYL). This selection is Dussel's prolegomenon to a philosophy of liberation, one where philosophical theory and everyday practice are linked to each other, to history, and to the global context.

APPENDIX: PHILOSOPHY AND PRAXIS[1]

Upon presenting a thought in English that originated in Spanish, I have to say with Kant that "despite the great wealth of our languages, the thinker often finds himself at a loss for the expression which exactly fits his concept."[2] But the difficulty in my presentation is not due only to language; it is much more due to the different points of view of the philosophical thinking of North Americans and Latin Americans, the daily realities of the two being so far apart.

A. Philosophy and Ideology

Philosophy is not only thinking demonstratively or scientifically.[3] It is also thinking critically and dialectically,[4] for it can think about its own principles. On the one hand, philosophy is not only to know (*Kennen*) objects or to have ontic knowledge (*Erkenntnis*) of the understanding (*Verstand*), but it is also an onto-logical or metaphysical knowledge (*Wissen*).[5] Inasmuch as it is a metaphysical knowledge (*Wissen*), it always has reference to praxis; because of its origin and destiny, it is also wisdom.

The inevitable reference to praxis, as we shall see—praxis understood in its fundamental meaning (as *Lebenswelt, ta endoxa,* as the total structure of the actions of an epoch)[6]—places philosophy on an ideological level, if by ideology is understood the systematic whole of ideas that explain, justify, and camouflage an entrenched praxis. All theoretical exercise has its own autonomy, but only a *relative* autonomy.[7] The relative autonomy of philosophy, in this instance, has reference to the concrete historical totality from which it emerges and to which it returns—everyday praxis. I shall take two classic examples, easily comprehended, to demonstrate that even in the case of the greatest philosophers, it is impossible to avoid a significant share of ideological "contamination."

A.1. Aristotle and Pro-Slavery Contamination

In his *Politics,* I, 1, the founder of logic tells us:

> Nature (*physis*) would like to distinguish between the bodies of freemen and slaves, making the one strong for servile labor, the other upright and altogether useless for such service. . . . It is manifest, then, that some men are by nature (*physei*) free, and others slaves, and that for these latter slavery is both expedient and right [1254b27–1255a21].

Noteworthy is the term "clear," "manifest" (*phaneron*), "evident," or "self-evident" (in German, *selbstverständlich*). Equally noteworthy is the certainty with which Aristotle attributes to nature the origin of the historicopolitical difference between the free man and the slave. The philosophical argument is totally contaminated by the ideological "daily evidence" of Hellenic slavery.

A.2. Thomas Aquinas and Macho Contamination

The example I shall give is essentially theological, but the argumentation is anthropological; we could say it belongs to philosophical anthropology. Talking about the transmission of original sin, Thomas Aquinas explains:

> Now it is manifest (*manifestum*) that in the opinion of philosophers the active principle of generation is from the father, while the mother provides the matter. Therefore, original sin is contracted, not from the mother, but from the father: so that, accordingly, if Eve, and not Adam, had sinned, their children would not contract original sin [*Summa Theologiae,* I–II, q. 81, ad 5c]. Accordingly we must assert that if we consider the conditions attaching to these persons, the man's sin is the more grievous, because he was more perfect than the woman [ibid., II-II, q. 163, ad 4c].

Again something is "manifest," evident, obvious. It does not matter that the argument is from authority; what matters is that it is accepted by all that the male gives Being to the child; the woman gives only the matter (ibid., III, q. 32, ad 4c). Man is superior to woman. The masculine (macho) ideology is the totality of ideas that justify the domination of the male over the female (sexually, economically, politically, and pedagogically), and it contaminates all the reasoning of Thomistic moral philosophy.

To say that ideological moments contaminate philosophical reasoning does not mean that such reasoning is invalidated. It only indicates that it is a human, fallible, finite, perfectible discourse. That is to say, it is not an absolute knowledge (*Wissen*). This is so because its reference to praxis is to concrete historical action, unfinished and ambiguous.

B. Dialectic between Philosophy and Praxis

Philosophy finds itself relatively determined by praxis. There is neither an absolute determination nor an absolute autonomy. These types of determination touch all the instances of theoretical exercise.

B.1. Determination on the Part of the Subject: Interests and Goals

The philosopher or subject of philosophical thinking (*PS* in fig 8.1) is not an "absolute I" as Fichte claimed,[8] but a finite subject, conditioned, relatively determined by the everyday world to everyday praxis, joined necessarily to a historical subject, to a social class, to a people, to a subject of basic practices.

Philosophical subjectivity (*PS*) clings to and depends upon (arrow *a*) the historical subjectivity (*HS*) that carries it. The *ego cogito* (I think) is first of all an *ego laboro* (I work), *ego opero* (I do), or *ego desidero* (I desire) of a group, of a people. It is true that one can make an abstraction and consider only the subject-object relationship (indicated by *t*), but it is only an abstraction—that is, taking the part for the whole (the philosophical subjectivity for the practical overall reality).

In the same manner, as proposed by classical thinking, the human end (*beatitudo*, *telos*) is the object of tendency (*bonum*) or appetite, which is identified with Being (*esse*). Today we would call such an end a practical interest (*PI*) of a projected undertaking of a social class (to which the philosopher belongs). The "interest" situates the theory in a practical manner in two ways: because it establishes (arrow *b*) the relevance or pertinence of the thematic object (*TO*) to be thought philosophically, or because it also grounds (arrows *c* and *a*), as a project, the practical totality of the class, nation, or group that constitutes the historical subject situated "under" the philosophical subject.

Because Being (*esse*) is identical to "interest" (*bonum*), it is the foundation of the intelligibility and pertinence of the thematic object, which, moreover, must be thought about because of practical exigencies of praxis itself. Throughout history, the themes of philosophy have sprung forth primarily because of the practical exigencies of the age in which the philosophers lived. If Hegel began his ethics or philosophy of right in the following manner, it was because the prevailing capitalist praxis clearly determined it—not absolutely, but sufficiently:

> Right is in the first place the immediate exterior being (*Dasein*), which freedom gives itself in an immediate way, i.e., possession (*Besitz*), which is property ownership [*Philosophy of Right*, §40].

That is, the thematic object that was imposed on Hegel as first in his practical philosophical discourse and as the first determination of "free will" is private property, the bedrock of the capitalism that is mirrored in his philosophy.

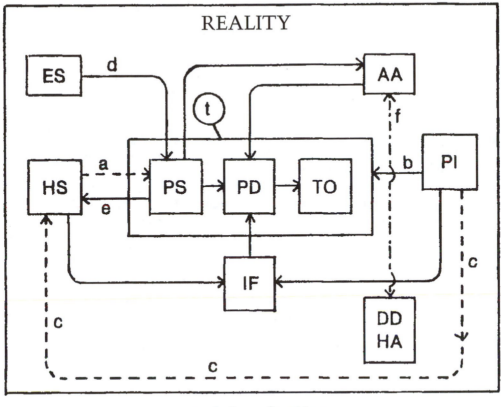

REALITY

- - - - - -→ determination
-—·—·—·—·→ practical opposition
————————→ other types of relationship

AA   academic apparatus
DD   dominant discourse
ES   empirical subject
HA   hegemonic apparatus
HS   historical subject
IF   ideological formation
PD   philosophical discourse
PI   practical interest
PS   philosophical subject
TO   thematic object

Figure: 8.1

B.2. Methodical and Categorical Exigencies

Praxis determines philosophy, although not absolutely, in a much more intimate manner in the constitution of philosophical discourse, be it because of the method chosen, or be it because of the necessity of constructing categories that adequately correspond to the practical *a priori* totality. In effect, if one chooses a reformist praxis or one that basically reaffirms the system in force, one will discard critical, holistic, or dialectical methods—and one will claim to discard them because they are naive, nonscientific, invalid. Karl Popper, with his methodical proposal of "falsifiability" of great precision,[9] falls into superficialities in his work *The Open Society and Its Enemies*, where he confuses dialectics with the predictability of future events.[10]

In the same manner, from the point of view of a practical option, the world (*Welt*) for Wittgenstein, comes to be identified with "the sum total of reality" (*Die gesamte Wirklichkeit*)[11] so that he says later on that the "feeling (*Gefühl*) [of] the world as a limited whole—it is this that is mystical."[12] For this reason *beyond* the world "it is impossible to speak about the will insofar as it is the subject of ethical attributes."[13] With this idea philosophical ethics is impossible: if "the *sense* of the world must lie outside the world" as that about which nothing can be said, one has to keep quiet on these topics.[14]

All these antidialectical, antiholistic thoughts are perfectly coherent to a praxis that reproduces the system. They are the philosophy of domination or of justification of oppression because they are anti-utopian—utopia here understood as the projected undertaking of liberation of the oppressed in the present system. It is a perfectly ideological scientific objectivity.[15]

The adoption of a dialectical method is demanded by a praxis of radical commitment to the oppressed.[16] Radical criticism is not exercised over the parts of the system; it confronts the totality in its entirety as a totality. If one "cannot speak about this" (*man nicht sprechen kann*), one would have to silence, by assassination, the millions and millions who cry out "I am hungry!" Does this "proposition" make sense? Those who believe that it does not have meaning should stop eating so that they can feel in their corporality the wound of hunger that has no reality because it is found beyond the system.

In the same manner, certain categories—"substance," for example—do not permit critical philosophical analysis of certain concrete historical situations of praxis. But the category of "totality," the fundamental category of dialectics, and that of exteriority[17] allow for a more adequate discourse because of a radicalization of meaning in the most material sense.[18]

The philosopher will not give in to the fear of losing a professorship, of being expelled from a country, or of being discriminated against because of a praxis that intrinsically challenges the dominant philosophical discourse. Affective-erotic subjectivity always articulates itself within social structures. The conduct of the petit bourgeois philosopher in systems of violence has been studied by Rozitchner.[19]

B.3. Philosophical Hegemony and Relative Autonomy

One fundamental aspect in the relationship between philosophy and praxis is almost always overlooked. There is no philosophical practice without an academic "apparatus" for instruction and learning. This has been true from the Academy and the Lyceum to the universities, periodicals, and conferences of today.[20] Needing to create a consensus, the dominant classes organize a hegemonic ideologico-academic apparatus. Philosophy plays a central role in the dominant ideological formation and within the hegemonic apparatus.[21]

From what has been said, we can conclude that all philosophy is determined by its dialectical relationship with praxis. It is clear that philosophy has its own autonomous theoretical status: no one denies the specificity of theoretical philosophical discourse. This autonomy, however, is not absolute (*simpliciter*) but relative (*secundum quid*). Within concrete, historical, integral reality, philosophy is relative to praxis because of its historical subjects (that is to say, the philosophical movement, apparatus, class, nation, epoch, etc.) and their interests. Philosophy is also relative to praxis because of the thematic objects, the method, and the categories it uses. Not to keep in mind these conditions of possibility, these relative determinations, is to make of philosophy a complete abstraction (*totum abstractum*), an ideological fetish that will be enshrined at the center of the hegemonic academic apparatus of the dominant classes in the developed countries. Thus a national and worldwide consensus will be created that will justify the capitalistic exploitation perpetrated by the so-called free or "Western and Christian" civilization.

C. Exigencies for a Philosophy of Liberation

I call philosophy of liberation the strictly philosophical discourse, the scientific-dialectical knowledge (*Wissen*), that gives thematic priority to the praxis of liberation *of the oppressed*. The oppressed are considered historically and socially as a class, geopolitically as a nation, sexually as repressed by macho ideology and practices, pedagogically as alienated and completely enclosed by an idolatrous fetishism. *Philosophy* of liberation also gives priority of origin and foundation to the liberation of philosophy from the naivety of its allegedly absolute autonomy as a theory. Philosophy *of liberation* is a theoretical knowledge (*Wissen*) articulated historically and concretely by the praxis of liberation of the oppressed—the first preconditioned for the possibility of such thinking. Far from agreeing that "all philosophy is a criticism of language,"[22] it affirms that philosophy is a criticism of oppression and a clarification of the praxis of liberation.[23]

C.1. Exigencies for a Philosophical Theory of the Praxis of Liberation of the Oppressed

The oppressed as "origin" and "space" that gives rise to critico-liberating philosophical discourse indicates that it is a practical, ethical discourse. The point of departure of this discourse is the human situation produced by the praxis of domination. That is, the practical precondition for the possibility of beginning a true discourse makes philosophy of praxis the first philosophy (*prima philosophia*). It is not a philosophy of any praxis whatsoever but of the praxis of *liberation*, the criterion or absolute tribunal of the truth of its discourse. Liberative orthopraxis permits a pertinent philosophical discourse that penetrates reality here and now.

The oppressed are the *poor* in political terms (person, class, nation), the *woman* in the macho sexual system, the child, youth, the *people* in the pedagogy of cultural domination. All the problems and topics of logic, philosophy of language, anthropology, and metaphysics acquire new light and new meaning when viewed from the absolute and nevertheless concrete (the opposite of universal) criterion that philosophy is the weapon of the liberation of the oppressed.

Sub lumine oppressionis, from the viewpoint of the oppressed, all ideology or philosophy of domination allows a glimpse into what it conceals—domination. Surpassing the horizon of Being of the system, philosophy of liberation reaches out to the exteriority of the other (the oppressed as other than the system), to the fount from which proceeds the light of being (the *Erkenntnissquelle* of Schelling).[24] Schelling, who was, in effect, Hegel's teacher, had indicated that beyond the Being (of all system) one can find the Other: "the originating cause is free." "The Lord of Being (*Herr des Seins*) is a much higher and more appropriate notion than the one that says that God is Being itself."[25] In the totality of the system (contrary to Wittgenstein, who thinks that "God does not reveal in the world"),[26] *in the world*, the self-revelation of the absolute Other takes place through the oppressed.[27] The very body, the corporality, the flesh of the oppressed (their hungry, tortured, violated bodies), when exposed (as the hero is "exposed" before the firing squad) within the system, is a subversion of the law and order that alienates them. It is the revelation of the Absolute in history as an epiphany, not only a phenomenon, an epiphany through the poor. The face (*pnín* in Hebrew, *prosopon* in Greek), the person, the corporality, the flesh (*basar*) of the poor is itself the originating word (*dabar*) from which arises the philosophy of liberation. Philosophy of liberation does not think about words; it thinks about reality.

Thus when the oppressed who struggle against the death that the system allots to them begin, through the praxis of liberation, the struggle for life, novelty irrupts in history beyond the Being of the system. A new philosophy, a positive one, necessarily makes its appearance. The novelty is not originally and primarily philosophical; it is originally and primarily historical and real; it is the liberation of the oppressed. It is secondarily a philosophical theory as a strategic instrument or weapon of liberation itself.

C.2. Exigencies on the Part of Historical Subjects, their Interests, and the Thematic Object

In the philosophy of liberation the coherent, organic articulation of the philosopher in union with a historical subject (class, women's liberation movement, culturally oppressed people; *HS* in Fig 8.1) is a decisive question. Concrete articulation from within a people is a *conditio sine qua non* for the philosophizing of liberation (arrow *e*). It is not some "experiment" that has to be conducted at a certain time. It is a permanent way of life, integrated into the everyday life of the philosopher under penalty of mere repetition, ideologization, loss of reference to the truth of reality—that is, to the actual, ever changing, historical manifestation of reality.[28]

The empirical subject (*ES* in Fig 8.1), who can be a member of the oppressed classes or a petit bourgeois by origin, is called to be an organic philosopher of liberation by a conversion to critical thinking (indicated by arrow *d*). The philosopher thus enters into a space of risk, anxiety, and danger, in a new lifestyle—that of philosophical subject (*PS*). To be a philosopher of liberation can mean losing one's freedom in prison, enduring the pain of torture, losing a professorship at a university, and perhaps being killed, given the situation in Latin America.

To be "organic" (arrow *e*) with the historical subject means to resolutely acquire a *class position* with an oppressed people; it means to become involved in and form part of the popular movement of the working class or of marginal groups, in movements for national liberation or that of women, or in groups organized for popular ideological, racial, or cultural struggle.

The philosopher elaborates the philosophical discourse (*PD*) of liberation on themes that must be grounded theoretically at the highest levels of abstraction in order to give to concrete political analysis all its practical effectiveness.[29] Only thus will it respond, on the one hand, to the necessity of clarifying to the utmost degree the class consciousness of the oppressed and, on the other hand, to the explicit philosophical formulation of the ideological formation (*IF*) of these classes. Philosophy of liberation is, to be precise, a philosophy that responds to the implicit content of the ideological formation of the oppressed and, in the final analysis, to the interests of their class, nation, sex. Philosophy of liberation is, then, a "weapon" of the oppressed; it thinks through and clarifies the most urgent themes; it organizes its own rational resources; it explains its articulations; it transforms itself into a standard of the ideological struggle against the dominant discourse (*DD* in Fig 8.1) of the system in force and against its hegemonic apparatus (*HA*). Of course, the philosophical antidiscourse also needs to start promoting its own (antihegemonic) academic apparatus (*AA*)—schools of philosophy, publications (books, magazines), symposia, and movements.[30] The antihegemonic apparatus can be expected to be the object of the violence of persecution, the sadism of oppressors.

The struggle (arrow *f* in Fig 8.1) between philosophy of domination and philosophy of liberation manifests on the theoretical level the violent class struggles provoked by domination. On this level, as on others, the philosophers of poor countries will need the solidarity of philosophers of wealthy countries, who are responsible for what their transnational corporations, their political leaders, and their armies cause outside their country's boundaries.

C.3. Method and Categories

Some of the exigencies at this level were mentioned in B.2, above. I shall now touch on other aspects. In the first place, if the dialectical or ontological method is accepted as the appropriate one to discover the meaning of the functional parts of a given system—a problem avoided by logical neopositivism, sociological functionalism, and various other philosophical positions—philosophy of liberation gives particular importance to the analectic moments of the dialectical process. In its essence, the dialectics of the dialectical method consists in the rational movement that passes from the part to the whole, or from a whole to a more extensive whole that includes it.[31] But the possibility of such passage—not the "Holy Thursday of reason" as Hegel would say, but the "Easter of reason"—

does not rest only on the negation of negation in totality (moment of negativity) and not even on the affirmation of totality (which would not "surpass" it with a radical metaphysical—not merely an ontological—surpassing [*Aufhebung*]). It is possible because of the affirmation of exteriority, which is more essential than is negation for a philosophy of the oppressed as an originating and a liberating fulfillment.

For example, the liberation of Nicaragua, as a process in which a nation dependent on the United States passes to being a free country (from a first totality to a second totality), does not take place only because of the negation of the oppression produced by capitalism (negation of negation). Nor is the process liberating only because of the affirmation of the democratic bourgeois potentialities of prerevolutionary Nicaragua. The liberation occurs also, metaphysically speaking, because of the affirmation of what Nicaragua is as *exteriority* (to capitalism), *as a totality* (what Nicaragua is, as an origination from the precapitalist, humane, heroic, and historic past; and what Nicaragua is today as a *proyecto*, a real utopia not contained even as a potentiality within bourgeois prerevolutionary Nicaragua).

The analectical moment of the dialectical method (anadialectical method) gives absolute priority to the *proyecto* of liberation of the other as new, as other, as distinct (and not only as different within the identity of the whole). In the final analysis, it can be affirmed that the analectic moment of dialectics is founded on the absolute anteriority of exteriority over totality, even to affirming the priority of the Absolute Other as creative origin over creation as a work, as a finite and therefore perfectible totality. The metaphysics of creation is the ultimate foundation (*Grund*) of political historical liberation (social revolutions), the erotic liberation of women, and the pedagogical liberation of the child and of the people. Beyond Being (if *Sein* is understood as the horizon of totality) *there is* reality; there one can find reality in its most consistent, future, and utopian horizon: anthropological exteriority (the other, the needy, the poor) or absolute exteriority (the absolute other, the Creator who appeals to the system through the epiphany of the poor when the system becomes lulled into a fetishistic, antidialectical "normalization").

In the same manner, a category such as face-to-face, which measures all practical human relationship as the origin and the end of history, gives sufficient light to interpret the injustice or alienation of the other as a mediation of the *proyecto* of the whole, from the immediacy where one lets the other be other than oneself in that other's real, metaphysical exteriority. From the experience of respect for and service to the other as other is judged every human political, pedagogical, or erotic relationship that is a "reifying instrumentalization" of the other as a mediation for one's own *proyecto*. The relevance or pertinency of both, and the method and categories used, depend on the articulation that the philosopher carries out with the praxis of liberation.

C.4. Political Space, Repression, and Antihegemonic Apparatus

Latin America today finds itself in an exceedingly complex situation. It is suffering the agonizing pains of giving birth to a new historical era. Philosophy of liberation is a theoretical and strategic product of a profound revolution that encompasses South and Central America and the Caribbean.

Philosophical thinking must have at least a certain modicum of freedom. When it lacks minimum freedom, philosophy emigrates; it exiles itself; it dies, and the body of the philosopher goes to jail, from Boethius to Gramsci (imprisonment is a form of dying), or to the cemetery (as my colleague from Mendoza, the philosopher Mauricio Lopez, and my philosophy student, Susana Bermejillo, a young woman beaten to death by undercover police in 1975).

C.4.1. Critical philosophical discourse has a growing political "space" in Brazil, Peru, Ecuador, Santo Domingo, and Panama, given the crisis of military dictatorships and the opening up to certain types of social democracies. The road is difficult; a long history of oppression and a lack of critical thought make the way difficult. The temptation of many is populism, because radical revolutionary positions are not "acceptable."

C.4.2. Philosophy of liberation is repressed today in Argentina, Uruguay, Chile, Bolivia, Paraguay, Haiti, El Salvador, Guatemala, and Honduras. Political "space" for critical thought is nonexistent. The military ideology of national security—learned in great part in the schools of the United States, such as West Point or the School of the Americas in Panama—does not tolerate, not even physically, the philosophical subjects of liberation or their dialectic and popular counterdiscourse. Repression reaches even to the psychosocial level, and torture is used as a means to persuade "anarchists" to return to the Western and Christian "order."[32] To be a philosopher of liberation in this situation is to be in mortal danger. In any event, the danger of accepting self-censorship (*autocensura*), or of holding hands with reformism or developmentalism (*desarrollismo*), is always there.

Those of us who are in exile, in the more ample political "space," develop our discourse of liberation with a twofold purpose: on the one hand, to fashion a clear and radical criticism of theoretical errors (such as populism in political philosophy) and, on the other hand, to set ourselves to the task of clarifying the great strategic themes that are expected to be the most relevant in the coming decades.

C.4.3. It seems, on the contrary, that the political "space" for philosophical thinking is closing in Colombia, where the military makes its presence felt more and more in national life as farmer and worker movements emerge. The philosophy of liberation grows there, and it still has possibility in populist and Christian thought, even if it has to be camouflaged. The situation is disquieting. Renowned social scientists have been imprisoned and tortured.

C.4.4. The philosophical discourse of liberation can be exercised with relative freedom in Mexico, Venezuela, Costa Rica, and Puerto Rico. That is, they are "spaces" of philosophico-critical productivity that can be "exported" to countries submerged in the most horrible repression or countries where a philosophy of liberation has not yet come to life. Again, it is at this level that the philosophers of developed countries can help us form a double front in a true "alliance for critical philosophy": on the front of the repressed countries (publishing critical works and sending them to countries we cannot enter, not even by means of books), and on the First World front (creating a trend of opinion favorable to critico-liberating thought developing in the countries of the Third World).

C.4.5. In the socialist process in Cuba and Nicaragua, philosophy of liberation, in the near future, will have to treat topics different from those in other countries where revolution is still a future event. The central thought to be explored within the situation of present growth in Cuba is not so much the political but the technologico-productive and ideological. On the one hand, the increase of productivity, development of productive forces, is in need of a philosophy of production, which I would call a philosophy of poiesis. In this manner, philosophy of liberation would open a new chapter, affirming that technology is not universal, is not absolutely autonomous, but that it corresponds to needs and requirements determined by the degree of development of social formation and by participation in the scientific-technological revolution.

A second fundamental question in the socialist Latin American countries is that of being able to formulate a new theory of religion. This theory would from the Marxist discourse where atheism as antifetishism and materialism as a last instance of worship (to offer to another a product of work) permit religion to be constituted as praxis and infrastructural work, as a positive and liberating structure. This question is a strategic one for the Latin American revolution, and for every other Third World revolution, because it would allow a whole people to be impelled, with a profound religious consciousness, into the liberating process, not only not denying its ties to religious transcendence but also relying on it to furnish absolute motivation for revolutionary praxis.

D. Toward an International Division of Philosophical Labor

Philosophy of liberation, as philosophy of the oppressed and for the oppressed, is not a task only for thinkers of the countries of the Third World. Philosophy of liberation can be exercised in all places and situations where there is oppression of person by person, class by class, racial minority by racial majority. Depending on the "space" where the discourse arises, diverse topics will be relevant. The themes can be different, but not the type of discourse, or its method, or its essential categories. In the United States it is possible to work out a philosophy of liberation from the experience of the oppression of the people by a system of consumption where the rationality of profit-making is beginning to show its true irrationality; from the suffering of the black and Hispanic minorities; from the humiliation of women not yet liberated; and specially from the ideological manipulation that conceals from the public what "the empire" does outside its boundaries to poor peoples that it impoverishes even more.

In the countries of the center, philosophy sometimes turns in upon itself and reduces its task to justifying itself (philosophy of language, of logic, etc.), without thinking through the great issues relevant to the final years of the twentieth century. In Asia and Africa philosophy concerns itself with other topics of liberation (dialogue with ancient cultures, authenticity, the question of neocolonialism). In Latin America, with differences from country to country, I have already sketched some thematic spheres within diverse political "spaces."

In conclusion, an international division of the philosophical labor, assigning to diverse groups and countries distinct tasks, would permit us to begin a fruitful dialogue where uniformity of themes would not be demanded, nor would certain thematic objects be spurned because they are not relevant to one or another group. Respect for the other's situation begins with respect for the other's philosophical discourse.

NOTES

1. An address given to the American Catholic Philosophical Association, Philadelphia, April 1980 (not included in the original Spanish edition of this book).

2. *Critique of Pure Reason*, A 312, B 368.

3. Edmund Husserl has already tried to show in his own way that it was necessary for philosophy to reach the level of science. See "Philosophy as a Rigorous Science" where he clarifies: "Philosophy, however, is essentially a science of true beginnings, or origins, of *rizōmata pantōn*" (*Phenomenology and the Crisis of Philosophy* (New York: Harper & Row, 1965), 146).

4. See my work *Método para una filosofía de la liberación* (Salamanca: Sígueme, 1974), 17ff. For Aristotle, dialectic is useful "for the philosophic sciences. . . . Further, it is useful in connection with the ultimate (*ta prota*) bases (*archon*) of each science; for it is impossible to discuss them at all on the basis of the principles peculiar to the science in question, since the principles are primary in relation to everything else, and it is necessary to deal with them through the generally accepted opinions (*endoxon*) on each point. This process belongs peculiarly, or most appropriately, to dialectic; for being of the nature of an investigation (*exetastike*) it lies along the path to the principles of all methods of inquiry" (*Topics* I, 2, 101a, 26b (Cambridge: Harvard University Press, 1960), 277–78).

5. Since Kant, "knowing" is of objects (*Erkenntnisse der Gegenstände, Critique of Pure Reason*, I, I, 3, A 139): knowing is of science; "rational faith" is of the Ideas. For Hegel, on the contrary, ontological knowledge (*Wissen*) is the intellectual act par excellence and is therefore philosophy. "This notion of philosophy is the self-thinking Idea, the truth aware of itself!" (*Encyclopedia*, 574; in Hegel's *Philosophy of Mind* (Oxford: Clarendon, 1971), 313). *Cognitio* or *cognoscere* is not *sapere* or *scire*, even in classical thought.

6. The later Husserl spoke more and more of the notion of "lived world" (*Lebenswelt*), which made ready for the concept of being-in-the-world (*in der Welt sein* of Heidegger) (*Die Krisis de europäischen Wissenschaften*, III; Husserliana VI (The Hague; Nijhoff, 1962), 105ff.). For Aristotle *ta endoxa* indicated everyday existential comprehension. By all means one will have to surpass the passive position (intellectual sight) of both notions to arrive at a notion of praxis in the sense of "structural totality of human actions" of a group, a social class, or a historical community. In this primary meaning, praxis *precedes* theory. It is *in* and *whence* theory arises. Praxis or the action decided on is *posterior* to the theoretical act and integrates itself as one moment in the totality of *a priori* praxis.

7. Theoretical exercise in its totality is suggested by classical thinkers: "There is a fourth order that reason in planning established in the external things which it causes" (Thomas Aquinas, *Commentary on the Nicomachean Ethics* (Chicago: Regnery, 1964), vol. 1, 6).

8. "The I posits itself . . . I as absolute Subject" (Fichte, *Grundlage der gessamten Wissenschaftslehre* [1794], vol. 1, 97).

9. *The Logic of Scientific Discovery* (New York: Harper & Row, 1968), 78ff.

10. Princeton University Press, 1966, 84ff.

11. Ludwig Wittgenstein, *Tractatus Logico-Philosophicus* (London: Routledge and Kegan Paul, 1961), 2.063, 8.

12. Ibid., 6.45, 13. This is precisely how the oppressed through practical totality feel the world (the system). But about this "feeling" of the oppressed, there is for Wittgenstein no philosophy.

13. Ibid., 6.423, 72.

14. Ibid., 6.41, 71. In this way it is impossible to pass complete judgment on the capitalist system as a whole, the task of dialectics. Popper and Wittgenstein will not make this critique that they discard or deny as holistic, foolish, or impossible. The reformist choice, justifying capitalism by claiming to demonstrate the impossibility of a way out (the critique of utopia and socialism limits itself by its own impossibility), becomes methodically antidialectical.

15. For a kind of journalistic example, see Noam Chomsky, "Objectivity and Liberal Scholarship," in *American Power and the New Mandarins* (New York: Vintage, 1969), 23ff.

16. From the time of Aristotle, "our programme was, then, to discover some faculty of reasoning about any theme put before us from the most generally accepted premises that there are. For that is the essential task of the art of discussion (dialectic) and of examination (peirastic)" ("On Sophistical Refutations," in *Basic Works of Aristotle* (New York: Random House, 1941), 183a37-bl, 210).

17. See Michael Theunissen, *Der Andere* (Berlin: Gruyter, 1965) and Emmanuel Levinas, *Totality and Infinity, an Essay on Exteriority* (Pittsburgh: Duquesne University Press, 1969).

18. By "matter" or "materialism" I understand not the indemonstrable affirmation that all is eternally *cosmological* matter (see. Engels, *Dialektik der Natur* (Berlin: Dietz, 1951)). This would be a *naive* materialism. I take "matter" and "materialism" in the practico-productive meaning: nature as *matter* (that with which) of human work. The "I work" is the *a priori* constituent of "matter" as a practico-productive (and not a cosmological) category. In this sense *material determination* (never absolute) is an instance that can never be left out of any historical anthropological consideration. On the other hand, "matter" refers to the Hebrew notion of "work-service-cult" (*habodah*); see G.W. Kittel, ed., *Theological Dictionary of the New Testament* (Grand Rapids: Eerdmans, 1971)—*diakonía, energemata*, etc. See my work, *Filosofía de la producción* (Mexico City: Universidad Metropolitana, 1984) and my preliminary study on Karl Marx, *Cuaderno tecnológicohistórico* (Universidad de Puebla, 1984).

19. Leon Rozitchner, in *Freud y los límites del individualismo burgués* (Buenos Aires: Siglo XXI, 1972), analyzes the subject as far as showing the determinations of the system in its most profound subjectivity. That is to say, "class struggle is included in human subjectivity as the nucleus of one's most individual existence," according to the Argentinian thinker.

20. See Christine Buci-Glucksmann, *Gramsci et l'Etat* (Paris: Fayard, 1975).

21. See Antonio Gramsci, *Quaderni del Carcere*, 19 (XXIII), II, no. 13 (Rome: Rinaudi, 1975), vol. I, 1250.

22. Wittgenstein, *Tractatus*, 4.0031, 19. That a philosophy of language is necessary and useful is not to be denied, but it is to be an "instrument" of philosophy and not its essence and ultimate finality. Aristotle already suggested that the art of rhetoric, which was the ultimate finality for the Sophists, was for the philosopher seeking truth only a means to avoid being confused by the Sophist: "As far as the choice of ground goes, the philosopher and the dialectician are making a similar inquiry, but the subsequent arrangement of material and the framing of questions are the peculiar province of the dialectician" (ibid., 675).

23. Besides the works cited in the talk by M. Christine Morkovsky, at the 1979 ACPA meeting, see my works, *Filosofía de la liberación* (Mexico City: Edicol, 1977), *Política*

(Bogotá: Editorial Nueva América, 1979), *Filosofía de la religión* (Bogotá: Editorial Nueva América, 1979), and my talk at the Third National Colloquy of Philosophy (Puebla, Mexico), "Filosofía, aparatos hegemónicos y exilio."

24. *Einleitung in die Philosophie der Offenbarung oder Begründung der positiven Philosophie*, in *Werke*, VI, B, 398.

25. "Erlanger Vorträge," in *Werke*, V, 305–6.

26. *Tractatus*, 6.432, 73.

27. See my work, *Religión* (Mexico City: Edicol, 1977).

28. Gramsci's notion of the "organic intellectual" is more or less the issue here, though in Latin America it includes concrete characteristics that we cannot take up in this short exposition. See Jürgen Habermas, *Theorie und Praxis* (Berlin: Suhrkamp, 1963). Lukacs explains that "organization is the form of mediation (*Vermittlung*) between theory and praxis" (*Werke*, vol. 2 [Neuwied, 1968], 475).

29. For example, the work of Alberto Parisi, *Filosofía y dialéctica* (Mexico City: Edicol, 1979) (on dialectical logic).

30. Our *Revista de filosofía latinoamericana* (Buenos Aires) was stopped in its second issue in 1975 by the military repression in Argentina. Eighteen of the thirty-two professors of philosophy in the philosophy department of the School of Philosophy and Letters at the National University of Cuyo, in Mendoza, Argentina, were expelled. The same thing occurred in the national universities of Salta, Tacumán, Córdoba, Rio IV, Rosario, Buenos Aires, La Plata, Bahía Blanca, Comahue, etc. The books published by Siglo XXI (which had published my work *Para una ética de la liberación latinoamericana*), by order of the government, were cut with a paper cutter, each into four parts (so they could not be sold even as waste paper). All these acts of vandalism were approved and justified by eminent rightist Catholic thinkers. Half of the students in the Department of Philosophy of Mendoza were expelled by the university, and they were not allowed to study in any university in the country. This is the policy that dependent capitalism advocates with regard to philosophy in Latin America. It is only one example.

31. Without any doubt the work of J. P. Sartre, *Critique de la raison dialectique* (Paris: Gallimard, 1960), aided in the rediscovery of "the matter of dialectic." I posed this problem in my work *Método para una filosofía de la liberación*, 162ff.

32. See the work of General Golbery do Couto e Silva (a West Point graduate), *Geopolítica do Brasil* (Rio de Janeiro: Olympic), 1967), 24–27.

9

Pedagogy of the Oppressed (1970)

Paulo Freire

Paulo Freire (Brazil, 1921–1997) was a Brazilian educator, a principal figure in twentieth-century popular education, and one of the pillars of critical pedagogy. In 1946, he began literacy courses for factory workers. In the mid-1950s, he accepted the offer of the University of Recife to teach the history and philosophy of education. His adult education activities with unions, church and student circles in Recife spread across Brazil leading to the "movement for popular education." At the beginning of the 1960s, the Catholic Church under the leadership of bishop Dom Helder Camara agreed to broadcast Freire's literacy programs on the radio. Political officials were also attracted to the successful methods of Freire. Supported by the mayor of Recife, Freire began an official literacy campaign in northeast Brazil at the start of the 1960s. In 1963, it was extended to the national level under president Goulart. Two million adult illiterates were included in it through 20,000 culture circles throughout the country. Out of these experiences Freire devised a new literacy method which he dubbed "education as practice of freedom." After the 1964 coup d'etat of the Brazilian military, his method was classified as subversive and thus prohibited, the literacy groups were shut down, and he was imprisoned and exiled. From 1964 to 1969 he was in Chile working for the Christian Democratic Agrarian Reform Movement. In 1969 he had a guest professorship at Harvard. During the 1970s, he was an advisor for education in developing countries, such as Cape Verde, Angola, and Guinea-Bissau, with the World Council of Churches in Geneva. In 1980, Freire was able to return to Brazil, where he taught at different universities, was active as an educational advisor and was increasingly engaged in party politics. He was a cofounder of the oppositional Workers' Party (PT) (1980), supervised PT's adults literacy project (1980–1986) and worked as Minister of Education for São Paulo (1988–1991). In subsequent years, he turned to issues of the environment, globalization, and neoliberalism in his addresses and publications. Freire's writings of education made him internationally known and sought after as a lecturer and advisor. Among the many honors he received there is the 1986 UNESCO Prize for Peace Education, nomination for the Nobel Peace Prize in 1993, and nearly thirty honorary doctorates. This selection from Freire's paradigmatic book represents the core of his approach to education as practice of freedom.

"BANKING" VS. "PROBLEM-POSING" CONCEPTS OF EDUCATION

A careful analysis of the teacher-student relationship at any level, inside or outside the school, reveals its fundamentally *narrative* character. This relationship involves a narrating Subject (the teacher) and patient, listening objects (the students). The contents, whether values or empirical dimensions of reality, tend in the process of being narrated to become lifeless and petrified. Education is suffering from narration sickness.

The teacher talks about reality as if it were motionless, static, compartmentalized, and predictable. Or else he expounds on a topic completely alien to the existential experience of the students. His task is to "fill" the students with the contents of his narration—contents which are detached from reality, disconnected from the totality that engendered them and could give them significance. Words are emptied of their concreteness and become a hollow, alienated, and alienating verbosity.

The outstanding characteristic of this narrative education, then, is the sonority of words, not their transforming power. "Four times four is sixteen; the capital of Pará is Belém." The student records, memorizes, and repeats these phrases without perceiving what four times four really means, or realizing the true significance of "capital" in the affirmation "the capital of Pará is Belém," that is, what Belém means for Pará and what Pará means for Brazil.

Narration (with the teacher as narrator) leads the students to memorize mechanically the narrated content. Worse yet, it to them into "containers," into "receptacles" to be "filled" by teacher. The more completely she fills the receptacles, the better a teacher she is. The more meekly the receptacles permit themselves to be filled, the better students they are.

Education thus becomes an act of depositing, in which the students are the depositories and the teacher is the depositor. Instead of communicating, the teacher issues communiqués and makes deposits which the students patiently receive, memorize, and repeat. This is the "banking" concept of education, in which the scope action allowed to the students extends only as far as receiving, filing. and storing the deposits. They do, it is true, have the opportunity to become collectors or cataloguers of the things they store. But in the last analysis, it is the people themselves who are filed away through the lack of creativity, transformation, and knowledge in this (at best) misguided system. For apart from inquiry, apart from the praxis, individuals cannot be truly human. Knowledge emerges only through invention and re-invention, through the restless, impatient, continuing, hopeful inquiry human beings pursue in the world, with the world, and with each other.

In the banking concept of education, knowledge is a gift bestowed by those who consider themselves knowledgeable upon those whom they consider to know nothing. Projecting an absolute ignorance onto others, a characteristic of the ideology of oppression, negates education and knowledge as processes of inquiry. The teacher presents himself to his students as their necessary opposite; by considering their ignorance absolute, he justifies his own existence. The students, alienated like the slave in the Hegelian dialectic, accept their ignorance as justifying the teacher's existence—but, unlike slave, they never discover that they educate the teacher.

The *raison d'être* of libertarian education, on the other hand, lies in its drive toward reconciliation. Education must begin with the solution of the teacher-student contradiction, by reconciling poles of the contradiction so that both are simultaneously teachers *and* students.

This solution is not (nor can it be) found in the banking concept. On the contrary, banking education maintains and even stimulates the contradiction through the following attitudes and practices, which mirror oppressive society as a whole:

(a) the teacher teaches and the students are taught;

(b) the teacher knows everything and the students know nothing;

(c) the teacher thinks and the students are thought about;

(d) the teacher talks and the students listen—meekly;

(e) the teacher disciplines and the students are disciplined;

(f) the teacher chooses and enforces his choice, and the students comply;

(g) the teacher acts and the students have the illusion of acting through the action of the teacher;

(h) the teacher chooses the program content, and the students (who were not consulted) adapt to it;

(i) the teacher confuses the authority of knowledge with his or her own professional authority, which she and he sets in opposition to the freedom of the students;

(j) the teacher is the Subject of the learning process, while the pupils are mere objects.

It is not surprising that the banking concept of education regards men as adaptable, manageable beings. The more students work at storing the deposits entrusted to them, the less they develop the critical consciousness which would result from their intervention in the world as transformers of that world. The more completely they accept the passive role imposed on them, the more they tend simply to adapt to the world as it is and to the fragmented view of reality deposited in them.

The capability of banking education to minimize or annul the students' creative power and to stimulate their credulity serves the interests of the oppressors, who care neither to have the world revealed nor to see it transformed. The oppressors use their "humanitarianism" to preserve a profitable situation. Thus they react almost instinctively against any experiment in education which stimulates the critical faculties and is not content with a partial view of reality but always seeks out the ties which link one point to another and one problem to another.

Indeed, the interests of the oppressors lie in "changing the consciousness of the oppressed, not the situation which oppresses them";[1] for the more the oppressed can be led to adapt to that situation, the more easily they can be dominated. To achieve this end, the oppressors use the banking concept of education in conjunction with a paternalistic social action apparatus, within which the oppressed receive the euphemistic title of "welfare recipients." They are treated as individual cases, as marginal persons who deviate from the general configuration of a "good, organized, and just" society. The oppressed are regarded as the pathology of the healthy society, which must therefore adjust these "incompetent and lazy" folk to its own patterns by changing their mentality. These marginals need to be 'integrated," "incorporated" into the healthy society that they have "forsaken."

The truth is, however, that the oppressed are not "marginals," are not people living "outside" society. They have always been "inside"—inside the structure which made them "beings for others." The solution is not to "integrate" them into the structure of oppression, but to transform that structure so that they can become "beings for themselves." Such transformation, of course, would undermine the oppressors' purposes; hence their utilization of the banking concept of education to avoid the threat of student *conscientização*.

The banking approach to adult education, for example, will never propose to students that they critically consider reality. It will deal instead with such vital questions as whether Roger gave green grass to the goat, and insist upon the importance of learning that, on the contrary, *Roger* gave green grass to the rabbit. The "humanism" of the banking approach masks the effort to turn women and men into automatons—the very negation of their ontological vocation to be more fully human.

Those who use the banking approach, knowingly or unknowingly (for there are innumerable well-intentioned bank-clerk teachers who do not realize that they are serving only to dehumanize), fail to perceive that the deposits themselves contain contradictions about reality. But, sooner or later, these contradictions may lead formerly passive students to turn against their domestication and the attempt to domesticate reality. They may discover through existential experience that their present way of life is irreconcilable with their vocation to become fully human. They may perceive through their relations with reality that reality is really a *process*, undergoing constant transformation. If men and women are searchers and their ontological vocation is humanization, sooner or later they may perceive the contradiction in which banking education seeks to maintain them, and then engage themselves in the struggle for their liberation.

But the humanist, revolutionary educator cannot wait for this possibility to materialize. From the outset, her efforts must coincide with those of the students to engage in critical thinking and the quest for mutual humanization. His efforts must be imbued with a profound trust in people and their creative power. To achieve this, they must be partners of the students in their relations with them.

The banking concept does not admit to such partnership—and necessarily so. To resolve the teacher-student contradiction, to exchange the role of depositor, prescriber, domesticator, for the role of student among students would be to undermine the power of oppression and serve the cause of liberation.

Implicit in the banking concept is the assumption of a dichotomy between human beings and the world: a person is merely *in* the world, not *with* the world or with others; the individual is spectator, not re-creator. In this view, the person is not a conscious being (*corpo consciente*); he or she is rather the possessor of *a* consciousness: an empty "mind" passively open to the reception of deposits of reality from the world outside. For example, my desk, my books, my coffee cup, all the objects before me—as bits of the world which surround me—would be "inside" me, exactly as I am inside my study right now. This view makes no distinction between being accessible to consciousness and entering consciousness. The distinction, however, is essential: the objects which surround me are simply accessible to my consciousness, not located within it. I am aware of them, but they are not inside me.

It follows logically from the banking notion of consciousness that the educator's role is to regulate the way the world "enters into" the students. The teacher's task is to organize a process which already occurs spontaneously, to "fill" the students by making deposits of information which he or she considers to constitute true knowledge.[2] And since people "receive" the world as passive entities, education should make them more passive still, and adapt them to the world. The educated individual is the adapted person, because she or he is better "fit" for the world. Translated into practice, this concept is well suited to the purposes of the oppressors, whose tranquility rests on how well people fit the world the oppressors have created, and how little they question it.

The more completely the majority adapt to the purposes which the dominant minority prescribe for them (thereby depriving them of the right to their own purposes), the more easily the minority can continue to prescribe. The theory and practice of banking education serve this end quite efficiently. Verbalistic lessons, reading requirements,[3] the methods for evaluating "knowledge," the distance between the teacher and the taught, the criteria for promotion: everything in this ready-to-wear approach serves to obviate thinking.

The bank-clerk educator does not realize that there is no true security in his hypertrophied role, that one must seek to live *with* others in solidarity. One cannot impose oneself, nor even merely co-exist with one's students. Solidarity requires true communication, and the concept by which such an educator is guided fears and proscribes communication.

Yet only through communication can human life hold meaning. The teacher's thinking is authenticated only by the authenticity of the students' thinking. The teacher cannot think for her students, nor can she impose her thought on them. Authentic thinking, thinking that is concerned about *reality*, does not take place in ivory tower isolation, but only in communication. If it is true that thought has meaning only when generated by action upon the world, the subordination of students to teachers becomes impossible.

Because banking education begins with a false understanding of men and women as objects, it cannot promote the development of what Fromm calls "biophily," but instead produces its opposite: "necrophily."

> While life is characterized by growth in a structured, functional manner, the necrophilous person loves all that does not grow, all that is mechanical. The necrophilous person is driven by the desire to transform the organic into the inorganic, to approach life mechanically, as if all living persons were things. . . . Memory, rather than experience; having, rather than being, is what counts: The necrophilous person can relate to an object—a flower or a person—only if he possesses it; hence a threat to his possession is a threat to himself; if he loses possession he loses contact with the world. . . . He loves control, and in the act of controlling he kills life.[4]

Oppression—overwhelming control—is necrophilic; it is nourished by love of death, not life. The banking concept of education, which serves the interests of oppression, is also necrophilic. Based on a mechanistic, static, naturalistic, spatialized view of consciousness, it transforms students into receiving objects. It attempts to control thinking and action, leads women and men to adjust to the world, and inhibits their creative power.

When their efforts to act responsibly are frustrated, when they find themselves unable to use their faculties, people suffer. "This suffering due to impotence is rooted in the very fact that the human equilibrium has been disturbed."[5] But the inability to act which causes people's anguish also causes them to reject their impotence, by attempting

> . . . to restore [their] capacity to act. But can [they], and how? One way is to submit to and identify with a person or group having power. By this symbolic participation in another person's life, [men have] the illusion of acting, when in reality [they] only submit to and become a part of those who act.[6]

Populist manifestations perhaps best exemplify this type of behavior by the oppressed, who, by identifying with charismatic leaders, come to feel that they themselves are active and effective. The rebellion they express as they emerge in the historical process is motivated by that desire to act effectively. The dominant elites consider the remedy to be more domination and repression, carried out in the name of freedom, order, and social peace (that is, the peace of the elites). Thus they can condemn—logically, from their point of view—"the violence of a strike by workers and [can] call upon the state in the same breath to use violence in putting down the strike."[7]

Education as the exercise of domination stimulates the credulity of students, with the ideological intent (often not perceived by educators) of indoctrinating them to adapt to the world of oppression. This accusation is not made in the naïve hope that the dominant elites will thereby simply abandon the practice. Its objective is to call the attention of true humanists to the fact that they cannot use banking educational methods in the pursuit of liberation, for they would only negate that very pursuit. Nor may a revolutionary society inherit these methods from an oppressor society. The revolutionary society which practices banking education is either misguided or mistrusting of people. In either event, it is threatened by the specter of reaction.

Unfortunately, those who espouse the cause of liberation are themselves surrounded and influenced by the climate which generates the banking concept, and often do not perceive its true significance or its dehumanizing power. Paradoxically, then, they utilize this same instrument of alienation in what they consider an effort to liberate. Indeed, some "revolutionaries" brand as "innocents," "dreamers," or even "reactionaries" those who would challenge this educational practice. But one does not liberate people by alienating them. Authentic liberation—the process of humanization—is not another deposit to be made in men. Liberation is a praxis: the action and reflection of men and women upon their world in order to transform it. Those truly committed to the cause of liberation can accept neither the mechanistic concept of consciousness as an empty vessel to be filled, nor the use of banking methods of domination (propaganda, slogans—deposits) in the name of liberation.

Those truly committed to liberation must reject the banking concept in its entirety, adopting instead a concept of women and men as conscious beings, and consciousness as consciousness intent upon the world. They must abandon the educational goal of deposit-making and replace it with the posing of the problems of human beings in their relations with the world. "Problem-posing" education, responding to the essence of consciousness—*intentionality*—rejects communiqués and embodies communication. It epitomizes the special characteristic of consciousness: being *conscious of*, not only as intent on objects but as turned in upon itself in a Jasperian "split"—consciousness as consciousness of consciousness.

Liberating education consists in acts of cognition, not transferrals of information. It is a learning situation in which the cognizable object (far from being the end of the cognitive act) intermediates the cognitive actors—teacher on the one hand and students on the other. Accordingly the practice of problem-posing education entails at the outset that the teacher-student contradiction to be resolved. Dialogical relations—indispensable to the capacity of cognitive actors to cooperate in perceiving the same cognizable object—are otherwise impossible.

Indeed, problem-posing education, which breaks with the vertical patterns characteristic of banking education, can fulfill its function as the practice of freedom only if it can overcome the above contradiction. Through dialogue, the teacher-of-the-students and the students-of-the-teacher cease to exist and a new term emerges: teacher-student with students-teachers. The teacher is no longer merely the-one-who-teaches, but one who is himself taught in dialogue with the students, who in turn while being taught also teach. They become jointly responsible for a process in which all grow. In this process, arguments based on "authority" are no longer valid; in order to function, authority must be *on the side of* freedom, not *against* it. Here, no one teaches another, nor is anyone self-taught. People teach each other, mediated by the world, by the cognizable objects which in banking education are "owned" by the teacher.

The banking concept (with its tendency to dichotomize everything) distinguishes two stages in the action of the educator. During the first, he cognizes a cognizable object while he prepares his lessons in his study or his laboratory; during the second, he expounds to his students about that object. The students are not called upon to know, but to memorize the contents narrated by the teacher. Nor do the students practice any act of cognition, since the object towards which that act should be directed is the property of the teacher rather than a medium evoking the critical reflection of both teacher and students. Hence in the name of the "preservation of culture and knowledge" we have a system which achieves neither true knowledge nor true culture.

The problem-posing method does not dichotomize the activity of the teacher-student: she is not "cognitive" at one point and "narrative" at another. She is always "cognitive," whether preparing a project or engaging in dialogue with the students. He does not regard cognizable objects as his private property, but as the object of reflection by himself and the students. In this way, the problem-posing educator constantly re-forms his reflections in the reflection of the students. The students—no longer docile listeners—are now critical coinvestigators in dialogue with the teacher. The teacher presents the material to the students for their consideration, and reconsiders her earlier considerations as the students express their own. The role of the problem-posing educator is to create, together with the students, the conditions under which knowledge at the level of the *doxa* is superseded by true knowledge, at the level of the *logos*.

Whereas banking education anesthetizes and inhibits creative power, problem-posing education involves a constant unveiling of reality. The former attempts to maintain the *submersion* of consciousness; the latter strives for the *emergence* of consciousness and *critical intervention* in reality.

Students, as they are increasingly posed with problems relating to themselves in the world and with the world, will feel increasingly challenged and obliged to respond to that challenge. Because they apprehend the challenge as interrelated to other problems within a total context, not as a theoretical question, the resulting comprehension tends to be increasingly critical and thus constantly less alienated. Their response to the challenge evokes new challenges, followed by new understandings; and gradually the students come to regard themselves as committed.

Education as the practice of freedom—as opposed to education as the practice of domination—denies that man is abstract, isolated, independent, and unattached to the world; it also denies that the world exists as a reality apart from people. Authentic reflection considers neither abstract man nor the world without people, but people in their relations with the world. In these relations consciousness and world are simultaneous: consciousness neither precedes the world nor follows it.

> La conscience et le monde sont dormés d'un même coup: extérieur par essence à la conscience, le monde est, par essence relatif à elle.[8]

In one of our culture circles in Chile, the group was discussing (based on a codification) the anthropological concept of culture. In the midst of the discussion, a peasant who by banking standards was completely ignorant said: "Now I see that without man there is no world." When the educator responded: "Let's say, for the sake of argument, that all the men on earth were to die, but that the earth itself remained, together with trees, birds, animals, rivers, seas, the stars . . . wouldn't all this be a world?" "Oh no," the peasant replied emphatically. "There would be no one to say: `This is a world.'"

The peasant wished to express the idea that there would be lacking the consciousness of the world which necessarily implies the world of consciousness. *I* cannot exist without a *non-I*. In turn, the *not-I* depends on that existence. The world which brings consciousness into existence becomes the world *of* that consciousness. Hence, the previously cited affirmation of Sartre: "*La conscience et le monde sont dormés d'un même coup.*"

As women and men, simultaneously reflecting on themselves and on the world, increase the scope of their perception, they begin to direct their observations towards previously inconspicuous phenomena:

> In perception properly so-called, as an explicit awareness [*Gewahren*], I am turned towards the object, to the paper, for instance. I apprehend it as being this here and now. The apprehension is a singling out, every object having a back-

ground in experience. Around and about the paper lie books, pencils, inkwells, and so forth, and these in a certain sense are also "perceived," perceptually there, in the "field of intuition"; but whilst I was turned towards the paper there was no turning in their direction, nor any apprehending of them, not even in a secondary sense. They appeared and yet were not singled out, were not posited on their own account. Every perception of a thing has such a zone of background intuitions or background awareness, if "intuiting" already includes the state of being turned towards, and this also is a "conscious experience," or more briefly a "consciousness of" all indeed that in point of fact lies in the co-perceived objective background.[9]

That which had existed objectively but had not been perceived in its deeper implications (if indeed it was perceived at all) begins to "stand out," assuming the character of a problem and therefore of challenge. Thus, men and women begin to single out elements from their "background awareness" and to reflect upon them. These elements are now objects of their consideration, and, as such, objects of their action and cognition.

In problem-posing education, people develop their power to perceive critically *the way they exist* in the world *with which* and *in which* they find themselves; they come to see the world not as a static reality, but as a reality in process, in transformation. Although the dialectical relations of women and men with the world exist independently of how these relations are perceived (or whether or not they are perceived at all), it is also true that the form of action they adopt is to a large extent a function of how they perceive themselves in the world. Hence, the teacher-student and the students-teachers reflect simultaneously on themselves and the world without dichotomizing this reflection from action, and thus establish an authentic form of thought and action.

Once again, the two educational concepts and practices under analysis come into conflict. Banking education (for obvious reasons) attempts, by mythicizing reality, to conceal certain facts which explain the way human beings exist in the world; problem-posing education sets itself the task of demythologizing. Banking education resists dialogue; problem-posing education regards dialogue as indispensable to the act of cognition which unveils reality. Banking education treats students as objects of assistance; problem-posing education makes them critical thinkers. Banking education inhibits creativity and domesticates (although it cannot completely destroy) the *intentionality* of consciousness by isolating consciousness from the world, thereby denying people their ontological and historical vocation of becoming more fully human. Problem-posing education bases itself on creativity and stimulates true reflection and action upon reality thereby responding to the vocation of persons as beings who are authentic only when engaged in inquiry and creative transformation. In sum: banking theory and practice, as immobilizing and fixating forces, fail to acknowledge men and women as historical beings; problem-posing theory and practice take the people's historicity as their starting point.

Problem-posing education affirms men and women as beings in the process of *becoming*—as unfinished, uncompleted beings in and with a likewise unfinished reality. Indeed, in contrast to other animals who are unfinished, but not historical, people know themselves to be unfinished; they are aware of their incompletion. In this incompletion and this awareness lie the very roots of education as an exclusively human manifestation. The unfinished character of human beings and the transformational character of reality necessitate that education be an ongoing activity.

Education is thus constantly remade in the praxis. In order to *be*, it must *become*. Its "duration" (in the Bergsonian meaning of the word) is found in the interplay of the opposites *permanence* and *change*. The banking method emphasizes permanence and becomes reactionary; problem-posing education—which accepts neither a "well-behaved" present nor a predetermined future—roots itself in the dynamic present and becomes revolutionary.

Problem-posing education is revolutionary futurity. Hence it is prophetic (and, as such, hopeful). Hence, it corresponds to the historical nature of humankind. Hence, it affirms women and men as beings who transcend themselves, who move forward and look ahead, for whom immobility represents a fatal threat, for whom looking at the past must only be a means of understanding more clearly what and who they are so that they can more wisely build the future. Hence, it identifies with the movement which engages people as beings aware of their incompletion—an historical movement which has its point of departure, its Subjects and its objective.

The point of departure of the movement lies in the people themselves. But since people do not exist apart from the world, apart from reality, the movement must begin with the human-world relationship. Accordingly, the point of departure must always be with men and women in the "here and now," which constitutes the situation within which they are submerged, from which they emerge, and in which they intervene. Only by starting from this situation—which determines their perception of it—can they begin to move. To do this authentically they must perceive their state not as fated and unalterable, but merely as limiting—and therefore challenging.

Whereas the banking method directly or indirectly reinforces men's fatalistic perception of their situation, the problem-posing method presents this very situation to them as a problem. As the situation becomes the object of their cognition, the naïve or magical perception which produced their fatalism gives way to perception which is able to perceive itself even as it perceives reality, and can thus be critically objective about that reality.

A deepened consciousness of their situation leads people to apprehend that situation as an historical reality susceptible of transformation. Resignation gives way to the drive for transformation and inquiry, over which men feel themselves to be in control. If people, as historical beings necessarily engaged with other people in a movement of inquiry, did not control that movement, it would be (and is) a violation of their humanity. Any situation in which some individuals prevent others from engaging in the process of inquiry is one of violence. The means used are not important; to alienate human beings from their own decision-making is to change them into objects.

This movement of inquiry must be directed toward humanization—the people's historical vocation. The pursuit of full humanity, however, cannot be carried out in isolation or individualism, but only in fellowship and solidarity; therefore it cannot unfold in the antagonistic relations between oppressors and oppressed. No one can be authentically human while he prevents others from being so. Attempting *to be more* human, individualistically, leads to *having more*, egotistically, a form of dehumanization. Not that it is not fundamental *to have* in order *to be* human. Precisely because it is necessary, some men's *having* must not be allowed to constitute an obstacle to others' *having*, must not consolidate the power of the former to crush the latter.

Problem-posing education, as a humanist and liberating praxis, posits as fundamental that the people subjected to domination must fight for their emancipation. To that end, it enables teachers and students to become Subjects of the educational process by overcoming authoritarianism and an alienating intellectualism; it also enables people to overcome their false perception of reality. The world—longer something to be described with deceptive words—becomes the object of that transforming action by men and women which results in their humanization.

Problem-posing education does not and cannot serve the interests of the oppressor. No oppressive order could permit the oppressed to begin to question: Why? While only a revolutionary society can carry out this education in systematic terms, the revolutionary leaders need not take full power before they can employ the method. In the revolutionary process, the leaders cannot utilize the banking method as an interim measure, justified on grounds of expediency, with the intention of *later* behaving in a genuinely revolutionary fashion. They must be revolutionary—that is to say, dialogical—from the outset.

NOTES

1. Simone de Beauvoir, *La Pensée de Droite, Aujord'hui* (Paris); ST, *El Pensamiento Político de la Derecha* (Buenos Aires, 1963), 34.

2. This concept corresponds to what Sartre calls the "digestive" or "nutritive" concept of education, in which knowledge is "fed" by the teacher to the students to "fill them out." See Jean-Paul Sartre, "Une idée fundamentale de la phénomenologie de Husserl: L'intentionalité," *Situations I* (Paris, 1947).

3. For example, some professors specify in their reading lists that a book should be read from pages 10 to 15—and do this to "help" their students!

4. Erich Fromm, *The Heart of Man* (New York, 1966), 41.

5. *Ibid.*, 31.

6. *Ibid.*

7. Reinhold Niebuhr, *Moral Man and Immoral Society* (New York, 1960), 130.

8. Sartre, *op. cit.*, 32.

9. Edmund Husserl, *Ideas—General Introduction to Pure Phenomenology* (London, 1969), 105–106.

III

DEPENDENCY THEORY: THE POLITICAL ECONOMY OF LATIN AMERICA

Open Veins of Latin America: Five Centuries of the Pillage of a Continent (1971)

Eduardo H. Galeano

Eduardo H. Galeano (b. Uruguay, 1940) is an Uruguayan journalist and writer. His works transcend orthodox genres, by combining documentary, fiction, journalism, political analysis, and history, and by incorporating nonliterary sources, songs, letters, newspaper advertisements, and oral tradition. Galeano began his career as a political writer when he was thirteen, publishing cartoons in El Sol, *the weekly paper of the socialist party in Uruguay. His first article was published in 1954. At the age of twenty, Galeano started his career as a journalist. He later wrote for the weekly journal* Marcha, *considered by Galeano to be "the most important Latin American publication in all of history," becoming editor-in-chief in 1961. In 1964 he became director of the daily newspaper* Época *and two years later became editor-in-chief at the University Press of Montevideo. As a result of the military coup of 1973, he was imprisoned and then forced to leave Uruguay. By that time he had published a novel and several books on politics and culture. In Argentina Galeano founded and edited the magazine,* Crisis, *described by him as showcasing "the best of Latin American literature, art, and popular culture." After the military coup of 1976 in Argentina his name was added to the lists of those condemned by the death squads and thus he moved to Spain. There he started to write his masterpiece,* Memoria del fuego, *a story of America, North and South, in which the characters are real historical figures, generals, artists, revolutionaries, workers, conquerors and the conquered. Galeano started with pre-Columbian creation myths and ended in the 1980s. At the beginning of 1985 he returned to Uruguay. Galeano has received several awards, among them Premio Casa de las Américas (1975, 1978) and the American Book Award (1989). In 1999 he received the first Cultural Freedom Prize from the Lannan Foundation in Santa Fe, New Mexico. The award was given for his courageous lifelong denunciation of injustice and defense of human rights. Since 2005 he has served as member of the advisory committee in the newly launched alternative, pan-Latin American TV station TeleSUR. This selection from Galeano's best known work explains the historical, cultural, economic, and political factors that created a structural exploitation of Latin America's resources and peoples by the global colonial powers since the fifteenth century.*

THE THIRTEEN NORTHERN COLONIES AND THE IMPORTANCE OF NOT BEING BORN IMPORTANT

In Latin America, private appropriation of land always came before its useful cultivation. The most backward aspects of the present property system are not the offspring of crises, but emerged in periods of great prosperity; inversely, periods of economic depression have tempered the voracity of the latifundistas in acquiring new acreage. In Brazil, for example, the decline of sugar and the virtual disappearance of gold and diamonds made possible, between 1820 and 1850, legislation providing that anyone who occupied land and made it produce acquired title to it. The rise of coffee as a new "king product" produced the 1850 Law of Lands, cooked to the taste of oligarchic politicians and military men and denying ownership of land to those who worked it when the great spaces of the interior, to the south and west, were being opened up. This law was subsequently "reinforced and ratified . . . by abundant legislation that decreed purchase as the only form of access to land, and created a civil registration system that would make it nearly impossible for a poor farmer to legalize his land, and stipulated as the sale value of the unoccupied government lands much higher price levels than the current ones for land already appropriated."[1]

U.S. legislation in the same period had the opposite aim: it was to promote the internal colonization of the country. Covered wagons rolled westward into virgin lands with pioneers who extended the frontier at the cost of slaughtered Indians. The Homestead Act of 1862 assured every family of ownership of a quarter section, a lot one-half mile square; each beneficiary committed himself to farm his parcel for a minimum of five years. The public domain was colonized with startling speed and the population grew and spread like a great oil smear. The fertile land that was to be had almost gratis drew European peasants like a magnet: they crossed the ocean and then the Appalachians onto the wide-open prairies. Thus it was free farmers who occupied the new central and western territories. As the country grew in extent and population, unemployment was avoided by the creation of farm jobs, and at the same time an internal market—the multitude of farmer-proprietors—was generated with substantial purchasing power to sustain industrial development.

In contrast, the rural workers who have pushed Brazil's frontier inland for more than a century have not been—and are not—free peasant families seeking a piece of land of their own, but (as Ribeiro notes) *braceros* contracted to serve latifundistas who have already taken possession of the great open spaces. The interior deserts have never been accessible, except in this way, to the rural population. Workers have hacked their way through the jungle with machetes to open up the country for the benefit of others. Between 1950 and 1960, sixty-five Brazilian latifundios absorbed a quarter of the new land brought under cultivation.

These two opposite systems of internal colonization reveal one of the most important differences between United States and Latin American development models. Why is the north rich and the south poor? The Rio Grande is much more than a geographical frontier. Is today's profound disequilibrium, which seems to confirm Hegel's prophecy of inevitable war between the two Americas, to be traced to U.S. imperialist expansion, or does it have more ancient roots? In fact, back in the colonial beginnings, north and south had already generated very different societies with different aims.[2] The *Mayflower* pilgrims did not cross the sea to obtain legendary treasures; they came mainly to establish themselves with their families and to reproduce in the New World the system of life and work they had practiced in Europe. They were not soldiers of fortune but pioneers; they came not to conquer but to colonize, and their colonies were settlements. It is true that a slave-plantation economy like Latin America's developed later south of the Delaware, but then was a difference: the center of gravity in the United States was from the outset the farms and workshops of New England, from which came the victorious armies of the Civil War. New England colonists, the original nucleus of U.S. civilization, never acted as colonial agents for European capitalist accumulation; their own development and the development of their new land, were always their motivation. The thirteen colonies served as an outlet for the army of European peasants and artisans who were being thrown off the labor market by metropolitan development. *Free* workers formed the base of that new society across the ocean.

Spain and Portugal, on the other hand, had an abundance of *subjugated* labor in Latin America. Enslavement of the Indians was followed by the wholesale transplantation of Africans. Through the centuries, a legion of unemployed peasants was always available to be moved to production centers: as precious metal or sugar exports rose and fell, flourishing centers coexisted with centers of decay, and the latter provided labor for the former. This structure persists to our time; today, as yesterday, it means low wage scales because of the pressure of the unemployed on the labor market, and frustrates the growth of an internal consumer market. But also in contrast to the northern Puritans, internal economic development was never the goal of the ruling classes of Latin American colonial society. Their profits came from outside; they were tied more to the foreign market than to their own domain. Landlords, miners, and merchants had been born to fulfill the mission of supplying Europe with gold, silver, and food. Goods moved along the roads in only one direction: to the port and overseas markets. This also provides the key to the United States' expansion as a national unit and to the fragmentation of Latin America. Our production centers are not interconnected but take the arm of a fan with a far-away vertex.

One might say that the thirteen colonies had the fortune of bad fortune. Their history shows the great importance of not being born important. For the north of America had no gold or silver, no Indian civilizations with dense concentrations of people already organized from work, no fabulously fertile tropical soil on the coastal fringe. It was an area where both nature and history had been miserly: both metals and the slave labor to wrest it from the ground were missing. Those colonists were lucky. Furthermore, the northern colonies, from Maryland to New England to Nova Scotia, had a climate and soil similar to British agriculture and produced exactly the same things. That is, as Sergio Bagú notes, they did not offer products *complementary* to the metropolis. The situation in the Antilles and the mainland Spanish-Portuguese colonies was quite different. Tropical lands produced sugar, tobacco, cotton, indigo, turpentine; a small Caribbean island had more economic importance for England than the thirteen colonies that would become the United States.

These circumstances explain the rise and consolidation of the United States as an economically autonomous system, one which did not drain abroad the wealth it produced. The ties between colony and metropolis were slender. In Barbados and Jamaica, on the other hand, only the capital necessary to replace worn-out slaves was reinvested. Thus it was not racial factors that decided the development of the one and the underdevelopment of the other: there was nothing Spanish or Portuguese about Britain's Antillean islands. The truth is that the economic insignificance of the thirteen colonies permitted the early diversification of their exports and set off the early and rapid development of manufacturing. Even before independence, North American industrialization had official encouragement and protection. And England took a tolerant attitude while it strictly forbade its Antillean islands to manufacture so much as a pin.

PROTECTIONISM AND FREE TRADE IN THE UNITED STATES: A SUCCESS DUE NOT TO AN INVISIBLE HAND

When the Triple Alliance was announcing Paraguay's imminent destruction in 1865, General Ulysses S. Grant was celebrating Lee's surrender at Appomattox. The Civil War brought victory to Northern industrialists—unblushing protectionists—over the free-trade cotton and tobacco planters of the South. Thus the outbreak of the war that sealed Latin America's colonial fate coincided with the end of the war that enabled the United States to consolidate its position as a world power. As the newly elected president said:

> For centuries England has relied on protection, has carried it to extremes, and has obtained satisfactory results from it. There is no doubt that it is to this system that it owes its present strength. After two centuries, England has found it convenient to adopt free trade because it thinks that protection can no longer offer it anything. Very well then, gentlemen, my knowledge of our country leads me to believe that within two hundred years, when America has gotten out of protection all that it call offer, it too will adopt free trade.[3]

Two and a half centuries earlier, adolescent English capitalism had sent to its North American colonies its men, its capital, its way of life, its incentives, and its projects. The thirteen colonies, safety valves for Europe's surplus population, soon turned to account the "handicap" of their poor soil and subsoil, and from early days developed an industrializing philosophy which the metropolis did little to discourage. In 1631 the recently arrived colonists in Boston launched a thirty-ton sloop, *Blessing of the Bay*, which they had built themselves, and from then on the shipping industry grew rapidly. White oak, abundant in to woods, was ideal for the framing and hulls; decks, bowsprits, and masts were made of pine. Massachusetts subsidized production of hemp for rigging and ropes, and also encouraged local manufacture of canvas and sails. To the north and south of Boston the coasts were dotted with prosperous shipyards. The colonial governments extended subsidies and premiums to all kinds of manufacture. There were incentives to promote the production of flax and wool, raw materials for crude fabrics which, if not over-elegant, were weatherproof and *national*. To exploit Lynn iron deposits, the first foundry went into operation in 1643; soon Massachusetts was supplying iron to the whole region. When the stimuli to textile production seemed insufficient, this colony opted for compulsion: in 1855 it imposed heavy penalties on any family failing to keep at least one spinning wheel continuously active. In the same period each county of Virginia had to select children for instruction in textile manufacture. It was also prohibited to export hides, so that these could be used domestically for making boots, belts, and saddles.

Economic historian Edward Kirkland wrote that the handicaps with which colonial industry must contend come from every direction except British colonial policy.[4] Indeed, three thousand miles' distance and the difficulties of communication made proscriptive legislation lose nearly all its force and favored the trend toward self-sufficiency. The Northern colonies sent no gold, silver, or sugar to England, while their consumption needs produced an excess of imports which had somehow to be checked. Trade across the ocean was light; hence development of local manufactures was indispensable for survival. England paid such scant attention to these colonies in the eighteenth century that they were able to introduce the latest metropolitan techniques into their factories, turning restrictive colonial pacts into scraps of paper. This was far from true of the Latin American colonies, which delivered their air, water, and salt to ascendant European capitalism and, in return, received a largesse of the finest and costliest luxury goods to pamper their ruling classes. The only expanding activities in Latin America were those oriented toward export, and so it continued in succeeding centuries: the economic and political interests of the mining and landlord bourgeoisie never coincided with the need for internal economic development, and businessmen were linked less with the New World than with foreign markets for the metals and foodstuffs they wanted to sell and with foreign sources of the manufactured articles they wanted to buy.

When the United States declared its independence, it had the same population as Brazil. The Portuguese metropolis—as underdeveloped as the Spanish—exported its underdevelopment to the colony. Throughout the eighteenth century, Brazil's economy had been orchestrated into the British symphony as imperial supplier of gold. This function was reflected in the colony's class structure. Unlike the United States, Brazil's ruling class was not made up of farmers, manufacturing entrepreneurs, and domestic businessmen. The chief interpreters of ruling-class ideals in the two countries, Alexander Hamilton and the Viscount de Cairú (one of the main figures influencing the opening of the ports in 1808), expressed the difference clearly. Both had been disciples, in England, of Adam Smith. But while Hamilton had become a champion of industrialization and a promoter of state protection for national industry, Cairú believed in the invisible hand that worked the magic of liberalism: *laissez faire, laissez passer, laissez vendre*.[5]

By the end of the eighteenth century, the United States had the world's second merchant fleet, consisting entirely of ships built in its own yards, and its textile and steel mills were in surging growth. Soon afterward its machine industry got under way, eliminating the need for its factories to buy capital goods abroad. The zealous *Mayflower* pilgrims had laid the foundations of a nation in the New

England countryside; along its coast of deep bays and great estuaries an industrial bourgeoisie had continuously grown and prospered. In this, as we have seen, the Antilles trade—including the sale of African slaves—had played a major role, but the U.S. achievement would not have happened if it had not been kindled from the outset by a fierce nationalist flame. George Washington had advised in his farewell address that the United States should pursue a lone course. Emerson proclaimed in 1837: "We have listened too long to the courtly muses of Europe. . . . We will walk on our own feet; we will work with our own hands; we will speak our own minds."[6]

Public funds broadened the internal market. The states built roads and railroads, bridges and canals. In mid-century, the state of Pennsylvania participated in launching more than one hundred and fifty mixed-economy enterprises, in addition to administering the $100 million invested in public works. The military operations which grabbed more than half of Mexico's territory also contributed substantially to the country's progress. But the state participated in the development process with more than capital investment and the military costs of expansion; in the North a tough protectionist policy had been inaugurated. The landlords of the South, on the contrary, were free traders. Cotton production doubled every ten years, and while it brought a large commercial income to the whole country and fed Massachusetts' modern textile mills, it depended above all on European markets. The Southern aristocracy, like that of Latin America, was primarily linked to the world market; 80 percent of the cotton spun in European mills came from the toil of Southern slaves. When abolition of slavery was added to Northern industrial protectionism, the contradiction set off the war. North and South confronted each other as two opposed worlds; two historical eras, two antagonistic philosophies of the national destiny. The twentieth century won this nineteenth-century war.

> Let every free man sing . . .
> Old King Cotton is dead and buried,

sang a poet of the victorious army. After General Lee's defeat, customs duties—which had been raised during the conflict to provide revenue and had remained in force to protect the industry of the victors—became sacred. Congress voted the ultra-protectionist "McKinley" tariff in 1890, and the Dingley Act further hiked customs duties in 1897. Soon afterward the developed countries of Europe felt obliged to erect customs barriers against the invasion of dangerously competitive U.S. manufactures. The word "trust" had been coined in 1882: petroleum, steel, foodstuffs, railroads, and tobacco were dominated by monopolies that advanced with giant strides.[7]

Before the Civil War Grant had participated in the plunder of Mexico; after it he was a protectionist president: all part of the same process of national affirmation. Northern industry was conducting the orchestra of history and, as political master of the state, seeing to its interests from the seat of power. The agricultural frontier moved westward and southward at the expense of Indians and Mexicans, but it was with small holdings, not latifundios, that it filled the new open spaces. The promised land not only attracted European peasants; masters of the most varied crafts and workers skilled in mechanics, metallurgy, and steel production also came from Europe to enrich the country's industrialization. By the end of the century the United States was the leading industrial power; in thirty years after the Civil War its factories had multiplied its production capacity by seven. It produced as much coal as Britain and twice as much steel, and had nine times as many miles of railroad. The center of the capitalist world was beginning to move.

After World War II the United States began to emulate Britain in exporting the doctrine of free trade and free competition, so that other people could consume. The International Monetary Fund and World Bank emerged together to deny to underdeveloped countries the right of protecting their national industries, and to discourage state action in those countries. Infallible curative properties were attributed to private enterprise. But the United States did not abandon an economic policy which still remains rigidly protectionist, and which listens carefully to the voice of history: in the North the disease was never confused with the remedy.

BOMBARDMENT BY THE INTERNATIONAL MONETARY FUND HELPS THE CONQUERERS TO LAND

Testifying before the parliamentary commission on the denationalization of Brazilian industry, two government ministers admitted that indigenously owned factories had been put at a disadvantage by the Castelo Branco regime's measure permitting the direct inflow of external credit. They were referring to the famous Order 289 of early 1965, which allowed foreign concerns operating in Brazil to get loans from abroad at 7 or 8 percent interest, with a government-guaranteed exchange arrangement in case the cruzeiro was devalued. Brazilian concerns had to pay almost 50 percent interest on credits they obtained—with difficulty—at home. The inventor of the measure, Roberto Campos, offered this explanation:

> Obviously the world is unequal. Some are born intelligent, some stupid. Some are born athletes, others crippled. The world is made up of small and large enterprises. Some die early, in the prime of life; others drag themselves criminally through a long useless existence. There is a basic fundamental inequality in human nature, in the condition of things. The mechanism of credit cannot escape this. To postulate that national enterprises must have the same access to foreign credit as foreign enterprises is simply to ignore the basic realities of economics.[8]

According to this brief but meaty "Capitalist Manifesto," the law of the jungle is the natural code governing human life; injustice does not exist, for what we know as injustice is merely an expression of the cruel harmony of the universe: poor countries are poor because . . . they are poor; our fate is written in the stars and we are born only to fulfill it. Some are condemned to obey, others are appointed to command. Some put their necks out and others put on the rope. The author of this theory was the creator of International Monetary Fund policy in Brazil.

As in other Latin American countries, application of IMF formulas opened the gates to let foreign conquerors into an already scorched land. From the end of the 1950s economic recession, monetary instability, the credit drought, and a decline in internal purchasing power all helped to capsize national industry and put it at the mercy of imperialist corporations. With the magical incantation of "monetary stabilization," the IMF—which not disinterestedly confuses the fever with the disease, inflation with the crisis of existing structures—has imposed on Latin America a policy that accentuates imbalances instead of easing them. It liberalizes trade by banning direct exchange and barter agreements; it forces the contraction of internal credits to the point of asphyxia, freezes wages, and discourages state activity. To this program it adds sharp monetary devaluations which are theoretically supposed to restore the currency to its real value and stimulate exports. In fact, the devaluations merely stimulate the internal concentration of capital in the ruling classes' pockets and facilitate absorption of national enterprises by foreigners who turn up with fistful of dollars.

In all Latin America, the system produces much less than the necessary monetary demand, and inflation results from this structural impotence. Yet the IMF, instead of attacking the causes of the production apparatus' insufficient supply, launches its cavalry against the consequences, crushing even further the feeble consumer power the internal market: in these lands of hungry multitudes, the IMF lays the blame for inflation at the door of excessive demand. Its stabilization and development formulas have not only failed to stabilize or develop; they have tightened the external stranglehold on these countries, deepened the poverty of the dispossessed masses—bringing social tensions to the boiling point—and hastened economic and financial denationalization in the name of the sacred principles of free trade, free competition, and freedom of movement for capital. The United States, which itself operates an enormous protectionist system—tariffs, quotas, internal subsidies—has never earned a glance from the IMF. Toward Latin America, on the other hand, the IMF is inflexible: for this it was brought into the world. As soon as Chile accepted the first IMF mission in 1954, the country swarmed with its "advisors"; and today most of the governments blindly follow its directives. The therapy makes the sick man sicker, the better to dose him with the drug of loans and investments. The IMF extends loans or flashes the indispensable green light for others to extend them. Born in the United States, headquartered in the United States, and at the service of the United States, the Fund effectively operates as an international inspector without whose approval U.S. banks will not loosen their purse strings. The World Bank, the Agency for International Development, and other philanthropic organizations of global scope likewise make their credits conditional on the signature and implementation of the receiving governments' "letters of intention" to the all-powerful Fund. All the Latin American countries put together do not have half as many votes as the United States in the direction of the policy of this supreme genie of world monetary equilibrium. The IMF was created to institutionalize Wall Street's financial dominion over the whole planet, when the dollar first achieved hegemony as international currency after World War II. It has never been untrue to its master.

It is true that the Latin American national bourgeoisie, with its vocation for living above its income, has done little to stop the avalanche of foreigners; but it is also true that imperialist corporations have used a bewildering range of demolition methods. With the IMF's preliminary bombardment facilitating the penetration, some enterprises were taken by a mere telephone call, after a sharp drop in the stock market, in exchange for a little oxygen in the form of shares, or by calling in some debt for supplies or for the use of patents, brand names, or technical innovations. Such debts, multiplied by currency devaluations—which oblige local enterprises to pay more in national currency for their commitments in dollars—thus become a death trap. Technological dependency costs dearly; the corporations' know-how includes expertise in the art of devouring one's neighbor. One of the last of the Mohicans of Brazilian national industry remarked shortly before the military government sent him into exile: "Experience shows that the profit from sales by a national enterprise often never reaches Brazil, but remains, bearing interest, in the financial market of the purchasing country."[9] The creditors collect by taking over the installations and machinery of the debtors. Banco Central del Brasil figures show that no less than one-fifth of new industrial investments in 1965, 1966, and 1967 was in reality a conversion of unpaid debts into investment.

On top of the financial and technological blackmail is the unfair "free" competition between strong and weak. As part of a global structure, the big-corporation affiliate can permit itself the luxury of losing money for a year, or two, or whatever is necessary. Prices fall, and it sits down to wait for the victim to surrender. The banks collaborate in the siege: the national enterprise is less solvent than it looked, supplies are denied it, and it soon raises the white flag. The local capitalist becomes a junior partner or functionary of his conquerors. Or else he brings off the most coveted feat—he retrieves his property in the form of shares in the foreign concern and ends his days as a well-heeled coupon-clipper. An eloquent story with regard to price "dumping" is that of Union Carbide's capture of the Brazilian tape factory, Adesite. Scotch Tape, part of the multitentacled Minnesota Mining and Manufacturing, began steadily lowering the price of its products in Brazil. Adesite's sales kept going down. The banks cut off credit. Scotch Tape continued lowering its prices—by 30 percent, then by 40 percent. Then Union Carbide appeared on the scene and bought the desperate Brazilian concern for a song. Later Union Carbide and Scotch Tape got together to share the national market: they divided up Brazil, taking half each, and agreed to digest what they had eaten by raising the price of tape by 50 percent. The antitrust law of the old Vargas days had been annulled years earlier.

The Organization of American States admits that the abundant financial resources of U.S. affiliates "in times of very low liquidity for national enterprises, has on occasion enabled some national enterprises to be acquired by foreign interests." In fact, the scarcity of financial resources, sharpened by the IMF-imposed contraction of internal credit, smothers local factories. But the same OAS document tells us that no less than 95.7 percent—80 percent in the case of manufacturing industries—of the funds U.S. enterprises require for their normal functioning and development in Latin America come from *Latin American* sources in the form of credits, loans, and reinvested profits.

TECHNOCRATS ARE BETTER HOLD-UP ARTISTS THAN MARINES

In taking out many more dollars than they bring in, the enterprises whet the region's chronic dollar hunger; the "benefited" countries are decapitalized instead of capitalized. And here the loan mechanism goes to work. International credit organizations are important in helping to dismantle the weak citadels of nationally capitalized industry and in solidifying neocolonial structures. "Aid" works like the philanthropist who put a wooden leg on his piglet because he was eating it bit by bit. The U.S. balance-of-payments deficit is the result of military spending and foreign aid, and is a critical sword of Damocles over U.S. prosperity. *At the same time*, it makes that prosperity possible: the Imperium sends forth its Marines to save its monopolists' dollars; more effectively, it sends its technocrats and loans to extend business and assume raw materials and markets.

At its global center of power the capitalism of our day exhibits a clear identity of interest between private monopolies and the state apparatus. Multinational corporations make direct use of the state to accumulate, multiply, and concentrate capital, to deepen the technological revolution, to militarize the economy, and by various means to assure success in the crusade to control the capitalist world. The Export-Import Bank (Eximbank), AID, and other smaller organizations function in this role, as do some purportedly international organizations in which the United States has unchallenged hegemony: the International Monetary Fund, its twin the International Bank for Reconstruction and Development (IBRD), and the Inter-American Development Bank (IDB). These assume the right to decide the economic policy of countries asking for credits, pouncing successfully on the countries' central banks and decisive ministers. They get hold of all the secret economic and financial data, draft and impose national laws, and ban or authorize steps proposed by governments whose course they chart down to the last detail.

International charity does not exist; it begins at home, for the United States as for everyone else. The role of foreign aid is primarily domestic—the U.S. economy aids itself—and it was defined by none other than Roberto Campos, when he was the ambassador for Goulart's nationalist government, as a program of broadening foreign markets to absorb U.S. surpluses and alleviate superproduction in U.S. exporting industries. In the early days of the Alliance for Progress, the U.S. Department of Commerce pointed to its successful creation of new businesses and job sources for private enterprise in forty-four states.[10] In January 1968, President Johnson assured Congress that more than 90 percent of U.S. foreign aid in 1969 would be applied to financing purchases in the United States, and that he had personally and directly intensified efforts to increase this percentage. In October 1969 cables sizzled with statements by Carlos Sanz de Santamaría, chairman of the Alliance's Inter-American Committee, who said in New York that the aid had turned out to be excellent business for the U.S. economy and for its treasury. After the disequilibrium of the U.S. balance of payments became critical at the end of the 1950s, loans were conditioned upon buying U.S. industrial goods, usually costing more than similar products from other countries. More recently, certain mechanisms were put into effect, among them "negative lists" to see that the credits are not used for exporting articles which the United States can sell on the world market under good competitive conditions without recourse to auto-philanthropy. Subsequent "positive lists" have made possible the sale through "aid" of certain U.S. manufactures at prices from 30 to 50 percent higher than the same goods from other sources.

"Tied aid" (so called by the OAS document cited earlier) bestows "a general subsidy on U.S. exports." In Brazil, "sales of U.S. capital exporters are faced with increasing competition from other exporters . . . [and] are at a serious disadvantage unless they can take advantage of the more liberal financing available under the various aid programs."[11] When, in a speech late in 1969, Richard Nixon promised to "untie" the aid, he referred only to the possibility of alternative purchases in Latin American countries. Such had been the case with the loans that the Inter-American Development Bank granted and charged to its Special Operations Funds. But experience shows that the United States—or the Latin American affiliates of its corporations—always ends up as the chosen supplier in the contracts. Loans from AID and Eximbank, and most of those from the IDB, also require that at least half of the shipments be made in U.S. bottoms. Freight rates on U.S. ships run as much as double those of other available shipping lines. The firms insuring the transported merchandise, and the banks through which the operations are effected, are also usually U.S. owned.

The OAS has made a revealing estimate of the extent of *real* aid received by Latin America. When chaff is separated from grain, one must conclude that a mere 38 percent of the *nominal* aid can be considered as *real* aid. Only one-fifth of the authorized total of loans for industry, mining, and communications, and compensatory credits, constitutes aid. In the case of Eximbank, the aid travels from south to north: the financing it extends, says OAS, means not aid but extra costs for the region in view of the inflated prices of U.S. articles exported via the bank.

Latin America provides most of flue ordinary capital resources of the IDB. But IDB documents carry the Alliance for Progress emblem in addition to its own insignia, and the United States is the only member country with veto power; the votes of the Latin American countries, in proportion to their contributions of capital, fall short of the two-thirds majority necessary for important resolutions. In his famous report to President Nixon in August 1969, Nelson Rockefeller admitted that "while the United States' veto power over IDB loans has not been used, the threat of its use for political purposes has influenced decisions." On most of the loans it extends, the IDB imposes the same conditions as do openly U.S. organs: the money must be spent on U.S. merchandise, at least half of which must be transported in ships flying the Stars and Stripes—and the Alliance for Progress is expressly mentioned in the publicity. The IDB determines the tariff and tax policy of the services it touches with its fairy wand: it decides how much must be charged for water and fixes the taxes for water mains and housing on the basis of proposals by U.S. consultants named with its gracious approval. It approves work plans, drafts the bidding terms, administers the funds, and keeps watch on how the job is done.[12] In the task of restructuring higher education in the region according to the standards of cultural neocolonialism, the IDB has played a fruitful role. Its loans to universities block the possibility of modifying laws and statutes without its knowledge and permission; at the same time, it imposes specific pedagogical, administrative, and financial reforms.[13] In the case of a difference of opinion the OAS' general secretary names the arbitrator.

Agency for International Development contracts not only mandate U.S. merchandise and freightage, but also ban trade with Cuba and North Vietnam and make the administrative tutelage of AID technicians obligatory. To compensate for the divergence of price between U.S. tractors or fertilizers and those more cheaply obtainable on the world market, the elimination of taxes and customs duties for products imported with credits is stipulated. AID aid includes jeeps and modern weapons for use by the police in safeguarding law and order in the countries concerned. Not for nothing is one-third of the credits payable immediately, while the other two-thirds are conditional on approval by the IMF—whose recipes normally kindle a fire of social agitation. And as if the IMF had not succeeded in dismantling all the mechanisms of sovereignty as one dismantles a watch, AID generally throws in the requirement of approval of specific laws and decrees. AID is the chief vehicle for Alliance for Progress funds. To cite but one example of the labyrinths of generosity, the Alliance's Inter American Committee got the Uruguayan government to sign a commitment whereby the income and expenditures of state bodies, and the official policy on tariffs, wages, and investments, would pass under the control of this foreign organization.[14] But the most pernicious conditions rarely appear in the published texts of contracts and commitments, and are hidden in secret codicils. The Uruguayan parliament never knew that in March 1968 the government had agreed to limit rice exports in that year so that the country could receive flour, corn, and sorghum under the U.S. agricultural surplus law.

Numerous daggers glint beneath the cloak of aid to poor countries. Teodoro Moscoso, who was chairman of the Alliance for Progress, confessed: "It may happen that the United States needs the vote of a particular country in the UN or the OAS, and it is possible that the government of that country [following the sacred tradition of Cold War diplomacy] may ask a price in exchange."[15] In 1962 the Haitian delegate to the OAS Punta del Este conference changed his vote in return for a new airport, and thus the United States got its majority in its attempt to expel Cuba.[16] Ex-director Miguel Ydigoras Fuentes of Guatemala said he had to threaten the United States with withholding his country's vote at Alliance for Progress conferences to make the United States keep its promise to buy more Guatemalan sugar.[17]

It might at first sight seem paradoxical that during the Goulart regime Brazil was the country most favored by the Alliance for Progress. But the paradox vanishes as soon as one realizes the internal distribution of the aid received: Alliance credits were sown in Goulart's path like explosive mines. Carlos Lacerda, governor of Guanabara and at that time leader of the extreme Right, got seven times more than all of the Northeast: Guanabara, with scarcely four million inhabitants, was thus able to create beautiful gardens for tourists on the shores of the world's most spectacular bay, while the Northeast remained the open sore of Latin America. In June 1964, after the coup d'état that successfully put Castelo Branco in power, Thomas Mann, Undersecretary of State for International Affairs and right arm of President Johnson, explained: "The United States distributed among the efficient governors of certain Brazilian states the aid that had been destined for the government of Goulart, thinking to finance democracy in this way; Washington gave no money for the balance of payments or the federal budget, because that could directly benefit the central government."[18] The U.S. administration had decided to deny any kind of cooperation to Belaúnde's government in Peru "unless it would give the desired assurances of following an indulgent policy towards the IPC. This Belaúnde refused to do and, as a result, by late 1965 he was still not receiving the share of Alliance for Progress funds that his government has earned the right to expect."[19] Later, as we know, Belaúnde compromised—and lost both oil and power: he had obeyed in order to survive. In Bolivia, U.S. loans did not provide a centavo for the country to build its own tin smelter, so that crude tin continued journeying to Liverpool and from there, smelted, to New York. "Aid" gave birth to a parasitic commercial bourgeoisie, inflated the bureaucracy, built large edifices and modern auto highways and other white elephants in a country that competes with Haiti for the highest rate of infant mortality in Latin America. The credits from the United States and its "international" organs denied Bolivia the right to accept Soviet, Czech, and Polish offers to create a petrochemical industry, extract and smelt zinc, lead, and iron, an install smelters for tin and antimony. At the same time, Bolivia we obliged to import products exclusively from the United States. When the *Movimiento Nacionalista Revolucionario* (MNR) government finally fell, its foundations eaten away by U.S. aid, U.S. Ambassador Douglas Henderson began to attend René Barrientos' cabinet meetings regularly.

The loans indicate as precisely as thermometers the general business climate of each country, and help clear political rain clouds or revolutionary storms from the blue sky of the millionaires. "The United States," announced a group of businessmen led by David Rockefeller in 1963, "will arrange its economic aid program in countries showing the greatest inclination to favor the investment climate, and will withdraw aid from other countries not showing a satisfactory performance."[20] The text of the foreign aid law provides categorically for the suspension of aid to any government that has "nationalized, expropriated, or acquired property or control of property belonging to any U.S. citizen, or any corporation, society, or association" that belongs not less than 50 percent to U.S. citizens.[21,22] Not for nothing does the Alliance for Progress Trade Committee include among its most distinguished members top executives of Chase Manhattan, National City Bank, Standard Oil, Anaconda, and Grace. AID clears the road for U.S. capitalists in many ways—for instance, by requiring approval of agreements guaranteeing investments against possible loss through wars, revolutions, insurrections, or monetary crises. In 1966, according to the U.S. Department of Commerce, U.S. private investors received these guarantees in fifteen Latin American countries, for one hundred projects involving more than $300 million, under the AID Investment Guaranty Program.[23]

ADELA is not a Mexican revolutionary song, but the name of an international investment consortium. It was started by First National City Bank, Standard Oil of New Jersey, and the Ford Motor Company. The Mellon group joined enthusiastically, and so did major European corporations because, as Senator Jacob Javits remarked, "Latin America provides an excellent opportunity for the United States to show, by inviting Europe to `enter,' that it does not seek a dominant or exclusive position."[24] In its 1968 annual report ADELA offered special thanks to the IDB for the parallel loans it had extended to promote the consortium's business in Latin America, and also saluted the performance along the same lines of the International Finance Corporation, an arm of the World Bank. ADELA is in continuous contact with both institutions to avoid duplication of effort and to evaluate investment opportunities.[25]

Many more examples of such holy alliances could be given. In Argentina, Latin American contributions to the resources of the IDB have served as very convenient loans benefiting such concerns as the Electric Bond & Share affiliate Petrosur (over $10 million for construction of a petro-chemical complex), and The Budd Company (Philadelphia) affiliate Armetal (to finance an auto parts plant). AID credits made possible the expansion of Richfield's chemical plant in Brazil, and Eximbank extended loans to ICOMI, a Bethlehem Steel affiliate in the same country. Also in Brazil, contributions from the Alliance for Progress and the World Bank enabled the Dutch Phillips' Industries to install Latin America's biggest complex of fertilizes factories in 1966. It all comes under the heading of "aid"—and all adds further to the weight of external debt on the countries so favored.

In the first days of the Cuban Revolution, Fidel Castro took the problem of rebuilding foreign currency reserves drained by the Batista dictatorship to the World Bank and the IMF; they replied that he must first accept a stabilization program, which implied—as it did everywhere else—the dismantling of the state and a freeze on structural reforms.[26] The World Bank and the IMF function in close harmony and for common ends; they were born together at Bretton Woods. The United States has one-fourth of the votes in the Work Bank: the twenty-two countries of Latin America have less than one tenth. The World Bank responds to the United States like thunder to lightning.

As the Bank explains it, most of the loans are for building roads and other communications links, and for developing sources of electrical energy, an essential condition for the growth of private enterprise. In effect, these infrastructure projects facilitate the movement of raw materials to ports and world markets and the progress of already denationalized industry in the poor countries. The World Bank believes that

> to the greatest extent practicable, competitive industry should be left to private enterprise. This is not to say that the Bank has an absolute bar against loans to government-owned industries, but it will undertake such financing only in cases where private capital is not available, and if it is satisfied, after thorough examination, that the government's participation will be compatible with efficient operation and will not have an unduly deterrent effect upon the expansion of private initiative and enterprise.

Loans are conditional upon application of the IMF stabilizing formula and prompt payment of the external debt, and are incompatible with policies of control of the enterprises' profits, "so restrictive that the utilities cannot operate on a sound basis, still less provide for future expansion."[27] Since 1968 the World Bank has to a considerable extent channeled its loans toward birth control promotion, educational plans, agrobusiness, and tourism.

Like all the other one-armed bandits of international high finance, the Bank is also an efficient instrument of extortion for the benefit of very specific circles. Its chairmen since 1946 have been prominent U.S. businessmen.

Eugene R. Black, chairman from 1949 to 1962, later became a director of several private corporations, one of which—Electric Bond & Share—is the world's top monopolist of electrical energy.[28] By chance or otherwise, in 1966 the World Bank made Guatemala accept a "gentlemen's agreement" with Electric Bond & Share as a condition for implementing the Jurún-Marinalá hydroelectric project: the agreement was to pay the firm a fat indemnity for possible damages in a river basin site which had been given it as a present some years earlier, and included a state commitment not to interfere with Electric Bond & Share in its fixing of electricity rates. By chance or otherwise, the World Bank, in 1967, made Colombia pay a $36 million indemnity to the Electric Bond & Share affiliate Compañía Colombiana de Electricidad for its old, recently nationalized machinery. The Colombian state thus bought what belonged to it—but the concession to the enterprise had run out in 1944. Three World Bank chairmen are stars in the Rockefeller power constellation. John J. McCloy, who presided from 1947 to 1949, moved on into a director's chair at Chase Manhattan Bank. His successor, Black, crossed the road in the opposite direction, coming from the Chase Manhattan board. Black was succeeded in 1963 by another Rockefeller man, George D. Woods. By chance or otherwise, the World Bank directly participates—with one-tenth of the capital and substantial loans—in the biggest Rockefeller venture in Brazil: South America's most important petrochemical complex, Petroquímica União.

More than half the loans Latin America receives come—after the IMF's green light—from private and official U.S. sources; international banks also provide an important percentage. The IMF and the World Bank put more and more pressure on Latin American countries to reshape their economies and finances in terms of payment of the foreign debt. But the fulfillment of commitments— the essence of international good conduct—gets more and more difficult and at the same time more necessary. The region is experiencing the phenomenon that economists call the "debt explosion." It is a strangulating vicious circle. Loans increase, investments follow investments, so that payments grow for amortization, interest, dividends, and other services. To pay off these debts, new injections of foreign capital are resorted to, generating bigger commitments, and so on and on. Servicing the debt consumes a growing proportion of income from exports, which in any case, due to the unremitting fall of prices, cannot finance the necessary imports; new loans to enable the countries to supply themselves thus become as indispensable as air to the lungs. In 1955 one-fifth of exports went for amortization, interest, and profit on investments; the proportion has kept growing and is approaching the explosion point. In 1968 these payments amounted to 37 percent of exports.[29] If Latin America continues resorting to foreign capital to fill the "trade gap" and finance the flight of profits on imperialist investment, by 1980 no less than 80 percent of the foreign currency will remain in foreign creditors' hands, and the total debt will be more than six times the value of exports. The World Bank had foreseen that in 1980 debt-servicing payments would completely cancel out the flow of new foreign capital to the underdeveloped world. But in fact the flow of new loans to Latin America in 1965 was already less than the capital drained out merely as amortization and interest to fulfill previous commitments.

THE ORGANIZED INEQUALITY OF THE WORLD MARKET IS UNCHANGED BY INDUSTRIALIZATION

The exchange of merchandise, along with loans and direct investments abroad, are the straitjacket of the international division of labor. Third World countries exchange rather more than one-fifth of their exports among each other, and three-quarters of their foreign sales are made to the imperialist centers whose tributaries they are. Most Latin American countries are identified in the world market with a single raw material or foodstuff.[30] Latin America has abundant wool, cotton, and natural fibers, and a traditional textile industry, but only a 0.6 percent share in European and U.S. purchases of yarns and fabrics. The region has been condemned to sell primary products to keep foreign factories humming; and it happens that those products "are mostly exported by strong consortiums with international connections, which have the necessary world-market relations to place their products under the most convenient conditions"[31]—the most convenient *for them*, suiting the interests of the buyer countries: that is to say, *at the lowest prices*. In international markets there is a virtual monopoly of demand for raw materials and of supply of industrial products, while suppliers of basic products, who are also buyers of finished goods, operate separately. The former, grouped around, and dominated by, the United States—which consumes almost as much as all the rest of the world—are strong; the latter are isolated and weak: the oppressed competing against the oppressed. The so-called free play of supply and demand in the so-called international market does not exist; the reality is a dictatorship of one group over the other, always for the benefit of the developed capitalist countries. The decision-making centers, where prices are fixed, are in Washington, New York, London, Paris, Amsterdam, Hamburg, in cabinet meetings and on the stock exchanges. It means little or nothing that international agreements have been signed to protect the prices of wheat (1949), sugar (1953), tin (1956), olive oil (1956), and coffee (1962). A glance at the descending curve of these products' relative value shows that the agreements have only been symbolic excuses offered by strong countries when the prices of the weak countries' products sank scandalously low. What Latin America sells gets constantly cheaper and—also in relative terms—what it buys gets constantly dearer.

For the price of twenty-two bullocks, Uruguay could have bought a Ford Major tractor in 1954; today more than twice as many are needed. A group of Chilean economists who made a survey for the trade unions calculated that, if the price of Latin American exports had risen since 1928 at the same rate as the price of imports, Latin America would have received $57 billion more for its sales abroad between 1958 and 1967 than it actually received.[32] Without going hack that far, and taking 1950 prices as a base, the United Nations estimates that due to exchange deterioration Latin America lost more than $18 billion in the decade 1955-1964. The fall continued after that. The "trade gap"—the difference between import needs and income from exports—will continue to widen if present external trade structures do not change, and each year the abyss gets deeper. If in the immediate future the region attempted to slightly step up its development pace over that of the past fifteen years—which has been snail-slow—the import needs it would confront would considerably exceed the foreseeable growth of its foreign currency income from exports. According to the Instituto Latinoamericano de Planificación Económica y Social, the trade gap will rise to $4.6 billion in 1975 and $8.3 billion in 1980. This last figure is no less than half the value of exports foreseen for that year. Thus the Latin American countries, hats in hand, will be knocking ever more desperately on the doors of international loan sharks.

Arghiri Emmanuel holds that the curse of low prices does not weigh upon particular products but upon particular countries.[33] After all, coal—until recently one of Britain's chief exports—is no less a raw material than wool or copper, and there is more labor in sugar than in Scotch whiskey or French wine. Sweden and Canada export timber, a raw material, at excellent prices. According to Emmanuel, the world market bases the trading inequality on the exchange of more work-hours in poor countries for less work-hours in rich countries: the key to the exploitation is that while there is an enormous difference between the wage levels of the poor and rich countries, it is not accompanied by differences of the same magnitude in the productivity of the work. It is the low wages that determine the low prices, says Emmanuel, not the reverse: the poor countries export their poverty—further impoverishing themselves in process—while the rich countries get the opposite result. According to Samir Amin, if the products exported by underdeveloped countries in 1966 had been produced by developed countries with the same techniques but with their much higher wage levels, the prices would have differed to such an extent that the developed countries would have received $14 billion more.[34]

Certainly the rich countries have used and are using tariff barriers to protect their high wage scales in areas in which they cannot compete with poor countries. The United States uses the IMF, the World Bank, and GATT (General Agreement on Tariffs and Trade) agreements to impose the free trade and free competition doctrine on Latin America, forcing the reduction of multiple exchanges, quotas, and import and export permits, and of tariffs and customs duties. But it in no way practices what it preaches. In the same way that it discourages state activity in other countries while protecting monopolies at home through a vast subsidy and privileged-price system, in its foreign trade the United States practices an aggressive protectionism with high tariffs and severe restrictions. Customs duties are combined with other taxes, and with quotas and embargoes. What would happen to the prosperity of Midwest cattlemen if the United States permitted access to its internal market—without tariffs and fanciful sanitary prohibitions—of better and cheaper meat from Argentina and Uruguay? Iron enters the U.S. market freely, but if it has been converted into ingots it pays $16 a ton, and the tariff rises in direct proportion to the stage of refinement. The same is true for copper and countless other products: let bananas be dried, tobacco cut, cacao sweetened, timber sawed, or dates stoned, and tariffs are implacably piled on them. In January 1969, the U.S. government ordered the suspension of purchases of Mexican tomatoes—which give jobs to 170,000 peasants in Sinaloa state—until Florida tomato growers got the Mexicans to raise the price to avoid competition.

But the most startling contradiction between theory and reality in the world market emerged in the open "soluble coffee war" in 1967. It then became clear that *only the rich countries* have the right to exploit for their own benefit the "natural comparative advantages" which theoretically determine the international division of labor. The sensationally expanding soluble coffee market is in the hands of Nestle and General Foods: before long, it is believed, these two will be supplying more than half the coffee consumed in the world. The United States and Europe buy coffee beans in Brazil and Africa, concentrate it in their industrial plants, and sell it worldwide in soluble form. Brazil, the biggest coffee producer, does not have the right to compete by exporting its own soluble coffee, thereby taking advantage of its obviously lower costs and providing an outlet for the surpluses which it once destroyed and now stores in state warehouses. Brazil only has the right to supply the raw material to enrich foreign factories. When Brazilian factories—a mere five in a world total of 110—began offering soluble coffee on the international market, they were accused of unfair competition. The rich countries yelled to high heaven and Brazil accepted a humiliating imposition: it placed a huge internal tax on its soluble coffee to put it out of the running in the U.S. market.

In erecting customs, tax, and sanitation barriers against Latin American products, Europe does not lag behind. The Common Market piles on import duties to defend the high internal prices of its agricultural products, and at the same time subsidizes those products in order to export them at competitive prices: it finances the subsidies with what it gets from the duties. Thus the poor countries pay their rich customers to compete against them. The price of a pound of sirloin in Buenos Aires or Montevideo is multiplied by five when it hangs from a butcher's hook in Hamburg or Munich. As a Chilean government delegate at an international conference justifiably complained: "The developed countries are willing to let us sell them jet planes and computers, but nothing that we have any likelihood of being able to produce."[35]

Imperialist investments in Latin American industry have in no way modified the terms of its international trade. The region continues to die as it exchanges its primary products for the specialized products of metropolitan economies. The expansion of sales by U.S. concerns south of the Rio Grande is concentrated in local markets, not in exports. Indeed, the proportion that is exported has tended to shrink: according to the OAS, U.S. affiliates exported 10 percent of their total sales in 1962 and only 7.5 percent three years later.[36, 37] Trade in Latin American industrial products only grows *inside* Latin America: in 1955, manufactures were 10 percent of the exchange among countries of the area; in 1966 the proportion had risen to 30 percent.

John Abbink, head of a U.S. technical mission in Brazil, had a prophetic moment in 1950: "The United States must he prepared to `guide' the inevitable industrialization of the undeveloped countries if we want to avoid the shock of intensive economic development outside U.S. aegis. . . . Industrialization, if not controlled in some way, would bring a substantial reduction of U.S. export markets."[38] Indeed, would not industrialization—even though teleguided from abroad—substitute national products for merchandise that each country previously had to import? Celso Furtado has noted that to the extent that Latin America advances in substitution for more complex imported products, "dependence on input from the head offices tends to increase." Between 1957 and 1964, the sales of U.S. affiliates doubled while their imports—apart from equipment—more than tripled. According to Celso Furtado, "This tendency would seem to indicate that 'substitutive' efficiency is a declining function of industrial expansion controlled by foreign countries."[39]

Dependence is not broken but undergoes a qualitative change: the United States today sells to Latin America a greater proportion more sophisticated and technologically higher-level products. "In the long run," the Department of Commerce says, "as Mexican industrial production goes up, opportunities are greater for additional U.S. exports of industrial raw materials or components. . . ."[40] Argentina, Mexico, and Brazil are very good customers for industrial machinery, electrical machinery, motors, equipment, and spare parts made in the United States. The affiliates of big corporations supply themselves from their head offices at deliberately inflated prices. As Ismael Viñas and Eugenio Gastiazoro have written about foreign auto concerns in Argentina: "Paying for these imports at very high prices, they sent funds abroad. The payments were often so large that the enterprises not only showed a loss (despite the prices for which cars were sold here), but began to go bankrupt, with rapid depreciation of shares held in the country. . . . The result was that of the twenty-two enterprises 'established,' ten now remain, some on the brink of bankruptcy."[41]

Thus for the corporations' greater glory their subsidiaries dispose of the scanty foreign currency of the Latin American countries. The operating plan of satellized industry does not differ much from traditional system of imperialist exploitation of raw materials. Antonio Garcia maintains that "Colombian" export of crude petroleum has in fact always been the physical transfer of crude oil from a U.S. oil field to refining, marketing, and consumption centers in United States, and "Honduran" or "Guatemalan" banana export a transfer by U.S. companies from certain colonial plantations to certain U.S. marketing and consumption areas.[42] But the "Argentine," "Brazilian," and "Mexican" factories—to mention only the most important—also occupy an economic space that has nothing to do with their geographical location. Along with many other threads, they make up an international web of corporations whose head offices transfer profits from one country to another, invoicing sales above or below the real prices according to the direction in which they want the profits to flow.[43] The mainsprings of external trade thus remain in the hands of U.S. or European concerns, which orient the countries' trade policies according to the criteria of governments and directorates outside Latin America. Just as U.S. affiliates do not export copper to the U.S.S.R., nor sell oil to Cuba, neither do they get raw materials and machinery from the cheapest and most convenient sources.

This efficient coordination of global activities, completely outside any "free play of market forces," is not of course translated into lower prices for local consumers, but into profits for foreign shareholders. The auto industry is a graphic example. Latin American countries offer an abundant and extremely cheap labor force and an official policy in every way favoring expansion of investments—free gifts of land, privileged electricity rates, state rediscounts to finance sales on credit, easily accessible money; and as if this were not enough, some countries have even exempted the companies from income or sales taxes. Control of the market is further facilitated in advance by the magical prestige attached, in the eyes of the middle classes, to makes and models promoted by global publicity campaigns. Yet far from making Latin American-produced cars cheaper than those produced in the companies' home countries, all these factors make them far more expensive. True, Latin American markets are much smaller; but it is also true that in these countries the corporations' appetite for profits is more leonine than anywhere else. A Ford Falcon made in Latin America costs three times as much as in the United States,[44] an Argentine-made Valiant or Fiat more than double its price in the United States or in Italy,[45] and the same goes for the relation between the Brazilian Volkswagen and its price tag in Germany.[46]

THE GODDESS TECHNOLOGY DOESN'T SPEAK SPANISH

Congressman Wright Patman considers that 5 percent of the shares in a big corporation can often suffice for an individual, family, or economic group to control it.[47] If 5 percent is enough to control one of the United States' mighty enterprises, what percentage is needed to dominate a Latin American enterprise? In fact, it can be done with less: the "mixed" company, one of the few remaining objects of pride for the Latin American bourgeoisie, merely adorns foreign power with a national capital participation that may constitute the majority but is never decisive over the foreign elements. Often the state itself goes into partnership with an imperialist enterprise which, thus transformed into a "national" concern, gets all the desirable guarantees and a cooperative—even an affectionate—climate. The "minority" participation of foreign capital is usually justified by the need for technical and patent transfers. The Latin American bourgeoisie, a bourgeoisie of merchants lacking any creative character, umbilically tied to the power of the land, prostrates itself before the goddess technology. If foreign shareholdings (however small) and technological dependence (rarely small) are evidence of denationalization, how many factories can really be considered national in Latin America? In Mexico, for example, foreign owners of the technology often demand shares in an enterprise, in addition to decisive technical and administrative controls, the sale of the product to specific foreign middlemen, and the importation of machinery and other goods from their head offices, in return for contracts to transmit patents or "know-how."[48] And not only in Mexico. Countries of the so-called Andean Group (Bolivia, Colombia, Chile, Ecuador, and Peru) have worked out a plan for common treatment of foreign capital in the area, stressing rejection of technology-transfer contracts that contain such clauses. But to countries that will not accept the plan, it proposes that foreign concerns holding patents should fix the prices of products resulting from the patents, or ban their export to specific areas.

The first system of patents to protect ownership of inventions was created almost four centuries ago by Sir Francis Bacon. Bacon liked to remark that "Knowledge is power," and it has since become clear how right he was. There is little universality in scientific universals; objectively they are confined within the frontiers of the advanced nations. Latin America does not apply the results of scientific research to its own advantage for the simple reason that it has none; consequently it is condemned to suffer the technology of the powerful, which attacks and removes natural raw materials, and is incapable of creating its own technology to sustain and defend its own development. The transplantation of the advanced countries' technology not only involves cultural—and, most definitely, economic—subordination. It has also been shown, after four and a half centuries' experience of proliferating modernized oases amid deserts of backwardness and ignorance, to resolve none of the problems of underdevelopment. This vast region of illiterates invests two hundred times less than the United States invests in technological research. There are less than one thousand computers in Latin America and fifty thousand in the United States; the electronic models and programming languages that Latin America supports are, of course, designed and created in the United States. Latin American underdevelopment is not a stage on the road to development, but the counterpart of development elsewhere; the region "progresses" without freeing itself from the structure of its backwardness and, as Manuel Sadosky points out, the "advantage" of not participating in progress with its own programs and goals is illusory.[49,50] The symbols of prosperity are symbols of dependence. Modern technology is received as railroads were received in the past century, at the service of foreign interests which model and remodel the colonial status of these countries. "What happens to us is what happens to a watch that loses time and is not regulated," Sadosky writes. "Although its hands continue moving forward, the difference grows between the time it shows and the real time."

On a small scale, Latin American universities turn out mathematicians, engineers, and programmers who can only find work in exile: we give ourselves the luxury of providing the United States with our best technicians and ablest scientists, who are lured to emigrate by the high salaries and broad research possibilities available in the north. At the same time, whenever a Latin American university or center of higher learning tries to stimulate the basic sciences, to lay the foundations for a technology that is not copied from foreign patterns and interests, a timely coup d'etat destroys the experiment on the pretext that it is an incubator of subversion. The University of Brasilia, crushed in 1964, was an example of this. And the truth is that the armor-plated archangels who guard the established order are not mistaken: an autonomous cultural policy, when it is genuine, requires and promotes deep changes in all existing structures.

The alternative is to depend on foreign sources: to imitate, apelike, the advances spread by the great corporations, which monopolize the most modern techniques of creating new products and improving the quality or reducing the cost of existing ones. The electronic brain has infallible methods of calculating costs and profits, and thus Latin America imports production techniques designed to economize on labor, although it has labor to spare and in several countries the unemployed may soon he the overwhelming majority. And thus our own impotence puts the progress of the region at the will or whim of foreign investors. For obvious reasons, control of the technological levers gives the multinational corporations a hold on other decisive levers of our economy. The head offices never, of course, give their affiliates the latest innovations or promote an independence which would not suit them. A survey made by *Business International* for the IDB concluded that "clearly the subsidiaries of international corporations operating in the region make no significant efforts in the direction of 'research and development.' In fact, most of them lack any department for this purpose and only in very rare cases take on the job of technical adaptation, while another small minority of enterprises—almost invariably located in Argentina, Brazil, and Mexico—undertake modest research activities."[51] Raúl Prebisch notes that "U.S. enterprises in Europe install laboratories and undertake research which helps strengthen the scientific and technical capacity of those countries, something that has not happened in Latin America," and makes a very serious point: "For lack of specialized knowledge ('know-how') on the part of national entrepreneurs, most of the transferred technology consists of techniques that are in the public domain hut are licensed as specialized knowledge."[52]

Technological dependence costs dearly in more ways than one: in hard-cash dollars, for instance, although the companies' versatile sleight-of-hand in declaring their remittances abroad makes the amount hard to estimate. Official figures nevertheless indicate that the dollar drain for technical aid to Mexico rose fifteen fold between 1950 and 1964, while in the same period new investments were not even doubled. Three-quarters of the foreign capital in Mexico today is in manufacturing industry, a rise from one-quarter in 1950. This concentration of resources in industry implies only a reflected modernization, using second-hand technology, for which the country pays as if it were the very latest. The auto industry has drained $1 billion from Mexico in one way or another, but a United Auto Workers leader wrote after touring the new General Motors in Toluca: "It was worse than archaic. Worse, because it was deliberately archaic, with the obsolescence carefully built in. . . . Mexico's plants are deliberately equipped with low-production machinery."[53,54] What should we say of the gratitude Latin America owes to Coca-Cola and Pepsi, which collect astronomical industrial licensing fees from their concessionaries for providing them with a paste that dissolves in water and is mixed with sugar and carbonation?

NOTES

1. Darcy Ribeiro, *The Americas and Civilization* (New York: Dutton, 1971), 211.

2. Lewis Hanke and other authors of *Do the Americas Have a Common History?* stretch their imaginations in vain trying to find parallels between northern and southern historical processes.

3. Quoted in Andre Gunder Frank, *Capitalism and Underdevelopment in Latin America* (New York and London: Monthly Review Press, 1967), 164, and retranslated from the Spanish.

4. Edward C. Kirkland, *A History of American Economic Life* (1932; reprint ed., New York: Appleton, 1969).

5. Celso Furtado, *The Economic Growth of Brazil* (Berkeley: University of California Press, 1963), 109.

6. Ralph Waldo Emerson, "The American Scholar," in *The Complete Essays and Other Writings of Ralph Waldo Emerson* (New York: Modern Library, 1950), 62-63.

7. The South became an internal colony of Northern capitalists. After the war, propaganda for spinning-mill construction in the two Carolinas, Georgia, and Alabama assumed the dimension of a crusade. But this was no victory for a moral cause, and no pure humanitarianism fathered the new industries; the South offered cheaper labor and power and soaring profits, sometimes amounting to 75 percent. Capital flowed from the North to tie

the South to the system's center of gravity. The tobacco industry, concentrated in North Carolina, was directly under the Duke trust, headquartered in New Jersey to take advantage of more favorable laws; in 1907 Tennessee Coal & Iron, which exploited Alabama's iron and coal, came under the control of U.S. Steel, which from then on arranged prices and thus eliminated irksome competition. At the beginning of our century the South's per capita income had fallen to half of what it was before the Civil War. [See C. Vann Woodward, *Origins of the New South, 1879-1913* (Baton Rouge: Louisiana State University Press, 1951).]

8. This testimony appeared in the report of a parliamentary commission investigating transactions between national and foreign enterprises, dated September 6, 1968. Soon afterward Campos published a curious interpretation of the Peruvian government's nationalist stance. According to him, the Velasco Alvarado government's expropriation of Standard Oil was mo more than an "exhibition of masculinity." The only objective of nationalism, he wrote, is to satisfy the human being's primitive need for hate. However, he added that "pride does not generate investments or increase the flow of capital . . ." [*O Globo*, February 25, 1969.]

9. Fernando Gasparian in *Correio da Manhã*, May 1, 1968.

10. *International Commerce*, February 3, 1963, 21.

11. *Ibid.*, July 17, 1967, 10.

12. For example, in Uruguay, the text of the contract signed on May 21, 1963, between the IDB and the Montevideo departmental government for the extension of water mains.

13. For example, in Bolivia, the text of the contract signed on April 1, 1966, between the IDB and San Simón University, Cochabamba, to improve the teaching of agricultural sciences.

14. This document was published in the daily *Ya* (Montevideo), May 28, 1970.

15. *Panorama* (Centro de Estudios y Documentación Sociales, Mexico), November-December 1965.

16. The Duvalier dictatorship was also promised, as a token of gratitude, a road out to the airport. Several authors agree that this was a case of bribery. [Irving Pflaum, *Arena of Decision: Latin American Crisis* (Englewood Cliff, N.J.: Prentice Hall, 1964); John Gerassi, *The Great Fear in Latin America* (New York: Macmillan, 1965)]. But the United States did not keep its promise to Haiti, and "Papa Doc" Duvalier, guardian of death in voodoo mythology, felt he had been swindled. The old sorcerer is said to have invoked the Devil's aid to bring vengeance on President Kennedy, and to have smiled contentedly when the bullets in Dallas felled the president.

17. Georgie Anne Geyer, in *Miami Herald*, December 24, 1966.

18. Statement to a House of representatives subcommittee, cited in Nelson Werneck Sodré, *História Militar do Brasil* (Rio de Janeiro, 1965).

19. Frederick B. Pike, *The Modern History of Peru* (New York: Praeger, 1967), 319.

20. David Rockefeller's daughter Peggy decided shortly afterward to go and live in a Rio de Janeiro *favela* called Jacarezinho. Her father, one of the world's richest men, went to Brazil to look after his multimillion-dollar affairs and personally visited the humble family house Peggy had chosen; he sampled the modest dinner and discovered with alarm that the house leaked and rats entered under the door. On his departure he left a check with a string of zeros on the table. Peggy lived there for some months, collaborating with the Peace Corps. The checks kept coming in, each one worth as much as the master of the house could earn by ten years' work. When Peggy finally left, the Jacarezinho house and family had been transformed. Never had the *favela* known such opulence. Peggy had come straight from heaven. It was like having won all the lotteries at once. The master of the house then became the mascot of the regime. TV and radio reportage, newspaper and magazine articles, publicity ran wild: the man was a model whom all Brazilians should

imitate. He had emerged from poverty thanks to his indomitable will to work and his capacity to save: look, look, he doesn't spend what he earns on booze, and now he has a TV, a refrigerator, new furniture, shoes for the kids! The propaganda left out one detail: the visit of Peggy, the fairy godmother. Brazil has ninety million inhabitants and the miracle had been performed for only one of them.

21. Hinckenlooper Amendment, Section 620 of the Foreign Assistance Act.

22. It is no accident that this legal text explicitly refers to measures adopted against U.S. interests "on January 1, 1962, or a later date." On February 16, 1962, Governor Leonel Brizola had expropriated the phone company, a subsidiary of ITT, in the Brazilian state of Rio Grande do Sul, and this had hardened relations between Washington and Brasilia. The firm did not accept the indemnity proposed by the government.

23. *International Commerce*, April 10, 1967, 44.

24. *NACLA Newsletter* (New York), May-June 1970.

25. ADELA Annual Report, quoted in *ibid*.

26. Harry Magdoff, *The Age of Imperialism* (New York: Monthly Review Press, 1968), 145-146.

27. World Bank, IFC, IDA, *Policies and Operations* (Washington, D.C., 1962).

28. According to Black, "Foreign aid stimulates the development of new overseas markets for U.S. companies and orients national economies toward a free enterprise system in which U.S. private firms can prosper." [Eugene R. Black, "The Domestic Dividends of Foreign Aid," *Columbia Journal of World Business*, no. 1, 1965, 23.]

29. ECLA, *Economic Survey of Latin America, 1968*, 1969.

30. In the three years 1966–1968, coffee earned Colombia 64 percent of its total export income, Brazil 43 percent, El Salvador 48 percent, Guatemala 42 percent, and Costa Rica 36 percent. Bananas earned 61 percent of its foreign currency for Ecuador, 54 percent for Panama, and 47 percent for Honduras. Nicaragua depended 42 percent on cotton, the Dominican Republic 56 percent on sugar. Meat, hides, and wool brought Uruguay and Argentina 83 percent and 38 percent respectively of their foreign currency. Copper was responsible for 74 percent of Chile's commercial income and for 26 percent of Peru's; for Bolivia tin represented 54 percent of the value of its exports, and 93 percent of Venezuela's foreign currency came from petroleum. [*Ibid.*]

As for Mexico, it "depends more than 30 percent on three products, more than 40 percent on five products, and more than 50 percent on ten products, mostly unmanufactured and having their main outlet in the U.S. market." [Pablo González Casanova, *La Democtacia en México* (Mexico, 1965).

31. Marco D. Poller, in INTAL/BID, *Los empresarios y la integración de América Latina* (Buenos Aires, 1967).

32. Central Única de Trabajadores de Chile, *América Latina, un mundo que ganar* (Santiago de Chile, 1968).

33. Arghiri Emmanuel, *Unequal Exchange* (New York: Monthly Review Press, 1972).

34. Samir Amin, *L'accumulation à l'échelle mondiale* (Paris, 1970).

35. *New York Times*, April 3, 1968.

36. OAS Secretariat-General, *El financiamiento externo para el desarrollo de la América Latina* (Washington, 1969); restricted document of the Sixth Annual Meeting of the Inter-American Economic and Social Council at the Ministerial Level.

37. A thorough survey of U.S. subsidiaries in Mexico, made for the National Chamber Foundation in 1969, showed that half the concerns answering the questionnaire were barred by their U.S. head offices from selling their products abroad. The affiliates had not been set up for that. [Miguel S. Wionczek, "La inversión extranjera privada en México: problemas y perspectivas," *Comercio exterior* (Mexico), October 1970.]

The relation between exports of manufactures and gross industrial product did not exceed 2 percent in 1963 in Argentina, Brazil, Peru, Colombia, and Ecuador; it was 3.7 percent in Mexico and 3.2 percent in Chile. [Aldo Ferrer in INTAL/BID, *Los empresarios*.]

38. *Jornal do Comercio* (Rio de Janeiro), March 23, 1950.

39. Celso Furtado, *Um projeto para o Brasil* (Rio de Janeiro, 1968).

40. *International Commerce*, April 24, 1967.

41. Ismael Viñas and Eugenio Gastiazoro, *Economía y dependencia, 1900–1918* (Buenos Aires, 1968).

42. Antonio García, "Las constelaciones del poder y el desarrollo latinoamericano," *Comercio exterior*, November 1969.

43. The mechanism is certainly not new. The Anglo meatpacking plant has always run at a loss in Uruguay in order to get subsidies from the state and pyramid the profits of its six thousand London butcher shops, where each pound of Uruguayan meat sells for four times the price at which Uruguay exports it. [Guillermo Bernhard, *Los monopolios y la industria frigorífica* (Montevideo, 1970)].

44. Statement made by President Salvador Allende as reported in Agence France Presse dispatch, December 12, 1970.

45. *La Razón* (Buenos Aires), March 2, 1970.

46. "Resultados de indústria automobilística," special study in *Cojuntura econômica*, February 1969.

47. *NACLA Newsletter*, April–May 1969.

48. Miguel S. Wionczek, "La transmission de la tecnología a los países en desarrollo: proyecto de un estudio sobre México," *Comercio exterior*, May 1968.

49. Manuel Sadosky, "América Latina y la computación," *Gaceta de la Universidad* (Montevideo), May 1970.

50. To illustrate the nature of the developmental illusion, Sadosky cites the testimony of an OAS specialist: "'The underdeveloped countries,' says George Landau, 'have some advantages over developed countries became when they introduce some new process or technique they usually select the most advanced of its type, and thus reap the benefit of years of investigation and the fruit of considerable investments that more industrialized countries had to make to achieve those results.'"

51. Quoted in Gustavo Lagos et al., *Las inversions multinacionales en el desarrollo y la integración de América Latina* (Bogota, 1968).

52. Raúl Prebisch, "La cooperación internacional en el desarrollo latinoamericano," *Desarrollo* (Bogota), January 1970.

53. Leo Fenster in *The Nation*, July 2, 1969.

54. The foreign affiliates are, however, far more modern than the national enterprises. For example, in the textile industry – one of the last bastions of national capital—the Degree of automation is abysmally low. According to ECLA reports, in 1962 and 1963 four European countries invested six times more in new equipment for their textile industries than all of Latin America invested for that purpose in 1964.

Change and Development—Latin America's Great Task: Report Submitted to the Inter-American Development Bank (1970)

Raúl Prebisch

Raúl Prebisch (Argentina, 1901–1986) was an Argentine economist known for his contribution to structuralist economics, in particular the Prebisch-Singer hypothesis that formed the basis of economic dependency theory. Originally defending the free-trade orthodoxy, after witnessing the 1930s collapse of the Argentine economy due to the Depression and the growing economic dominance of the U.S., Prebisch converted to protectionism and the economics of John Maynard Keynes. From 1923 to 1948 he was professor of political economy at the National University of Buenos Aires. He was the mastermind behind the founding of the Central Bank of Argentina and its first Director-General (1935–1943). From 1948 to 1963 he was Executive Secretary of the United Nations Economic Commission for Latin America (ECLA). Under his leadership ECLA became the center of Third World activism in the UN, giving birth to the Latin American school of structuralist economics. At ECLA, Prebisch became firmly associated with import substitution industrialization (ISI), in which a nation isolates itself from trade and tries to industrialize using only its domestic market as an engine. Between 1964 and 1969 he served as the founding Secretary-General of the United Nations Conference on Trade and Development (UNCTAD). Selected for his unparalleled reputation, he tried to forge UNCTAD into a body advocating the case of the whole developing world. His approach to development took a more trade-focused approach, advocating preferential access to the markets of developed countries and regional integration—building up trade between peripheral countries. From 1969 to 1972 he was Director-General of the United Nations Latin American Institute for Economic and Social Planning. After 1972 he remained a United Nations economic advisor. In 1975 he became editor-in-chief of the newly created CEPAL (ECLA) Review. In 1983 he returned to Argentina to collaborate with the newly elected democratic government of Raúl Alfonsín at the end of the seven-year period of military dictatorship. This selection presents a report with general policy recommendations on a process of economic development in Latin America, marked by unevenness, sluggishness, excessive dependence on external financial support, and hostage to the shortsightedness and immediatism of the policies and interests of the international community and the local business elites.

INTRODUCTION

The Lack of the Required Degree of Dynamism

Spurious Absorption of Manpower

This report is geared to action. For the Latin American countries can no longer put off the decision to take deliberate steps to influence the course of their economic and social development if they are to overcome serious handicaps which the passage of time is more likely to aggravate than to remedy.

In reality, the region has not as yet been able to cope with the contradictions which the march of science and technology brings in its train along with the far-reaching possibilities of human welfare that it opens up.

These contradictions, whose implications have become increasingly apparent in the last two decades, include the inconsistency between the population explosion and the factors limiting capital formation. For this and other reasons, only a part of the economically active population is productively absorbed. A very high proportion constitutes redundant manpower in the rural areas, where the surplus labor force has been and still is large; and the migrants from the rural areas who constantly pour into the bigger towns merely shift the scene of their redundancy.[1] In their new environment, they needlessly swell the motley ranks of the services sector, in which a substantial proportion of the natural increase in the urban labor force itself is also skirmishing for jobs. Thus the result is a spurious rather than a genuine absorption of manpower, if not unemployment pure and simple.

This phenomenon is characteristic of the Latin American economy's lack of the required degree of dynamism. Its rate of development has been too slow to meet the peremptory demands deriving from the population explosion, and a huge amount of human potential is wasted in one way or another, to the detriment of economic growth, equitable income distribution, and social harmony.

Disparities in income distribution date back for centuries in Latin America, and privilege is deeply rooted in the region's history. During the phase of outward-looking development which preceded the world depression of the 1930's, no solution of the problem was forthcoming; on the contrary, the increases in income which development brought in its train, and which in many countries were substantial, were concentrated in the few hands that already held land and wealth in their grasp. Since then, in the phase of development which has continued up to the present time, the effects of the process have undeniably been more widely spread out; although it is also true that new patterns of concentration of wealth and income have emerged. Those at the top of the social pyramid have conspicuously prospered; the urban middle strata, too, have increased in size and have raised their level of living, although less than might have been the case, and far from enough to satisfy their growing consumption aspirations. But the benefits of development have hardly touched the broad masses relegated to the lower income strata. The percentage of the population represented by the last-named groups may possibly have diminished, although precise data to substantiate such an assertion are lacking. In any event, they still constitute as much as about 60 percent of Latin America's total population, both in rural and in urban areas, although the proportions vary from one country to another. They would seem to have decreased in relative terms; but at the same time the gap between the lower and upper strata has widened.

Nor is this all. The advances made in mass communication techniques—almost inconceivable in bygone days—are giving rise to new phenomena, the scope of whose implications defies prediction. The broad masses of Latin America's rural population, formerly cut off by the illiteracy which debarred them from access to books and newspapers, are swiftly becoming receptive to the radio and the television, which bring them nearer and nearer to the beguiling mirage of city life. Beguiling at first, only to prove later on a hotbed of tormenting frustration: the frustration bred of social marginality in the larger towns.[2] It is not just a matter of consumption aspirations. There is something of greater social and political significance. The rural and urban masses are awakening to consciousness of their long-forgotten dignity as human beings, of their pathetic relegation to ways of life long left behind by the peoples of the developed countries.

The social integration of these stranded masses is of primary importance. It is a question of fair distribution. Let there be no misunderstanding, however. Redistribution measures alone will not suffice. The income distribution pattern is defective, and could undoubtedly be amended to some extent in existing circumstances. But there will be no substantial and lasting improvement unless the rate of development is speeded up.

Economic considerations are not necessarily at variance with social needs, but when growth is sluggish, distribution is almost always unsatisfactory. The practice of social equity calls for a vigorous rate of development, as well as for the political art of distribution, a delicate business in itself.

The Occupational Structure and the Waste of Human Potential

It is common knowledge that the migration of manpower from the countryside to the towns has always been a spontaneous product of development, whatever the economic and social system in force; and equally well-known is the importance of the dynamic role that industry, construction, and mining[3] are called upon to play in the productive absorption of the labor force from the rural areas. In Latin America they have failed to do their part in this respect, at any rate during the last two decades. Only two countries are exceptions to the rule, and for very different reasons in each case.

If the production of goods in all these nonagricultural activities absorbs fewer people than it should, and employment in services increases disproportionately, a serious imbalance inevitably supervenes: the proportion of the labor force that wishes to consume such goods expands beyond all reasonable bounds, while the proportion that produces them shrinks to an abnormal extent.

The scale on which this is happening is truly disconcerting; an approximate idea of it can be obtained from a glance at fig 11.1, which clearly shows how the

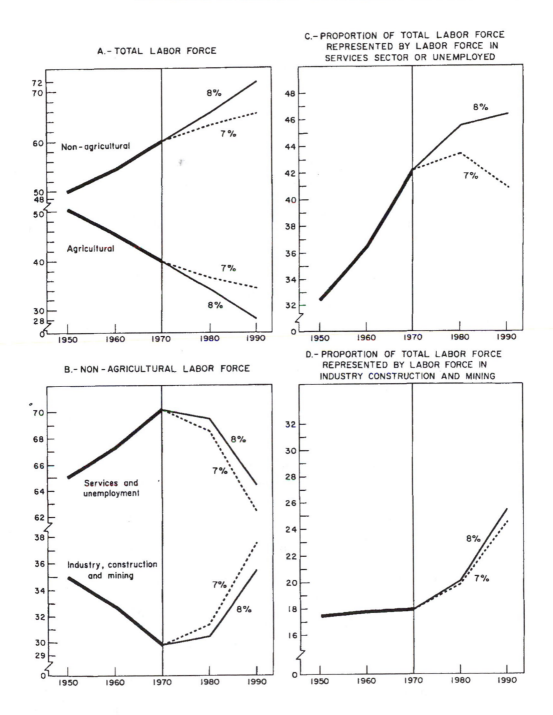

Figure 11.1: Group of Countries Considered: Distribution of the Labor Force (percentages). *Source:* ECLA, on the basis of official data.

proportion of the economically active population working in the industry group steadily declines instead of rising, whereas the opposite is the case in the services sector, where the spurious absorption of redundant manpower occurs, and part of the labor force is left jobless altogether. It is essential to correct this distortion of the occupational structure by reversing the trends described.

The mere correction of the occupational structure of the labor force would have highly important consequences. Suffice it to reflect that the attainment of this objective, by means of a more rapid rate of capital formation and the fulfillment of other requirements, would mean that the annual growth rate of the aggregate product would have risen to 7 percent by the end of the current decade, instead of the average of 5.2 percent recorded in 1950–1969. The average annual growth rate of the per capita product would thus increase from 2.5 percent to 3.9 percent. Even so, it would take a very long time and a still more rapid rate of growth of the aggregate product for the lack of dynamism to be remedied completely.

Exceptional significance attaches to this projection. It must be borne in mind that for demonstration purposes the calculation was based on the assumption—afterward discarded—that neither in agriculture nor in the industry group would the growth rate of the product per worker be more rapid than in the past. To achieve these remarkable results, productive occupation of the redundant manpower migrating from the rural areas would be enough.

The explanation of this vital fact is well-known. In agriculture, the average product per active person is very low, or purely nominal; and the employment of former agricultural workers in the industry group, where the average product per active person is much higher, suffices in itself to bring about an appreciable rise in the product of the whole economy.

The problem of the enormous loss of income sustained by the Latin American countries on this account derives not only from that proportion of the active population which leaves the agricultural sector and is not productively absorbed elsewhere, but also from the redundant manpower remaining in agriculture. The reduction of the agricultural labor force will have to continue as the product per worker increases through more efficient use of the land and through technical progress. Hence it will become even more imperatively necessary to give powerful impetus to the development of the industry group.

The idea of placing the emphasis on agriculture and paying little attention to industry is dying hard; but is is indefensible in the light of the foregoing considerations. The industry group needs to develop much more intensively than before in order to fulfill one of its principal dynamic functions, as well as to provide the manufactured goods required for speeding up development.

Incidentally, the exodus of agricultural workers is inevitable if the level of living of the rural masses is to be raised. What is not inevitable is the appalling congestion in the big towns, due mainly to this population shift. In this as in other respects, the Latin American countries are suffering some of the drawbacks of the development process in advance, long before they have reaped its benefits. In the present instance, the disadvantage they have to combat is that of overconcentration in the larger towns. This again is not an ill that can be left to remedy itself. Quite the contrary. It will have to be tackled with a determination of which no categorical evidence has yet been given by the Latin American countries—not even by those in which this social evil is most flagrant.

Social Integration and the Domestic Market

The social integration of the lower income groups in the course of development must now be understood in its true significance, as a highly important element in a process of structural change which would considerably improve the income levels of the groups in question. As has already been stated, these lower strata comprise about 60 percent of the population of Latin America. Victimized as they are by the social inequity with which the economic system operates, the consumption of the members of these groups is meager in relation to their rapidly multiplying numbers. According to conjectural estimates, not even as much as 20 percent of the total supply of manufactured goods reaches their hands.

The integration of these lower strata is a pressing social necessity. It is also an economic need, for it will extend the frontiers of Latin America's industrial development process. This is the only alternative that the dynamics of development affords. The growth of industry can no longer depend, as it did before, on import substitution alone. The fruit has been squeezed too hard by now for the flow of juice to be as plentiful as at first. New solutions, new markets must now be sought. There is a potential market of which scarcely any advantage is taken: that of the underprivileged masses. But their social integration is the only means of opening it up.

The frontiers of industrial expansion will be extended, inasmuch as the absorption of redundant manpower in industry—together with the improvement of the income levels of the rural population—will generate a considerable and continuing demand for manufactured goods, and will also give a vigorous fillip to demand for agricultural products, at present largely pent up by the poverty of the lower income groups. Thus agriculture and industry will derive a more powerful stimulus from their reciprocal demand and will give each other mutual support, propagating their growth throughout the rest of the economy.

Such is the significance of the social integration of the underprivileged masses. The task is one that cannot be postponed, but this does not mean that it can be accomplished independently of others. It is frequently argued that this internal social integration must first be achieved, and then industrial integration at the Latin American level. A great mistake. Internal integration calls for the acceleration of development. And for that a sine qua non is the integration of the dynamic industries at the Latin American level, in default of which it will be impossible to ease the external constraint that is slowing up economic expansion. This in no way belittles the importance of other measures designed to assist in correcting regional disequilibria within individual countries themselves.

The Progress of Science and Technology, and Its Contradictions

Clearly, then, development must be speeded up. The task is much more difficult than that with which the advanced countries were faced in their own development process. For although the spectacular progress achieved by science and technology in the developed countries opens up broader prospects of human betterment for the Latin American countries—of which full advantage must be taken to further our development—it is in fact attended by grave contradictions which did not arise in former times, or at any rate not to such a marked degree. The population explosion, of course, is one of the striking consequences of the progress in question. In order to cope with it, capital formation on a very large scale is required, both because of the increasing numbers for whom work must be provided, and because the technology originating in the great industrial centers entails a steadily rising capital/worker ratio.

This difficulty is aggravated by another of the effects of scientific and technical progress, which unremittingly militates against capital formation. The higher income strata in the Latin American societies are prone to imitate the living patterns of their counterparts in the developed countries; and thanks to the ever-increasing might of mass communication media, these living patterns are forcing their way into the lower income groups, whose members are incessantly confronted with the alluring image of a consumer society to which their strained means deny them access.

Thus, the advance of science and technology has conflicting implications which are likely to widen the disparity between population growth and capital formation. Moreover, it adversely affects Latin America's export trade and helps to generate the persistent tendency toward an external bottleneck.

The Acceleration of Development and the Obstacles in its Way

The March of Ideas in the International Field

The conflicting implications of scientific and technological progress partly explain why the dynamic impetus of the Latin American economy falls short of what is required. They are reflected in a number of internal and external factors which, within the context of the existing economic and social structure, have done much to hold back the development process. In the present report, however, the accent is placed on the internal factors of development, whose fundamental importance we do not always explicitly acknowledge when these problems are discussed at the international level. It is essential to restore the balance, although what is said of them here will certainly help—praise be!—to rekindle the flames of controversy.

With regard to the external factors that cramp development and the action that can be taken to influence them, controversy is already bearing fruit. Ideas which were considered inadmissible until only a short time ago are now infiltrating into circles where they used to be labeled unrealistic, if not flagrantly irresponsible. Such ideas, which had been evolving and establishing themselves in the developing countries, and particularly in Latin America, were crystallized in the United Nations Conference on Trade and Development (UNCTAD), and are now among the many important concepts and recommendations embodied in the Pearson Report.[4] Thus they are endorsed by the moral authority and intellectual prestige of the Report's authors, who deserve great credit for their sponsorship. The only trouble is that in the meantime some of these ideas have been left behind by the demands of an increasingly complicated set of circumstances. This, however, does not detract from the great significance of the document. Highly important, likewise, is the recent report on the Second Development Decade prepared by the United Nations committee of experts under the chairmanship of Professor Jan Tinbergen.[5] He is one of the few eminent economists in the northern hemisphere who long ago grasped the nature of these problems and the need to tackle them on the basis of a carefully concerted strategy. A man of deep convictions, Professor Tinbergen will beyond all doubt continue his unflagging work of persuasion. Another noteworthy report is that prepared by Professor Isaiah Frank,[6] who had already adopted a highly constructive approach to these questions. A report still more recently submitted to the United States Government[7] also vigorously defends some of the primary aspirations of the developing countries, although unfortunately it does not set up a target for financial cooperation.

Thus, more and more outstanding figures in the advanced countries are espousing the cause of effective international cooperation in the development of the Third World. As far as they are concerned, we have no need to preach to the converted. But the progress achieved on the intellectual plane does not warrant complacency. Considerable energy will still have to be expended if the conviction felt by men like these is to be communicated to the policy-makers who have to take the major decisions which international cooperation entails. The path is beset with formidable obstacles, and in my view it will be difficult, if not impossible, to forge ahead unless the efforts made in this direction are given definite support.

This does not mean mere praise and appreciation. The Latin American countries must give manifest proof of their unhesitating determination to effect basic structural changes and adopt new attitudes, and to apply a rigorous and socially meaningful discipline of development; and this determination must be reflected in a strategy with clearly defined objectives. Such is the firm foundation on which international cooperation should rest.

The time has come to shake off the all too common habit of attributing the inadequacy of Latin America's rate of development to external factors alone, as though there were no major internal stumbling blocks in the way. We must fully recognize our own responsibility. While development strategy is undeniably our countries' own internal business, it is equally true that international cooperation policy is an internal affair of the advanced countries; "at the international level" is only an abstract term. In reality, development calls for a number of convergent measures which must be adopted by both groups of countries if it is universally acknowledged that the problem is common to all.

There can be no more convincing proof of the need for such convergent action than the testimony of past experience. In reviewing it here, the aim has been to draw lessons from it rather than to demarcate areas of responsibility. The matter is of such importance that it is worth while to insert a few remarks here, in anticipation of its fuller treatment in a later chapter.

Financial Cooperation and Internal Development Policy

International financial cooperation has failed to play as dynamic a role as might have been expected, not only because its volume has been insufficient and its terms unsatisfactory, but also because of basic flaws in the development policy of the Latin American countries themselves.

Owing to this combination of external and internal factors, the funds received from abroad have not served to promote more intensive mobilization of the region's own resources. The direct effects of investment of these funds are not denied; but in none of the countries on which data were available for the purposes of the present study[8]—and which account for nearly 90 percent of Latin America's total product—has the coefficient of investment with domestic resources increased to any marked extent. On the contrary, it has tended to decrease in the region as a whole, and in some of the individual countries the decline is striking. But part of the explanation lies in the neglect of internal measures which might effectively have counteracted the unfavorable influence of this and other external factors.

The burden of amortization and reimbursement of foreign capital has been very heavy, and so has that of interest, although to a lesser degree. It is estimated that total annual service payments on public international funds alone are equivalent to 19 percent of the debt outstanding. There is no economy in existence—however great its potential—that could withstand such pressure with impunity. And it addition, account must be taken of the adverse effects of the deterioration in the terms of trade which has taken place during the greater part of the last two decades. These outflows have represented a heavy drain on internal investment resources. All these issues are discussed in due course in the present report, together with the question of private foreign investment.

Suffice it to point out here that private foreign investment, along with its favorable aspects, involves a number of problems which, in order to work out ways and means of living in economic and political harmony with the developed countries, must be examined from a completely objective viewpoint. In the context of these problems, it is impossible to disregard the concern aroused in Latin America by certain forms of foreign investment which in some cases have an adverse effect on the balance of payments; in others, instead of helping Latin American enterprise to make up its financial and technological leeway, they are more liable to keep it indefinitely at a disadvantage; and in others again, they introduce new patterns of dependence which are at variance with the fundamental concept of autonomy in development.

It is only fair to recognize that the unfavorable impact of such situations on the coefficient of investment with domestic resources might have been less if the persistently expansionist trend of consumption—especially in the higher and middle income groups—had been restrained.

In short, for international financing to have played the dynamic role expected of it, it would have had to be granted on a much larger scale and on reasonable terms; and internal measures would have had to be adopted to ensure the progressive growth of investment with domestic resources.

The decisive importance of this latter requisite must be stressed from the outset. Latin America has not succeeded in dealing satisfactorily with its capital formation problem. If the next few years are to witness a transition to a satisfactory rate of development, investment with domestic resources will have to increase faster than consumption. To allow a considerable external debt to pile up, without energetically promoting the mobilization of the region's own resources until the point was reached at which they could fully meet capital formation requirements, would be to invite deplorable consequences.

Unless Latin America makes a strenuous investment effort, it will be unable to remedy the economy's lack of dynamism and the social ills inherent in it. External cooperation is important, but only as a means of supplementing and stimulating internal action, not as a substitute for it. Any other formula is inconceivable and, moreover, would be self-defeating from the economic standpoint and politically inadmissible.

Of great importance also is the role that financial resources from abroad are called upon to play in the gradual elimination of the external bottleneck. Here again they have failed to do their part. On the contrary, the burden of interest and amortization payments makes matters worse, since it has shown a disquieting increase in proportion to the purchasing power of exports and the saving of foreign exchange achieved through import substitution.

For this and other reasons, resolute action in respect to foreign trade is essential. The great industrial centers have left the countries of Latin America, like the other developing countries, to drift along as best they can. They have made no basic moves to offset the adverse influence exerted by their technical progress, directly or indirectly, on Latin America's export trade. Rather, they have erected what in some instances are formidable barriers. But this is yet another case in which the blame must not be laid solely on external factors, for Latin America could have done much more than it has to relieve the external bottleneck. Export opportunities have often been missed because of the negative effects of certain measures, or for want of a policy of steady encouragement.

Still more serious is the waste of Latin America's considerable intraregional trade potential. It is true that the expansion revealed by the relevant figures is by no means negligible; but at the same time, little has been done in the field of industrial integration agreements relating to the intermediate and capital goods for which demand tends to boom as development advances.[9]

The Latin American countries have left undone many of those things which they ought to have done in the past 20 years. And the developed countries—in particular the United States—have failed to do what might have been expected of them. There has been a want of concerted action reflecting—without the slightest suggestion of pressure from above or of paternalism—a definite consensus with respect to the attainment of certain development objectives and the nature, scale, and scope of the measures required for attaining them. This is the unequivocal lesson of the past. The inadequate and incompatible measures that have been adopted at the international level cannot be called strategy. To transfer far less resources than are needed and yet be in a hurry to recover them is manifestly inconsistent; and so is hampering the export trade which must provide the means of making interest and amortization payments and meeting the large-scale import requirements attendant upon the development process.

Nowadays all this can be clearly seen. Formerly, perhaps, it was not so plain. Hence the value of past experience. To fail to take advantage of it in facing the future would be inexcusable today. The present report, I hope, will help to guard against such neglect. It is motivated not only by a hankering for elucidation—a worthwhile end in itself—but, above all, by the conviction that the Latin American countries can no longer put off deciding in favor of deliberate and farsighted action to influence the forces of development. They must draw up their own strategy and define their common denominators and their patterns of concerted action, both in the sphere of their relations with the developed countries and in that of their relations with one another, where much of great importance can and must be done.

Time Is No Panacea

The acceleration of development demands sweeping changes in structures and in mental attitudes. They are essential if technical progress is to be assimilated, its advantages turned to account, its contradictions resolved, and its adverse effects counteracted; and essential also for the promotion of social mobility, both for its own sake and because it too is one of the indispensable requirements of technological progress. Social mobility is not merely a matter of general education and technical training; it is a basic question of structures.

I think it my duty to speak very frankly in this report. Latin America stands in need of the changes to which I refer—with all due acknowledgment of the reforms already introduced—and it likewise needs a development discipline which has rarely existed, and when it has been applied has seldom lasted long.

Such a discipline is indispensable in order that the region may enter upon a new stage of development, since the dynamic impetus of the present phase has gradually slackened. Powerful expansionist forces exist, but they are being obstructed; a determined effort must be made to clear the way for them. What has been achieved by virtue of these forces is no good reason for going on as hitherto. There is no room for complacency in Latin America. It is often displayed in face of striking evidence of progress. The impressive growth of the region's cities, their remarkable degree of modernization, the development and diversification of their industries are sometimes taken as irrefutable proof of an encouraging process of development. It is forgotten, however, that the urban activities have shown themselves incapable of fully and productively absorbing the manpower increment, and that this and other circumstances are generating increasingly acute social tensions. It is forgotten, likewise, that the progress made in urban areas has not spread to the countryside and that, on the contrary, it is the countryside that is invading the towns. The emissaries of this movement are people who have broken loose from their own economic and social constellations without becoming properly incorporated into the urban setting. All they do is to transfer their poverty-stricken way of life to the wretched shanty towns in which the marginal population of the cities takes refuge.

The progress of the urban areas should promise a steady improvement in conditions of well-being which have been attained only in part, and their extension to those broad strata of the population to which they have not yet spread in any appreciable measure.

If all these ills are to be remedied, it is essential to accelerate development. This report will have served its purpose if it carries conviction of the necessity and possibility of doing so: a conviction which must be implanted both inside and outside Latin America.

The developed countries do not always understand this need to speed up the rate of development. It has averaged 5.2 percent yearly over the past two decades, with wide intercountry disparities. This figure cannot be described as modest in itself, since it is similar to that recorded in recent times by the developed countries in the private-enterprise group. What is more, their rates of development in the past were usually lower than those of Latin America.

Why such impatience, then? Why try to force the pace of events? If the countries now at advanced stages of development took a long time to get where they are, why should not the Latin American countries keep to the same rhythm? Cannot time perhaps solve their problems too?

Questions such as these are frequently asked at international meetings and in academic discussions, although less often than used to be the case. I hope the answer may be found in the present report. For it is highly important that in international circles—and particularly in the United States—full awareness of Latin America's problem should exist. It is a problem that we shall have to solve ourselves, in one way or another; but it so happens that the way matters a great deal, and may be considerably influenced by the international cooperation policy pursued in the coming decades. The economy's lack of the required dynamism cannot be made good by the mere passage of time. And the longer the time that is allowed to go by, the harder this weakness will be to cure, and the greater will be the social and political cost, or, in a word, the cost in human terms.

Development Options and International Cooperation

Immediatism at the International Level

The times we live in do not seem particularly favorable to a policy of international cooperation. Immediatism—that is, the desire (very understandable from the political standpoint) to show quick results—generally prevails over long-term policy in the Latin American countries, and has also predominated in the attitude of the developed countries toward international cooperation. There is something more in this than short-term pressures exerted by narrow economic or political interests. It is an increasingly striking fact that countries which have made giant strides in technology have not managed to forestall the attendant evils. Too much trust has been placed in the spontaneous forces of the economy, and there has been a want of farsighted policies capable of overriding the interaction of those forces where they could not operate effectively. They can do much, but not everything. This is being recognized nowadays; and the idea of consciously looking ahead, which used to be entertained very little or not at all, is progressively gaining ground. But it has not yet extended to relationships with the developing countries; it is not being crystallized in a policy of genuine international cooperation.

It was not foresight that motivated certain attitudes which favored the developing countries during the iciest spell of the Cold War. They found expression mainly in temporary expedients, seldom dictated by a broad strategy in which economic and social development played a basic and continuing part.

It is certainly true that the Cold War has had its repercussions in Latin America. But it would be a grave mistake to ascribe to them the role that events themselves have been playing, and will continue to play to an ever-increasing extent if the rate of development remains the same as in the past. I have no belief whatever in the incoercible determinism of events, for the simple reason that there is great development potential in this part of the world: a potential that consists of human as well as natural resources. Creativeness abounds, and finds expression in a wide variety of ways. Latin America has great vitality. But its creative impulses are held in check, and their power to stimulate economic expansion is fettered.

Herein lie the great problem and the great open question with which Latin America is faced. The problem is that of releasing these expansionist forces by means of changes in structures and mental attitudes, and taking conscious and deliberate steps to influence them. And the open question is whether this will be done in time, and whether it will be possible to rely upon an equally timely, as well as energetic and enlightened, policy of international cooperation.

Two Forms of Development

The transition from a relatively low rate of development with little social significance to one which will give the economy the requisite dynamic impetus and will be socially meaningful entails a considerable effort: an effort to bring about structural changes and to adopt an authentic development discipline, especially in respect of capital formation and the promotion of foreign trade. This is inevitable. If strong opposition to a conscious and deliberate discipline is put up, development by coercion in one form or another will be the ultimate outcome. For frustration is no alternative, whether it be the frustration of a policy of laissez-aller or the frustration of populism. One good point about the latter is that it has uncovered major social ills and has aroused legitimate aspirations for the social integration of the masses. In the absence of strong convictions, however, and in default of a well-knit system of ideas, populism resorts to the unfailing device of using emotion in order to exalt charismatic figures. It sidesteps difficult problems and puts immediatism in respect of income redistribution before the need for overall changes, before the basic solutions demanded by development.

Populism, therefore, is not an acceptable alternative to a development discipline. Such a discipline is an essential requisite for the considerable capital formation effort required in order to give the economy the additional dynamism it needs. It is not conceivable—must less desirable—that this should be done mainly with foreign capital. A great internal effort will be an imperative and inescapable necessity. Will it be possible without recourse to compulsion?

The reply depends not only upon the political art of development, the ability to tackle basic problems and combine immediate expedients with long-term measures, but also upon international cooperation. In a strategy for the acceleration of development there is a difficult but decisive initial phase: that of preparing the economy for the capital formation process to be put into effect without undue tensions. What is needed is a large-scale contribution of financial resources from abroad, to stimulate the rapid expansion of the economy through the utilization of idle or inefficiently used resources and other internal measures converging toward the same goal. Obviously, when the economy expands in this way, it becomes less difficult to promote capital formation without sacrificing consumption beyond certain limits.

This is the initial dynamic role of international financial cooperation: to act as a spur to domestic capital formation. With that end in view, the terms on which it is extended would have to be very different from those offered in the past.

I have no wish to put forward arguments in this report which might appear to detract from its sobriety. But I cannot attempt to hide the growing concern felt in Latin America, and among the enlightened men of the northern hemisphere to whom I have referred, with respect to the turn taken by this cooperation. I have reflected a great deal on this matter and have discussed it with people who view the facts with objective impartiality. In these discussions one question invariably arises: will the Latin American countries be able to avoid coercive methods of capital formation if external financing does not make a much bigger contribution on appropriate terms?

The experience of the socialist countries has always been followed with great interest in Latin America, although in recent times this interest has also extended to private-enterprise countries which have attained very high rates of development, in particular Japan. Perhaps the most important feature of the experience in question has been the method of capital formation. Needless to say, Marx had envisaged a different process of radical transformation of the system, one which would be ineluctably brought about by the determinism inherent in the evolution of capitalism, once a large amount of capital had been accumulated and the whole machinery of production had been concentrated in a few hands. In the specific experience of the socialist countries it was precisely this substantial accumulation of capital which did not exist, and the want had to be supplied at considerable social and political cost. In reality, socialism has been a method of development rather than a method of transforming an advanced economy.

The gradual aggravation of the ills besetting the Latin American economy is, of course, creating a propitious atmosphere for ideologies which advocate transforming the system, root and branch. But irrespective of such ideologies, the course of events might lead to the socialist method of development even if that had not been the original intention of those who set themselves to strengthen the dynamic impetus of the economic system.

The Underlying Political Assumptions

If external financing were not obtained on a large enough scale and at the right time, consumption—or its expansion—would inevitably have to be more tightly restricted in order to speed up the rate of development.[10] There would seem to be a possibility of doing this. The Latin American countries are not making the savings effort which their average per capita income would allow. And the distribution of this income is such that the restriction of consumption in the upper strata might enable the investment coefficient to be appreciably increased. The problem is quite simple from the statistical standpoint, but very difficult in actual fact. The power structure is undoubtedly a major obstacle, although not an insuperable one, since it might conceivably be changed through the political process. Even so, there would be room for doubt as to the possibility of too drastically restricting the consumption of the higher income groups without arousing strong opposition, cloaked or overt, weakening investment incentives, and precipitating the flight of capital abroad on a far greater scale than at present.

If this were to happen, if the operation of the economy were thus distorted, events themselves might impel the State to take over the very sources of income of the upper strata by a process of socialization—of the major enterprises, at least—even if no ideological considerations were involved. Ideologies would come later to justify *faits accomplis* and strengthen their significance.

This brings us to the heart of the matter. I do not wish to reiterate the time-honored arguments with respect to State enterprise. It is a different aspect of the question that I want to stress. The fact that those who had gained political power realized the need to consolidate their authority by managing public enterprises efficiently would not necessarily mean that they could do so within the ordinary system of party politics. The pressure of electoral interests has always been a factor militating against the satisfactory operation of the State machinery in Latin America. What is more, in some countries where public enterprises used to operate at a reasonable level of efficiency, the economy's lack of the required degree of dynamism has induced the State to overstaff them, to the detriment of the efficiency previously achieved.

Hence a question of decisive importance arises: whether the determination to ensure the success of this experiment is compatible with periodic party strife, with each party's constant restless anxiety—by no means inevitable—to buttress its position by granting immediate benefits which generally conflict with basic solutions. Unless this and other defects are corrected in time, nobody would have cause for wonder—however much for regret—whether the sheer force of economic circumstances succeeded in imposing patterns of political organization which, while tending to give continuity to the groups in power, would at the same time permit them a freedom of action which they would not otherwise enjoy.

These considerations do not apply solely to issues of economic management. Any system which fails to imbue the economy with the required degree of dynamism, and to promote more equitable income distribution, will have irrevocably forfeited the right to survive. The requisite remedial measures entail substantial economic and social outlays and investment. It would be hazardous to conjecture whether the savings capacity which the higher income groups are at present wasting would or would not be sufficient to meet all these requirements. It might well prove necessary to tap the resources of lower income strata, where the new ruling groups, however great their power and their moral justification, might encounter a serious obstacle: the very understandable need to put the satisfaction of pressing consumption aspirations before capital formation.

It would be unthinkable, of course, to inflict further hardship on the rural population that ekes out so precarious a livelihood, or on the underprivileged masses that have not been incorporated into the urban development process. Consequently, it would have to be the middle strata of society that were drawn into the savings effort. Given their propensity to adopt new consumption patterns, it would be very hard to curb their aspirations, and still more difficult, in case of need, to lower their present standards of consumption.

Thus the same question arises as before: can the consumption of the middle strata conceivably be affected without recourse to compulsion? Could the restrictions be persistently maintained under the system of ordinary party politics?

The objective study of these problems calls for a very explicit definition of the underlying political assumptions, especially when supreme importance is attached to the progressive strengthening of certain values and objectives which, despite setbacks and compromises in the course of the political development process, continue to hold up an ideal image as the goal of the long journey that still lies ahead of Latin America.

This is where international cooperation could play a very significant part by helping to make the initial phase of transition to a higher rate of development less hard and to prevent it from entailing the sacrifice of political convictions formerly regarded as sacrosanct. This phase of transition is inevitable whether the economic and social system merely undergoes changes or is transformed altogether, and whether the process is carried out by design or dictated by the force of circumstances themselves.

Inescapable Necessities

In any event, no system will have sufficient intrinsic virtue to evade certain necessities imposed by hard fact. A case in point is that of foreign trade. The tendency toward disequilibrium might perhaps be mitigated, but could not be corrected altogether unless the structure that hampers the export trade were progressively modified. Even socialist economies of enormous size, like the Soviet Union, have not found it possible to dispense with foreign trade; on the contrary, they are making strenuous endeavors to expand it.

Still more intensive is the effort that must be made by smaller socialist countries, such as those of Eastern Europe, with respect to trade not only with the Soviet Union, but also with the rest of the world, and particularly with the developed capitalist countries.

Where Latin America is concerned, the cost of import substitution must count for much in economic calculations, in the requirements of a rational approach, irrespective of the economic and social system in force. And the need to expand industrial as well as primary exports must arise in any event, and so must the necessity of promoting the integration of basic industries within the framework of regional or subregional agreements.

Competition, too, is an essential requisite in any case. It would not be indispensable for a country that was content to continue using its resources inefficiently, as is the general rule in Latin America at present. How, then, could productivity be rapidly increased and the levels of living of the masses improved? There is a stage at the start when enthusiasm for the construction of a new order might serve as a powerful spur to more efficient production. But later comes the need to introduce competition, with the stimulus it provides and the economic incentives attendant upon it. This is what is happening in the socialist countries at present: socialist competition in a market system which, despite its limitations, is called upon to play an important role from the standpoint both of the consumer and of the efficiency of enterprises. As I see it, socialist competition does not represent a swing back in the direction of capitalism but, rather, a quest for new modus operandi compatible with the collective ownership of the means of production.[11]

Development and "Developmentism"

All the above are issues which cannot be shirked at the present time. For Latin America must blaze new trails, must shake off the burden of the past, must shun ideological preconceptions. The lack of the required degree of dynamism is not an episodic phenomenon, but the outward and visible sign of the critical state of the phase of development which began with the great world depression of the 1930's. This phase has long since served its turn, and is now generating another crisis—and a notable one at that—especially among those of the rising generation who are beginning to concern themselves with economics and the social sciences: the crisis of "developmentism." As with all the terms that spring up in the course of ideological discussion, there is some confusion about the meaning of "developmentism." Perhaps it may be interpreted as the refusal to believe that major changes are necessary in order to accelerate the present pace of development, and the trust that social disparities will gradually be smoothed out by the dynamics of development itself. The essential thing is to develop; then we shall see! Such attitudes as these jar on the social conscience of the younger generation and of others who have long left youth behind.

Nor is this all. While those who mistrust "developmentism" do not deny the value of technology as a means of freeing mankind from the agelong burden of heavy labor, the subordination of the human factor to technology causes them extreme concern. Prevalent among them, too, is the idea of a genuinely national effort incompatible with old or new forms of dependence, in economic affairs as in intellectual life and cultural patterns. They would like to tackle the problems of man and society as a whole; and without underrating the importance of a healthy economy, they do not see it as an end in itself, but as a means—one of the means—of attaining the fullness of living, of drawing nearer to the inaccessible goal of human excellence.

It is a salutary crisis, which leads to the restatement of the problem, to a reexamination of its terms, to discussion of where the Latin American societies are going and where they ought to go: all essential prerequisites for conscious and deliberate action to influence the manifold forces of the economic and social complex. This is no light task. The easy way out afforded by privilege and makeshift expedients is no longer conceivable. Can it be that the new generations are seeking that of clinging to makeshift methods, despite the increasing intricacy of the problems they have to solve? Or do they fully recognize the imperative need for calculation and rationality in face of the constant advances of science and technology: the need to take advantage of this progress to improve the lot of the Latin American population and to fulfill designs extending beyond the economic system? Emotional impulses often override calculation. Emotion has generated great collective movements and has led men to perform memorable feats. But it would not have been possible to get very far without rationality as well. Whether the aim is to introduce such changes in the system as will give it dynamic force, or to replace it with another, rationality is in any case indispensable in man's great adventure of development.

NOTES

1. In the present report, the terms "redundant" and "redundancy" will be applied to the manpower that could be dispensed with, even on the basis of the techniques in current use, without a resulting decrease in production of goods and services. With technical progress, of course, the redundant labor force tends to grow larger, and in order to absorb it the rate of development must be speeded up.

2. The serious phenomenon of urban marginality originates largely in the cities themselves. But it has been greatly aggravated by the exodus of rural population, mainly people who in one way or another were socially integrated in their places of origin. There is a manifest link between the increase of marginality and the incapacity of urban activities to absorb the population increment in productive employment.

3. For the sake of simplicity, this group of activities will henceforth be referred to as "the industry group."

4. See *Partners in Development: Report by the Commission on International Development* (New York: Praeger Publishers, 1969).

5. See *Committee for Development Planning: Report on the Sixth Session (5–15 January 1970)*, United Nations document E/4776, Economic and Social Council, 49th session, supplement No. 7.

6. See Committee for Economic Development, Assisting Development in Low-Income Countries: Priorities for U.S. Government Policy (September, 1969).

7. *US Foreign Assistance in the 1970's* (Washington, March 1970), a report which a group headed by the distinguished banker Rudolf Peterson has submitted to President Nixon. (Mimeographed.)

8. These countries are Argentina, Brazil, Chile, Colombia, Guatemala, Mexico, Peru, Uruguay, and Venezuela.

9. It is a very encouraging circumstance that in the Cartagena Agreement signed by the members of the Andean Group, special importance is attached to measures of this kind.

10. This point will be discussed later. Suffice it here to draw attention to the necessity of ensuring that the restriction of consumption does not adversely affect productive activities.

11. I make no claim that this view of the role of incentives is universally shared by technical experts in this field. Perhaps I may be permitted a personal reminiscence here. When Comandante Ernesto "Che" Guevara was the head of the Cuban delegation to the General Assembly of the United Nations, he was good enough to come to see me in my office in New York, a few months before he left Cuba forever. We had met in 1961 at the Punta del Este conference, and had established cordial relations in Geneva at the first session of UNCTAD in 1964. At the time of the interview to which I refer, there was a great deal of talk about Liebermann in the Soviet Union and about the system of market prices and incentives which he advocated. Since I asked him for his opinion, Comandante Guevara, who was given to reasoning dispassionately and weighing his words with care, strongly emphasized the sacrifice which the revolution in Cuba had represented, and for that very reason rebutted Liebermann's theory, which he regarded as contrary to the essence of socialism and its design of bringing about a radical change in the motives of human action.

12

Dependency and Development in Latin America (1971)

Enzo Faletto and Fernando Henrique Cardoso

Enzo Faletto (Chile, 1935–2003) was a Chilean sociologist, historian, and econo-mist—an iconic figure of the Latin American school of critical sociology. From 1967 to 1972 he taught sociology and journalism at the University of Chile and from 1968 he was professor at the Latin American School of Sociology of the Latin American Social Sciences Institute (FLACSO). From 1973 to 1990 he was advisor at the United Nations Commission for Latin America and the Carib-bean, with ties to FLACSO. From 1990 until his death, he returned as Professor of the University of Chile.

Fernando Henrique Cardoso (b. Brazil, 1931) is a Brazilian sociologist, pro-fessor, and former president of Brazil. In 1953 he started teaching at the Univer-sity of São Paulo. After the 1964 military coup, Cardoso was exiled, spending the next four years in Chile and France. From 1982–1986 he was president of the International Sociological Association. The author of numerous books and ar-ticles, Cardoso is internationally known for his intellectual accomplishments in the social sciences, for which he has received many national and international honors. But Cardoso is equally known and honored for his achievements in Brazilian politics. In 1986 he cofounded the Brazilian Social Democratic Party and was president-elect of Brazil for two consecutive terms from 1995 to 2003. Currently he is cochair of Inter-American dialogue, professor-at-large at Brown University, and president of the Fernando Henrique Cardoso Institute.

This selection from the best known book in dependency theory explains some of the key points of the theory such as its notion of development as a so-cial process, its critique of notions of modernity and processes of modernization, and its account of the relationship between a global socioeconomic structure and differential processes and rates of development between central and periph-eral regions of the world.

COMPREHENSIVE ANALYSIS OF DEVELOPMENT

Development is itself a social process. To the economic assumption that under-development leads to development through the creation of a dynamic domestic sector capable of generating both self-sustained growth and the transfer of the "decision-making center," some authors have added a sociological interpretation of the transition from traditional to modern societies.

Traditional and Modern Societies

It is argued that Latin American societies belong to a structural type generally called "traditional," which is giving way to another type of society called "modern."[1] It would appear that before becoming modern a society enters an intermediate, hybrid pattern called "structural dualism," and that this pattern is characteristic of "developing" countries.[2]

This scheme is a reincarnation of the classical "community-society" dichotomy formulated by Tönnies. It is open to criticism from two points of view. On the one hand, the concepts of "traditional" and "modern" are neither broad enough to cover all existing social situations nor specific enough to distinguish the structures that define the ways of life of different societies. On the other hand, these concepts do not show how the different economic stages (for example, underdevelopment or development through exports or through import substitution, etc.) are linked to the various types of social structure that are attributed to "traditional" and "modern" societies.

With this kind of characterization it continues to be impossible to explain the transition from one type of society to another. In fact, change in social structures, far from being only a cumulative process of incorporating new "variables," involves a series of relations among social groups, forces, and classes, through which some of them try to impose their domination over society.[3]

In purely economic terms, the degree of development of a production sector can be analyzed through a group of variables—the relation between the number of workers and capital, industrial output per added capital, and so forth—that reflect the process of structural diversification of the economy. Using this analysis as a base, the structure of society is deduced principally from the pattern of income distribution and the structure of employment. However, this strictly economic analysis can only be related to political and social development by looking beyond the social structure to its process of formation and to the social forces exerting pressure to maintain or change it.

Analyses that relate development to modern society and underdevelopment to traditional society are too simple. Development and modernization are not necessarily related just because domination in developed societies excludes "traditional groups." It may happen that a society modernizes its patterns of consumption, education, and so forth without a corresponding advance in development, if by development we understand less dependency and self-sustained growth based on the local capital accumulation and on the dynamism of the industrial sector.

Social Change: External Models, Demonstration Effect, and Specific Situations

In almost all theories of modernization it is assumed that the course taken by political, social, and economic systems of Western Europe and the United States foretells the future for the underdeveloped countries. The "development process" would consist in completing and even reproducing the various stages that characterized the social transformation of these countries.[4] Therefore, the historical variations, the specificities of each situation of underdevelopment, have little value for this type of sociology.

It would be naive to assume that Latin America is in the nineteenth century while the developed countries are in the twentieth. More frequently, the underdeveloped countries are described as being "backward" in certain aspects of their structure although not in others. Thus, labor unions in countries like Brazil and Argentina became national and influenced decisions on wage levels during a phase that was abnormal by comparison with what had occurred in the countries of "early development." Accelerated urbanization in Latin America, which has come before industrialization, has helped to spread expectations and forms of political behavior that encourage greater participation of the masses in the power game before there is autonomous economic growth based on a domestic market. Such popular demands to share in the decisions affecting consumption are considered by many authors a "precocious" datum in the development process of Latin America.

It has been suggested that, because this level of participation is supposedly similar to that of the central countries, it might serve as a kind of bridge tending to approximate the social patterns and value orientations of the underdeveloped societies to those of the developed, modernizing them, even if not assuring similar levels of economic growth. This, broadly speaking, is what has come to be called the "demonstration effect": the modernization of consumption patterns, implying some degree of income improvement for urban population.

In an economic analysis, the "demonstration effect" assumes that the economy will be modernized through consumption and that ultimately modernization alters the production system in such a way that it may deviate from the "stages" of industrialization characteristic of advanced countries. But since investments depend to a large extent on domestic savings, the modernizing pressure of consumption can act also as a brake on development: it may stimulate the importation of consumer goods orienting the utilization of savings to the payment of external producers, as well as induce investment in sectors that are not basic to the economy.

On the other hand, the "demonstration effect" has not been thought of only in economic terms. Presumably, the pressures to modernize consumption are also pressures to change other aspects of human behavior—in the political and social areas—before diversification of the production system is completed. It should be stressed that the "demonstration effect" took place, at least until the sixties in the case of Latin America, because there was a minimum participation of the people in the political process. Sociological analysis should explain this measure of modernization to avoid simplistic interpretations that take "demonstration effect" by itself as "causal" explanation of the developing process. This kind of approach amounts to saying that the dynamism of underdeveloped societies derives from external factors and that the structural particularities in underdeveloped countries produce forms of development that are deviant cases when compared with classic stages of growth.

Rather than stressing the consequences of the "demonstration effect" or of other exogenous variables as a "modernizing factor" in the functioning of the economic system or in the behavior of social groups, it is important to study the historical-structural contexts in which such a process is generated since they reveal the very meaning of such modernization. We have therefore emphasized the specifics of the Latin American situation as principal conditioning factors in the development process. In this approach, the "demonstration effect" is incorporated into the analysis as a subordinate explanatory element. It is more basic for us to describe the relations among social groups at the national level, which of course also depend on linkages between the economic system and the international political blocs.

Structure and Process: Reciprocal Determination

To analyze development properly, we must consider in their totality the "historic specificities," both economic and social, underlying the development processes at the national and international levels. Within given structural situations, we must understand the conflict between social movements that "are set in motion" by social classes in developing societies. Our approach must examine not only structural conditions and the ideologies of the social movements, but also their relations and their reciprocal determination.

How can we link the economic and social components of development in an analysis of the behavior of social groups? First of all, every economic link is, by itself, a social link. Capital itself is the economic expression of a social relation; it requires the existence of a set of persons working by wage—selling its labor force—and another group owning machines and money to buy raw material and to pay wages and salaries. On the other hand, such an "economic" relation supposes not only exploitation—and thus social mechanisms to assure domination—but some degree of stability and recurrence in the relations of exploitation. Then this form of relation has a structure. Nevertheless, if structures already built appear as a mechanism that promotes the "natural" reinforcement of a given social order, they have in fact been built as a result of social struggles and are, in that sense, a historical product. Consequently, economic relations and the social structures on which they are based have to be studied as a process through which different classes try to sustain, preserve, or change interests rooted in social structures. Development results therefore from the interaction and struggles of social groups and classes that have specific ways of relating to each other. The social and political structure is modified insofar as new social classes and groups succeed in imposing their interests on or accommodating them to previous dominant classes in society.

Social change depends on historical alternatives. In the tensions between groups with divergent interests and directions, it finds the filter through which the purely economic influences have to pass.[5]

Our basic theoretical problem is how to determine what forms the structures of domination will adopt, because through these structures the dynamics of class relations may be understood. Political institutions at a given moment can only be fully understood in terms of the structures of domination because these express the class interests behind political organization. These structures also make it possible to follow the process of change at the political-institutional level. Significant historical changes in the process of Latin American development have always been accompanied, if not by a radical alteration of the structure of domination, at least by the adoption of new forms of relations and, consequently, of conflict between classes and groups. In that sense, the oligarchical period characteristic of the export economy drive was replaced, for instance, by the "populist" period of soaring industrialization oriented toward internal markets. In the case of economically dependent countries, the explanation of structures of domination involves establishing the links that may exist between internal and external determinants. These links should not be understood in terms of a mechanical and immediate determination of the internal by the external: it is important to delineate the interconnections between these two levels, suggesting the ways through which external factors are interwoven with internal ones.

The concept of dependence tries to give meaning to a series of events and situations that occur together, and to make empirical situations understandable in terms of the way internal and external structural components are linked. In this approach, the external is also expressed as a particular type of relation between social groups and classes within the underdeveloped nations. For this reason, it is worth focusing the analysis of dependence on its internal manifestations.

Because the purpose of this essay is to explain the economic processes as social processes, it is necessary to find a theoretical point of intersection where economic power is pressed as domination, that is to say, as politics. An economic class or group tries to establish through the political process a system of social relations that permits it to impose on the entire society a social form of production akin to its own interests; or at least it tries to establish alliances or to control the other groups or classes in order to develop an economic order consistent with its interests and objectives. The modes of economic relations, in turn, set the limits of political action.

Thus the topics to be dealt with are the economic factors conditioning the world market; the structure of the national production system and the kind of linkage it has developed with the external market; the historical-structural shape of such societies, with their ways of assigning and maintaining power; and above all, the political-social movements and processes that exert pressure toward change, and their respective orientations and objectives. Direct analysis of the main socio-political processes in underdeveloped or developing societies is an immense and limitless task. Nevertheless, there are certain topics that, although of a particular character, throw light on the overall situation. In particular, it is illuminating to look for the points where the economic system intersects with the social system, which will indicate the links and dynamics that affect the possibility of development.

By and large, the problems of social control of production and consumption are the axis of a sociological analysis of development viewed from this perspective. The sociological interpretation of economic change requires analysis of tensions between social groups which reveal what supports the economic and political structure.

Although it is now fashionable to analyze "decision-making mechanisms" from this angle, no sociological view of the problem of development can be reduced to this approach, because it misses the point that is crucial for us: social forces and structural determinants behind political processes. Development always alters the social system of domination as it changes the organization of production and consumption. It cannot be reduced to changes at the institutional level or to the analysis of actors' value orientations. This view of the problem encourages us to analyze the political behavior of social classes that maintain control at the structural level and those that oppose such control. Moreover, it moves us to consider the value orientations that give the action its framework of reference, not at the individual level, but at the cultural one, as ideologies.

Underdevelopment, Periphery, and Dependence

The historical specificity of the situation of underdevelopment derives from the relation between "peripheral" and "central" societies. Underdeveloped countries must be distinguished from those without development: the latter are economies and peoples—fast disappearing—that do not have market relations with the industrialized countries. As for underdevelopment, in some situations the linkage between the peripheral economies and the world market can be described as "colonial," whereas in others the peripheral economies belong to "national societies." In the latter case some peripheral countries already had a national society when they formed links with the more developed dominant centers, while others were colonies that became nations but without any change in their situation of underdevelopment.

In any event, the situation of underdevelopment came about when commercial capitalism and then industrial capitalism expanded and linked to the world market nonindustrial economies that went on to occupy different positions in the overall structure of the capitalist system. Thus, there exists among the developed and underdeveloped economies a difference, not only of the stage or the state of the production system, but also of function or position within the international economic structure of production and distribution: some produce industrial goods; others, raw material. This requires a definite structure of relations of domination to assure an international trade based on merchandise produced at unequal levels of technology and cost of labor force.

The concept of underdevelopment, as it is usually employed, refers to a type of economic system with a predominant primary sector, a high concentration of income, little diversification in its production system, and above all, an external market far outweighing the internal. This concept will not suffice.

Understanding the historicity of the underdevelopment situation requires more than just an indication of the structural characteristics of underdeveloped economies. It is necessary to analyze how the underdeveloped economies were linked historically to the world market and how internal social groups defined the outward-directed relations implicit in underdevelopment. Dependence on the sociopolitical level also began historically with the expansion of the economies of the early capitalist countries. In extreme cases of dependence, decisions affecting the production or consumption of a given economy are taken in terms of the growth and interests of the developed economies; a typical example is the economy based on a colonial enclave.

The foregoing argument suggests that the distinction between "central" and "peripheral" economies has greater social significance than that between developed and underdeveloped economies. The former can incorporate immediately the idea of unequal positions and functions within the same structure of overall production. Nonetheless, it would not be sufficient or correct to replace the concepts of development and underdevelopment with those of a central and a peripheral economy, or—as if it were a synthesis of both—with those of an autonomous and a dependent economy. These concepts differ as much in their dimensions as in their theoretical meaning. The idea of dependence refers to the conditions under which alone the economic and political system can exist and function in its connections with the world productive structure. The idea of underdevelopment refers to the degree of diversification of the production system without emphasizing the patterns of control of decisions on production and consumption, whether internal (socialism, capitalism, etc.) or external (colonialism, periphery of the world market, etc.). The ideas of "center" and "periphery" stress the functions that underdeveloped economies perform in the world market, but overlook the socio-political factors involved in the situation of dependence.

A society can undergo profound changes in its production system without the creation of fully autonomous decision-making centers. Such was the case when Argentina and Brazil ended the process of import substitution and began the production of capital goods. They had attained a degree of economic maturity, even—as happened to some extent in Argentina—in income distribution. In spite of that, not only is its industrial sector controlled from abroad, but it plays a complementary and subordinated role from the standpoint of the international capitalist system. A national society can achieve a certain autonomy of decision without thereby having a production system and an income distribution comparable to those in the central developed countries or even in some peripheral developing countries. This can occur, for example, when a country breaks its ties with a given system of domination without incorporating itself totally into another (Yugoslavia, China, Algiers, Egypt, Cuba, and even Revolutionary Mexico).

Since there need not be an immediate connection between the diversification of the economic system and the formation of autonomous decision-making centers, analyses should define not only the degree of economic diversification and social differentiation reached by countries that are being integrated into the world market, but also the manner in which this integration was achieved historically. Such an approach calls for great caution in interpreting how the economy of Latin America has developed and its society has been modernized.

Various authors have emphasized development as an "unforeseen result" in Latin America. Some countries, for example, when planning the defense of their principal export product, carried out a currency devaluation policy that had the indirect and not altogether intended consequence of creating favorable conditions for industrial growth. Nevertheless, it would be difficult to claim that the economic diversification achieved in this way—during market fluctuations and without a program for increasing autonomy and changing class relations—can alone substantively alter the relations of dependence. The political sphere of social behavior necessarily influences the form of the development process.

Thus, in a global interpretation of development, arguments based solely on market incentives and reactions do not suffice to explain industrialization and the economic process. Such incentives or mechanisms to defend the economy can only begin an industrialization process; its continuation requires changes favorable to development in the international market and, still more essential, elements favorable to a broader measure of autonomy within the socio-political game of the developing countries.

What we seek are the characteristics of the national societies that express relations with the outside. The internal sociopolitical factors—linked naturally to the dynamic of the hegemonic centers—are precisely the ones that may produce policies taking advantage of the "new conditions" or new opportunities for economic growth. Similarly, it is the internal forces that give sociopolitical scope to the "spontaneous" diversification of the economic system. For example, the traditional dominant groups initially may oppose handing over their power of control to the new social groups that appear with industrialization, but they also may bargain with them, thereby altering the social and political consequences of development. National economic groups are connected with external groups in different ways and with different consequences before and after the development process begins. Moreover, the internal system of political alliances is often modified by international alliances.

We cannot accurately discuss the development process just from a strictly economic angle when our stated objective is to understand the formation of the national economies. Nor, for purposes of description, is it enough to analyze the behavior of variables—such as productivity, savings, and income rates, and consumption and employment functions—since these depend on structural factors and the historical process of change.

In the "colonial enclave" situation, the political subordination of the colony highlights the fact that the economic system is directly bound to the political system. On the other hand, when development takes place in "national states," the economic aspect becomes more visible; the political and social hegemony becomes less visible, but continues to influence whatever opportunities for development may appear in the market.

If it is accepted that market influences by themselves neither explain development nor guarantee its continuity or direction, then the behavior of social groups and institutions becomes crucial to the analysis of development.

"National Underdevelopment"

In situations of extreme colonial dependency local history is almost reduced to a reflection of what happens in a metropolis. However, the decision by local forces to rebel against colonialism and to create a nation implies an attempt to influence local history according to local values and interests. Economic links with external markets still impose limits to decisions and actions even after independence. The contradiction between the attempt to cope with the market situation in a politically autonomous way and the de facto situation of dependency characterizes what is the specific ambiguity of nations where political sovereignty is expressed by the new state and where economic subordination is reinforced by the international division of labor and by the economic control exerted by former or new imperialist centers. From a sociological viewpoint, here is perhaps the core of the problem of national development in Latin America.

"National underdevelopment" is a situation of objective economic subordination to outside nations and enterprises and, at the same time, of partial political attempts to cope with "national interests" through the state and social movements that try to preserve political autonomy. Ideological components play some role in the perception of what "national interest" means, as well as in the rationalization about the possibility of the existence of nation-states that have submitted to foreign interests and pressures.

One of the aims of comprehensive analyses of the national development process is to determine the links between social groups that in their behavior actually tie together the economic and political spheres. Insofar as, by definition, links of economic dependency imply a relationship between local and external classes, states, and enterprises, the analyses of local social and political groups must include the connections with international partners. Some local classes or groups sustain dependency ties, enforcing foreign economic and political interests. Others are opposed to the maintenance of a given pattern of dependency. Dependence thus finds not only internal "expression," but also its true character as implying a situation that structurally entails a link with the outside in such a way that what happens "internally" in a dependent country cannot be fully explained without taking into consideration the links that internal social groups have with external ones. Dependence should no longer be considered an "external variable"; its analysis should be based on the relations between the different social classes within the dependent nations themselves.

This analysis does away with the idea that class relations in dependent countries are like those of the central countries during their early development. At the beginning of the development process in the central countries, market forces generally act as arbiter in the conflict of interests between the dominant groups. Thus, economic rationality, measured in money, was made a norm of society; and consumption and investment were limited by the growth of the economic system. Expansion of the system was due to a dynamic group that controlled investment decisions and imposed upon the entire society an orientation based on its own interests. The rising economic class possessed efficiency and consensus in capitalistic terms.

It was believed that the ruling groups expressed the general interest and that the market functioned adequately as a mechanism to satisfy general and particular interests. Other groups that exerted pressure in order to share in the fruits of "progress" and in decision-making were ignored. Only long after the initial stage of industrialization did the popular classes participate politically and socially in the industrial societies.[6]

The national economies in the countries of "early growth" succeeded in part because they were consolidated at the same time that the world market expanded, so that these countries came to occupy the leading positions in the system of international domination. From this scheme it is evident that "early

development," although a very broad and imprecise term, is significantly different from what has occurred in Latin America.

It has been assumed that the peripheral countries would have to repeat the
evolution of the economies of the central countries in order to achieve development. But it is clear that from its beginning the capitalist process implied
an unequal relation between the central and the peripheral economies. Many
"underdeveloped" economies—as is the case of the Latin American—were incorporated into the capitalist system as colonies and later as national states, and
they have stayed in the capitalist system throughout their history. They remain,
however, peripheral economies with particular historical paths when compared
with central capitalist economies.

Capitalism should be studied in the hope, not of finding how its history
may repeat at a later date in the peripheral countries, but of learning how the
relation between peripheral and central was produced. Although it is possible to
distinguish in the economic history of Latin America the periods of mercantile,
industrial, and financial capitalism, it is important for us to make clear what the
relation of dependence meant in each of these phases. It would be senseless to
seek how far or how close Latin American economies are from "mercantilism,"
"industrialism," or "finance" forms of capitalism. They belong to the same international capitalistic system as central economies do. Consequently the history
of central capitalism is, at the same time, the history of peripheral capitalism.
But specific links between dependent and central economies could have been
different in each of the above periods. The same can be argued vis-à-vis analyses
about competitive or monopolistic trends in the development of capitalism and
its effects on peripheral economies.

During these different phases of the capitalist process, the Latin American
countries depended on various countries that acted as centers and whose economic structures influenced the nature of the dependence. For example, Great
Britain's economic expansion required some measure of development in the peripheral economies, since it relied on them to supply raw materials. Furthermore,
these same economies were part of the market for its manufactured products.
It was therefore necessary for Latin American production to achieve a certain
degree of growth and modernization. The United States economy, on the other
hand, had its own natural resources as well as a domestic market that permitted
it a more autonomous development in respect of the peripheral economies; in
some cases it even competed with the countries producing raw materials. The
relation of dependence thus came to denote control of the development of other
economies both in the production of raw materials and in the possible formation
of other economic centers. The vitalizing role of the United States in the Latin
American economies was therefore less important (prior to the formation of the
present multinationals) than the role performed by English capitalism.

The developing countries are by no means repeating the history of the developed countries. Historical conditions are different. When the world market was
created along with development, it was thanks to the action of the "bourgeoisie
conquérante." Now, development is undertaken when capitalist market relations already exist between both groups of countries and when the world market
is divided between the capitalist and socialist worlds. What at first glance may

appear to be deviant forms of the classic development pattern are simply not. When we recognize this, the present socioeconomic system in dependent countries may become understandable.

Types of Linkage Between the National Economies and the Market

The rupture of what historians call the "colonial pact" and the early expansion of European industrial capitalism were the dominant historical features in the formation of the "new nations" in the nineteenth century. Expansion of the central industrialized economies, first of England and later of the United States, was carried out in the presence of the economic and social systems established by the preceding colonial expansion. Conversely, peripheral national economies fed into the different phases of the capitalist process. The development of a nation exporting a widely consumed product would differ according to whether the phase of capitalism was predominantly competitive or predominantly monopolistic. In the first case, chances are more favorable for local producers to find a place in the market. In the latter case, international monopolies usually try to control local production. In the same way, a country whose economy had been that of a colony of settlement, largely self-sufficient and using abundant labor, would differ from an exploitation colony that was more strictly exploited from the outside: after independence, the former could more easily organize an internal political-administrative apparatus to promote and carry out a "national policy." Furthermore, the physical foundation of a country's economy—for example, the type and possibilities of land occupation or the type of available mineral wealth—would influence the nature of its link with the world market after the period of national formation.

When Latin America emerged from its colonial dependence and entered a period of dependence on Great Britain, Britain sought support from national producers of export commodities who, because of the growth of their economic base—already under way in the colonial situation—could effect a new accommodation with emergent dominant forces at world level. Thanks to this they gained, if not absolute control, at least a privileged position in local structures of power.

In the passage from British to United States hegemony, new factors came into play: growth of the exporting groups was accompanied by a significant growth of the urban sectors of the economies, especially industry. Although the new form of dependence had explanations outside the nation—it reflects the expansion of industrial corporations at the world level—internal class relations made it possible and gave it shape. The growth of the dependent economic system within the nation was determined, within limits, by the capacity that the internal systems of alliance between classes and groups and the hegemonic position of these alliances over society had to assure economic expansion. The pressure of the masses in recent years to incorporate themselves into the political system has spurred the dynamism of the prevailing economic form: dominant groups have expanded internal markets, and thus it is possible for them to absorb social pressures from below.

During this "nationalist-populist" period, the popular classes often allied with the new economically dominant groups tried to impose their participation and came into conflict with the systems of alliance existing among landlords and exporting sectors of the earlier situation.

The industrial group at first appeared in a marginal situation. Nevertheless, it was the only group in the new urban sectors that possessed a real economic base. As the one group that could absorb the urban popular sectors in a productive way, it was strategically situated to establish terms of alliance or compromise with the rest of the social system. This also accounts for its importance in the period following the crisis of the agroexport system.

Toward a Comprehensive Analysis of Development

There is no doubt that an analysis is needed to redefine, within the context of development, the meaning and functions of social classes and of the alliances they establish to maintain a structure of power and to generate social change and economic growth.

In developing but dependent countries, social structures reflect the double edge of the economic system: its external links and internal roots. Thus, social dynamics and social conflicts usually express both kinds of interests and pressures, those that derive from external influences and those that are national. Yet, as we stressed before, foreign interests have internal expression through the action of groups and persons who represent them or have advantages in their presence. It is not necessarily foreign interests that are represented or sustained by "modernizing elites." "Traditional" groups—for instance, large landlords—are often the main sustaining force for foreign interests. On the other hand, after the industrialization of peripheral economies under the control of multinational corporations, previous industrializing spurts have gained continuity and have considerably expanded. This implies the growth of urban working classes, as well as the diversification of social stratification. New middle-class groups—technicians, private and public employers, people devoted to the service sector, professionals, and so forth—have gained strength in society. The strong participation of the state in the economic process of growth has enlarged the participation of bureaucracies and of the military in Latin American societies. All together these processes show the complexity of the situation of underdevelopment. It gives rise to activities of social groups corresponding to the patterns of "industrialized mass societies"—as in the case of urban patterns of mass consumption vis-à-vis mass media influence on mass behavior—and at same time to others in which social norms typical of "class situations" prevail. The latter can be seen in the style of political confrontation in crises situations, as well as in the shape and functions of workers unions. Corporatist components of the political system indeed redefine class behavior, as is notorious in the case of unions under authoritarian regimes in Latin America. Sometimes even "state situations" (in the Weberian sense) have importance in the understanding of conflicts and accommodations that prevail: "traditional" sectors of middle and upper classes protect themselves through mechanisms of social identification—clubs, professional associations, and so forth—that are based not on direct economic or market interests but on specific forms of socialization and defense of privileges based on degrees of education, family origin, and shared values.

If we admit that those factors of differentiation and complexity are intermixed with the above mentioned multiple links with external societies and economic interests, it is not difficult to see the reasons why analyses of dependency need theoretical efforts to stress specificities.

The social and economic transformations that alter the internal and external aspects of the underdeveloped and dependent societies are actually political processes that, in present historical conditions, do not always favor national development. Our analysis of social development always assumes the possibility of stagnation and heteronomy. To determine the possibilities of success, it is necessary to analyze not only structure but also the action of social forces—both those that tend to maintain the status quo and those that exert pressure for social change—as well as the "value orientations" or ideologies that are associated with social actions and movements. Since these forces are interrelated and express a market situation with various possibilities of growth, analysis is complete only when the economic and the social have their reciprocal determinations defined at the internal and external levels.

NOTES

1. This analytical approach stressing the passage from a traditional to a modern society is related specifically to Latin America by R. Redfield in *The Folk Culture of Yucatan* (Chicago: University of Chicago Press, 1940). B. Hoselitz later gives it a decidedly sociological orientation in *Sociological Factors in Economic Development* (Glencoe: Free Press, 1960) and applies it to Latin America in *Contribution to the First International Conference in Economic History: Stockholm, 1960* (The Hague: Mouton & Co., 1960). Gino Germani is possibly the Latin American who has best set forth this approach in, for example, his *Política y sociedad en una época de transición* (Buenos Aires: Paidós, 1962). It should be noted that Talcott Parsons, *The Social System* (Glencoe: Free Press, 1951), and Robert K. Merton, *Social Theory and Social Structure* (Glencoe: Free Press, 1949), have decisively influenced the formulation of this type of development analysis. Furthermore, Daniel Lerner, in *The Passing of Traditional Society: Modernizing the Middle East* (Glencoe: Free Press, 1958), states in more general terms—that is, not oriented toward the problem of development—the traditionalism and modernism approach in an analysis of the processes of social change. The psychological aspects of the passage from traditionalism to modernism are discussed by Everett Hagen, in *On the Theory of Social Change* (Homewood: Dorsey Press, 1962), and by David McClelland, in *The Achieving Society* (Princeton: Van Nostrand, 1961).

2. For the concept of structural dualism in this context, see Jacques Lambert, *Le Brésil: structure sociale et institutions politiques* (Paris: 1953), and from the viewpoint of an economist, Albert O. Hirschman, *The Strategy of Economic Development* (New Haven: Yale University Press, 1958).

3. See for example Peter Heintz, *Análisis contextual de los países latino-americanos* (Berkeley: mimeographed edition).

4. See especially W. W. Rostow, *The Stage of Economic Growth, A Non-Communist Manifest* (Cambridge: Cambridge University Press, 1962); Wilbert Moore, *Economy and Society* (New York: Doubleday, 1955); Clark Kerr, et al., *Industrialism and Industrial Man* (Cambridge: Harvard University Press, 1960).

5. For an analysis of this point of view, see F. H. Cardoso, *Empresário industrial e desenvolvimento econômico no Brasil* (São Paulo: Difusão Europeia do Livro, 1964), chaps. 1 and 2.

6. See Alain Touraine, "Industrialisation et conscience ouvrière a São Paulo," *Sociologie du Travail* (April 1961).

13

The Structure of Dependence (1970)

Theotonio Dos Santos

Theotonio Dos Santos (b. Brazil, 1936) is a noted Brazilian social scientist. He has been professor at the universities of Brasilia, Chile, and the National Autonomous University of Mexico (UNAM). He was exiled from Brazil after the 1964 military coup. From 1965 to 1973 he was in Chile where he directed the Center for Socio-Economic Studies at the University of Chile. After the 1973 Chilean military coup, he moved to Mexico where he stayed until 1980 directing the Post-graduate Economics Division of the Institute of Economic Studies of the UNAM. After 1980 he returned to Brazil, where he currently is Subject Coordinator of UNESCO's United Nations University on Global Economy and Sustainable Development, and Professor of Economics at the Fluminense Federal University in Rio de Janeiro. Dos Santos has taught and lectured at many international universities and has written numerous articles and books. This selection is the best known brief exposition of dependency theory in the United States.

This paper attempts to demonstrate that the dependence of Latin American countries on other countries cannot be overcome without a qualitative change in their internal structures and external relations. We shall attempt to show that the relations of dependence to which these countries are subjected conform to a type of international and internal structure which leads them to underdevelopment or more precisely to a dependent structure that deepens and aggravates the fundamental problems of their peoples.

I. WHAT IS DEPENDENCE?

By dependence we mean a situation in which the economy of certain countries is conditioned by the development and expansion of another economy to which the former is subjected. The relation of interdependence between two or more economies, and between these and world trade, assumes the form of dependence when some countries (the dominant ones) can expand and can be self-sustaining, while other countries (the dependent ones) can do this only as a reflection of that expansion, which can have either a positive or a negative effect on their immediate development.[1]

The concept of dependence permits us to see the internal situation of these countries as part of world economy. In the Marxian tradition, the theory of imperialism has been developed as a study of the process of expansion of the imperialist centers and of their world domination. In the epoch of the revolutionary movement of the Third World, we have to develop the theory of laws of internal development in those countries that are the object of such expansion and are governed by them. This theoretical step transcends the theory of development which seeks to explain the situation of the underdeveloped countries as a product of their slowness or failure to adopt the patterns of efficiency characteristic of developed countries (or to "modernize" or "develop" themselves). Although capitalist development theory admits the existence of an "external" dependence, it is unable to perceive underdevelopment in the way our present theory perceives it, as a consequence and part of the process of the world expansion of capitalism—a part that is necessary to and integrally linked with it.

In analyzing the process of constituting a world economy that integrates the so-called "national economies" in a world market of commodities, capital, and even of labor power, we see that the relations produced by this market are unequal and combined—unequal because development of parts of the system occurs at the expense of other parts. Trade relations are based on monopolistic control of the market, which leads to the transfer of surplus generated in the dependent countries to the dominant countries; financial relations are, from the viewpoint of the dominant powers, based on loans and the export of capital, which permit them to receive interest and profits; thus increasing their domestic surplus and strengthening their control over the economies of the other countries. For the dependent countries these relations represent an export of profits and interest which carries off part of the surplus generated domestically and leads to a loss of control over their productive resources. In order to permit these disadvantageous relations, the dependent countries must generate large surpluses, not in such a way as to create higher levels of technology but rather superexploited manpower. The result is to limit the development of their internal market and their technical and cultural capacity, as well as the moral and physical health of their people. We call this combined development because it is the combination of these inequalities and the transfer of resources from the most backward and dependent sectors to the most advanced and dominant ones which explains the inequality, deepens it, and transforms it into a necessary and structural element of the world economy.

II. HISTORIC FORMS OF DEPENDENCE

Historic forms of dependence are conditioned by: (1) the basic forms of this world economy which has its own laws of development; (2) the type of economic relations dominant in the capitalist centers and the ways in which the latter expand outward; and (3) the types of economic relations existing inside the peripheral countries which are incorporated into the situation of dependence within the network of international economic relations generated by capitalist expansion. It is not within the purview of this paper to study these forms in detail but only to distinguish broad characteristics of development.

Drawing on an earlier study, we may distinguish: (1) Colonial dependence, trade export in nature, in which commercial and financial capital in alliance with the colonialist state dominated the economic relations of the Europeans and the colonies, by means of a trade monopoly complemented by a colonial monopoly of land, mines, and manpower (serf or slave) in the colonized countries. (2) Financial-industrial dependence which consolidated itself at the end of the nineteenth century, characterized by the domination of big capital in the hegemonic centers, and its expansion abroad through investment in the production of raw materials and agricultural products for consumption in the hegemonic centers. A productive structure grew up in the dependent countries devoted to the export of these products (which Levin labeled export economies;[2] other analysis in other regions[3,4]), producing what ECLA has called "foreign-oriented development" (*desarrollo hacia afuera*).[5] (3) In the postwar period a new type of dependence has been consolidated, based on multinational corporations which began to invest in industries geared to the internal market of underdeveloped countries. This form of dependence is basically technological-industrial dependence.[6]

Each of these forms of dependence corresponds to a situation which conditioned not only the international relations of these countries but also their internal structures: the orientation of production, the forms of capital accumulation, the reproduction of the economy, and, simultaneously, their social and political structure.

III. THE EXPORT ECONOMIES

In forms (1) and (2) of dependence, production is geared to those products destined for export (gold, silver, and tropical products in the colonial epoch; raw materials and agricultural products in the epoch of industrial-financial dependence); i.e., production is determined by demand from the hegemonic centers. The internal productive structure is characterized by rigid specialization and monoculture in entire regions (the Caribbean, the Brazilian Northeast, etc.). Alongside these export sectors there grew up certain complementary economic activities (cattle-raising and some manufacturing, for example) which were dependent, in general, on the export sector to which they sell their products. There was a third, subsistence economy which provided manpower for the export sector under favorable conditions and toward which excess population shifted during periods unfavorable to international trade.

Under these conditions, the existing internal market was restricted by four factors: (1) Most of the national income was derived from export, which was used to purchase the inputs required by export production (slaves, for example) or luxury goods consumed by the hacienda and mine-owners, and by the more prosperous employees. (2) The available manpower was subject to very arduous forms of superexploitation, which limited its consumption. (3) Part of the consumption of these workers was provided by the subsistence economy, which served as a complement to their income and as a refuge during periods of depression. (4) A fourth factor was to be found in those countries in which land and mines were in the hands of foreigners (cases of an enclave economy): a great part of the accumulated surplus was destined to be sent abroad in the form of profits, limiting not only internal consumption but also possibilities of reinvestment.[7] In the case of enclave economies the relations of the foreign companies with the hegemonic center were even more exploitative and were complemented by the fact that purchases by the enclave were made directly abroad.

IV. THE NEW DEPENDENCE

The new form of dependence, (3) above, is in process of developing and is conditioned by the exigencies of the international commodity and capital markets. The possibility of generating new investments depends on the existence of financial resources in foreign currency for the purchase of machinery and processed raw materials not produced domestically. Such purchases are subject to two limitations: the limit of resources generated by the export sector (reflected in the balance of payments, which includes not only trade but also service relations); and the limitations of monopoly on patents which leads monopolistic firms to prefer to transfer their machines in the form of capital rather than as commodities for sale. It is necessary to analyze these relations of dependence if we are to understand the fundamental structural limits they place on the development of these economies.

1. Industrial development is dependent on an export sector for the foreign currency to buy the inputs utilized by the industrial sector. The first consequence of this dependence is the need to preserve the traditional export sector, which limits economically the development of the internal market by the conservation of backward relations of production and signifies, politically, the maintenance of power by traditional decadent oligarchies. In the countries where these sectors are controlled by foreign capital, it signifies the remittance abroad of high profits, and political dependence on those interests. Only in rare instances does foreign capital not control at least the marketing of these products. In response to these limitations, dependent countries in the 1930's and 1940's developed a policy of exchange restrictions and taxes on the national and foreign export sector; today they tend toward the gradual nationalization of production and toward the imposition of certain timid limitations on foreign control of the marketing of exported products. Furthermore, they seek, still somewhat timidly, to obtain better terms for the sale of their products. In recent decades, they have created mechanisms for international price agreements, and today UNCTAD and ECLA press to obtain more favorable tariff conditions for these products on the part of the hegemonic centers. It is important to point out that the industrial development of these countries is dependent on the situation of the export sector, the continued existence of which they are obliged to accept.

2. Industrial development is, then, strongly conditioned by fluctuations in the balance of payments. This leads toward deficit due to the relations of dependence themselves. The causes of the deficit are three:

a) Trade relations take place in a highly monopolized international market, which tends to lower the price of raw materials and to raise the prices of industrial products, particularly inputs. In the second place, there is a tendency in modern technology to replace various primary products with synthetic raw materials. Consequently the balance of trade in these countries tends to be less favorable (even though they show a general surplus). The overall Latin American balance of trade from 1946 to 1968 shows a surplus for each of those years. The same thing happens in almost every underdeveloped country. However, the losses due to deterioration of the terms of trade (on the basis of data from ECLA and the International Monetary Fund), excluding Cuba, were $26,383 million for the 1951–1966 period, taking 1950 prices as a base. If Cuba and Venezuela are excluded, the total is $15,925 million.

b) For the reasons already given, foreign capital retains control over the most dynamic sectors of the economy and repatriates a high volume of profit; consequently, capital accounts are highly unfavorable to dependent countries. The data show that the amount of capital leaving the country is much greater than the amount entering; this produces an enslaving deficit in capital accounts. To this must be added the deficit in certain services which are virtually under total foreign control—such as freight transport, royalty payments, technical aid, etc. Consequently, an important deficit is produced in the total balance of payments; thus limiting the possibility of importation of inputs for industrialization.

c) The result is that "foreign financing" becomes necessary, in two forms: to cover the existing deficit, and to "finance" development by means of loans for the stimulation of investments and to "supply" an internal economic surplus which was decapitalized to a large extent by the remittance of part of the surplus generated domestically and sent abroad as profits.

Foreign capital and foreign "aid" thus fill up the holes that they themselves created. The real value of this aid, however, is doubtful. If overcharges resulting from the restrictive terms of the aid are subtracted from the total amount of the grants, the average net flow, according to calculations of the Inter-American Economic and Social Council, is approximately 54 percent of the gross flow.[8]

If we take account of certain further facts—that a high proportion of aid is paid in local currencies, that Latin American countries make contributions to international financial institutions, and that credits are often "tied"—we find a "real component of foreign aid" of 42.2 percent on a very favorable hypothesis and of 38.3 percent on a more realistic one.[9] The gravity of the situation becomes even clearer if we consider that these credits are used in large part to finance North American investments, to subsidize foreign imports which compete with national products, to introduce technology not adapted to the needs of underdeveloped countries, and to invest in low-priority sectors of the national economies. The hard truth is that the underdeveloped countries have to pay for all of the "aid" they receive. This situation is generating an enormous protest movement by Latin American governments seeking at least partial relief from such negative relations.

3. Finally, industrial development is strongly conditioned by the technological monopoly exercised by imperialist centers. We have seen that the underdeveloped countries depend on the importation of machinery and raw materials

for the development of their industries. However, these goods are not freely available in the international market; they are patented and usually belong to the big companies. The big companies do not sell machinery and processed raw materials as simple merchandise: they demand either the payment of royalties, etc., for their utilization or, in most cases, they convert these goods into capital and introduce them in the form of their own investments. This is how machinery which is replaced in the hegemonic centers by more advanced technology is sent to dependent countries as capital for the installation of affiliates. Let us pause and examine these relations, in order to understand their oppressive and exploitative character.

The dependent countries do not have sufficient foreign currency, for the reasons given. Local businessmen have financing difficulties, and they must pay for the utilization of certain patented techniques. These factors oblige the national bourgeois governments to facilitate the entry of foreign capital in order to supply the restricted national market, which is strongly protected by high tariffs in order to promote industrialization. Thus, foreign capital enters with all the advantages: in many cases, it is given exemption from exchange controls for the importation of machinery; financing of sites for installation of industries is provided; government financing agencies facilitate industrialization; loans are available from foreign and domestic banks, which prefer such clients; foreign aid often subsidizes such investments and finances complementary public investments; after installation, high profits obtained in such favorable circumstances can be reinvested freely. Thus it is not surprising that the data of the U.S. Department of Commerce reveal that the percentage of capital brought in from abroad by these companies is but a part of the total amount of invested capital. These data show that in the period from 1946 to 1967 the new entries of capital into Latin America for direct investment amounted to $5,415 million, while the sum of reinvested profits was $4,424 million. On the other hand, the transfers of profits from Latin America to the United States amounted to $14,775 million. If we estimate total profits as approximately equal to transfers plus reinvestments we have the sum of $18,983 million. In spite of enormous transfers of profits to the United States, the book value of the United States's direct investment in Latin America went from $3,045 million in 1946 to $10,213 million in 1967. From these data it is clear that: (1) Of the new investments made by U.S. companies in Latin America for the period 1946–1967, 55 percent corresponds to new entries of capital and 45 percent to reinvestment of profits; in recent years, the trend is more marked, with reinvestments between 1960 and 1966 representing more than 60 percent of new investments. (2) Remittances remained at about 10 percent of book value throughout the period. (3) The ratio of remitted capital to new flow is around 2.7 for the period 1946–1967; that is, for each dollar that enters $2.70 leaves. In the 1960's this ratio roughly doubled, and in some years was considerably higher.

The *Survey of Current Business* data on sources and uses of funds for direct North American investment in Latin America in the period 1957–1964 show that, of the total sources of direct investment in Latin America, only 11.8 percent came from the United States. The remainder is in large part the result of the activities of North American firms in Latin America (46.4 percent net income, 27.7 percent under the heading of depreciation), and from "sources located abroad"

(14.1 percent). It is significant that the funds obtained abroad that are external to the companies are greater than the funds originating in the United States.

V. EFFECTS ON THE PRODUCTIVE STRUCTURE

It is easy to grasp, even if only superficially, the effects that this dependent structure has on the productive system itself in these countries and the role of this structure in determining a specified type of development, characterized by its dependent nature.

The productive system in the underdeveloped countries is essentially determined by these international relations. In the first place, the need to conserve the agrarian or mining export structure generates a combination between more advanced economic centers that extract surplus value from the more backward sectors, and also between internal "metropolitan" centers and internal interdependent "colonial" centers.[10] The unequal and combined character of capitalist development at the international level is reproduced internally in an acute form. In the second place the industrial and technological structure responds more closely to the interests of the multinational corporations than to internal developmental needs (conceived of not only in terms of the overall interests of the population, but also from the point of view of the interests of a national capitalist development). In the third place, the same technological and economic-financial concentration of the hegemonic economies is transferred without substantial alteration to very different economies and societies, giving rise to a highly unequal productive structure, a high concentration of incomes, underutilization of installed capacity, intensive exploitation of existing markets concentrated in large cities, etc.

The accumulation of capital in such circumstances assumes its own characteristics. In the first place, it is characterized by profound differences among domestic wage-levels, in the context of a local cheap labor market, combined with a capital-intensive technology. The result, from the point of view of relative surplus value, is a high rate of exploitation of labor power.[11]

This exploitation is further aggravated by the high prices of industrial products enforced by protectionism, exemptions and subsidies given by the national governments, and "aid" from hegemonic centers. Furthermore, since dependent accumulation is necessarily tied into the international economy, it is profoundly conditioned by the unequal and combined character of international capitalist economic relations, by the technological and financial control of the imperialist centers by the realities of the balance of payments, by the economic policies of the state, etc. The role of the state in the growth of national and foreign capital merits a much fuller analysis than can be made here.

Using the analysis offered here as a point of departure, it is possible to understand the limits that this productive system imposes on the growth of the internal markets of these countries. The survival of traditional relations in the countryside is a serious limitation on the size of the market, since industrialization does not offer hopeful prospects. The productive structure created by dependent industrialization limits the growth of the internal market.

First, it subjects the labor force to highly exploitative relations which limit its purchasing power. Second, in adopting a technology of intensive capital use, it creates very few jobs in comparison with population growth, and limits the generation of new sources of income. These two limitations affect the growth of the consumer goods market. Third, the remittance abroad of profits carries away part of the economic surplus generated within the country. In all these ways limits are put on the possible creation of basic national industries which could provide a market for the capital goods this surplus would make possible if it were not remitted abroad.

From this cursory analysis we see that the alleged backwardness of these economies is not due to a lack of integration with capitalism but that, on the contrary, the most powerful obstacles to their full development come from the way in which they are joined to this international system and its laws of development.

VI. SOME CONCLUSIONS: DEPENDENT REPRODUCTION

In order to understand the system of dependent reproduction and the socioeconomic institutions created by it, we must see it as part of a system of world economic relations based on monopolistic control of large-scale capital, on control of certain economic and financial centers over others, on a monopoly of a complex technology that leads to unequal and combined development at a national and international level. Attempts to analyze backwardness as a failure to assimilate more advanced models of production or to modernize are nothing more than ideology disguised as science. The same is true of the attempts to analyze this international economy in terms of relations among elements in free competition, such as the theory of comparative costs which seeks to justify the inequalities of the world economic system and to conceal the relations of exploitation on which it is based.[12]

In reality we can understand what is happening in the underdeveloped countries only when we see that they develop within the framework of a process of dependent production and reproduction. This system is a dependent one because it reproduces a productive system whose development is limited by those world relations which necessarily lead to the development of only certain economic sectors, to trade under unequal conditions [9], to domestic competition with international capital under unequal conditions, to the imposition of relations of superexploitation of the domestic labor force with a view to dividing the economic surplus thus generated between internal and external forces of domination.[13]

In reproducing such a productive system and such international relations, the development of dependent capitalism reproduces the factors that prevent it from reaching a nationally and internationally advantageous situation; and it thus reproduces backwardness, misery, and social marginalization within its borders. The development that it produces benefits very narrow sectors, encounters unyielding domestic obstacles to its continued economic growth (with respect to both internal and foreign markets), and leads to the progressive accumulation of balance-of-payments deficits, which in turn generate more dependence and more superexploitation.

The political measures proposed by the developmentalists of ECLA, UNC-TAD, BID, etc., do not appear to permit destruction of these terrible chains imposed by dependent development. We have examined the alternative forms of development presented for Latin America and the dependent countries under such conditions elsewhere.[14] Everything now indicates that what can be expected is a long process of sharp political and military confrontations and of profound social radicalization which will lead these countries to a dilemma: governments of force which open the way to facism, or popular revolutionary governments, which open the way to socialism. Intermediate solutions have proved to be, in such a contradictory reality, empty and utopian.

NOTES

This work expands on certain preliminary work done in a research project on the relations of dependence in Latin America, directed by the author at the Center for Socio-Economic Studies of the Faculty of Economic Science of the University of Chile. In order to abridge the discussion of various aspects, the author was obliged to cite certain of his earlier works. The author expresses his gratitude to the researcher Orlando Caputo and Roberto Pizarro for some of the data utilized and to Sergio Ramos for his critical comments on the paper.

1. Theotonio Dos Santos, *La crisis de la teoría del desarrollo y las relaciones de dependencia en América Latina*, Boletín del CESO, 3 (Santiago, Chile, 1968), 6.

2. I. V. Levin, *The Export Economies* (Harvard Univ. Press, 1964).

3. Gunnar Myrdal, *Asian Drama* (Pantheon, 1968).

4. K. Nkrumah, *Neocolonialismo, última etapa del imperialismo* (Siglo XXI, México, 1966).

5. CEPAL, *La CEPAL y el Análisis del Desarrollo Latinoamericano* (Santiago, Chile, 1968).

6. Theotonio Dos Santos, *El nuevo carácter de la dependencia*, CESO (Santiago, Chile, 1968).

7. Paul Baran, *Political Economy of Growth* (Monthly Review Press, 1967).

8. Consejo Interamericano Económico Social (CIES) O.A.S., Interamerican Economic and Social Council, External Financing for Development in L.A. *El Financiamiento Externo para el Desarrollo de América Latina* (Pan-American Union, Washington, 1969).

9. *Ibid.*, II-33.

10. Andre G. Frank, *Development and Underdevelopment in Latin America* (Monthly Review Press, 1968).

11. On measurements of forms of exploitation, see Pablo Gonzalez Casanova, *Sociología de la explotación* (México, Siglo XXI, 1969).

12. Cristian Palloix, *Problemes de la Croissance en Economie Ouverte* (Maspero, Paris, 1969).

13. On economic surplus and its utilization in the dependent countries, see Paul Baran, *Political Economy of Growth* (New York: Monthly Review Press, 1967).

14. Theotonio Dos Santos, *La dependencia económica y las alternativas de cambio en América Latina*, Ponencia al IX Congreso Latinoamericano de Sociología (México, Nov., 1969).

14

Guide to the Perfect Latin American Idiot (1996)

Plinio Apuleyo Mendoza, Carlos Alberto Montaner and Alvaro Vargas Llosa

Plinio Apuleyo Mendoza (b. Colombia, 1932) is a Colombian journalist and writer. He started his journalist career in Venezuela, where he directed the magazines Elite *and* Momento. *In 1959 he returned to Colombia to direct the Cuban press agency Prensa Cubana. From the 1970s until 1987, Mendoza lived in Paris as cultural attaché of the Colombian Embassy and as editor-in-chief of the magazine* Libre, *bringing together the best writers of the so-called Latin American boom. Upon his return to Colombia, he directed radio and television programs and was columnist for the daily newspaper* El Tiempo. *As a journalist he covered the country's hotspots of guerrilla and narcotraffiking activity, as a consequence he received several death threats. From 1993 to 1995 he was the Colombian Ambassador in Italy. Currently he is a columnist for the* Revista Semana, *which he cofounded, and director of the radio show* Desafíos RCN. *Mendoza has written numerous fiction and nonfiction books and was awarded the Simón Bolívar National Journalism Prize.*

Carlos Alberto Montaner (b. Cuba, 1943) is a Cuban journalist and writer. After being imprisoned in 1961, at age 17, for his opposition to the Cuban communist government, he escaped and went into exile, living in Madrid, Spain since 1970. Montaner's syndicated weekly column is published in dozens of newspapers all around the world, making him one of the most widely read and influential Spanish-speaking columnists. In 1990 he founded the Cuban Liberal Union with the purpose of enabling a transition to freedom and democracy in Cuba. Since 1992 he has been vice president of the Liberal International, an international organization of liberal political parties, based in London. Montaner has written numerous books, received many awards, and taught at several universities.

Alvaro Vargas Llosa (b. Peru, 1966) is a Peruvian journalist and writer. He is a senior fellow and director of The Center on Global Prosperity at the Independent Institute, and a nationally syndicated columnist and radio and television commentator. He was recently appointed Young Global Leader 2007 by the World Economic Forum in Davos. Since the age of 15, Vargas Llosa has devoted himself to journalism in print, television, and radio. He is the author of several books and the recipient of numerous awards. Vargas Llosa was the press spokesman for the

240

presidential campaign of the Democratic Front in 1990 in his native Peru and an Advisor on International Relations for the presidential campaign of Perú Posible in 2001. He lectures widely on world economic and political issues.

This selection is the most widely read liberal-libertarian response to dependency theory in Latin America, aiming to debunk the basic tenets of this theory.

WE'RE POOR: IT'S THEIR FAULT

The underdevelopment of poor countries is historically the result of the enrichment of others. Ultimately, our poverty is due to exploitation in which we are victims of the world's rich countries.

As this statement shows, which could be uttered by our idiot, the blame for what happens to us is never our own. Somebody else—a business, a country, a person—is always responsible for our condition. We love being incompetent with a clear conscience. We take morbid pleasure in believing that we are the victims of some injustice. We exercise imaginary masochism and fantasize about suffering, not because poverty in Latin America is imaginary—it's quite real for the shantytowns of Lima, Rio, and Oaxaca—but rather because we love to blame some evil villain for our shortcomings. Mr. Smith, an executive of a lightbulb factory in Wisconsin, is a reprobate subjecting us to hunger, a highway robber responsible for the miserable $1,000 annual per capita income in Honduras (yes, even our macroeconomic data is conveniently tallied in dollars; how nice!). Mrs. Wayne, a real estate agent in Miami, who covets others' possessions, is capable of the worst injustices, such as keeping 12 million Peruvians out of a formal job. Mr. Butterfly, a computer-chip manufacturer in New York, lives a life of torment thinking about the Hell that awaits him in the afterlife because he owes his million-dollar enterprise to the Guadalupe-Hidalgo Treaty, which in 1848 stole more than half of Mexico's territory and gave it to the United States.

If this onanism of suffering were original, it might actually be nice, one of many other elements in our political folklore. But it's imported from Europe, specifically from a line of thought that at the beginning of the twentieth century tried to justify why the Marxist revolutionary prediction concerning wealthy countries failed, arguing that capitalism would survive thanks to imperialism. This brilliant idea gained even more strength with the independence movement of the postwar era, when all of the colonies that were freed from their rulers believed it was necessary to despise the wealth of the rich in order to feel more independent. Respectable figures such as Pandit Nehru and Nasser, and later some distinguished thugs who took over certain African governments, expanded *urbi et orbe* the cult against the rich. Latin America—always so original—made this its personal mantra and incorporated it into the deepest crevices of academia, politics, communications, and the economy. We Latin Americans made contributions to the esoteric theories of dependency, and figures such as Raúl Prebisch and Henrique Cardoso gave them intellectual respectability.

For starters, poor Marx must be jumping up and down in his grave with these theories. He never supported such an idea. Rather, he praised colonialism as a way of accelerating the arrival of capitalism in underdeveloped countries, this being an indispensable step toward communism. Few men have so vigorously sung the modernizing glory of capitalism as Marx (even without seeing Napoleon on a CD-ROM or faxing a letter to his friend Engels). It would never have occurred to the intellectual father of the cult against the rich that Latin America's poverty was directly proportional to, and caused by, the wealth of the United States or Europe.

No one has christened this ideology as well as the Venezuelan Carlos Rangel: "Third worldism." And no one has better defined its mission than France's Jean-François Revel: "Third worldism's objective is to blame and, if possible, destroy developed societies, not to develop those lagging behind."

Simple logic should suffice to invalidate the statement that our poverty is the wealth of the rich, since it's obvious that if wealth is created and not something that already exists, one country's prosperity is not the result of another's wealth being stolen. If services (which constitute three-fourths of today's U.S. economy) do not use raw materials from Latin America or anywhere else, how, without using magic, could those services be the result of the plundering of our natural resources? If the United States' annual $6 trillion economy is eight times greater than the three major Latin American economies combined (the "giants" Brazil, Mexico, and Argentina), in order for the aforementioned premise to be true, it would have to be shown that at some time these three economies jointly, for example, produced eight times more than they do today, and, when added together, the giant three's production reached a number similar to $6 trillion. If we delve a little into the past, we'll see that $6 trillion is as strange a concept for our current or past economies as solitude is for the Chinese or Hell for the Eskimos.

One could argue that this is not a fair comparison since the United States did not exactly steal everything that it produces but rather it pocketed the necessary resources and then built its own wealth from them. But this argument would invalidate the entire premise that our poverty is due to the exploitation that made us victims, since the exploitation concept rests completely on the idea that wealth is not made but distributed. If it does not exist, it is created, and if it is created, no country's wealth is another's poverty. Even the worst colonial government from the Renaissance era until today has brought the victim country tools of knowledge or technology, providing them some development (at least economically if not politically or intellectually). What would Latin America's economy be today in comparison to wealthy countries if we had not had contact with "the white man's" economies? It's hard to believe that the combined production of Mexico, Brazil, and Argentina would be only eight times less than that of the United States. Peruvians will probably continue patting themselves on the back for the agricultural virtues of the terraced hillsides, a noteworthy invention of the pre-Columbian period but not exactly the forerunner of, for example, the steam or internal-combustion engine (to mention just two rather antiquated capitalist inventions).

Does this mean that there was no plundering during the colonial era or any imperialist injustices during the times of the republic? Yes, there was, but that has as much to do with our current state of underdevelopment as the relationship our intellectuals have with common sense. When our *criollos* confronted the royal Spanish armies (made up of Indians) and cut ties with the motherland, as a region we were much wealthier than the United States, and that was after the pillaging of the colonial era had ended. Furthermore, Spain squandered the gold it carried off on useless European wars instead of using it productively. Therefore, unless we want to go back to grade school, we cannot attribute Spain's current relative prosperity to its previous wealth. Some Peruvian accountant, with patriotic patience, has calculated in present-day numbers the sum of all the gold plundered in the colonial era (this calculation could not have come at a more opportune time than for the 1992 World Exposition in Seville). Spain and Portugal, colonial powers par excellence, are among the poorest countries in the European Union, while Germany, the continent's great driving force, was not a colonial power (not to mention the fact that Germany began its development at the beginning of the twentieth century and from then on has survived colonialist adventures such as Hitler's, which brought the country, economically speaking, many more problems than benefits). The colonialism practiced by the former USSR did not succeed in developing any country. The Cuban economy, deprived of suckling the Soviet teat for its subsidy of more than $5 billion a year, is now begging for outside currency, creating a mystical cult of spine-chilling dimensions to the Dollar God, headed by General Castro himself.

When people talk about the responsibility of colonialism and the exploitation of the weaker countries by the stronger, the reference is usually made to recent centuries. This is a convenient trap. By focusing only on the modern age, it is easy to ignore that colonialism is as old as humanity itself. As far as we know, no part of the world that conquered another, either in antiquity or during the Middle Ages, achieved development comparable to capitalism.

Among the countries to achieve development in recent times have been some that did not possess any important natural resources or conquer any other country. At the end of the Korean conflict, South Korea was left stripped of all industry, since this was all in North Korea. Singapore had no natural resources and lacked cultivable land. In a few decades both South Korea and Singapore (it's becoming quite boring always citing the tigers, but what else can we do?) achieved an economic boom that Latin American countries, much richer in raw materials, have not attained. The countries of the Commonwealth of Independent States (the former Soviet Union) have, on the other hand, all the natural resources in the world and are still suffocating from underdevelopment.

For the first thirty years of the twentieth century, Argentina was an economic world power, much more advanced than many European countries that today have surpassed it. In the decades since then, no one can claim, without embarrassing himself, that Argentina has been a victim of colonialism and significant exploitation. Latin America's recent history is full of virtuous revolutions, such as Mexico's, Bolivia's National Revolutionary Movement, Juan Velasco's revolution in Peru, and Fidel Castro's in Cuba. All rebelled against economic imperialism and selling out to the bourgeoisie. At the end of this process, none of the four countries was better off than before it began. It can be said that in Mexico's case there was relative improvement only when the Revolution, as pliable as putty, conveniently changed its principles and sold itself out to the bourgeoisie.

Since neither resources nor endless incomes are considered wealth, it would be of no use to divide the prosperity of the United States among all Latin Americans—because it would evaporate immediately. Simply transferring this wealth would not solve the basic problem, namely, how to create it. If Latin Americans were to retain the per capita income of the United States, keeping in mind that we have a little less than twice the number of inhabitants in the United States, each would receive around $10,000 annually. If we appropriated this income every year, at the end of five years our situation would not be much better than the current one since the money would not have created businesses or needed job opportunities. Of course the option to invest the money is ruled out since this would contradict the axiom that wealth is not made but stolen. We would not have left underdevelopment behind. In the meantime, our neighbors to the north would be faced with two options for that five-year period: praise the virtues of autophagia or—something more palatable—get to work and try to double the appropriated annual income, currently at $21,000, so the Americans would be able to again enjoy a similar income.

Multinational companies are plundering our wealth and creating a new type of colonialism.

One has to ask why world powers like the United States, Europe, and Japan would plunder our wealth by such strange means as internationalization instead of something more expeditious like sending in an army. It's a mystery why these thieves in search of others' fortunes spend so much money performing studies, building factories, transporting machinery, technology, and managers, promoting products, distributing goods, and employing workers, not to mention paying the customary bribes (an indispensable component of operating costs). What's even more bizarre is actually how in many of these situations profitable returns often cause these enemies of our prosperity to spend even more money to expand production. Why don't they just avoid all these costly charades and send in their military forces and carry off our cornucopia once and for all?

For one simple reason: a multinational corporation is not a government but a business, completely incapable of using physical force against any country. Even though in the past a confrontation with a United States international company in Latin America could have brought about military retaliation, that has not happened for decades. Companies come when they are allowed to come and go when they are forced to leave. The odd thing is that they keep coming to our countries despite the many times in the recent past that our governments have forced them to pack up their belongings and leave. With strange stubbornness foreign capital returns to the place where it has received the worst treatment. It enjoys a good beating. It's more masochistic than some of the Marquis de Sade's protagonists.

A multinational company is not a charity fund, of course. It does not give away money to the country it invests in, precisely because that is what it does— it *invests*, an activity that cannot be separated from the perfectly respectable goal of making a profit. If General Motors or Coca-Cola devoted itself to constructing the entire costly production line referred to earlier in this chapter, and didn't expect to get a cent of profit from it, respect for them would be lost ipso facto.

If they dedicated themselves to philanthropy, they themselves would disappear in no time.

Rather, what these companies do is look for profits. The whole world operates on the expectation of making a profit. Our entire modern structure rests on this foundation. Even genetic engineering and biotechnology, which ultimately are nothing more than manipulative experiments on human and animal genes, in the long run can only yield their desired medical results if the companies that invest fortunes in scientific research believe they will be able to turn a profit. That's why today there exists something so controversial as the patent for human genes. Maybe someday genetic engineering will produce a Latin American intellectual capable of understanding that the quest for profit is healthy and ethical.

It is important for us—and within the intellectual reach of even the most mentally challenged patriot—that these businesses already established in our countries earn profits. Moreover, it would be good if they made billions and, if possible, trillions of dollars. These companies bring in money, technology, and employment, and any profits that they receive will come from being able to sell the goods and services that they produce. If these goods are sold within the country, the local market grows. If they are exported, the country has succeeded in securing a venue for its local products, which otherwise it would not have had. Therefore, our countries profit from a firm's decision to maintain as well as expand its investment in the nation where it has established its business. For any two-legged creature with the ability to reason, all of this should be easier to digest than lettuce.

Major automakers have, for example, announced that they would like for Brazil to be something like the second industrial automotive capital in the Western Hemisphere. What does this mean? It means they want to double their automobile production, which would require these multinational giants to invest a total of $12 billion. Volkswagen, the Satan of the steering wheel, exploiter of our people, devourer of our gold, will inject into that unfortunate country—oh, the horror of it all!—S2.5 billion in order to increase its production to one million vehicles. Ford, the bloodthirsty Moloch on whose altar we sacrifice our children, has announced another $2.5 billion investment. And so it goes. General Motors, a company that was without a doubt created to defile our honor and deprive us of our soul, hates us so much that it employs 100,000 Mexicans, Colombians, Chileans, Venezuelans, and Brazilians. The French company Carrefour, a true imperial Napoleon of foreign capital, inflicted 21,000 jobs onus in Argentina and Brazil, less than half the number mercilessly imposed on us by Volkswagen in Argentina, Brazil, and Mexico.

Until 1989, there was what we in Latin America called "capital flight." In the end, though, the money our own capitalists withdrew exceeded the amount of investment dollars that came to us from outside Latin America's borders. For that year specifically, the "flight" (what lunacy using such foul-sounding police terminology to talk about the economy) totaled around $28 billion. The situation five years later was just the opposite. In 1994, some $50 billion arrived in Latin America all wrapped up in a bow with a card attached reading "foreign capital." Therefore, the "plundering" is recent. Never in the postcolonial history of Latin America was there any such deluge of foreign capital. This, considering that 1994 experienced a decrease in foreign investment of around 30% compared with the previous year, due to the fickleness of Mexican policies, which resulted in even more investment reductions in 1995. Moreover, these investment ups and downs show that there is no guarantee that our markets will attract foreign money. Just like a flirtatious woman, money will make you beg.

A quick look at the 500 largest companies in Latin American shows—oh! oh!—that less than half of them are foreign. In 1993, only 151 of the 500 were foreign, which means that 349 of the largest companies in Latin America were—are—companies that our patriots call "national." In this era of openness to foreign capital, from general imperialism and sell-outs to the bourgeoisie, it seems that still not even half the companies handling the most money come from our enemies' shores; instead they come from our own. What does this mean? First of all, if someone is plundering our wealth, the primary plunderers are not foreign multinational companies. Second, when an economy is opened to foreign capital local investments also benefit, provided that there are some minimally attractive conditions. It doesn't matter whether the business is foreign or domestic; the general movement of the economy pushes the country forward into the area where firms, foreign and domestic, operate. Third, our problem is still—despite everything—how to get more foreign capital to come in instead of go out as it has been, leaving us for other areas (Asia, for example). If we could blame someone for economic imperialism, it's our own Latin American companies that are inundating the very same Latin American countries. A veritable avalanche of Latin American investments is moving through many countries between the Rio Grande and the Straits of Magellan. This is what allows the Chileans to manage private pension funds in Peru, for example, or Chile's Embotelladora Andina to buy the Coca-Cola bottling company in Rio de Janeiro, or Televisa to acquire a television station in Santiago. We cannot blame the developed countries anymore for monopolizing foreign investments; we ourselves have become compulsive foreign investors in Latin America.

Not long ago our problem was not foreign capital but rather the lack of it. Today, we should regret that there is not $100 or even $200 billion of foreign investment. Our problem isn't that 15% of all Japanese foreign investments are going to Latin America, but rather that only 15% and not 40 or 50% is headed our way. At the beginning of the 1990s, 15% of Spain's foreign capital investments came *to Latin America*. What should upset us is that our mother country didn't invest more.

Much of the foreign capital goes into the securities markets, but takes off as soon as a hair-raising crisis appears (such as the devaluation of the Mexican peso at the beginning of 1995, with its consequent "tequila effect" in countries such as Argentina, or the squabble between Peru and Ecuador that same year). This means that those dollars still do not have enough confidence in us; they are only dipping their toes in our waters. This being the case, how can anyone complain about any pillaging? The problem is that those investments do not stay. Aren't many of those dollars speculative, you may ask? Yes, but that's the nature of dollars. They make our economy breathe and even provide capital for our own companies. By the way, the macroeconomic effect of those dollars is no small matter; many times they compensate for our trade deficits, helping to avoid massive devaluation that would cause inflation to shoot up. And lastly, foreign investments spread confidence to other foreigners with well-lined pockets.

Foreign investments alone have not rescued any country from its misery; this will not be possible unless a strong national market, with domestic savings and investments within a free society, is developed. But in this world of frenzied global competition, foreign investments are a way of being pulled into the modern age. The progressives of this world would like to take us back to the autarkic communities of the Dark Ages. Progressivism is science fiction turned into politics: tourism to the past.

Our poverty is closely tied to the progressive deterioration of the terms of trade. It is extremely unfair that we have to sell our raw materials at low prices and buy industrial products and manufactured capital goods from rich countries at high prices. A new, more equitable economic order is needed.

It's also not fair that the sky is blue and that iguanas are ugly critters. The difference is that we can't do anything about these natural injustices. But for man-made ones we can, as long as an "I didn't do it" look isn't the response to every blunder committed by our leaders. It seems that, in Latin America, trade is a form of serfdom that we are subjected to by the great powers; this after almost two centuries of independence. We forget that toward the end of the nineteenth century—in 1880, for example—many decades after the Monroe Doctrine, Latin America's participation in world trade was similar to that of the United States. Until 1929, many years after any American military marauding took place in our lands and after the Platt Amendment was passed (a limitation on Cuban sovereignty imposed by the U.S. Congress in 1901), our countries' export quota was 10% of the world total, a number not the least bit inconsequential for nations enslaved by the emerging power from the North and by traditional powers from beyond the Atlantic. In those times, when our military and political vulnerability was much greater with respect to the great powers, our ability to export was, comparatively speaking, better than today's. The world needed our goods and, in the global commercial market, we meant something. The economic benefits we received from those sales were considerable because, since our products were highly valued in the eyes of the buyer, the demand—and consequently the prices—were respectable. How can we blame the rich countries that Latin American products ceased being as valuable as they were in the first half of the twentieth century? How is economic imperialism to blame that the products we offer on the world market are less appealing now since buyers' needs have changed?

Immediately after the war, when the international trade organization called GATT was born (now replaced by the World Trade Organization), the bulk of the world's trade was in raw materials (which we had a lot of) and manufactured goods (which for some reason we had no desire to produce). Today, this has changed drastically as the service industry has blown into our lives like a hurricane. Services now constitute a fourth of the entire world's trade and soon will be a third. In countries such as the United States, services already account for three-fourths of the economy, which makes any statement that America's prosperity is related to its trading terms with Latin America ridiculous. In a world where the service industry rules, our products become less attractive with each passing minute. Therefore, our lament shouldn't be that they buy from us low and sell to us high, but rather that, if we follow our lazy attitude of essentially exporting the things nature generously dropped in our laps, we will become completely dispensable as suppliers of goods on the international market. The threat, dear idiots, is not serfdom but insignificance.

We should be grateful that this transition from an industrial economy to a service economy has been relatively recent. We should be grateful that this has made it possible for our traditional products to still excite a few well-to-do palates for some decades, allowing us to play our small role in the world's growing postwar trade (trade has grown tenfold since the creation of GATT). Trade has been one of the factors responsible for the fact that Latin America's per capita income grew 162% between 1960 and 1982. If the service economy had made its phantasmagoric appearance a few decades earlier, these figures—which have certainly not solved our poverty problem—would probably have been much lower for our area of the Western Hemisphere. Surprisingly, the equivalent of $7 billion is generated annually in regions where raw materials and traditional commodities still dominate exports, as is the case in Central America. That figure is Lilliputian in comparison to exports from the small Asian giants with smaller geographic surfaces and fewer resources spewing forth from the earth. But the figures are high if you keep in mind how really insignificant those products, which make even this figure possible, are in the present-day economy. It's hardly serious to claim, on the threshold of the twenty-first century, to be somebody important in the world by waving a banana in one hand and a coffee bean in the other.

Except in very unusual cases where one trade partner aims the barrel of a gun at another, the poverty or wealth of our countries (concerning exports) has depended primarily on our ability to produce what others want to buy. Furthermore, in many cases we have "restricted" rich countries, barricading our economies inside veritable tariff fortresses. While their markets were semi-open, ours were closed. This allowed us in 1990 to have a trade surplus of $26 billion for the entire region—a huge chasm of export revenues over import costs. No one sent in the big guns to open our tariff-cemented walls, and evidently neither did they retaliate as is done today, for example, with Washington attacking Japan in revenge for its trade deficit. The powerful economies were not sufficiently open then, nor are they now. But in commercial trade there was no colonialist use of force; Latin America could block the influx of many exports from the rich countries and assure that its own exports brought in a few billion dollars, even in an international economy that relied less on raw materials.

Let's look for a moment at what happened in commercial trade between us and the despised United States. In 1991, when Latin American countries began to boldly open up their economies to imports—what the idiot calls "tariff disarmament"—our lives were filled with consumer goods from those powerful countries that previously caused us to lose so much sleep. It just so happens, however, that the United States also receives many of our products. As a result, in that year Latin America exported a total of 873 billion, while it imported a total of $70 billion. Where is the commercial imperialism? Where are the "unfair trading terms"? Commercially speaking, in the 1990s, Latin America profited from the U.S. market just as the United States has with the Latin American market. Half of Latin America's exports go to the United States. If the United States wanted to do without our exports, it could do so easily. But the effect for us would be devastating—since we haven't developed any domestic markets capable of sustaining the growth of those products which today have a venue through the export pipeline (albeit insufficient in comparison to the ideal or to other areas of the world). Each time an American regulation obstructs Latin American products from being imported (Colombian flowers, for example), we shriek like magpies. We complain about the trading terms, but when that trade is threatened we become hysterical. So what do we want? Do we want them to buy our products or not? It's true that since 1991 the United States has exported more to Latin America than to Japan. But it's because we want it to be that way, not because we have a gun pointed at our head. Finally, we are the beneficiaries of these imports. We acquire consumer goods at lower prices and in many cases of better quality. The United States is of course not the only powerful country that buys our products and, incidentally, slips dollars into our economies. In 1991, our exports to Spain increased 20% while our markets received only 4% of Spain's exports. Who is "exploiting" whom? If we didn't export those amounts to the United States and Spain, we would be much poorer than we already are.

A curious defect in our political experts and economists has prevented them from seeing that the solution to the diminishing importance of raw materials is to diversify the economy, to begin producing things more in tune with the reality that has made our traditional products as passé as the rationalizations of those who believe low prices are caused by a world conspiracy. Countries like Mexico are showing that diversification is feasible. In 1994, 58% of Mexican exports were metal products, machinery, industrial and automotive spare parts, and electronic equipment. The state-controlled oil company, Pemex, today contributes only 12% to Mexico's total exports, when in 1986 oil constituted 80%. Similarly who would dare say, without getting tongue-tied, that Mexico's problem is the sale of cheap raw materials and the purchase of expensive manufactured products?

Of the ten Latin American companies with the highest sales in 1993, only four—that is, less than half—sell raw materials. The others are in the automotive industry, business, telecommunications, and electricity. In 1994, the Latin American company leading in sales was not a business offering raw materials but telecommunications. Latin America's economy, although still very dependent on raw materials, is becoming diversified. As long as this continues, the problem will be overcome, a problem not caused by any conspiracy but by changes in the world reality, namely raw materials no longer being a seducer of markets.

Does this mean that we should toss our raw materials into the ocean? No, it means that we shouldn't rely on them—but let's profit from them as much as we can. Often incompetence has prevented us from making a sufficient profit from the use of those raw materials. How much oil and gold remain to be found? Probably a lot. If we hadn't waited so long to bring in investors willing to run the risk of development, we would have more oil to sell. Here then, one arrives at the conclusion that trading raw materials for manufactured products is just as unfair as our needing imperialist investors to extract the raw materials from the places where nature has buried them. Panama is eagerly exploring its subsoil for gold and copper. Today, mining constitutes 5% of its economy, and the authorities believe that it could reach 15% by the year 2005. Who is responsible for the mining industry comprising only 5% and not 15% of Panama's economy today? Our illustrious intellectuals and politicians would undoubtedly say that it's the multinationals' fault since they didn't offer their services earlier to come and find the gold and copper.

There are, however, Latin American raw materials that, in addition to being exploited, exploit the rich. Oil has been a plentiful and valuable commodity in some countries. Those countries form part of the international cartel called OPEC (Organization of Petroleum Exporting Countries), which one fine day in 1973 decided to increase its prices astronomically, bringing the powerful countries whose industries needed this source of energy to their knees. A country like Venezuela has so exploited the price of its petroleum resources that between the 1970s and 1990s it received the "meager" sum of $250 billion! What did it do with the money? What it did is much more responsible for the poverty in Venezuela than the prices the world has paid for the Saudi-Venezuelan oil those twenty years.

Another way of escaping the claws of imperialist civilization is for Latin American countries to do business with each other. In 1994, for example, almost a third of Argentina's exports ended up in Brazil, its partner in the common market Mercosur. A third of the pharmaceutical products bought in Brazil, a total of $5 billion (everyone knows that in Brazil the pharmacy is as popular as the church), are manufactured by Latin American companies. Some countries in the area have set in motion a vast project for an interconnecting natural gas pipeline, a network that will he worth billions of dollars when finished. Is anyone threatening to invade the territories south of the Rio Grande in any of this? Are Tokyo, Berlin, or Washington decreeing the selling price *manu militari*?

Unfortunately, Latin America is once again beginning to prevent the import of products from the infamous shores of prosperity. The process, slow but menacing, is dictated by the fallacious notion that a good part of our inability to rapidly create prosperous local economies is the voluminous influx of imports that causes trade imbalances. After its financial crisis in January 1995, Mexico immediately raised its tariffs. Argentina, affected by this shot of "tequila," did the same, and its government proposed that all Mercosur countries raise the tariffs on products coming from outside the borders of the member nations. Latin America continues to place many restraints on foreign trade—even on areas where tariffs have been lowered—by using open-ended or veiled regulations that increase the price of imports. (One shouldn't forget that the tariffs themselves, despite being lower than before, continue to penalize the consumer.) The psychosis created by the traumatic devaluation of the Mexican peso has placed the trade deficit at the top of many Latin American countries' list of enemies. The only problem: the Mexican crisis was not caused by that deficit. It was caused by a lack of political confidence (the result of the prevailing system) and the capricious fixing of the Mexican peso at levels no longer justified by market reality. A trade deficit in itself is not bad. It just means that there are more imports than exports, and imports benefit consumers. Deficits can put pressure on the money supply if there are no other resources for bringing in dollars to offset the effects of trade imbalances on the balance of payments. In which case, to avoid greater problems, it's best to let the currency reflect the real price. To equalize the trade balance, the solution is not to punish consumers but to export more.

If any criticism can be made against rich countries, it's not that they are imposing unfair trading terms but that they are still not opening up their economies enough. And they are even placing barriers to letting many of our products enter. For example, it costs the twenty-four richest countries in the world $250 billion a year to protect their farmers from competition. Our political charlatans should be ceaselessly denouncing this type of nonsense. Any damage done by the rich to the poor, in the global economy, is because they don't dare let us compete in their markets on equal terms. The rest—trade stipulations based on the price of outgoing raw materials and incoming manufactured products—belongs to our idiots' idle fantasy and the ideological Paleolithic era in which they continue to exist.

There will be no more poverty when the put an end to the economic differences characterized by our societies.

The only thing that makes any sense in this axiom is that poverty and economic differences exist in our countries. There is not a single society without economic differences, especially in countries where they have adopted policies of equality predicated by Marxists. We have very poor societies. But they are not the poorest in the world. Our per capita income is five times greater than that of southern Asia and six times greater than that of black Africa. Even so, half of our people are submerged beneath what in economic jargon is called (invoking geometry to refer to the matters of the stomach) the "poverty line." It's also true that there are economic disparities. In the streets of Lima or Rio de Janeiro it's not difficult to cross from opulence to destitution within a few yards. Some Latin American cities are veritable monuments to economic contrasts.

But here stop the neurons of him who uttered the memorable sentence preceding these lines. As for the rest, logic is overwhelming: there will be no poverty when there are no economic differences. Does this mean that when everyone is poor there won't be poverty? Every government having proposed abolishing poverty has through its "equalizing" methods succeeded—effectively, we might add—in reducing many of the disparities, not because everyone has become rich but because almost everyone has become poor. Not *everyone* has become poor of course—the elite ruling class managing these socialist policies has always become rich. In Latin America we are experts on this. Think of Nicaragua's Sandinista experience. What did the boys in olive green accomplish when they proposed to obliterate poverty by putting an end to differences? A 90% drop in the average wage. Wouldn't you know, though, that the authors of that heroic deed saved themselves from the classless society; they all helped themselves to grand properties and amassed enviable capital resources. Popular wit christened this pillaging with the ironic name "the piñata." In Peru, Alan García planned to do something similar. The result: while the capital resources of those governing grew in bank accounts in tax havens all over the world, the money belonging to the Peruvian people turned to dust. So for whoever had 100 *intis* in the bank when Alan García assumed power, barely 2 *intis* remained by the end of his term. In Bolivia, Hernando Siles Zuazo, although less predatory than the Sandinistas or García in Peru, turned the banking industry into a circus. In order to withdraw small sums of money from the bank you had to go to the financial institution with potato sacks, since it was impossible to carry in your hands or pockets all the bills needed for minor expenses. The list goes on, but this suffices to demonstrate that Latin America's recent history has specifically proved what a government can accomplish when it proposes to break the backs of the rich in order to straighten the backs of the poor.

For starters, in our countries it's the government, or more exactly the state, who is rich. The richer our governments, the greater their inability to create societies where wealth extends to many citizens. Incredible cases have been recorded, one being the wealth acquired by Venezuelan oil: $250 billion in twenty years. That is certainly wealth. No private Latin American enterprise has generated such a fortune in postcolonial history. What became of this wave of prosperity controlled by a government that said it was acting on behalf of the poor?

There are more such cases. The Cuba of "social justice," whose government proposed banishing poverty from the Caribbean island once and for all by expropriating from the rich to avenge the poor, received subsidies totaling $100 billion from one Soviet government after another over the course of three decades. In Cuba, though, the government has been the rich one. Have you seen the living conditions of the Cuban people improve thanks to the money the government received on their behalf? Revolutionary ineptitude has caused even the wealth of the governing rich to reach such low levels that only the most intimate circles of power can retain a monetary fortune. In Brazil, the largest company is not private but government-owned. How could it be any other way in the country where Getulio Vargas instilled the idea that government was the engine of wealth? Are the inhabitants of the barren Sertão backwoods or the starving children of the shantytowns in Rio aware of the money that Petrobrás generates for them? How much of the wealth represented by Brazil's 147 public companies is accessible to them? In revolutionary Mexico, which ended when Porfirio Díaz sold out to the bourgeoisie, the oil company, the leading business in the country, had a net worth of $35 billion and annual profits of nearly a billion dollars. Have the Mexicans in Chiapas seen one peso of that treasure?

The richest of them all, the government, dedicates its money to everything but the poor (except during election time). The money goes to pay political cronies, enlarge surreptitious bank accounts, finance inflation, and for stupid expenses like armaments. The Third World—a concept more suitable for Steven Spielberg than for the world's political and economic reality—spends on armaments four times the amount of foreign investments made in Latin America. A large percentage of these expenditures comes from our region's public coffers. Governments calling themselves defenders of the poor become rich and spend the money—whatever monies they don't steal—on things that never benefit the poor. A small portion is allocated for the poor in the form of subsidies and social programs but is soon eaten up by the inflation that results from government expenditures.

There are still insufficient examples of failed policies defending the poor in Latin America that would prevent socialist escapades from running rampant continentwide. Costa Rica, a country whose democracy sets an example for all Latin America, is seeing how in the mid-1990s its social-democratic government increased public spending by 18%. The result: inflation and economic stagnation. A policy weighted down by good intentions—to help the downtrodden—is accomplishing just the contrary: making the poor even poorer. As usual in a climate of this type, it's the rich who are best protected against an economic crisis fueled by the friendly government that calls itself a partner to the poor.

Experience teaches us that the best way to help the poor is to not try to defend them. No genetic defect is forcing our poor to be that way. Moreover, whenever Latin Americans have had the opportunity to create wealth in the few societies where they are permitted to do so, they have. For several countries—Mexico, the Dominican Republic, Peru, and El Salvador, to name just a few—an essential source of foreign currency is the money sent back home to the poor from relatives living abroad. Most of these relatives didn't go in search of work carrying personal checkbooks in their backpockets. In a short time they succeeded in making a living overseas, some with great success, others less successfully but with enough money to be able to help those they left behind. The most remarkable example of Latin Americans living successfully in exile is the Cubans. After several years of exile, the Cubans in the United States—some 2 million, including the second generation—produce $30 billion worth of goods and services per year, while the 10 million Cubans on the island produce only one-third that amount. Are there any biological defects in the Cubans on the island that prevent them from generating as much wealth as those elsewhere? Some cerebral defect? Unless some phrenologist can prove otherwise, there is no difference between the brains of those on or those off Cuba. There is simply a different institutional climate.

Enthusiasm is beginning to build concerning the activity of our stock markets and the improvement of our macroeconomic numbers. Latin America, however, is far from breaking free from its straightjacket of poverty because, among other reasons, it still doesn't invest or save enough. In 1993, investments in these unfortunate lands totaled some 18% of the GDP. In "developing" Asian countries—another gem in the secret language bureaucrats of international economy use—the figure is 30%. This was not the first time in the twentieth century's history that our economies have grown. It has happened before and yet poverty did not decrease significantly because of it. For example, we grew at a respectable rate of 4.5% between 1935 and 1953 and 5% between 1945 and 1955. None of this gave the poor access to wealth-creating ventures, or introduced free institutions that would defend property rights and the sanctity of contracts, or reduced the cost of doing business, facilitated competition, or eliminated monopolistic privileges—all indispensable factors in a market economy.

When our countries have an institutional climate that favors enterprise, attracts investment, and stimulates saving, and when success is not limited to those who swarm around the government like flies to receive monopolies (most privatization in Latin America is a monopolistic concession on payment of a bribe), then our poor will stop being poor. This doesn't mean that the rich will cease being rich. In a free society wealth is not measured in relative terms but in absolute ones, not collectively but individually. It wouldn't help anyone to distribute the net worth of the rich in each of our countries among the poor. The sum each would receive would be small and wouldn't guarantee future subsistence since the distribution would have completely wiped out the existing wealth. If we were to divide the estimated $12 billion net worth of Mexico's telecommunications company, Telmex, among the 90 million Mexicans, each would receive the monumental sum of . . . $133! It's more to the Mexicans' advantage for this business to continue employing 63,000 people and generating juicy profits of $3 billion a year, keeping the company operating and expanding.

The culture of envy believes that by taking away the yachts belonging to the Azcárragas (Mexico) and the Cisneros (Venezuela), or the jets owned by groups like Bunge y Born (Argentina), Bradesco (Brazil), and Luksic (Chile), Latin America would be a much fairer place. Maybe the fish in the sea where the Azcárragas and the Cisneros sail, or the clouds where Lázaro de Mello Brandao and Octavio Caraballo's planes fly, would appreciate a little less disruption by these "intruders." Maybe our idiots would sleep better, or pat themselves on the back, or their elated joy of revenge would get their adrenaline flowing. But there can be no doubt that Latin America's poverty would not be alleviated one bit. The philosophy of economic revanchism—what Von Mises called "the Fourier complex"—is due more to one's resentment of one's own condition than to the idea that justice is a kind of natural law of compassion relentlessly carried out against the "haves" in favor of the "have-nots." True, our rich, with few exceptions, are rather uncouth and ostentatious, common and arrogant. So what! Social justice is not a code of conduct, a British boarding school with a matron who slaps the wrist of anyone who misbehaves. It's a system, a sum of institutions arising from a culture of freedom. Until this culture exists among us, it will be a "members-only" club. To open the doors to this club we don't have to close it down but instead change the rules of the game.

The strange thing about capitalism is that the key to its success lies in the disparities, making it by far the best economic system. The best, which is to say, fairer, more equal. What incentive does a Cuban have to produce more if he knows he'll never be entitled to private ownership of the means of production, nor to reap the benefits of his efforts, and he'll forever be a sheep in an indistinguishable flock behind a despotic shepherd? If the incentive for this disparity disappears, the overall product and wealth in its entirety also disappear and what remains to be distributed is therefore even less.

The key to capitalism is that capital growth exceeds population growth. With time, what seemed like a luxury for the few becomes mass consumption. How many Dominicans considered poor today have a radio and television? For a poor person in the Middle Ages, comparable items were inconceivable luxuries. Sooner or later, capitalism makes commonplace those objects that were initially flaunted by the rich. This is no consolation to minimize the terrible effects of poverty. It's simply a demonstration that the most restrictive capitalism, enriching a few, also enriches others, although very slightly. The freest capitalism, one that abides under an equal rule of law for all, does the same thing but multiplied a hundredfold.

Free capitalism is one that does not accept the existence of oligarchies sheltered by power. Although the word "oligarchy" has a special place in the perfect Latin American idiot's dictionary, it's not an invention of his but rather an ancient term used by Greek philosophers. Yes, there are oligarchies in Latin America. They are no longer oligarchies of landowners and ranchers; instead they are industrial oligarchies and business groups that have prospered under protectionist power. To eliminate these oligarchies one doesn't have to eradicate their external manifestations—their money—but rather the system that made them possible. If these oligarchies, faced with coming of age, and being emancipated from state tutelage, continue to fatten their bank accounts then . . . long live the rich!

There is yet another explanation for our poverty: foreign debt is strangling Latin America's economies, and the great international banking industry is profiting from its usurious interest rates.

Foreign debt doesn't amount to a hill of beans. The best demonstration of this is that today anyone who has even the slightest understanding of the economy is not concerned about it, despite the fact that the region's total debt is greater now than in previous years, when the continent's political song and dance was limited to the tune of the $550 billion debt. Until recently, nothing titillated our politicians more or better induced Pavlovian reactions in our intellectuals' salivary glands than the foreign debt.

The debt is nothing more than the result of Latin American supplications to foreign governments and banks that began in the 1960s with a fervor that belies our traditional cult of "dignity" and continued throughout the 1970s. Latin America's total debt went from $29 billion in 1969 to $450 billion in 1991 as the region from Mexico to Patagonia turned into a zoo of white elephants that provided no returns to the people in whose name the grandiose public works were undertaken. The banks, burgeoning with dollars to be used wherever possible and whose existence was justified by the interest earned from the loans being issued, joyfully greased our machinery of public life. Can the banks be criticized for giving us the resources our imploring hands requested? Let's pretend that the international community had not given us the loans. What would we have been saying then? Instead of being a "usurious bank" it would have been a "racist," "stingy," or "voracious" bank. The banks only gave us what we asked for, not what the gun-toting imperialists made our governments accept. Looking back at it now, however, Latin America would no doubt have retained greater government control if the world had been less acquiescent to our insatiable begging. The largest Latin American debtor is not a private businessman but the government. There is not one Latin American country where the government doesn't owe at least half of the foreign debt.

Interest rates are high, you say? Interest rates are like elevators or ocean tides. Sometimes they go up, and sometimes they go down. If it's agreed that the debt will be subject to flexible interest rates, no one can shoot the banker when one day he raises the rates because the market set them there. At the beginning of the 1980s the United States raised its interest rates to fight inflation. Was the Reagan administration's decision to fight inflation a Machiavellian conspiracy craftily planned to make Latin America's debt seem more unwieldy than it already was? Proof of Latin America's magic realism is that there is a legion of people capable of believing this.

If the conspiracy were true, the imperialists got their just deserts. In 1982, a memo from Mexico was sent directly to Washington with a simple message: We cannot continue paying the debt. We all know what came afterward: a financial cataclysm. The vengeance of Latin America's history of suffering remained forever indelible in a brief paragraph on a piece of official paper. The consequences were not a medieval-style punishment for the borrower who confessed that he could not repay. Instead, there was an overall crisis in the world financial system. Another characteristic of the somniferous affair of Latin America's foreign debt is how countries can stop paying their debts whenever they wish without incurring any significant reprisals, except for difficulties in taking out new loans. (What nerve!) Thanks to Mexico's capricious decree, nine of the top ten American banks were on the verge of becoming insolvent, and no one retaliated against the catalyst of the crisis. Consequently, the debt became a double-edged sword. On the one hand, there was a threat to the Latin American economy since it owed money to the lenders. On the other hand, it kept the creditors hanging, their solvency partly relying on the myth that the debt will one day be repaid in full. The golden rule with debts is never to say that the loan will not be repaid, even though payments may already have stopped. The world of international finance is mind-boggling. The world banking industry is a fraternity of simpletons lending clients money so they can repay the previous debt that was borrowed to pay the debt prior to that one.

Accompanying Latin America's debt is the assurance of impunity. Each time arrears accumulate, especially now in times of economic growth, the banks are very tolerant. Between 1991 and 1992, $25 billion in arrears had accumulated. Did any bank or government say a word about it? Quite the contrary: while the arrears were accumulating the United States forgave more than 90% of the bilateral debt owed by Guyana, Honduras, and Nicaragua; 70% of that owed by Haiti and Bolivia; 25% of Jamaica's debt; and 4% of Chile's debt.

As for the trade debt, with a little bit of imagination—this premise being an optimistic one—and a playful nature, its structure can he molded like clay. The first country to figure this out was Bolivia, which in 1987, after having reduced its inflation, asked for money to buy out its entire trade debt at 11% of its value. So, without complaining or groaning, almost like magic, Bolivia reduced its total debt from $1.5 billion to $259 million. Then came Mexico, thanks to the Brady plan. In February 1990, it convinced the good-hearted commercial bankers to convert the debt to guaranteed negotiable bonds. Where was the trick? Easy, those bonds were 65% of the value of the debt instruments. It convinced another group of bankers to exchange its debt for guaranteed bonds with a 6.5% yield. With a single blow, using numbers instead of insults, Mexico slashed the debt it owed. Since then, most Latin American countries have "restructured" their debts—a nasty term simply meaning that the tyrants in the world banking industry forgave a huge percentage of these countries' debts in exchange for the remaining debt to be paid off on mutually convenient terms, which (in the context of minimally sensible economic policy) means easy. In 1994, for example, Brazil changed its payment timetable and structure to $52 billion, sweeping $4 billion of principal and $4 billion in interest under the rug. Recently Ecuador, the unfortunate victim of global racketeering, succeeded in reducing its debt principal by 45% through restructuring and simply exchanging smiles with its creditors. In the first quarter of 1995, Panama had nearly reached a similar agreement. Reducing one's debt with commercial banks is much easier than snatching the billfold from an unsuspecting tourist arriving at Lima's Jorge Chávez airport.

The debt is such an unimportant topic of discussion between the international community and Latin America that the debt instruments are being revalued on the secondary market. Plainly said, this simply means that the world thinks that a good macroeconomic situation in Latin America gives them reason to believe our countries will continue making future partial payments, since Latin America is solvent. Moreover, the current trend is that private companies, which offer stocks and bonds on the international stock markets, hold much of the new debt. The world is again accepting the myth that someday the debt will be paid off. And since we all know that the financial world is the land of hopes as much as reality, the key is not paying off the debt but rather believing that it will be paid off, believing in the simple fantasy that repayment is possible. The only thing missing in these trade-debt situations is sticking one's tongue out at the creditor. In government-to-government debts, one just needs to shake hands with a group of bureaucrats meeting under the aristocratic title of the *Club de Paris*, something already accomplished by many countries.

If Latin America's foreign debt were strangling the continent's economies, it would not be possible for many of these countries to have billion-dollar reserves as they have today. Nor, of course, could they attract the volatile migratory capital—"swallow" capital, as it's known in Spanish—that comes to Latin American stock markets to earn fabulous, fast-moving profits in national company stocks whose yields regurgitate such returns.

Without a doubt, paying the debt is a burden. For Bolivia it means allocating a little more than 20% of its export dollars to service its debt. For Brazil it's 26%. None of this is pleasant (remembering that these are inevitable consequences of our governments' irresponsibility), but the payments are spread out in installments in accordance with each country's ability to pay. Besides that, a normal relationship with the financial community allowed a country such as Mexico to receive an astronomical international aid package at the beginning of 1995 in order to rescue itself from its own incompetence and for Argentina to protect itself from the ensuing "tequila effect" with credits from the imperialists.

For years foreign debt was the great excuse, absolving Latin America's conscience of any blame. This excuse was so attractive that our politicians—for example, Fidel Castro and Alan Garcia—swore in public that they would not pay the debt while secretly continuing to pay it. Alan García, the prince of demagogy, made famous the refrain "ten percent" (indicating he wouldn't pay more than 10% of the total amount of export sales). But in the end he paid more than his predecessor, Belaunde Terry, who never publicly objected to his obligations to the bank and still reduced the payments substantially. As for Fidel Castro, a champion veteran of anti-Western causes, he tried to start a debtor's club, a kind of insolvency union, to confront the powerful and refuse to pay. Shortly afterward it was discovered that he was one of the most punctual payers of his debt to the capitalist banks, at least until 1986 when he declared bankruptcy and stopped making payments altogether. Bankers should be told to find those specimens in a continent's political fauna that roar the loudest against usurious banks and foreign debt because those species will, without a doubt, be their most exemplary clients.

The International Monetary Fund's demands are plunging our people into poverty.

Funditis, like the Ebola virus, is a virus that causes hemorrhaging and diarrhea. The hemorrhaging and diarrhea caused by funditis, less degrading than those caused by the Ebola virus, are verbal. This particular virus attacks the brain. Its victims, who are found by the thousands throughout Latin America, discharge a torrent of words day and night, clamoring against the common enemy of Latin American nations and underdevelopment in general: the International Monetary Fund. They lose many hours of sleep, foam at the mouth, and blow smoke out their ears, obsessed by the creature that lives only to snatch away the last crust of bread from the lips of the emaciated child in the slums. Marches, demonstrations, proclamations, coup d'etats, countercoups. How many political lamentations have paid homage to hatred for the International Monetary Fund! For the "progressives," this institution became in the 1980s what United Fruit was a few decades earlier: the flagship of imperialism. Not only poverty but also earthquakes, floods, and cyclones are all spawned by the Fundist's plans, a perfect glacial conspiracy designed by its managing director. Is there anything that the IMF is not capable of doing? Maybe precipitating a South American defeat in the final round of the Soccer World Cup, but it's best not to test the IMF.

What exactly is this monster that devours impoverished countries? Is it an army? An extraterrestrial? A nightmare? Where does it get its power to inflict hunger, sickness, and helplessness on Latin America's downtrodden? It's truly quite sad to reveal what the International Monetary Fund really is. Far from the fantastic mythology that has been woven around it, it's simply a financial institution created as part of the Bretton-Woods accord during the uncertainty immediately following the Second World War when the world was pulling its hair out trying to solve the problem of how to dig itself out of the economic hole into which the misfortunes of war had put it. The agency was to function as a conduit for funds that were paid in and then directed toward a specific destination according to monetary needs. Over time, the IMF began sending the bulk of its funds to countries today known as "underdeveloped." Those funds did not come from some philanthropic volunteer's imagination but from the economic giants. Latin America became one of the areas where the IMF would try to ease the financing problems faced by certain governments.

Were our governments obligated to accept the IMF? It was an impossible and heroic task to stop the Monetary Fund's troops from entering our countries, right? It was so impossible and so heroic that we didn't have to do a thing. All we had to do was not ask for help and, if it was offered, slam the door right in its face. In fact, many of our governments did just that. Others signed letters of intent with this agency and then blew off the agreement.

Some governments have sought aid from the IMF contingent upon certain macroeconomic policies—conditions which were actually negotiated with the applicant country. These dynamics ("I will give you money, but I would like you to take certain steps so that this aid has some meaning") are the result of a decision made by the donor countries. The IMF will help certain governments in exchange for a certain rigor in administering public finance. No one has a pistol pointed at his head, forcing him to accept the conditions. Nor does anyone have the right to appropriate someone else's funds (this part is usually forgotten by our patriots who bellow against the frigid—and rather devoid of sex appeal—Mr. Camdessus, the managing director of the IMF). Our barking at the Fund is simply because this institution doesn't give away dollars (which don't even belong to it in the first place).

In many cases, not accepting the IMF as a mediator has made the defiant country an enemy of the other financial institutions and of some major governments donating foreign aid. Is this unusual? Governments and banks, which are not forced by any natural or human law to provide social assistance, much less charity, prefer some type of guarantee, especially after the cataclysmic effects of the debt crisis at the beginning of the 1980s. Therefore, although it's always in the hands of the country to decide whether it wants a little *fundistic* push out of paralysis, it can suffer the consequences of not complying with the Fund's agreement insofar as it can find deafer ears at other financial organizations. Peru's Alan García did this (and he was not the only one).

Is the IMF the answer to Latin America's problems? Anyone who believes this deserves to have a privileged entry in the idiots' registry. This simple method of aiding government accounts in exchange for a little restriction on fiscal spending in order to contain inflation is not going to create vigorous societies where wealth flourishes like flowers in the spring. Furthermore, adopting certain fiscally disciplined measures without opening and deregulating stale economies is what has contributed greatly to liberalism's association with the IMF over these past years and, incidentally, has established the equation that states: the more IMF, the greater the poverty. Thanks to this, the history of the IMF is the story of how the most boring man—its managing director—has become the most hated man.

The IMF is neither the key to prosperity nor the ticket to success. To attribute these false characteristics to the Fund is one way of deepening the hatred for this agency, since no macroeconomic policy tied to the IMF's fiscal mathematics will ever suffice to solve the problem of poverty. These solutions are not found in the stiff, well-dressed IMF officer's briefcase; they were not yet even born when the reasons for our postcolonial failure manifested themselves. Only the institutions of the country in question can produce that miracle.

Our countries will never be free as long as the United States participates in our economies.

Peruvians call a tortuous relationship between a husband and wife *amor serrano;* the greater the abuse, the greater the love between them. The greatest sign of love is a slap, a karate kick, or a head bash. There is nothing more touching, sentimental, or exciting than a beating. Between Latin Americans and the United States there is *amor serrano*. As we saw previously, no one defined this relationship from the Latin American's point of view better than the Uruguayan José Enrique Rodó: USA-mania. This refers to the maddening fascination for everything American, a fascination that is both healthy and envious, as much holy in essence as vile in form. We all have a *gringo* inside of us and we would all love to grab a *gringo* by the scruff of his neck. Throughout the twentieth century, we always defined Latin Americans in contrast to the United States. It's admiration rather than laughter that Fidel Castro provokes when, without allowing his beard to tremble, he denounces the bombardment of microbes from American laboratories destined for his country. The last bombardment, according to the General, provoked an epidemic of optical neuritis on the island. All of us have a Yankee spying on us from under the bed. Reclined on the psychiatrist's couch a star-spangled red, white, and blue flag emerges from our subconscious before any shame for our own past.

The worst Yankee offenses have, of course, been military. The only thing our patriots forget to add is that the United States' interventionist mistakes and defeats have probably been more significant than its victories. It was never able to overthrow Fidel Castro or the Sandinistas; it had to support Perón; and three years of criminal acts by Cedras, François, and Constant had to pass before its troops could finally land on Haiti, that veritable nuclear power in the hemisphere. And it was in Haiti where the Americans ran into danger when they faced a highly sophisticated and powerful resistance when attempting to place Aristide in the seat of power. The United States has also been accused of economic corruption. From American universities where our patriotic redeemers hold professorships or from research institutions financed by *gringo* foundations they pontificate: "We are an economic colony of the United States." They assure us that the submission inflicted on this hemisphere's Latinos by the Americans is the main reason for our inability to become part of civilization. We believe that we are the slaves and whores of the empire.

A quick look at this common truism unfortunately conjures up an incredible fantasy. For starters, half a century of anti-American sentiment has been very profitable for us. Hating the United States is the world's best business. The returns: economic and military assistance (the direct offspring of the *amor serrano* relationship) totaling $32.6 billion between 1946 and 1990. El Salvador, Honduras, Jamaica, Colombia, Peru, and Panama have each received billions of dollars. On loan? No, as a gift. For each rhetorical missile that has left our intellectual arsenals, one financial missile has been fired from the other side. No other country in history has so rewarded the intellectuals, politicians, and countries that hate it as has the United States. Politically speaking, anti-imperialism is the most profitable way of making love.

To what extent does the United States stick its nose into our business? To say "a lot" is what the *gringos* call "wishful thinking." The truth is that we have much less of an impact on Washington than we think. Both times in Latin America's postcolonial history when our countries were caught in the crossfire, our only importance was geopolitical, as part of the "influence zone." The first time was in the nineteenth century, around the time of our independence, when the United States fought European powers in order to establish its political sovereignty on these shores. Economic issues were not even discussed, since the United States was not in a position to do so. Until World War I, a century after the Monroe Doctrine, it was England who invested more than the United States in Latin America. The second time was of course during the Cold War, when communism established several beachheads on the continent. But not even then did the United States take an overwhelming economic interest in the countries south of its borders. Its priority was geopolitical, not economic. The numbers scream louder than the *criollo's* anti-American vocal cords. In the 1950s, American investments in our countries barely totaled $4 billion. In the 1970s, it was $11 billion, microscopic sums in today's world. In more recent times the only sure thing is that the United States has become quite disinterested in Latin America (and in all underdeveloped countries). In all these years only 5% of U.S. investments have gone to foreign markets and only 7% of its products have been exported. Seventy-five percent of its investments have gone to developed countries, not south of the Rio Grande. The Aristotelian enslavement that America's international companies have allegedly imposed on us does not make sense simply because until just yesterday, sales and investments in the United States have been ten times greater within its own territory than in the entire Third World combined.

These numbers will slowly change as the economic opening currently happening in traditionally uncivilized areas of the world begins to attract the corporate giants from other areas, in light of the lower costs and market growth in these countries. Latin America is gradually becoming one of those areas of interest. But this phenomenon is so recent—and cannot yet be categorized amid our continent's combined economic profits—that assessing the absence of freedom in our countries in terms of American economic colonialism is, politically speaking, one of the most painful displays of unrequited love.

How can our countries be important to the imperialist monsters when General Motors, Ford, Exxon, Wal-Mart, AT&T, Mobil, and IBM each have annual sales greater than any Latin American country except Brazil, Mexico, and Argentina? How are we to believe that we are vital to the strategic plans of economic imperialism when General Motors' sales are three times larger than Peru's total production? It's precisely because General Motors is obsessively oriented to the U.S. market that their sales fell sharply in 1994. If this company had its sales radius focused a little more on the benefits of imperialism, it would be less vulnerable to any shrinking of its sales in the United States.

In the mid-1990s the American presence in our economy, as well as the presence of other capital exporting countries, began to grow. This is significant. First, because money and technology from stronger countries are helping to boost our dormant markets. Second, because with the powerful nations competing for our markets, our consumers become the beneficiaries. Third, because finally our whiny anti-imperialists will be partially correct. Although economic imperialism was at one time in a position to function as a mini-state within Central American territory (the United Fruit Company and its military backing in Guatemala in 1954, for example), there are many more examples of our governments expropriating imperialists or expelling intruders who naively came to invest because the American military was ordered to support the dominant position of some international company in Latin America. It should also be stated that no expropriation of or prohibition directed against American investments was ever in itself a motive for the United States to send in the Marines. What better illustration is there than the Cuban revolution, which expropriated from dozens of American companies and citizens? And what about Fidel Castro's constant howls in favor of lifting the American trade embargo? Isn't this the best example of how economic imperialism is a fantasy? How can denouncing economic imperialism be compatible with continual pleas for the U.S. economy to stop ignoring—that being exactly what an embargo is—this Caribbean nation?

IV

GUERRILLA REVOLUTION AND SOCIALIST UTOPIA

Socialism and Man in Cuba (1965)[1]

Ernesto "Che" Guevara

Ernesto "Che" Guevara (Argentina, 1928–Bolivia, 1967) was an Argentine doctor, Marxist thinker, and Cuban and international guerrilla revolutionary. After traveling through Latin America and volunteering in a Peruvian leprosarium in 1952, he became aware of the severe state of poverty and injustice pervading Latin America. In 1953 he went to Guatemala to try to participate in and learn from President Jacobo Arbenz's progressive government efforts to improve the economic conditions in Guatemala. Once Arbenz's government was overthrown in 1954 in a CIA-backed military coup, he traveled to Mexico, where he joined Fidel Castro's 26th of July Revolutionary Movement. In 1956 he went to Cuba to initiate the guerilla struggle to overthrow Fulgencio Batista's regime. In 1959 the Batista government was overthrown and a nationalist-communist government was established, where Guevara was named President of the National Bank of Cuba. In 1961 he was appointed Minister of Industries with the task of restructuring the Cuban economy. In 1964 he decided to leave Cuba to devote himself to the international revolutionary struggle. He traveled to Congo in 1965 to initiate guerrilla operations there but with no success. Finally, in 1967, he lead guerrilla operations in Bolivia, where he was captured and executed by the Bolivian military, aided by the CIA and U.S. Special Forces. This selection represents the best-known ethical reflection on socialism in Latin America, arguing for the need for an inner revolution following an external one, leading to the emergence of a new kind of human being, who can provide long-term sustenance and give real social meaning to socialism, once the external political and economic structures are in place.

Dear *Compañero*:

I am finishing these notes during my trip through Africa, stimulated by the desire to fulfill, though tardily, my promise to you. I shall deal with the theme of the title as I believe it will be interesting to your Uruguayan readers.

It is common to hear from capitalistic spokesmen, as an argument in the ideological struggle against socialism, the statement that this social system or the period of socialist construction which Cuba has entered is characterized by the abolition of the individual for the sake of the state. I shall not try to refute this assertion on a merely theoretical basis, but shall attempt to establish the facts as they are experienced in Cuba and to add some general comments of my own. First, I shall outline a brief history of our revolutionary struggle before and after taking power.

As is known, July 26, 1953, is the precise date when the revolutionary actions were initiated which would eventually lead to triumph in January 1959. A group of men led by Fidel Castro in the dawn hours of that day attacked the Moncada Barracks in Oriente Province. The attack was a failure, and the failure became a disaster. The survivors wound up in prison and after a subsequent amnesty again undertook the revolutionary struggle.

During this process when there existed only the seeds of socialism, man was the fundamental factor. On him we relied, individualized, specific, with first and last name, and on his capacity for action depended the success or failure of a given mission.

Then the phase of guerrilla struggle began. It developed in two distinct environments: the people, a dormant mass yet in need of mobilization, and the vanguard, the guerrilla, the generator of revolutionary consciousness and enthusiasm. This vanguard was the catalyst which created the subjective conditions for victory. Throughout the proletarianization of our thought and the revolution that was taking place in our habits and our minds, the individual was the fundamental factor. Every fighter of the Sierra Maestra who achieved a high rank in the revolutionary forces had a history of notable achievements to his credit. Based on these, he attained his rank.

This was the first heroic stage in which men vied to achieve a place of greater responsibility, of greater danger, and without any other satisfaction than that of fulfilling their duty. In our work in revolutionary education we return often to this instructive theme. In the attitude of our fighters, we could glimpse the man of the future.

Total commitment to the revolutionary cause has been repeated at other times during our history. Throughout the October Crisis and the days of hurricane Flora, we saw acts of exceptional sacrifice and courage performed by all of our people. From an ideological viewpoint, our fundamental task is to find the formula which will perpetuate in daily life these heroic attitudes.

In January 1959, the revolutionary government was established with the participation of the various members of the submissive bourgeoisie. The presence of the Rebel Army as the fundamental factor of force constituted the guarantee of power. Serious contradictions arose which were resolved in the first instance in February 1959, when Fidel Castro assumed the leadership of the government in the post of prime minister. This process culminated in July of the same year with the resignation of President Urrutia due to pressure from the masses.

Into the history of the Cuban came a personage with clearly defined features which would systematically reassert itself: the masses. This multidimensional entity is not, as is sometimes pretended, the sum of the elements of one category (reduced to the same uniformity by the system imposed) acting as a docile herd. It is true that it follows its leaders, primarily Fidel Castro, without vacillating. But the degree to which he has earned this trust corresponds precisely with his ability to interpret the desires and aspirations of the people and with his sincere endeavor to fulfill the promises made.

The masses participated in the agrarian reform and in the difficult task of managing state enterprises, they went through the heroic experience of Playa Girón, forged themselves in combat against the different groups of CIA armed bandits, lived through one of the most important self-definitions in modern times during the October Crisis, and today work on toward the construction of socialism.

Looking at things from a superficial viewpoint, it would seem that those who speak about the subordination of the individual to the state are correct; the masses perform with unequaled enthusiasm and discipline the tasks assigned by the government be they of an economic, cultural, defensive, or athletic nature. Generally the initiative comes from Fidel or those in the revolutionary high command and is explained to the people, who make it their own. At other times local experience which is thought to be valuable is picked up by the party and the government and generalized following the same procedure.

However, the state makes mistakes at times. When this occurs, the collective enthusiasm diminishes due to a quantitative diminishing that takes place in each of the elements that make up the collective and work becomes paralyzed until it is reduced to an insignificant magnitude. This is the time to rectify the error.

That is what happened in March 1962, due to the sectarian line imposed on the party by Aníbal Escalante.

It is evident that the mechanism is not sufficient to assure a sequence of sensible measures. What is missing is a more structured relationship with the masses. We must improve this in years to come but for now, in the case of the initiatives arising on the top levels of government, we are using an almost intuitive method of listening to the general reactions in the face of the problems posed.

Fidel is a master at this, and his particular mode of integration with the people can only be appreciated by seeing him in action. At the great mass meetings, one can observe something like the dialogue of two tuning forks whose vibrations summon forth new vibrations each in the other. Fidel and the masses begin to vibrate in a dialogue of increasing intensity until it reaches an abrupt climax crowned by cries of struggle and of victory.

For one who has not lived the revolutionary experience, it is difficult to understand the close dialectical unity that exists between the individual and the mass, in which both are interrelated, and the mass, as a whole composed of individuals, is in turn interrelated with the leader.

Under capitalism, phenomena of this sort are observed when politicians appear who are capable of popular mobilization; but if it is not an authentic social movement, in which case it is not completely accurate to speak of capitalism, the movement will have the same lifespan as its promoter or until the popular illusions imposed by the rigors of capitalism are ended. In this type of society, man is directed by a cold mechanism which habitually escapes his comprehension. The alienated man has an invisible umbilical cord which ties him to the whole society: the law of value. It acts on all facets of his life, shaping his road and destiny.

The laws of capitalism, invisible and blind for most people, act on the individual even though he is not aware of them. He sees only a horizon that appears infinite. This is how capitalistic propaganda presents it, pretending to extract from the "Rockefeller" story—whether it is true or not—a lesson of the possibility of success. Yet the misery which necessarily accumulates in order that an example of this sort arise and the sum total of vileness resulting from a fortune of this magnitude do not appear in the picture. It is not always possible to clarify these concepts for the popular forces. (It would be fitting at this point to study how the workers of the imperialist countries gradually lose their international class spirit under the influence of a certain complicity in the exploitation of the dependent countries and how this fact at the same time wears away the masses' spirit of struggle within their own country, but this is a topic which is not within the intention of these notes.)

In any case the path is very difficult and apparently an individual with the proper qualities can overcome it to achieve the final goal. The prize is glimpsed in the distance; the road is solitary. Moreover, this is a race of wolves: One can only arrive by means of the failure of others.

I shall now attempt to define the individual, this actor in the strange and passionate drama that is the building of socialism, in his twofold existence as a unique being and as a member of the community.

I believe that the simplest way to begin is to recognize his unmade quality: man as an unfinished product. The prejudices of the past are carried into the present in the individual's consciousness and a continual effort has to be made in order to eradicate them. It is a twofold process. On the one hand, society acts with its direct and indirect education; and on the other, the individual submits himself to a conscious process of self-education.

The newly forming society has a hard competition with the past. This is so not only on the level of individual consciousness, with the residue of a systematic education oriented toward the isolation of the individual, but also on the economic level where, because of the very nature of the transitional period, mercantile relationships persist. *Mercancía*[2] is the economic cell of capitalistic society; as long as it exists, its effects will be felt in the organization of production and, hence, in the individual's consciousness.

In Marx's scheme, the period of transition was conceived as the result of the explosive transformation of the capitalist system destroyed by its own contradictions; subsequent reality has shown how some countries which constitute the weak branches detach themselves from the capitalist tree, a phenomenon foreseen by Lenin. In those countries, capitalism has developed sufficiently for its effects to be felt in one way or another on the people, but it is not its own inner contradictions that explode the system after having exhausted all of its possibilities. The struggle for liberation against a foreign oppressor, misery provoked by strange accidents such as war, whose consequences make the privileged classes fall upon the exploited, and liberation movements to overthrow neocolonial regimes are the habitual unchaining factors. Conscious action does the rest.

In these countries there has not been a complete education, for social work and wealth through the simple process of appropriation is far away from the reach of the masses. Underdevelopment on the one hand and the usual flight of capital to the "civilized" countries on the other make a rapid change impossible without sacrifice. There is still a long stretch to be covered in the construction of an economic base, and the temptation to take the beaten path of material interest as the lever of accelerated development is very great.

There is the danger of not seeing the forest because of the trees. Pursuing the wild idea of trying to realize socialism with the aid of the worn-out weapons left by capitalism (the market place as the basic economic cell, profit making, individual material incentives, and so forth), one can arrive at a dead end. And one arrives there after having traveled a long distance with many forked roads where it is difficult to perceive the moment when the wrong path was taken. Meanwhile, the adapted economic base has undermined the development of consciousness. To construct communism simultaneously with the material base of our society, we must create a new man.

This is why it is so important to choose correctly the instrument for the mobilization of the masses. That instrument must be of a fundamentally moral nature, without forgetting the correct utilization of material incentives, especially those of a social nature.

As I have stated before, it is easy to activate moral incentives in times of extreme danger. To maintain their permanence, it is necessary to develop a consciousness in which values acquire new categories. Society as a whole must become a gigantic school.

In general the phenomenon is similar to the process of the formation of a capitalist consciousness in the system's first stage. Capitalism resorts to force but also educates the people in the system. Direct propaganda is carried out by those who explain to the people the inevitability of the class system, whether it be of divine origin or due to the imposition of nature as a mechanical entity. This appeases the masses, who find themselves oppressed by an evil impossible to fight.

This is followed by hope, which differentiates capitalism from the previous caste regimes that offered no way out.

For some, the caste system continues in force: the obedient will be rewarded in the afterlife by the arrival in other wonderful worlds where the good are requited, and thus the old tradition is continued. For others, innovation: the division of classes is a matter of fate, but individuals can leave the class to which they belong through work, initiative, and so on. This process, and that of self-education for success, must be deeply hypocritical; it is the interested demonstration that a lie is true.

In our case, direct education acquires much greater importance. Explanations are convincing because they are true; there is no need for subterfuge. It is carried out through the state's educational apparatus in the form of general, technical, and ideological culture, by means of bodies such as the Ministry of Education and the party's information apparatus. Education takes among the masses, and the new attitude that is patronized tends to become a habit; the masses incorporate the attitude as their own and exert pressure on those who still have not become educated. This is the indirect way of educating the masses, as powerful as the other one.

But the process is a conscious one; the individual receives a continuous impact from the new social power and perceives that he is not completely adequate to it. Under the influence of the pressure implied in indirect education, the individual tries to accommodate to a situation which he feels is just while recognizing that his lack of development has impeded him in doing so until now. He educates himself.

In this period of the construction of socialism, we can see the new man being born. His image is as yet unfinished; in fact, it will never be finished, for the process advances parallel to the development of new economic forms. Discounting those whose lack of education makes them tend toward the solitary road, toward the satisfaction of their ambitions, there are others who, even within this new panorama of overall advances, tend to march in isolation front the accompanying mass. What is important is that men acquire more awareness every day of the need to incorporate themselves into society, and, at the same time, of their importance as motors of that society.

They no longer march in complete solitude along lost paths toward distant longings. They follow their vanguard constituted of the party, of the most advanced workers, of the advanced men who move along bound in close communion to the masses. The vanguard has their sight on the future and its rewards, but these are not envisioned as something individual; the reward is the new society where men will have different characteristics—the society of communist man.

The road is long and full of difficulties. Sometimes it is necessary to retreat, having lost the way; at times, because of a rapid pace, we separate ourselves from the masses; and on occasion, because of our stow pace, we feel the close breath of those who follow on our heels. In our ambition as revolutionaries, we try to move as quickly as possible, clearing the path, understanding that we receive our nourishment from the masses and that they will advance more rapidly if we encourage them by our example.

In spite of the importance given to moral incentives, the fact that there exist two principal groups (excluding, of course, the minority fraction of those who do not participate for one reason or another in the construction of socialism) indicates the relative lack of development of social consciousness. The vanguard groups are ideologically more advanced than the mass. The latter is acquainted with the new values, but insufficiently. Whereas in the former a qualitative change occurs which permits them to make sacrifices as a function of their vanguard character, the latter see only by halves and must be subjected to incentives and pressures of some intensity; it is the dictatorship of the proletariat operating not only over the defeated class but also individually over the victorious class.

All of this entails, for its total success, a series of revolutionary institutions. The image of the multitudes marching toward the future fits the concept of institutionalization as a harmonic unit of canals, steps, dams, well-oiled apparatus which make the march possible, which will permit the natural selection of those who are destined to march in the vanguard and who will dispense rewards and punishments to those who fulfill their duty or act against the society under construction.

The institutionalization of the Revolution has still not been achieved. We are searching for something new which will allow perfect identification between the government and the community as a whole, adjusted to the peculiar conditions of the building of socialism and avoiding to the utmost the commonplaces of bourgeois democracy transplanted to the society in formation (such as legislative houses, for example). Some experiments have been carried out with the aim of gradually creating the institutionalization of the Revolution, but without too much hurry. Our greatest restraint has been the fear that any formal aspect might separate us from the masses and the individual, making us lose sight of the ultimate and most important revolutionary ambition: to see man liberated from his alienation.

Notwithstanding the lack of institutions (which must be overcome gradually), the masses now make history as a conscious aggregate of individuals who struggle for the same cause. The individual's possibilities for expressing himself and making himself heard in the social apparatus are infinitely greater, in spite of the lack of a perfect mechanism to do so.

It is still necessary to accentuate his conscious, individual, and collective participation in all the mechanisms of direction and production and tie them in with the idea of the need for technical and ideological education, so that the individual will grasp how these processes are closely interdependent and their advances parallel. He will thus achieve total awareness of his social being, which is equivalent to his full realization as a human creature, having broken the chains of alienation.

This will be translated concretely into the reappropriation of his nature through freed work and the expression of his own human condition through culture and art.

In order for it to attain the characteristic of being freed, work must acquire a new condition; man as a commodity ceases to exist and a system is established which grants a quota for the fulfillment of social duty. The means of production belong to society and the machine is only the front line where duty is performed. Man begins to liberate his thought from the bothersome fact that presupposes the need to satisfy his animal needs through work. He begins to see himself portrayed in his work and to understand its human magnitude through the created object, through the work carried out. This no longer entails leaving a part of his being in the form of labor, power, soul, which no longer belong to him, but rather it signifies an emanation from himself, a contribution to the life of society in which he is reflected, the fulfillment of his social duty.

We are doing everything possible to give work this new category of social duty and to unite it to the development of technology, on the one hand, which will provide the conditions for greater freedom, and to voluntary labor on the other, based on the Marxist concept that man truly achieves his full human condition when he produces without being compelled by the physical necessity of selling himself as a commodity.

It is clear that work still has coercive aspects, even when it is voluntary; man as yet has not transformed all the coercion surrounding him into conditioned reflexes of a social nature, and in many cases he still produces under the pressure of the environment (Fidel calls this moral compulsion). He still has to achieve complete spiritual re-creation in the presence of his own work, without the direct pressure of the social environment but bound to it by new habits. That will be communism.

The change in consciousness is not produced automatically, just as it is not produced in the economy. The variations are slow and not rhythmic; there are periods of acceleration, others are measured, and some even involve a retreat.

We must also consider, as we have already pointed out, that we are not before a pure transition period such as that envisioned by Marx in the *Critique of the Gotha Program*, but rather a new phase not foreseen by him—the first period in the transition to communism or in the construction of socialism.

This process takes place in the midst of a violent class struggle; and elements of capitalism are present within it, which obscure the complete understanding of the essence of the process.

If to this be added the scholasticism that has delayed the development of Marxist philosophy and impeded the systematic treatment of the period in which the political economy has as yet not been developed, we must agree that we are still in diapers and it is urgent to investigate all the primordial characteristics of the period before elaborating a far-reaching economic and political theory.

The resulting theory will necessarily give preeminence to the two pillars of socialist construction: the formation of the new man and the development of technology. In both aspects we have a great deal to accomplish still, but the delay is less justifiable regarding the conception of technology as the basis: here it is not a matter of advancing blindly, but rather of following for a considerable stretch the road opened up by the most advanced countries of the world. This is why Fidel harps with so much insistency on the necessity of the technological and scientific formation of all of our people and especially of the vanguard.

In the field of ideas that lead to nonproductive activities, it is easier to see the division between material and spiritual needs. For a long time man has been trying to free himself from alienation through culture and art. He dies daily in the eight and more hours during which he performs as a commodity in order to be resuscitated in his spiritual creation. But this remedy bears the germs of the same disease: Ile is a solitary being who seeks communion with nature. He defends his oppressed individuality from the environment and reacts to esthetic ideas as a unique being whose aspiration is to remain immaculate.

It is only an attempt at flight. The law of value is no longer a mere reflection of production relations; the monopoly capitalists have surrounded it with a complicated scaffolding which makes of it a docile servant, even when the methods employed are purely empirical. The superstructure imposes a type of art in which the artist must be educated. The rebels are dominated by the apparatus, and only exceptional talents are able to create their own work. The remaining ones become shamefaced wage-workers, or they are crushed.

Artistic experimentation is invented and is taken as the definition of freedom. But this "experimentation" has limits which are imperceptible until they are clashed with, that is to say, when the real problems of man and his alienation are dealt with. Senseless anguish or vulgar pastimes are comfortable safety valves for human uneasiness; the idea of making art a weapon of denunciation and accusation is combatted.

If the rules of the game are respected, all honors are obtained—the honors that might be granted to a pirouette-creating monkey. The condition is to not attempt to escape from the invisible cage.

When the Revolution took power, the exodus of the totally domesticated took place; the others, revolutionaries or not, saw a new road. Artistic experimentation gained new impulse. However, the roots were more or less traced, and the concept of flight was the hidden meaning behind the word freedom. This attitude, which was a reflection in consciousness of bourgeois idealism, was frequently maintained in the revolutionaries themselves.

In countries which have gone through a similar process, there was an attempt made to combat these tendencies with an exaggerated dogmatism. General culture became something like a taboo, and a formally exact representation of nature was proclaimed as the height of cultural aspiration. This later became a mechanical representation of social reality created by wishful thinking, the ideal society, almost without conflict or contradiction, that man was seeking to create.

Socialism is young and makes mistakes. We revolutionaries many times lack the knowledge and the necessary intellectual audacity to face the task of the development of the new human being by methods distinct from the conventional ones, and the conventional methods suffer from the influence of the society that created them. (Once again the topic of the relation between form and content appears.) Disorientation is great, and the problems of material construction absorb us. There are no artists of great authority who also have great revolutionary authority.

The men of the party must take this task on themselves and seek the achievements of the critical objective: to educate the people.

What is then sought is simplification, what everyone understands, what the functionaries understand. True artistic experimentation is annulled and the problem of general culture is reduced to the assimilation of the socialist present and the dead (and therefore not dangerous) past. As such, socialist realism is born on the foundation of the art of the last century.

But the realistic art of the nineteenth century is also class art, perhaps more purely capitalist than the decadent art of the twentieth century, where the anguish of alienated man shows through. In culture, capitalism has given all that it has to give and all that remains of it is the announcement of a bad-smelling corpse—in art, its present decadence. But why endeavor to seek in the frozen forms of socialist realism the only valid recipe? "Freedom" cannot he set against socialist realism because the former does not yet exist and it will not come into existence until the complete development of the new society. But at all costs let us not attempt to condemn all post-mid-nineteenth-century art forms from the pontifical throne of realism. That would mean committing the Proudhonian error of the return to the past, and strait-jacketing the artistic expression of the man who is being born and constructed today.

An ideological and cultural mechanism which will permit experimentation and clear out the weeds that shoot up so easily in the fertilized soil of state subsidization is lacking.

In our country, the error of mechanical realism has not appeared, but rather the contrary. This has been because of the tack of understanding of the need to create the new man who will represent neither nineteenth-century ideas nor those of our decadent and morbid century. It is the twenty-first-century man whom we must create, although this is still a subjective and unsystematic aspiration. This is precisely one of the fundamental points of our studies and our work; to the extent that we make concrete achievements on a theoretical base or vice versa, that we come to theoretical conclusions of a broad character on the basis of our concrete studies, we will have made a valuable contribution to Marxism-Leninism, to the cause of mankind.

The reaction against nineteenth-century man has brought a recurrence of twentieth-century decadence. It is not a very grave error, but we must overcome it so as not to leave the doors wide open to revisionism.

The large multitudes of people are developing themselves, the new ideas are acquiring an adequate impetus within society, the material possibilities of the integral development of each and every one of its members make the task ever more fruitful. The present is one of struggle; the future is ours.

To summarize, the culpability of many of our intellectuals and artists lies in their original sin; they are not authentic revolutionaries. We can attempt to graft elm trees so they bear pears, but simultaneously we must plant pear trees. The new generations will arrive free of original sin. The possibility that exceptional artists will arise will be that much greater because of the enlargement of the cultural field and the possibilities for expression. Our task is to keep the present generation, maladjusted by its conflicts, from becoming perverted and perverting the new generations. We do not want to create salaried workers docile to official thinking or "scholars" who live under the wing of the budget, exercising a freedom in quotation marks. Revolutionaries will come to sing the song of the new man with the authentic voice of the people. It is a process that requires time.

In our society the youth and the party play a large role. The former is particularly important because it is malleable clay with which the new man, without any of the previous defects, can be constructed.

They receive treatment which is in consonance with our ambitions. Education is increasingly more complete, and we do not forget the incorporation of the students into work from the very first. Our scholarship students do physical work during vacation or simultaneously with their studies. In some cases work is a prize, in others it is an educational tool; it is never a punishment. A new generation is being born.

The party is a vanguard organization. The best workers are proposed by their comrades for membership. The party is a minority, but the quality of its cadres gives it great authority. Our aspiration is that the party become a mass one, but only when the masses have attained the level of development of the vanguard, that is, when they are educated for communism. Our work is aimed at providing that education. The party is the living example; its cadres must be lecturers of assiduity and sacrifice; with their acts they must lead the masses to end the revolutionary task, which entails years of struggle against the difficulties of construction, class enemies, the defects of the past, imperialism.

I would like to explain now the role played by the personality, man as the individual who leads the masses that make history. This is our experience, and not a recipe.

Fidel gave impulse to the Revolution in its first years, he has given leadership to it always and has set the tone; but there is a good group of revolutionaries developing in the same direction as the maximum leader and a great mass that follows its leaders because it has faith in them. It has faith in them because these leaders have known how to interpret the longings of the masses.

It is not a question of how many kilograms of meat are eaten or how many times a year someone may go on holiday to the seashore or how many pretty imported things can be bought with present wages. It is rather that the individual feels greater fulfillment, that he has greater inner wealth and many more responsibilities. In our country the individual knows that the glorious period in which it has fallen to him to live is one of sacrifice; he is familiar with sacrifice.

The first ones came to know it in the Sierra Maestra and wherever there was fighting; later we have known it in all Cuba. Cuba is the vanguard of America and must make sacrifices because it occupies the advance position, because it points out to the masses of Latin America the road to full freedom.

Within the country the leaders must fulfill their vanguard role; and it must be said with all sincerity that, in a true revolution, to which one gives oneself completely, from which one expects no material compensation, the task of the vanguard revolutionary is both magnificent and anguishing.

Let me say, with the risk of appearing ridiculous, that the true revolutionary is guided by strong feelings of love. It is impossible to think of an authentic revolutionary without this quality. This is perhaps one of the greatest dramas of a leader; he must combine air impassioned spirit with a cold mind and make painful decisions without flinching one muscle. Our vanguard revolutionaries must idealize their love for the people, for the most sacred causes, and make it one and indivisible. They cannot descend, with small doses of daily affection, to the places where ordinary men put their love into practice.

The leaders of the Revolution have children who do not learn to call their father with their first faltering words; they have wives who must be part of the general sacrifice of their lives to carry the Revolution to its destiny; their friends are strictly limited to their comrades in revolution. There is no life outside it.

In these conditions, one must have a large dose of humanity, a large dose of a sense of justice and truth, to avoid falling in dogmatic extremes, into cold scholasticism, into isolation from the masses. Every day we must struggle so that this love of living humanity is transformed into concrete facts, into acts that will serve as an example, as a mobilizing factor.

The revolutionary, ideological motor of the Revolution within his party, is consumed by this uninterrupted activity that has no other end but death, unless construction be achieved on a worldwide scale. If his revolutionary eagerness becomes dulled when the most urgent tasks are realized on a local scale, and if he forgets about proletarian internationalism, the revolution that he leads ceases to be a driving force and it becomes a comfortable drowsiness which is taken advantage of by our irreconcilable enemy, by imperialism, which gains ground. Proletarian internationalism is a duty, but it is also a revolutionary need. This is how we educate our people.

It is clear that there are dangers in the present circumstances. Not only that of dogmatism, not only that of the freezing up of relations with the masses in the midst of the great task, but there also exists the danger of weaknesses in which it is possible to fall. If a man thinks that in order to dedicate his entire life to the Revolution, he cannot be distracted by the worry that one of his children lacks a certain product, that the children's shoes are in poor condition, that his family lacks some very necessary item, beneath this reasoning the germs of future corruption are allowed to filter through.

In our case we have maintained that our children must have, or lack, what the children of the ordinary citizen have or lack; our family must understand this and struggle for it. The Revolution is made through man, but man must forge clay by day his revolutionary spirit.

Thus we go forward. At the head of the immense column—we are neither ashamed nor afraid to say so—is Fidel, followed by the best party cadres and, immediately after, so close that their great strength is felt, come the people as a whole, a solid conglomeration of individualities moving toward a common objective: individuals who have achieved the awareness of what must be done, men who struggle to leave the domain of necessity and enter that of freedom.

That immense multitude is ordering itself; its order responds to an awareness of the need for order; it is no more a dispersed force, divisible in thousands of fractions shot into space like the fragments of a grenade, trying through any means, in a fierce struggle with their equals, to attain a position that would give them support in the face of an uncertain future.

We know that we have sacrifices ahead of us and that we must pay a price for the heroic act of constituting a vanguard as a nation. We, the leaders, know that we must pay a price for having the right to say that we are at the head of the people who are at the head of America.

Each and every one of us punctually pays his quota of sacrifice, aware of receiving our reward in the satisfaction of fulfilling our duty, conscious of advancing with everyone toward the new man who is glimpsed on the horizon.

Allow me to attempt to come to some conclusions:

We socialists are more free because we are more fulfilled; we are more fulfilled because we are more free.

The skeleton of our freedom is formed, but it lacks the protein substance and the draperies; we shall create them.

Our freedom and its daily sustenance are the color of blood and are swollen with sacrifice.

Our sacrifice is a conscious one; it is the payment for the freedom we are constructing.

The road is long and unknown in part; we are aware of our limitations. We shall make the twenty-first-century man, we ourselves.

We shall be forged in daily action, creating a new man with a new technology.

The personality plays the role of mobilization and leadership insofar as it incarnates the highest virtues and aspirations of the people and is not detoured.

The road is opened up by the vanguard group, the best among the good, the party.

The fundamental clay of our work is the youth; in it we have deposited our hopes and we are preparing it to take the banner from our hands.

If this faltering letter has made some things clear, it will have fulfilled my purpose in sending it.

Accept our ritual greetings, as a handshake or an "Ave María Purísima."

Patria o muerte

NOTES

1. Letter addressed to Carlos Quijano, editor of *Marcha* (Montevideo), March 1965. *Verde Olivo* (Havana), April 11, 1965, 14-18, 66.

2. *Mercancía*: There is no precise translation of this term into English. It has the connotation of goods for sale, commodities, merchandise, but it could also mean market relationships. Eds.

16

Problems and Principles of Strategy (1969)

Carlos Marighella

Carlos Marighella (Brazil, 1911–1969) was a Brazilian communist politician, revolutionary theoretician, and guerrilla organizer, who founded the National Liberation Action (ALN) organization and led it in an armed struggle to promote communism in Brazil, after he was expelled from the Brazilian Communist Party for "pro-Cuban" sympathies in 1967. His tactics, especially as espoused in his underground classic, Minimanual of the Urban Guerrilla, *inspired various urban guerrilla organizations, such as the Italian Red Brigades, the German Red Army Faction, and the Provisional Irish Republican Army. Throughout his life he was imprisoned several times and finally was executed by police in an ambush in São Paulo, Brazil. This selection explains some of Marighella's main ideas about guerrilla warfare, such as the relationship between and roles of urban and rural guerrilla, and the distinction between strategy and tactics within a revolutionary movement.*

The most important problem of the Brazilian revolution is that of strategy, and regarding this—the sense in which it should be directed—there exists no complete accord among revolutionaries. Our organization has adopted a determined strategic concept through which it has been oriented, but it is evident that other organizations have different viewpoints.

The concepts and principles expressed here refer, therefore, to those questions about which our organization can give an opinion acquired from experience. For us the strategy of the Brazilian revolution is guerrilla warfare. Guerrilla warfare forms part of revolutionary people's warfare. In "Some Questions About the Brazilian Guerrillas" we have already established the principles that orient our strategy, and for those who wish to know them it is sufficient to refer to the mentioned work. To the principles already enumerated there, we would like to add some others which will help form an idea of our strategic concepts regarding the Brazilian revolution.

Study and application of these principles by revolutionary groups combined with the personal experience of militants will contribute to a better comprehension not only of the desired objectives of our struggle, but also of the fundamental means to reach them. The following are the strategic principles to which we refer:

THE STRATEGY OF THE NATIONAL LIBERATION ACTION

1. In a country like Brazil, where a permanent political crisis exists resulting from a deepening of the chronic structural crisis together with the general crisis of capitalism and where, as a consequence, military power has been established, our strategic principle is to transform the political crisis into an armed struggle of the people against military rule.

2. The basic principle of revolutionary strategy under the conditions of a permanent political crisis is to release, in the city as well as in the countryside, such a volume of revolutionary action that the enemy will be obliged to transform the political situation into a military one. Then dissatisfaction will reach all the strata of society, and the military will be held absolutely responsible for all failures.

3. The main aim of revolutionary strategy in the transformation of the permanent political crisis into an armed struggle and of the political situation into a military solution, is to destroy the bureaucratic-military machine of the state and replace it with the people in arms.

4. To destroy the bureaucratic-military apparatus of the Brazilian state, revolutionary strategy starts from the premise that that apparatus, within the conditions of the permanent political crisis that characterizes the national situation, entails ever closer relations with the interests of North American imperialism. This machine cannot be destroyed unless the main blow is aimed against North American imperialism, which is the common enemy of humanity and primarily of the Latin American, Asian, and African peoples.

5. Our conception of revolutionary strategy is global both in the sense that its main function consists in countering the global strategies of North American imperialism and in the sense that the political and military strategies exist and act as one, rather than as two separate entities. At the same time, tactical functions are subordinate to strategy, and there exists no possibility of their employment outside of this subordination.

6. Given the global character of our strategy, in undertaking the struggle for the overthrow of the military, we must take into account as a strategic principle the radical transformation of the class structure of Brazilian society toward the goal of socialism. North American imperialism is our principal enemy and we must transform the struggle against it into a national liberation and antioligarchic action.

   Thus, in the face of revolutionary attacks, the military will be compelled to come to the defense of North American imperialism and of the Brazilian oligarchy and will become publicly discredited. On the other hand, with the overthrow of military power and the annihilation of its armed forces, we shall expel the North Americans and destroy the Brazilian oligarchy, eliminating the obstacles in the road to socialism.

STRATEGIES OF URBAN AND RURAL STRUGGLE

1. The urban struggle acts as a complement to the rural struggle, and thus all urban warfare, whether from the guerrilla front or from the mass front (with

the support of the respective supply network), always assumes a tactical character.

2. The decisive struggle is the one in the strategic area (i.e., the rural area) and not the one that evolves in the tactical area (i.e., the city).

3. If by some mistake, urban guerrilla warfare were to be conducted as the decisive struggle, the strategic conflict in the rural area of the peasantry would become relegated to a secondary level. Noting the weak or nonexistent participation of the peasantry in the struggle, the bourgeoisie would take advantage of such circumstances to suborn and isolate the revolution; it will try to maneuver the proletariat which, lacking the support of its fundamental ally, the peasantry, will try to preserve untouched the bureaucratic-military apparatus of the state.

4. Only when the reactionary armed forces have already been destroyed and the military-bourgeois state cannot continue to act against the masses, can a general strike in the city be called which, in combination with guerrilla struggle, will lead to victory. This principle, derived from that which affirms that the primary end of revolutionary struggle is the destruction of the military-bureaucratic apparatus and its substitution with the people in arms, is employed to prevent the bourgeoisie from subverting the general strike and resorting to a coup d'etat in order to seize the initiative from the revolutionaries and cut their road to power.

STRATEGY OF THE URBAN GUERRILLA

1. Because the city is the complementary area of struggle, the urban guerrilla must play a tactical role in support of the rural guerrilla. We must make of the urban guerrilla therefore an instrument for the destruction, diversion, and containment of the armed forces of the dictatorship in order to avoid their concentration of repressive operations against the rural guerrilla.

2. In the process of unleashing the urban guerrilla, the forms of struggle that we employ are not those of mass struggle, but those of small armed groups supplied with firepower and dedicated to the battle against the dictatorship. Seeing that the firepower of the revolutionaries is directed against their enemies, the masses, who until then were powerless before the dictatorship, will look upon the urban guerrillas with sympathy and lend them their support.

3. The forms of struggle that characterize the urban guerrilla are guerrilla tactics and armed actions of all types, actions of surprise and ambush, expropriations, seizure of arms and explosives, revolutionary terrorist acts, sabotage, occupations, raids, punishment of North American agents or police torturers, in addition to flash meetings, distribution of leaflets, painting of murals by armed groups, etc.

4. The infrastructure of the urban and rural guerrillas have common points: the training and specialization of the guerrilla; physical conditioning; self-defense; the utilization of professional skills; the technical preparation of homemade weapons; the development of firepower and training for its handling; information networks; means of transportation and communication; medical

resources and first aid. Our aim is to rely on both infrastructures, in order not to be reduced to one or the other guerrilla forms, and to combine the two correctly.

5. Revolutionaries engaged in guerrilla warfare give enormous importance to the mass movement in the urban area and to its forms of struggle, such as acts of restitution, strikes, marches, protests, boycotts, etc. Our strategic principle with respect to the urban mass movement is to participate in it with the objective of creating an infrastructure for armed struggle by the working class, students, and other forces: to employ urban guerrillas and to unleash their operations through the use of armed mass groups.

STRATEGY OF THE RURAL GUERRILLA

1. Peasant struggles resulting from demands against landlords, or from the organization of rural syndicates, will develop into armed clashes and in this sense are positive. However, without firepower the peasants will be crushed by the forces of reaction. It is unlikely that rural guerrillas will emerge, in a strategic sense, out of peasant conflicts. The Brazilian peasantry has a very limited political consciousness and its tradition of struggle does not reach farther than mysticism or banditry; its experience of class struggle under the direction of the proletariat is recent and limited.

   Under the present conditions of the country, dominated by the dictatorship, the strategic struggle in the rural area will develop from a guerrilla infrastructure emerging among the peasantry. Seeing in their midst the emergence of a firepower that combats the landlords and does not violate their interests, the peasants will support and participate in guerrilla warfare.

2. The main strategic principle of guerrilla struggle is that it can neither have any consequence nor any decisive character in revolutionary warfare unless it is structured and consolidated in an armed alliance of workers and peasants united with students. Such an alliance, supplied with growing firepower, will give the guerrillas firm foundations and advance their cause. The armed alliance of the proletariat, peasantry, and the middle class is the key to victory.

3. Rural guerrilla warfare is decisive because, in addition to the extreme mobility possible in the interior of the country, it leads to the formation of the revolutionary army of national liberation which can be built from an embryo constituted by the armed alliance of workers and peasants with students. The peasants, without whom the revolution cannot reach its ultimate consequences, are impossible to incorporate into the urban guerrilla.

4. In no event should the Brazilian guerrilla defend areas, territories, regions, or any base or fixed position. If we were to do such, we would permit the enemy to concentrate its forces in campaigns of annihilation against known and vulnerable targets.

5. The Brazilian rural guerrilla should always be mobile. Similarly, the urban guerrilla ought to be extremely mobile and never stage an occupation without meticulously organizing a retreat. Revolutionary warfare in Brazil is a war of movement, whatever the circumstances.

6. The guerrilla plays the principal strategic role in revolutionary warfare, and its political objective is the formation of a revolutionary army of national liberation and the seizure of power. In the revolutionary struggle we must avoid the distortion of this political objective and prevent the guerrilla, urban or rural, from transforming itself into an instrument of banditry, or unifying with bandits or employing their methods.

ORGANIZATIONAL STRATEGY

1. The continental size of the country, the varying strategic importance of its areas, and the principle of diversity of revolutionary action combine with other factors to determine the existence or emergence of multiple revolutionary centers with regional coordination. Such revolutionary centers will dedicate themselves to implementing a guerrilla infrastructure to unleash the revolutionary struggle and dispose freely of political and tactical action at the regional level.
2. The strategic direction and global tactics of our organization—i.e., the unified political and military direction—will not emerge at once. Such leadership is formed through a permanent process in which armed struggle assumes the fundamental form of guerrilla warfare, going from the strategic field to the tactical and vice versa, until affirming itself in a group of men and women identified with revolutionary action and capable of carrying it to its ultimate consequences.
3. The revolutionary unity of our organization exists in terms of the strategic, tactical, and organic principles that we have adopted and not in terms of names or personalities. It is this identity of ideology, theory, and practice which will ensure that unconnected revolutionaries in various parts of the country will perform acts that will identify them as belonging to the same organization.

Sixth Declaration of the Selva Lacandona (2005)

Zapatista Army of National Liberation

Zapatista Army of National Liberation (EZLN) is an armed revolutionary group based in Chiapas, one of the poorest states of Mexico. The group was founded in 1983 by nonindigenous members of the FLN guerrilla group from Mexico's urban North together with indigenous inhabitants of the remote Las Cañadas/ Selva Lacandona regions in eastern Chiapas. It went public in 1994, simultaneously with the signing of the North American Free Trade Agreement (NAFTA) between the United States and Mexico, which they categorically oppose. Their social base is mostly indigenous, but they also have supporters in urban areas of Mexico, as well as internationally. Their spokesperson and military commander, although not their leader, is Subcomandante Marcos, himself not an indigenous Mayan. The Zapatistas see themselves as the ideological heirs of Emiliano Zapata, the most progressive proponent of the Mexican Revolution (1910–1920), and of five hundred years of indigenous resistance against imperialism. Some consider the Zapatista movement the first "post-modern" revolution: an armed revolutionary group that has abstained from using violence since their 1994 uprising was countered by the overpowering military might of the Mexican Federal Army, surviving instead by garnering support from Mexican and international civil society, through the use of the internet to disseminate information and to enlist the support of nongovernmental organizations (NGOs) and solidarity groups. Internationally, they portray themselves as part of the wider anti-globalization, antineoliberalism movement, but like other indigenist-popular movements, their local focus is on control over their own resources, particularly land, the right to govern themselves according to their own customs, and living in peace without government interference. This selection is the EZLN's latest manifesto explaining their history, their present situation, their current view of the world and Mexico, their short-term and long-term goals—locally, nationally, and internationally—and the means that they will use to achieve those goals. It provides a rare glimpse into the collective mind of a dynamic, indigenist-popular movement.

This is our simple word which seeks to touch the hearts of humble and simple people like ourselves, but people who are also, like ourselves, dignified and

282

rebel. This is our simple word for recounting what our path has been and where we are now, in order to explain how we see the world and our country, in order to say what we are thinking of doing and how we are thinking of doing it, and in order to invite other persons to walk with us in something very great which is called Mexico and something greater which is called the world. This is our simple word in order to inform all honest and noble hearts what it is we want in Mexico and the world. This is our simple word, because it is our idea to call on those who are like us and to join together with them, everywhere they are living and struggling.

I – WHAT WE ARE

We are the zapatistas of the EZLN, although we are also called "neo-zapatistas." Now, we, the zapatistas of the EZLN, rose up in arms in January of 1994 because we saw how widespread had become the evil wrought by the powerful who only humiliated us, stole from us, imprisoned us and killed us, and no one was saying anything or doing anything. That is why we said "*Ya Basta!,*" that no longer were we going to allow them to make us inferior or to treat us worse than animals. And then we also said we wanted democracy, liberty and justice for all Mexicans although we were concentrated on the Indian peoples. Because it so happened that we, the EZLN, were almost all only indigenous from here in Chiapas, but we did not want to struggle just for our own good, or just for the good of the indigenous of Chiapas, or just for the good of the Indian peoples of Mexico. We wanted to fight along with everyone who was humble and simple like ourselves and who was in great need and who suffered from exploitation and thievery by the rich and their bad governments here, in our Mexico, and in other countries in the world.

And then our small history was that we grew tired of exploitation by the powerful, and then we organized in order to defend ourselves and to fight for justice. In the beginning there were not many of us, just a few, going this way and that, talking with and listening to other people like us. We did that for many years, and we did it in secret, without making a stir. In other words, we joined forces in silence. We remained like that for about 10 years, and then we had grown, and then we were many thousands. We trained ourselves quite well in politics and weapons, and, suddenly, when the rich were throwing their New Year's Eve parties, we fell upon their cities and just took them over. And we left a message to everyone that here we are, that they have to take notice of us. And then the rich took off and sent their great armies to do away with us, just like they always do when the exploited rebel—they order them all to be done away with. But we were not done away with at all, because we had prepared ourselves quite well prior to the war, and we made ourselves strong in our mountains. And there were the armies, looking for us and throwing their bombs and bullets at us, and then they were making plans to kill off all the indigenous at one time, because they did not know who was a zapatista and who was not. And we were running and fighting, fighting and running, just like our ancestors had done. Without giving up, without surrendering, without being defeated.

And then the people from the cities went out into the streets and began shouting for an end to the war. And then we stopped our war, and we listened to those brothers and sisters from the city who were telling us to try to reach an arrangement or an accord with the bad governments, so that the problem could be resolved without a massacre. And so we paid attention to them, because they were what we call "the people," or the Mexican people. And so we set aside the fire and took up the word.

And it so happened that the governments said they would indeed be well-behaved, and they would engage in dialogue, and they would make accords, and they would fulfill them. And we said that was good, but we also thought it was good that we knew those people who went out into the streets in order to stop the war. Then, while we were engaging in dialogue with the bad governments, we were also talking with those persons, and we saw that most of them were humble and simple people like us, and both, they and we, understood quite well why we were fighting. And we called those people "civil society" because most of them did not belong to political parties, rather they were common, everyday people, like us, simple and humble people.

But it so happened that the bad governments did not want a good agreement, rather it was just their underhanded way of saying they were going to talk and to reach accords, while they were preparing their attacks in order to eliminate us once and for all. And so then they attacked us several times, but they did not defeat us, because we resisted quite well, and many people throughout the world mobilized. And then the bad governments thought that the problem was that many people saw what was happening with the EZLN, and they started their plan of acting as if nothing were going on. Meanwhile they were quick to surround us, they laid siege to us in hopes that, since our mountains are indeed remote, the people would then forget, since zapatista lands were so far away. And every so often the bad governments tested us and tried to deceive us or to attack us, like in February of 1995 when they threw a huge number of armies at us, but they did not defeat us. Because, as they said then, we were not alone, and many people helped us, and we resisted well.

And then the bad governments had to make accords with the EZLN, and those accords were called the "San Andrés Accords" because the municipality where those accords were signed was called "San Andrés." And we were not all alone in those dialogues, speaking with people from the bad governments. We invited many people and organizations who were, or are, engaged in the struggle for the Indian peoples of Mexico, and everyone spoke their word, and everyone reached agreement as to how we were going to speak with the bad governments. And that is how that dialogue was, not just the zapatistas on one side and the governments on the other. Instead, the Indian peoples of Mexico, and those who supported them, were with the zapatistas. And then the bad governments said in those accords that they were indeed going to recognize the rights of the Indian peoples of Mexico, and they were going to respect their culture, and they were going to make everything law in the Constitution. But then, once they had signed, the bad governments acted as if they had forgotten about them, and many years passed, and the accords were not fulfilled at all. Quite the opposite, the government attacked the indigenous, in order to make them back out of the struggle, as they did on December 22, 1997, the date on which Zedillo ordered the killing of 45 men, women, old ones and children in the town in Chiapas called ACTEAL. This immense crime was not so easily forgotten, and it was a demonstration of how the bad governments color their hearts in order to attack and assassinate those who rebel against injustices. And, while all of that was going on, we zapatistas were putting our all into the fulfillment of the accords and resisting in the mountains of the Mexican southeast.

And then we began speaking with other Indian peoples of Mexico and their organizations, and we made an agreement with them that we were going to struggle together for the same thing, for the recognition of indigenous rights and culture. Now we were also being helped by many people from all over the world and by persons who were well respected and whose word was quite great because they were great intellectuals, artists and scientists from Mexico and from all over the world. And we also held international *encuentros*. In other words, we joined together to talk with persons from America and from Asia and from Europe and from Africa and from Oceania, and we learned of their struggles and their ways, and we said they were "intergalactic" *encuentros*, just to be silly and because we had also invited those from other planets, but it appeared as if they had not come, or perhaps they did come, but they did not make it clear.

But the bad governments did not keep their word anyway, and then we made a plan to talk with many Mexicans so they would help us. And then, first in 1997, we held a march to Mexico City which was called "of the 1,111" because a *compañero* or *compañera* was going to go from each zapatista town, but the bad government did not pay any attention. And then, in 1999, we held a *consulta* throughout the country, and there it was seen that the majority were indeed in agreement with the demands of the Indian peoples, but again the bad governments did not pay any attention. And then, lastly, in 2001, we held what was called the "march for indigenous dignity" which had much support from millions of Mexicans and people from other countries, and it went to where the deputies and senators were, the Congress of the Union, in order to demand the recognition of the Mexican indigenous.

But it happened that no, the politicians from the PRI, the PAN and the PRD reached an agreement among themselves, and they simply did not recognize indigenous rights and culture. That was in April of 2001, and the politicians demonstrated quite clearly there that they had no decency whatsoever, and they were swine who thought only about making their good money as the bad politicians they were. This must be remembered, because you will now be seeing that they are going to say they will indeed recognize indigenous rights, but it is a lie they are telling so we will vote for them. But they already had their chance, and they did not keep their word.

And then we saw quite clearly that there was no point to dialogue and negotiation with the bad governments of Mexico. That it was a waste of time for us to be talking with the politicians, because neither their hearts nor their words were honest. They were crooked, and they told lies that they would keep their word, but they did not. In other words, on that day, when the politicians from the PRI, PAN and PRD approved a law that was no good, they killed dialogue once and for all, and they clearly stated that it did not matter what they had agreed to and signed, because they did not keep their word. And then we did not make any contacts with the federal branches. Because we understood that dialogue and negotiation had failed as a result of those political parties. We saw that blood did not matter to them, nor did death, suffering, mobilizations, *consultas*, efforts, national and international statements, *encuentros*, accords, signatures, commitments. And so the political class not only closed, one more time, the door to the Indian peoples, they also delivered a mortal blow to the peaceful resolution—through dialogue and negotiation—of the war. It can also no longer be believed that the accords will be fulfilled by someone who comes along with something or other. They should see that there so that they can learn from experience what happened to us.

And then we saw all of that, and we wondered in our hearts what we were going to do.

And the first thing we saw was that our heart was not the same as before, when we began our struggle. It was larger, because now we had touched the hearts of many good people. And we also saw that our heart was more hurt, it was more wounded. And it was not wounded by the deceits of the bad governments, but because, when we touched the hearts of others, we also touched their sorrows. It was as if we were seeing ourselves in a mirror.

II – WHERE WE ARE NOW

Then, like the zapatistas we are, we thought that it was not enough to stop engaging in dialogue with the government, but it was necessary to continue on ahead in the struggle, in spite of those lazy parasites of politicians. The EZLN then decided to carry out, alone and on their side ("unilateral," in other words, because just one side), the San Andrés Accords regarding indigenous rights and culture. For 4 years, since the middle of 2001 until the middle of 2005, we have devoted ourselves to this and to other things which we are going to tell you about.

Fine, we then began encouraging the autonomous rebel zapatista municipalities—which is how the peoples are organized in order to govern and to govern themselves—in order to make themselves stronger. This method of autonomous government was not simply invented by the EZLN, but rather it comes from several centuries of indigenous resistance and from the zapatistas' own experience. It is the self-governance of the communities. In other words, no one from outside comes to govern, but the peoples themselves decide, among themselves, who governs and how, and, if they do not obey, they are removed. If the one who governs does not obey the people, they pursue them, they are removed from authority, and another comes in.

But then we saw that the Autonomous Municipalities were not level. There were some that were more advanced and which had more support from civil society, and others were more neglected. The organization was lacking to make them more on a par with each other. And we also saw that the EZLN, with its political-military component, was involving itself in decisions which belonged to the democratic authorities, "civilians" as they say. And here the problem is that the political-military component of the EZLN is not democratic, because it is an army. And we saw that the military being above, and the democratic below, was not good, because what is democratic should not be decided militarily, it should be the reverse: the democratic-political governing above, and the military obeying below. Or, perhaps, it would be better with nothing below, just completely level, without any military, and that is why the zapatistas are soldiers so that there will not be any soldiers. Fine, what we then did about this problem was to begin separating the political-military from the autonomous and democratic aspects of organization in the zapatista communities. And so, actions and decisions which had previously been made and taken by the EZLN were being passed, little by little, to the democratically elected authorities in the villages. It is easy to say, of course, but it was very difficult in practice, because many years have passed—first in the preparation for the war and then the war itself—and the political-military aspects have become customary. But, regardless, we did so because it is our way to do what we say, because, if not, why should we go around saying things if we do not then do them.

That was how the Good Government Juntas were born, in August of 2003, and, through them, self-learning and the exercise of "govern obeying" has continued.

From that time and until the middle of 2005, the EZLN leadership has no longer involved itself in giving orders in civil matters, but it has accompanied and helped the authorities who are democratically elected by the peoples. It has also kept watch that the peoples and national and international civil society are kept well-informed concerning the aid that is received and how it is used. And now we are passing the work of safeguarding good government to the zapatista support bases, with temporary positions which are rotated, so that everyone learns and carries out this work. Because we believe that a people which does not watch over its leaders is condemned to be enslaved, and we fought to be free, not to change masters every six years.

The EZLN, during these 4 years, also handed over to the Good Government Juntas and the Autonomous Municipalities the aid and contacts which they had attained throughout Mexico and the world during these years of war and resistance. The EZLN had also, during that time, been building economic and political support which allowed the zapatista communities to make progress with fewer difficulties in the building of their autonomy and in improving their living conditions. It is not much, but it is far better than what they had prior to the beginning of the uprising in January of 1994. If you look at one of those studies the governments make, you will see that the only indigenous communities which have improved their living conditions—whether in health, education, food or housing—were those which are in zapatista territory, which is what we call where our villages are. And all of that has been possible because of the progress made by the zapatista villages and because of the very large support which has been received from good and noble persons, whom we call "civil societies," and from their organizations throughout the world. As if all of these people have made "another world is possible" a reality, but through actions, not just words.

And the villages have made good progress. Now there are more *compañeros* and *compañeras* who are learning to govern. And—even though little by little—there are more women going into this work, but there is still a lack of respect for the *compañeras*, and they need to participate more in the work of the struggle. And, also through the Good Government Juntas, coordination has been improved between the Autonomous Municipalities and the resolution of problems with other organizations and with the official authorities. There has also been much improvement in the projects in the communities, and the distribution of projects and aid given by civil society from all over the world has become more level. Health and education have improved, although there is still a good deal lacking for it to be what it should be. The same is true for housing and food, and in some areas there has been much improvement with the problem of land, because the lands recovered from the *finqueros* are being distributed. But there are areas which continue to suffer from a lack of lands to cultivate. And there has been great improvement in the support from national and international civil society, because previously everyone went wherever they wanted, and now the Good Government Juntas are directing them to where the greatest need exists. And, similarly, everywhere there are more *compañeros* and *compañeras* who are learning to relate to persons from other parts of Mexico and of the world. They are learning to respect and to demand respect. They are learning that there are many worlds, and that everyone has their place, their time and their way, and therefore there must be mutual respect between everyone.

We, the zapatistas of the EZLN, have devoted this time to our primary force, to the peoples who support us. And the situation has indeed improved some. No one can say that the zapatista organization and struggle has been without point, but rather, even if they were to do away with us completely, our struggle has indeed been of some use.

But it is not just the zapatista villages which have grown—the EZLN has also grown. Because what has happened during this time is that new generations have renewed our entire organization. They have added new strength. The *comandantes* and *comandantas* who were in their maturity at the beginning of the uprising in 1994 now have the wisdom they gained in the war and in the 12 years of dialogue with thousands of men and women from throughout the world. The members of the CCRI, the zapatista political-organizational leadership, is now counseling and directing the new ones who are entering our struggle, as well as those who are holding leadership positions. For some time now the "committees" (which is what we call them) have been preparing an entire new generation of *comandantes* and *comandantas* who, following a period of instruction and testing, are beginning to learn the work of organizational leadership and to discharge their duties. And it also so happens that our *insurgentes*, *insurgentas*, militants, local and regional *responsables*, as well as support bases, who were youngsters at the beginning of the uprising, are now mature men and women, combat veterans and natural leaders in their units and communities. And those who were children in that January of '94 are now young people who have grown up in the resistance, and they have been trained in the rebel dignity lifted up by their elders throughout these 12 years of war. These young people have a political, technical and cultural training that we who began the zapatista movement did not have. This youth is now, more and more, sustaining our troops as well as leadership positions in the organization. And, indeed, all of us have seen the deceits by the Mexican political class and the destruction which their actions have caused in our *patria*. And we have seen the great injustices and massacres that neoliberal globalization causes throughout the world. But we will speak to you of that later.

And so the EZLN has resisted 12 years of war, of military, political, ideological and economic attacks, of siege, of harassment, of persecution, and they have not vanquished us. We have not sold out nor surrendered, and we have made progress. More *compañeros* from many places have entered into the struggle so that, instead of making us weaker after so many years, we have become stronger. Of course there are problems which can be resolved by more separation of the political-military from the civil-democratic. But there are things, the most important ones, such as our demands for which we struggle, which have not been fully achieved.

To our way of thinking, and what we see in our heart, we have reached a point where we cannot go any further, and, in addition, it is possible that we could lose everything we have if we remain as we are and do nothing more in order to move forward. The hour has come to take a risk once again and to take a step which is dangerous but which is worthwhile. Because, perhaps united with other social sectors who suffer from the same wants as we do, it will be possible to achieve what we need and what we deserve. A new step forward in the indigenous struggle is only possible if the indigenous join together with workers, *campesinos*, students, teachers, employees . . . the workers of the city and the countryside.

III – HOW WE SEE THE WORLD

Now we are going to explain to you how we, the zapatistas, see what is going on in the world. We see that capitalism is the strongest right now. Capitalism is a social system, a way in which a society goes about organizing things and people, and who has and who has not, and who gives orders and who obeys. In capitalism, there are some people who have money, or capital, and factories and stores and fields and many things, and there are others who have nothing but their strength and knowledge in order to work. In capitalism, those who have money and things give the orders, and those who only have their ability to work obey.

Then capitalism means that there a few who have great wealth, but they did not win a prize, or find a treasure, or inherited from a parent. They obtained that wealth, rather, by exploiting the work of the many. So capitalism is based on the exploitation of the workers, which means they exploit the workers and take out all the profits they can. This is done unjustly, because they do not pay the worker what his work is worth. Instead they give him a salary that barely allows him to eat a little and to rest for a bit, and the next day he goes back to work in exploitation, whether in the countryside or in the city.

And capitalism also makes its wealth from plunder, or theft, because they take what they want from others, land, for example, and natural resources. So capitalism is a system where the robbers are free and they are admired and used as examples.

And, in addition to exploiting and plundering, capitalism represses because it imprisons and kills those who rebel against injustice.

Capitalism is most interested in merchandise, because when it is bought or sold, profits are made. And then capitalism turns everything into merchandise, it makes merchandise of people, of nature, of culture, of history, of conscience. According to capitalism, everything must be able to be bought and sold. And it hides everything behind the merchandise, so we don't see the exploitation that exists. And then the merchandise is bought and sold in a market. And the market, in addition to being used for buying and selling, is also used to hide the exploitation of the workers. In the market, for example, we see coffee in its little package or its pretty little jar, but we do not see the *campesino* who suffered in order to harvest the coffee, and we do not see the *coyote* who paid him so cheaply for his work, and we do not see the workers in the large company working their hearts out to package the coffee. Or we see an appliance for listening to music like cumbias, rancheras or corridos, or whatever, and we see that it is very good because it has a good sound, but we do not see the worker in the *maquiladora* who struggled for many hours, putting the cables and the parts of the appliance together, and they barely paid her a pittance of money, and she lives far away from work and spends a lot on the trip, and, in addition, she runs the risk of being kidnapped, raped and killed as happens in Ciudad Juárez in Mexico.

So we see merchandise in the market, but we do not see the exploitation with which it was made. And then capitalism needs many markets . . . or a very large market, a world market.

And so the capitalism of today is not the same as before, when the rich were content with exploiting the workers in their own countries, but now they are on a path which is called Neoliberal Globalization. This globalization means that they no longer control the workers in one or several countries, but the capitalists are trying to dominate everything all over the world. And the world, or Planet Earth, is also called the "globe," and that is why they say "globalization," or the entire world.

And neoliberalism is the idea that capitalism is free to dominate the entire world, and so tough, you have to resign yourself and conform and not make a fuss, in other words, not rebel. So neoliberalism is like the theory, the plan, of capitalist globalization. And neoliberalism has its economic, political, military and cultural plans. All of those plans have to do with dominating everyone, and they repress or separate anyone who doesn't obey so that his rebellious ideas aren't passed on to others.

Then, in neoliberal globalization, the great capitalists who live in the countries which are powerful, like the United States, want the entire world to be made into a big business where merchandise is produced like a great market. A world market for buying and selling the entire world and for hiding all the exploitation from the world. Then the global capitalists insert themselves everywhere, in all the countries, in order to do their big business, their great exploitation. Then they respect nothing, and they meddle wherever they wish. As if they were conquering other countries. That is why we zapatistas say that neoliberal globalization is a war of conquest of the entire world, a world war, a war being waged by capitalism for global domination. Sometimes that conquest is by armies who invade a country and conquer it by force. But sometimes it is with the economy, in other words, the big capitalists put their money into another country or they lend it money, but on the condition that they obey what they tell them to do. And they also insert their ideas, with the capitalist culture which is the culture of merchandise, of profits, of the market.

Then the one which wages the conquest, capitalism, does as it wants, it destroys and changes what it does not like and eliminates what gets in its way. For example, those who do not produce nor buy nor sell modern merchandise get in their way, or those who rebel against that order. And they despise those who are of no use to them. That is why the indigenous get in the way of neoliberal capitalism, and that is why they despise them and want to eliminate them. And neoliberal capitalism also gets rid of the laws which do not allow them to exploit and to have a lot of profit. They demand that everything can be bought and sold, and, since capitalism has all the money, it buys everything. Capitalism destroys the countries it conquers with neoliberal globalization, but it also wants to adapt everything, to make it over again, but in its own way, a way which benefits capitalism and which doesn't allow anything to get in its way. Then neoliberal globalization, capitalism, destroys what exists in these countries, it destroys their culture, their language, their economic system, their political system, and it also destroys the ways in which those who live in that country relate to each other. So everything that makes a country a country is left destroyed.

Then neoliberal globalization wants to destroy the nations of the world so that only one Nation or country remains, the country of money, of capital. And capitalism wants everything to be as it wants, in its own way, and it doesn't like what is different, and it persecutes it and attacks it, or puts it off in a corner and acts as if it doesn't exist.

Then, in short, the capitalism of global neoliberalism is based on exploitation, plunder, contempt and repression of those who refuse. The same as before, but now globalized, worldwide.

But it is not so easy for neoliberal globalization, because the exploited of each country become discontented, and they will not say well, too bad, instead they rebel. And those who remain and who are in the way resist, and they don't allow themselves to be eliminated. And that is why we see, all over the world, those who are being screwed over making resistances, not putting up with it, in other words, they rebel, and not just in one country but wherever they abound. And so, as there is a neoliberal globalization, there is a globalization of rebellion.

And it is not just the workers of the countryside and of the city who appear in this globalization of rebellion, but others also appear who are much persecuted and despised for the same reason, for not letting themselves be dominated, like women, young people, the indigenous, homosexuals, lesbians, transsexual persons, migrants and many other groups who exist all over the world but who we do not see until they shout *ya basta* of being despised, and they raise up, and then we see them, we hear them, and we learn from them.

And then we see that all those groups of people are fighting against neoliberalism, against the capitalist globalization plan, and they are struggling for humanity.

And we are astonished when we see the stupidity of the neoliberals who want to destroy all humanity with their wars and exploitations, but it also makes us quite happy to see resistances and rebellions appearing everywhere, such as ours, which is a bit small, but here we are. And we see this all over the world, and now our heart learns that we are not alone.

IV – HOW WE SEE OUR COUNTRY WHICH IS MEXICO

Now we will talk to you about how we see what is going on in our Mexico. What we see is our country being governed by neoliberals. So, as we already explained, our leaders are destroying our nation, our Mexican Patria. And the work of these bad leaders is not to look after the well-being of the people, instead they are only concerned with the well-being of the capitalists. For example, they make laws like the Free Trade Agreement, which end up leaving many Mexicans destitute, like *campesinos* and small producers, because they are "gobbled up" by the big agroindustrial companies. As well as workers and small businesspeople, because they cannot compete with the large transnationals who come in without anybody saying anything to them and even thanking them, and they set their low salaries and their high prices. So some of the economic foundations of our Mexico, which were the countryside and industry and national commerce, are being quite destroyed, and just a bit of rubble—which they are certainly going to sell off—remains.

And these are great disgraces for our Patria. Because food is no longer being produced in our countryside, just what the big capitalists sell, and the good lands are being stolen through trickery and with the help of the politicians. What is happening in the countryside is the same as Porfirismo, but, instead of *hacendados*, now there are a few foreign businesses *which* have well and truly screwed the *campesino*. And, where before there were credits and price protections, now there is just charity . . . and sometimes not even that.

As for the worker in the city, the factories close, and they are left without work, or they open what are called *maquiladoras*, which are foreign and which pay a pittance for many hours of work. And then the price of the goods the people need doesn't matter, whether they are expensive or cheap, since there is no money. And if someone was working in a small or midsize business, now they are not, because it was closed, and it was bought by a big transnational. And if someone had a small business, it disappeared as well, or they went to work clandestinely for big businesses which exploit them terribly, and which even put boys and girls to work. And if the worker belonged to his union in order to demand his legal rights, then no, now the same union tells him he will have to put up with his salary being lowered or his hours or his benefits being taken away, because, if not, the business will close and move to another country. And then there is the "microchangarro," which is the government's economic program for putting all the city's workers on street corners selling gum or telephone cards. In other words, absolute economic destruction in the cities as well.

And then what happens is that, with the people's economy being totally screwed in the countryside as well as in the city, then many Mexican men and women have to leave their Patria, Mexican lands, and go to seek work in another country, the United States. And they do not treat them well there, instead they exploit them, persecute them and treat them with contempt and even kill them.

Under neoliberalism which is being imposed by the bad governments, the economy has not improved. Quite the opposite, the countryside is in great need, and there is no work in the cities. What is happening is that Mexico is being turned into a place where people are working for the wealth of foreigners, mostly rich *gringos*, a place you are just born into for a little while, and in another little while you die. That is why we say that Mexico is dominated by the United States.

Now, it is not just that. Neoliberalism has also changed the Mexican political class, the politicians, because they made them into something like employees in a store, who have to do everything possible to sell everything and to sell it very cheap. You have already seen that they changed the laws in order to remove Article 27 from the Constitution so that *ejidal* and communal lands could be sold. That was Salinas de Gortari, and he and his gangs said that it was for the good of the countryside and the *campesino*, and that was how they would prosper and live better. Has it been like that? The Mexican countryside is worse than ever and the *campesinos* more screwed than under Porfirio Diaz. And they also say they are going to privatize—sell to foreigners—the companies held by the State to help the well-being of the people. Because the companies don't work well and they need to be modernized, and it would be better to sell them. But, instead of improving, the social rights which were won in the revolution of 1910 now make one sad . . . and courageous. And they also said that the borders must be opened so all the foreign capital can enter, that way all the Mexican businesses will be fixed, and things will be made better. But now we see that there are not any national businesses, the foreigners gobbled them all up, and the things that are sold are worse than those that were made in Mexico.

And now the Mexican politicians also want to sell PEMEX, the oil which belongs to all Mexicans, and the only difference is that some say everything should be sold and others that only a part of it should be sold. And they also want to privatize social security, and electricity and water and the forests and everything, until nothing of Mexico is left, and our country will be a wasteland or a place of entertainment for rich people from all over the world, and we Mexican men and women will be their servants, dependent on what they offer, bad housing, without roots, without culture, without even a Patria.

So the neoliberals want to kill Mexico, our Mexican Patria. And the political parties not only do not defend it, they are the first to put themselves at the service of foreigners, especially those from the United States, and they are the ones who are in charge of deceiving us, making us look the other way while everything is sold, and they are left with the money. All the political parties that exist right now, not just some of them. Think about whether anything has been done well, and you will see that no, nothing but theft and scams. And look how all the politicians always have their nice houses and their nice cars and luxuries. And they still want us to thank them and to vote for them again. And it is obvious, as they say, that they are without shame. And they are without it because they do not, in fact, have a Patria, they only have bank accounts.

And we also see that drug trafficking and crime has been increasing a lot. And sometimes we think that criminals are like they show them in the songs or movies, and maybe some are like that, but not the real chiefs. The real chiefs go around very well dressed, they study outside the country, they are elegant, they do not go around in hiding, they eat in good restaurants and they appear in the papers, very pretty and well dressed at their parties. They are, as they say, "good people," and some are even officials, deputies, senators, secretaries of state, prosperous businessmen, police chiefs, generals.

Are we saying that politics serves no purpose? No, what we mean is that THAT politics serves no purpose. And it is useless because it does not take the people into account. It does not listen to them, it does not pay any attention to them, it just approaches them when there are elections. And they do not even want votes anymore, the polls are enough to say who wins. And then just promises about what this one is going to do and what the other one is going to do, then it's bye, I'll see you, but you don't see them again, except when they appear in the news when they've just stolen a lot of money and nothing is going to be done to them because the law—which those same politicians made—protects them.

Because that's another problem, the Constitution is all warped and changed now. It's no longer the one that had the rights and liberties of working people. Now there are the rights and liberties of the neoliberals so they can have their huge profits. And the judges exist to serve those neoliberals, because they always rule in favor of them, and those who are not rich get injustice, jails and cemeteries.

Well, even with all this mess the neoliberals are making, there are Mexican men and women who are organizing and making a resistance struggle.

And so we found out that there are indigenous, that their lands are far away from us here in Chiapas, and they are making their autonomy and defending their culture and caring for their land, forests and water.

And there are workers in the countryside, *campesinos*, who are organizing and holding their marches and mobilizations in order to demand credits and aid for the countryside. And there are workers in the city who do not let their rights be taken away or their jobs privatized. They protest and demonstrate so the little they have isn't taken away from them and so they don't take away from the country what is, in fact, its own, like electricity, oil, social security, education.

And there are students who don't let education be privatized and who are fighting for it to be free and popular and scientific, so they don't charge, so everyone can learn, and so they don't teach stupid things in schools.

And there are women who do not let themselves be treated as an ornament or be humiliated and despised just for being women, but who are organizing and fighting for the respect they deserve as the women they are.

And there are young people who don't accept their stultifying them with drugs or persecuting them for their way of being, but who make themselves aware with their music and their culture, their rebellion.

And there are homosexuals, lesbians, transsexuals and many ways who do not put up with being ridiculed, despised, mistreated and even killed for having another way which is different, with being treated like they are abnormal or criminals, but who make their own organizations in order to defend their right to be different.

And there are priests and nuns and those they call laypeople who are not with the rich and who are not resigned, but who are organizing to accompany the struggles of the people.

And there are those who are called social activists, who are men and women who have been fighting all their lives for exploited people, and they are the same ones who participated in the great strikes and workers' actions, in the great citizens' mobilizations, in the great *campesino* movements, and who suffer great repression, and who, even though some are old now, continue on without surrendering, and they go everywhere, looking for the struggle, seeking justice, and making leftist organizations, nongovernmental organizations, human rights organizations, organizations in defense of political prisoners and for the disappeared, leftist publications, organizations of teachers or students, social struggle, and even political-military organizations, and they are just not quiet and they know a lot because they have seen a lot and lived and struggled.

And so we see in general that in our country, which is called Mexico, there are many people who do not put up with things, who do not surrender, who do not sell out. Who are dignified. And that makes us very pleased and happy, because with all those people it's not going to be so easy for the neoliberals to win, and perhaps it will be possible to save our Patria from the great thefts and destruction they are doing. And we think that perhaps our "we" will include all those rebellions.

V – WHAT WE WANT TO DO

We are now going to tell you what we want to do in the world and in Mexico, because we cannot watch everything that is happening on our planet and just remain quiet, as if it were only we who were where we are.

What we want in the world is to tell all of those who are resisting and fighting in their own ways and in their own countries, that you are not alone, that we, the zapatistas, even though we are very small, are supporting you, and we are going to look at how to help you in your struggles and to speak to you in order to learn, because what we have, in fact, learned is to learn.

And we want to tell the Latin American peoples that we are proud to be a part of you, even if it is a small part. We remember quite well how the continent was also illuminated some years ago, and a light was called Che Guevara, as it had previously been called Bolivar, because sometimes the people take up a name in order to say they are taking up a flag.

And we want to tell the people of Cuba, who have now been on their path of resistance for many years, that you are not alone, and we do not agree with the blockade they are imposing, and we are going to see how to send you something, even if it is maize, for your resistance. And we want to tell the North American people that we know that the bad governments which you have and which spread harm throughout the world is one thing—and those North Americans who struggle in their country, and who are in solidarity with the struggles of other countries, are a very different thing. And we want to tell the Mapuche brothers and sisters in Chile that we are watching and learning from your struggles. And to the Venezuelans, we see how well you are defending your sovereignty, your nation's right to decide where it is going. And to the indigenous brothers and sisters of Ecuador and Bolivia, we say you are giving a good lesson in history to all of Latin America, because now you are indeed putting a halt to neoliberal globalization. And to the *piqueteros* and to the young people of Argentina, we want to tell you that, that we love you. And to those in Uruguay who want a better country, we admire you. And to those who are *sin tierra* in Brazil, that we respect you. And to all the young people of Latin America, that what you are doing is good, and you give us great hope.

And we want to tell the brothers and sisters of Social Europe, that which is dignified and rebel, that you are not alone. That your great movements against the neoliberal wars bring us joy. That we are attentively watching your forms of organization and your methods of struggle so that we can perhaps learn something. That we are considering how we can help you in your struggles, and we are not going to send euro because then they will be devalued because of the European Union mess. But perhaps we will send you crafts and coffee so you can market them and help you some in the tasks of your struggle. And perhaps we might also send you some pozol, which gives much strength in the resistance, but who knows if we will send it to you, because pozol is more our way, and what if it were to hurt your bellies and weaken your struggles and the neoliberals defeat you.

And we want to tell the brothers and sisters of Africa, Asia and Oceania that we know that you are fighting also, and we want to learn more of your ideas and practices.

And we want to tell the world that we want to make you large, so large that all those worlds will fit, those worlds which are resisting because they want to destroy the neoliberals and because they simply cannot stop fighting for humanity.

Now then, what we want to do in Mexico is to make an agreement with persons and organizations just of the left, because we believe that it is in the political left where the idea of resisting neoliberal globalization is, and of making a country where there will be justice, democracy and liberty for everyone. Not as it is right now, where there is justice only for the rich, there is liberty only for their big businesses, and there is democracy only for painting walls with election propaganda. And because we believe that it is only from the left that a plan of struggle can emerge, so that our Patria, which is Mexico, does not die.

And, then, what we think is that, with these persons and organizations of the left, we will make a plan for going to all those parts of Mexico where there are humble and simple people like ourselves.

And we are not going to tell them what they should do or give them orders.

Nor are we going to ask them to vote for a candidate, since we already know that the ones who exist are neoliberals.

Nor are we going to tell them to be like us, nor to rise up in arms.

What we are going to do is to ask them what their lives are like, their struggle, their thoughts about our country and what we should do so they do not defeat us.

What we are going to do is to take heed of the thoughts of the simple and humble people, and perhaps we will find there the same love which we feel for our Patria.

And perhaps we will find agreement between those of us who are simple and humble and, together, we will organize all over the country and reach agreement in our struggles, which are alone right now, separated from each other, and we will find something like a program that has what we all want, and a plan for how we are going to achieve the realization of that program, which is called the "national program of struggle."

And, with the agreement of the majority of those people whom we are going to listen to, we will then engage in a struggle with everyone, with indigenous, workers, *campesinos*, students, teachers, employees, women, children, old ones, men, and with all of those of good heart and who want to struggle so that our Patria called Mexico does not end up being destroyed and sold, and which still exists between the Rio Grande and the Rio Suchiate and which has the Pacific Ocean on one side and the Atlantic on the other.

VI – HOW WE ARE GOING TO DO IT

And so this is our simple word that goes out to the humble and simple people of Mexico and of the world, and we are calling our word of today:

Sixth Declaration of the Selva Lacandona

And we are here to say, with our simple word, that . . .

The EZLN maintains its commitment to an offensive ceasefire, and it will not make any attack against government forces or any offensive military movements.

The EZLN still maintains its commitment to insisting on the path of political struggle through this peaceful initiative which we are now undertaking. The EZLN continues, therefore, in its resolve to not establish any kind of secret relations with either national political-military organizations or those from other countries.

The EZLN reaffirms its commitment to defend, support and obey the zapatista indigenous communities of which it is composed, and which are its supreme command, and—without interfering in their internal democratic processes—will, to the best of its abilities, contribute to the strengthening of their autonomy, good government and improvement in their living conditions. In other words, what we are going to do in Mexico and in the world, we are going to do without arms, with a civil and peaceful movement, and without neglecting nor ceasing to support our communities.

Therefore . . .

In the World . . .

1. We will forge new relationships of mutual respect and support with persons and organizations who are resisting and struggling against neoliberalism and for humanity.

2. As far as we are able, we will send material aid such as food and handicrafts for those brothers and sisters who are struggling all over the world.

In order to begin, we are going to ask the Good Government Junta of La Realidad to loan their truck, which is called "Chompiras," and which appears to hold 8 tons, and we are going to fill it with maize and perhaps two 200 liter cans with oil or petrol, as they prefer, and we are going to deliver it to the Cuban Embassy in Mexico for them to send to the Cuban people as aid from the zapatistas for their resistance against the North American blockade. Or perhaps there might be a place closer to here where it could be delivered, because it's always such a long distance to Mexico City, and what if "Chompiras" were to break down and we'd end up in bad shape. And that will happen when the harvest comes in, which is turning green right now in the fields, and if they don't attack us, because if we were to send it during these next few months, it would be nothing but corncobs, and they don't turn out well even in tamales, better in November or December, it depends.

And we are also going to make an agreement with the women's crafts cooperatives in order to send a good number of *bordados*, embroidered pieces, to the Europes which are perhaps not yet Union, and perhaps we'll also send some organic coffee from the zapatista cooperatives, so that they can sell it and get a little money for their struggle. And, if it isn't sold, then they can always have a little cup of coffee and talk about the antineoliberal struggle, and if it's a bit cold then they can cover themselves up with the zapatista *bordados*, which do indeed resist quite well being laundered by hand and by rocks, and, besides, they don't run in the wash.

And we are also going to send the indigenous brothers and sisters of Bolivia and Ecuador some nontransgenic maize, and we just don't know where to send them so they arrive complete, but we are indeed willing to give this little bit of aid.

3. And to all of those who are resisting throughout the world, we say there must be other intercontinental *encuentros* held, even if just one other. Perhaps December of this year or next January, we'll have to think about it. We don't want to say just when, because this is about our agreeing equally on everything, on where, on when, on how, on who. But not with a stage where just a few speak and all the rest listen, but without a stage, just level and everyone speaking, but orderly, otherwise it will just be a hubbub and the words won't be understood, and with good organization everyone will hear and jot down in their notebooks the words of resistance from others, so then everyone can go and talk with their *compañeros* and *compañeras* in their worlds. And we think it might be in a place that has a very large jail, because what if they were to repress us and incarcerate us, and so that way we wouldn't be all piled up, prisoners, yes, but well-organized, and there in the jail we could continue the intercontinental *encuentros* for humanity and against neoliberalism. Later on we'll tell you what we shall do in order to reach agreement as to how we're going to come to agreement. Now that is how we're thinking of doing what we want to do in the world. Now follows . . .

In Mexico . . .

1. We are going to continue fighting for the Indian peoples of Mexico, but now not just for them and not with only them, but for all the exploited and dispossessed of Mexico, with all of them and all over the country. And when we say all the exploited of Mexico, we are also talking about the brothers and sisters who have had to go to the United States in search of work in order to survive.

2. We are going to go to listen to, and talk directly with, without intermediaries or mediation, the simple and humble of the Mexican people, and, according to what we hear and learn, we are going to go about building, along with those people who, like us, are humble and simple, a national program of struggle, but a program which will be clearly of the left, or anti-capitalist, or antineoliberal, or for justice, democracy and liberty for the Mexican people.

3. We are going to try to build, or rebuild, another way of doing politics, one which once again has the spirit of serving others, without material interests, with sacrifice, with dedication, with honesty, which keeps its word, whose only payment is the satisfaction of duty performed, or like the militants of the left did before, when they were not stopped by blows, jail or death, let alone by dollar bills.

4. We are also going to go about raising a struggle in order to demand that we make a new Constitution, new laws which take into account the demands of the Mexican people, which are: housing, land, work, food, health, education, information, culture, independence, democracy, justice, liberty and peace. A new Constitution which recognizes the rights and liberties of the people, and which defends the weak in the face of the powerful.

TO THESE ENDS . . .

The EZLN will send a delegation of its leadership in order to do this work throughout the national territory and for an indefinite period of time. This zapatista delegation, along with those organizations and persons of the left who join in this Sixth Declaration of the Selva Lacandona, will go to those places where they are expressly invited.

We are also letting you know that the EZLN will establish a policy of alliances with non-electoral organizations and movements which define themselves, in theory and practice, as being of the left, in accordance with the following conditions:

Not to make agreements from above to be imposed below, but to make accords to go together to listen and to organize outrage. Not to raise movements which are later negotiated behind the backs of those who made them, but to always take into account the opinions of those participating. Not to seek gifts, positions, advantages, public positions, from the Power or those who aspire to it, but to go beyond the election calendar. Not to try to resolve from above the problems of our Nation, but to build FROM BELOW AND FOR BELOW an alternative to neoliberal destruction, an alternative of the left for Mexico.

Yes to reciprocal respect for the autonomy and independence of organizations, for their methods of struggle, for their ways of organizing, for their internal decision-making processes, for their legitimate representations. And yes to a clear commitment for joint and coordinated defense of national sovereignty, with intransigent opposition to privatization attempts of electricity, oil, water and natural resources.

In other words, we are inviting the unregistered political and social organizations of the left, and those persons who lay claim to the left and who do not belong to registered political parties, to meet with us, at the time, place and manner in which we shall propose at the proper time, to organize a national campaign, visiting all possible corners of our Patria, in order to listen to and organize the word of our people. It is like a campaign, then, but very otherly, because it is not electoral.

Brothers and sisters:

This is our word which we declare:

In the world, we are going to join together more with the resistance struggles against neoliberalism and for humanity.

And we are going to support, even if it's but little, those struggles.

And we are going to exchange, with mutual respect, experiences, histories, ideas, dreams.

In Mexico, we are going to travel all over the country, through the ruins left by the neoliberal wars and through those resistances which, entrenched, are flourishing in those ruins.

We are going to seek, and to find, those who love these lands and these skies even as much as we do.

We are going to seek, from La Realidad to Tijuana, those who want to organize, struggle and build what may perhaps be the last hope this Nation—which has been going on at least since the time when an eagle alighted on a nopal in order to devour a snake—has of not dying.

We are going for democracy, liberty and justice for those of us who have been denied it.

We are going with another politics, for a program of the left and for a new Constitution.

We are inviting all indigenous, workers, *campesinos*, teachers, students, housewives, neighbors, small businesspersons, small shop owners, micro-businesspersons, pensioners, handicapped persons, religious men and women, scientists, artists, intellectuals, young persons, women, old persons, homosexuals and lesbians, boys and girls—to participate, whether individually or collectively, directly with the zapatistas in this NATIONAL CAMPAIGN for building another way of doing politics, for a program of national struggle of the left, and for a new Constitution.

And so this is our word as to what we are going to do and how we are going to do it. You will see whether you want to join.

And we are telling those men and women who are of good heart and intent, who are in agreement with this word we are bringing out, and who are not afraid, or who are afraid but who control it, to then state publicly whether they are in agreement with this idea we are presenting, and in that way we will see once and for all who and how and where and when this new step in the struggle is to be made.

While you are thinking about it, we say to you that today, in the sixth month of the year 2005, the men, women, children and old ones of the Zapatista Army of National Liberation have now decided, and we have now subscribed to, this Sixth Declaration of the Selva Lacandona, and those who know how to sign, signed, and those who did not left their mark, but there are fewer now who do not know how, because education has advanced here in this territory in rebellion for humanity and against neoliberalism, that is in zapatista skies and land.

And this was our simple word sent out to the noble hearts of those simple and humble people who resist and rebel against injustices all over the world.

Democracy!

Liberty!

Justice!

From the mountains of the Mexican Southeast.

Clandestine Revolutionary Indigenous Committee—General Command of the Zapatista Army of National Liberation.

Mexico, in the sixth month, or June, of the year 2005.

V

FROM SOCIALIST REVOLUTION TO DEMOCRACY, NEOLIBERALISM, AND GLOBALIZATION: POST–COLD WAR SOCIAL AND POLITICAL THOUGHT

18

Cultures of Politics, Politics of Culture: Re-Visioning Latin American Social Movements (1998)

Evelina Dagnino (b. Brazil, 1945) is a Brazilian political scientist and professor of Political Science at the University of Campinas, São Paulo, Brazil. She has been visiting professor at Yale University in the United States and Göteborg University in Sweden. She has several books and articles published in several countries on the relations between culture and politics, social movements, civil society and participation, democracy and citizenship. Currently she is involved in a comparative project on democratization and the relationships between civil society and political society in Latin America. This selection is a well-known representative of the shift in Latin America from a Marxist political economy discourse, emphasizing the relationship between politics and the economy, to a Gramscian cultural politics discourse, emphasizing the relationship between culture and politics. In it Dagnino explores the role of contemporary Latin American social movements in redefining the relationships between culture and politics, and in defining the operational meanings and scope of democracy and citizenship in Latin America, in general, and Brazil, in particular.

CULTURE, CITIZENSHIP, AND DEMOCRACY: CHANGING DISCOURSES AND PRACTICES OF THE LATIN AMERICAN LEFT

Democracy and Citizenship: The Cultural Politics of Social Movements

As in most Latin American societies, political struggle in Brazil today is being waged around alternative designs for democracy. As stated in the Introduction to Alvarez et al. 1998, "Fundamentally in dispute are the parameters of democracy—to be sure, the very boundaries of what is to be properly defined as the political arena: its participants, its institutions, its processes, its agenda, and its scope." Social movements have been deeply involved in this struggle since the very beginning of the resistance to the authoritarian regime in the early 1970s.

Although the positive role of social movements in the transition to democracy has been largely acknowledged by analysts, since the return to civilian rule in 1985 their actual or potential contribution to the expansion and deepening of democracy has been questioned. In discussing this questioning,[1] conveyed by both mainstream theorists of "democratic consolidation" and some social movements analysts, I suggested that it has been based on a predominant focus on the institutional dimension of the democratic process: Social movements are presented either as irrelevant to and even destabilizing for democratic institutionalization or as incapable of adjusting to the new formal representative political arenas. What these objections may fail to acknowledge is precisely the existence of dispute among alternative conceptions of democracy and the political arena. As an emphasis on institutional "engineering" and consolidation has monopolized most of the intellectual efforts of analysts of the process of democratization in Latin America (and a great deal of the energies of its political technocrats), other crucial dimensions of the process, valued by those historically excluded from traditional representative democracy, are often disregarded.

The basic question I would like to address in this section is how social movements in Brazil have been contributing to resignifying the relations between culture and politics in their democratizing struggles. There are clear points of confluence between the main process of renovation on the Left and the political directions indicated by the struggles of social movements. In fact, such a confluence results from the intermingling of influences that takes place within a common ethical-political field.

The notion of a social movement's ethical-political field has been developed in order to account for the production and circulation of "a common field of references and differences for collective action and political contestation" (Baierle 1992, 19). In recent analyses of social movements' collective actions, such a notion has been connected to the emergence of "webs," or networks of social movements, to indicate the collective construction that results from this articulation of social movements of various kinds with other sectors and organizations, such as political parties, leftist organizations, the Catholic Church, scientific groups, nongovernmental organizations (NGOs), trade unions, and so on (Alvarez 1993; Alvarez and Dagnino 1995; Doimo 1995; Teixeira 1995; Scherer-Warren 1993). Through the interchange of discourses and practices, "an active process of elaboration which reflects the dynamics of multiple emergent concrete practices of struggle and their internal conflicts" takes place in these webs, configuring a distinctive ethical-political field.[2]

I will argue first that social movements have advanced a conception of democracy that transcends the limits both of political institutions as traditionally conceived and of "actually existing democracy." The distinctive feature of this conception, which points toward the extension and deepening of democracy, is the fact that it has as a basic reference not the democratization of the *political regime* but of society as a whole, including therefore the cultural practices embodied in social relations of exclusion and inequality. Second, I will argue that the operationalization of this conception of democracy is being carried out through a redefinition of the notion of citizenship and of its core referent, the notion of rights. Finally, I will suggest that this societal emphasis does not imply, as some of the early literature on social movements argued, a refusal of political institutionality and the state but rather a radical claim for their transformation.

As social movements do not constitute homogeneous social actors or political subjects but indeed are characterized by heterogeneity and diversity, the conceptions discussed here are not to be taken as representative of the whole multiplicity of social movements existing today in Brazil. If it is true that a certain tendency to mystify their collective actions as incarnations of political virtue and bearers of all the new hopes for social transformation on the Left must be critically assessed, this should not be done at the expense of denying or obscuring the molecular changes that result from social movements' practice.

The adoption of an alternative perspective in examining the cultural politics of social movements and assessing the scope of their struggles for the democratization of society seeks to highlight the less visible and often neglected implications of these struggles. Emphasizing cultural implications implies the recognition of the capacity of social movements to produce new visions of a democratic society insofar as they identify the existing social ordering as limiting and exclusionary with respect to their values and interests. Fragmentary, plural, and contradictory as they may be, these cultural contestations are not to be seen as by-products of political struggle but as constitutive of the efforts by social movements to redefine the meaning and the limits of the political itself.

For the excluded sectors of Brazilian society, the perception of the political relevance of cultural meanings embedded in social practices is part of their daily life. As an exemplary case that can be easily generalized for Latin America as a whole, Brazilian society is one in which economic inequality and extreme levels of poverty have been only the most visible aspects of the unequal and hierarchical organization of social relations as a whole, what can be called *social authoritarianism*. Class, race, and gender differences constitute the main bases for a social classification that has historically pervaded Brazilian culture, establishing different categories of people hierarchically disposed in their respective "places" in society. Underneath the apparent cordiality of Brazilian society, the notion of *social places* constitutes a strict code, very visible and ubiquitous, in the streets and in the homes, in the state and in society, which reproduces inequality in social relations at all levels, underlying social practices and structuring an authoritarian culture.[3]

The perception of the need for cultural changes as a fundamental element in the process of democratization has been obviously crucial to women, homosexuals, blacks, and other groups. A great part of their political struggle, in fact, is directed toward confronting this authoritarian culture. Yet, if the recognition of their struggles as cultural politics is more acceptable, there is still resistance to acknowledging their meaning in reconfiguring society as a whole and to redefining the political they imply.

What is seldom recognized, however, is the fact that urban popular movements reached this same understanding of the intermingling of culture and politics as soon as they realized that what they had to struggle for was not only their social rights, housing, health, education, and so on but their very right to have rights. As part of the authoritarian, hierarchical social ordering of Brazilian society, to be poor means not only to endure economic and material deprivation but also to be submitted to cultural rules that convey a complete lack of recognition of poor people as subjects, as bearers of rights. In what Telles (1993) called the incivility embedded in that tradition, poverty is a sign of inferiority, a way of being in which individuals lose their ability to exercise their rights. This cultural deprivation imposed by the absolute absence of rights, which ultimately expresses itself as a suppression of human dignity, then becomes constitutive of material deprivation and political exclusion.[4]

In this sense, the struggle for rights, for the right to have rights, exposed what had to be a political struggle against a pervasive culture of social authoritarianism, thus setting the stage for the urban popular movements to establish a connection between culture and politics as constitutive of their collective action. This connection has been a fundamental element in establishing a common ground for articulation with other social movements that are more obviously cultural, such as ethnic, women's, gay rights, ecological, and human rights movements, in the search for more egalitarian relations at all levels, helping to demarcate a distinctive, enlarged view of democracy.

A fundamental instrument used by social movements in the struggle for democratization in recent times has been the appropriation of the notion of citizenship, which operationalizes their enlarged view of democracy. The origins of the present redefined notion of a new citizenship can be partially found in the concrete experience of social movements in the late 1970s and 1980s. For urban popular movements, the perception of social needs, *carências*, as rights represented a crucial step and a turning point in their struggle.[5] For other social movements such as the ecological movement and those led by women, blacks, homosexuals, and others, the struggle for the right to equality and to difference found clear support in the redefined notion of citizenship. A significant part of this common experience was the elaboration of new identities as subjects, as bearers of rights, as equal citizens.

This turning point represented a rupture with the predominant strategies of political organization of the popular sectors characterized by favoritism, clientelism, and tutelage. Such strategies, still alive, of course, find support in and reinforce the dominant authoritarian culture insofar as they do not confront its systems of classification and exclusion and its basic hierarchies, thus legitimating the maxim, as put by Teresa Sales: "In Brazil either you give orders or you plead" (*"No Brasil ou bem se manda ou bem se pede"*), expressing an oligarchic conception of politics that still obstructs the political organization of the excluded and that enlarges the political autonomy of the elites (see Alvarez et al. 1998, 18).

A broader emphasis on the extension and deepening of democracy came to reinforce the concrete experience of social movements as a struggle for equal rights. Such an emphasis, as already discussed, was connected not only to the new political and theoretical status that the question of democracy had acquired throughout the world but also to the crisis of the authoritarian regime in Brazil and the new directions taken by the Brazilian, and Latin American, Left.

In recent years the use of the term "citizenship" has spread increasingly throughout Brazilian society. As the redefined notion continued to underlie popular struggles and the political practices of parties such as the PT (Partido dos Trabalhadores) and NGOs such as those associated with the Brazilian Association of Nongovernmental Organizations (ABONG), citizenship is squarely behind solidarity campaigns aimed at the mobilization of the middle classes, such as the Ação da Cidadania contra a Fome, headed by Herbert de Souza-Betinho, or associations of progressive entrepreneurs such as CIVES (Associação Brasileira de

Empresarios pela Cidadania). The term "citizenship" also began to be reappropriated by neoliberal sectors and even by conservative traditional politicians, with obviously very different meanings and intentions.[6]

Neoliberal versions of citizenship, created in connection with the implementation of policies of economic and social adjustment now prevailing throughout Latin America, have been particularly energetic in their attempts to redefine "the political domain and its participants—based on a minimalist conception of both the state and democracy" (see the Introduction to Alvarez et al. 1998). On the one hand, neoliberalism works with a view of citizenship as an alluring individual integration to the market. On the other, it systematically operates for the elimination of consolidated rights, transforming their bearers/citizens into the new villains of the nation, privileged enemies of political reforms intended to shrink state responsibilities. Moreover, social expenditures are directed toward the reversion of that major step in the organization of social movements that made possible the very emergence of the new citizenship, the definition of needs as rights: Transformed into public charity for the needy, the *carentes*, governmental social expenditures are decided without any real participation by civil society (Oliveira 1996).

The symbolic dispute around the meaning of citizenship attests to its political relevance and to the importance attributed by the different contenders to the redefinitions deployed by social movements. Such a dispute also requires an effort to clarify the notion referred to here as the "new citizenship."

A first crucial and distinctive element in this notion comes from the very conception of democracy it intends to operationalize: The new citizenship seeks to implement a strategy of democratic construction, of social transformation, that asserts *a constitutive link between culture and politics*. Incorporating characteristics of contemporary societies such as the role of subjectivities, the emergence of social subjects of a new kind and of rights of a new kind, and the broadening of the political space, this strategy acknowledges and emphasizes the intrinsic character of cultural transformation with respect to the building of democracy. In this sense, the new citizenship includes cultural constructions such as those underlying social authoritarianism as fundamental political targets of democratization. It is therefore my argument here that the redefinition of the notion of citizenship, as formulated by social movements, expresses not only a *political strategy* but also a *cultural politics*.

To assert the notion of citizenship as a political strategy (Wiener 1992) means to emphasize its character as a historical construct that expresses concrete interests and practices not previously defined by a given universal essence. In this sense, its contents and meanings are not previously defined and limited but constitute a response to the dynamics of real conflicts and the political struggle lived by a particular society at a given historical moment. Such a historical perspective poses a need to distinguish the new citizenship of the 1990s from the liberal tradition that coined this term at the end of the eighteenth century. Emerging as the state's response to claims from excluded social sectors, the liberal version of citizenship ended up essentializing the concept, in spite of the fact that it today performs functions entirely different from those that characterized its origin.

In a very preliminary way, it is possible to indicate some points that clarify this distinction. There is a similarity in the vocabulary that expresses common references, the most obvious being the very question of *democracy* and the notion of *rights*, central elements in both conceptions. But beyond this similarity, it is necessary to identify to what extent the political differences that emerge from different historical contexts are also expressed as conceptual differences.

1. The first point refers to the very notion of *rights*. The new citizenship assumes a redefinition of the idea of rights, and the point of departure is the conception of *a right to have rights*. This conception is not limited to legal provisions, access to previously defined rights, or the effective implementation of abstract, formal rights. It includes the invention and creation of *new* rights, which emerge from specific struggles and their concrete practices. In this sense, the very determination of the meaning of "right" and the assertion of some value or ideal as a "right" are themselves objects of political struggle. The right to autonomy over one's own body, the right to environmental protection, the right to housing, are examples (intentionally very different) of this creation of new rights. In addition, this redefinition comes to include not only the right to equality but also the right to difference, which specifies, deepens, and broadens the right to equality.[7]

2. The second point, which implies the right to have rights, is that the new citizenship, contrary to older conceptions, is not linked to the strategy of the dominant classes and the state for the gradual political incorporation of excluded sectors for the purpose of greater social integration or as a legal and political condition necessary for the installation of capitalism.[8] The new citizenship requires the constitution of active social subjects (political agents), defining what they consider to be their rights and struggling for their recognition; it is even *thought of* as consisting of this process. In this sense, it is a strategy of the non-citizens, of the excluded, to secure a citizenship "from below."

3. The third point is the idea that the new citizenship transcends a central reference in the liberal concept, the claim to access, inclusion, membership, and belonging to an already given political system. What is at stake, in fact, is *the right to participate in the very definition of that system, to define what we want to be members of*, that is to say, the invention of a new society. The recognition of the right to citizenship, as defined by those who today in Brazil are excluded from it, points toward radical transformations in our society and in its structure of power relations. Recent political practices inspired by the new citizenship, such as those emerging in the cities governed by the Partido dos Trabalhadores/ Frentes Populares, where popular sectors and their organizations have provided space for the democratic control of the state through the effective participation of citizens in power, help to visualize future possibilities.

The Participatory Budget Council (Conselho do Orçamento Participativo) of Porto Alegre, which began in 1989, is probably the most successful of these alternative democratic experiments (see Baierle, in Alvarez et al. 1998). But Porto Alegre is only one example among many. There is in Brazil today a proliferation of microexperiments that cannot be ignored since they reveal important possibilities of change as a result of the building of citizenship (Alvarez and Dagnino 1995). In addition, these experiences point to the efforts of social movements themselves to adjust to democratic institutionality. This has implied a qualitative change in their practices that challenges some well-known interpretations of the character of their political participation, such as the predominance of corporate interests that would force social movements to compete among themselves for state resources, or to develop a clientelistic relationship with the state or whoever could meet their demands, or even to move *against* the State.

It is not contradictory to emphasize these experiences of popular intervention in the state after having emphasized the importance of civil society and cultural transformation as crucial spaces of political struggle for the building of citizenship. These experiences show changes not only in the modes of decision-making within the state but also in the forms of relationship between state and society. In addition, there is no doubt that they express and contribute to reinforcing the existence of citizens-subjects and of a culture of rights that includes the right to be a coparticipant in city government. Moreover, this kind of experience contributes to the creation of public spaces, where private and common interests, specificities, and differences can be exposed, discussed, and negotiated (see Telles and Paoli, in Alvarez et al. 1998).

There are obviously real difficulties for the popular sectors in playing this new role. Most of the difficulties refer to inequalities in terms of information, uses of language, and technical knowledge. Nevertheless, they are not serving as an excuse to eliminate the new role for popular sectors but are being challenged in concrete practices.

4. The emphasis on the process of the constitution of subjects, on "becoming a citizen," on the diffusion of a "culture of rights," poses again the question of a democratic culture mentioned above and points to an additional, crucial distinction: the *broadening of the scope* of the new citizenship, the meaning of which is far from limited to the formal and legal acquisition of a set of rights and therefore to the political-judicial system. The new citizenship is a *project for a new sociability*: not only an incorporation into the political system in a strict sense, but a more egalitarian format for social relations at all levels, including new rules for living together in society (for the negotiation of conflicts, a new sense of a public order and public responsibility, a new social contract, and so on). A more egalitarian format for social relations at all levels implies the "recognition of the other as a subject bearer of valid interests and of legitimate rights" (Telles 1994b, 46; see also Telles and Paoli, in Alvarez et al. 1998). It also implies the constitution of a public dimension of society where rights can be consolidated as public parameters for the interlocution, debate, and negotiation of conflicts, making possible the reconfiguration of an ethical dimension of social life. Such a project unsettles not only social authoritarianism as the basic mode of social ordering in Brazil but also more recent neoliberal discourses that establish private interest as the measure for everything, denying alterity and hence obstructing the possibilities for an ethical dimension of social life.[9]

5. This broadened conception of citizenship implies, in contrast to the liberal view, that citizenship is no longer confined within the limits of the relationship with the state or between the state and the individual but must be established within civil society itself. The process of building citizenship as the affirmation and recognition of rights is, especially in Brazilian society, a process of transformation

of practices rooted in society as a whole. Such a political strategy implies moral and intellectual reform: a process of social learning, of constructing new kinds of social relations, implying, obviously, the establishment of citizens as active social subjects. But also, for society as a whole, this strategy requires learning to live on different terms with these emergent citizens, who refuse to remain in the places that were socially and culturally defined for them. This is one point in which the radicality of citizenship as cultural politics seems quite clear.

Some of the results from a survey on democratic culture and citizenship in which I participated in Campinas, São Paulo, in 1993, may help to substantiate the analytical arguments developed above addressing the conceptions of citizenship and democracy deployed by social movements. The research was intended to investigate to what extent perceptions that emphasize the democratization of social relations as a whole, especially a refusal of social and cultural practices responsible for social authoritarianism, would be present in different sectors of organized civil society. One additional motivation underlying this research was that the emphasis on the need for cultural changes today in Brazil, where the worsening of economic inequalities, hunger, and extreme poverty has transformed social authoritarianism into social apartheid, violence, and genocide, has been often considered inappropriate. However, when the economic crisis determines what tends to be a certain "economic reductionism" in the analysis of the question of democracy, emphasizing the cultural dimension of citizenship seemed even more important.[10] Thus, I particularly wanted to investigate how the connection between social authoritarianism as a historical model of social ordering in Brazil and the present situation of deprivation lived by the majority of the population, which seemed clear at the theoretical level, was perceived by political leaders of civil society.

Fifty-one members of organized sectors of civil society were interviewed: both urban popular movements and social movements of a wider character (such as women's, black, and ecological movements), workers' and middle-class trade unions, entrepreneurs' associations, and elected members of the São Paulo City Council (*vereadores*). The survey included a question asking the interviewees to select, from a list, which quality was most important for a country to be considered democratic. The alternatives were:

- There are several political parties.
- All have food and housing.
- Whites, blacks, men, women, rich, and poor are all treated equally.
- People can participate in unions and associations.
- People can criticize and protest.

My expectation was that social and economic equality would be overwhelmingly chosen, given the critical economic situation at that time and the economic claims that characterize the political activities of the associations surveyed. However, 58 percent of the sample selected equal treatment for whites, blacks, men, women, rich, and poor as most important (see table 18.1). What these results indicate is that the existence of social authoritarianism and the hierarchization of social relations is perceived, more than economic inequality or the absence of

Table 18.1 Dimensions of Democracy: Responses to the Question: "In your opinion, what is the most important thing for a country to be considered democratic?"

	Entrepreneurs	Middle-Class Unions	Workers' Unions	Urban Movements	Wider Social Movements	City Council Members	General Sample
Mentioned as Most Important:							
Political parties	12.5	12.5	—	—	—	14.3	5.8
Food and housing	12.5	25.0	10.0	11.1	20.0	14.3	15.4
Equal treatment	50.0	50.0	60.0	66.7	70.0	42.9	57.7
Particip. in unions and associations	12.5	—	10.0	22.2	—	14.3	9.6
Freedom of expression	12.5	12.5	10.0	—	10.0	14.3	9.6
Mentioned as Second Most Important:							
Political parties	12.5	12.5	—	11.1	—	14.3	7.7
Food and housing	25.0	37.5	10.0	22.2	40.0	28.6	26.9
Equal treatment	25.0	12.5	10.0	11.1	20.0	14.3	15.4
Particip. in unions and associations	12.5	12.5	30.0	11.1	20.0	14.3	17.3
Freedom of expression	25.0	37.5	60.0	22.2	10.0	14.3	28.8
Total	100.0	100.0	100.0	100.0	100.0	100.0	100.

Source: Research Cultura Democrática e Cidadania.

freedom of expression and party and union organization, as a serious obstacle to the building of democracy.

The distribution of this preference among the various sectors interviewed is also very significant; it seems to be most important to social movements, to whose experience the emergence of the notion of a new citizenship is clearly associated. Even urban popular movements, certainly the sector most penalized by economic inequality within the sample, stressed an egalitarian code for social relations as the most important dimension of democracy. Entrepreneurs and members of the middle-class unions, sectors certainly less affected by the cultural practices of social authoritarianism, nevertheless clearly identified its consequences for the democratization of society. Elected members of the City Council, where more conservative parties form the majority, seem to be the least sensitive to the egalitarian dimension of democracy. Significantly, social movements of both kinds as well as workers' unions clearly stated their position about the diminished importance of political parties to democracy by ignoring this category altogether.

This data seems to indicate that the classical dimensions of liberal democracy—freedom of expression and organization and the existence of political parties—are perceived as already ensured and that the emphasis should now be placed on the need to deepen and extend democracy. The deeply rooted existence of social authoritarianism as the dominant cultural mode of social relations at various levels of society and, secondarily, economic inequality (which received 15 percent of the first-place votes) constitute the two, clearly connected, central questions around which the struggle of social movements for citizenship is organized today in Brazil.

Open-ended questions enabled us to collect qualitative data that confirmed the perception of members of subaltern organizations of the contradiction between existing authoritarian cultural practices that permeate social relations at all levels and the building of citizenship and a democratic society. Asked whether or not they were treated as citizens, members of social movements of both kinds and of workers' trade unions revealed very different perceptions in relation to the two other sectors interviewed. While middle-class interviewees and entrepreneurs stressed activities such as "paying taxes," "having a profession," "voting," or even "having money" as evidence of their citizenship (63 and 75 percent of these sectors, respectively, considered themselves treated as citizens), members of social movements and trade unions stressed that their nonexistence as citizens was related to the ways they were treated socially: A great majority of them mentioned disrespect, discrimination, and prejudice as part of their daily experience in the city; referred to their status as "second-class citizens"; and complained of mistreatment because of their race or because they were not dressed well. The state was repeatedly mentioned as being responsible for this treatment, mainly through references to police abuse and to the absence of basic services to the poor. Although 90 percent of the interviewees from these sectors affirm that they are not treated as citizens, they do consider themselves as such (wider social movements, 80 percent; urban popular movements, 90 percent; workers' trade unions, 60 percent), primarily because they "struggle for their rights."

Another set of questions in the study referred to the nature of politics (who engages in politics, who *should* engage in politics, and so on). The data showed that members of social movements and trade unions have an extended conception of the political arena; they indicated their belief that civil society and its organizations, including the social movements and trade unions themselves, are crucial terrains and agents of democratization, but that they had yet to be acknowledged as such by the official public sphere.[11]

The emphasis on civil society and on the cultural practices that underlie social relations as arenas of the struggle of social movements for democratization shall not be understood as a limiting choice that would exclude, again, the state and political institutionality as secondary arenas. The concrete experience of social movements in the transition to democracy in Brazil is full of examples that show this dichotomy to be false (Alvarez and Dagnino 1995).

This research showed that members of social movements, in contrast to much of the Brazilian population, have a very positive view of political institutions. Whereas both members of urban movements and of black, women's, and ecological movements clearly value political parties (89 and 80 percent, respectively), national surveys showed that 52 percent of the general population considered that "political parties only divide people"; only 35 percent saw them as "indispensable to democracy"; 61 percent believed that "parties only defend interests of politicians"; and 50 percent believed that "political parties make political participation more difficult."[12] In addition, members of both urban popular movements and wider social movements identify themselves or are affiliated with political parties (89 and 70 percent, respectively); consider voting an important instrument of participation in society; and would vote even if it were not mandatory (78 and 80 percent, respectively).

This positive view of traditional institutional mechanisms, however, is not a complacent one. This approach to institutional channels of political participation in representative democracy is far from implying the abandonment of the critical perspective that underlies the very emergence of social movements. It coexists with a clear demand for the improvement of the democratic content of such mechanisms, both through transformations in the political culture that would redefine their present significance and through the creation of new mechanisms that may expand and deepen the limits of actually existing democracy. Thus, when none of the members of social movements and trade unions mentioned the existence of parties as significant indicators of democracy (while members of entrepreneurial and middle-class associations did), they seem to be saying not only that the existence of political parties is not a sufficient or relevant indicator of democracy but that parties, such as those currently in existence in Brazil, do not constitute guarantees of democracy. In addition, for these sectors, dissatisfaction with political parties is not passive. Thus, the elimination of clientelistic and personal relations as criteria in electoral choices, the strengthening of relations between elected representatives and voters, and the adoption of mechanisms of control over elected representatives in order to ensure their accountability were pointed out both as motivating concrete practices executed by members of social movements and as examples of their demands for formal, functioning democratic institutions.

These statements suggest that social movements, in emphasizing the transformation of authoritarian social relations and cultural practices throughout civil society as fundamental in building democracy, are not selecting exclusive targets or turning their backs on political institutions. On the contrary, they perceive that their cultural politics can extend into formal representative political arenas.

In theoretical terms, the perspective explored here is certainly not intended to reproduce the compartmentalization and hierarchization of the multiple dimensions of democracy and its forms of struggle. In fact, it was exactly against the "schizophrenia" of political analysis of democratization—which segregates the institutional from the noninstitutional, the state from civil society, the political from the cultural—that I decided to work toward a theoretical framework that was able to take into account this complex multiplicity without obscuring what appeared to me as concrete and crucial aspects of the collective action of social movements.

In enacting an enlarged view of democracy and operationalizing this view in terms of a struggle for citizenship, social movements also convey an alternative vision of what counts as political in Latin American societies (see Slater, in Alvarez et al. 1998). The very existence of social movements has unsettled dominant notions of political subjects and spaces, as the theoretical redefinitions carried out by the Left's renovation showed. As they enter the dispute among the different blueprints for democracy, social movements, along with other political actors sharing the same perspective, offer new parameters for that dispute and react against reductionist conceptions of both democracy and politics itself. In politicizing what is not conceived of as political, in presenting as public and collective what is conceived of as private and individual, they challenge the political arena to enlarge its own boundaries and broaden its agenda. It is my contention that the cultural effects of such efforts upon this dispute and upon the social imaginary must be recognized as political, beyond the assessment of other successes or failures that may result from them.

NOTES

I would like to thank Raul Burgos for his generous bibliographical help and valuable insights for the discussion of the Latin American Left; Sonia Alvarez for a most stimulating and rewarding intellectual *parceria* from which emerged several of the ideas discussed here; and the Conselho Nacional de Desenvolvimento Científico e Tecnológico, CNPq, for its research support.

1. See Alvarez and Dagnino 1995.

2. "As the `discursive matrix' analyzed by Sader (1988) in the origins of the social movements in the 1970s, an ethical-political field refers to distinctive "ways of approaching reality which imply different attributions of meaning," deriving from the "elaboration of experiences previously silenced or interpreted differently" (Sader 1988, 19). The openness to include the new, for which there were not previous categories, can then be seen as a defining characteristic of an ethical-political field. This suggests, on the one hand, its internal plurality and nonhomogenous nature, and on the other hand, its oppositional character with respect to existing political fields, especially the dominant one" (Alvarez and Dagnino 1995, 14).

3. Referring to the historical rooting of authoritarianism will not obscure its constant renovation and reelaboration, with the emergence of new forms of exclusion and violence through which this deeply rooted mode of social ordering becomes adapted to the transformations engendered by the modernization, and postmodernization, of Brazilian society. Thus, if recent legislation proscribed the generalized existence of "service elevators" reserved for "noncitizens" (employees, domestic maids, but very often just plainly black people), the closing of streets to public transit in middle- and upper-class neighborhoods for alleged security reasons is already a pervasive habit in large cities.

4. Urban popular movements' perceptions of the intermingling of these different dimensions of exclusion and deprivation and how they affect each other first became evident to me through the experience of the Assembléia do Povo, an early (1979) *favelado* movement in Campinas, São Paulo. At the beginning of their struggle for the "right to the use of the land," their first public initiative was to ask the media to publicize the results of their own survey of the *favelas*, in order to show the city that they were not idle people, marginals, or prostitutes, as *favelados* were considered to be, but decent working citizens. See Dagnino 1995.

5. See Miguel Díaz-Barriga, in Alvarez et al. 1998, for the meaning attributed by Mexican colonas to "*necesidad.*"

6. See Verónica Schild, in Alvarez et al. 1998, for how this appropriation is taking place in Chile with respect to the women's movement.

7. For a discussion of citizenship and the connections between the right to difference and the right to equality, see Dagnino 1994.

8. For other conceptions of citizenship deployed by dominant classes in recent Brazilian history, see the notions of *cidadania regulada* ("regulated citizenship") (Santos 1979), *cidadania concedida* ("citizenship by concession") (Sales 1994), and also Carvalho 1991.

9. For Vera Telles (1994a), the absence of these public and ethical dimensions, which leaves the moral codes of private life as the only available spaces for the formulation and solution of daily individual and collective dramas, is certainly behind the criminality, vigilante justice, police violence, and various kinds of prejudices that plague our [Brazilian] uncivil society.

10. Ironically, this "economic reductionism" is sustained not only by the traditional Left but also by neoliberals trying to solve social inequality by reducing poverty to supportable levels.

11. There were additional questions about whether or not the interviewees perceived themselves and their organizations as political actors, and about who engages in politics in Brazil today and who should engage in politics.

12. This information is drawn from CESOP (Centro de Estudos de Opinião Pública, Universidade Estadual de Campinas, São Paulo): DAT/BR90, Mar-00219, 1990.

REFERENCES

Alvarez, Sonia E. 1993. "'Deepening Democracy': Popular Movement Networks, Constitutional Reform, and Radical Urban Regimes in Contemporary Brazil." In *Mobilizing the Community: Local Politics in the Era of the Global City*, ed. R. Fischer and J. Kling. Newbury Park, Calif.: Sage Publications.

Alvarez Sonia E. and Evelina Dagnino. 1995. Para Além da Democracia Realmente Existente: Movimentos Sociais, a Nova Cidadania e a Configuração de Espaços Públicos Alternativos: Paper presented at the Nineteenth Annual Meeting of the Associaçao Nacional de Pos-Graduaçao e Pesquisa em Ciencias Sociais (ANPOCS), Caxambu, Minas Gerais, Brazil.

Baierle, Sérgio Gregório. 1992. "Urn novo principio ético-político: pratica social e sujeito nos movimentos populares urbanos em Porto Alegre nos anos 80." Master's thesis, Universidade Estadual de Campinas, São Paulo.

Carvalho, José Murilo de. 1991. *Os Bestializados*. São Paulo: Companhia das Letras.

Dagnino, Evelina. 1994. "Os Movimentos Sociais e a Emergência de uma Nova Noção de Cidadania." In *Anos 90: Política e Sociedade no Brasil*, ed. E. Dagnino. São Paulo: Brasiliense.

———. 1995. "On Becoming a Citizen: The Story of D. Marlene." In *International Yearbook of Oral History and Life Stories*, ed. R. Benmayor and A. Skotnes. Oxford: Oxford University Press.

Doimo, Ana Maria. 1995. "A Vez e a Voz do Popular: Movimentos Sociais e Participação Política no Brasil Pós-70" Rio de Janeiro: Relume-Dumará/ANPOCS.

Sader, Eder. 1988. *Quando Novos Personagens Entraram em Cena*. São Paulo: Paz e Terra.

Sales, Teresa. 1994. "Raízes da Desigualdade Social na Cultura Brasileira." *Revista Brasileira de Ciências Sociais* 25: 26–37.

Santos, Wanderley G. dos. 1979. *Cidadania e Justiça*. São Paulo: Editora Campus.

Scherer-Warren, Ilse. 1993. *Redes de Movimentos Sociais*. São Paulo: Loyola.

Teixeira, Ana Cláudia Chaves. 1995. "Movimentos Sociais e a Construção de uma Cultura Democrática." Universidade Estadual de Campinas, São Paulo. Mimeographed.

Telles, Vera da Silva. 1993. "Pauvretté et Citoyenneté, dilémme du Brèsil Contemporaine." *Problèms de Amérique Latine* 9: 73–85.

———. 1994a. "A Sociedade Civil e a Construção de urn Espaço Público." In *Anos 90: Política e Sociedade no Brasil*, ed. E. Dagnino. São Paulo: Brasiliense.

———. 1994b. "Sociedade Civil, Direitos e Espaços Públicos." *Polis* 14: 43–53.

Wiener, Antje. 1992. "Citizenship, New Dynamics of an Old Concept: A Comparative Perspective on Current Latin American and European Political Strategies." Paper presented at the Seventeenth International Congress of the Latin American Studies Association, September, Los Angeles.

19

Utopia Unarmed: The Latin American Left After the Cold War (1993)

Jorge G. Castañeda

Jorge G. Castañeda (b. Mexico, 1953) is a Mexican writer, political scientist, university professor, and politician. He has taught at Mexico's National Autonomous University (UNAM), Princeton University, and the University of California at Berkeley, and written numerous books. He is the former foreign minister of Mexico (2000–2003) and was a presidential hopeful in Mexico's 2006 elections. Currently, he is Global Distinguished Professor of Politics and Latin American and Caribbean Studies at New York University and a regular columnist for the Mexican daily Reforma, The Los Angeles Times, *and* Newsweek International. *This selection argues for a redefinition of nationalism in Latin America within the present context of globalization and U.S. economic and political hegemony in the continent. Castaneda's proposal reaffirms the relevance of the nation-state as main coordinating agent in a process of regional economic (and perhaps political) integration among economic equals.*

REFORMULATING NATIONALISM: LONGITUDINALLY AND REGIONALLY

I

Because nation-building in Latin America is incomplete, and the cause of social change inseparable from redeeming the nation for the "people," the left in Latin America has no choice but to remain nationalistic. The goal of constructing nations to which millions of excluded Latin Americans (the overwhelming majority of the population, in contrast to Western Europe and North America, where the excluded exist but represent a minority) can belong is as valid and urgent as ever. And much of the left's nationalism will continue to be directed towards the United States, as it lingers awhile as the sole great power in the region or the world and new shapes of and reasons for American involvement in the hemisphere replace old ones. But as the parameters and definition of the nation under construction change, the way in which that nationalism must also evolve has yet to be determined. Before proposing a new nationalism for the left, it is worth examining how the traditional trappings of U.S. intervention, which underpinned much of the region's nationalism and many of the conflicts of the past fifty years, are replaced by other, newer forms.

In the immediate aftermath of the Cold War's conclusion, a substitute for anti-Sovietism in the United States' policy toward Latin America rapidly emerged: drug enforcement and, to a lesser but growing extent, immigration. After the evil (Soviet-Communist) empire to the east, the evil (drug-producing, migrant-generating) slum to the south.[1] As American national security is redefined in the post-Cold War era, new links are established between instability, change, and certain policies in Latin America, and their effects on U.S. welfare. While the causal relationship between revolution (or reform) and drugs or immigration is not evident or simple, it can be theoretically, albeit convolutedly, posited, as in the cases of Peru and Colombia.

The emergence of drugs as an important facet of U.S. policy in the region did not start with the thaw in East-West relations. Drug enforcement had played a significant role in U.S. policy toward Mexico, the Andean countries, Colombia, and Cuba for a number of years. And that role had already been sharply "interventionist," providing pretexts and motivations for United States involvement in the domestic affairs of many Latin American nations. This was the rationale for the longstanding presence of Drug Enforcement Administration agents in Mexico, and also for new forms of highly intrusive cooperation (including counterinsurgency).

The most disquieting trend in this respect may well have been the argument whereby Washington affirmed the unilateral right to prosecute individuals beyond U.S. national jurisdiction. There was a precedent in American purported counterterrorist actions in the Middle East, and the extension of U.S. law beyond American borders. The United States would use whatever means were necessary to bring to justice whomever it considered a criminal, no matter where the suspect was found or his or her political or diplomatic status. It followed that international conventions, principles of common law, and foreign legislation and judicial systems were all superseded by U.S. authority.

The February 28, 1990, decision by the Supreme Court in *United States v. Urquídez Verdugo* established a legal precedent in this regard. Chief Justice William H. Rehnquist and five other justices ruled that search and seizure operations conducted abroad by U.S. law enforcement agents, military personnel, or other government agencies against foreigners should not be restricted by the provisions of the Fourth Amendment of the Constitution. Thus the Court determined that constitutional rights meant to protect Americans from the abuses of power of their government were not applicable to foreigners abroad.

Simultaneously, the Justice Department issued an internal legal opinion authorizing its agents acting abroad to abduct foreigners in order to bring them to trial in the U.S.[2] The document, drafted by Attorney General William Barr, stated that the President and the attorney general had the "inherent constitutional power" to order the capture of fugitives abroad. It affirmed that "the extraterritorial enforcement of United States laws is becoming increasingly important in order to protect vital national interests."[3]

This policy was first applied in two nearly simultaneous cases: the 1989 invasion of Panama and subsequent arrest of Manuel Antonio Noriega, and the kidnapping of Dr. Humberto Alvarez Machain in Mexico in February of that same year. Alvarez Machain was abducted from his home in Guadalajara by bounty hunters contracted by the Drug Enforcement Administration, which wanted him brought to trial for his presumed involvement in the 1985 torture and murder of DEA agent Enrique Camarena in Mexico. Although Washington's explicit participation in the Alvarez Machain case was initially less evident than in Noriega's, Attorney General Richard Thornburgh's statements and actions clarified the Justice Department's stand on the issue. When a federal judge in Los Angeles ruled that Alvarez Machain's kidnapping violated the U.S.-Mexican Extradition Treaty and ordered him set free, the department took the case to the Supreme Court. In June 1992 the Court ruled in the Bush administration's favor, and against Alvarez Machain, Urquídez Verdugo, and the Mexican government, legalizing their abduction and just about anyone's, in the opinion of many legal scholars. Alvarez Machain was freed and returned to Mexico in December 1992 after the judge presiding over his case ruled there was insufficient evidence to present to the jury for deliberation. But the issue was not laid to rest; behind the Noriega affair and the Alvarez Machain case lay the same reasoning: limitations on other nations' sovereignty and the extraterritorial extension of U.S. law enforcement capability and justice were deemed valid practices in the war against drugs.[4]

Many believed that American insistence on drug enforcement was simply a disguise for further U.S. domination. A *Washington Post*/ABC News poll taken in February 1990 in Colombia showed that 65 percent of those interviewed "suspect the drug war is a U.S. attempt to control their government."[5] But only with the coming of the drug age in American domestic politics and the elimination of other ideological justifications for U.S. policy in Latin America did drugs acquire their full importance in hemispheric relations. Although the Bush administration paid lip service to the principle of parity between supply and demand as the drug crisis's root cause, supply-directed policies were easier, cheaper, and more popular, though undeniably less effective.

It was no accident that the Panama invasion was at least subliminally presented as a drug-motivated action and that its popularity in the United States—in addition to Noriega's own villainous image—was due largely to the perception of Noriega as a drug dealer. The first U.S. intervention in Latin America without Cold War packaging was also the first attempt by the United States to justify the use of force abroad on the grounds of drug enforcement. There were sufficient other examples to prove conclusively that drugs had become far more than simply another item on the inter-American agenda. These instances ranged from sending U.S. military detachments to Bolivia in 1987 to the escalation of the DEA presence in the Upper Huallaga Valley in Peru.[6] They included the construction of a second base and the signing of U.S.-Peruvian military agreements with a joint drug enforcement, counterinsurgency focus, the growing militarization of the Southwest U.S.–Mexican border and the enhanced role of U.S. armed forces in patrolling the Caribbean drug routes.[7]

Immigration has not yet achieved the same urgency or implications, and the absence of a domestic consensus in the United States leaves open the possibility that it might not ever attain such levels of import. In addition, its emotional impact is not yet in the same league as drugs. Nevertheless, as the effects of two significant trends of the 1980s began to bite, immigration was likely to acquire significant foreign policy implications. The unintended effects of the 1986 U.S. Immigration Reform and Control Act and the fully foreseeable consequences of ten years of Latin American economic stagnation—extensive unemployment, falling wages, and the ensuing mass exodus to the north—began to make themselves felt in the 1990s.

Widespread and continuing documentation of undocumented aliens rapidly emerged as one of the most important and immediate impacts of the Simpson-Rodino Immigration Bill. As a result of the law's amnesty and family reunification provisions, together with other mechanisms and the special agricultural worker clauses that permitted the legal entry of individuals previously employed in the harvest of perishable agricultural produce, nearly 3 million formerly undocumented Mexicans regularized their migratory status.

Similarly, ten years of economic stagnation in Latin America, coupled with the "new," fashionable free-market policies that included low real wages as a major competitive advantage, contributed to maintaining or increasing the magnitude of the flow north, not only from Mexico but from many other countries. For years, Mexican and American researchers had been compiling data showing that the single most important contributing factor to immigration—illegal or not—was the wage differential.[8] The unemployed do not emigrate: they lack the money to pay the cost of doing so. Those who leave tend to be individuals who already have jobs, either in rural areas, or, more frequently today, in large cities, and who choose to leave them in search of higher wages elsewhere. As long as the wage differential between the United States and Mexico, for example, averaged roughly eight to one, enterprising young Mexicans of all social strata were going to continue their trek north. In 1990 the Mexican minimum wage was 55 cents an hour, whereas its counterpart in California, where fully half of all undocumented Mexican immigrants make their home, was $4.75 an hour. Similarly, a tenured university professor in Mexico, Brazil, or Argentina, with a Ph.D. and recognized publications, took home at most $1,000 per month in the early nineties (and often much less), yet could often make between $5,000 and $6,000 or more per month, after taxes, in a major American university.

As the consequences of these trends took hold, reasons became stronger for fearing that immigration would occupy a growing role in U.S. foreign policy toward migration-generating countries, as opposed to being a domestic issue with sporadic, secondary foreign implications. If immigration began to be perceived as a significant threat to U.S. welfare, national security (defined, inevitably, in a new sense), and even national identity, the same causes could well produce analogous effects. The problem's roots would again be found abroad and hypothetical solutions would increasingly be localized in countries of origin. The United States had already pressured Mexico with regard to so-called third-country immigration, that is, the transit of undocumented emigrants from Central America, South America, and Asia through Mexico to the United States. It also demanded that several Central American nations be more forthcoming in deterring migratory flows north by controlling highways, airports, train stations, and bus terminals, to hold the line as far south as possible, with each country limiting migration from its neighbor to the south, whatever the domestic costs.

If Latin authorities prove unwilling or unable to comply, intrusive U.S. cooperation could follow.

For these reasons, and for all of the deeper, more historical ones outlined above, the left's updating cannot involve discarding the nationalist agenda or forsaking the nation-building tasks that are still pending. More than ever today, the social situation in Latin America resembles the type of "social apartheid" pattern that constitutes the very antithesis of nation-building: the gap between rich and poor, whites and others, included and excluded, is greater than at any time in the past twenty years, and getting worse. At the same time the temptations and pressures from abroad on Latin authorities to step away from the nationalist stances of the past are also more intense than before. The need to secure scarce funding, to appear responsible and "mature," and to conform to post-Marxist, postsocialist globalization fads are all powerful constraints, forcing sensible politicians from the center and right-of-center into antinationalist stances they would not otherwise adhere to.[9] Both motives—the yawning domestic chasms in Latin American society, and the "denationalization" of elites—are powerful incentives for the left to retain a nationalism so unfashionable in these times, yet so necessary.

The conclusion of the Cold War means the cloture of a certain form of United States anti-Communism in Latin America. This in turn implies that the nationalist stances and policies that Latin America may devise and sustain will not propagate the type of excessive reaction in the United States that tended to occur in the past. In particular, such developments open the way for an affirmation of sovereignty in areas that are fundamental to Latin America (and to any country), while at the same time not infringing upon the type of economic relationships that the transformation of the world economy is undoubtedly provoking. Thus the first chapter of the left's new nationalism must be the restatement and assertion of sovereignty on issues involving domestic non-economic affairs. The left should strive to oppose the new forms of intervention that run contrary to its principles, while accepting new commitments to abide by international standards on issues that are consonant with those principles. It should continue to reject any foreign involvement in drug enforcement, immigration control, and extraterritorial law enforcement of any sort. But conversely, the left should embrace the notion that on matters such as human rights, the environment, labor rights and consumer protection, and the monitoring of clean elections, international obligations and cooperation enhance nation-building, not the other way around. This mixed, more principled, and at the same time more pragmatic stance becomes possible.

Yet changes such as these solve neither the question of unfinished national construction in Latin America, the issue of continuing forms of U.S. intervention in the hemisphere, nor the problem of greater constraints placed on Latin American sovereignty and autonomy by international economic factors. These can range from actual stringent requirements to obtain substantial if costly and ephemeral funding, to the ideological constraint of having to conform to fashionable ideologies or policies in order to qualify for always disappointing volumes of resources.[10]

Likewise, the ongoing relevance of nationalism to the left's agenda does not address the question of the type of nationalism or the translation into policy of a broader nationalist aspiration in the post-Cold War, post-Marxist world. Crafting a new nationalist response is one of the chief challenges the left must face today. Needless to say, that challenge can only be met over time and across the hemisphere. But certain ideas or general trends can be sketched out here. The left's "new nationalism" has to be reformed in two directions: with regard to whom it is targeted against, and in the institutional level or tier from which it emanates.

The first point, that different sectors of the left have discovered often intuitively in recent years, is that directing nationalist passions or policies toward the United States is a contradictory affair. There is almost always someone, or a given political sector in the United States, opposed to his or her government's policy and far more supportive of a Latin American aspiration than of a U.S. one. This unconscious, superficial sensation has rarely led to a more conceptual approach. It is high time it did, as conditions for it seem uncommonly favorable at the end of the Cold War.[11] Although this overhaul of Latin American nationalism must by no means be limited to the United States and should extend to Western Europe and elsewhere, particularly in view of the older ties between the Latin American left and European socialists, it is inevitably centered on the U.S. What follows must be read as an indication of what the left must accomplish in relation to the world as a whole, but the emphasis here is placed on the United States.

It has been a long time since U.S. politics stopped at the water's edge. At least from the Vietnam War onward, various segments of American public opinion have adopted differing or opposing viewpoints with respect to those of their government on various foreign policy issues. Once a distinct stance has been adopted, the next step, i.e., fighting to convert it into government policy, or at least attempting to change the prevailing, contrary course, has been only a matter of time. Since Jane Fonda's trip to Hanoi, but undoubtedly more often and significantly since then, other countries and slices of the political spectrum outside the United States have enjoyed access to American support and sympathy of diverse sincerity and conviction, expediency and opportunism.

In the case of the Latin American left, although Fidel Castro unearthed several American politicians and intellectuals critical of U.S. policy toward Cuba and its revolution during the sixties and seventies, the convergence of sensibilities stopped there. While the Cuban Interest Section in the U.S. capital was on occasion adept at "working Washington," it was selling such "unwanted goods" that it rarely made much headway. The Cuban interface with Washington never transcended itself, failing to become a true alliance with specific goals, tactics to achieve them, and a strategy to frame them. No change of U.S. policy on Cuba was perceived as likely or realistic as late as 1992—and in consequence there was scant margin for an alliance. The Chilean left and center-left also underwent a similar experience, although greater skill and sensitivity on the part of the Chileans, and the existence of at least minimal stakes in the United States, justified the effort.

But the advent of Ronald Reagan and the antipathy he evoked in many liberal American quarters, together with the sympathy the Sandinista Revolution initially awakened in many grass roots, semi-left-wing circles, laid the ground for a much clearer convergence and the beginnings of an alliance, if only of convenience. During the 1980s it was clear to the Sandinistas that "Washington," the "United States," "*el imperialismo americano,*" and even "*el yanqui, enemigo de la humanidad*" was a far more heterogeneous and double-edged notion than originally suspected. The most important opposition to Reagan's support for the contras originated in the United States itself. It included liberals and church groups, left-wing "*sandalistas*" (the name given to American and Western European radicals who traveled to Central America in search of the perfect revolution), and middle-of-the-roaders mobilized by their respect for the rule of law and outraged by Reagan's neglect of it, whatever their opinion of the Sandinistas. The Sandinistas learned to "work Washington," and though they were never as skilled at it, or as conspiratorial in forging alliances with such strange bedfellows as former House Speaker Jim Wright or Connecticut senator Christopher Dodd as the Reagan administration charged, they achieved a great deal.[12] Mainly, they understood that the most effective ally, if not the most reliable friend, that practically anyone in Latin America with a U.S. agenda could seek was to be found within the United States.

A similar convergence, and much more rewarding alliance, was slowly established by the Salvadorean left—all shapes and sizes mixed together. Again, the ties in question were much less intimate and collusive than many conservatives in Washington imagined. CISPES, or the Committee in Solidarity with the People of El Salvador, was undoubtedly linked closely to the FMLN, and its positions were much more sympathetic a priori to the Salvadorean insurgents than independently arrived at. But CISPES itself was only a small part of a much broader coalition, or more accurately, of a wider area of encounter, convergence, and occasional common effort. The radius of this circle stretched from influencing the U.S. Congress's votes on aid to El Salvador to prosecuting Salvadorean death squad members for the murders, diversely, of American nuns, local Jesuits, or human rights activists.

Other activities included fund-raising, securing access to the U.S. media, and building bridges between the Salvadorean left and that part of the U.S. establishment that would have any truck with it. They also extended to organizing encounters between guerrilla leaders and American members of the foreign policy elite, the most important of which was perhaps the one organized by former American ambassador to El Salvador Robert White and his International Center for Development Policy, in Cocoyoc, Mexico, in July of 1989. They paved the way for the exchanges that began to take place between the Bush administration and the FMLN in 1992.

The Salvadorean left—like the Sandinistas before it, and like, somewhat later, Cuauhtémoc Cárdenas's involvement in the Free Trade debate in the United States and Canada—thus began, in practice, to redefine the profiles and contours of the left's new nationalism. On a higher plane of abstraction, this nationalism had to be premised on one fundamental assumption. While there undeniably did exist an American central government and all the fragmentation of power in the world could not water down its existence and its capacity to greatly affect the destinies of most Latin American countries and people, the U.S. political system did provide a large margin of action to those who wanted to take their case to the American public.

Sometimes the "natural" ally of the Latin American left would be the "liberal" faction of the establishment and its friends in the media, academia, Hollywood, and Washington. These interlocutors were more powerful and entrenched in American society and politics than others, but they were generally less involved in the substance of issues and more fickle in their friendship. On other occasions only the grass roots groups in the U.S. would prove willing to establish close ties with certain sectors of the left in Latin America: church activists, human rights groups, radical environmentalists, progressive faculty—in sum, the solidarity network. This faction was usually more devoted and loyal but less influential, although at the margin it could wield considerable power. At other stages still, U.S. labor, mainstream environmental organizations, and consumer associations would become the logical interlocutors for the Latin American left in the United States: this was the case of the "fair-trade" type of coalition that developed between Canadian, American, and Mexican groups in the course of the early 1990s free-trade negotiations.

What this all meant was that the fault line for left-wing nationalism in Latin America should not run between the United States and the nations of the hemisphere, but rather across them. The new, "longitudinal" nationalism of the left should not be directed against the United States, but against specific policies put in practice by the U.S. government and deemed pernicious to the national interests of a given country in the region. The goal of the new nationalism, then, lay not in opposing the United States but in building coalitions in the United States, as well as domestically, in favor of certain policies and against others. It is less "attitudinal," and more policy-oriented.

As the effects of the end of the Cold War continue to make themselves felt, there will undoubtedly be fewer Americans willing to tolerate many of the traditional tenets of their country's policies toward Latin America.[13] As the left engages in debate, confrontation, and the search for convergences with diverse interlocutors in the United States, it will find that people in a growing number of walks of American life will be willing to listen, sometimes agree, and on occasion, put a shoulder to the wheel. And, as the fall of socialism and the disappearance of a Communist or Soviet threat to American (in)security has its effect and the costs of winning the Cold War come to the fore, the political center of gravity in the United States will in all likelihood shift. It will surely bring more and, most importantly, different sectors in contact with the policies and attitudes that affect Latin America. Regardless of whether time brings greater involvement or growing indifference on the part of the United States as a whole in relation to Latin America, it is safe to say that there will always be sufficient room to move in and interest to work upon. Granted, the margin of maneuver will always be contradictory and subject to severe constraints that could easily shatter inordinate expectations. Americans will always have their own priorities, which is as it should be as long as politics in the world remain essentially national in nature. Whoever has attempted to forge a lasting bond with a U.S. member of Congress or the editor of an American news organization cannot be too cynical or enthusiastic about their loyalty and attention span. The Latin American left should head for Washington and the heartland with its eyes wide open and scant illusions. But that is the landfall it should seek.

Since, as most of the left and a good portion of the right have traditionally thought, many of the most important decisions affecting Latin America are made in Washington, then that is where the left should leave its mark. It should lobby, speak, write, and study in the United States, as it has already begun to do. The number of visits by leftists of all persuasions to U.S. campuses, editorial boards, Committees on Foreign Relations, radio talk shows, and ethnic neighborhoods is rising exponentially. It is both fitting and expected that two of the smallest nations in the hemisphere, Nicaragua and El Salvador, because they were among the most affected, and the two largest, Brazil and Mexico, because of their very size, were where the left first and most vigorously began to forge this new nationalism. For example, Lula took his 1989 Brazilian presidential campaign to New York and Washington in the spring of that year: a blue-collar worker from Pernambuco and the suburbs of São Paulo discussed economic policy with the notables of the U.S. Council of Foreign Relations.

Later, the poorest nation in the hemisphere also got involved: when overthrown Haitian president Jean-Bertrand Aristide saw his attempts to return to office endangered by American indifference, he "took his case directly to the American people,"[14] benefiting from two specific strong suits the Haitian left had going for it in the United States: the large Haitian immigrant community and Aristide's Church connections, both of which allowed him to organize meetings, speeches, and travel across the United States. Other leaders of the left enjoyed these same connections, or others: Cárdenas relied on a powerful Michoacán community in California and Washington State; the FMLN, on the large Salvadorean community in Washington, D.C., Los Angeles, and San Francisco, together with its Jesuit contacts between the Universidad Centroamericana and the Society of Jesus in the United States. Even Sendero Luminoso had its supporters among some Peruvian émigrés. And the Sandinistas benefited from similar associations with other religious orders.

The left must sustain and intensify its efforts to build American constituencies for change in the hemisphere. They are decisive when the left is out of power and seeking to equalize the conditions whereby it competes—respect for human rights, election monitoring, a free press, union and labor rights, etc. These American alliances are equally or more significant when the left is in power, becoming bulwarks for the type of social and economic change it wishes to accomplish, and that cannot be carried out without support *in* Washington, if not support *from* Washington. These constituencies are not necessarily identical to each other, and on occasion they run at cross-purposes. The best way to lobby the International Monetary Fund or the World Bank is not necessarily through solidarity groups, grass roots Church activists, and American left-wing academic faculty. However, these pillars of support are indispensable if the left in Latin America is to succeed in governing. Not only must it not blame Washington for failing, but it must ensure that political and cultural forces in the United States contribute emphatically to its success.

Latin American networking with the United States is not new, of course. The military, the business community, academics, and the new, business-school and economics-educated technocracies of the hemisphere have been pursuing it for some time. The left lagged behind largely because it was a prisoner of its traditional outlook: if the enemy was the United States as country and monolith, its citizens, while not all enemies, could hardly become allies other than at a purely personal level. Thus networking of this sort is new for the left, because in practice it implies a totally different mind-set. The United States as an all-encompassing, uniformly and universally evil entity becomes unthinkable once parts of it become valuable allies in any given endeavor.

The entire nationalist issue becomes vertical, following a North-South axis, rather than horizontal, dividing entire nations. On many clear-cut issues regarding the defense of national sovereignty—American intervention, drugs, immigration—groups, governments, or organizations of the left will discover that they have more in common with many sectors of the United States than with groups or elements in their own countries. And on many social, economic, environmental, and human rights issues, they will find that their interlocutors in the United States, from the grass roots to Capitol Hill, can be more firm and loyal backers than domestic interests that, more often than not, will in fact be their enemies. Evidently this means opening up to the rest of the world: the Latin American cannot seek to influence Washington politics, in alliance with myriad American groups, without accepting that this gives many foreign entities a lever and a right to sway Latin politics. Likewise, the left will have to understand that this different type of nationalist politics entails outside oversight and accountability, sometimes against a government's will. But the left cannot have its enchilada and eat it too.

A refashioning of Latin American nationalism can find encouragement in a trend that resembles what has been described above, but is nonetheless a distinct process. This is what has been called the birth of global civil society, which acquired considerable relevance at the 1992 Rio de Janeiro Earth Summit. The proliferation of nongovernmental organizations that took place in Latin America in recent years has been matched and outpaced in fact by a similar phenomenon throughout the world. NGOs in Europe, North America, and, to a lesser extent, in Asia have become increasingly active and have begun to network across the globe. In this way, on issues such as the environment and human rights, but also in broader economic policy matters, a emerging web of groups and relationships has been woven across borders and traditional, state-to-state international relations. As one advocate and scholar of these trends has noted, the process involves:

> exertions of influence on state and market forces that will produce a degree of voluntary restructuring of international relations and the existence, in rudimentary but evolving form, of an ensemble of norms, actors, tactics, identities that underpins international relations with a reality that can be called international civil society.[15]

Groups such as Greenpeace, Amnesty International, and the Brandt, Palme, Brundtlandt, and Nyeyere-South commissions are all examples of this emerging process. While it should not be overstated or idealized in terms of its strength or representativity, something along the lines of an international civil society is beginning to come forth, and the Latin American left, which has been part of this process, should support it and find encouragement in it, even if on occasion it involves sovereignty loss or implies forging alliances with groups from the North whose motivations are impeccably honest but who do not necessarily control the effects of their intentions. If the South is coming North in so many ways, and if—as many authors, politicians, and poets believe—the key to change in the South, and specifically in Latin America, lies in change in the U.S., the left from the South should look and, whenever possible, head North.

II

This cross-cutting, longitudinal nationalism, emphasizing causes and their natural allies more than permanent enmities and immutable goals, dovetails neatly with the second facet of what the left's new nationalism should consist of. Economists can argue endlessly—and they do—about whether the post-Cold War world is breaking up into trade blocs (probably not), and whether regionalism and economic integration is the wave of the present and future.[16] But in Latin America, after years of failures, disappointments and formalism, certain serious efforts at regional integration are finally under way.[17]

The left, while mostly opposing attempts to develop forms of economic integration with richer, industrialized nations, should take up the banner of regional economic integration in general, and of a certain type in particular. It should do so because regional integration represents an intermediate solution between a largely unsustainable status quo and a highly harmful progression toward the dissolution of sovereignties and economic and social options for the developing nations. This maiming of the latter's national autonomy is occurring through their subordinate inclusion in wealthy nations' economic spheres of influence, at a juncture when the rivalries and conflicts between the great powers have not yet acquired a paradigmatic, ideological connotation. Conserving the nation-state as the prime area of economic activity appears impossible; joining one of the three large economic spheres of influence at a time of great flux and under conditions of gaping disparities and overwhelming weakness cannot be a desirable option, even if some resignedly accept it. Regional economic integration is a halfway house that possesses intrinsic merits and is preferable to existing alternatives. It can be either a lasting solution or a steppingstone to a better world, when it arrives.

Mercosur in the Southern Cone (uniting Brazil, Argentina, Uruguay, and Paraguay, and soon Bolivia), the reborn Central American Common Market, and the Colombian-Venezuelan economic integration process are all regional initiatives that the left should not only support, but take the lead in promoting and strengthening, as long as they meet a number of conditions and are steered in a certain direction. There are various reasons for doing so. To begin with, the left should encourage these processes because in many cases—with the possible exceptions of Brazil, Mexico, and Argentina—there is a problem of economic viability among many Latin American nations. Even regarding the "big three," it is unclear whether under conditions of economic globalization, single nations with one currency, one market, a national business community, and an autonomous economic policy are viable propositions. Continental integration could be such a slow and arduous process that it would implicitly postpone any real enlargement of economic space almost indefinitely. On the contrary, regional economic integration broadens markets, provides economies of scale, enhances regional autonomy, and concentrates trade and investment among equals, diverting it from other, far more economically powerful partners.

There is a trade-off involved: more economic relationships among equals slows the pace of technological advancement and could deter foreign investment and curtail competition and modernization induced from abroad. But as worldwide competition increases with or without trading pacts, and now that the transfer of technology is possible from many sources, it would seem that the benefits of greater economic exchange among equals outweigh the disadvantages of restricting flows with unequals.

Moreover, the trade-off today is not between integration and economic stagnation but rather between integration among (relative) equals and the integration of small fish with bigger ones. The three groups mentioned, even in the case of a refurbished Central American Common Market with the hypothetical inclusion of Mexico and the Caribbean, are economic integration strategies among essentially equal partners. That is their strength and their weakness: because they are relatively equal, their economies are not terribly complementary; but because of their similarities, few nations can truly impose their will on others. Brazil is the exception. Even Mexico would have found itself in a stronger negotiating stand when it decided to seek a free-trade agreement with the United States had it pursued a policy of regional economic integration previously; it didn't, partly because of the wars of Central America and political divergence, partly because the country's powers-that-be were unconvinced.

At the same time, the formation of these regional groupings protects nations from the more intrusive, potentially damaging integration processes being proposed by the United States, which essentially boil down to opening local markets to American exports and concentrating trade with the least competitive of the world's trading zones. This does not mean that Latin American integration should be based exclusively on import substitution industrialization (ISI), as it was in the past. As we shall see, the question of trade liberalization versus protectionism has been framed incorrectly. Regional economic integration in Latin America today can be different both from ISI integration of the distant past and from Reagan-Bush free-trade dogma of the recent past and lingering present.

President Bush's Enterprise for the Americas Initiative rested on three singularly slender pillars: investment promotion (without tax subsidies), aid via debt reduction (along Brady Plan lines), and the elimination of trade barriers (essentially already low tariffs). It demanded in return large-scale trade liberalization in Latin America, foreign investment regime reform, and privatization. According to two American economists, "The underlying bargain in the Bush initiative appears to exchange relatively small amounts of new money for quite substantial policy reforms."[18] The reciprocity on the part of the United States with regard to trade and the static gains arising from free trade between many Latin American nations and the United States are both small. Most Latin American exports to the United States enter under low or nonexistent tariffs,[19] and most nontariff barriers are not really included in free-trade agreements, as the Mexican and Canadian precedents tend to prove. Moreover, with regard to dynamic gains—i.e., investment and credit from the United States and third countries, as well as ensuing increases in exports—the outlook is also mixed. As for policy reform, this is a synonym for policy convergence with what has been called the "Washington consensus":[20] a list of instructions derived from the perceived workings of the American economy that has not proved in recent years to be the best suited to dictate recipes to the rest of the world.

There are sound reasons for most of Latin America to be wary of economic integration with the United States. The first is that with the exception of Mexico and Venezuela most of the larger Latin economies have quite diversified trade ties with the rest of the world: the average of their trade concentration with the United States is in the 20–25 percent range. Free-trade agreements with the United States, either individually or collectively, would divert their trade from other countries, exactly the opposite of what they have been attempting for years. But most importantly, as even a study carried out by two World Bank experts was forced to acknowledge,

> Overall, full Free-Trade Agreement preferences would raise Latin American exports only 8 or 9 percent. . . . U.S. trade gains, particularly for highly protected transport and machinery products, are likely to be considerably greater than those for Latin America in the U.S. market.[21]

But if the left takes up the banner of regional economic integration and a new regional nationalism emphasizing cooperation within the new areas and competition with those outside, how would it differentiate itself from other zones of the political spectrum? To begin with, it need not distinguish itself from everybody: the left's nationalism today, as on occasions in the past, should unite countries, not further divide them. Secondly, the banner of regional economic integration is inevitably contrary, even in the case of Mexico, to the cause of hemispheric economic integration or the creation of a free-trade zone "from Alaska to the Antarctic," both euphemisms for the creation of a United States zone of economic influence where the battered U.S. economy could curtail competition with its European and Japanese rivals.

Most importantly, though, regional economic integration is not a blank sheet upon which nuances and details, as well as broader philosophical currents, leave no lasting imprint. The left should not only favor regional economic integration, but should push mainly for a certain type of regional economic integration. As we shall underline later, there are substantive differences between the types of "capitalisms" prevailing in the modem world—i.e., between the American, radical free-market type, the Rhineland social market economy, and the Japanese, hyper-*dirigiste* cultural model. Consequently, there are also terribly important distinctions between a "leave-it-to-the-market," laissez-faire notion of integration, along the lines of the U.S.-Canadian Free Trade Agreement of 1988, and similar to the North American Free Trade Agreement, or NAFTA, as the conservative Bush, Mulroney, and Salinas governments negotiated it, on the one hand, and the European Community model, on the other. Likewise, there are various, contending options within the EC: more or less "social," more or less regulated, slower or more rapid, more or less political. The EC, whose underlying philosophy dates back to the late 1940s and the first European institutions—the Steel and Coal Community, the Euratom, the Benelux—was first conceptualized in the 1958 Treaty of Rome and in myriad subsequent enlargements and is a highly regulated, planned, socially centered form of integration with a strong role for the state.

It implies an important—indeed, decisive—common external tariff, common subsidies—in the case of the Common Agricultural Policy—and a regulating mechanism for channeling public funds—often on a massive scale—from the wealthier regions to the poorer ones: the Italian Mezzogiorno in the sixties, Ireland in the late seventies, and Spain, Portugal, and Greece in the eighties and nineties. It includes labor mobility, a central bureaucracy—"Brusselles," as it came to be known, and reviled but respected, throughout Europe—common environmental norms, consumer protection standards, and occupational safety and health considerations. The social charter, which was not laid down as such until late in the game, encountered multiple obstacles to its application. But this was less important than elsewhere because of the relatively high degree of harmonization that already existed in Western Europe regarding social issues. The principle of a social charter and harmonization was ever present, as the need to harmonize was acutely felt in order to stop firms from one country "running away" to another to circumvent regulations or lower costs by cutting wages. Most of the harmonization was mid-level: not up to the most stringent standards, but not down towards the most lax.

All of these features must be part and parcel of the regional economic integration the Latin American left should be proposing when it is in opposition, and implementing when it is in office. The left's blueprint for regional economic integration should not only exclude the United States, Europe, or Japan, but should be accomplished in a manner that is, in particular, diametrically opposed to the American free-market "old-fashioned way." Instead, the strategy should include: compensatory financing funded by windfall profit taxes and duties, labor mobility, a common external tariff to protect sectors of industry and agriculture that are jointly considered strategic and worthy of support, subsidies and credit facilities in order to make them competitive, in a business-government alliance and industrial policy along East Asian lines, a social charter or its equivalent and an environmental charter that harmonize up, not down, and include financing provisions for the adoption of superior norms in one area or another, common subsidies and expenditures for research and development, and dispute settlement mechanisms open to all interested parties and relevant issues. These characteristics are all the more desirable and necessary given the far greater regional, economic, and social, as well as ethnic, disparities that exist within and among most of the hemisphere's nations. Leaving these imbalances and historical differences to the market will simply accentuate them, not gradually wear them down.

This said, the European example should not be idealized or stripped of the infinite problems it has encountered. The Economic Community has been roundly criticized, from the left and from the right, for countless deficiencies, inadequacies, failed commitments, and unfulfilled promises. Some regret its bureaucratic excess: the Brussels Commission having transformed itself into a regulatory nightmare. Many more accuse it of not being sufficiently regulated or socially and environmentally aware, or fair, no matter how great the contrast between its institutions and inspiration on the one hand, and those of the United States on the other.[22] It has also been faulted from both the left and the right for the total absence of a political chapter and lack of definition on supranationality.[23]

Despite its marked contrasts with the Anglo-Saxon, conservative free-market paradigm—amply demonstrated by Margaret Thatcher's constant, lost battles over restricting the community's encroachment into social, political, and legal realms—the EC is certainly not a perfect model of social, regulated, planned, environmentally sound, and politically democratic and accountable integration. But it is a space in constant flux: it can be more or less social and regulated, more or less accountable, more or less democratic. The farther developed the political institutions, the more rigid the regulatory framework; the more stringent the social clauses, the greater the possibilities of transforming Europe into a more humane, democratic, fair, and historically meaningful enterprise. This, and not so much in its specific aspects or presently functioning mechanisms, is why it is an example for Latin America.

The items on the above regional agenda are not far-fetched; they have been included either in some legal instruments or in proposals made by mainstream economists in the United States. Thus the June 1986 Argentine-Brazilian Economic Cooperation and Integration Programme (the antecedent of the Mercosur agreement) foresaw the signing of numerous protocols, many of which were concluded during the first three years of the accord, on matters including capital goods, wheat, agroindustries, binational firms, and those creating an Investment Fund and a common currency. While these did not all proceed at the same pace, they indicated the type of integration these countries were seeking. In March 1991, Paraguay and Uruguay joined Argentina and Brazil to create a South American Common Market by December 31, 1994. The four countries agreed to remove all nontariff barriers, promote gradual tariff reductions, and progressively eliminate exemptions for intraregional trade. This acceleration of the initiative responded to two factors: the rapid rise in intra-Mercosur trade (from $2.2 billion in 1987 to $4.9 billion in 1991)[24] and to the political necessity of both Brazil and Argentina to move forward quickly. They also decided to negotiate a common external tariff.[25]

It is true, of course, that many of these noble intentions will remain just that: wishful thinking in a continent where it has been a rampant feature of economic and social, regional and international theory and practice. But this type of integration, involving industrial policy coordination, sectoral planning, investment funds, and external tariffs, as opposed to the laissez-faire model, is firmly rooted in Latin America. If the left is able to transcend its traditional resistance to any supranational scheme and position itself firmly in favor of this approach, it will both place itself squarely in the mainstream of traditional hemispheric doctrine and simultaneously differentiate itself from much of the right, the United States, and the international financial community's agenda.

Moreover, thanks to this kind of economic integration, the regional-federalist impulse that Latin America needs can become a reality: as the level of decision-making rises supranationally, it also makes state or local decision-making more plausible and effective. This view also converges with a broader trend, formulated elsewhere and for other areas, perhaps still far off for Latin America, yet already relevant for its future:

a confederal union of semi-autonomous communities smaller than nation-states, tied together into regional economic associations and markets larger than nation-states—participatory and self-determining in local matters at the bottom, representative and accountable at the top.[26]

But only through considerable resource transferring mechanisms can the risk that greater local autonomy inevitably entails be reduced. Otherwise, it reproduces and aggravates existing disparities. The poorer regions of each country, and of the entire hemisphere, require funding from the richer ones if they are ever to escape from their prostration. Without regional integration, this will never come about.

If the left should favor those facets of regional economic integration that make it "kinder and gentler," it should also favor ratcheting up the noneconomic domains in which integration takes place. Grass roots regional integration and the creation of regional political, social, and legal institutions should gradually fill the intermediate void created by economic globalization. If Europe failed in any one way, it may well have been by proving incapable of keeping the political, economic, and social levels of integration reasonably abreast of each other. Instead, it let the economic agenda jump far ahead, leaving the political and social ones lagging behind. The European left was partly to blame for this failure, as it convinced itself of the inevitability of a united Europe only late in the game.[27]

In Latin America, the time may have come for building regional political institutions and legal mechanisms of a supranational appellate nature, above and beyond national jurisdictions. Little has been actually accomplished in this direction, and new steps taken along this road are not progressing speedily, to say the least. But the left now has a tradition of understanding how most of the time, in most places, certain supranational initiatives—on human rights, election monitoring, judicial review and due process, labor rights and environmental protection—favor its causes, not those of its opponents. If deeper, more participatory and broader democracy favors the left, as many believe it does, then the greater its supranational facets, the better. With one condition, though: that it remain among equals and be sufficiently regional and close enough to home to make a difference. Otherwise, the new supranational institutions would simply become another distant, detached bureaucracy and authority in a continent that has suffered through too many such estrangements.

This new nationalist program must be presented to the left's supporters through an original political discourse that starts by telling the truth. The truth in this respect means, to begin with, that there can be no elevation of sovereignty, no regional integration, economic or otherwise, without a certain reduction in national autonomy. Regional institutions cannot be created without the abdication of a given amount of sovereignty by each member; moreover, those abdications, even if the process is only economic at the outset, will not remain exclusively economic in nature. Economic integration leads to political and cultural convergence, and generates indisputable constraints on national policymaking. It makes no sense for the Latin American left to strive for regional integration and then to state that the political and cultural costs will be nil or that there are no trade-offs involved. On the contrary, the more political the process, the better for the left, if it is a democratic politicization that takes place. As a French philosopher wrote recently about Europe: "Not every state is democratic; but a nonstate, by definition, cannot be democratized."[28]

Similarly, it would be meaningless for the left to maintain that a socially progressive, environmentally harmonized, regulated, planned, and fair model of integration is totally devoid of internal contradictions and unintended consequences. In fact, the entire process is intrinsically ambivalent, and many of the social clauses, economic protection, or sovereignty-saving provisions not only fail to function adequately but occasionally produce results that are the exact opposite of those pursued. Harmonization does not always lead up the ladder; sometimes it entails a lowering of standards. Compensatory financing can help but often does not achieve the desired aims: the Italian Mezzogiorno has improved its desperate situation of the 1950s largely because it has been emptied of its inhabitants, and the sums funneled into it over the past three decades are disproportionate to the difference they made. The left in Latin America, here too, has to go forward with its eyes wide open, and with a healthy dose of skepticism and dampened expectations.

Lastly, there is, of course, a Mexican question in this respect, or more accurately, a Mexican exception. Although President Bush's Enterprise of the Americas initiative addressed the entire hemisphere, and smaller Latin American nations have negotiated trade agreements of one sort or another with the United States, only Mexico has truly embarked on a full-fledged process of economic integration with a "nonequal": the United States. Thus for the Mexican left, the issue was couched in different terms: to be initially in favor or against economic integration not with the rest of the region, or even with the United States together with other nations previously integrated in a Meso-American, Caribbean Basin Common Market, but alone with Washington. As the debate was framed in Mexico at the time, it was difficult, if not impossible, for the Mexican left not be against the Free Trade Agreement as signed.[29]

Then, once it became clear that this course was irrevocably chosen or imposed, the left was faced with the option of struggling to overturn it, or redirecting it in a fashion more conducive to its principles and ethics, and to its perception of the national interest. Thus, up to a point, the platform suggested above for the rest of the left was not totally applicable to Mexico. In fact, however, the Mexican left's new nationalist banner should also be based on regional economic integration, precisely of the type outlined previously, and even more so. If any country should strive to make its integration more regulated, more noneconomic, more planned and subsidized, encompassing more areas such as labor mobility, compensatory financing, industrial policy, environmental soundness, it is Mexico in its integration with the United States. But this should be conditional on its accomplishment within a regional framework—i.e., with Central America and the Caribbean—and in a strong, lasting alliance with those sectors in the United States and Canada that for different but equally valid reasons want to transform the existing NAFTA.

An example of the novelty, difference, and viability of this approach is provided by the proposal for a North American Development Bank and Adjustment

Fund, presented by three American economists in 1991.[30] The bank would be an intergovernmental institution, capitalized by paid-in shares of its three member governments and would raise funds by selling bonds on the international market. The proposal borrowed explicitly from the European Regional Development Fund and the European Social Fund set up to deal with adjustment costs incurred by the inclusion in the Common Market of less developed areas such as Ireland, Portugal, Greece, and Spain. It is a typical *dirigiste*, interventionist idea. Its purpose would be as follows:

> The investment bank would focus on long-term development projects in: physical infrastructure that would facilitate improved trade, such as roads, bridges, ports, railroads, border facilities, and integrated border development; social infrastructure aimed at improving trade performance, such as technical assistance, worker training, collaborative research, educational exchanges, research and development. . .; investment projects aimed at promoting sustainable rural development, given increased trade and the need to manage labor market integration; investment projects for environmental improvements, including establishing institutions for monitoring, enforcement, cleanup and adoption of new technologies; institutional development aimed at improving the operation of capital and labor markets to facilitate efficient, equitable and environmentally sound integration across the three countries. The assistance fund would focus on short-to-medium term financing to help affected communities adjust to changes emanating from the establishment of a North American FTA . . . including plant closures, labor retraining and conversion investment"[31]

Needless to say, none of the three governments negotiating the Free Trade Agreement paid the proposal any heed, initially the Mexican government least of all.[32] Its inclusion in the negotiations, like that of labor mobility, might have slowed down the entire process, but the rush was much more the Salinas administration's than that of the nations involved. Moreover, Mexican opposition leader Cuauhtémoc Cárdenas had previously presented a similar, though less technically elaborated idea in a speech at the Americas Society in New York.[33] Again, the issue was less whether any of these schemes were actually put in practice than whether they were mainstream ideas that stemmed from concrete precedents elsewhere and specific needs in the cases in question.[34] They also ran counter to the way things were being pursued by the conservative, right-of-center regimes in power in the three countries as the NAFTA negotiations went forward.

The left as a whole has already begun to move in this direction. For example, virtually all the Salvadorean ex-guerrilla groups favor a process of Central American economic integration: "In the same way a regional war was fought, we can now proceed to implement democratic transformations on a regional scale, combining them with a process of regional economic integration, and remove the remaining dictatorships."[35] A Latin American left-of-center coordinating group known as the São Paulo Forum comprising virtually all of the organizations examined in the previous chapters, held a meeting in Lima in February of 1992 devoted to economic integration. The conference agreed that:

A long-term alternative for Latin America has, as a fundamental premise, the strengthening of processes of integration among the countries of the region. . . . This implies restructuring, in favor of the peoples of the region, the existing mechanisms of regional integration such as the Andean Pact, Mercosur, and the Central American Common Market. Items such as the regulation and control of foreign capital, the establishment of norms governing investment, taxation, the environment, and transfers of technology should be included.[36]

While the rhetoric remains largely unchanged, the content is different. A few years ago, the very notion that the Latin American left could subscribe to the idea of restructuring existing mechanisms of integration would have been virtually inconceivable.

In the end, the Latin American left's nationalism, new or old, must be above all a function of its hope and struggle to "give back the nation to the people," or more accurately, to give the millions of excluded citizens of the hemisphere the nation they never had. This nationalism is at least as much part of a domestic agenda as it is of an international one. It means extending the democratization process begun throughout Latin America in the 1980s far beyond its present limits in every country. Without bringing a majority of the people into the nation, the nationalism of the few—the intellectual elite, the urban, professional middle class, the impoverished lower middle class of urban schoolteachers, students, and part-time workers—will never attain a true constituency. Nationalism in Latin America today has to become once again, as it was in a distorted and often authoritarian, but nonetheless inclusive, way in the 1930s and 1940s, a force for incorporating the excluded into the nation. But this time it has to do so democratically.

NOTES

1. The other, better though perhaps excessively European metaphor that has been used appears in the title of one of the more insightful books written on the North-South question in the aftermath of the Cold War: Jean-Christophe Rufin's *L'Empire et les Nouveaux Barbares* (Paris: Editions JC Lattès, 1991). The metaphor states: "The ideological revolution occurring in Rome after the fall of Carthage is comparable to that which today has substituted the East-West confrontation with a world dominated by a North-South opposition. . . . Yes, a new unification of the North is possible, by defining its values by their opposites, by that which runs contrary to them or threatens them. The emergence of the South in the role of the new barbarians achieves this goal. . . . This is the pact: on one side, security for the North, a form of eternity, and on the other, the simple abandonment of justice." Pp. 13, 18, 208.

2. The Mexican Foreign Ministry requested a clarification from the United States regarding the Supreme Court ruling and the Executive's interpretation. No reply was ever made public; there may well have never been a reply at all. For the effects of the *Urquídez Verdugo* ruling for Mexico and Latin America, see Adolfo Aguilar Zinser, *Siempre!*, March 29, 1990.

3. *Washington Post*, August 14, 1991.

4. One analyst linked the principle of extraterritoriality to the Noriega affair from the very beginning. "The administration also moved to make 'hardball' legal. At the Justice Department, Assistant Attorney General William P. Barr asserted that U.S. law

enforcement officers could make an arrest in a foreign country even if the foreign government did not grant permission. Barr and other officials explained that such powers were necessary to combat narco-traffickers and terrorists. . . . To some legislators, Barr's claim represented a dramatic and dangerous change in policy and was nothing less than a license to kidnap. . . . Representative Don Edwards (D-Califomia) said: 'I can think of no law passed by the Congress or any provision of the Constitution that licenses the United States to be an international outlaw.' " Kevin Buckley, *Panama: The Whole Story* (New York: Simon and Schuster, 1991), 221.

5. *Newsweek* (Latin American edition), February 19, 1990.

6. According to one critical source: "[Given the limits established by the Pentagon on U.S. troop involvement] the U.S. military involvement in the drug war in the Andes is expanding sharply. The administration has approved plans . . . for a host of new drug-related activities in the Andes. In recognition of the increasingly diffuse and flexible cocaine trade, the plans foresee expanded U.S. military operational support for security forces in Central America and the rest of South America. . . . The military component of the Andean strategy is historically, doctrinally and operationally linked to U.S. counterinsurgency strategy." Washington Office on Latin America, "Clear and Present Dangers: The U.S. Military and the War on Drugs in the Andes," Washington, D.C., October 1991, 21, 43.

7. The extent to which this process evoked memories of previous forms of American intervention was highlighted in a *Newsweek International* investigative report published at the outset of 1992, "The Newest War": "A two-month *Newsweek* inquiry has documented a Pentagon drug war, parts of it secret, that has quietly escalated to dimensions greater than most Americans yet realize. It involves thousands of U.S. and Latin troops, at a cost of more than a billion dollars per year." *Newsweek International*, January 13, 1992, 6–11.

8. According to an oft-quoted American study of Mexican migration, in Los Altos de Jalisco (a strong emigration-generating area for nearly 100 years) in 1976, 77 percent of interviewed migrants stated that the main reason for leaving Mexico was to improve their income; only 9 percent gave unemployment as a reason. Wayne Cornelius, "Mexican Migration to the United States: Causes, Consequences, and U.S. Responses," Center for International Studies, Massachusetts Institute of Technology, Cambridge, Mass., 1978 (mimeo). According to a Mexican and an American expert, "The determining factor [in migration] is the difference between the wages that Mexican workers receive in the two countries." Manuel García y Griego and Mónica Verea, *México y Estados Unidos frente a la migración de los indocumentados* (Mexico City: UNAM, 1988), 56.

9. An interesting example of how this paradoxical process unfolded in the early nineties emerges from a *New York Times* account of a visit to Capitol Hill by Peruvian president Alberto Fujimori in September 1991. House of Representatives Western Hemisphere Sub-Committee chairman Robert Torricelli was quoted as saying: "Peru is a nation facing an almost complete security, economic and health collapse. . . . Fujimori represents a real balance between the legitimate interests of the United States and his own people." In the midst of collapse, for an elected leader to be qualified as striking a "balance" between the interests of his people and those of another power is a remarkable situation, particularly since those who elected him did not do so for him to represent, even only partly, the interests of that other power. Governments have fallen for less reason than this in Latin America; in the post-Cold War days, times had obviously changed. *New York Times*, September 24, 1991, A3.

10. Less than a month after an attempted coup that nearly toppled him, Venezuelan president Carlos Andrés Perez made the following confession: "The economic reforms [I have implemented] were done partly as a result of pressure from international lending agencies." He made this statement to a group of external advisers (headed by Henry Kiss-

inger) who strongly urged him to persevere in his free-market policies. *La Jornada* (Mexico City), March 22, 1992, front page.

11. An initial attempt to devise such an approach, not for the left in particular but for Mexican policy in general, can be found in Jorge G. Castañeda, "La larga marcha de la politica exterior de México," *Nexos* (Mexico City), no. 101, April 1986, reprinted in Castañeda, *México: El futuro en juego* (Mexico City: Joaquín Mortiz Editores, 1987).

12. Alan Fiers, a former CIA official and a key witness it r Iran-Contra trials was quoted by the *New York Times* on September 20, 1991 as testifying that conversations between Sandinista leaders and Democratic members of the U.S. Congress were tapped by the CIA. *A tout seigneur, tout honneur*.

13. Some scholars link the end of the Cold War with the development of an "internationalized politics . . . i.e., the involvement of international organizations, foreign states and internationally based nongovernmental groups in the so-called domestic politics of a country. . . . There has been a significant broadening of the types and number of groups penetrating Latin American societies. . . . Classic types have been joined by a wide range of advocacy groups, nongovernmental organizations and international agencies. These . . . organizations have formed what has been called 'issue network.'" Douglas Chalmers, "The Internationalized Politics of Institution Building in Latin America," paper presented at a Joint Conference of the Institute of Latin American Studies (Columbia University) and the Centro de Estudios sobre América, Havana, July 4, 1992.

14. Barbara Crossette, *New York Times*, March 10, 1992.

15. Richard Falk, "New Dimensions in International Relations and the Birth of Global Civil Society," paper presented at the Nobel jubilee Symposia, Oslo, December 8-9, 1992, p. 2.

16. "The recent discussion of regionalism ['The world is fragmenting into rival trading blocs'] has serious flaws. First . . . it has rested on a view of underlying trade patterns that is highly misleading. Under several different definitions of the relevant regions, interregional trade is growing as fast or faster than intra-regional trade. . . . A second point is that the discussion of regionalization has tended to overlook the status of the United States as, in effect, a member of several regions at the same time. . . . A third weakness is that the discussion has been focused on trade issues, ignoring the growing internationalization of investment flows. . . . Finally, a number of studies have placed too much weight on the role of political decisions in structuring trade flows." Albert Fishlow and Stephen Haggard, "The United States and the Regionalization of the World Economy," Research Programme on Globalization and Regionalization, OECD, Paris, January 1992 (mimeo), 13.

17. The first Latin American trade grouping, the Latin American Free Trade Association (or ALALC) was founded in 1960. It died a silent death in 1982, never having amounted to much.

18. Ibid., 30.

19. "In 1989 a quarter of U.S. imports from Brazil entered the U.S. duty-free under the Most Favored Nation clause (MFN), an additional 16 percent received the benefits of the Generalized System of Preferences (GSP), and the remaining 59 percent paid generally low tariffs." Roberto Bouzas, *A U.S.-Mercosur Free Trade Area: A Preliminary Assessment*, FLACSO, Documentos e Informes de Investigación no. 143, Buenos Aires, November 1991, 11.

20. The term was coined by John Williamson and includes "agreements" by what the distinguished economist refers to as "the political Washington of Congress and senior members of the administration, and the technocratic Washington of the international financial institutions, the economic agencies of the U.S. government, the Federal Reserve Board, and the think tanks." The "consensus" refers to ten areas: fiscal discipline, public expenditure priorities, tax reform, financial liberalization, exchange rates, trade liberalization, foreign direct investment, privatization, deregulation, and property rights. Cf.

John Williamson, "The Progress of Policy Reform in Latin America," in *Latin American Adjustment: How Much Has Happened*, ed. J. Williamson (Washington, D.C.: Institute for International Economics, 1990), 358–378.

21. Refik Erzan and Alexander Yeats, "Free Trade Agreements with the United States: What's in It for Latin America," World Bank Policy Research Working Paper, WPS 827, January 1992, inside cover summary.

22. In the words of a none-too-left-wing critic (a businessman and economics journalist): "In the last analysis, it is the American philosophy that is carrying the day, but taken to the extreme. . . . The risk is that the great new market will function in a permanent state of imbalance, without regulation or counterweights." Alain Minc, *La Grande Illusion* (Paris: Grasset, 1989), 115, 119.

23. "The state in Europe today is neither national nor supranational, and this ambiguity instead of fading with time is getting worse. In practice, this means that on the economic and financial side, as well as on the legal and social one, in the distribution of power between the level of "national states" and that of the community institutions, there is a constant redundancy, a constant competition among institutions." Etienne Balibar, *Les Frontières de la Démocratie* (Paris: La Découverte, 1992), 186. Balibar does come from the left: he was a member of the French Communist Party until 1981 and has continued to sustain markedly left-of-center stances.

24. "The New World's Newest Trade Bloc," *Business Week*, May 4, 1992, 50.

25. Bouzas, op. cit., 5.

26. Benjamin R. Barber, "Jihad vs. McWorld," *Atlantic Monthly*, March 1992, 63.

27. "Economic citizenship has led to the emergence of a bizarre 'homo europeanus' that represents the most Marxist of beings: only his economic rights make him a European, and not his culture, his roots and his right to vote. What a paradox: a Greek doctor can settle in Lyons and compete freely for patients with his French colleagues, but he cannot elect the local mayor, much less his congressman." Minc, op. cit., 108. The Maastricht Treaty of 1991 in fact provides for electoral rights for all European nationals across the community.

28. Balibar, op. cit., 190.

29. Not that this process was unforeseen or that a nuanced position on the issue of integration was not staked out by center-left academics years before: "Opposition to formal economic integration with the United States is widespread in Mexico, yet it rings increasingly hollow. Many Mexicans favor the changes the economy is undergoing, but fear their consequences; many support the premises of economic integration, but oppose the political and cultural changes they may lead to. A substantial part of the nation's political, intellectual and even entrepreneurial establishment is against greater economic ties with the United States, but believes the growth of such ties may be inevitable. The question for Mexico is thus changing from 'Is integration desirable?' to 'Is it reversible, and if not, what are its consequences for Mexico; can it be successfully administered and can Mexico get the most out of it?'" Jorge G. Castañeda, "Sliding Toward Economic Integration," in Robert Pastor and Jorge G. Castañeda, *Limits to Friendship: The United States and Mexico* (New York: Knopf, 1988), 241.

30. Albert Fishlow, Sherman Robinson, and Raúl Hinojosa-Ojeda, "Proposal for a Regional Development Bank and North American Adjustment Fund," *Mexico Policy News*, Consortium for Research on Mexico, San Diego State University Institute for Regional Studies of the Californias, no. 7, winter 1992, 16–18.

31. Ibid., 17.

32. In the course of his adjusting to the new situation arising from Bill Clinton's election, President Salinas de Gortari flirted with the idea of compensatory financing and a regional bank. See the *Wall Street Journal*, December 7, 1992.

33. Cárdenas stated that: "In an economic integration process such as the one currently under way, the more disadvantaged economy inevitably has to make more and costlier adjustments. It also suffers more dislocations in the short-term. . . . The disparities between the three economies [Canada, the United States, and Mexico] mean that, over and above the market-induced funds that could come as a consequence of the FTA, Mexico will require substantial funding to finance, first, the adjustment process, including needed investments in infrastructure and education in order to absorb additional new investments; second, the harmonization of norms, and third, the provisions of a social charter. We know that financing is not easy, but making the fundamental disparity of the three economies the cornerstone of the agreement means making compensatory financing its centerpiece." Cuauhtémoc Cárdenas, "A Continental Development and Trade Initiative," Council of the Americas/Americas Society, New York, February 8, 1991.

34. Similarly, in a speech at the Institute for International Economics in Washington on July 27, 1991, House Democratic Majority Leader Richard Gephardt proposed an environmental tax for inclusion in the NAFTA, to finance environmental harmonization.

35. Joaquin Villalobos, interview with the author, Mexico City, September 5, 1991.

36. Documento Final, Seminario/Taller sobre Integración y Desarrollo Alternativo, organizado por los Movimientos y Partidos del Foro de São Paulo, Lima, February 26–29, 1992. More than twenty papers were presented specifically on the three regional integration initiatives, mostly critical of their current status, and proposing alternatives within the existing mechanisms.

20

The Market Turn Without
Neoliberalism (1999)

Carlos Salinas de Gortari and Roberto Mangabeira Unger

*Carlos Salinas de Gortari (b. Mexico, 1948) was president of Mexico from 1988
to 1994. Previously he was professor of economics at the National Autonomous
University of Mexico (UNAM) and held several government posts, including
minister of the Bureau of Planning and Budget from 1982 to 1987. During his
term as president, Salinas undertook a large scale neoliberal restructuring of the
Mexican economy that included reversing land reform legislation, privatizing
the Mexican Bank and state-owned corporations and industries, and, most importantly, negotiating the North American Free Trade Agreement (NAFTA) with
the United States and Canada. Currently Salinas lives in self-imposed exile in
Ireland due to family scandals, involving fraud and corruption, related to his
years as president of Mexico.*

*Roberto Mangabeira Unger (b. Brazil, 1947) is a Brazilian social theorist,
law professor, and one of the founders of the Critical Legal Studies movement.
Unger has long been active in Brazilian and Latin American politics, as a political candidate, activist, and advisor. He is founding member, major ideologue,
and vice president of the Brazilian Republican Party. Currently he is minister
of the Special Bureau of Long Term Actions in the Worker Party government
of Brazilian president Luis Inácio Lula da Silva. Since 1970 he has been a law
professor at Harvard University and since 2004 a member of the American
Academy of Arts and Sciences. The author of numerous books, Unger is also a
regular contributor to the* Folha de São Paulo, *a Brazilian newspaper with the
largest circulation of any newspaper in Latin America.*

*This selection critically examines the dominant neoliberal model of economic
and social development and the standard social-democratic alternative, arguing
instead for a third alternative, especially in underdeveloped countries; an alternative that does not rely so heavily and exclusively on global capital markets.*

The world financial crisis provides an opportunity to rethink the way forward to freedom and prosperity all over the planet, in richer countries as well as
in poorer ones. The essential meaning of the crisis is that in an age of financial
volatility, scarcity, and skepticism, most countries will have to walk on their
own legs more than their governments and elites had wanted or expected.

In societies as different as Russia and Brazil, the call has gone out for a mobilization of national resources. The global capital market has been revealed as no savior, and the plain truth that countries must first help themselves in order to profit from help from abroad has been painfully driven home.

But what does the mobilization of national resources require? The economies hit most severely by the crisis need to reinvent the arrangements connecting finance with the real economy. They need to make their prospects for sustained and socially inclusive growth less dependent on the whims of finance.

How can they achieve such goals without retreating behind protectionist barriers, into economic isolation? Or without resorting to a style of inadequately inclusive export-driven growth, brokered among political and business elites, that deprives most of the population of its benefits?

To put the matter this way is to recognize that today's financial crisis does what crisis has always done: It makes more urgent and obvious a need that existed before it arose. In much of the world, the search was already under way for an alternative to what has come to be called neoliberalism, an alternative that would make the market shift—the global turn to markets—more people-friendly than it has been so far. The search was more anxious in the developing countries, especially in those that have made the strongest commitment to joining the world economy. These are the same countries that have suffered most from the ravages of the world financial crisis. It is nevertheless a worldwide search. Everywhere people are asking whether the market revolution will lift up the many or merely enrich the few.

THE CRISIS RECONSIDERED

Unlike the crisis of the 1930s, today's crisis began in peripheral rather than central economies. Japan's remains the only major economy to have been shaken until now. The issues nevertheless transcend their origins. Academic debate has thus far focused on the secondary and the superficial: whether to limit financial volatility through exchange and capital controls or to persist in the opening of the global economy to free flows of capital, and whether to extend or scale back bailouts by multilateral financial agencies like the International Monetary Fund. However, the larger meaning of the crisis lies in the questions it raises about some of the most basic features of the path taken by the commitment to market-oriented economies.

Saving and production, the money economy and the real economy, continue to be weakly connected in contemporary societies. The production system finances itself through retained earnings. Much of the productive potential of saving gets squandered in financial speculation and irresponsibility. Money gains to investors bear an uncertain relation to real gains to people in jobs, consumption, and production. As the financial markets ride the rollercoaster of boom and bust, mania and panic, they can do real harm to the real economy. Can we diminish these evils by reshaping market economies in ways that draw saving and production, finance and industry, money and the real economy closer together? This is not a question that pure economic analysis can hope to answer, for the answer depends crucially on the different ways we can reorganize the market economy in fact—reorganize it, not just regulate it.

The development of a global economy has been informed by an unquestioned and almost unconscious doctrine of sharp contrasts in the steps by which capital and labor should gain the right to cross national frontiers. According to this doctrine, capital should win unrestricted freedom of movement right now and all at once. Labor should stay within the nation-state until, thanks to the gradual equalization of productivity and wages throughout the world, it no longer needs to move. The international financial crisis, however, casts suspicion on this selective view of economic freedom. It invites us to ask whether it might not be better for capital and labor to win freedom together, but to win it in small, incremental steps.

The Bretton Woods organizations have not only championed free capital movement. They have also espoused pre-Keynesian monetary and fiscal orthodoxy in the service of worldwide convergence toward the economic and political institutions now established in the North Atlantic democracies and especially in the United States. They have mixed up the minimalist and necessary job of helping to keep the world economy open with the maximalist and controversial attempt to impose on all countries in need of their help a particular route to freedom and prosperity. The crisis, along with the unhappy role of the Bretton Woods organizations in its genesis and correction, strengthens the case for insisting upon international organizations open to diversity of vision and direction.

THE NEED FOR AN ALTERNATIVE

The world wants a progressive alternative, not a withdrawal into protectionism and populism. This alternative should join open markets to social solidarity, and do so through innovations in the ways free polities, societies, and economies are organized. Unlike conventional, institutionally conservative social democrats, we must not hesitate to experiment with new institutional arrangements for representative democracies, market economies, and independent civil societies.

Social assistance, although indispensable, is less vital than community organization. Success in securing for the individual the economic and cultural equipment he needs to function as an effective worker and citizen counts for more than a rigid equality of resources. Rebuilding practices and institutions to strengthen the individual and collective capacities to tinker and to transcend is what matters most of all.

A program like the one outlined here marks a direction rather than designing a blueprint. One of us comes to the statement of this program from a commitment to "social liberalism," the other from an effort to explore radically democratic alternatives to contemporary institutions. We unite in support of a proposal that appeals to the skeptical as well as to the hopeful, and to the radicals of the center as well as to the heretics of the left.

The effort is timely because all over the world there has been a turn to the market economy. Is this market project really a conversion to the doctrine often labeled neoliberalism? The widespread turn to markets need not and should not mean adherence to the neoliberal program, nor require national governments to kowtow to international finance.

When we look more closely at each of the planks making up the worldwide platform of the market program, we discover that each lends itself to two readings. One recommends the familiar recipes of economic and political orthodoxy; the other anticipates a project that is as supportive of markets as it is open to institutional reform, even if the reform must be radical.

The first reading—call it neoliberalism—has the advantage of easy reference. It is the project of convergence toward the institutions and practices most characteristic of the North Atlantic economies. The Asian model has lost its aura. European social democracy is on the defensive and anxious to rescue a modicum of social protection from the rush to American-style "flexibility." The American version of the market economy, softened by a little more social protection than Americans have been willing to allow, has become the presumed goal of worldwide convergence. This is neoliberalism. If everything in today's economics manuals were true, the pathway this project lays out would be the preferred route to prosperity and democracy. In fact, it would be the only one.

The second reading—call it the alternative—has the benefit of giving shape to something most of humanity wants: economic freedom and economic progress without social disinheritance. However, it is not simply an attempt to juxtapose the heritage of the welfare state and the familiar devices of economic flexibility. It is a productivist as well as a redistributivist program. It seeks to anchor its social commitments in the daily routines of economic life. It recognizes that, in much of the world, social progress continues to require rapid and persistent as well as inclusive economic growth. Moreover, it takes seriously the connection between economics and politics.

The goal is a deepening of democracy as well as a quickening of trial and error in economic, social, and political life; an economy more open to diversity of practices and institutions as well as of technologies and, therefore, better able to combine the two clashing and overlapping requirements of economic progress cooperation and innovation; a polity more energized and, therefore, more oriented to the repeated practice of structural reform; and a society more evenly organized outside government and, therefore, more capable of generating different conceptions of its future and of acting upon them. Democratic deepening and democratic experimentalism are the watchwords of this alternative. Cumulative, sustained, and motivated institutional innovation is its master tool.

The neoliberal version of the market economy may favor the interests of big international businesses and transactions, weakening the practical and conceptual instruments of deviation from the one true way. However, the neoliberal program suits almost no one else. The world will remain restless under the sway of a doctrine leaving so little room for opposing interests and visions.

Consider how each of the major proposals we associate with the market turn looks different according to whether we interpret it from the standpoint of neoliberalism or from the perspective of the alternative.

FREE TRADE: CAPITAL AND LABOR

According to the established understanding of the market turn, free trade means that capital, together with goods and services, should be free to roam the world. Labor should remain locked up within the nation-state or within blocs of relatively homogeneous nation-states such as the European Union. If enough capital moves from capital-rich to capital-poor countries, wages will converge and workers will no longer need to move.

The trouble, however, is that the vast majority of capital continues to stay at home. The relatively small amount that goes abroad does more to divide workers and frustrate governments than to raise wages. Long-lasting inequalities of returns to labor between rich and poor countries coexist with disruptive financial instability.

There is an alternative. Capital and labor should win freedom to cross national frontiers together and step by step. We need constraints on speculative financial trading across frontiers as well as more effective regulation of domestic financial institutions, selective controls on short-term capital flows, and international agreements among national governments, national labor movements, and multilateral organizations to make more migration possible and to minimize its disruptive effects. Instead of arrangements like the *bracero* program between Mexico and the United States (for migrant agricultural workers) or the inland colonies of the old South Africa, we need understandings and deals among the labor unions of the participating countries. Only then can the shared freedom of capital and labor be socially and politically as well as economically feasible.

In principle, transnational investment, together with the growth of international trade, could achieve much of the economic effect of migration if enough such investment took place quickly enough. However, it will not. If it did, with the necessary speed and in the requisite amounts, its political and economic consequences would be even more destabilizing than those of the gradual but paired progress of mobility for capital and labor.

Let labor begin to move freely—that is a doctrine right for an age committed to making economic freedom available to all. The difficulties of establishing this principle are real. The benefits extend far beyond economics to changes in the role of national differences. More open to outsiders, nations should begin to define themselves less by the traditions they have inherited than by the distinct ways of life they may yet forge. The role of nations in a world of democracies is to embody moral specialization within humanity. Such a world recognizes that the roots of a human being lie as much in the future as in the past.

PRIVATIZATION, REGULATION, AND PRIVATE-PUBLIC PARTNERSHIP

Neoliberalism tells governments to get out of the business of producing through public enterprises. It advises them to give free rein to the decentralized trial and error of the market, the unrivaled wealthmaker. According to this neoliberal view, government should focus on what it can accomplish best: provide security, education, and basic health care or fallback health insurance;

regulate business; and soften the social pain of economic adjustment by developing social safety nets.

We should reconsider this advice in the light of a striking feature of contemporary economies. Rich and poor countries alike are being torn apart by a deepening division between advanced and backward sectors of the economy. Traditional dual theories of development fail to illuminate the contemporary significance of this division. A worldwide network of productive vanguards has increasingly become the commanding force in the world economy. Advanced sectors of each economy, characterized less by huge financial resources or physical capital than by flattened hierarchies, cooperative competition, and permanent innovation, trade people, ideas, and practices as well as products, resources, and services.

In each economy, the division between vanguards and rearguards has become the chief source of inequality and exclusion. If the majority of the population remains arrested in a productive rearguard, no amount of welfare assistance through conventional tax-and-transfer techniques will suffice to ensure greater equality and inclusion.

The advanced sectors barely need government to prosper on their traditional favored terrain. Governmental initiative becomes necessary when we want to help overcome the division between productive vanguards and rearguards, generalizing vanguardist practices in the economy as a whole. Arm's-length regulation is then no longer enough.

We need partnership between government and business, but not in the form of comprehensive industrial and trade policy formulated by a centralized bureaucracy. We need a radical expansion of venture capital, commercial credit, and technical assistance for start-up companies and small and medium-sized enterprises, but not subsidies or credit allocation according to plan and preconception. The goal is to redesign and expand the market, not to trump it in favor of bureaucratic dogmas and political clienteles. At present, the venture-capital industry of California and Massachusetts dwarfs venture capital in the rest of the world. What should be a central concern of finance remains, almost everywhere, a marginal activity.

We need to fashion for the economy as a whole a decentralized and participatory alliance between public actions and private initiative. It is the kind of alliance that succeeded in organizing family-size agriculture from the mid-nineteenth to mid-twentieth century in countries as different as the United States and Denmark.

The solution, according to this alternative reading of the market turn, is to establish between governments and firms an intermediate level of organization: funds, banks, extension services, with a mixed public and private character, financially responsible and market competitive. Some funds might take equity stakes in the firms with which they deal, while preserving their independence and allowing the firms to keep theirs. Others might eventually become the financial and technical centers of little confederations of businesses that both compete and cooperate with one another. From these contrasting styles of association between funds and firms, many varieties of private and nongovernmental social property might develop, coexisting experimentally within the same market economy. There is not one market regime. There are many.

SAVING AND PRODUCTION

Neoliberalism emphasizes the need to discipline public spending and to raise public-sector saving through budgetary discipline. However, neoliberals have been complacent or fatalistic about private thrift and sanguine about the use of foreign capital to make up for shortfalls of national saving. Moreover, they have been willing to leave the relationship between saving and production to take care of itself through the present system of banks and stock markets.

The alternative proposal to develop the market program takes a different stand on each of these issues. Consider that last one first. Today, in mature market economies, the production system largely finances itself: A decisive majority of funds invested in production comes from retained earnings. Both initial public offerings and venture capital remain sideshows in the financial markets. Trades in these markets are supposed to contribute—mainly indirectly—to the financing of production, and indeed they do. However, it requires no primitive contrast between sterile and productive investment to admit that much of the productive potential of saving continues to be squandered.

The market-friendly alternative to neoliberalism insists upon tightening the link between saving and production. It wants to do so in one way by reforming the established system of banks and stock markets—for example, by extending the facilities for local and cooperative financial institutions able to take up the undone work of the start-up investor. It proposes to do so in another way by building, alongside this system, a second bridge between saving and production—for example, pension funds regulated to act as venture capitalists and turnaround financiers, with risks pooled and, when possible, securitized. The point again is not to replace the market but to reorganize it in ways that make it more experimental and, in a real sense, more of a market. What looks like a subsidy—trumping the market—may turn out to be an initial move in an effort to redesign the market, opening it to greater variety of agents and arrangements. Experience, not analysis, establishes the difference.

We learned from Keynes that supply fails to ensure its own demand. Now we must add the other half: Demand fails to guarantee its own supply. Demand management will often prove inadequate to generate supply expansion. One reason is that an increase of demand may appear unsustainable to those who must make the decision to produce more, the point emphasized by the monetarist critique of Keynesianism. It is, however, subsidiary to another, more basic consideration. This reason would be too obvious to mention did it not play so uncomfortable a role in economic theory.

The owners and managers of productive business are not a corps of social functionaries dedicated to bringing the greatest possible satisfaction to consumers. Their aim is to make money and rise in the world, not to act at the beck and call of buyers with increased spending power. Sometimes they may think they can make more money by selling more or better goods and services to consumers who have more resources with which to buy them. At least as often, however, other tacks will seem more enticing; for example, selling the same goods and services at higher prices and waiting to see what the competition does, or putting spare time and cash into financial speculation.

The more production depends for its funding on retained earnings—the portion firms keep from their profits rather than distributing to shareholders—and the less new and small businesses enjoy reliable sources of external finance, the greater is the likelihood that the supply response will be weak. Approaches to full employment will then fail to result in sustainable, noninflationary growth.

To provide the resources for a vast expansion of venture capital and decentralized commercial credit, we may need to increase private as well as public saving in many economies. We can do so through a scheme for the public organization of compulsory private saving, such as saving for retirement. Arrangements for compulsory private saving should make the saving obligation steeply proportional to personal income. This obligation should be combined at the lower levels of the income scale with its inverse: guaranteed minimum income, substituting for the salaries of those who cannot work and supplementing the salaries of those who do work but receive the lowest incomes. The funds receiving such compulsory saving payments should be independently managed. They should operate both within the financial markets and, as venture capitalists, outside them.

TAXES, WELFARE, AND GRASSROOTS PARTICIPATION

The market turn is supposed to require a commitment to low taxes as well as to social safety nets. The message is to protect saving and investment through a tax system that depends primarily on consumption. It is also to ease the extremes of economic insecurity through the modest, targeted social entitlements that such fiscal discipline may allow.

In rich and poor countries alike, conservatives defend consumption-oriented taxation with low tax rates. Social democrats support income-oriented taxation at rates steeply proportional to earnings. They hope against hope that political and economic forces will allow them to raise enough revenue to fund generous, comprehensive social entitlements.

There is nothing in the idea of a market economy or in the agenda of a democratic market turn that should commit us to minimize taxes and social rights. The market cannot create its own foundations: people with the health and education needed to become effective workers and citizens.

A central paradox of the neoliberal take on the market turn is that its benefits would be greatest and its dangers smallest where an earlier history of reform and revolution has overcome the extremes of inequality. In today's Latin America, for example, neoliberalism might be least beneficial in the most unequal countries, such as Brazil and Mexico. It might be less dangerous to countries that have seen a protracted succession of conflicts and reforms strike down extreme inequality. However, the combination of a long, painful revolutionary history and a neoliberal epilogue is not one on which we can act. No one could or would choose it. The task of an alternative understating of the market project is to supply the practical equivalent to this impossible combination.

One component of such an alternative is a commitment to consumption-based taxation at competitive high rates. This commitment results from the juxtaposition of three ideas.

First, the national government in a divided and hierarchical society needs high tax revenues in order to play its part in solving society's problems. It is unlikely to be able to give people the means with which to develop themselves if it (and the other levels of government together) fails to take in at least 30 percent of gross domestic product (GDP).

Second, the most important lesson to be learned from contemporary fiscal experience is that redistribution takes place much more on the spending side than on the revenue-raising side of the budget. What matters in the short run is the aggregate level of tax revenue and the capacity-enhancing character of social spending.

Third, the transaction-based taxation of consumption, preferably through a comprehensive value-added tax (VAT) at a flat rate, supplies the most effective way to raise revenue while minimizing the negative impact on incentives to work, save, and invest. In many developing countries, where gasoline consumption is concentrated in the highest income brackets, an aggressive gasoline and luxury surtax may prove an especially effective way to supplement the VAT, combining as it does, a redistributive effect with a consumption focus. After we have secured high revenues by such means, we can hope to increase, little by little, the direct and steeply progressive taxation of each taxpayer's expenditures.

A high level of social spending, sustained by a growth-friendly style of taxation, can help ensure both the fiscal discipline and the investment in people and their capacities that every country, rich or poor, needs.

Where should the money go? In developing countries, or in the poorer sectors of richer countries, children and their ties to families, schools, and local communities should be the priority. The school can often provide a setting in which children receive medical and dental support, eye care, food supplements, and even proper hygiene, as well as education. The school should recognize children as the little prophets they are, giving them access to contrasting ideas and experiences rather than speaking as the obedient voice of the local community or the national bureaucracy.

As countries become richer, the core package of social rights should develop into a social inheritance. All citizens should inherit from society a minimal fund of resources, made available at turning points in their lives, such as receiving a higher education, starting a family, or opening a business. Imagine, for example, a basic social-endowment account set up for each individual. Such an account could vary upward according to two countervailing principles: increments responding to special needs by predetermined criteria and increments rewarding special capabilities, competitively demonstrated.

The relationship of these core rights and benefits to the unquiet experiments of a more vibrant democracy and a more diversified market economy is like the relationship between the love a parent feels for a child and the willingness of the child to run risks for the sake of transformation and self-transformation. People must be economically and culturally equipped to act as effective citizens and workers. They must also feel secure in a haven of protected vital interests if they are to face instability and innovation without fear.

Money, however, is not enough. It is not even the main pillar sustaining the alternative. The effective enjoyment of social rights depends on social action and social organization. Local communities must organize to participate in the design and implementation of assistance programs.

In many countries, both rich and poor, millions of children live in single-parent families. The weakening of the family often takes place against a background of community disorganization. In such a circumstance, welfare assistance to maintain these children in their family and school lacks its most important ally—community associations able to take over some of the responsibilities of fractured and overwhelmed families. Offering help in ways that trigger community association becomes the key to successful child support.

Popular organization and decentralization of decisions become crucial to ensure efficiency and equity in social spending. If this strategy of participatory community engagement is not to degenerate into the delegation of governmental power to local bosses and activists, access to all but the most basic social benefits should be made conditional upon broad-based community organization.

HIGH-ENERGY DEMOCRACY

The market turn is widely thought to be associated with democracy. But what kind? Neoliberals like democracy as long as democratic arrangements do not go too far toward arousing popular political energy. They hold out hope for the reciprocal reinforcement of economic and political freedoms. However, they also worry about the "excesses" of grass-roots democracy, which, they believe, threaten to arouse unrealizable expectations and generate self-defeating policies. Politics, they think, should not get too exciting before people get rich. After people get rich, they will doubtless find other matters more exciting.

The trouble is that the low-energy, limited democracy implied by this way of thinking favors a selective neoliberalism, more congenial to plutocratic lobbies than to small-time entrepreneurs. Such a program will, for example, be more anxious to sell off government enterprises than to break up private oligopolies. The masses of ordinary people, forgotten by this policy, will seek political revenge against it. A costly swing between economic orthodoxy and economic populism is the likely result.

The alternative version of the market turn requires a more energetic style of democracy than now prevails in the North. A commanding idea in those countries is that politics should become small, so that people can become big. However, small politics make people small too, starving the institutional renewal that represents the lifeblood of democracy. An experimental economy and an organized society can flourish only in the climate of an energized polity.

High-energy democracy requires constitutional arrangements that favor the rapid resolution of deadlocks among the political branches of government (for example, through plebiscites and anticipated elections, called by either political branch for both branches) and the heightening of organized civic engagement (for example, through rules of mandatory voting, public financing of free access of political parties, and social movements to the mass media). Such a program mixes elements of representative and direct democracy. It wants democratic politics once again to become a contest of visions, not the benevolent management of a world without options. It is a contest requiring a resilient, vigilant, organized, civil society.

THE ALTERNATIVE: THE EMPOWERED WORKER-CITIZEN AND THE DEMOCRATIZED MARKET ECONOMY

One way to grasp the sense of the alternative is to move away from familiar controversies about the role of government in the economy and to place this proposal in a fresh context. This context is the debate now taking place throughout the world about industrial renewal and its implications for relations between workers and managers. We can distinguish three voices in this controversy.

The first position—call it the conservative managerial program—has the initiative. It translates neoliberalism into the everyday realities of work and business. Its complaint is that present work arrangements are both too rigid and too conflictual. In the name of flexibility, it wants to minimize restraints upon managerial discretion to move people and resources around. However, it also wants to enhance cooperation on the job, turning work into teamwork.

It manages the tension between these two planks in its platform using devices such as the segmentation of the labor force. A core of relatively stable workers benefits from efforts at industrial cooperation and reskilled jobs. The unemployed, temporary workers at home and workers in foreign countries bear the brunt of "flexibility."

The second program is the conventional social-democratic response to managerial reform. It wants to restrain managerial discretion, turning present jobs and benefits into vested rights. It also proposes to broaden the range of "stakeholders" to whom managers should account: workers, consumers, and local communities as well as legal owners.

This social-democratic program suffers from two great defects. It restrains innovation. Moreover, it takes for granted, and reinforces, an underlying division between insiders and outsiders. Its worker beneficiaries are typically a relatively privileged group holding jobs in the highly skilled and capital-rich parts of the economy.

The third position is the extension of the alternative presented in these pages into a distinct proposal for industrial renewal. Instead of vested rights for the insiders, it wants to enhance the economic and cultural endowment of all workers. It seeks to ensure that everyone—outsiders as well as insiders—will have the means with which to thrive in the midst of instability. Instead of "stakeholding" by multiple constituencies, holding one another ransom, it wants radically to decentralize and democratize access to productive resources and opportunities. The ideas about financial reform mentioned earlier represent a first step in this direction.

The goal is not to regulate the market economy but to democratize it. We cannot, however, hope either to develop or to maintain the institutions of a democratized market economy without drawing upon the capabilities created by community organization and civic engagement. The alternative program of industrial renewal can begin without broader political and social reforms, but it cannot continue without them.

Would-be progressives today lack a program. Typically, their program is the program of their adversaries, with a discount. Abandoning hope in an alternative, they have resigned themselves to the humanization of the inevitable. They want to soften or slow down what they cannot replace or reimagine.

Thus, in the United States some Democrats look backward, nostalgically, to the New Deal, clinging to social entitlements without social participation and organization, while other Democrats look sideways to the Republican agenda, seeking to superimpose a little bit of social concern upon a great deal of market orthodoxy. European social democrats fail to combine their ever weaker redistributive commitments with a productive vision or with an institutional view of how both to democratize the market economy and to deepen political democracy.

In the postcommunist societies, an empty contrast between "shock therapy" and gradual reform reduces national debate to a discussion about different rates of progression along the same trajectory. This abdication sets the stage for the crudest forms of nationalist resentment and populist reaction. In some of the major developing countries of the South, centralized industrial and trade policy in the style of the Asian economies has sometimes been offered as the sole feasible alternative to neoliberal rectitude—one discredited formula against another.

Many countries have been happy to turn their backs on inflationary populism, import-substituting protectionism, and loss-making public production. Few of these countries, however, are ready to welcome the denationalization of industry, the widening of social and economic inequalities, and the submission of national governments to financial fashions as the wave of the future.

Improving the life chances of individuals, sustaining families within organized and therefore capable communities, and encouraging the powers of nonconformist insight and innovation in every field of social experience—these achievements are what count at the end of the day. To care about people, however, we must be experimental about institutions.

The focus of conflict and debate in the world is changing. The old opposition between state and market is dead or dying. It is being replaced by a new rivalry among the alternative institutional forms of representative democracies, market economies, and free civil societies. (The most influential economic heresy of the twentieth century—Keynesianism—shares with the tradition of English political economy a poverty of institutional imagination. We need another heresy, free of that flaw.)

Reforms undertaken in the name of the market economy can start us down more than one road of reinvigorating political, economic, and social freedom. One of these roads turns people into enemies of markets because it turns markets into enemies of people. Another road leads to a society reconciling more decentralized and diversified economies with more intense democracies, and productive innovation with social solidarity.

21

The Other Path: The Economic Answer to Terrorism (1986)

Hernando de Soto

Hernando de Soto (b. Peru, 1941) is a Peruvian economist known for his work on the informal economy. De Soto has served as an economist for the General Agreement on Tariffs and Trade (GATT), as president of the Executive Committee of the Intergovernmental Council of Copper Exporting Countries (CIPEC), as CEO of Universal Engineering Corporation (continental Europe's largest consulting engineering firm), as a principal of the Swiss Bank Corporation Consultant Group, and as a governor of Peru's Central Reserve Bank. De Soto was Peruvian president Alberto Fujimori's personal representative and principal advisor (1990–1992). President Alan Garcia hired de Soto in 2006 to lobby the U.S. Congress for passage of the Peru–United States Free Trade Agreement. De Soto founded Peru's Institute for Liberty and Democracy (ILD) in 1980, considered by many to be one of the world's most influential think tanks. As ILD president, de Soto has been focused on designing and implementing capital formation programs to empower the poor in Africa, Asia, Latin America, Middle East, and former Soviet Nations. Since 2005 he also cochairs, with former United States secretary of state Madeleine Albright, the Commission on Legal Empowerment of the Poor, the first global organization to focus specifically on the link between exclusion, poverty, and law. The commission is independent of government influence, is hosted by the United Nations Development Programme (UNDP), and contributes to the United Nations Millennium Development Goals. This selection is the best summary of de Soto's version of neoliberal economic development theory and its application to the case of the economic empowerment of the Peruvian poor.

NEW PREFACE (2002)

"Boooom!!!" The massive explosion hit at 8:00 P.M. on July 20, 1992, while many of us were still working at the Instituto Libertad y Democracia (ILD) offices in Miraflores, a suburb of Lima. The blast was so powerful that it smashed walls and windows, sending splinters of glass, metal, and furniture shooting through rooms like jet-propelled daggers. It was a car bomb, and the explosion hurled the car's engine across the property, destroying everything in its way until it crashed into the wall of a neighbor's house some one hundred meters to the rear of our building. For miles around, a huge mushrooming cloud could be seen rising above our devastated headquarters.

It was not the first time we had been the target of terror. The Shining Path, which had been terrorizing Peru since 1980, considered the ILD their intellectual nemesis. They had bombed our offices before, shot at our automobiles, and threatened our people. That nagging feeling that there is bound to be a next time saved many lives. Three minutes before the bomb went off, we heard the familiar cracking of the gunfire directed at our building intended to force our security guards to take cover behind the outer walls protecting the ILD so that a group of Shining Path commandos could deliver a much more deadly package—in this case, according to the police investigation, a car containing four hundred kilos of dynamite and ammonium nitrate. The warning shots gave us precious seconds to dive for cover and avoid the deadly debris that soon was hurtling through our offices.

Some, however, were not so lucky. According to the press, three people died in the attack and nineteen were wounded. Among the wounded, Edilberto Mesías, an ILD security guard who had taken a bullet in the stomach, crawled to a nearby hospital and managed to survive. Marco Tulio Ojeda, a policeman assigned to the ILD, heroically rushed to the car to try to tear out the bomb's burning fuse but was seconds too late: the car blew and Marco was immediately killed. By the time the twenty of us who were inside the building got up from the floor, shook off the glass, metal, and dust, and rushed outside to assess the damage, we found a Franciscan priest already administering last rites to some of the victims lying on the sidewalk, innocent passersby who had been killed by the gunfire and explosion.

It was a tragic moment. All of us were stunned by the violence of it and saddened by the innocent lives lost. But nobody was surprised. In fact, some of us were convinced that this attack was another sign that we were actually winning our intellectual war against the Shining Path. The most optimistic among us was Mariano Cornejo, the guru of our think tank, who rushed into the remains of my office fifteen minutes after the explosion. Living just a few blocks away from the ILD, Mariano knew who the target was as soon as he heard the explosion. "What more proof do we need that we have the Shining Path on the run?" he asked me. "They have run out of arguments. They can only make statements with gunpowder. They don't know what to do anymore."

Mariano was referring to the fact that the ILD had openly taken on the Shining Path five years before, when we published *The Other Path* in Peru. As the title indicates, the book was an intellectual challenge to the terrorists. Based on solid fieldwork and hard facts, the book puts forward a much more realistic picture of poverty in Peru and a more effective alternative to remedy underdevelopment and injustice than that proposed by the terrorists.

Why Did the Shining Path Spend So Much of Their Explosives on a Think Tank?

The Shining Path described themselves as a Maoist movement. To Bernard Aronson, the U.S. assistant secretary of state for Latin America, they were "the bloodiest and most murderous guerrilla group ever to operate in the Western hemisphere." Aronson saw Sendero (the Path), as the terrorists were called in Peru, as the Latin American version of the Cambodian Khmer Rouge. "Latin America has seen violence and terror," he told the U.S. Congress, "but none like Sendero's . . . and make no mistake, if Sendero were to take power, you would see this century's third genocide." Peru would enter history, in other words, alongside Nazi Germany and Pol Pot's Cambodia.

Since it began operating in 1980, Sendero had mobilized some eighty thousand subversives in a war that killed over twenty-five thousand people. This made the terrorist group, according to Carlos Tapia, one of Peru's principal experts on violence, the nation's most important political party. It was certainly the most destructive, paralyzing the Peruvian judicial system by threatening judges and freeing prisoners from jails; displacing over 2 million Peruvians from their homes and sending a million more fleeing into voluntary exile; terrorizing entire villages and cities where they executed, tortured, and scalped people alive in public; and taking control of a substantial part of Peru's coca-growing regions.

As early as 1984, I became convinced that the Shining Path would never be eliminated as a political option without first being defeated in the world of ideas. Like many, 1 felt that Sendero's major strength stemmed from its intellectual appeal to those excluded by the system and its ability to generate a political cause for natural leaders, whether in universities or shantytowns. Sendero's chief, Abimael Guzman, was a former philosophy professor at the University of Huamanga in the south-central Andes of Peru. His strategy was no mystery: he wanted to bully the intellectual opposition into silence, capture the people's imagination, and create a revolutionary argument "secure from all refutation," as the French Marxist thinker Georges Sorel (1847-1922) would have said.

Many Peruvian intellectuals spoke and wrote against violence in general and participated in candle-carrying marches calling for peace, in general. Few, however, dared attack Sendero publicly by name. In fact, the name "Sendero" itself inspired such fear that it was uttered only in a whisper. This expansive wave of terror allowed Guzman to appear invincible, an alpha male that few intellectuals were prepared to mess with. By terrorizing his critics into silence, the murderous professor had more than enough rhetorical space to advance his "revolutionary message" within Peruvian society.

To prove to my compatriots that there was nothing magical or superior in Sendero's proposal for a new society, I titled my book *El Otro Sendero*, The Other Path. Though I had written a straightforward book about development and not terrorism, I organized the text to counter the Shining Path's well-worn fare against liberal democracy and capitalism, dealing with their arguments one by one, starting with the assumption—obviously false to anyone who bothered to walk through the streets of Lima—that poor Peruvians were a social class naturally disposed against markets and democracy.

When *The Other Path* was published in Latin America in 1987, its success went way beyond our wildest dreams. Already the best-selling book ever in Peru, it quickly became a number one bestseller throughout Latin America. In an unusual effort to make the book's findings and arguments accessible to those with little time or inclination to read any book, the editors of Peru's most popular tabloid newspaper, *Ojo*, summarized *The Other Path* in a sixteen-page special supplement and distributed it nationwide. Newspapers and magazines throughout the country ran stories about the book; many of its principal arguments were broadcast in radio jingles or in TV spots and sketches, and it was even featured in comic strips. The book was also discussed in public squares in shantytowns from northern to southern Peru. In this way the book's message reached deep into the ranks of the people excluded from the mainstream.

The message of *The Other Path* traveled so well that Guzman continually attacked the book in his essays and speeches. Sendero's newspaper, *El Diario*, warned that *The Other Path* was distancing young people from terrorist activities and undercutting recruitment. Guzman himself wrote, "It is clear that the objective of *The Other Path* is to deceive and mislead the masses. . . . It directly targets young people, who are the driving force of society. . . . It leads the young away from the people's war."

That night, after the bomb attack, Mariano Cornejo was convinced that the ILD had totally stripped away Sendero's intellectual leadership. By 1992, *The Other Path* had been distributed and discussed so extensively in Peru that it reached an audience exceeding that of Guzman and his supporters literally by millions. It demonstrated so clearly that Sendero's proposals did not respond to the needs of the poor that dozens of poor people's organizations grouping hundreds of thousands of persons openly announced in newspaper advertisements that they had committed themselves to following the other path. Thus Guzman, who had generally not bothered to attack researchers and intellectuals who disagreed with him, decided to make the ILD the principal civilian target of his violence. Surely that alone sent a message to all of Peru that even Guzman knew his ideas were bankrupt. That night Mariano and I agreed that Guzman's image had gradually evolved from a defender of the poor to a bloodthirsty, gun-toting reactionary who murdered people who proposed ideas more effective than his own.

The Power of Good Class Analysis

[*The Other Path*] contains facts, numbers, and historically based analyses that shatter all the hypotheses on which radical antimarket and antidemocracy thinkers like Guzman base their class diagnosis. In their place, *The Other Path* makes the following major points

1. Most Peruvians are not proletarians (i.e., blue-collar workers) ready to rise against business. They are emerging entrepreneurs working outside the legal system. Legally employed proletarians make up less than 4.8 percent of the Peruvian population.
2. The real revolutionary class in Peru is made up of the micro, small, and medium-sized entrepreneurs who during the last half of the twentieth century began migrating from rural areas to towns and cities to work in the fragmented market economies of the informal or "extralegal" sector.
3. These extralegal entrepreneurs are hardly a small and marginal sector of Peruvian society. Together with their extended families, they are the

majority—around 60–80 percent of the nation's population. They construct seven out of every ten buildings; they have built and they own 278 out of Lima's 331 markets; they operate 56 percent of all businesses of the nation; they retail over 60 percent of all foodstuffs; and they operate 86 percent of all the buses. For some forty years, these people have been trying to convert themselves into an entrepreneurial class resembling more the self-reliant American settlers of the eighteenth and nineteenth centuries than the cowed proletarians who lived in Abimael Guzman's blinkered imagination. Peru's extralegal entrepreneurs are not timid shoeshine boys who run for cover when they see the police. They are forceful pioneers.

4. These entrepreneurs want to live under the rule of law. The proof: even though they are forced to operate outside the Peruvian legal system, they have made their own rules, which in [*The Other Path*] I call "extralegal law." For them, the market economy and capital are not "bourgeois prejudices" or "culturally alienating concepts" but goals that they and their informal organizations strive to reach. I describe how their spontaneously created rules do not reflect a feudal, tribal, or communist system, but rather a market economy.

5. Contrary to the arguments of Sendero, the Communist Manifesto, and today's most violent critics of the market, most Peruvians do not lack property. On the contrary, they own assets with a replacement value in excess of US$80 billion—fourteen times greater than the value of foreign direct investment in Peru. Collectively, and unconsciously, Peru's entrepreneurial majority has begun a market and social revolution against economic poverty and legal oppression many times more significant and more powerful than the program that the Shining Path wanted to ram down the throats of Peruvians at gunpoint.

6. The principal enemy of these entrepreneurs is the existing legal system, which excludes them. Based on real case histories and simulations, [*The Other Path*] demonstrates that in Peru, for example, it takes a new entrepreneur thirteen years to overcome the legal and administrative hurdles required to build a retail market for food that would help take vendors off the street; twenty-one years to obtain authorization to construct a legally titled building on wasteland; twenty-six months to get authorization to operate a new bus route, and nearly a year, working six hours a day, to gain the legal license to operate a sewing machine for commercial purposes.

7. In the face of such obstacles, new entrepreneurs hold their assets outside the law and therefore do not have access to the facilitative devices that a formal legal system should provide to help them organize and leverage resources. Because they have no secure property rights and cannot issue shares, they cannot capture investment. Because they have no patents or royalties, they cannot encourage or protect innovations. Because they do not have access to contracts and justice organized on a wide scale, they cannot develop long-term projects. Because they cannot legally burden their assets, they are unable to use their homes and businesses

to guarantee credit. Now stop and ask yourself: if European and American businessmen did not have access to the limited liability systems and insurance policies that the law allows, how many risks would they run? How much capital would they accumulate without legally created paper that can represent value? How many resources would they be able to pool without legally recognized business organizations that can issue shares? How often would Europeans or Americans choose bankruptcy and try to start all over again if the law did not allow them to convert their debts into shares?

8. There *is* class warfare in Peru, to be sure. But the main line bisecting Peruvian society today is not a horizontal one dividing entrepreneurs from workers, where those above make themselves rich with the surplus value from the poorly paid work of those below. For the moment, the principal dividing line is a vertical frontier, to the right of which are politicians, bureaucrats, and businessmen who profit and live off the government's favor and to the left of which are legal and extralegal producers who are excluded from favor.

9. Because the poor cannot hold assets or trade within the law, they cannot be part of the global economy either. How can you fill in a bill of lading if you don't have a legal address or an officially recognized business? How can you move an asset in the international market place if it is not fixed in a formal property system? Obviously you cannot, and that is why the excluded will not benefit very much from globalization. Moreover, can you understand what the poor feel when a foreign investor comes into their country with clear legal property rights that can be enforced both nationally and internationally, while they have none? Do you think they will sympathize with globalization, or do you think they will feel it is exclusive and unfair?

10. The economic system oppressing most Peruvians is not democratic capitalism but mercantilism. *The Other Path* demonstrates that democratic capitalism, as it is known in the West today, has not really been tried in Peru—or, for that matter, in most places outside the West. Mercantilism can be defined as the supply and demand for monopoly rights by means of laws, regulations, subsidies, taxes, and licenses. The fallout of these privileges creates a wall of legal barriers that exclude the poor. Mercantilism is a politicized and bureaucratized environment dominated by privileged redistributive combines that prevailed in Europe before and during the Industrial Revolution before the rise of democratic capitalism. Strongly opposed by the great eighteenth-century economist Adam Smith and all the classical economists who followed him, and buried by the triumph of capitalism in the West, mercantilism nevertheless continues to be the predominant economic system in twenty-first-century Peru. The nation's mercantilist elites find it culturally impossible to believe or understand that today's impoverished masses could become the most important source of prosperity for Peru.

11. In its own way, Sendero also holds a mercantilist viewpoint, since it believes that prosperity can only be brought about from above, through

government elites. Like eighteenth-century European mercantilists, Sendero has little faith in ordinary people or individual responsibility. No less condescending than the traditional elites they claim to despise, the terrorists believe that, left to their own devices, the poor would produce only more poverty, hunger, disease, and death.

12. The poor are voting against the mercantilist system with their feet. In Peru, for example, they are either walking into the fragmented and incipient market economies of the extralegal sector or migrating in millions to capitalist countries.

13. If its legal system is reengineered to provide everyone the tools for entrepreneurship, Peru will eventually thrive. If Peruvians do not find a way of incorporating the excluded into an open economy, the excluded will be vulnerable to being railroaded into extreme economic alternatives, especially during a recession or war, as in Russia in 1917 and around the world after World War II. Alternatively, mercantilism and its privileges can continue, at least for a while, but only at the cost of prolonged repression and unhappy citizens.

The Other Path illustrates how the poor have become a new class of entrepreneurs and why and how they organize themselves outside the law. It makes the case that social and political peace will not be possible until all of those who know that they are excluded feel they have a fair chance to achieve the standards of the West. *The Other Path* sets the scene for reform. It was also a landmark in the ILD's own development from a traditional "think tank" to the "think and *acting*" organization that we became in the 1990s, first in Peru then worldwide.

Beating the Terrorists Requires Listening to the Excluded

The publicity around *The Other Path*, along with press reports on ILD fieldwork, created a major stir in Peru. We had pointed out with facts and figures that the millions of people whom elite Peruvians viewed as unruly squatters and urban pests were actually enterprising citizens who were carrying the nation's economy on their backs. It was a revelation that turned the ILD into a major player in Peruvian politics. Felipe Ortiz de Zevallos, one of Peru's top pundits and pollsters, wrote in the *Wall Street Journal* in 1990 about the "enormous influence" of the ILD in Peru. Local polls indicated that ILD influence in the nation was surpassed only by the president, the armed forces, and the Catholic Church. Between 1984 and 1995, even president of Peru called on the ILD to help change the country.

This unusual partnership between an independent research organization and Peru's heads of state began in 1984, when President Fernando Belaúnde Terry invited me to his offices and told me that the ILD's work had "gotten under the nation's skin" (*agarró carne*) and asked what the next steps should be. A reply was urgent, he noted, because Sendero continued to grow.

I explained to the president that if the majority of Peruvians worked outside the law—in the extralegal sector—the inescapable conclusion was that the nation's people viewed the law, and the government that was trying to enforce it, as hostile to their interests. If he wanted Peruvians to avoid the temptations of the terrorists, he would have to show the people that working within the law was in their interest. ILD research had already demonstrated that due to bad law, the poor were facing huge entry and operational costs and were missing some of the crucial institutions needed to create prosperity. The president's primary concern should be to reform the legal system.

That would be no small task. By our count, the Peruvian central government had issued more than 700,000 laws and regulations since 1947. The question was, how does one find out which laws are bad and don't work and which have to be modified? Reading laws as they are written gives no clue to how they will work in practice. The Peruvian government had reviewed the legal texts many times, using the most prestigious foreign consulting firms, but nonetheless was unable to make it easier for the poor to enter the legal system.

In the face of this labyrinth of Peruvian norms, we needed to find some criteria for where to cut and where to build. The only people who could provide us with such criteria for reform were the excluded themselves. We were like the dentist who cannot begin without asking the patient which tooth hurts. The poor not only knew where the problems were, but they also knew what institutions and services were missing—the very ones the local communities and terrorists were busily trying to provide by default. For too long, the Peruvian government had been acting on the basis of outdated theories and prejudices and with little access to hard facts. We needed to know what was really going on in our streets and fields if we were to discover how to put the official law in line with how people actually lived and worked. Arid to find that out, we had to enable government to do what few governments in history have ever done: listen carefully to the excluded.

Over the next decade, until 1995, the ILD designed rules, procedures, and organizations to help the government listen to its own people. We not only found out where some of the major bottlenecks in the system were located, but we also learned to devise solutions, build institutions, and draft, promote, and then implement major legislation and reform projects. During that period, the ILD initiated some four hundred major laws and regulations and managed one of the world's largest property-creation projects.

One of the first instruments the ILD created for government to use in listening to people was the "Prepublication Legislative Decree" obliging the executive branch to publish in draft form any law and regulation that it wanted to enact (including an estimate of the costs and benefits of the proposed norm for Peruvian society). Citizens and the press would now be in a position to scrutinize the government's intentions and provide it with feedback to ensure that any new norm was suitable for ordinary citizens.

Another measure was to campaign for and finally create Peru's first "ombudsman" to represent the interests of citizens, first in the attorney general's office in 1986 and then as an independent office created by the new Constitution in 1993. Under contract with the attorney general's office, we set up special offices and, with the help of the press, put out a call for grievances. During the first month, we received complaints from 153 civic organizations representing some 300,000 individuals. The most notable result was that more than half of the grievances were about difficulties people had gaining legal title to real estate—in the form of houses, offices, factories, or agricultural land—and the obstacles they faced when trying to initiate and operate their businesses. Over the years, the other listening and feedback mechanisms that we set up for government continued to lead us to the conclusion that the primary concern of the poor was how to gain legal access to property, either in the form of real estate or business, or how to leverage it.

Interestingly, Sendero had reached that same conclusion. In its 1986 war plan, "Rematar el gran salto con sello de oro," Sendero had begun titling land, homes, and businesses throughout Peru to win the favor of poor people. They were simply following what Mao Zedong did in the 1940s in China and what Ho Chi Minh did in Vietnam in the 1960s. In the rural areas, they were awarding and enforcing property rights in Huánuco, Huallaga, and the Sierra de la Libertad. In cities like Lima, they were organizing squatting and property titling in shantytowns like Raucana, Vitarte, and Huaycán. Further research told us that one of the primary functions of terrorists in the Third World—what buys them acceptance—is protecting the possessions of the poor, which are typically outside the law. In other words, if government does not protect the assets of the poor, it surrenders this function to the terrorists, who then can use it to win the allegiance of the excluded.

Clearly, one way to put terrorists out of business is for the government to assume its modern role as the enforcer of property rights. This line of reasoning allowed us to lobby government to accept our proposal for bringing the poor into the legal system. What originally moved us, however, was not a military objective but our conviction that the property system was crucial to development. As we listened to the poor and analyzed what they were missing, my ILD colleagues and I began to realize that property is more than just ownership; it is the hidden architecture that organizes the market economy in every Western nation. Without a legal property system, efforts to create a sustainable market economy are doomed to fail, as I have argued at length in my new book, *The Mystery of Capital: Why Capitalism Triumphs in the West and Fails Everywhere Else.*

The connection between the formal property system and the creation of wealth is something that the rich nations of the West take for granted. But this essential connection became clear to us only when we realized that in spite of owning houses and businesses, most Peruvians could not generate wealth because their assets were held outside the legal property system. And thus in numerous articles and pamphlets, posters and TV spots, the ILD argued that without property institutions and organizations, a modern market economy cannot work. Why? Because ownership cannot be certain, addresses cannot he systematically verified, assets cannot be described according to standard business practices, people cannot be made to pay their debts, authors of fraud and losses cannot be easily identified. As a result, buildings and land cannot be used to guarantee credit or contracts. Ownership of businesses cannot be divided and represented in shares that investors can buy. Without property law, capital itself is impossible to create because the instruments that store and transfer value, such as shares of corporate stock, patent rights, promissory notes, bills of exchange, and bonds, are all determined by the architecture of legal relationships with which a property system is built.

Gaining this insight not from books but by talking to the poor and observing how they lived, we were able to design and implement a legal property system around the objective interests of the poor themselves. The legal devices we created worked because we made sure that they were compatible with the principles that the poor already used in the extralegal economy. More importantly, by relying on the poor for rule making and support, the Peruvian government could now push for reform, but not in the name of a foreign ideology, philosophers the people had never heard of, or the dictates of an international financial institution. They could institute major reforms in the name of the nation's poor. This allowed us to convert (at least for a while) the transition to capitalism and liberal democracy into what it should always be—a truly humanist cause, a genuine war against exclusion, rooted in the best interests of the nation. This provided the Peruvian head of state with a formidable argument: "The majority of the nation's population is cut off from the official market economy and access to capital as starkly as apartheid once separated white and black South Africans and we are going to correct that."

By 1990, after six years of listening to the poor, the ILD was actually in a position to help them. We put into place all the legislation and mechanisms required to bring into the law most extralegal real estate and businesses. On the real estate side, we brought down the administrative time needed to record the property of the poor from more than a dozen years to one month, and cut the costs by 99 percent. By 1995, such reforms had brought into the legal system some 300,000 owners whose property on average at least doubled in value. Twenty-five credit institutions began giving loans to these now legal owners. By 2000, some 1.9 million buildings on urban land had entered the legal system, about 75 percent of the extralegal market.

On the business side, we cut the cost of entering business from some three hundred days down to one. We also put registration offices in the right places and made the government bureaucracy more user-friendly for small entrepreneurs. By 1994, over 270,000 formerly extralegal entrepreneurs had entered the legal economy, creating over half a million new jobs and increasing tax revenues by US$1.2 billion.

In 1991, in Peru's northern jungle areas, the ILD began organizing the legal recognition of existing coca farmers. In gratitude for being allowed to enter the legal system and have the right to gain legal title to their assets, the farmers provided the Peruvian government with most of the information and maps required to flush out terrorists, as well as drug traffickers, from the area. As the farmers switched to legal crops, Peru's participation in the international cocaine market began gradually to descend from 60 percent to 25 percent.

These reforms, along with change in the nation's macroeconomic policies, also initiated by the ILD even before President Fujimori's inauguration in 1990, gave Peru very high growth rates—including the world's highest (12 percent) in 1994.

We also tried to make the Peruvian government more accountable to the people and, although laws drafted by the ILD for access to public information did not pass, authorities incorporated ILD principles into the 1993 Constitution, the rules governing the consumer protection agency, the Civil Procedural Code, and the law for citizen participation.

To deal with queues, paperwork, and all the excessive bureaucratic procedures that waste everyone's time in developing countries like Peru, we presented a legislative proposal for "administrative simplification" that was debated in public hearings throughout the country and was unanimously approved in Congress by all political parties. To make it as convenient as possible for people to file their complaints about excessive bureaucracy, we put bright yellow boxes in the ILD headquarters, in several government offices, and in all the radio, television, and newspaper outlets. When an astonishing or outrageous story came their way, the media were encouraged to take up the cause, creating the kind of public pressure that was impossible for politicians to ignore.

The complaints were dealt with in a publicly televised tribunal every two weeks, on Saturday morning. Managed by the ILD and presided over by the president of the republic, these "Administrative Simplification Tribunals" racked up ratings that would have been the envy of any entertainment series; Peruvians sat in front of their TV sets amazed to see hundreds of the kinds of knots that were strangling their lives untied. The time previously required to fulfill hundreds of different kinds of official procedures, including obtaining a passport, applying to university, and getting a marriage license, was cut across the board at least seventy-five percent. To get a marriage license, which used to take 720 hours of bureaucratic hassles, was reduced to 120 hours—thus helping women secure their rights as marriage partners. The same law that created these procedures also contained the mechanisms that allowed government to carry out most of the structural adjustment reforms required to insert Peru into the global economy.

The ILD worked to make the administration of justice more accessible to the poor by proposing various low-cost arbitration procedures to help parties sort out their conflicts in a quick, inexpensive, and fair way out of court. The ILD also modified the Penal Procedure Code to release untried prisoners who had already served jail terms that were longer than those set by law for the crimes they had allegedly committed. In 1990–1991, the first year of the program, four thousand prisoners were released—30 percent of the prisoners behind bars without trial—proving to the Peruvian population that government was serious about reform.

All in all, these and hundreds of other reforms helped put the Peruvian government in better standing with its citizens. To help draft pertinent legislation and regulation, the ILD continually incorporated extralegal customary principles that common people understood, respected, and obeyed. The ILD held hundreds of public hearings, involving thousands of people representing informal organizations throughout the country, so that each law would be grounded in reality and Peruvians would understand that the government was taking them seriously.

Our quick success connecting the concerns of grassroots Peruvians with legal reform was confirmed by no less an authority on the people than Sendero chief Guzman. "The ILD is a source of legislation," he wrote in 1991. "They make laws. They themselves draft laws and have them enacted." Competition was not what the Sendero leader was looking for, so he redoubled his efforts to knock us out of the game by taking shots at my car, trying to kill me at home, and setting off bombs on our office doorstep.

That Sendero was targeting the ILD for using the legal system to give the poorest of the poor a stake in the political and economic life of Peru was a curious way to win the hearts and minds of Peruvians, most of whom, after all, were poor. My colleague Mariano Cornejo was right. Guzman had run out of arguments; our work had helped undermine the appeal of terrorism among Sendero's prime constituency—the excluded. Shortly after the July 1992 bombing of our headquarters, Abimael Guzman was arrested as a result of the outstanding work of the Peruvian police, especially Colonel Benedicto Jimenez Bacca, who had been tracking Guzman for years. Thanks to this major police coup, Sendero's cell-based organization was quickly dismantled and, by 1993, most of the hit squads were identified and captured, including the seventeen-person cell that had been trying to assassinate us. This was the last of many successful battles waged against Sendero by millions of Peruvians. Sendero was defeated in the Andean countryside by farmer organizations led by brave people like Hugo Huillca, in the coca-growing regions by heroic peasant leaders like Walter Tocas, and by enlightened military leaders like General Alberto Arciniega, who brought the government closer to the farmers. In the cities, urban leaders like Maria Elena Moyano and Michel Azcueta, from Villa El Salvador, organized resistance against their incursions.

There were many heroes in Peru's war against terrorism, both inside and outside of government. That history remains to be written. What is certain is that Sendero lost because the excluded rejected terrorism. The goal of the excluded was to improve their lives, and to this end they became convinced that there was a better path than the one offered by terrorists.

Unhappily for us, Sendero's bombs were replaced by political minefields. The majority of our reforms had been initiated during the last years of Alan Garcia's government (1985–1990) and with his support. Most of the actual reform programs, however, were fully implemented under the first government (1990–1995) of Alberto Fujimori, who publicly stated that his reason for entering politics in the first place was that he had discovered his constituency in *The Other Path*. In fact, our reforms pretty much set the scene for Fujimori's role as a leader during that period. As Peru's premier historian, Pablo Macera, put it: "Fujimori was unaware [when he became president in 1990] that he was going to be the vehicle of a dynamic renovation project which had the ILD at one extreme and Abimael Guzman at the other."[1]

While President Fujimori publicly applauded the successes that the ILD brought to his government, in private he was annoyed by our high public opinion ratings for designing and implementing institutional reforms. Initially, the president seemed happy that we were in charge of explaining the reforms to the public because he was not yet comfortable as a political communicator. In retrospect, publicly taking the leadership of the projects was a political mistake on my part because it gave Fujimori's enemies the opportunity to needle him incessantly for nearly two years about the rumor that the ILD was actually running Peru. As flattering as such publicity might have been, it was clear that we, an independent think tank, would not be allowed to outshine the president for long. Our days as a government partner were numbered. Finally, in 1992, I resigned as his principal adviser and personal representative, and in 1996, the ILD ceased running government projects.

The Lessons from Peru's Successful War Against Terrorism

The ILD did not set out to take on the terrorists. Our goal was to figure out ways of bringing the majority of Peruvians into a legal system that had traditionally shut them out and thus stunted the nation's economic development. We never had any intention of joining the war. Like the historian Arnold Toynbee, I firmly believe that war is not only tragic but a total waste of human energy. But if you happen to be committed to development and helping the poor, and in time of war you are caught in crossfire, you had better try to understand what is happening and why. Our participation taught us much about the politics of exclusion and development in today's circumstances.

What I have come to understand is that today, a massive social and economic revolution is taking place in the developing world that rivals the Industrial Revolution in the West that gave rise to market capitalism. In the last forty years, some 4 billion people, who had been living in the hinterlands of developing countries and former Soviet nations, have abandoned their traditional way of life. They are moving away from small, isolated communities toward a larger and more global division of labor in the expanding markets that both Adam Smith and Karl Marx had seen emerging in the West two hundred years ago and that are now struggling to emerge outside the West.

These people clustering around big towns and migrating by the hundreds of millions to larger cities are the newest players in the global scene. Over the past four decades, for example, the population of Peru's capital city of Lima has increased sixfold; Port-au-Prince, Haiti's capital, has increased at least fifteen times during the same period; the population of Ecuador's Guayaquil has also increased eleven times. The underground economies in Russia and the Ukraine now account for 50 percent of GDP; the black market in Georgia generates a whopping 62 percent. The International Labor Organization reports that since 1990, 85 percent of all new jobs in Latin America and the Caribbean have been created in the extralegal sector. In Zambia, only 10 percent of the workforce is legally employed. From Peru to the Philippines, these extralegal workers and entrepreneurs are improving their lives. They now read, travel, and have radios and televisions. As a result, they know that the westernized elites of their nations live well, and they too aspire to that good life.

The economic potential is clearly there. Although the new migrants of the developing and postcommunist world live in shantytowns and are horribly poor by Western standards, they are not without assets. The ILD's work over the past twenty years has revealed the extraordinary entrepreneurial potential of the people of the Third World. According to our estimates, over the last forty years, these people have created more than US$10 trillion of wealth, a value ninety times greater than all bilateral foreign aid and forty times larger than international development loans received by undeveloped nations, and a value larger than the size of the world's twenty largest stock markets.[2]

The difference between today's industrial revolution and that which began in the West over two hundred years ago is that this new revolution is roaring ahead much faster and transforming the lives of many more people. Britain supported just 8 million people when it began its 250-year progression from the farm to the laptop computer. Indonesia is making that same journey in only four decades—with a population of more than 200 million. Is it any wonder that Indonesia's institutions have been slow to adapt? But adapt they must. A tide of humanity has moved from isolated communities and households to participate in ever widening circles of economic and intellectual exchange. It is this tide that has transformed Jakarta, Mexico City, São Paolo, Nairobi, Bombay, Shanghai, and Manila into megacities of 10, 20, 30 million and overwhelmed their political and legal institutions.

Instead of helping them, the law excludes them. It is this legal lag that produces a pervading sense of alienation—of being a class apart. And it is this extreme class differentiation that gives rise to terrorists who will always be around to champion the cause of the excluded. In Peru, the intellectual and political leaders of Sendero were willing to resort to terror to take power because they perceived that a majority of Peruvians were totally unhappy with the status quo. Sendero felt that the strength of this sentiment could be harnessed and channeled to subvert the existing political and economic systems.

Some have argued that the appearance of small enclaves of prosperous economic sectors in the midst of large undeveloped or informal sectors marks the dawn of an uneven but nevertheless inevitable and easy transition to capitalist systems. I do not buy this. The existence of prosperous enclaves in a sea of poverty conceals an abysmal retardation in many nations' capacities to create channels of communication with these excluded and to make available the underpinnings of the rule of law by providing formal property rights to the majority of its citizens. This becomes an invitation for political minorities to form terrorist movements with a view to capturing these large constituencies.

What we did in Peru, by making important parts of the rule of law accessible for all people, was deprive Sendero, to a great extent, of the isolated nooks and crannies it needed to hide in and to operate from. We were able to find out just in the nick of time that people don't rebel because they are poor but because they are excluded from the system. To give people a stake in the economy, to prove to them that government is in the business of including them in formal society, is to put the terrorists out of business.

Ten years have now passed since Sendero's political defeat and five years since the ILD stopped working for the Peruvian government. There was a war and, as patriotic Peruvians, we decided that it was an opportunity to start important reforms. Still based in Lima, we are now working in other developing countries to bring the excluded into the legal economy on a purely technical basis. We work as an independent nongovernmental organization that assists governments in discovering and sizing up their extralegal economies. Once that research is completed, we help the country pull together all the dispersed extralegal systems that function outside the legal economy under one rule of law in one consistent network of legal devices. We try to create legal systems where the assets of all citizens can be securely held and moved to their best possible use. Our general recipes are summarized in figures 21.1 and 21.2 (PROFORM and BUSFORM), located at the end of this chapter.

Since I stopped working for Peru, I am no longer involved in the politics of reform. However, using hindsight, I would like to take the opportunity of writing this preface for the new edition of *The Other Path* to draw some useful conclusions.

In spite of the lives lost and the terrible suffering, it is morally correct to get involved in reforming your nation's institutions when terror strikes. For some recurring historical reason, possibilities for change are frequently initiated by a crisis, many times by violence. Rudolph von Jhering, the great nineteenth-century German jurist, argued that the rule of law is not a preset order—it arises from conflict and as the legal system responds to circumstances. If you are committed to economic development in your country, should terror suddenly erupt, you cannot just stand on the sidelines claiming that you are an economist or a lawyer or businessman without any expertise in political violence. You have an obligation to use your professional training to try to understand the economic and legal reasons why poor people take up arms and then identify ways of using that bitterness and anger against the status quo to create an efficient legal system under which everyone can prosper.

It would be wonderful if economic development could always be initiated in peacetime when an enlightened leader decided it was time to boost all his people to a superior standard of living. And if it doesn't, you need to channel the desire for change in the right direction; you need to use the despair and suffering to build hope, and you need to learn how to divert the concerns that breed terror to creating peace and wealth. You need to get involved. Otherwise, how can you live with yourself?

I am convinced that we received overwhelming support from the poor in our reforms because our actions were geared not to preserving the status quo but to changing it. Make no mistake: the poor don't like the present. What they want is change, and they want it badly.

You can initiate institutional reforms only if they are championed by the head of state. And the reform process will continue only if the head of state sticks with the program. In developing and ex-communist countries, only the head of state and his immediate entourage can command the attention and garner the overwhelming political support required to wipe out the willful inertia of the status quo. Elites and bureaucracies are initially inclined to resist even small changes. Any decision as far-reaching as creating a legal property system, which will include and emancipate the poor, is essentially political and should be put in the hands of the head of state right from the start.

Keeping the head of state with the program is a major challenge for any reformer, as we found out in Peru, where the enemies of the reforms sought to dampen the president's commitment to change by continually labeling us as potential political rivals. It was a mistake for us as a think tank to get into the political front lines of the reforms. When Presidents Garcia and Fujimori called, I should have found ways to make sure the limelight was always on the president. Or perhaps I should have accepted Fujimori's proposal to become his first prime minister and build within the government an elite team to lead the reforms. My initial belief that an independent think tank could carry out the reforms on its own, without a political commitment to the government, was sheer illusion. It is the head of state himself, and the politicians he trusts, who should implement the reform process to make sure that those who take the political risks get the credit. That is why the ILD has no problems in working abroad, where we operate as hired technocrats, foreigners without any political involvement.

The legal reform process required to bring the extralegal entrepreneurs into one official legal framework is essentially a cultural exercise: adapting Western market and corporate law to the vibrant cultures and customs of the new entrepreneurs of the developing and former Soviet countries.

What about the famous "clash of cultures" according to which many people in developing nations just don't have cultural traits that would allow them to succeed? Arguments about the cultural reasons for economic success operate a bit like the tourist industry: they concentrate on the differences between people and totally miss what they have in common. Granted, it is amusing to read that Americans will never get along with Chinese and Koreans because Asians have been eating dogs for the last five thousand years—the pets of Charlie Brown and Dennis the Menace. The Japanese continue to enjoy eating "Free Willy" the whale, while the French insist on eating horses. And Tiger Woods keeps winning by eating his Wheaties.

Those who are serious about solving the world's conflicts will find it more useful to focus on real-life political achievements in bringing cultures together efficiently: the accession procedures in the European Union, for example. From World War I to the end of World War II, Europe had no shortage of "cultural gurus" writing that Europeans would never find peace. People who cultivated grapes and drank wine could never get along with those who preferred beer. Such cultural differences, the argument went, doomed the Christian nations of Europe to eternal warfare. Notice the echo in the equally absurd claims of various authors today claiming that Islam is fated to battle the "infidel" West. These make amusing bedside reading, but surely more interesting and relevant are the stories of how European legal craftsmen—set in motion by political leaders such as Robert Schumann of France, Alcide DeGasperi of Italy, and Konrad Adenauer of Germany—used the law to reorganize isolated pieces of European culture until they were all able to fit comfortably together.

Rather than succumb to this pessimistic culturalist literature and repeat absurd claims, I prefer to point to real evidence regarding the work of people like Jean Monnet, the father of European integration, who hunkered down to examine under the microscope the legal details of different European laws and institutions. And what did they find under the microscope?

That in spite of their differences, Europeans had much in common. By looking at culture through the legal prism, the Europeans found ways to build bridges between different cultures. As a result, the very nations that fewer than sixty years ago broke the record for wartime carnage have come together in a European Union that shares a parliament, market, and common currency. *E pluribus unum*—in spite of the different cultures.

The only way you can deal with culture when you are in politics, without being railroaded in a specific direction by unconscious prejudices, is to deconstruct the large inimical concepts that come from examining different cultures into legal categories where the hooks and loops that allow different cultures to hang together can be found. When it comes to culture, the devil is in the details, and you can only catch him by the tail with legal tweezers.

The study of cultures need not be a breeding ground for creating myths or stimulating conflict. That only helps terrorism. If you want to find out how cultures can be brought together, read the documents leading to the formation of any international organization, the European Union, or the evolving law of the United States, or read figures 21.1 and 21.2, or give the ILD a call.

You cannot sell expanded markets and capitalism to the poor outside the West using Western paradigms. It is no use telling people in Haiti or Ghana how General Electric transformed itself from a successful American company with $25 billion in sales in 1980 to an almost $200 billion international conglomerate twenty years later. You have to represent progress to people using case histories that come from their own social environment. That is what *The Other Path* tries to do: it organizes in descriptive form and puts into numbers a reality so recognizable to Third Worlders that most of them can understand what it is that they are doing collectively and what their real options are to survive and achieve prosperity in the context of a market economy formally governed by the rule of law.

The final and most important lesson I learned is that the excluded hold the key to victory. They are the overwhelming majority, and it is they who are looking for change most fervently. Few people in the developing world are unaware of how well their counterparts live in the market democracies of the West. If governments create the legal property tools that they require for their enterprises to prosper, they will become part of the legal expanded market. If governments do not take them seriously as economic agents, if governments see them only as a nuisance or passive recipients of charity, the resentment among the poor against the status quo will only increase. Enter the terrorists, eager to exploit this hostility against the state, encouraging the poor to focus on their exclusion rather than on their aspirations to resemble the affluent citizens of the market democracies of the West.

The poor want only what everyone reading this book wants: a secure, prosperous life for themselves and their children. *The Other Path* is the story of how the poor in one country are spontaneously creating a market society. They are on the right track. Do we help them create the legal framework to achieve that goal by themselves or do we ignore their economic aspirations and, by default, open an opportunity for terrorism?

Hernando de Soto
Lima, Peru
May 2002

NOTES

1. Pablo Macera as quoted by Dennis Falvy "Pensamiento Macera," *La Republica*, July 2000.

2. Hernando de Soto, *The Mystery of Capital: Why Capitalism Triumphs in the West and Fails Everywhere Else* (New York: Basic, 2000), esp. chaps. 2–4.

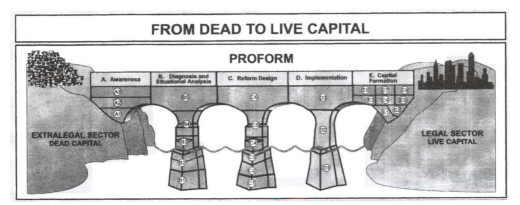

Figure 21.1

A. AWARENESS

Raising awareness about:

A.1 The importance of property law in capitalism

A.2 The stake of the poor in capitalism

A.3 The role of leadership in each country

B. DIAGNOSIS AND SITUATIONAL ANALYSIS

B.1 Identify, locate and classify extralegal assets (dead capital).

- Develop local recruitment specifications to penetrate extralegal sector.
- Locate economic sectors and geographic areas where extralegal activities are most prevalent.
- Identify the ways in which property rights are held and exercised by the different informal settlements and areas.
- Determine causes for the accumulation of extralegal assets so as to develop workable typologies.

B.2 Quantify the actual and potential value of extra legal assets (dead capital).

- Develop appropriate methodologies to estimate the value of extralegal assets using existing information and data gathered in the field.
- Customize criteria to gather and process information and to confirm results.
- Establish the importance of the value of extra legal assets.

B.3 Analyze the interaction of the extralegal sector with the rest of society.

- Research the relevant links between government and extralegal assets.
- Research the relevant links between legal businesses and extralegal assets.

- Identify processes where government has already successfully dealt with extralegal assets.

B.4 Identify the extralegal norms that govern extralegal property.

- Detect and decode the extralegal norms that define the manner in which property rights are held and exercised by the different extralegal communities in the country.
- Identify points where the extralegal norms, informal customs and practices conflict or coincide with the law.

B.5 Identify the principal institutional obstacles to transform informally held assets into more productive formal property and determine the costs of extra legality to the country:

- The costs to the extralegal sector
- The costs to the legal business sector
- The costs to government

C. REFORM DESIGN

Design of a comprehensive program of reforms containing alternative options to formalize informal assets in the urban sector on a massive and nationwide scale, including:

C.1 Ensure that the highest political level assumes responsibility for capitalization of the poor.

C.2 Put into operation agencies that will permit rapid change.

- Identify and connect with the capitalization process the different institutions that presently govern property rights or impinge upon their ability to generate surplus value.
- Design, obtain approval for, and put into operation agencies that will permit the rapid introduction of changes in the diverse processes required for capitalization.
- If possible, create a single organization having the sole mandate to capitalize assets and decentralize offices to provide services throughout the country.
- Ensure that the capitalization process both incorporates the political priorities of the government and reflects a consensus within society that makes the process easily enforceable.

C.3 Remove administrative and legal bottlenecks.

- Calculate the costs of capitalizing extralegal assets, including: requirements for permits at all levels of government, requirements for and the amount of pay-

ments for these permits, the number of forms and other documents required, requirements that cannot be met in practice, all other transaction costs, including time delays.
- Remove administrative and legal bottlenecks by identifying and modifying the institutions, statutes and practices that create unnecessary red tape.

C.4 Build consensus between legal and extralegal sectors.

- Determine the points where extralegal norms coincide with the law so as to be able to draft statutes that recognize acceptable extralegal proofs of ownership with the support of extralegal communities.
- Ensure that in the draft legal norms that incorporate extralegal property do so without compromising the level of security that the existing legal order now provides property that is duly recorded and effectively controlled so as to obtain acquiescence of the legal sector.

C.5 Draft statutes and procedures that lower the costs of holding assets legally below those of holding them extralegally.

- Enact the statutes required for all property in a country to be governed by one consistent body of law and set of procedures.
- Broaden the definition of proofs of ownership to suit the new process, and consolidate into administratively manageable packages the statutes and procedures that will govern the capitalization process.
- Consolidate dispersed legislation into a single law.
- Develop institutions and procedures that permit economies of scale for all the activities which constitute the process of capitalization.
- Create an expedient and low-cost alternative to squatting and other forms of extralegal appropriation.
- Consolidate process and respect for the law by establishing incentives and disincentives aimed at encouraging legal and discouraging extralegal conveyance.
- Design and implement administrative or private processes, to substitute judicial processes, where suitable, so as to encourage settlement of disputes within the law.

C.6 Create mechanisms that will reduce risks associated with private investment, including credibility of titles and nonpayment for public services.

D. IMPLEMENTATION

D.1 Design and implement field operation strategy, procedures, personnel, equipment, offices, training and manuals that enable government to recognize and process individual property rights in the extralegal sector.

- Design mechanisms to obtain the massive participation of the members of extralegal settlements for the purpose of reducing the costs of capitalization.
- Carry out training courses for the organization of capitalization brigades that reflect the types of extralegality they will encounter.

- Develop manuals that explain to the leaders and the people of extralegal settlements the ways in which they can participate in the selection and collection of proofs of ownership.
- Prepare for capitalizing extralegal communities:
  i) Identify and train local promoters within each community
  ii) Implement a local promotional campaign within each community
  iii) Educate each community about the proofs of ownership required
  iv) Train local leaders to record ownership information on registration forms
  v) Identify and train private verifiers to certify information collected by the community
- Gather and process information on physical assets:
  i) Obtain or prepare maps showing the boundaries of individual parcels (where necessary prepare digital base maps to record boundary information)
  ii) Verify that maps showing individual parcels correspond with what is on the ground
  iii) Enter the maps into the computer system
- Gather and process ownership information:
  i) Gather ownership information and record on registration forms
  ii) Verify that ownership rights are valid under the new law
  iii) Enter the ownership information into the computer system
  iv) Officially register the ownership rights
  v) Hand out certificates to the beneficiaries at a public ceremony

D.2 Implement communications strategies using appropriate media to encourage participation of the extralegal sector, support in the business community and the government sector, and acquiescence among those with vested interests in the status quo.

- Conduct a campaign for each particular type of community in the extralegal sector to encourage their participation in the process.
- Devise mechanisms that show beneficiaries of capitalization process that their assets are protected by the same institutional framework that protects the rights of private investors, both domestic and foreign. This will give these owners a reason to respect contracts governed by the formal legal order.
- Conduct a campaign for each legal community that may feel vulnerable.
- Design the means of communicating to legal sector the benefits of capitalization, emphasizing the reduction in risks and making it clear that capitalization will neither affect existing property rights nor compromise the rights of third parties.
- Conduct a campaign for professionals with vested interests in property definition, explaining their future role and increased involvement within an expanded legal sector after capitalization.

D.3 Re-engineer the record keeping organizations and registration processes so that they can pull together all the economically useful descriptions about a country's extralegal assets and integrate them into one data/knowledge based computer system.

- Structure the organization of the registry and its internal work flows, simplify the registration processes, establish specifications for automating information, design and implement a quality control system, select and train personnel, and establish procedures to ensure that the registry can handle a massive national program of capitalization.
- Construct GIS based systems to provide spatial analytical capabilities.
- Establish control mechanisms to guarantee that the cost of enrollment and registration services are sufficiently efficient and cost effective that its users will not be motivated to slip back into extralegality.
- Insert descriptions of features of extralegal property holdings into customized, computer-friendly registration forms where they can be differentiated, recorded and managed in one computer environment.
- Break down the information that is traditionally contained in deeds into simple categories that can be entered into computer software and be systematized for easy access, after having effected a legally approved streamlining of existing information gathering procedures.
- Facilitate the update of computerized property information by placing data input centers close to the beneficiaries. The purpose is to cut down on the transportation and transaction costs of legally registering property and property-related business and keeping their status legal.

E. CAPITAL FORMATION

E.1 Coordinate joint operations between real estate and business formalization.

E.2 Create facilitative law for assisting capitalization with: burdening of ownership documents against credit, issuing of shares to obtain equity, and accessing risk reducing mechanisms, such as insurance, refinement of limited liability institutions, procedures to enter into and enforce contracts, accessing entrepreneurial information.

E.3 Identify and reduce new obstacles that affect the poor. This includes arranging mechanisms to remove additional obstacles in coordination with other government agencies.

E.4 On an ongoing basis, cut costs and increase benefits of entering the formal sector.

E.5 Provide legal access to assets by building alternatives to squatting, illegal subdivisions, and extralegal enterprises.

E.6 Create a communications strategy tailored to each segment of society.

E.7 Relate formalization to capital formation; identification systems; national security; collections systems for credit, rates and taxes; housing and infrastructure; insurance and other value added information services.

E.8 Assess the impact on credit and investment for extralegals by reviewing the availability of specific services such as: personal banking (checking and savings accounts), credit and mortgage applications, issuance and registration of bonds and shares and security interests, merger and change of legal status, personal or business insurance, bankruptcy and mortgage foreclosure.

© ILD

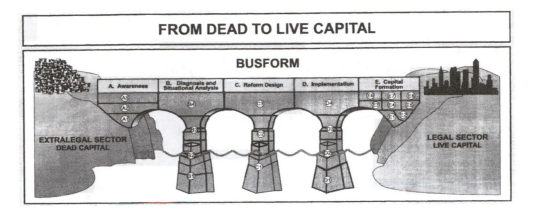

Figure 21.2

A. AWARENESS

Raising awareness about:

A.1 The importance of property law in capitalism

A.2 The stake of the poor in capitalism

A.3 The role of leadership in each country

B. DIAGNOSIS AND SITUATIONAL ANALYSIS

B.1 Define and assess the impact of the extralegal business sector.

- Define the extralegal business sector and determine its magnitude.
- Identify the different kinds of extralegal businesses and their origins.
- Locate the geographic areas and sectors where extralegality is most active.
- Research the relevant links between government and extralegal businesses.
- Research the relevant links between legal and extralegal businesses.
- Identify processes where government has already successfully dealt with extralegal business.

B.2 Determine the costs of extralegality to the extralegal sector.

Examine the costs of extralegality, by determining the degree to which extralegal businesses need to but cannot:

- Constitute a business organization capable of: defining rules and responsibilities that are legally enforceable among associates and third parties; distributing risk, pooling capital and making otherwise impossible associations viable through shares; bringing together diverse resources required to address business opportunities; and providing for succession
- Define the limits of financial risk and liability
- Reduce risks by using legal institutions such as insurance, hedging and futures markets

- Expand to achieve economies of scale, increase sales by using overt advertising, or invest significantly in capital goods (any of which would increase the risk of being detected by authorities)
- Access legal credit, which is much cheaper than extralegal credit
- Protect against inflation and theft by reducing reliance on cash-based transactions
- Use instruments of exchange such as bills of lading, warrants, letters of credit, etc.
- Export or import through legal ports of entry
- Contract with public entities
- Capture the value of reputation and other elements of goodwill
- Be accountable and contract for infrastructure services (electricity, water, sewerage, telecommunications, etc.)

B.3 Determine the costs of extralegality to the state, society and the business sector.

Examine the costs of extralegality, by determining the degree to which government and society cannot:

- Increase the tax base and tax collection
- Improve and expand access to publicly or privately supplied infrastructure services (electricity, water, sewerage, telecommunications, etc.)
- Increase opportunities for capital formation through securitization of assets
- Improve access to information by the business community for investment decisions, marketing, etc.
- Increase the number of legal jobs (which enjoy social benefits)
- Increase the revenues of social programs (social security, pension funds, health care, housing funds, etc.) to improve or expand their services and to contribute to the development of capital markets
- Improve access to information required to set better economic and social policies
- Protect third-parties from extralegal liabilities by guaranteeing debentures with property

B.4 Determine the costs of formalizing and staying in business.

Calculate the costs of formalizing different lines of business by establishing actual enterprises or analyzing case examples. This involves determining:

- Requirements for permits at all levels of government
- Requirements for and the amount of payments for these permits
- The number of forms and other documents required
- Requirements that cannot be met in practice
- All other transaction costs, including time delays

C. REFORM DESIGN

C.1 Introduce institutional reform that enables massive business formalization and realizes the associated benefits.

- Prepare a draft law for business formalization, so that: the costs of legality are obviously lower than those of extralegality; provisions are made to ensure that all of the benefits of legality are accessible; and all of the required government agencies and functions are in place to implement and administer formalization.
- Restructure the functions and procedures of government agencies to suit the needs of formalization by: accepting applications at face value and introducing ex-post controls; reviewing all procedures in order to eliminate those which are unnecessary and to reduce the costs of those that are directly relevant; streamlining decision making by delegating procedural authority to the front line while strengthening senior executive oversight and control; using public input and feedback to guide institutional reform and future adjustments.
- Introduce the law and/or regulations that enable massive business formalization and allow benefits to government and society in general to be realized.
- Create an authority responsible for managing the entire formalization process.

C.2 Streamline public administration by adapting successful local and international practices.

- Eliminate regulatory requirements that are not directly relevant to creating a business.
- Eliminate requirements to comply with unnecessary, redundant and costly red tape, which survives out of inertia or because it generates additional fees as well as bribes.
- Simplify access to administrative services (avoid queues by using mail, phone, fax, etc.).
- Assign as much as possible of the administrative burden borne by applicants to a streamlined public service.
- Perform legal certification ex-post.
- Where necessary, delegate responsibility for administrative work and legal authorizations, generally assigned to an exceedingly small group of high-ranking executive officers, to a greater number of lower-ranking officers. In this way, top managers are free to concentrate on planning, organizing, and facilitating the work of the offices under their administration, while more public servants will be authorized to attend to and resolve citizens' requests directly.

C.3 Modernize information systems and integrate exchange of information among relevant authorities.

- Design computer systems adapted to the streamlined formalization process, and information networks linking the various public entities involved.
- Decentralize administrative procedures for formalization to the local level for more effective access, and integrate the resulting information into a national network.
- Achieve faster processing of documentation by optimizing public service standards.

D. IMPLEMENTATION

D.1 Implement systems to encourage public input and feedback, and integrate this information to improve the formalization process.

- Implement a system to obtain public input and feedback: in person; through suggestion boxes; or by mail, phone or fax.
- Involve the Head of State or high-ranking political authorities in resolving complaints, through public declarations or by directly calling attention to offenders.
- Define and implement a communications strategy for publicity and media involvement in explaining the advantages of business formalization and encouraging the public contribution of solutions.

D.2 Implement more effective ex-post controls by government.

- Replace ex-ante controls that burden applicants with selective ex-post controls that reduce queues, time delays, paperwork and corruption.
- Introduce legal sanctions for misrepresentation. Rigorously punish cases of fraud or false allegations, identified through sampling, with appropriate administrative, civil and penal measures.

D.3 Accept applications from people seeking to formalize businesses at face value ex-ante.

- Issue immediate authorization to operate, once applications are documented through affidavits containing all of the information necessary to exercise expost control.

D.4 Administer a program to ensure that the greatest benefits are achieved from formalization for both government and society.

- Administer ex-post controls.
- Implement an evolutionary program of product standards that encourage rather than discourage the transition from extralegality to legality.
- Enhance and accelerate the benefits of formalization to society by implementing services and programs that increase revenues, including those from taxation.
- Expand access to and the availability of infrastructure services.
- Increase access to credit and opportunities for capital formation through securitization.
- Reduce risks of doing business through insurance and other institutions.
- Provide business training and extension services to new legal entrepreneurs.

E. CAPITAL FORMATION

E.1 Coordinate joint operations between real estate and business formalization.

E.2 Create facilitative law for assisting capitalization with: burdening of ownership documents against credit, issuing of shares to obtain equity, accessing risk reducing mechanisms (like insurance), refinement of limited liability institutions, procedures to enter into and enforce contracts, accessing entrepreneurial information.

E.3 Identify and reduce new obstacles that affect the poor. This includes arranging mechanisms to remove additional obstacles in coordination with other government agencies.

E.4 On an ongoing basis, cut costs and increase benefits of entering the formal sector.

E.5 Provide legal access to assets by building alternatives to squatting, illegal subdivisions, and extralegal enterprises.

E.6 Create a communications strategy tailored to each segment of society.

E.7 Relate formalization to capital formation; identification systems; national security; collections systems for credit, rates and taxes; housing and infrastructure; insurance and other value added information services.

E.8 Assess the impact on credit and investment for extralegals by reviewing the availability of specific services such as: personal banking (checking and savings accounts), credit and mortgage applications, issuance and registration of bonds and shares and security interests, merger and change of legal status, personal or business insurance, bankruptcy and mortgage foreclosure.

Index

260, 318–21; protectionism and free trade, 178–81; public opinion compared to policy, 322–27; trade regulations, 248–49

United States v. Urquídez Verdugo, 318

universities and subversion, 195

University Reform, 9–10

Uraguay, agreements of, 331

urban and rural struggles, 278–80

urban areas, 204–5, 210

urban popular movements, 305–6, 311–12, 314n4

Valle Espinoza, Eduardo ("Owl-Eyes"), 6, 26–27

value-added taxes (VAT), 348

vanguard groups, 270–72, 274–76, 345

Vargas Llosa, Alvaro, 240–61

VAT (value-added taxes), 348

Venezuela, 252, 336n10

venture-capital industry, 345

Viking transmitters, 59–67

violence, 38–44, 63, 293–94. *See also* Tlatelolco Massacre

wage differentials and immigration, 320

war against terrorism. *See* Instituto Libertad y Democracia (ILD)

wealth: in BEC discussions, 139–47; creation of, 242–44; from oil, 252; ruling classes, 251

white gloves, 24, 28–29

Wittgenstein, Ludwig, 152

women's issues: in Christian Church, 118–19; discrimination, 149; EZLN struggles, 287–88; as guerrilla minority, 79–80; International Women's Tribunal, 50–57

working poor, 54–56

World Bank, 188–89

world relations: cultural studies, 367–68; impact on productive structure, 237–38; views on Tlatelolco Massacre, 19; zapatistas' solidarity, 295–96. *See also* international issues

writers of radio programs, 74–75

Yaser ("Menéndez y Pelayo"), 75–76

young people, 10, 288–89

Zamora Vértiz, Marta, 22

Zapatista Army of National Liberation (EZLN): goals, 295–97; history, 282–86; means for attaining goals, 297–300; progress, 286–89; views on capitalism, 289–92; views on Mexico, 292–95

About the Editor

Iván Márquez was born in San Juan, Puerto Rico in 1965. He studied biology and philosophy at the University of Puerto Rico at Río Piedras and received a PhD in philosophy from Indiana University at Bloomington in 1995. He has taught at Indiana University at Bloomington, California State University at Fresno, and University of Puerto Rico at Cayey. Currently, he is associate professor in the Department of Philosophy at Bentley College in Waltham, Massachusetts. He has published articles in social and political philosophy, ethics, metaphysics, epistemology, philosophy of education, and Latin American social and political thought.